A Tale of Two Narratives

The Holocaust and the Nakba are foundational traumas in Israeli–Jewish and Palestinian societies and form key parts of each respective collective identity. This book offers a parallel analysis of the transmission of these foundational pasts in Israeli–Jewish and Palestinian societies by exploring how the Holocaust and the Nakba have been narrated since the signing of the 1993 Oslo Accords. The work exposes the existence and perpetuation of ethnocentric victimhood narratives that serve as the theoretical foundations for an ensuing minimization – or even denial – of the other's past. Three established realms of societal memory transmission provide the analytical framework for this study: official state education, commemorative acts, and mass mediation. Through this analysis, the work demonstrates the interrelated nature of the Israeli–Palestinian conflict and the contextualization of the primary historical events, while also highlighting the universal malleability of mnemonic practices.

GRACE WERMENBOL is a Middle East-focused analyst for the U.S. government and a non-resident scholar at the Washington-based Middle East Institute. She holds a Ph.D. from St Antony's College, University of Oxford, where her research focused on the Israeli–Palestinian conflict. She is the recipient of numerous academic grants and awards, including from the University of Oxford, the Council of British Research in the Levant, the University of Cambridge's Woolf Institute, and the Dutch Prins Bernhard Foundation.

T0381878

Cambridge Middle East Studies

Editorial Board

Cambridge Middle East Studies has been established to publish books on the nineteenth- to twenty-first-century Middle East and North Africa. The series offers new and original interpretations of aspects of Middle Eastern societies and their histories. To achieve disciplinary diversity, books are solicited from authors writing in a wide range of fields including history, sociology, anthropology, political science, and political economy. The emphasis is on producing books affording an original approach along theoretical and empirical lines. The series is intended for students and academics, but the more accessible and wide-ranging studies will also appeal to the interested general reader.

A list of books in the series can be found after the index.

A Tale of Two Narratives

*The Holocaust, the Nakba, and the
Israeli–Palestinian Battle of Memories*

Grace Wermenbol

CAMBRIDGE
UNIVERSITY PRESS

Shaftesbury Road, Cambridge CB2 8EA, United Kingdom

One Liberty Plaza, 20th Floor, New York, NY 10006, USA

477 Williamstown Road, Port Melbourne, VIC 3207, Australia

314–321, 3rd Floor, Plot 3, Splendor Forum, Jasola District Centre, New Delhi – 110025, India

103 Penang Road, #05–06/07, Visioncrest Commercial, Singapore 238467

Cambridge University Press is part of Cambridge University Press & Assessment, a department of the University of Cambridge.

We share the University's mission to contribute to society through the pursuit of education, learning and research at the highest international levels of excellence.

www.cambridge.org
Information on this title: www.cambridge.org/9781108794404

DOI: 10.1017/9781108885430

© Grace Wermenbol 2021

This publication is in copyright. Subject to statutory exception and to the provisions of relevant collective licensing agreements, no reproduction of any part may take place without the written permission of Cambridge University Press & Assessment.

First published 2021
First paperback edition 2022

A catalogue record for this publication is available from the British Library

Library of Congress Cataloging-in-Publication data
Names: Wermenbol, Grace, 1990- author.
Title: A tale of two narratives : the Holocaust, the Nakba, and the Israeli-Palestinian battle of memories / Grace Wermenbol.
Description: Cambridge, United Kingdom ; New York, NY : Cambridge University Press, 2020. | Series: Cambridge Middle East studies | Includes bibliographical references and index.
Identifiers: LCCN 2020037768 (print) | LCCN 2020037769 (ebook) | ISBN 9781108840286 (hardback) | ISBN 9781108794404 (paperback) | ISBN 9781108885430 (epub)
Subjects: LCSH: Jewish-Arab relations. | Arab-Israeli conflict–Historiography. | Holocaust, Jewish (1939-1945)–Historiography. | Israel-Arab War, 1948-1949–Historiography. | Collective memory–Israel. | Group identity–Israel. | Israel–Ethnic relations.
Classification: LCC DS119.7 .W45735 2020 (print) | LCC DS119.7 (ebook) | DDC 956.9405–dc23
LC record available at https://lccn.loc.gov/2020037768
LC ebook record available at https://lccn.loc.gov/2020037769s

ISBN   978-1-108-84028-6   Hardback
ISBN   978-1-108-79440-4   Paperback

Cambridge University Press & Assessment has no responsibility for the persistence or accuracy of URLs for external or third-party internet websites referred to in this publication and does not guarantee that any content on such websites is, or will remain, accurate or appropriate.

In loving memory of my father.

A world that can be explained even with bad reason is a familiar world. But, on the other hand, in a universe suddenly divested of illusions and lights, man feels an alien, a stranger. His exile is without remedy since he is deprived of the memory of a lost home or the hope of a promised land. —Albert Camus, *The Myth of Sisyphus*

And, of course, people are interested only in themselves. If a story is not about the hearer he will not listen. And I here make a rule – a great and lasting story is about everyone or it will not last. The strange and the foreign is not interesting – only the deeply personal and familiar.
—John Steinbeck, *East of Eden*

Contents

Figures

Tables

Acknowledgments

The realization of this work would not have been possible without the support of several individuals and organizations; they are, therefore, directly responsible for any merits this book might be deemed to possess. I would like to thank *Het Prins Bernhard Cultuurfonds, The Anglo-Israeli Foundation, The Sir Richard Stapley Educational Trust, The Council for British Research in the Levant,* and *The University of Oxford* for their generous financial assistance in the execution of my research. I am also grateful to my editors at Cambridge University Press: Daniel Brown, Atifa Jiwa, and, at the preliminary and final stages, Maria Marsh for overseeing the transformation of this work from doctoral thesis to academic manuscript. As the culmination of a six-year project, this work benefited from the input and counsel of many individuals. In Jerusalem, Dalia Kerstein assisted me in scouring Israeli and Palestinian phone books and, perhaps more importantly, provided me with steadfast company during my explorations of the city's culinary scene. From Oxford and, subsequently, Oklahoma, Andrew Porwancher offered continual encouragement as I completed my doctoral work and embarked on this book project. My sincere gratitude also goes out to my colleagues and academic mentors who helped me during various stages of the project and whose names – and influence – are interspersed throughout this work. In particular, I would like to convey my utmost appreciation to my doctoral supervisors: Professor Eugene Rogan and Dr. Zoe Waxman. Their intellectual guidance during my time in Oxford, in addition to their consistent positive reinforcement during our many meetings, allowed me to bring this project to successful fruition. This work equally benefited from the input of several academics who provided critical insight during the research and writing process; I would like to thank Professor Avi Shlaim, Professor Nicholas Stargardt, Professor Walter Armbrust, Professor Gilbert Achcar, and Professor Yaacov Yadgar for offering their time and feedback. Finally, I would like to thank my family and my partner for their unwavering support – both in person and from afar.

A Note on Transliteration

For transliteration of Modern Standard Arabic and Hebrew, this work follows the American Library Association-Library of Congress System[1] with two exceptions: First, where established English names of people, places, and institutions exist, English-language spelling is applied and, second, this work uses "tz" rather than "ts" for the Hebrew letter tzadi. For the list of characters of Modern Standard Arabic and Hebrew, see below.

Arabic

Consonants	Romanization	Consonants	Romanization
ا	omit	ض	ḍ
ب	b	ط	ṭ
ت	t	ظ	ẓ
ث	th	ع	ʻ (ayn)
ج	j	غ	gh
ح	ḥ	ف	f
خ	kh	ق	q
د	d	ك	k
ذ	dh	ل	l
ر	r	م	m
ز	z	ن	n
س	s	ة ، ه	h
ش	sh	و	w
ص	ṣ	ي	y

---

[1] Randall K. Barry, *ALA-LX Romanization Tables: Transliteration Schemes for Non-Roman Scripts* (Washington, DC: U.S. Library of Congress, 1991), 4, 52.

Vowels	Diphthongs
˙	a
ʾ	u
.	i
ا	ā
ـِى	á
ـُو	ū
ـِى	ī
ـَو	aw
ـَى	ay

Hebrew

Consonants	Romanization	Consonants	Romanization
א	ʾ (alif) or disregarded	ל	l
ב	b	מ (final ם)	m
ב	v	נ (final ן)	n
ג	g	ס	s
ד	d	ע	ʿ (ayn)
ה	h	פ (final ף)	p
ו	v (only if a consonant)	פ (final ף)	f
וו	v (only if a consonant)	צ (final ץ)	tz
ז	z	ק	ḳ
ח	ḥ	ר	
ט	ṭ		sh
י		שׂ	ś
כ (final ך)	k	ת	t
כ (final ך)		ת	t

Vowels	Romanization
ַ	a
ָ	a or o
ֶ	e
ֵ	e
ִ	i
ֹ	o
ֻ	u
	e
	ai
	e
	i
	o
	u
	e or disregarded
	a
	e
	o

Abbreviations

ADRID	Association for the Defense of the Rights of the Internally Displaced
AMAN	Coalition for Accountability and Integrity
CMIP	Center for Monitoring the Impact of Peace
CPJ	Committee to Protect Journalists
DFLP	Democratic Front for the Liberation of Palestine
DOP	Declaration of Principles on Interim Self-Government Arrangements
GDP	Gross Domestic Product
ICC	International Criminal Court
IDF	Israeli Defense Forces
IDP	internally displaced Palestinian
JNF	Jewish National Fund
MDHH	Memorial Day to the Holocaust and Heroism
MEMRI	Middle East Media Research Institute
MK	Member of Knesset
MOE	Ministry of Education
NGO	nongovernmental organization
NSC	Nakba and Steadfastness Committee
OT	occupied territories
PA	Palestinian Authority
PCBS	Palestinian Central Bureau for Statics
PCDC	Palestinian Curriculum Development Center
PDFLP	Popular Democratic Front for the Liberation of Palestine
PFLP	Popular Front for the Liberation of Palestine
PLC	Palestinian Legislative Council
PLO	Palestinian Liberation Organization
PMW	Palestinian Media Watch
PNA	Palestinian National Authority
PNC	Palestinian National Council

POW	prisoner of war
PPP	Palestinian People's Party
UNESCO	United Nations Educational, Scientific and Cultural Organization
UNRWA	United Nations Relief and Works Agency for Palestine Refugees in the Near East
USHMM	United States Holocaust Memorial Museum

Introduction

With the Israeli-Palestinian conflict raging on into its eighth decade, by now, we are well-accustomed to reoccurring reports discussing the latest flare-up in violence. The vicissitudes of the Mideast conflict continue to dominate the international policy agenda, undeterred by the numerous failed attempts at reconciliation and the resulting entrenchment of the peace-adverse status quo. Despite the primary conceptualization of the conflict as a territorial dispute over borders and designated state territory, the interminable state of political confrontation and violence has had a profound effect on both Palestinian and Israeli-Jewish society. Palestinians and Israelis' worldview, past and present, has been affected by – and in turn influences – the ongoing dispute. This study is concerned with the usage of primary historical narratives as a means of group identity-formation and as a means of contextualizing and justifying political acts. In doing so, this book exposes the social taming of societies' pasts. The resulting tales of empowerment seek to demonstrate the justness of today's cause and culminate in a rejection of the opponent's foundational narrative.[1] The pasts inferred here are the Holocaust and the Nakba, which have turned into primary formative events among the two groups engaged in an intractable conflict.[2]

---

[1] Robert Rotberg, "Building Legitimacy through Narrative," in *Israeli and Palestinian Narratives of Conflict: History's Double Helix*, ed. Robert Rotberg (Bloomington: Indiana University Press, 2006), 1.

[2] A work published by Amos Goldberg and Bashir Bashir in 2015, dedicated to "examining the possibility of a joint engagement with the Holocaust and the Nakba as [the] two traumatic national identities of Palestinians and Jews in Israel and Palestine," fell subject to public scrutiny because it was wrongly deemed to compare both events. Amos Goldberg and Bashir Bashir, *The Holocaust and the Nakba: Memory, National Identity and Jewish-Arab Partnership* (Jerusalem: The Van Leer Jerusalem Institute and Hakibbutz Hameuchad), 2015, 7 (in Hebrew).

See Ben-Dror Yemeni, "The Disgraceful Link Drawn between the Holocaust and the Nakba," *Ynet News*, July 29, 2015, www.ynetnews.com/articles/0,7340,L-4695275,00.html, accessed December 18, 2019.

This work's simultaneous deliberation of the Holocaust and the Nakba[3] does not mean conflating or equating them: one cannot compare mass extermination by an external, third party with mass, episodic displacement.[4] Such an equation would not only be historically – and ethically – erroneous, but would equally fail to recognize the divergence in historical culpability. Indeed, Germany is chiefly responsible for the Holocaust.[5] The state of Israel is, on the other hand, in large part responsible for the Nakba and its persistence.[6] Both events are, nevertheless, historically tied together. The founding of the state of Israel as a post-Holocaust haven for Jews meant[7] disestablishing the Palestinians from their homes; the state's subsequent confiscation of land and property, in addition to the purposeful destruction and reappropriation of Palestinian towns and localities, has all but precluded Palestinians' return.[8] This historical connection is not indicative of a causal link, as has been promulgated by, inter alia, the late Palestinian writer Emile Habibi,[9] but rather a contextual link. A more relational linkage does exist: as dominant national metanarratives, the Holocaust and the Nakba have bolstered exclusive identities within the two groups, both centering on unique claims of ongoing victimhood and loss and a consequential devaluation – if not denial – of the other's catastrophe.[10] Despite the obvious differences in political circumstances and national rights among Palestinians – as a stateless people – and Israelis, the foundational traumas continue to constitute open wounds. Their explicit "presentness," as this study demonstrates, centers on diverging concerns and perspectives through the application of a similar syntax of binary opposition and ethnocentrism.

[3] This work will adopt the English rendition of the word Nakba; the final ة (نكبة), as such, will be presented without the "h," with the sole exception of transliterated work.
[4] Nadim Khoury, "Postnational Memory: Narrating the Holocaust and the Nakba," *Philosophy and Social Criticism* 46 (2019): 5.
[5] Ibid.   [6] Ibid.
[7] Edward W. Said, "Invention, Memory, and Place," *Critical Inquiry* 26:2 (2000): 183.
[8] According to Khoury, a third of the Zionist forces "that ethnically cleansed Palestinian villages and towns" were Holocaust survivors, and many of these survivors were given abandoned Palestinian property unjustly seized after the promulgation of absentee laws. Nadim Khoury, "Holocaust/Nakba and the Counterpublic of Memory," in *The Holocaust and the Nakba: A New Grammar of Trauma and History*, ed. Amos Goldberg and Bashir Bashir (New York: Columbia University Press, 2018), 117.
[9] See, for instance, Habibi's 1986 article, entitled "Your Holocaust, Our Catastrophe," in which he argued that "If not for your – and all of humanity's – Holocaust in World War II, the catastrophe that is still the lot of my people would not have been possible." Emile Habibi, "Your Holocaust, Our Catastrophe," *Politica* 8 (1986): 26, 27 (in Hebrew).
[10] See Bashir Bashir and Amos Goldberg, "Introduction: The Holocaust and the Nakba: A New Syntax of History Memory and Political Thought," in Goldberg and Bashir, *A New Grammar of Trauma and History*, 1–42.

The Holocaust and the Nakba as Foundational Pasts

Scholarly application of (post)memory theory has convincingly demonstrated that both Palestinians and Israeli-Jews are shaped by traumatic events that preceded their birth, leading the Nakba (Arabic: grievous catastrophe)[11] and the Holocaust to respectively become the major component of the contemporary identity of Palestinians and Israeli-Jews despite more than seventy years that have passed since the foundational events took place.[12] Surveys and studies conducted among the Israeli-Jewish population since the early 1990s consistently show that the early dialectical process of exclusion and appropriation has given way to an entire third generation, which, irrespective of family heritage and origin, has had the Holocaust narrative etched into its consciousness. This narrative dictates, as indicated in a 2009 survey, that remembering the Holocaust's particularistic and ethnocentric meaning – captured by Yoram Taharlev in his popular 1970s song, *ha-'olam kulo negdenu* (Hebrew: the entire world is against us)[13] – constitutes the most important guiding principle for the adult population, far outweighing the committal to Jewish solidarity and Jewish existence in Israel.[14] Most people in Israel, as a result, do not identify with Yehuda Elkana's universalistic appeal that a Holocaust should "never happen again."[15] Instead, they identify with the Zionist lesson of the Holocaust which dictates "it should never happen to us again."[16]

Much like the Holocaust in Israeli-Jewish collective memory and, according to some, in response to Israeli memory discourse,[17] the

---

[11] Throughout this work I use the term Holocaust to refer to the systematic murder of approximately six million Jews at the hands of the Nazis and their collaborators between 1939 and 1945. Application of the neutral designation "the 1948 War" will be used to infer the period between the outbreak of the unofficial civil war in November 1947 and the signing of the final armistice agreement with Syria at the close of the official war in July 1949. The Palestinian conception of the war as a catastrophe will be applied when invoking Palestinian collective memory of the war and its aftermath.

[12] Lila Abu-Lughod and Ahmad H. Sa'di, "Introduction: The Claims of Memory," in *Nakba: Palestine, 1948, and the Claims of Memory*, ed. Lila Abu-Lughod and Ahmad H. Sa'di (New York: Columbia University Press, 2007), 21; Yair Auron, *Israeli Identities: Jews and Arabs Facing the Self and the Other* (New York/Oxford: Berghahn Books, 2012), 145.

[13] Auron, *Israeli Identities*, xviii.

[14] In 2009, 98.1 percent of the respondents stated that the Holocaust is a guiding principle in their life. Yechiel Klar, Noa Schori-Eyal, and Yonat Klar, "The 'Never Again' State of Israel: The Emergence of the Holocaust as a Core Feature of Israeli Identity and Its Four Incongruent Voices," *Journal of Social Issues* 69 (2013): 126.

[15] Yehuda Elkana, "A Plea for Forgetting," *Haaretz*, March 2, 1988, 13.

[16] Auron, *Israeli Identities*, xviii. Emphasis added.

[17] Adoption of Israeli-Jewish Holocaust mnemonic rituals include the sounding of a siren and the observance of a two-minute silence on Nakba Day.

Nakba constitutes a foundational event for the Palestinians.[18] Although Palestinians had various forms of identity before 1948,[19] the Nakba has become "a key narrative"[20] not only for those directly affected but for subsequent generations as well, leading the "loss of Palestine"[21] to become "a shared national identity."[22] Both inside the 1948 borders and in the West Bank – the principal geographical focus areas in this work – the 1948 War left its imprint on the two emerging categories of Palestinians: *Filasṭiniu al-dākhil* (Arabic: the internal Palestinians)[23] and *Filasṭiniu al-shatāt or al-khārij* (Arabic: the Palestinian refugees of the diaspora), as they are known in the national discourse. Inside the 1948 borders, the Haifa Declaration of 2007 issued by the "sons and daughters of the Palestinian Arab people who remained in our homeland despite the Nakba" thus casts the Nakba as a "formative event," which defines "our citizenship and our relationship to the state of Israel [in view of] the setback to our national project."[24] In a similar fashion, the Palestinian Declaration of Independence issued in 1988 by the Palestinian Liberation Organization (PLO) positions the Nakba as the lens through which to view the Palestinian people's struggle for nationhood; in spite of "the willed dispossession and expulsion from their ancestral homes [the Palestinian people] never faltered and never abandoned its conviction in its rights of Return and independence."[25] As is evident from these documents, the Nakba among these communities represents an

---

[18] Gilbert Achcar, Ahmad Sa'di, Lila Abu-Lughod, Meir Litvak, and Esther Webman are among the few who have noted symmetries between the role of the Holocaust and the Nakba among Israelis and Palestinians, including similarities in terminology. Thus, as Achcar notes, symmetries between the various terms include: "Shoah/Nakba, displaced person/refugee, Law of Return/Right of Return [...]." Gilbert Achcar, *The Arabs and the Holocaust* (New York: Metropolitan, 2010), 23.

[19] Abu-Lughod and Sa'di, "Introduction," 4; Rashid Khalidi, *Palestinian Identity: The Construction of Modern National Consciousness* (New York: Columbia University Press, 2010), 7, 20.

[20] Saloul Ihab, *Catastrophe and Exile in the Modern Palestinian Imagination: Telling Memories* (New York/Basingstoke: Palgrave Macmillan, 2012), 3.

[21] The Nakba not only represents the loss of "the homeland," but also "the disintegration of society, the frustration of national aspirations, and the beginning of a hasty process of destruction of Palestinian culture." Ahmad H. Sa'di, "Catastrophe, Memory and Identity: Al-Nakbah as a Component of Palestinian Identity," *Israel Studies* 7:2 (2002): 175.

[22] Ibid., 177.

[23] According to a survey conducted in 2008, the 1948 War consisted the most formative event for contemporary Palestinian identity inside Israel, with 33 percent of respondents self-identifying with reference to the war. Tamir Sorek, *Palestinian Commemoration in Israel: Calendars, Monuments and Martyrs* (Stanford: Stanford University Press, 2015), 206, 207.

[24] Mada al-Carmel, *The Haifa Declaration* (Haifa: Mada al-Carmel, 2007), 7, 8, 14.

[25] Yehuda Lukacs, ed., *The Israeli-Palestinian Conflict: A Documentary Record 1967–1990* (Cambridge: Cambridge University Press, 1992), 412.

"eternal present,"[26] for, as Lila Abu-Lughod and Ahmad Sa'di state: "the past is neither distant nor over [and] exile is neither transitional nor transitory; it is an inherited state."[27]

Theorizing Collective Memory

The Nakba's "presentness," similarly to the Holocaust, is an outcome of intergenerational familial and cultural transmission. In the context of the aforementioned post-memory theory, this "present continuous" can be related to the affix "post," which does not necessarily indicate an "adopt [ion] of [an]other's [memories] as one's own,"[28] but rather, the transmission of the emotional and personal effects related to the original memories.[29] As Taharlev's song continues, "We have learned it from our forefathers and we will teach it to our children and grandchildren."[30] Crucially, family, even in its most intimate moments, is entrenched in the society that surrounds it, where it is shaped by public structures and shared stories and images that inflect the transmission of familial remembrance. Moreover, while communicative memory is dependent on original exposure to the historical event, cultural or collective memory transmission allows for a conveyance of narratives to individuals based on group membership rather than familial heritage or generational belonging.[31] Indeed, with regard to the group memories at hand, I will demonstrate that the contemporary prominence of the Nakba and the Holocaust, which exists among both the descendants of affected and unaffected families, has relied on what Maurice Halbwachs in his landmark study of 1925 defined as *cadres sociaux*. Halbwachs, evidencing the influence of his teacher, the social theorist Émile Durkheim,[32] argued

[26] Sa'di, "Catastrophe, Memory and Identity," 177.
[27] Abu-Lughod and Sa'di, "Introduction," 10, 19.
[28] Marianne Hirsch, "The Generation of Post-Memory," *Poetics Today* 29:1 (2008): 114.
[29] Ernst van Alphen, "Second-Generation Testimony, Transmission of Trauma, and Postmemory," *Poetics Today* 27:2 (2006): 473–488.
[30] Cited in Ilan Peleg, ed., *Victimhood Discourse in Contemporary Israel* (Lanham, MD: Lexington Books, 2019), 3.
[31] In his book *Das kulturelle Gedächtnis*, Jan Assmann differentiates between two kinds of collective memory: communicative memory and cultural memory. Communicative memory is biographical and factual and is located within a generation of contemporaries who witness an event as adults and who can pass on their bodily and affective connection to that event to their descendants. Cultural memory views individuals as part of social groups with shared belief systems that frame memories and shape them into narratives and scenarios. Jan Assmann, *Das kulturelle Gedächtnis* (München: Verlag C.H. Beck, 1992), 36, 37 (in German).
[32] Émile Durkheim, "The Elementary Forms of Religious Life," in *The Collective Memory Reader*, ed. Jeffrey K. Olick, Vered Vinitzky-Seroussi, and Daniel Levy (New York; Oxford: Oxford University Press, 2011), 136.

that group membership – as a social milieu – provides the materials for memory and prods individuals into recalling certain events, including those that have never been experienced in a direct sense.[33]

The dual role ascribed to individuals, as members of social groups that draw strength from individuals' behavior and, simultaneously, as individuals that constitute social groups, means that Halbwachs acknowledged the relationship between the individual and the social group.[34] Yet Halbwachs' apt analysis of a practical construction of group memories in line with contemporary societal needs is underpinned by the less-than-adequate conception of the formation of these memories as passive materializations of the group's present concerns based on an unambiguous consensus which does not require any active mobilization.[35] Far from a spontaneous retrieval by individual group members, however, recollection of the past is an active, constructive process, and one which is mostly orchestrated from above.[36] Thus, this book conceives of collective narratives as those which, while reflecting the social group and affirmed by its members, are actively constructed and imparted on behalf of elite societal institutions.[37] The resulting hegemonic[38] narrative can be deemed a compromise, unifying the political and societal outlook and designs of the elite and the subjective reality of the "community of memory."[39]

The incorporation of post-modern individualist theory requires an important revision of the unitary Durkheimian approach, namely the transformation of Halbwachs' schema to schemata as a means of indicating an individual's simultaneous belonging to numerous societal groups.

[33] Jeffrey Olick, "Collective Memory: The Two Cultures," *Sociological Theory* 17:3 (1999): 335.
[34] As Halbwachs stated: "One may say that the individual remembers by placing himself in the perspective of the group, but one may also affirm that the memory of the group realizes and manifests itself in individual memories." Maurice Halbwachs, "The Collective Memory," in Olick, Vinitzky-Seroussi, and Levy, *Collective Memory*, 139–142; Olick, "Collective Memory," 342.
[35] Maurice Halbwachs, *On Collective Memory*, trans. Lewis A. Coser (Chicago: Chicago University Press, 1992), 40.
[36] Barry Schwartz, "The Social Context of Communication: A Study in Collective Memory," *Social Forces* 61:2 (1982): 374.
[37] Daniel Bar-Tal and Gavriel Salomon, "Israeli-Jewish Narratives of the Israeli-Palestinian Conflict: Evolvement, Contents, Functions and Consequences," in Rotberg, *Israeli and Palestinian Narratives of Conflict*, 19, 20.
[38] Hegemonic is used here in the way it was put forward by Antonio Gramsci, namely a prominent set of ideas in society that the vast majority of the people cannot even contemplate to challenge. Cited in Peleg, *Victimhood Discourse*, 4.
[39] Julie Ne'eman Arad, "The Shoah as Israel's Political Trope," in *Divergent Jewish Cultures: Israel and America*, ed. Deborah Dash Moore and S. Ilan Troen (New Haven: Yale University Press, 2001), 193.

Moreover, the pluralist conception of collective memory allows for the coexistence of alternative memories and, of most relevance to this study, rival memories among a social group bound in a cultural schema.[40] The materialization of the former is evidenced with reference to diverging in-group narratives. In the case study on Israeli-Jewish collective memory, deviant narratives can be found among individual Israeli-Jews who seek to challenge the normative Israeli usage of the Holocaust and, as Elkana put it, "eradicate the domination of this historical memory over our life."[41] Rather than amending the collective memory of the in-group, rival memories in existence among Palestinians living within the 1948 borders and Israeli-Jews – constituting a social group based on geographical perimeters, citizenship, and, to a large extent, the Hebrew language – challenge the very historical foundations of the other's collective memory, thereby indicating that an ethnic in-group alliance defines the community of Nakba and Holocaust memory.

Silencing the Other's Past

Collective memory is by definition subjective, as historical narratives in the service of the collective must facilitate the crystallization of a common consciousness through the creation of an orderly metanarrative of the past constructed in the service of the present.[42] It follows that mnemonic narratives need not reflect the historical truth, and instead they favor a narrative that is functional for a group's existence.[43] As a result, I am not so much concerned with the historical particularities of the Holocaust and the 1948 War; rather, I am principally interested in the exclusionary memories of these events and their endurance to this day. This singular focus equally means that this work pertains to describing the exclusionary identity practices that derive from and – in turn – sustain the dominant metanarratives while foregoing an in-depth analysis of the counter-narratives promoted by individuals and organizations in both societies. Nevertheless, nonconformist messages are featured throughout this book, offering important insights into nuanced attempts – and, where relevant, their failure – at envisioning an alternative reality in which the relationship between Israeli-Jews and Palestinians is not bound by the logic of ethnonationalism.[44]

---

[40] Peter Burke, "History as Social Memory," in Olick, Vinitzky-Seroussi, and Levy, *Collective Memory*, 191.
[41] Elkana, "Plea for Forgetting."
[42] Adil Manna and Moti Golani, *Two Sides of the Coin: Independence and Nakba 1948* (Dordrecht: Republic of Letters, 2011), 5.
[43] Rotberg, "Building Legitimacy," 4.   [44] Khoury, "Postnational Memory," 2.

Part and parcel of selecting functional collective narratives worth remembering is its antithetical process, because, as Ernest Renan contended, "Forgetting, I would even go so far as to say historical error, is a crucial factor in the creation of a nation."[45] By emphasizing the plasticity of memory construction, Renan, of course, alluded to cultural demarcation practices within national groups in Europe; yet, in conflicts "social silencing" does not only denote forgoing incompatible in-group memories, but also the opponent's master narrative(s).[46] Typically, the delegitimization and dehumanization of the out-group center on the simultaneous de-emphasis and erasure of the other's suffering to justify the in-group's own moral standing and provide a coping mechanism in a situation of interminable strife.[47] As in other national conflicts in which the opposing sides are members of different ethnic groups, the psychological dimension of the Israeli-Palestinian conflict manifests in a subversion of the other's narrative of suffering and a lack of recognition of the most fundamental traumas framing the conflict, including by the current leadership.[48] For instance, in 2018, Palestinian Authority President Mahmoud Abbas delivered what he called a "history lesson" in a speech broadcast live on Palestinian TV. During the 90-minute remarks, Abbas suggested that the Holocaust was the fault of Jews themselves, further claiming "that animosity toward Jews was not because of their religion but because of their social activities."[49] Abbas' Israeli counterpart has equally engaged in Nakba trivialization. More than ten years earlier, then opposition leader Benjamin Netanyahu said that including the word "Nakba" in Israeli

---

[45] Ernest Renan, "What Is a Nation," in Olick, Vinitzky-Seroussi, and Levy, *Collective Memory*, 80.

[46] Efrat Ben-Ze'ev, "Social Silence: Transference, De-sensitization and de-focusing among Israeli Students," in *Zoom In: Palestinian Refugees of 1948, Remembrances*, ed. Sami Adwan et al. (Dordrecht: Institute of Historical Justice and Reconciliation and Republic of Letters Publishers, 2011), 165–175.

[47] Bar-Tal and Salomon, "Israeli–Jewish Narratives of the Israeli–Palestinian Conflict," 24.

[48] Shifra Sagy, Avi Kaplan, and Sami Adwan, "Interpretations of the Past and Expectations for the Future among Israeli and Palestinian Youth," *American Journal of Orthopsychiatry* 72:1 (2002): 27.

[49] Abbas has long been accused of denying or undermining the Holocaust. His doctoral thesis, executed in the former Soviet Union, questioned whether the death toll of six million Jews might have been inflated, and he argued that Zionists and Nazis worked together to send Jews to present-day Israel. However, in 2003 Abbas said that the Holocaust was "a terrible, unforgivable crime against the Jewish nation, a crime against humanity that cannot be accepted by humankind"; in 2014, he issued a statement in which he called the Holocaust "the most heinous crime to have occurred against humanity in the modern era." See Siobhán O'Grady, "Palestinian President Says Jewish Behavior Caused the Holocaust, Sparking Condemnation," *The Washington Post*, May 2, 2018, www.washingtonpost.com/news/worldviews/wp/2018/05/02/palestinian-president-says-jewish-behavior-caused-the-holocaust-sparking-condemnation/, accessed February 23, 2020.

textbooks was tantamount to spreading propaganda, paving the way for the term's ban by the Israeli Ministry of Education in 2009 and other cultural restrictions outlined in this work.[50]

In addition to polls conducted among Palestinians living inside the 1948 borders and Israeli-Jews on attitudes towards the other's foundational trauma, reconciliatory attempts by individual civilians on both sides and the ensuing societal responses shed light on the materialization of mnemonic delegitimization efforts. In May 2009, Sammy Smooha published his index of Jewish-Palestinian relations, which found that despite public exposure to the Holocaust, 40.5 percent of Palestinian citizens in Israel claimed that the Holocaust never occurred, a 12.5 percentile rise from Smooha's 2006 polling.[51] Attempts to expose Palestinians to the Holocaust have largely been met with rejection,[52] as evidenced in the reactions to Khalid Mahameed's homemade Holocaust museum. Founded in 2005 in his law office in Nazareth, Mahameed sought to "help Palestinians understand the source of Israeli behavior," which according to the lawyer "is grounded on a Holocaust victimhood memory." Mahameed's personal initiative[53] fell on deaf ears, as, in his own words, the Palestinian community engaged in "a total boycott" of his exhibition.[54] In a similar fashion, an educational trip organized to

---

[50] Reuters, "Israel Bans Use of Palestinian Term 'Nakba' in Textbooks," *Haaretz*, July 22, 2009, www.haaretz.com/1.5080524, accessed February 24, 2020.

[51] According to Smooha, Holocaust denial cuts across sectors within the Palestinian population and is espoused by 37.1 percent of those with high-school education and 56.4 percent of Negev Bedouin. Smooha's research question regarding the Holocaust reads as follows: "I believe that there was a Holocaust in which the Nazis murdered millions of Jews." Possible responses included: disagree; inclined to disagree; inclined to agree; agree. Of the respondents, 40.5 percent disagreed or were inclined to disagree. Auron, *Israeli Identities*, 139.

[52] Not all exposure attempts are met with rejection. See, for instance, a 1997 *Maariv* article for a discussion of workshops for Palestinian students and teachers at Kibbutz Lohamei Hagetaot. Karni Am-Ad, "Saour and Ibrahim," *Maariv*, May 5, 1997 (page number unknown).

[53] Interview conducted with Khalid Mahameed on August 3, 2016. Also see Charles A. Radin, "Muslim Opens Holocaust Museum in Israel," *The Boston Globe*, May 6, 2005, http://archive.boston.com/news/world/middleeast/articles/2005/05/06/muslim_opens_holocaust_museum_in_israel/, accessed January 12, 2020.

[54] Four years later, Mahameed also held a Holocaust exhibit in the small West Bank village of Naalin to understand Jews' "defense mechanism deriving from [...] the Holocaust." This initiative was heavily criticized too, both by Israelis and Palestinians. For the former, the simultaneous presentation of the Nakba side-by-side to the Holocaust as a way to "explain the Shoah to Palestinians by passing through their own narrative and identity" drew accusations of conflation. Lorenzo Kamel and Daniela Huber, "The De-Threatenization of the Other: An Israeli and a Palestinian Case of Understanding the Other's Suffering," *Peace & Change* 37:3 (2012): 374–376; Roi Mandel, "Naalin Holds Holocaust Exhibit," *Ynet*, January 27, 2009, www.ynetnews.com/articles/0,7340,L-3662822,00.html, accessed January 12, 2020.

Auschwitz in 2014 by a former professor of Al-Quds University, Mohammed Dajani, resulted in a public dismissal of his "normalization efforts." As part of a history program, Dajani took twenty-eight students from East Jerusalem and the West Bank to Auschwitz in order to "challenge the denial of the Holocaust, which is both historically and morally wrong and, through a failure to understand the other's psychic, impedes the peace process."[55] While implicit threats had been conveyed to Dajani and the participants prior to the trip, upon the return from Poland, Dajani came under particular scrutiny from the Palestinian Authority (PA) and the university's faculty who demanded his resignation. The accusation leveled at him was treason and "selling out to the Jews" as he and his students had chosen to study the Holocaust rather than the Palestinian tragedy: the Nakba.[56]

Left-wing Israeli organizations dedicated to exposing their fellow citizens to the Nakba find themselves accused of the same perfidious conduct. Zochrot (Hebrew: remembering), an Israeli NGO established in 2002 amidst the ongoing turmoil of the Second Intifadah to raise awareness of the Nakba among the broad Israeli-Jewish public, has been accused of conducting "anti-Israeli" and "traitorous activities" equal to "commemorating [the] pain of Nazi casualties."[57] Objections to the dissemination of the Palestinian narrative have not remained confined to the public (media) sphere;[58] rather, as will be discussed in Chapters 2 and 4 of this work, appointed officials have attempted to thwart the Nakba's invocation among Israeli-Jews and Palestinians living inside Israel. In 2001, the minister of education, Limor Livnat, declared that she was considering awarding extra funding to "Arab schools" that were considered "loyal to the state." One of the ways in which schools

---

[55] Interview conducted with Mohammed Dajani on March 17, 2016.

[56] William Booth, "Palestinian University Students' Trip to Auschwitz Causes Uproar," *The Washington Post*, April 12, 2014, www.washingtonpost.com/world/middle_east/palestinian-university-students-trip-to-auschwitz-causes-uproar/2014/04/12/c162ba42-c27d-11e3-9ee7-02c1e10a03f0_story.html?hpid=z5, accessed March 10, 2016.

[57] Jo Roberts, *Contested Land, Contested Memory: Israel's Jews and Arabs and the Ghosts of Catastrophe* (Toronto, ON: Dundurn Press, 2013), 227. Also see Itamar Inbari, "The Palestinian Nakba Is Coming to the Streets of Israel," *NRG/Maariv*, May 14, 2007, www.nrg.co.il/online/1/ART1/581/574.html, accessed September 6, 2017; Eitan Bronstein, "Im Tirtzu Targets Zochrot for Promoting the Return of Palestinian Refugees," *Zochrot*, http://zochrot.org/en/article/53843, accessed September 6, 2017.

[58] For another example, see a 2018 report by *Haaretz*, which found that Israel's art scene has made conscious efforts to whitewash the Nakba by refusing to use the term – or any terminology which would indicate "the 'catastrophe' endured by the Palestinians" – to ensure the "erasure of consciousness that Israel is forcing upon the Palestinians." Rona Sela, "Israel's Art Scene Is Whitewashing the Nakba," *Haaretz*, December 28, 2018, www.haaretz.com/israel-news/.premium-israel-s-art-scene-is-whitewashing-the-nakba-1.6787625?=&ts=_1547149605080, accessed January 10, 2019.

could exhibit disloyalty, according to Livnat, was by commemorating Nakba Day.[59] In the same year, newly appointed Minister of National Infrastructure Avigdor Lieberman instructed the ministry's functionaries to avoid any contact with public figures who participated in Nakba commemorations. Lieberman justified his decision by a need to "punish public figures who turn Independence Day into a day of Holocaust."[60] Although there is no evidence that either policy was officially implemented, these statements provided fertile ground for the most extreme materialization of a mnemonic determent: the 2011 Nakba Law. With the introduction of this law, which constituted the culmination of a ten-year legal struggle to prevent Nakba commemoration, the government is authorized to withhold funding from state-sponsored groups and institutions in Israel that engage in the promotion and commemoration of the Palestinian Nakba. The law also enables a broader interpretation: in 2019, Tel Aviv University utilized the law to ban a student-organized lecture on campus to mark Nakba Day, marking the first time the Nakba Law was invoked by an academic institution to restrict political activity.[61] In defense of his party's bill (Yisrael Beiteinu) (Hebrew: Israel our home), Knesset Member David Rotem claimed that the law[62] was necessary because, as he stated: "When we are at war against a harsh enemy,

---

[59] Tamar Trabelsi, "Livnat to Arab Schools: Give Loyalty – Get Money," *Ynet/Yedioth Ahronot*, August 19, 2001, www.ynet.co.il/articles/0,7340,L-1029929,00.html, accessed August 22, 2017.

[60] Analogies between Nakba commemoration and Nazism also were made in 2012, when Education Minister Gideon Saar and Knesset Member Alex Miller sought to prevent a Nakba assembly from being held at Tel Aviv University, because, as the latter proclaimed, "today there is 'Yizkor' for Nakba casualties and tomorrow there will be 'Yizkor' for Nazi soldiers." Sorek, *Palestinian Commemoration in Israel*, 156, 157.

[61] Students had been barred from organizing Nakba commemoration events prior to this, too. In 2014, for instance, the University of Haifa penalized a group of students for "illegally organizing events (dedicated to) the commemoration of the 66th anniversary of the Nakba." Shira Kadari-Ovadia, "Israeli University Cancels Event Marking Nakba Day, Citing Violation of Law," *Haaretz*, May 16, 2019, www.haaretz.com/israel-news/.premium-in-first-israeli-university-bans-political-event-citing-violation-of-nakba-law-1.7250174, accessed January 12, 2020; Anonymous, "The Student Front: The University of Haifa Punishes Two Students for Commemorating the Nakba," *Kul al-Arab Online*, September 18, 2014, www.alarab.com/Article/636726, accessed March 12, 2020.

[62] According to the amended law, the minister of finance is authorized to halt funding for organizations that support the commemoration the Nakba. Officially termed the Budget Foundations Law, it is more commonly known as the Nakba Law. Israeli state-funded organizations found guilty of violating the Nakba Bill can be fined up to three times the sponsorship they previously received, with further penalties imposed for consistent breaches. Brendan Ciaran Browne, "Transitional Justice and the Case of Palestine," in *Research Handbook on Transitional Justice*, ed. Cheryl Lawther, Luke Moffett and Dov Jacobs (Cheltenham/Northampton: Edward Elgar Publishing, 2010), 503.

we will legislate laws that will prevent him from hurting us."[63] For Palestinian-Israelis, the law not only constitutes an attempt to erase their past, but equally is, as Joint List leader and Hadash Chairman Ayman Odeh stated, "Point of proof that the Nakba – the erasure of Palestinians, along with our history, language and stories – is not a single historical event. It is a continuing phenomenon."[64] Indeed, it is wholly unsurprising that official societal marginalization of the Nakba has led to a situation in which despite the emergence of revisionist historiography, 40.8 percent of Israelis continue to uphold the traditional Zionist account of the 1948 War, which dictates that "the Palestinians fled willingly because of fear and pressure from Arab leaders," and 30 percent express resentment when faced with the Palestinian narrative of the same events.[65]

Victimhood Narratives and Their Exclusionary Manifestations

The subversion of the other's foundational narrative, while sustained and reinforced by the intractable Israeli-Palestinian conflict, is premised on the existence of exclusive victimhood[66] identities. The exclusionary bases of Palestinian and Israeli victimhood narratives, much like the original scenes of the watersheds and the principal actors, differ. Thus, in the case of the Israeli-Jewish narrative, the invocation of an exclusive Jewish victimhood is not unique to Israeli society; instead, as Jean-Michel Chaumont pointed out, "The absolute singularity of the Shoah" has

---

[63] Ilan Peleg and Dov Waxman, *Israel's Palestinians: The Conflict Within* (Cambridge: Cambridge University Press, 2011), 128.

[64] Ayman Odeh, "Israel Celebrates Its Independence, We Mourn Our Loss," *The New York Times*, April 18, 2018, www.nytimes.com/2018/04/18/opinion/israel-independence-palestine-nakba.html, accessed March 12, 2020.

[65] Rafi Nets-Zehngut and Daniel Bar-Tal, *The Israeli-Jewish Collective Memory of the Israeli-Arab/Palestinian Conflict* (Rep. N.p.: International Peace Research Association, 2008), 222; Shibley Telhami, *The World through Arab Eyes: Arab Public Opinion and the Reshaping of the Middle East* (New York: Basic Books, 2013), 63.

[66] According to Ilan Peleg, collective victimhood combines five mutually supportive convictions: (1) A sense that the victimized group is the target of systematic and relentless persecution; (2) The conviction that the persecution is permanent and unchangeable, a constant and not a variable (although its intensity may change across time and space); (3) The belief that the persecution is completely unrelated to the actions of the targeted in-group and that it is exclusively the product of actions taken by the out-group (it is therefore assumed that the persecuted in-group cannot impact that victimization); (4) The notion that the persecutors include many, most or even all members of the out-group; (5) The perception that the persecuted group the collective victim, is in a unique situation, different than any other group. In the eyes of the victim, its condition of victimhood is highly particularistic and definitely not universal. Peleg, *Victimhood Discourse*, 2, 3.

been proclaimed by Jews and non-Jews alike to be "incomparable and incommensurable to every other event, both past, present, and future."[67] While comparability, as Charles Maier notes, does not exculpate or diminish the horror of Nazi crimes, uniqueness is perceived as a crucial issue.[68] As the "ultimate symbol of evil and human criminality,"[69] the Holocaust has emerged – particularly in the West[70] – as the indisputable yardstick against which other atrocities can be measured, but never equalized.[71] An exceptionalist reading of the Holocaust does not demand the accordance of special victimhood;[72] nevertheless, a transnational recognition of ultimate victimhood can confer, and lead to an appropriation of, special moral authority. Holocaust victimhood has, as a result, been endowed with a singular hierarchy unafforded to victims of other injustices, rendering it more powerful in the Israeli-Palestinian battle of memories. Aware of this crucial asymmetry, Edward Said noted that Palestinians "have had no Holocaust to protect [them] with the world's compassion."[73] Indeed, although the Holocaust constitutes a "global memory"[74] that does not exclusively belong to one nation or people,[75]

---

[67] Jean-Michel Chaumont, *La concurrence des victimes: Génocide, identité, reconnaissance* (Paris: La Découverte, 2010), 1, 2 (in French).

[68] Charles Maier cited in Dominick LaCapra, *Representing the Holocaust: History, Theory, Trauma* (Ithaca/London: Cornell University Press: 1994), 44, 45.

[69] Bashir and Goldberg, "Introduction," 6, 7.

[70] Peter Novick, "The Holocaust Is Not – and Is Not Likely to Become – A Global Memory," in *Marking Evil: Holocaust Memory in the Global Age*, ed. Amos Goldberg and Haim Hazan (Oxford/New York: Berghahn Books, 2015), 52.

[71] This societal yardstick is not necessarily indicative of scholarship over the past four decades. Since the infamous *Historikerstreit* of the 1980s, when German historians debated the integrated study of German totalitarianism in the twentieth century, the national-martyrological view of the Holocaust has been taken by new ideas that seek to challenge the traditional historiography. Recent theoretical approaches, as outlined by Daniel Blatman, thus seek to combine Holocaust studies with genocide studies and incorporate the Holocaust into a broader history of the twentieth century. See Daniel Blatman, "Holocaust Scholarship: Towards a Post-Uniqueness Era," *Journal of Genocide Research* 17:1 (2015): 21–43.

[72] The exceptionalist historian Alan S. Rosenbaum, for instance, argues that while any presumption about the uniqueness of the Holocaust may be entirely warranted, it does not in any manner diminish or still the certain moral authority that must be accorded to other groups whose members have also been forced to endure unspeakable atrocities during their histories. Alan S. Rosenbaum, "Introduction to the First Edition," in *Is the Holocaust Unique? Perspectives on Comparative Genocide*, ed. Alan S. Rosenbaum (New York: Routledge, 2009), 3.

[73] Edward Said, *After the Last Sky: Palestinian Lives* (New York: Columbia University Press, 1999), 17.

[74] Bashir and Goldberg, "Introduction," 6, 7.

[75] Tom Segev cited in Aleida Assman and Sebastian Conrad, "Introduction," in *Memory in a Global Age: Discourses, Practices and Trajectories*, ed. Aleida Assman and Sebastian Conrad (New York: Palgrave Macmillan, 2010), 8.

as the self-declared "legatee of" and "spokesman for"[76] the Holocaust, Israel continues to invoke the supremacy of Jewish victimhood during the Second World War – and the emergence of a new Amalek – to context-ualize contemporary objectives and political outlooks.

Chaumont's claim that a "concurrence des victimes" is founded on the banalization of other victims' suffering to a certain degree elucidates the materialization of an exclusive Palestinian victimhood.[77] Part and parcel of the basis for this exclusionary narrative is what Azmi Bishara termed "the Zionist instrumentalization [and appropriation] of the Holocaust,"[78] creating the notion of a "package deal" whereby "accepting the Jewish Holocaust mean[s] accepting Israel's right to be a colonial-settler state."[79] Yet, rather than solely emphasizing an under-standing of Israeli-Jewish usage and conceptions of the Holocaust as the foundation for an exclusive Palestinian victimhood, I argue that the existence of a Palestinian exclusionary narrative primarily derives from the group's perceived ongoing marginalization at the hands of the Israelis, leading to a "screen[ing] out [of] the suffering of [the] enemy."[80] In other words, the minimization of Israeli-Jewish victim-hood as a result of the persistent conflict informs the creation of an exclusive Nakba victimhood rather than vice versa, because, as the Palestinian journalist Jamil Hamad noted, "When the Palestinians talk about the Holocaust, they can't take the Holocaust as an isolated issue and talk about it – it's impossible. They have to link it [to] the political developments and military developments [...] in Palestine."[81]

Conversely, it is the primary conception of an exclusive Jewish victim-hood that dictates an ensuing subversion of the Palestinian narrative, further demonstrated in several socio-psychological studies executed among the Israeli-Jewish population. Studies conducted by Alon Lazar and Tal Litvak Hirsch (2009) and Johanna Ray Vollhardt (2013) evi-dence that hostile attitudes towards Palestinians and, through an inhib-ition of empathy, a disregard of their suffering derive from a Zionist understanding of the Holocaust. This Zionist understanding of the

---

[76] Novick, "Holocaust," 49.

[77] Meir Litvak and Esther Webman, "Perceptions of the Holocaust in Palestinian Public Discourse," *Israel Studies* 8:3 (2003): 131.

[78] Azmi Bishara, "The Arabs and the Holocaust. The Analysis of a Problematic Conjunctive Letter," *Zmanim* 53 (1995): 54 (in Hebrew).

[79] Joseph Massad, "Palestinians and Jewish History: Recognition or Submission?," *Journal of Palestine Studies* 30 (2000): 53; Raef Zreik, "When Does a Settler Become a Native? (With Apologies to Mamdani)," *Constellations* 23 (2016): 360.

[80] David K. Shipler, *Arab and Jew: Wounded Spirits in a Promised Land* (London: Bloomsbury, 1989), 343.

[81] Cited in ibid., 344.

Holocaust is characterized by two dialectical themes.[82] Within this narrative, a unique Jewish victimhood status based on the perception of the diaspora as an inherently hostile environment for Jews coexists with a defensive in-group narrative, which demands "never to be a victim again."[83] The existence of these victimhoods elucidates the repudiation of the Palestinian narrative. In their 2008 work, Julia Chaitin and Shoshana Steinberg thus asserted that the transgenerational experience of being a (unique) victim stymies connecting to "the suffering of others, especially if those others continue to be defined as 'the enemy'."[84]

Consistent framing of the violent confrontations in the Middle East in the context of the European watershed means that any self-acknowledgment as a victimizer is impeded by the perseverance and invocation of the radically incompatible Zionist Holocaust victimhood narrative. Accordingly, the 1948 War and its outcome are viewed as a pure and untainted act of historical justice that changed the historical course of the Jewish people.[85] Through past and present invocation of the Holocaust and its implications for Israeli-Jewish self-understanding, this book also sheds light on the perceived threat of another Holocaust, this time at the hands of their neighbors. In his memoir, entitled "A Tale of Love and Darkness," the late author Amos Oz identified the potential sociological effects of viewing today's Palestinians as "Nazis in disguise" by noting that: "When we look at them, we do not see fellow victims either; we see not brothers in adversity but pogrom-making Cossacks, bloodthirsty anti-Semites [...] as though our European persecutors have reappeared here in the Land of Israel, put keffiyehs on their heads, and grown moustaches, but they are still our old murderers."[86]

While the persistence of Israeli and Palestinian exclusionary narratives provides a solid explanatory cognitive schema in interminable conflict, the "battle of memories," as the acclaimed Palestinian poet Mahmoud Darwish termed it,[87] also actively contributes to the conflict's continuation.

---

[82] Johanna Ray Vollhardt, "'Crime against Humanity' or 'Crime against Jews'? Acknowledgment in Construals of the Holocaust and Its Importance for Intergroup Relations," *Journal of Social Issues* 69:1 (2013): 144–161; Alon Lazar and Tal Litvak Hirsch, "Cultural Trauma as a Potential Symbolic Boundary," *International Journal of Politics, Culture, and Society IJPS* 22:2 (2009): 183–190.

[83] Klar, Schori-Eyal, and Klar, "The 'Never Again' State of Israel," 139.

[84] Julia Chaitin and Shoshana Steinberg, "You Should Know Better: Expressions of Empathy and Disregard among Victims of Massive Social Trauma," *Journal of Aggression, Maltreatment, and Trauma* 17:2 (2008): 197–226.

[85] Manna and Golani, *Two Sides of the Coin*, 14.

[86] Amos Oz, *A Tale of Love and Darkness* (London: Vintage Books, 2005), 330.

[87] Cited in Gil Hochberg, *In Spite of Partition: Jews, Arabs, and the Limits of Separatist Imagination* (Princeton: Princeton University Press, 2007), 119.

The reciprocal relationship between collective narratives and intractable conflicts means that group members, inculcated by their own in-group narrative, anticipate the worst from the adversary and react accordingly, leading to a prolonging of the actual conflict.[88] As a result, although certainly not the only condition for reconciliation, changes in the collective narratives are a necessary precondition to the resolution of the Israeli-Palestinian conflict; one part of this process is learning about the rival group's collective narrative.[89] The required "unequivocal acknowledgment of the suffering of the Jews and recognition of the suffering of the Palestinians on the part of the Israelis,"[90] importantly, does not necessitate a utopian-style adoption of the other's narrative by the in-group, but rather acknowledging the validity of the other's narrative as a legitimate position not to be rejected solely based on its belonging to the out-group. Crucially, the propagation of Israeli and Palestinian collective narratives "free of ethnocentrism,"[91] which would allow for exposure to the other's narrative, depends on changes in the in-group's narrative and, simultaneously, a thorough comprehension of its perseverance. Though previous scholarship has convincingly identified exclusive victimhood identities[92] among Palestinians and Israeli-Jews as a root cause for the ensuing "battle of memories" or "battle of

---

[88] As Daniel Bar-Tal notes, "long-standing intractable conflicts deeply involve society members, who develop a socio-psychological repertoire of beliefs, attitudes and emotions (about) their own group, about the rival, and about the desired solution. Eventually this repertoire becomes an investment in the conflict, because its supports and fuels its continuation. It is frozen and resistant to change and thus inhibits deescalation of the conflict and its peaceful resolution." Daniel Bar-Tal, *Intractable Conflicts: Socio-Psychological Foundations and Dynamics* (New York: Cambridge University Press, 2013), 16, 17; Rotberg, "Building Legitimacy," 5.

[89] Bar-Tal and Salomon, "Israeli-Jewish Narratives of the Israeli-Palestinian Conflict," 31, 40.

[90] Meir Litvak and Esther Webman, *From Empathy to Denial: Arab Responses to the Holocaust* (London: Hurst, 2011), 17. For similar appeals see Achcar, *Arabs*, 275, 279; Said, "Invention," 183; Ilan Pappé, "Fear, Victimhood, Self and Other: On the Road to Reconciliation," in *Across the Wall: Narratives of Israeli-Palestinian History*, ed. Ilan Pappé and Jamil Hilal (London: I.B. Tauris, 2010), 167; Yair Auron, "Letter to a Palestinian Reader: Holocaust, Resurrection and Nakba," *Haaretz*, May 8, 2014, www.haaretz.com/opinion/.premium-1.589454, accessed October 15, 2015.

[91] Litvak and Webman, "Perceptions of the Holocaust," 133.

[92] See Shipler, *Arab and Jew*; Massad, "Palestinians and Jewish History," 52–67; Edna Shoham, Neomi Shiloah and Raya Kalisman, "Arab Teachers and Holocaust Education: Arab Teachers Study Holocaust Education in Israel," *Teaching and Teacher Education* 19:6 (2003): 609–625; Ilan Pappé, *The Ethnic Cleansing of Palestine* (Oxford: Oneworld, 2006); Ronit Lentin, Co-*memory and Melancholia: Israelis Memorialising the Palestinian Nakba* (Manchester: Manchester University Press, 2010).

victimhoods,"[93] a solid understanding of the inter- and transgenerational conveyance of these exclusionary narratives, to date, is lacking. By conducting a parallel analysis of the collective transmission of these exclusive narratives, I, therefore, seek to address a scholarly void while safeguarding against any claims of comparisons between the historical events themselves.

Structural Make-up and Methodology

Attempts to institutionalize group narratives are characterized by two important features which inform the examined collective societal realms. A successful institutionalization process – meaning that the beliefs of the narrative are widely held by society members who acquire and store this repertoire as part of their socialization from an early age – depends on a wide societal application and expression in cultural products and the narrative's appearance in educational materials.[94] The former, which can include exposure to and, of particular importance, active engagement in media products and commemoration activities, governs the parallel examination of collective mnemonic activities and mass mediation dedicated to the Nakba and the Holocaust in, respectively, Parts II and III of this work. Educational socialization efforts, a significant element of narrative institutionalization due to the narrative's dissemination to a society's younger generation, the perceived authority of textbooks, and compulsory school attendance, will constitute the first examined collective realm of exclusive Nakba and Holocaust transmission.

An array of pre-formulated research questions seeks to guide the analysis of the development and maintenance of exclusionary group narratives in the three case studies. The main question addresses the qualitative nature of exclusionary victimhood narratives by examining *how* the collective transmission of the Nakba and the Holocaust propagates exclusive victimhood narratives in the post-Oslo era. By emphasizing the societal dynamics of identity- and narrative-formation, I discuss to what extent the collective narratives mirror and instrumentalize contemporary social and political concerns. In doing so, I seek to find out

[93] For works invoking this battle of memory, see Hochberg, *In Spite of Partition*, 119; Edward Said, *The End of the Peace Process: Oslo and After* (London: Granta, 2000); Said, "Invention," 175–192; Ilan Gur-Ze'ev, *Destroying the Other's Collective Memory* (New York: Peter Lang, 2003); Litvak and Webman, *From Empathy to Denial*; Achcar, *Arabs*; Pappé and Hilal, *Across the Wall*; Yair Auron, *The Holocaust, the Resurrection and the Nakba* (Ramallah: Madar Press, 2013).
[94] Adopted from Bar-Tal and Salomon, "Israeli-Jewish Narratives of the Israeli–Palestinian Conflict," 33, 34.

whether the exclusionary marginalization of the out-group's victimhood narrative coincides with a political deterioration in the Israeli-Palestinian peace process.

In order to answer the above research questions, I principally rely on historic material, including textbooks, mnemonic institutions' archives, and newspaper articles. In addition, Part II incorporates participant observation of mnemonic rituals and institutions dedicated to commemorating the Holocaust and the Nakba as a means of shedding light on the sought experiential effects on mnemonic participants. The results of this observational research are consistently supported by historical documentation in order to ensure the institutions and their employees' vision aligns with the findings of participatory study. The three case studies also include semi-structured interviews with representatives of the realm under examination, which shed light on the societal relevance of the transmitted narrative. These interviews contribute to understanding the findings originating from observational and primary source research, so that while these methodological categories provide the "how," the interviews seek to shed light on the "why."[95] Crucially, individuals' candid participation in this work should not be equated to a (passive) sanctioning of victimhood narratives and their exclusionary manifestations. Memory agents involved in the creation of collective mnemonics do not necessarily seek the emergence of an ensuing marginalization of the out-group's foundational narrative. Nevertheless, part and parcel of this work is to reveal, in Foucauldian terms, the framework of hidden mechanisms that shape the emergence of exclusive victimhoods and, consequently, the actions and outlooks of those influenced by these narratives. Moreover, interviews conducted with memory agents testify to the contemporary dominance of the second-generation – as the custodians of the first generation – in vertical (transgenerational) and, to a lesser extent, intergenerational (horizontal) memory transmission.[96]

---

[95] Adopted from Samira Alayan, "The Holocaust in Palestinian Textbooks: Differences and Similarities in Israel and Palestine," *Comparative Education Review* 60:1 (2015): 87.

[96] Since the early 2000s, memory scholars have paid attention to this horizontal characteristic of collective memory. For example, Lila Abu-Lughod and Ahmad Sa'di's 2007 work argued that individuals' memories adjust to each other, what Lilliane Hammer (2005) termed the "canonization" of stories. A similar argument was made by Eva Hoffman in 2004. Hoffman draws a line between "the postgeneration as a whole and the literal second generation in particular" and argues that while intergenerational vertical identification of a child and a parent occurs within the family, intergenerational horizontal identification makes the child's position more broadly available to other contemporaries in society. Abu-Lughod and Sa'di, "Introduction," 7; Eva Hoffman, *After Such Knowledge: Memory, History, and the Legacy of the Holocaust* (New York: Public Affairs, 2004), 187.

As the formulation of the research questions suggests, this book is accompanied by both temporal and geographical constraints. The geographical focus within the Palestinian case studies lies on the territories occupied in 1967 (East Jerusalem and the West Bank) and the Palestinian community inside the 1948 border. Yet, rather than amalgamating these areas into one uniform study, this work differentiates between the respective Palestinian communities through revealing the particularities of Nakba discourse as a reflection of the community's historic mnemonic traditions and, of particular relevance, the community's past and present political interaction with the Israeli state. Consequently, while not challenging the existence of a uniform Palestinian perception of the Nakba as a foundational event, this study does distinguish between the communities' instrumentalization of the event, highlighting the varying societal and political circumstances and aspirations since 1948.

Changes in the political organization in the Palestinian communities and the consequential exposure to authoritative collective narratives equally inform this work's temporal focus on the post-Oslo period, which here designates the twenty-two years between May 4, 1994 and May 15, 2016. The latter date constitutes the sixty-eighth anniversary of the Nakba and the eighteenth annual staging of the "March of Return," described at length based on participant observation in Chapter 4, while the former date represents the signing of the 1994 Cairo Agreement, officially called the Agreement on the Gaza Strip and the Jericho Area. The 1994 Gaza–Jericho Agreement, a follow-up treaty to the Oslo I Accord, facilitated, for the first time, the establishment of a Palestinian Ministry of Education and, through the right of administrative self-government, an independent Palestinian media in the West Bank and East Jerusalem, free from Israeli (military) censorship. The Oslo Accords had an equally profound effect on mnemonic practices, this time not resulting from the (interim) state-building process, but as a consequence of what the Syrian poet Nizar Qabbani in 1995 referred to as: "[stealing] from us the memory of the orange trees [and leaving] a sardine can called Gaza and a dry bone called Jericho."[97] The "capitulation of Oslo" invoked in Qabbani's poem,[98] meaning the PA's postponement of the refugee issue to final status negotiations,[99] not only influenced Nakba mnemonics within the 1967 areas,

---

[97] Cited in Meron Benvenisti, *Sacred Landscape: The Buried History of the Holy Land since 1948* (Berkeley: University of California Press, 2000), 267.

[98] Ibid., 267.

[99] These were to begin no later than the beginning of the third year of the interim period. Ghassan Khatib, *Palestinian Politics and the Middle East Peace Process* (London/New York: Routledge, 2010), 95.

but also inside Israel under the organized leadership of *al-muhajjarīn fī al-dākhil* (Arabic: the refugees inside [the 1948 borders]). The Oslo Peace Accords, conversely, did not impact domestic governance in Israel, and the three collective mnemonic spheres under review – the realms of Israeli state education, official state(-like) commemoration, and mass media – have existed since the establishment of the state. Nevertheless, the three case studies attest to the fact that the collective usage of historical narratives reflects particular contemporary political and social concerns, which demand a modification and reconceptualization of prior mnemonic trends. The final section of this work, for instance, evidences a materialization of a Holocaust ritual in Israeli mass media on *Yom ha-Shoah* (Hebrew: Holocaust Memorial Day) since the mid-1990s, characterized by traditional Holocaust symbolism and prescriptive commemorative reminders.

To examine the evolution and perpetuation of the narratives under review, I have divided the three case studies in an equal amount of parts, each divided into two separate chapters on Israeli-Jewish and Palestinian society and the transmission of the respective group narrative.

Part I, entitled "The Textbook of Memory," concentrates on the exclusive educational transmission of the Nakba and the Holocaust through an analysis of history textbooks published between 1994 and 2014. The simultaneous incorporation of modern European and Middle Eastern history in textbooks means that both chapters not only include an analysis of the transmission of their own foundational narratives, but also, in contrast to subsequent parts, provide a comprehensive examination of the presentation – or indeed lack of – the other's foundational history. Interviews conducted with education officials, including former ministers of education, and a review of educational policies and historiographical and political developments in the time period under examination are used to contextualize the textbooks' content.

Part II, bearing the title "The Landscape of Memory," similarly to Part I, emphasizes the vertical transmission of exclusionary victimhoods through its emphasis on (semi-)official mnemonic practices. Differentiating between physical and non-physical mnemonics, the two chapters that make up this part offer an examination of abstract mnemonic acts, namely the annual observation of official memorial days, and non-abstract year-round visits to dedicated memory sites, which include mnemonic institutions and, in the Palestinian case study, collective return visits to former Palestinian localities. This part's distinction between abstract and non-abstract mnemonic practices is a testimony to the physical disparity that has arisen due to the difference in governance within the two communities under review. For the Palestinian community inside the 1948 borders, the minority's inability to construct a Nakba memory site has transformed the historical act of familial visitations to destroyed localities into a collective mnemonic ritual, which, through the perception of a contemporary manifestation of an ongoing Nakba, aims to confront Israeli palimpsest practices – what Sari Hanafi terms "spaciocide"[100] – and expose the experienced political and cultural marginalization.

Finally, Part III, entitled "Scoop on the Past," constitutes an in-depth examination of anniversary journalism. By offering an overview of annual media output dedicated to the commemoration of the Holocaust and the Nakba in the largest Israeli and Palestinian media outlets, the two chapters incorporated in this part reveal how both societies have shaped their worldview over the last two decades. Indeed, mass media's reflection of readers' interests – and by extension society's pulse – provides insight into the analogical instrumentalization of the Nakba and the Holocaust, whereby the invocation of the past contextualizes the present and forms a yardstick in the interpretation of present-day concerns. The interpretation of mass media as a reflection of society's ideological framing also testifies to the complexity of "agenda-setting," as producer and consumer can, at times, be one. Media professionals' conveyance of received mnemonic narratives to their readers, particularly among the second and third generation, thus demonstrates that it is not solely media consumers who are exposed to a horizontal and vertical mediated transmission, but equally the very agents behind the news.

---

[100] Sari Hanafi, "Spacio-Cide: Colonial Politics, Invisibility and Rezoning in Palestinian Territory," *Contemporary Arab Affairs* 2:1 (2009): 106–121.

1   The Post-Oslo Period
A Historical Overview

As this book goes to print, the Israeli–Palestinian peace process is mori-
bund. The post-Oslo period in which this study is situated thus both
refers to the buoyancy of a potential reconciliation in the immediate wake
of the 1993 Oslo Peace Accords and the subsequent demise of a viable
two-state solution. As evidenced in the paragraphs below, perceptions of
the formulation of the Oslo Accords and, more importantly, their key
successes and failures will largely depend on the party under examination, making the peace agreement – similarly to other historical events –
a subject of narrative dissent. Rather than provide the reconciliatory
framework and confidence-building measures to address past grievances,
as was intended through the interim nature of the 1993 agreement, the
post-Oslo period therefore witnessed an ongoing irreconcilability of key
narratives. This chapter offers both a holistic understanding of the political and societal impact of these historic accords and an overview of the
key events that were influenced by – and affected – subsequent implementation and interpretations of the Oslo peace agreements. The events
highlighted in this chapter do not provide an exhaustive analysis of
Israeli-Jewish or Palestinian politics in the post-Oslo era; however, they
do seek to render formative insights into the societal underpinnings that
explain the rise and persistence of exclusionary identity politics that form
the main interest of this work.

The Declaration of Principles

On September 13, 1993, United States President Bill Clinton presided
over one of the most famous handshakes in modern history. On the
White House lawn, Prime Minister Yitzhak Rabin and the Palestinian
Liberation Organization Chairman Yasser Arafat were determinedly
ushered towards one another by the American president. The "dramatic

image,"[1] as the *New York Times* celebrated the handshake, marked the announcement of the Declaration of Principles (DOP) for a political settlement of the Israeli–Palestinian conflict.[2] The DOP, or in full the "Declaration of Principles on Interim Self-Government Arrangements," constituted the culmination of months of secret meetings in Oslo sponsored by the Norwegian government between the Tunis-based Palestinian Liberation Organization, headed by Arafat, and the Israeli government.

The signing of the DOP, known as Oslo I, marked the first of some nine agreements[3] that were negotiated and signed over the period of the next six years. These agreements are cumulatively referred to as the Oslo Accords. While the Interim Agreements dealt with the establishment of a Palestinian Interim Self-Government Authority[4] in parts of the West Bank and Gaza, the foundations for Oslo I and subsequent negotiations lay in the principle of mutual recognition. Four days prior to the public White House ceremony, Arafat and Rabin had exchanged letters of mutual recognition.[5] The achieved mutual recognition went beyond a departure in prior negotiation policies. During a secret signing ceremony in Oslo in August 1993, Uri Savir, head of the Israeli delegation, told his

---

[1] Elaine Sciolino, "The Ceremony: After Decades as Enemies, Arafat and Rabin Will Meet," *The New York Times*, September 12, 1993.

[2] Noam Chomsky, "The Oslo Accords: Their Context, Their Consequences," in *The Oslo Accords: A Critical Assessment*, ed. Petter Bauck and Mohammed Omer (Cairo: The American University in Cairo Press, 2017), 1.

[3] They are: (1) Letters of Mutual Recognition between Israel and the PLO – September 9 and 10, 1993; (2) Declaration of Principles on Interim Self-Government Arrangements ("Oslo-I") – September 13, 1993; (3) (Paris) Protocol on Economic Relations – April 29, 1994; (4) Agreement on Gaza Strip and the Jericho Area (the "Cairo Agreement") – May 4, 1994; (5) Agreement on Preparatory Transfer of Powers and Responsibilities – August 29, 1994 (additional agreement, August 28, 1995); (6) Israeli–Palestinian Interim Agreement on the West Bank and the Gaza Strip ("Oslo-II") – September 28, 1995; (7) Protocol Concerning the Redeployment in Hebron – January 15, 1996; (8) Wye River Memorandum – October 23, 1998; (9) Sharm el-Sheikh Memorandum – September 4, 1999. Shamir Hassan, "Oslo Accords: The Genesis and Consequences for Palestine," *Social Scientist* 39:7/8 (July–August 2011): 6.

[4] Nathan Brown, *Palestinian Politics after the Oslo Accords: Resuming Arab Palestine* (Berkeley: University of California Press, 2003), 12/13.

[5] Israel recognized the PLO as the legitimate representative of the Palestinian people and no longer considered it a terrorist organization. The PLO for its part recognized Israel's right to exist in peace and security and undertook to annul the articles of the Palestinian Covenant that rejected Israel's right to exist, to accept Resolutions 242 and 338 of the UN Security Council, to renounce the path of terrorism and violence, and to conclude the conflict by peaceful means. Uri Ben-Eliezer, *Old Conflict, New War: Israel's Politics toward the Palestinians* (New York: Palgrave Macmillan, 2012), 36.

interlocutors that the agreements marked "a new dawn for the two peoples plagued by historical tragedies."[6]

The Israeli Road to Oslo

Israel's engagement in the Oslo process was not simply the result of a new-found political will. For the Israeli government, the bypass to the Turkish road,[7] as Israeli negotiator Yossi Beilin termed the bilateral negotiation track in Washington DC, marked a long-held policy reversal. Since 1967, all Israeli governments had strongly opposed engaging in negotiations with the PLO, considered a terrorist organization. As the PLO represented primarily the Palestinian diaspora, it was also assumed that the PLO would not compromise on a "right of return" for millions of refugees and their families.[8] By 1992, however, the Israeli political and societal landscape had changed significantly. Four factors, in particular, were decisive in explaining the shift in Israeli policy. First, in the summer of 1988, Israel was faced with the absence of the hitherto preferred negotiating partner: Jordan. The loss of "the Jordanian option" in the summer of 1988, a result of Jordan's renouncement of its claim to the West Bank, forced Israel to "develop a Palestinian option."[9] With the outbreak of a Palestinian uprising in the late 1980s, many Israelis also, for the first time, became confronted with the Palestinians' plight and the moral costs of the ongoing occupation.[10] The military suppression methods adopted by the dominant Israeli army in the wake of the outbreak of the First Intifadah in December 1987 effectively reversed the image of David and Goliath, a powerful narrative adopted in the wake of the 1948 War to showcase Israel's miraculous victory at the hands of "an Arab Goliath"[11] – and one that had begun to be challenged with Israel's

---

[6] David Makovsky, *Making Peace with the PLO: The Rabin Government's Road to the Oslo Accord* (Boulder/San Francisco/Oxford: Westview Press, 1995), 220.

[7] Yossi Beilin, *Touching Peace: From the Oslo Accord to a Final Agreement* (London: George Weidenfeld & Nicholson, 1999), 268.

[8] Jonathan Rynhold, "Cultural Shift and Foreign Policy Change: Israel and the Making of the Oslo Accords," *Cooperation and Conflict* 42:4 (December 2007): 423/424.

[9] Shimon Peres, *Battling for Peace* (London: George Weidenfeld & Nicholson, 1995), 375.

[10] In the Gaza Strip, for example, slightly more than 5,000 recently arrived settlers living amid a population of 1.2 million Palestinians dominated a fifth of the land, used 30 percent of the water, prevented local economic development, blocked Palestinians from traveling on the roads, and deprived most of them of access to the sea. Ben-Eliezer, *Old Conflict, New War*, 31.

[11] Nur Masalha, *The Palestine Nakba: Decolonising History, Narrating the Subaltern, Reclaiming Memory* (London: Zed Books, 2012), 69, 70.

1982 invasion of Lebanon. Simultaneously, the Intifada challenged the sustainability of the status quo as the uprising not only put a strain on the Israeli economy but also posed a threat to Israelis' daily life and personal security, leading to a shift in public opinion. Polls conducted in the wake of the Intifadah thus showed that opposition to territorial compromise and direct negotiation with the PLO had declined dramatically.[12]

The altered perception of reality was closely related to the end of the Cold War. With the collapse of the Soviet Union, Israel's value as a "strategic asset" to the United States[13] was eroded.[14] Simultaneously, while the demise of the Soviet Union brought an end to the military and political patronage to Arab states, Israel continued to perceive a military threat from states on the periphery, principally Iran and Iraq, and, closer to home, from the military group Hamas.[15] In his memoirs on the Oslo Accords, Beilin notes that from the early 1990s, there was a growing fear that Hamas was "liable to take over the entire Palestinian camp."[16] The Oslo track, in Beilin's estimation, accordingly had the additional purpose of "preventing the domination by Hamas."[17]

Undoubtedly, the fourth and most decisive factor for the emergence of the Oslo process was the June 1992 election. Yitzhak Rabin, the leader of the Labor Party, effectively harnessed the burgeoning change in public opinion to the Intifadah and the Gulf War and the related fatigue from ongoing conflict. Rabin, who ran against the backdrop of the above-mentioned unfolding political events, promised voters to use the "window of opportunity" as "an end to bereavement, tears and pain"[18] With Rabin's election in 1992, Israelis, therefore, enabled, if ever so narrowly,[19] the creation of a government that dismissed Likud's former offer of "peace

---

[12] Before the Intifadah, around 20 percent of Israelis were willing to negotiate with the PLO if it recognized Israel and renounced terrorism. Following the Intifadah, this number rose, reaching a majority of the public in 1993. Rynhold, "Cultural Shift and Foreign Policy Change," 426; Hassan, "Oslo Accords," 67.

[13] For the United States, as Seth Anziska explains, the end of the Cold War and the victory in the Persian Gulf facilitated the Bush administration's move to begin negotiations in 1991. Moreover, the fall of the Soviet Union also helped embed an alternative view of the PLO as a Soviet proxy and the Palestinians as undeserving of statehood. Seth Anziska, *Preventing Palestine: A Political History from Camp David to Oslo* (Princeton: Princeton University Press, 2018), 268, 299.

[14] Hassan, "Oslo Accords," 67.   [15] Beilin, *Touching Peace*, 269.   [16] Ibid., 269.

[17] Ibid., 270.   [18] Ben-Eliezer, *Old Conflict, New War*, 35.

[19] The outcome of the June elections enabled Rabin to form a coalition government headed by Albor, which had won 44 seats, with Meretz (12 seats) and the ultra-orthodox Shas party (6 seats), which lead to a narrow majority of 62 seats in the 120-member Knesset. Ami Ayalon, ed., *Middle East Contemporary Survey, Volume XVI 1992* (Boulder/Oxford: Westview Press, 1995), 124.

for peace,"[20] and instead sought to make peace with the Palestinians on the basis of compromise.[21]

The Palestinian Road to Oslo

Israel's interlocutors during the peace negotiations had also faced crucial external and internal political and social developments in the pre-Oslo years. The Palestinian Liberation Organization, an umbrella organization founded in 1964 to represent the worlds' Palestinians, was in a weakened position in 1993 as a result of challenges to the organization's political leadership and the changing geopolitics of the Middle East in the post-Cold War era. One particular challenge to the PLO – led by Arafat – was the Palestinian uprising that erupted in Gaza in 1987 and quickly spread throughout the Occupied Territories (OT). This Intifadah proved a surprise to the PLO's leadership, which had been installed in Tunis following Israel's 1982 invasion of Lebanon.[22] Initiated and orchestrated by the "internal Palestinians" to oppose the occupation, the Intifadah, in the words of Geoffrey Watson, was a social revolution within Palestinian society.[23] Its attempt to challenge traditional forms of hierarchy and domination thus went hand in hand with a clear denunciation of the PLO's recent strategic shift away from military confrontation toward diplomacy.[24]

The PLO's alienation from Palestinian national politics and its failure to exert control over the events in the West Bank and Gaza signaled an immediate threat to the organizations' ability to influence Palestinian society, a menace which was heightened due to the politicization of groups within the OT. The Palestinian-American journalist Lamis Andoni reported that in the pre-Oslo years, the PLO was "facing the worst crisis since its inception [as] Palestinian groups – except for Fatah – and independents are distancing themselves from the PLO [and the] shrinking clique around Yasser Arafat."[25] Hamas and other Islamist groups, whose organizational strength and popularity in the OT had assumed substantial proportions by the early 1990s, formed the principal

---

[20] Mark Rosenblum, "Netanyahu and Peace: From Sound Bites to Sound Policies?" in *The Middle East and the Peace Process*, ed. Robert O. Freedman (Gainesville: University Press of Florida, 1998), 35.
[21] Peres, *Battling*, 375.
[22] Geoffrey R. Watson, *The Oslo Accords: International Law and the Israeli-Palestinian Peace Agreements* (Oxford/New York: Oxford University Press, 2000), 37, 38.
[23] Ibid., 38.   [24] Chomsky, "Oslo Accords," 3.   [25] Cited in ibid., 6.

Palestinian groups to challenge the PLO's leadership.[26] For the PLO, the increasing popularity of these groups threatened its claim of "expressing the people's wishes and speaking on their behalf."[27] As Seth Anziska notes, the desire to place the PLO back at the heart of the national struggle and restore political legitimacy, in addition to the leadership's disconnect from daily life under Israeli occupation, influenced Arafat's decision to sign on to an interim agreement – a "Faustian bargain" in Anziska's words – that would constrain sovereignty.[28]

The changing geopolitical trends in the immediate aftermath of the Cold War provide a direct causal link to the PLO's push toward the historic accord of 1993. For the PLO, similarly to the Israelis, the collapse of the USSR signaled far-reaching changes. As Peter Ezra Weinberger points out, whereas the Israelis were uncertain if they would continue to receive U.S. military and economic assistance in the new global climate, the PLO had completely lost the political and logistical support of its superpower patron: Russia.[29] The PLO could also no longer count on the financial and diplomatic support that had long been provided by Saudi Arabia and Kuwait due to Arafat's support for Saddam Hussein in the Gulf War. At the same time, this conflict, which lasted from 1990 to 1991, severely weakened the conventional fighting capabilities and nuclear potential of Iraq,[30] the only regional state that hitherto had been capable of rivaling Israeli military strength.[31]

While the above-mentioned developments created a clear interest for the PLO to enter into negotiations, it is important to note that by the early 1990s, internal Palestinian politics and external geopolitical factors generated viable conditions for peace negotiations. From as early as 1973, PLO officials were steadily moving toward diplomacy rather than armed struggle, which had shaped the movement in its early years.[32] By late 1988, the PLO had already taken steps in anticipation of holding direct talks with the Israelis. In November of that year, during a meeting of the quasi-parliamentary Palestinian National Council (PNC) in Algiers, the PLO renounced terrorism[33] and recognized the state of

---

[26] Mark A. Tessler, *A History of the Israeli–Palestinian Conflict* (Bloomington: Indiana University Press, 1994), 755.

[27] Mahmoud Abbas, *Through Secret Channels* (Reading: Garnet, 1995), 11.

[28] Anziska, *Preventing Palestine*, 282, 285.

[29] Peter Ezra Weinberger, "Co-opting the PLO: A Critical Reconstruction of the Oslo Accords, 1993–1995" (PhD Diss., London School of Economics, 2002), 17.

[30] Ibid., 18, 19.   [31] Tessler, *History*, 754.   [32] Anziska, *Preventing Palestine*, 289.

[33] This was followed by a speech from Arafat to the UN General Assembly and a subsequent press conference explicitly recognizing Israel's right to exist in peace and security and denouncing all forms of terrorism. Hassan, "Oslo Accords," 66.

Israel,[34] both preconditions for dialogue that had been set by the Americans in 1975.[35] Following the ejection of Iraq from Kuwait, America, for its part, was in a position to respond to the newly established PLO policy by committing itself to the conclusion of the Israeli–Palestinian conflict. Yet the success of the first Iraq war, which established "what we say goes" in the triumphant words of late President George H. W. Bush, could not be replicated in the 1991 Madrid Peace conference.[36] The negotiations, held between Israel and the "internal Palestinians," proved inconclusive, in part due to the interwoven nature of the bilateral and multilateral negotiation tracks.[37] In this context, the Norwegian bilateral track, first proposed by Arafat in 1979,[38] provided the PLO, in the words of the journalist Andoni, with the opportunity to assert its authority, "especially amid signs that the Israeli government could go the extra ten miles by talking directly to the PLO, thus salvaging for it the legitimacy it is losing internally."[39]

Public Reaction to the Oslo Accords

As previously noted, the Oslo I Accord was the first of several agreements that were made between mid-September 1993 and September 1999 following the exchange of letters of mutual recognition. This historic recognition "[of] their mutual and political rights," as the declaration's preamble read, was a first step toward "an end to decades of confrontation and conflict."[40] Yet the ultimate goal of the 1993 Declaration of Principles went

---

[34] It simultaneously declared an independent Palestinian state in the West Bank and Gaza and explicitly accepted both UN General Assembly Resolution 181 of 1947, the so-called "partition solution" calling for a two-state solution to the conflict and UN security council resolution 242, which demanded an Israeli withdrawal from occupied land in exchange for peace. The PLO declaration, which accepted the overwhelming international consensus on a diplomatic settlement, was virtually the same as the two-state solution brought to the Security Council in January 1976 by Egypt, Syria, and Jordan, and vetoed by the United States in 1980. Makovsky, *Making Peace with the PLO*, 8, 9; Chomsky, "Oslo Accords," 2.

[35] In 1975 Secretary of State Henry Kissinger formalized the PLO's marginalization with a 1975 ban on official engagement with the PLO that demanded an end to violence and the acceptance of UN resolutions that recognized Israel. Hassan, "Oslo Accords," 72; Anziska, *Preventing Palestine*, 289.

[36] Chomsky, "Oslo Accords," 1.   [37] Peres, *Battling*, 371.

[38] Hilde Henriksen Waage, "Norway's Role in the Middle East Peace Talks: Between a Strong State and a Weak Belligerent," *Journal of Palestine Studies* 24:4 (Summer 2005): 7.

[39] Cited in Chomsky, "Oslo Accords," 7.

[40] Israeli Ministry of Foreign Affairs, "Declaration of Principles," www.mfa.gov.il/mfa/foreignpolicy/peace/guide/pages/declaration%20of%20principles.aspx, accessed October 15, 2018.

beyond an end to strife, and the declaration further called for the achievement of "a just, lasting and comprehensive peace settlement and historic reconciliation through the agreed political process."[41]

Opinion polls conducted after the 1993 Oslo Accords showed a mixed reaction to the peace agreement. Both the Israeli administration and the PLO obtained legislative approval of the agreements fairly quickly. The Israeli Knesset, following a contentious debate, approved the accord on September 23, 1993 by a vote of 61–50;[42] the PLO central council in Tunis ratified the accord a few months later, on October 11 of that year. In Israeli and Palestinian society, however, public response to the accord diverged and was subject to change. An opinion poll held immediately after the signing of the DOP showed that 60 percent of Israelis supported the accord.[43] Two years later, only 37 percent of the public gave their support to the Interim Agreement.[44] These numbers cannot be seen in a vacuum; they are intimately connected to the public's security concerns. Thus, in December 1994, following suicide bombings perpetrated by Hamas,[45] 47 percent of respondents stated that Israel's security situation had worsened due to the peace process. The percentage of Jewish-Israeli respondents ranking peace as the most important issue also experienced a significant drop in the wake of Oslo I, dropping from 40 percent in June 1992 to 29 percent in January 1995.[46]

Reaction to the Oslo Accords among Palestinians within the Occupied Territories was also mixed, both among the public and among Islamist and left-wing political parties. Arafat encountered opposition from Hamas and Islamic Jihad groups that rejected the peace process in its entirety and vehemently opposed the Oslo Accords.[47] While supporting a

---

[41] Watson, *Oslo Accords*, 41.

[42] On the Israeli side, opposition came from the right-wing parties and all the religious parties. The vote in their favor in the Knesset or the Israeli Parliament obtained a majority of only one (61), with 50 opposed, including Ariel Sharon, and eight abstentions, including Ehud Barak, then a labor minister. Hassan, "Oslo Accords," 69.

[43] Tessler, *History*, 754.

[44] Nimrod Rosler, "Leadership and Peacemaking: Yitzhak Rabin and the Oslo Accords," *International Journal of Intercultural Relations* 54 (2016): 63.

[45] These attacks, according to the Israeli Ministry of Foreign Affairs, "undermined efforts to reach a peace accord." For a list of the dates and places of the attacks, see Galit M. Ben-Israel and Marina Shorer-Zeltser, "Telling a Story by Dry Statistics: Suicide Terror Attacks in Israel: (1993–2000)," in *Contemporary Suicide Terrorism: Origins, Trends and Ways of Tackling it*, ed. Tatiāňa Dronzina and Rachid El Houdaïgui (Amsterdam: IOS Press BV, 2012), 54. Israeli Ministry of Foreign Affairs, "The Real Face of Hamas," http://mfa.gov.il/MFA/ForeignPolicy/Issues/Pages/The-real-face-of-Hamas.aspx, accessed October 15, 2018.

[46] Rosler, "Leadership and Peacemaking," 63; Beilin, *Touching Peace*, 3.

[47] Hassan, "Oslo Accords," 69.

peace process with Israel, the Left in the Palestinian Territories, primarily consisting of the Popular Front for the Liberation of Palestine (PFLP) and the Democratic Front for the Liberation of Palestine (DFLP), opposed the Oslo Accord because of the absence of the mention of Palestinian statehood.[48] Even those close to Arafat did not refrain from criticizing the accord. Faisal Husseini, the unofficial PLO observer during the Madrid Negotiations and later the Palestinian National Authority's unofficial foreign minister, said that the accord "is definitely not the beginning that our people were looking for."[49] The Palestinian delegation head at Madrid, Abdel Shafi, was critical of the PLO's leadership for accepting an agreement that would permit Israel to continue its settlement program, "annexation and Judaization" of Jerusalem, and its "economic hegemony" over Palestinians.[50] Mahmoud Darwish, who had written the Palestinian Declaration of Independence in 1988, was equally critical of the accords and resigned from the PLO executive committee in August 1993, criticizing the agreement's fundamental ambiguity and its abandonment of core Palestinian interests. As the national poet exclaimed: "We have taken two generations to their death in the project of liberation and independence, and now it appears we are abandoning them completely."[51]

The results of public opinion polls conducted among Palestinians in the wake of the DOP were equally divergent. Varies polls, including one commissioned by CNN and French TV, reported that 66.4 percent of the 15,000 Palestinians surveyed in the West Bank and Gaza supported the accords, whereas only 29.3 percent expressed opposition.[52] According to another poll, 52 percent of the public supported the agreement while 35 percent were against it.[53] Similarly, reports on the population's response to the agreement, a further indication of the public mood, lacked uniformity. Research by Mark Tessler claims that the response was a jubilant one, as he wrote that "Palestinians celebrated throughout the West Bank and Gaza, flying flags that had previously been banned and

---

[48] Article I of the DOP states that the end result of the process is to be "a permanent settlement based on Security Council Resolutions 242 and 338." Resolutions 242 and 338 say nothing at all about Palestinian rights, apart from a reference to a "just settlement of the refugee problem." Chomsky, "Oslo Accords," 8.
[49] Lawrence Joffe, "Faisal Husseini," *The Guardian*, May 31, 2001, www.theguardian.com/news/2001/jun/01/guardianobituaries.israel, accessed October 15, 2018.
[50] Clyde Haberman, "Major Figures on Both Sides Questioning Israel–P.L.O. Talks," *The New York Times*, April 26, 1994, A00011.
[51] Mahmoud Darwish, "Resigning from the PLO Executive Committee," in *The Israel-Arab Reader: A Documentary History of the Middle East Conflict*, ed. Walter Laqueur and Barry Rubin (New York: Penguin Books, 2016), 373, 374.
[52] Tessler, *History*, 754.   [53] Ben-Eliezer, *Old Conflict, New War*, 37.

displaying T-shirts and posters with pictures of Yasir Arafat over slogans calling for peace."[54] Conversely, Youssef Ibrahim, who reported for the *New York Times*, found that PLO representatives "were pelted with stones by Palestinian youths as they rode into [Jericho] in Israeli army jeeps."[55]

Implementing the Oslo Accords

The DOP foresaw that the agreement's completion would occur following a five-year transitional period. During this interim period, the declaration called for a gradual transfer of power from Israel to the PA, which would begin upon the Israeli army's withdrawal from the Gaza Strip and Jericho area. Permanent status negotiations on the most difficult – and controversial – issues, namely Jerusalem, final borders, Israeli settlements, the Palestinian refugee issue, and security arrangements, were to begin two years after the Israeli withdrawal from Jericho and Gaza, which occurred on May 4, 1994.[56] Crucially, the declaration stipulated in Article V of the DOP that "the two parties agree that the outcome of the permanent status negotiations should not be prejudiced or preempted by agreements reached for the interim period."[57] Simply put, while the objective was defined, the end result and the path to its implementation were left ambiguous in the declaration.

The transfer of power, according to the DOP, was to take place in four stages. The first stage consisted of an Israeli withdrawal from Jericho and Gaza, which would facilitate the second stage: the transfer of some civil authority and responsibility to the Palestinian Authority. The PA's authority, as specified in the declaration's articles, was to extend over "the West Bank and Gaza Strip territory, except for issues that will be negotiated in the permanent status negotiations: Jerusalem, settlements, military locations, and Israelis."[58] The third stage was to constitute an interim agreement on the implementation of the DOP while the final and

---

[54] Tessler, *History*, 754.   [55] Chomsky, "Oslo Accords," 7.
[56] Watson, *Oslo Accords*, 41.
[57] Makovsky, *Making Peace with the PLO*, 206; Israeli Ministry of Foreign Affairs, "Declaration of Principles," www.mfa.gov.il/mfa/foreignpolicy/peace/guide/pages/declaration%20of%20principles.aspx, accessed October 15, 2018.
[58] Israeli Ministry of Foreign Affairs, "Declaration of Principles," www.mfa.gov.il/mfa/foreignpolicy/peace/guide/pages/declaration%20of%20principles.aspx, accessed October 15, 2018. According to the 1994 Agreement on the Gaza Strip and Jericho Area, "Israeli military forces and civilians may continue to use roads freely within the Gaza Strip and the Jericho area." Israeli Ministry of Foreign Affairs, "Agreement on Gaza Strip and Jericho Area," www.mfa.gov.il/mfa/foreignpolicy/peace/guide/pages/agreement%20on%20gaza%20strip%20and%20jericho%20area.aspx, accessed October 15, 2018.

most complicated stage involved an agreement of "permanent status arrangement" – or a final settlement of the aforementioned final status issues.[59]

Implementation of the first stage of the declaration took longer than anticipated. Although the Israeli administration and the PLO had obtained legislative approval of the agreements, talks between the two parties to implement the declaration dragged on for months, and the withdrawal process was delayed until April 4, 1994, when the Israeli army, the Israeli Defense Forces (IDF), began withdrawing from their headquarters in Jericho and Gaza. Exactly a month later, the PLO and Israel met in Cairo, where they signed the Agreement on Gaza Strip and the Jericho Area. This "Cairo Agreement" called for a full Israeli withdrawal from these territories within a period of three weeks.[60] The Gaza–Jericho agreement further established a Palestinian self-governing entity, called the Palestinian Authority – also known as the Palestinian National Authority (PNA) – to which Israel had agreed to transfer limited civil authority. In the wake of his return to Gaza after twenty-seven years of exile, Arafat, as president of the PA, and Israel signed an agreement on August 29, 1994 providing for the transfer of six spheres of civil authority to the PA: education and culture, health, social welfare, tourism, direct taxation, and VAT on local production. Under this agreement, fully titled the "Agreement on Preparatory Transfer of Powers and Responsibilities," the PA's power over these spheres extended beyond Gaza and Jericho; it encompassed the entire West Bank, except that it did not extend to "Jerusalem, settlements, military locations and, unless otherwise provided in this Agreement, Israelis."[61]

The next major step in implementing the Oslo I Accord took place on September 28, 1995, when PLO and Israeli delegates traveled to Taba and – four days later – Washington to sign the Interim Agreement of the Declaration of Principles, better known as Oslo II. Oslo II sought to provide the tools to challenge the dichotomous nature of in-conflict societies and help both group members overcome psychological barriers inhibiting progress toward peace.[62] The interim agreement thus required both Israel and the Palestinians to pay due regard to "internationally-accepted norms ... of human rights" and to collaborate on security matters.[63] The Palestinians were equally obliged to amend the

---

[59] Watson, *Oslo Accords*, 41/2.   [60] Ibid., 42.
[61] Ibid., 43, 44; Israeli Ministry of Foreign Affairs, "Agreement on Preparatory Transfer of Powers and Responsibilities," www.mfa.gov.il/mfa/foreignpolicy/peace/guide/pages/agreement%20on%20preparatory%20transfer%20of%20powers%20and%20re.aspx, accessed October 15, 2018.
[62] Rosler, "Leadership and Peacemaking," 55, 56.   [63] Watson, *Oslo Accords*, 45/4.

Palestinian National Charter by removing anti-Semitic and anti-Israeli clauses.[64] Oslo II also provided a key legal framework that was intended to supersede previous agreements and become the basis for subsequent negotiations and the preliminary of an eventual comprehensive peace agreement. Built on the foundations of Oslo I, Oslo II contained an interim agreement on the West Bank and the Gaza Strip, which stipulated that these territories constituted one territorial unit – with the exclusion of Jerusalem – and that the boundaries still had to be drawn.[65] Oslo II further rendered control over the majority of the Palestinian population to the PA.[66] The IDF was to retain security control over 73 percent of the West Bank and its 140 Jewish settlements, which were to remain under Israeli jurisdiction.[67]

The interim agreement laid down important legal principles for the mechanisms of Palestinian self-government in the Palestinian Territories. Oslo II called for the creation of an elected eighty-two-person Palestinian council to supersede the earlier-established PA. It further stipulated that a president – designated *ra'īs*[68] in Arabic – would be elected to serve as head of a twenty-four-person executive authority, most of whose members would come from the council and all of whom would be appointed by the president. In the aftermath of the first elections in January 1996, PLO Chairman Arafat presided over a newly formed Palestinian executive authority while Arafat's Fatah faction made up the majority of members of the new council.[69]

In order to allow for the Palestinian self-government in compliance with principles of Oslo II, the Israeli redeployment in the West Bank, similarly to the transfer of power, was to be completed in four phases. The first phase, which was to be finalized before the elections of the Palestinian council, involved redeployment from populated areas in the West Bank. The three further redeployments of Israeli troops to "specified military locations" would take place at six-month intervals.[70] Despite Israel's

---

[64] The United Nations Information System on the Question of Palestine, *Chronological Review of Events Relating to the Question of Palestine: Monthly Media Monitoring Review* (UNISPAL, January 1998).

[65] Hassan, "Oslo Accords," 69.

[66] The interim agreement superseded the Gaza–Jericho agreement and the agreement on transfer of civilian responsibility though most provisions of those agreements were incorporated into the text or annexes of the interim agreement.

[67] Ben-Eliezer, *Old Conflict, New War*, 42/3.

[68] Although the official language of the Oslo accords has always been English, the Arabic word *ra'īs* (Arabic: رئیس) was chosen as a compromise between the Palestinian preference for president and the Israeli preference for chairman, a term that would not so clearly connote a head of state. Watson, *Oslo Accords*, 45.

[69] Ibid., 46.   [70] Ibid., 45.

withdrawal of forces from six[71] urban areas by the end of 1995, Israeli withdrawal from Hebron was postponed for almost a year, thereby also delaying the subsequent disengagement, which was contingent on the completion of the first withdrawal phase.

The deadlock over Hebron was broken on January 15, 1997, when Israel, now led by Benjamin Netanyahu, and the PLO signed the Protocol Concerning Redeployment in Hebron. This protocol provided that Israeli forces would retain control of the section of the city populated by Jewish settlers as well as the area containing the Tomb of the Patriarchs, a holy place for Muslims and Jews alike.[72] Following a rescheduling of "further redeployment" to March 1997, the peace process, once again, came to halt. This time, Palestinian leaders charged Israel with prejudging the status of East-Jerusalem, an issue reserved for final status negotiations, following the Israeli government's announcement to construct housing in East Jerusalem.[73]

After an additional eighteen-month standstill during which important deadlines were missed, the parties agreed to resume negotiations. At the Wye River Resort in Eastern Maryland, the Jordanian King Hussein and President Clinton forged a breakthrough. The resulting Wye River Memorandum, signed on October 23, 1998, set forth a detailed timeline to fulfill and concretize the obligations agreed upon during the interim agreement.[74] Rather than simply calling on Israel to redeploy to "specified military locations," the memorandum defined the specific size of the first two of three deployments. The Palestinians, in turn, were obliged to take concrete steps to outlaw and combat terrorist organizations, to prohibit illegal weapons, to prevent incitement of violence, to cooperate in security and law enforcement matters, and to amend their charter.[75]

While PNC did amend its charter by deleting provisions[76] calling for the destruction of Israel and other anti-Israel references,[77] the Netanyahu government – following the first redeployment – charged the PA with failing to fulfill its obligations on terrorism and security, once again derailing the

---

[71] These were: Jenin, Nablus, Tulkarem, Kalkilya, Ramallah, and Bethlehem.
[72] Ibid., 48.   [73] Ibid., 49.   [74] Ibid., 52.   [75] Ibid.
[76] For instances of anti-Israel statements, see, for example, the Palestinian charter of 1964 and 1968, which says "The liberation of Palestine from the Arab viewpoint is a national duty to repulse the Zionist, imperialist invasion from the great Arab homeland and to purge it from the Zionist presence." Palestinian Ministry of Information, *The Palestinian Charter* (Palestine Ministry of Information, June 1999).
[77] Rosenblum, "Netanyahu and Peace," 55; Deborah Sontag, "Clinton in the Mideast: The Overview; Clinton Watches as Palestinians Drop Call for Israel's Destruction," *The New York Times*, December 15, 1998, www.nytimes.com/1998/12/15/world/clinton-mideast-overview-clinton-watches-palestinians-drop-call-for-israel-s.html, accessed October 15, 2018.

redeployment. Upon taking office in May 1999, Netanyahu's successor, Labor politician Ehud Barak, made one final push toward a final agreement.[78] On September 4, Barak's administration concluded a new agreement with the PLO at the Egyptian Red Sea resort of Sharm el-Sheikh. According to the Sharm el-Sheikh Memorandum, Israel agreed to resume withdrawals according to a new schedule; the memorandum also codified Barak's goal of reaching a final status agreement by the fall of 2000, a year-and-a-half after the original deadline set in Oslo I.[79] With the outbreak of the Second Intifadah in September of 2000 in the West Bank, however, the peace process came to another standstill, and the deadlines offered in the memorandum were never met.

The Failures of the Oslo Accords Explained

The picture perfect handshake on the White House lawn was, as indicated above, hardly suggestive of the years that followed the signing of the DOP. Indeed, the effective state of war after two decades of peace negotiations is, as Sean F. McMahon notes, paradoxical for the dominant reading of the Oslo Process.[80] Yet an analysis of the ideological framework and diplomatic power dynamics accompanying the Norwegian-led negotiations and the accord's resulting legal composition – both its interim nature and its adoption of constructive ambiguity principles – provide insight into the accord's hitherto failure. Yehouda Shenhav, Bashir Bashir, and Nadim Khoury convincingly argue that the deliberations' adoption of the "language of 1967"[81] – or a solution premised on the borders of the Green Line – eliminated chances for sincere dialogue through sentencing the origins of the conflict, and Palestinians' watershed around which they shape their memory of the conflict as well as the vista for its resolution, to oblivion.[82] In a 2010 article, former chief Palestinian negotiator Saeb Erekat emphasized the continued importance of the Nakba to the conflict, stating that future negotiations need to include Israeli "recognition of Palestinian refugee rights and its agreement to provide reparation and meaningful refugee choice in the exercise of these rights [as this] will mark

---

[78] Watson, *Oslo Accords*, 52, 53.
[79] Anthony H. Cordesman, *The Israeli–Palestinian War: Escalating to Nowhere* (Westport, CT/London: Praeger Security International, 2005), 8.
[80] Sean F. McMahon, *The Discourse of Palestinian–Israeli Relations: Persistent Analytics and Practices* (New York/London: Routledge Taylor & Francis Group, 2010), 150.
[81] Yehouda Shenhav, *Beyond the Two-State Solution: A Jewish Political Essay* (Cambridge: Polity Press, 2012), 1, 2.
[82] Ibid.

the beginning of a new reality [and] lead to a lasting peace."[83] Conversely, in the words of Raef Zreik, the Oslo framework dictated that "the problem was one of the occupation of 1967, as though it all started then; no refugees, no Nakba [and] one may argue that Israel wanted to close the file of 1948 without opening it in the first instance; to buy 1948 with the currency of 1967."[84] The imposition of a "hegemonic epistemology"[85] centered on 1967 as a watershed did not only neutralize history and memory, but also reduced Palestine geographically to the territories of the West Bank and the Gaza Strip and the Palestinians politically to the residents of these territories.[86] Paradoxically, the Oslo Accords thus placed the issue of national narratives on the political agenda – and in the public space – only to impose two "partitioned narratives, mirroring the territorial separation along the Green Line."[87] It is the replication of this same asymmetrical power structure in the accord and its dependency on confidence-building measures that allowed the politics of the post-Oslo era to challenge the practical implementation of a final status agreement.[88]

The peace deal's replication of the material power structures cannot be understood without examining the role of the Norwegian intermediaries. The Norwegians, as Hilde Henriksen Waage illustrates, saw themselves as suitable agents to promote conflict resolution because of the country's international status as a small, impartial actor due to its own strategic oil resources and because of its strong links of support for both Israel and the PLO. Nevertheless, Norway's move from facilitator to active mediator in April 1993[89] led to a replication of the power dynamics in favor of Israel,

---

[83] In this same article, Erekat also noted that "The fact that Israel bears responsibility for the creation of the refugees is beyond argument (and) al-Nakba or 'the catastrophe,' is the seminal Palestinian experience and source of our collective identity." Saeb Erekat, "The Returning Issue of Palestine's Refugees," *The Guardian*, December 10, 2010, www .theguardian.com/commentisfree/2010/dec/10/israel-palestine-refugee-rights, accessed August 16, 2016.

[84] Zreik, "Settler Become a Native," 361.

[85] Bashir Bashir, "Neutralizing History and Memory in Divided Societies: The Case of Making Peace in Palestine/Israel," in *The Goodness Regime*, ed. by Jamana Manna and Sille Storihle (New York, Berlin: Strenberg Press, 2016), 26.

[86] Ibid. Also see Ingrid Baukhol, "Security and Fear in Israeli and Palestinian Conflict Narratives: A Social-Psychological Study" (MA thesis, University of Gothenburg, 2015), 9. Baukhol argues that the breakdown in Israeli–Palestinian negotiations can, at least partially, be blamed on the fact that the negotiations during the 1990s did not take socio-psychological aspects into consideration.

[87] Khoury, "Holocaust," 126.   [88] Weinberger, "Co-opting the PLO," 47.

[89] When Johan Holst took over as Norway's foreign minister in April 1993, he began virtually to run the Oslo process, moving Norway's involvement from "facilitator" to active "mediator." Moreover, Haage points out, PLO leaders (including Arafat, as far back as 1979) had tried to interest Norway in mediation between the two parties. Hilde Henriksen Waage, "Postscript to Oslo: The Mystery of Norway's Missing Files," *Journal of Palestine Studies* 38:1 (2008): 60.

both within the negotiations and in the resulting accord. As a weak, third-party without the diplomatic leverage of a superpower, Norway was forced to play by the rules of the stronger party – Israel[90] – if it wanted to play a role in the process.[91] Documents written by officials involved in the peace negotiations reveal that the Norwegian foreign minister's role was that of persuading the Palestinians to accept what they were being offered by Israel by "softening the position of Arafat" to the Israeli viewpoint.[92] The role adopted by Norway was not dictated by sympathy for Israel; neither was it because the Norwegians necessarily agreed with the positions put forward. Rather, as Beilin noted, the Norwegian foreign minister was prepared "to do anything in his power to prevent the talks from collapsing"[93] in a bid to promote the country as an effective conflict mediator on the world stage and to protect its role in the process.[94]

The Role of Constructive Ambiguity in the Peace Process

The asymmetrical power structure present during the negotiations was reflected in the end product.[95] While the structure of the Oslo accord aimed to give basic satisfiers to the Palestinian, it provided no institutional mechanisms to advance their positions on final status issues;[96] neither did it offer a concrete termination of the interim phase or a clause terminating the accord.[97] As Anziska notes, Arafat's acceptance of limited self-rule through the establishment of an interim PA diluted central elements of the Palestinian national struggle and virtually guaranteed Israel's continued settlement expansion in the territories, further eroding the basis of what might emerge as a sovereign, independent nation-state.[98]

The theoretical concept driving the interim structure of the accord was based on the need for "constructive ambiguity." As Shamir Hassan explains, the underlying foundation driving the initial agreement on principles was that the two sides were not yet ready for a full peace

---

[90] As Dennis Ross remarked: "Norway had to embrace the Israeli position. It would be no deal otherwise." Given the asymmetry of power, Norway could either play this role or not play. It chose to play. Cited in Waage, "Norway's Role in the Middle East Peace Talks," 19.

[91] Waage, "Postscript to Oslo," 63.

[92] Waage, "Norway's Role in the Middle East Peace Talks," 14.   [93] Ibid.

[94] Peace-making became one of the country's chief exports, with Norwegians becoming involved in peace processes from Guatemala and Columbia to Sudan, from Sri Lanka to Cyprus and former Yugoslavia. Waage, "Postscript to Oslo," 55.

[95] Weinberger, "Co-opting the PLO," 17.   [96] Ibid., 20.

[97] Watson, *Oslo Accords*, 248.   [98] Anziska, *Preventing Palestine*, 299, 300.

38 The Post-Oslo Period: A Historical Overview

agreement and, therefore, "an interim period was needed during which to build mutual trust."[99] With the limited agenda of the Oslo Accords and the postponement of final status issues, it was also the intention that attitudes would soften, making compromise more likely.[100] In his work *Irreversible Peace*, the political scientist Jonathan Stevenson[101] argues that "the maintenance of peace does not depend on any written agreement or visions of permanence (for these diverge), but on the political process engendered by [a] peace process itself," thereby also providing the theoretical foundations for proponents of the trust-building measures encompassed in the Oslo Accords.[102] Yet as the asymmetry of power was preserved and reproduced in the agreement, any progress – or the evaluation of the confidence-building progress – depended largely on Israel's assessment of the Palestinian performance.[103]

The Oslo agreement's interim nature – or the "decision not to decide"[104] – was in many regards a continuation of the architecture of the Camp David Accords, which called for full autonomy for the Palestinians within a transitional period of five years without offering the defined mechanisms, or territorial definition, for Palestinian statehood.[105] Indeed, although Israel's willingness to engage in final status negotiations down the road was considered a significant concession,[106] the process of constructive ambiguity meant that the terms were more favorable to the Israelis. By situating the agreement on nebulous ground in which multiple outcomes were deemed available, Elyakim Rubinstein, chief negotiator for the Israelis, pointed out that the accord allowed for the option of Israeli sovereignty over the territories[107] – in direct contravention with what the Palestinians desired as the final outcome: a

---

[99] Hassan, "Oslo Accords," 67, 68.
[100] Each side viewed this as a major concession on its part – for the Israelis that they would even agree to discuss those three issues; for the PLO, that they would be willing to defer them for several years. Makovsky, *Making Peace with the PLO*, 141.
[101] Conversely, Aaron Klieman argues that "proper construction of agreements and the careful precise wording of declarations, protocols, or binding treaty accords has its own cogency." Aaron S. Klieman, *Constructive Ambiguity in Middle East Peace-Making* (Tel Aviv University, Tami Steinmetz Center for Peace Research, 1999), 12.
[102] Jonathan Stevenson, "Irreversible Peace in Northern Ireland?," *Survival* 42:3 (2002): 19.
[103] Waage, "Norway's Role in the Middle East Peace Talks," 17, 18.
[104] Anziska, *Preventing Palestine*, 301.
[105] As Anziska argues: "The link between Camp David, the autonomy talks, and the Oslo Accords is almost entirely absent (but) in the view of former Israeli Knesset member and political Naomi Chazan, Camp David indirectly curtailed ... the prospects of territorial compromise in the West Bank and Gaza." Anziska, *Preventing Palestine*, 301.
[106] Waage, "Norway's Role in the Middle East Peace Talks," 17.
[107] Rosenblum, "Netanyahu and Peace," 36.

Palestinian state.[108] While the DOP set in motion the end of Israeli rule over the Palestinian Territories, an Israeli clause incorporated in the agreement thus would enable ongoing settlement expansion before permanent status negotiations.[109] The shelving of the most contentious issues, which chiefly reflected Palestinian national interests, constituted a clear strategic win for Israel as it was able to use the interim arrangement to drive a self-envisioned conclusion and create what the forensic architect Eyal Weizman has called "prosthetic sovereignty."[110] For the Palestinians, the Israeli formalization of a clear ceiling to Palestinian self-rule – based on a non-territorial definition of autonomy, not viable statehood – not only exacerbated conditions on the ground, but equally revealed the difficulty in Palestinians' attempts to "negotiate their own way out of occupation."[111]

Palestinian Politics in the Wake of Oslo

The characterization of Palestinian politics as solely a product of the conflict with Israel risks, as Nathan Brown has previously noted, doing a disservice to those involved in working for change and "seriously miscasting the issues."[112] Nevertheless, any analysis of the Palestinian politics in the post-Oslo era cannot escape the political context laid down in the wake of the 1993 Oslo Accords, which led to a measure of self-government in the Occupied Palestinian Territories – albeit one which continued to be heavily constricted. Indeed, with the signing of the Oslo Accords, Palestinians living in Gaza and the West Bank were exposed to a new political reality.[113] The newly founded PA was accorded some jurisdiction over the 2.5 million Palestinians living in these areas; however, the extent of authority depended on administrative divisions according to the Oslo II Accords, which divided the West Bank into Areas A, B, and C.[114] While the resulting institution-building in Areas

---

[108] Ashrawi was certain that Israelis would exploit their powers as occupiers "to the hilt" so that by the time final status negotiations discussing Palestinian statehood began, Israel would be left with great sections of Palestinian territory. Hanan Ashrawi, *This Side of Peace* (New York: Touchstone, 1995), 261.

[109] Anziska, *Preventing Palestine*, 263.

[110] Eyal Weizman cited in Anziska, *Preventing Palestine*, 284   [111] Ibid., 304.

[112] Brown, *Palestinian Politics after the Oslo Accords*, 5.

[113] George Giacaman, "In the Throes of Oslo: Palestinian Society, Civil Society and the Future," in *After Oslo: New Realities, Old Problems*, ed. George Giacaman and Dag Jørund Lønning (London: Pluto Press, 1998), 4.

[114] Watson, *Oslo Accords*, 243.

A and B,[115] which administer full civil control and – in Area A – security control to the PA, were the direct outcome of the peace accords, the foundations for Palestinian government had been laid in the preceding decades and were distinctly rooted in a Palestinian and broader Arab context.[116] As will become evident in section one of this work, in the realm of education, Palestinian officials examined Arab countries' educational systems and relied heavily on the Jordan education system in the West Bank as a practical interim solution during the formation of Palestinian textbooks. Perceiving the replication of Arab state-building principles across Palestinian society, Brown has argued that the 1993 accords were not perceived as the source of Palestinian institution-building or legitimacy by Palestinians, but rather as a necessary means to obtain Israeli and international recognition.[117]

The 1996 democratic elections ratified in the accords offer a prime example of the historical foundations of post-Oslo institutions and, simultaneously, provide insight into the current political rift between Hamas and Fatah. In January 1996, for the first time, democratic elections were held for the Palestinian Legislative Council. The PLO, which had been established in 1964 and the words of Abbas constituted "the offspring of the Arab regimes,"[118] won sixty-eight out of eighty-eight seats. For Uri Ben-Elzier, the PLO's decisive 1996 victory is indicative of Palestinian society's support for peace and rejection of "the terrorist ways of Hamas."[119] Nevertheless, this statement precludes an understanding of the political role of opposition parties in the wake of the Oslo Accords. Palestinian opposition parties were paralyzed as a result of the Oslo agreements. Not only had they found themselves outside the realm of peace negotiations due to their unwillingness to "follow the lead of Yasser Arafat,"[120] but most – especially those on the Left – also did not join the election for the Palestinian Legislative Council in 1996 and were

---

[115] The accords confer on the Palestinians jurisdiction only over the territory of Areas A and B, plus functional jurisdiction over a wide variety of matters in Area C – but not over any matters in Jerusalem. See articles IX–XVII–XVIII in Israeli Ministry of Foreign Affairs, "The Israeli–Palestinian Interim Agreement on the West Bank and the Gaza Strip (Oslo II)," www.mfa.gov.il/mfa/foreignpolicy/peace/guide/pages/the%20israeli-palestinian%20interim%20agreement.aspx, accessed October 15, 2018.

[116] Since signing the first Oslo Accord in 1993, Brown argues that the Palestinian leadership has sought to ground institutional development not in the agreements with Israel, but instead in the much older process of state building in the Arab world. Where Palestinian antecedents were insufficient or needed to be updated, PNA officials tended to turn to the examples set by Arab countries, especially Jordan and Egypt. Brown, *Palestinian Politics after the Oslo Accords*, 14, 8.

[117] Ibid., 7.   [118] Abbas, *Through Secret Channels*, 11.

[119] Ben-Eliezer, *Old Conflict, New War*, 48.   [120] Giacaman, "In the Throes of Oslo," 4.

unable to stop or influence the political direction.[121] At the same time, the opposition was not able to mobilize public support to influence the political process from their position outside the Arafat-dominated system.[122]

Palestinian political institutions' widespread corruption practices further complicated the administrative ability of regulatory control and oversight. In 1997, the PNA's General Control Institute published a report – dubbed the "Corruption Report" – for the PLC in which it detailed administrative and accounting irregularities in most ministries and agencies. A wide range of misconduct was uncovered. As Brown previously demonstrated, some of the misdeeds involved inefficiency, such as unclear policies and responsibilities and inadequate monitoring in many government offices; some involved wasteful extravagance, such as renting overly lavish offices and furniture.[123] At times the corruption was personal and small scale, and included overuse of international telephone lines and personal use of ministry cars, while at other times the corruption was on a larger scale and – in an overt display of crony capitalism – involved padding the pockets of business elites.[124] Two years after the publication of the PNA study, in June 1999, a report co-sponsored by the American Council on Foreign Relations and chaired by Michel Rocard, the former French prime minister, found similar instances of corruption in the upper echelons of the Palestinian authority.[125] In its criticism of Palestinian political institutions, the report noted that the PA's interdependence on the peace process – and thus its direct interlocutor – had weakened concern for "budgetary priorities and undermined proper regard for human rights and the rule of law," further stating that the PA's limited power "affects the development and functioning of its executive, legislative, and judicial branches of government."[126]

In the report's aftermath, Arafat's wariness of internal dissent became clear. In November 1999, twenty prominent Palestinians signed a petition condemning the authority's corruption and abuse of its own citizens. Arafat responded by throwing most of the dissidents in jail.[127] Almost

---

[121] Ibid., 8.   [122] Ibid., 13.
[123] Elliot Abrams, "Corruption in the Palestinian Authority," *Council on Foreign Relations*, April 5, 2018, www.cfr.org/blog/corruption-palestinian-authority, accessed October 15, 2018.
[124] Brown, *Palestinian Politics after the Oslo Accords*, 108.   [125] Ibid., 1.
[126] Michel Rocard, Henry Siegman, Yezid Sayigh, and Khalil Shikaki, *Independent Task Force Report: Strengthening Palestinian Public Institutions* (New York: Council on Foreign Relations, 1999), 25.
[127] Edward W. Said, *The End of the Peace Process: Oslo and After* (New York Vintage Book, 2001), xiv.

twenty years later, Palestinian society remains marred by corruption, as highlighted in yearly reports published by the Coalition for Accountability and Integrity (AMAN). In its 2017 report, AMAN discusses the PA's squandering of public funds.[128] The report revealed that the PA spent about $11 million on the PLC; however, half of that money went to salaries for the Palestinian lawmakers even though the parliament has failed to play a tangible role due to the decade-long dispute between Fatah and Hamas.[129]

One of the accusations leveled at Arafat by his critics centered on Israel's ongoing dominance over Palestinian society and its perceived consolidation of control over the Occupied Territories during the interim period.[130] This complex system of cooptation, as Weinberger termed the existing Palestinian sub-sovereignty arrangement,[131] provided Israel with the means to bring the PLO into a position of substantial authority, albeit under an Israeli-dictated aegis.[132] Invoking a powerful figure of controversy, Sheik Na'ef Rajoub, imam of Dura and brother of Jibril Rajoub, head of the Palestinian Preventative Security Organization, even suggested in 1996 that Oslo was turning Arafat into an Antoine Lahad, a Lebanese national who fell subject to national criticism in his home country following his collaboration with – and subsequent move to – Israel.[133]

Israel's continual control over daily Palestinian life – and thereby the extent of Palestinian statehood – in the post-Oslo years is perhaps best illustrated with reference to restrictions on individuals' movement. The limitations of statehood are obvious for a Palestinian attempting to travel from Gaza to Ramallah in the West Bank. Travel between the Occupied Territories, and inside the West Bank itself, involves going through

---

[128] Coalition for accountability and Integrity-AMAN, *Tenth Annual Report Integrity and Combating Corruption Palestine 2017* (Ramallah: Aman, 2017), 67, 68.

[129] As the report notes, "It is the right of citizens to inquire about the feasibility of these expenses without tangible results of the role of the PLC, and its failure to hold sessions that include members of Parliament in the West Bank and Gaza, in accordance with the law." Ibid., 68.

[130] Edward Said, in a similar vein, noted that Oslo's fatal flaw was that it provided a framework that perpetuated Israeli control over the Occupied Territories. Cited in Hassan, "Oslo Accords," 70; Weinberger, "Co-opting the PLO," 11.

[131] Weinberger, "Co-opting the PLO," 15.   [132] Ibid., 11.

[133] Lahad headed the pro-Israel militia, the South Lebanon Army from 1984 until 2000, which fought the PLO and later Hezbollah during the Lebanese civil war. Following Israel's withdrawal of Southern Lebanon in 2000, Lahad fled to Israel. Laleh Khalili, *Time in the Shadows: Confinement in Counterinsurgencies* (Stanford: Stanford University Press, 2013), 110; Ada Ushpiz, "Alas, the Authority Has Finished Us," *Haaretz*, August 9, 1996, B2.

Israeli-manned security checkpoints, which were introduced to the land-scape in the 1990s.[134] As such, Palestinian movement is dependent on Israeli permission.[135] The geographic land division that has emerged in the West Bank also reflects the limitations of Palestinian sovereignty; the territory under Palestinian civil control and security authority amounts to only 18 percent of the land.[136] With the fate of Israeli settlements and borders confined to final status negotiations, about seven discontinu-ous Palestinian islands have emerged which are surrounded by Israeli-controlled territory and bypass roads designated for Israeli settler usage.[137]

Israeli Politics in the Post-Oslo Era

Whereas the establishment of a Palestinian state depended on the struc-ture, interpretation, and implementation of the Oslo agreements, the accords would stand to affect the Israeli borders, not its existence.[138] At the same time, the interim nature of the accords and their intended constructive ambiguity meant that post-Oslo internal politics – and cor-responding changes in public opinion – largely dictated the extent of the accords' implementation. The slew of Hamas-perpetrated bombings inside Israel in the years following Oslo I, for instance, constituted a formidable challenge to the peace camp. Baruch Goldstein's massacre of twenty-nine Palestinians in the Cave of the Patriarchs in Hebron in February 1994 was a crucial turning point. Prior to the massacre, as a general rule, Hamas attacked military targets, not civilians. However, in retaliation for the Hebron attack by the Brooklyn-born Jewish settler, the movement launched a series of devasting suicide bombings inside Israel, killing dozens of civilians.[139] These suicide bombings, which occurred from 1994 onwards and were categorized as "Arab terror," led many Israelis to once again adopt the dichotomous characterization of "us" versus "them."[140] As one reader in the daily newspaper *Yedioth Ahronot* wrote: "Why do we need these Arabs, the solution is one: driving them out."[141] In the wake of the Goldstein massacre and the extreme violence

---

[134] Helga Tawil-Souri, "Qalandia Checkpoint: The Historical Geography of a Non-Place," *Jerusalem Quarterly* 42 (2010): 32.

[135] Brown, *Palestinian Politics after the Oslo Accords*, 14.

[136] The Wye River Agreement signed in October 1998 was supposed to give Palestinians about 10 percent more land but was never implemented. Said, *End of the Peace Process*, xv; 294.

[137] Ibid., xv.   [138] Giacaman, "In the Throes of Oslo," 5.

[139] Michael I. Karpin, *Imperfect Compromise: A New Consensus among Israelis and Palestinians* (Washington, DC: Potomac Books, 2013), 121.

[140] Ben-Eliezer, *Old Conflict, New War*, 44.   [141] Cited in ibid.

it precipitated, the vociferous expression of these views became com-monplace.[142] A *New York Times* article of 1994 described these chal-lenges to the peace process, noting that there was a growing fraction of those who "shared the passions that drove Goldstein," or as one the interviewees put it, "If he stopped these so-called peace talks, then he is truly holy because this is not real peace."[143]

Even though the terrorist attacks in Israel were the work of Hamas and Islamic Jihad, opponents of the peace process sought to persuade the public that they presented formidable proof that the Palestinians did not want peace and that the PA was incapable of executing control over its people.[144] Blame was also attributed to the Israeli Left and its leaders.[145] Anti-Oslo demonstrations were marked by declarations of incitement against Rabin. On October 5, 1995, one of these rallies saw demonstra-tors flocking to Zion Square in the center of Jerusalem, where partici-pants screamed "Death to Rabin," burned his portrait and distributed a photomontage showing the prime minister in an SS uniform.[146] Rabin also received incendiary pushback from his contemporary political opponents. Likud Leader Benjamin Netanyahu accused Rabin of estab-lishing a "Palestinian terrorist state" and compared Oslo to Neville Chamberlain's appeasement of Adolf Hitler, telling Foreign Minister Peres: "You are even worse than Chamberlain. He imperiled the safety of other people, but you are doing it to your own people."[147] Ariel Sharon, a member of the Likud opposition, was similarly disparaging, utilizing the same historical framework to call Rabin a "traitor who was behaving like a Nazi [...]."[148]

---

[142] On February 25, 1994, extremist Jewish settler Baruch Goldstein opened fire on Muslims praying in Hebron's Tomb of the Patriarchs, a site holy to both faiths, killing twenty-nine Palestinians before being beaten to death by enraged survivors. Riots ensued across the territories and, facing intense domestic pressure, Arafat suspended the implementation talks and called for the dismantling of the Jewish settlement in Hebron housing some 400 Israelis. Rabin refused, citing an agreement in the DOP that the disposition of settlements would be discussed only in final status negotiations slated to begin no more than two years after the completion of Gaza-Jericho implementation talks. Makovsky, *Making Peace with the PLO*, 146.
[143] Clyde Haberman, "Hundreds of Jews Father to Honor Hebron Killer," *The New York Times*, April 1, 1994, A00010.
[144] Ben-Eliezer, *Old Conflict, New War*, 44.
[145] An announcer on Arutz, a far-right radio station, by the name of Adir Zik branded Rabin a traitor. A weekly called *hashavu'a* (Hebrew: this week) declared that the day would come when Rabin and Peres would stand trial or be sent to an asylum for the insane. Ibid., 45, 47.
[146] Ibid., 45.   [147] Cited in Anziska, *Preventing Palestine*, 286.
[148] Anita Miller, Jordan Miller, and Sigalit Zetouni, *Sharon: Israel's Warrior-Politician* (Chicago: Academy Chicago Publishers and Olive Publishing, 2004), 188.

The peace process received another major blow on November 4, 1995, when Rabin was assassinated by Yigal Amir, a staunch opponent of the peace process. The commission of inquiry that was appointed to investigate the assassination focused on the security breaches that enabled the assassin to carry out the murder. Less attention was paid to the extensive incitement and the toxic political climate that led up to the assassination. Amir claimed to have been influenced by a steady stream of rabbinic and political messages declaring the "illegitimacy" of those who "hand over territories."[149] In an interview with Israel's Channel 10 in 2008, Amir further indicated that his "decision to kill the prime minister" was driven by the above-cited Sharon, "who said this agreement will result in disaster."[150] Indeed, through his action, Amir wanted to halt the Israeli withdrawal and transfer of power in six cities in the West Bank, which had been ratified in Oslo II two months prior.

Contrary to Amir's goals, Rabin's successor, Shimon Peres, solemnly declared that the assassination would not bring an end to the peace process.[151] Following his assumption of the role of prime minister in November 1995, Peres expedited the peace process by accelerating the withdrawal from major Palestinian cities in the West Bank and by engaging in intensive peace talks with Syria. Peres was not an unlikely proponent of the peace process; he was a critical component to the Oslo Accords, as he – together with Beilin – persuaded Rabin to move toward peace with the Palestinians and thereby challenged opposition from members of Israel's right wing.[152] By continuing the withdrawal from population centers in the West Bank (except Hebron), Peres enabled the Palestinians to hold the first-ever national elections for the PLC on January 20, 1996 in the West Bank and Gaza.[153] Following these elections,[154] the Israeli government conditioned the additional withdrawal on a series of security moves on the Palestinian side. Thus, Peres demanded that the PA crack down on terrorism[155] and rescind parts of the Palestinian charter that were in violation of the Oslo agreements;[156] all Islamic militias had to be declared

---

[149] Ben-Eliezer, *Old Conflict, New War*, 45
[150] Raanan Ben-Zur, "Rabin Killer: Sharon Affected My Decision," *Ynet Online*, October 10, 2018, www.ynetnews.com/articles/0,7340,L-3615595,00.html, accessed January 4, 2019.
[151] Ibid., 46.   [152] Robert O. Freedman, "Introduction," in Freedman, *Middle East*, 2.
[153] Ibid., 1.   [154] Rosenblum, "Netanyahu and Peace," 37.   [155] Ibid., 38.
[156] During a news conference held in Jericho in January 1998, senior PLO negotiator Saeb Erakat commented on the issue: "The PNC will not reconvene. It convened in 1996 and cancelled the articles which contradicted the mutual letters of recognition.... After receiving our clarifications there was an American understanding of our position regarding the PNC charter and security issues." The United Nations Information

illegal and disarmed.[157] As part of its anti-terrorism measures, the Israeli government imposed a total closure[158] on the West Bank and Gaza to stop the movement of people and goods into Israel from territories governed by the PA, which "cantonized the West Bank's 1.3 million Palestinians into their 465 villages and towns [...]."[159]

Doves and Hawks: Confronting the Peace Process

Despite Peres' desire to further the implementation of the 1993 accords, the peace process received a further setback in late February and March 1996, when a series of terrorist attacks by Hamas and Islamic Jihad against Israelis challenged the objectives of the "generation of peace."[160] The terrorist attacks countered expectations of a long-term security and welfare that would coincide with the peace process – a failure which proved one of the great challenges for Labor's election campaign in 1996.[161] The crux of the electoral debate centered on the 1993 Oslo Accords and Labor's "land for peace" approach.[162] Netanyahu, Peres' opponent during the elections, leveraged the public's security concerns by attacking the Labor government for "subcontracting" Israelis' security to the PLO and the PA. The Likud leader vowed that, if elected, he would put "security first" and create a "secure peace," even if it would take longer.[163] While his attempt to honor previous agreements and

System on the Question of Palestine, *Chronological Review of Events Relating to the Question of Palestine: Monthly Media Monitoring Review* (UNISPAL, January 1998).

[157] Rosenblum, "Netanyahu and Peace," 39.

[158] According to the UN Office of the Special Coordinator in the OT, the Israeli closure policy, including Peres' "total closure" after the February–March bombings, cost the PA in the West Bank and Gaza about $800 million in 1996. About $300 million of this was lost to wages and $500 million was lost Gross Domestic Product (GDP). Prior to the first closure in March 1993, the number of Palestinians from the territories working in Israel exceeded 120,000. The closure following the February–March suicide terrorism cost 50,000 Palestinian jobs in the West Bank and Gaza, approximately one third of the estimated 150,000-member labor force. Rosenblum, "Netanyahu and Peace," 41, 42.

[159] Ibid., 39.   [160] Ben-Eliezer, *Old Conflict, New War*, 48.

[161] The 1996 election constituted the first direct popular election of the prime minister. In Israel's thirteen previous elections, the leader of the party receiving the largest number of Knesset seats became prime minister. Don Peretz and Gideon Doron, "Israel's 1996 Elections: A Second Political Earthquake?," *The Middle East Journal* 50:4 (Autumn 1996): 530.

[162] Ibid., 532.

[163] Likud billboards among Israeli highways had a simple message "Peres will divide Jerusalem." Netanyahu, conversely, used the campaign slogan "Peace with Jerusalem." Roger Friedland and Richard Hecht, *To Rule Jerusalem* (Berkeley/Los Angeles, CA: Berkeley University Press, 2000), 504; also see Keren Neubach, *Campaign 96* (Tel Aviv: Yediot Ahronot, 1996), 180 (in Hebrew).

continue the peace process sought to win over doves in the electorate, Netanyahu also garnered support among those who opposed the peace process and believed that Peres would "divide Jerusalem."[164] Ami Ayalon, head of the Shabak, the general security service, for instance, noted that Amir could not be seen "as a passing phenomenon," further claiming that "there are many people in this country who identify with the assassin's act, who would in fact be ready to do the same in a given political situation."[165]

With Netanyahu's election in 1996, the political shortcomings of the peace agreement came to the fore. Since the Oslo agreements incorporated to-be-agreed principles rather than a concrete roadmap to peace, the new Israeli government was able to read and interpret the agreement in line with its own inclinations.[166] Despite his campaign pledges of peace with security, Netanyahu quickly made it clear that he was far less interested in the peace process than his predecessor had been.[167] Netanyahu, in the words of Ben-Eliezer, did everything he could to slow down the Oslo process and avoid honoring Israel's commitments by stalling the promised redeployment from Hebron.[168] In late September 1996, the hawkish policies of the Netanyahu government led to a direct confrontation between the Israeli army and armed Palestinian police, providing a further challenge to the security cooperation envisaged in the Oslo Accords. The Israeli prime minister had secretly arranged for the opening of a secret tunnel connecting the Western Wall Plaza with the Muslim Quarter, where the al-Aqsa and Dome of the Rock mosques are located.[169] The "rock of our existence," as Netanyahu termed the tunnel, proved a sore in Arafat's eyes. The head of the PA declared that the opening of the tunnel violated the peace process, as it constituted an attempt to make East Jerusalem Jewish. The violence that subsequently engulfed Jerusalem and the West Bank led to the loss of dozens of Israeli and Palestinian lives; for the first time since the Oslo Accords, Palestinian police clashed with Israeli security forces.[170]

Upon taking office, Netanyahu also embarked on a program of enlarging Jewish settlements in the West Bank as part of a carefully orchestrated

---

[164] Ben-Eliezer, *Old Conflict, New War*, 48.   [165] Ibid., 48.
[166] Azmi Bishara, "Reflections on the Realities of the Oslo Accords," in Giacaman and Lønning, *After Oslo*, 212.
[167] Freedman, "Introduction," 1.
[168] Ben-Eliezer, *Old Conflict, New War*, 49; 73; Chemi Shalev, a Maariv correspondent, was more forgiving, claiming at the time that "for every Palestinian infraction there is an Israeli infringement." Rosenblum, "Netanyahu and Peace," 56; *Mideast Mirror, Israel Section* June 19, 1996 (Mideast Mirror, 1996), 14.
[169] Freedman, "Introduction," 2.   [170] Rosenblum, "Netanyahu and Peace," 66.

reciprocal relationship with the increasingly powerful settler movement that offered the Likud leader a political lifeline in times of need.[171] During his first trip to Washington in July 1996, he claimed that the settler population had increased by 50 percent under the previous government; Likud, he declared to President Clinton, could not be "expected to do less than the labor government."[172] Indeed, following this visit, the government's settlement policy pushed forward. In early August, the cabinet decided to discontinue Labor's prior settlement freeze, thereby ending what Netanyahu termed "the discrimination against Jewish settlements in Judea, Samaria and the Gaza Strip."[173] During the signing of the Hebron agreement in January 1997, Netanyahu provided further reassurance to settlers that they would not be impacted by the peace agreement, stating that "there is not and will not be a Palestinian state ... No foreign sovereignty will arise between the Jordan and the sea. The Jewish presence and Jewish settlement throughout Judea and Samaria will live, prosper, and exist for all time."[174]

After three years in office, Netanyahu was defeated by the new leader of the Labor party, Ehud Barak. While Barak styled himself as Rabin's successor by proffering a message of moderation and commitment towards the peace process, he adopted similar policies to his Likud predecessor. To satisfy the military-religious component of Israeli society who had felt their needs ignored by Rabin, Barak sought to find a compromise that would allow illegal outposts in the West Bank to remain following a peace agreement.[175] Under Barak's rule, the number of settlements also continued to grow. By 2000, seven years after the signing of the DOP, the number of settlers in the territories had doubled, to 200,000.[176] The status of Jerusalem similarly remained unnegotiable; beyond a few sacred places in the old city, the Palestinians were to settle with authority over Abu Dis as their capital.[177]

---

[171] Ben Caspit, *The Netanyahu Years*, trans. Ora Cummings (New York: Thomas Dunne Books, 2012), 112, 205; Colin Schindler, *The Rise of the Israeli Right: From Odessa to Hebron* (London: Cambridge University Press, 2015), 341, 342.

[172] National Archives and Records Administration, *Public Papers of the Presidents of the United States, William J. Clinton* (Washington: United States Government Printing Office, 1996), 1093.

[173] Subsequently, on August 11, Minister of Defense Yitzhak Mordechai announced that he had eased procedures for obtaining building permits in the West Bank and Gaza and had approved a request by settlers to set up 300 hundred mobile homes in settlements. That same day, Eli Suissa, the minister of interior, pledged $5 million in immediate aid as compensation for past financial burdens the settlers had to bear "as a result of the Israeli–Palestinian agreements." Rosenblum, "Netanyahu and Peace," 63, 64.

[174] Ben-Eliezer, *Old Conflict, New War*, 50.   [175] Ibid., 73.   [176] Ibid., 76.

[177] Said, *End of the Peace Process*, xv.

With the election of Barak, a former chief of general staff, the IDF took on a more central role in Israeli politics and the peace process.[178] Indeed, Brigadier General Zvi Fogel, the chief of staff of the Southern Command at the time, noted that with the building of army strongholds in Gaza, "the IDF set in motion an irreversible process that would culminate in a collision with the Palestinians."[179] At the same time, Ben-Eliezer points out that the IDF continued to humiliate the Palestinians in everyday life, particularly at checkpoints.[180] These actions, which affected Palestinians' living conditions and the security forces' perception of Israeli behavior, Fogel explained were "not intended to end without a confrontation … [they] actually led to the confrontation."[181] Amos Gilad, the contemporary head of the Research Division in Military Intelligence, also conveyed an ambiguous message of duality. Despite the fact that the continued security coordination between Israel and the PA reduced levels of terrorism following the major terrorist attacks of 1996, Gilad "persuaded" the military and political leadership alike that "there is no Palestinian partner."[182] The effects were clear: following the Camp David Agreement of mid-July 2000, 50.4 percent of Israelis affirmed that they had grown more pessimistic since Camp David regarding the chances of peace with the Palestinians.[183] Arafat, Barak stated, was "no partner for peace." The Israelis, conversely, according to Barak, had "no cause to blame our-selves. Our hands are clean. We have turned every stone and were prepared to discuss almost every possible idea in order to explore whether the other side is prepared to pursue the road of peace."[184] At the same time, Barak faced significant public opposition to the negoti-ations, rendering doubt on his own ability to garner enough national support for the initiative. Thus, on July 17, some 200,000 people demonstrated in Rabin Square against the Camp David Summit invok-ing "the destruction of the state, [the] Auschwitz borders, [the] Holocaust that was and the Holocaust to come."[185]

---

[178] Ben-Eliezer, *Old Conflict, New War*, 50, 51.   [179] Ibid., 76.   [180] Ibid.
[181] Ibid., 79.   [182] Ibid.
[183] Ephraim Ya'ar and Tamar Herman, "Peace Index – August 2000," *Peaceindex*, August 2000, www.peaceindex.org/files/peaceindex2000_8_3.pdf, accessed December 13, 2018.
[184] Israeli Ministry of Foreign Affairs, "Statement by Prime Minister Ehud Barak-07-Oct-2000," www.mfa.gov.il/mfa/pressroom/2000/pages/statement%20by%20prime%20minister%20ehud%20barak%20-%2007-oct-20.aspx, accessed October 15, 2018.
[185] Idith Zertal and Akiva Eldar, *Lords of the Land: The War over Israel's Settlements in the Occupied Territories, 1967–2007* (New York: Nation Books, 2007), 177, 178.

The Camp David Negotiations

In a 2009 interview, Barak admitted that he had gone to Camp David, the site of the historic peace accord between Egypt and Israel, with the knowledge that the talks would not result in a final agreement and aware of the fact that Arafat would organize an uprising in September.[186] For Barak, the negotiations predominantly constituted important optics, allowing the prime minister to show the world that Israel had done all it could to reach a peace agreement while placating President Clinton who sought to conclude his presidency with a historic peace agreement.[187] Barak's perception of Arafat and Palestinian responsibility for the impasse[188] resonated with right-wing activists who claimed that Oslo was a Palestinian deception and that the Palestinians had no other intention than to destroy Israel.[189] The reality, of course, was more complicated. The Palestinians were suspicious about Israel's intentions to conclude final status talks as little had changed since the Oslo Accords.[190] Moreover, even if Barak had not insisted on a dichotomous all-or-nothing approach, which dictated that "nothing is agreed upon, until everything is agreed upon,"[191] Arafat did not have the public support to accept any offer that would be considered detrimental to the Palestinians. In fact, most Palestinians called on Arafat not to accept the – solely verbal – offers[192] made by his interlocutors, viewing them as insufficient and ambiguous: the proposals were silent on the question of

---

[186] The Americans also blamed the Palestinians for the failure of the talks, saying that Arafat's explanations for the failure were inadequate, if not fraudulent: "Why do you say that you were not offered even 90% of the territories, when you were offered 97% of them?" Dennis Ross asked. Ross also mentioned, as the Israeli delegations claimed, that the Palestinians did not bring any offer from their side, even though they were asked to do so, and that they just said "no" to every Israeli or American offer. Ben-Eliezer, *Old Conflict, New War*, 77.

[187] Ibid., 75.

[188] Suleyman Demirel et al., *Sharm El-Sheikh Fact-Finding Committee Report "Mitchell Report"* (The Michell Committee, 2001), 7.

[189] Ben-Eliezer, *Old Conflict, New War*, 78.   [190] Ibid., 76.

[191] Gilad Sher, *Within Reach: The Israeli-Palestinian Peace Negotiations, 1999-2001* (Tel Aviv: Miskal-Yedioth Ahronoth Books and Chemed Books, 2001), 20, 197, 406 (in Hebrew).

[192] Ben-Eliezer, *Old Conflict, New War*, 77. At the summit, Israel offered to establish a sovereign Palestinian state encompassing the Gaza Strip, 92 percent of the West Bank, and some parts of East Jerusalem. In return, it proposed the annexation of Jewish neighborhoods (settlements) in East Jerusalem. Israel also asked for several security measures, including early warning stations in the West Bank and an Israeli presence at Palestinian border crossings. In addition, it would accept no more than a token return of Palestinian refugees under a family reunification program. After the failure of the summit, Israeli and Palestinian negotiators continued to meet in small groups in August and September 2000. Jeremy Pressman, "Visions in Collision: What Happened at Camp David and Taba?," *International Security* 28:2 (2003): 8. Also see Deborah

refugees, the land exchange was unbalanced, and much of East Jerusalem was to remain under Israeli sovereignty.[193] From the perspective of the PLO, Camp David "represented nothing less than an attempt by Israel to extend the force it exercises on the ground to negotiations [and] the attempts to allocate blame on the Palestinian side only added to the tension on the ground."[194]

The Second Intifadah

The confrontation expected by Barak came at the end of September, when Ariel Sharon, the representative of the Likud opposition, visited the holy site in Jerusalem known to Jews as the Temple Mount and to Muslims as Haram al-Sharif.[195] With his visit, Sharon wanted to make it clear that "the Temple Mount is the holiest place for Jews in the world and that the Arabs must recognize the Jews' legitimate historic rights there."[196] Sharon's decision to affirm "the right of every Jew to visit the Temple Mount"[197] fit a historic pattern set by the former military commander, which – similarly to the Jerusalem mayor Teddy Kollek – sought to guarantee the Jewish nature of Jerusalem.[198] Following the Oslo peace accords, Sharon had been active with Amana, the settlement arm of Yesha,[199] in creating a blueprint for massive settlement expansion in

Sontag, "And Yet So Far: A Special Report; Quest for Mideast Peace: How and Why It Failed," *The New York Times*, July 26, 2001, a1.

[193] Robert Malley and Hussein Agha, "Camp David: A Tragedy of Errors," *The Guardian*, July 19, 2001, www.theguardian.com/world/2001/jul/20/comment, accessed January 19, 2019.

[194] Demirel et al., *Sharm El-Sheikh*, 7.   [195] Ben-Eliezer, *Old Conflict, New War*, 80.

[196] Ibid.

[197] Yossi Beilin, *The Path to Geneva: The Quest for a Permanent Solution, 1996-2003* (New York: RDV Books, 2004), 191.

[198] Following a U.S.-supported UN resolution referring to Jerusalem as "occupied," Kollek stated: "The solution is to bring as many immigrants to the city as possible and make it an overwhelmingly Jewish city, so they will get it out of their heads that Jerusalem will not be Israel's capital." Roger Friedland and Richard Hecht, *To Rule Jerusalem* (London: University of California Press, 2000), 444.

[199] The Yesha Council, which was formed in 1980 as an umbrella organization to represent the twenty-four local councils in non-annexed territories, has been at the forefront of settler political mobilization; it also is involved in lobbying the government and the state on settlement issues and construction and in opposition to diplomatic initiatives that involve ceding any land. Amana, formed in 1978 as the settlement arm of Gush Emunim, is recognized by the state as a legal construction and settlement agency, which primarily constructs settlements in the West Bank. It can compete in state tenders and has received land for construction from the Settlement Division of the World Zionist Organization. Oded Haklai, "The Decisive Path of State Indecisiveness: Israel in the West Bank in Comparative Perspective," in *Settlers in Contested Lands: Territorial Disputes and Ethnic Conflicts*, ed. Oded Haklai and Neophytos Loizides (Stanford: Stanford University Press, 2015), 34, 35.

the West Bank.[200] Prior to this, as housing minister, Sharon had sought to implement the idea of a "Greater Jerusalem" through the expropriation of Palestinian lands in East Jerusalem and the construction of new Jewish neighborhoods surrounding the Palestinian population core in East Jerusalem.[201] An experienced politician, Sharon was highly attentive to the changing disposition of the Israeli public and the political and economic frustrations simmering in the territories.[202] His visit, which was coordinated with Barak, thus all but guaranteed a heated Palestinian reaction the next day, the most important day of the week for Muslims: Friday.[203]

Following Sharon's visit, disturbances spread across the West Bank and inside Israel; the accompanying violence led to a loss of lives on both sides. In early October 2000, clashes between Palestinians protesting the heavy-handed Israeli reaction in the territories and the police led to the death of thirteen Palestinian citizens of Israel, fueling the isolation[204] of Palestinian citizens in an increasingly polarized society.[205] On October 12, in the aftermath of the lynching of two Israeli reserve soldiers in Ramallah, the IDF – for the first time since the Oslo Accords – attacked PA institutions in Gaza and Ramallah. Chief of Staff Mofaz claimed in early 2001 that these actions in the territories were justified as the PA had become a "terrorist authority" engaged in "a full-fledged war."[206] With Israel being subjected to suicide bombings from October onwards, it was not difficult to persuade the public and the political leadership that Israel's way of life and existence was under threat, or as

---

[200] Rosenblum, "Netanyahu and Peace," 47,   [201] Friedland and Hecht, *Rule*, 444.

[202] Ami Pedahzur, *The Triumph of Israel's Radical Right* (New York: Oxford University Press, 2012), 166; Beilin, *Path to Geneva*, 191.

[203] Ben-Eliezer, *Old Conflict, New War*, 81.

[204] For a discussion of the effects of the October 2000 protests on cooperation between Israeli-Jews and Palestinian and Palestinian perceptions of their (equal) rights in Israel, see Dan Rabinowitz and Khawla Abu-Baker, *Coffins on Our Shoulders: The Experience of the Palestinian Citizens of Israel* (Berkeley: University of California Press, 2005), 136, 137.

[205] The events led to the publication of various reports, including by a commission established in the wake of the October 2000 clashes, the Orr Commission. Published in September 2003, the Orr commission demanded police reform and prosecution of the police officers involved in the deaths of the Palestinian citizens. The failure to bring the police officers to trial remains an open wound as evidenced by Barak's belated apology in July 2019. In response to an op-ed written by Meretz parliament member Esawi Frej titled "Things that Barak Needs to Say," the former Labor party leader apologized for his role in the violent thwarting of the protests. See Grace Wermenbol, "The Ongoing Political Divide," *The Middle East Institute*, September 16, 2019, www.mei.edu/publications/ongoing-divide-palestinian-participation-israeli-elections, accessed January 19, 2020.

[206] Ibid., 95.

Deputy Chief of Staff Ya'alon declared: "[This is] Israel's most important military campaign since 1948."[207]

While the suicide bombings, which were spearheaded by Hamas, had
initially be confined to the territories and had been aimed at the army,
from early 2001 onwards, the attacks were almost exclusively aimed at
Israeli civilians and perpetrated inside Israeli towns and cities, leading
Netanyahu to state that "today the whole nation knows that [the settlement of] Kedumim is no different from Tel Aviv."[208] Importantly, this
change in strategy played into the hands of the settlers and anti-Oslo
proponents. For the first-named group, the unmitigated targeting of
Israelis meant that they were able to seek legitimization for their
project by arguing that Palestinians considered every Jew an enemy.
The violence also allowed opponents of the Oslo process to effectively
argue that peace with the PA would be impossible by claiming the
authority's implication with terrorism. "Oslo," thousands of members
of militaristic-religious society shouted during a demonstration at the
Knesset, needed to be buried "before Oslo buries Israel."[209]

In the wake of the eruption of the Intifadah, the United States created
the Mitchell Committee to investigate the causes of violence. Even
though the Mitchell Report, which was published in April 2001, did
cast doubt on the extent and effectiveness of the PA's renunciation of
terrorism, it found no hard evidence implicating the PA in terrorist
activities.[210] Nevertheless, the narrative proved tenacious. Faced with
continuous terror attacks, with dozens of Israelis killed throughout the
latter months of 2001 – dubbed Black September[211] – and the first
months of 2002, the Israeli government even categorized the PA as a
"terrorist authority."[212] For Israel's most important ally, the existing
geopolitical circumstances were particularly crucial to its support for
the Jewish state and its official re-evaluation of its peace partner.
Engaged in a global war of terror in the aftermath of the 9/11 attacks,
the Bush administration couched the Intifadah as an additional theatre
in the war on terror. In June 2002, President Bush thus called on
the Palestinians to "elect new leaders, leaders not compromised by

---

[207] Ibid., 103.   [208] Ibid., 100.   [209] Ibid., 98.
[210] The report stated that in order to rebuild confidence, the PA should "make clear through
concrete action to Palestinians and Israelis alike that terrorism is reprehensible and
unacceptable, and that the PA will make a 100 percent effort to prevent terrorist
operations and to punish perpetrators. This effort should include immediate steps to
apprehend and incarcerate terrorists operating within the PA's jurisdiction." Demirel
et al., *Sharm El-Sheikh*, 2; Dennis J. Deeb, *Israel, Palestine, and the Quest for Middle East
Peace* (Lanham: University Press of American, 2013), 25–28.
[211] Ben-Eliezer, *Old Conflict, New War*, 116.   [212] Ibid., 124.

terrorism," as a means of demonstrating its commitment "to peace [...] with us or against us."[213]

Bush's comments came in the wake of an Israeli military offensive aimed at curbing the escalating terror attacks inside Israel and the Palestinian Territories and a failure by his own secretary of state, Colin Powell, to secure a cease-fire and halt hostilities.[214] On March 29, 2002, in the midst of ongoing terror attacks inside Israel and the Palestinian Territories and two days after a devastating suicide attack on an Israeli hotel in Netanya left twenty-eight dead, Israel launched the largest military offensive in the West Bank since the 1967 War. The ongoing global war against terror proved an important contextualization for Operation "Defensive Shield" (Hebrew: *Mivtz'a ḥomat magen*). In a televised address to the nation on March 31, Prime Minister Sharon noted that "the State of Israel is in a war, a war against terror," further noting that "we must wage an uncompromising fight [as] it is impossible to compromise with someone who is prepared – like the suicide-bombers on the streets of Israel's cities and at the World Trade Center in the United States."[215] Beyond rooting out "terrorist activities [and] infra-structures,"[216] the offensive was aimed at establishing a new security reality favorable to Israel and isolating Arafat,[217] who according to Sharon operated "a strategy of terror" and was "an obstacle to peace in the Middle East."[218] The message was clear: besieged in his Ramallah compound by IDF, the Palestinian Authority chairman would not be on the receiving end of Israel's "outstretched hand."[219]

---

[213] "President Bush Calls for New Palestinian Leadership," The White House, https://georgewbush-whitehouse.archives.gov/news/releases/2002/06/20020624-3.html, accessed December 13, 2018.

[214] Shaul Shay, "Ebb and Flow versus The Al-Aqsa Intifadah: The Israeli-Palestinian Conflict, 2000–2003," in *Never-Ending Conflict: Israeli Military History*, ed. Mordechai Bar-On (Mechanicsburg: Stackpole Books, 2004), 237.

[215] Israeli Ministry of Foreign Affairs, "PM Sharon-s Address to the Nation-31-Mar-2002," https://mfa.gov.il/MFA/PressRoom/2002/Pages/PM%20Sharon-s%20Address%20to%20the%20Nation%20-%2031-Mar-2002.aspx, accessed January 19, 2020.

[216] Israeli Ministry of Foreign Affairs, "Cabinet Communique-28-Apr-2002," https://mfa.gov.il/MFA/PressRoom/2002/Pages/Cabinet%20Communique%20-%2028-Apr-2002.aspx, accessed January 20, 2020.

[217] Shaul Mofaz, "Operation Defensive Shield: Lessons and Aftermath," The Washington Institute for Near East Policy, June 18, 2002, www.washingtoninstitute.org/policy-analysis/view/operation-defensive-shield-lessons-and-aftermath, accessed January 19, 2020.

[218] Israeli Ministry of Foreign Affairs, "PM Sharon's Address to the Nation-31-Mar-2002," https://mfa.gov.il/MFA/PressRoom/2002/Pages/PM%20Sharon-s%20Address%20to%20the%20Nation%20-%2031-Mar-2002.aspx, accessed January 19, 2020.

[219] Israeli Ministry of Foreign Affairs, "Cabinet Communique-28-Apr-2002," https://mfa.gov.il/MFA/PressRoom/2002/Pages/Cabinet%20Communique%20-%2028-Apr-2002.aspx, accessed January 19, 2020.

Operation Defensive Shield, which officially ended on April 21, successfully reduced Palestinian militancy – albeit at a high cost to civilian life and Palestinian infrastructure.[220] Nevertheless, Israel's objective of ending the Intifadah remained unmet[221]; and Israel's most "important confrontation since the War of Independence"[222] continued to claim large numbers of victims on both sides. The Intifadah, which continued until 2005, led to the deaths of 6,500 Palestinians. Nearly 40,000 Palestinians suffered injuries. On the other side, the number of Israeli deaths amounted to 1,200 and about 8,000 were wounded.[223] The disparity in numbers was discussed in various contemporaneous reports. The aforementioned Mitchell report, for instance, found that the IDF had used excessive and lethal force against unarmed civilians, further stating that there was "no evidence on which to conclude that ... the Government of Israel made a consistent effort to use non-lethal means to control demonstrations of unarmed Palestinians."[224] A report published by Amnesty International in 2002 was similarly critical of Israel's military strategy, claiming that the Israeli government accepted illegal killings and offered the IDF immunity from punishment.[225]

While the Israeli public at large agreed with Barak that "there is no one to talk to,"[226] his political and military strategy to counter the ongoing Palestinian violence was considered inadequate. As a result, Barak gradually lost his coalition, leading to the collapse of his government. In line with coalition partners' demand,[227] early elections were held in February 2001. The hawkish Likud leader Sharon came out as the clear winner, obtaining 62 percent of the vote in the direct elections for prime minister,

---

[220] In a UN report published in the aftermath of the offensive, the fact-finding body noted that "combatants on both sides put civilians in danger," further documenting extensive physical damage to Palestinian Authority civilian property, including heavy destruction of Arafat's compound. The World Bank estimated that reconstruction costs for physical and institutional damage to Palestinian Authority civilian infrastructure resulting from the incursions in the West Bank in March and April 2002 would total $361 million. United Nations, *Report of the Secretary-General Prepared Pursuant to GA Resolution ES-10/10 (Report on Jenin) (A/ES-10/186)* (UN General Assembly, July 2002).

[221] Beverley Milton-Edwards, *The Israeli-Palestinian Conflict: A People's War* (New York: Routledge, 2009), 158.

[222] Yalon cited in Tikva Honig-Parnass, "Zionism's Fixation: War without End," in *Readings on Israel, the Palestinians, and the U.S. War on Terror*, ed. Tikva Honig-Parnass and Toufic Haddad (Chicago: Haymarket Books, 2007), 129.

[223] Ben-Eliezer, *Old Conflict, New War*, 221.   [224] Demirel et al., *Sharm El-Sheikh*, 8.

[225] Amnesty International, *Report 2002* (London: Amnesty International Publications, 2002), 134, 135.

[226] Ben-Eliezer, *Old Conflict, New War*, 99.

[227] Stewart Ain, "Barak's Gov't near Collapse," *Times of Israel*, June 16, 2000, https://jewishweek.timesofisrael.com/baraks-govt-near-collapse/, accessed February 15, 2020.

to Barak's 38 percent.[228] Sharon, who had promised to crush the
Intifadah, was perceived by many Israelis as a more steadfast leader with
a clear strategy – one that included doing away with the Oslo Accords.
According to the new prime minister, Arafat was the enemy of the
people, a terrorist with "blood on his hands." The "foolish" Oslo
Accords, Sharon concluded, had to be replaced by a war to eradicate
terrorism.[229]

During the so-called "war for the war,"[230] Sharon implemented far-
reaching policies that sought to re-orchestrate relations between the
Palestinians and the Israelis. Faced with a continual wave of terrorist
attacks, a public movement petitioned the new government in 2001 to
build a separation fence along the historic Green Line. The initial concept, which was ratified by the government on June 3, 2002, put forward
a "security separation" in the form of a 350-kilometer long continuous
barrier, which would include trenches, force deployments, a wall where
needed, and other security apparatus.[231] In contrast to the initial plans,
the building of the barrier, which commenced in 2002, did not follow the
Green Line. Instead, a more eastward route was adopted, ensuring that
settlements and other strategic geographic and logistical locations would
fall on the Israeli side of the fence.[232]

Both in Israeli and international courts, the legality of the fence – and
particularly its damage to local Palestinian inhabitants – was considered
following petitions by inhabitants of Palestinian villages, where daily life
had become obstructed by the fence. Whereas security grounds effectively marred early petitions by a number of villages,[233] in July 2004, in an
advisory opinion, the International Criminal Court (ICC) in the Hague
challenged the fence's security aspect and called on Israel to dismantle
what had already been built and financially compensate the Palestinians
who had been injured by its construction.[234] Invoking the right of self-
defense enshrined in the UN charter, the government of Israel, which is
not a member of the ICC,[235] rejected the opinion and declared it would
continue to build the fence.[236]

---

[228] Thomas G. Mitchell, *Likud Leaders: The Lives and Careers of Menahem Begin, Yitzhak
Shamir, Benjamin Netanyahu and Ariel Sharon* (Jefferson: McFarland & Company,
2015), 145–146.
[229] Ben-Eliezer, *Old Conflict, New War*, 101, 102.   [230] Ibid., 86.   [231] Ibid., 177.
[232] Ibid., 178.   [233] Ibid., 179.
[234] "International Court of Justice Finds Israeli Barrier in Palestinian Territory Is illegal,"
UN News, https://news.un.org/en/story/2004/07/108912-international-court-justice-
finds-israeli-barrier-palestinian-territory-illegal, accessed December 13, 2018.
[235] It is worth noting that Israel, as a non-member of the court, does not accept
ICC jurisdiction.
[236] Ben-Eliezer, *Old Conflict, New War*, 183.

The Israeli government's stance was supported by its own courts. A month prior to the ICC's finding, the High Court rejected the petition by the Palestinian Beit Surik village council that the fence primarily constituted a political rather than a military project. Nevertheless, in a landmark ruling, the Israeli High Court did stipulate that "the relationship between the injury to the local inhabitants and the security benefit from the construction of the separation fence along the route, as determined by the military commander, is not proportionate."[237] As a result, the authorities were obliged to re-plan the remaining route of the barrier to ensure minimal injury to the fabric of life of the local inhabitants. The new route was made public in February 2005. The route laid out Israel's plan to annex approximately 7–9 percent of the West Bank and the Jordan Rift Valley by building the fence, as compared to 20 percent under the original route. Rather than bringing tens of thousands of Palestinians into Israeli territory, the new route allowed Sharon to annex about 75 percent of settlers to Israel – nearly a quarter of a million people.[238] By including large settlement blocs, the new route still did not follow the Green Line; it also continued to entail large-scale land expropriation and the creation of demarcated Palestinian enclaves while demarcating what Justice Minister Tzipi Livni termed "Israel's future border."[239]

Withdrawing from Gaza: Ending the "War of the Settlers"

An important reason driving Sharon's ability to move ahead with what Ben-Eliezer terms his "delimitation strategy" was the lack of American pressure in light of Israel's promise of an imminent withdrawal from the Gaza Strip, a densely populated area of merely 360 square kilometers that is home to 1.8 million Palestinians.[240] Dov Weisglass, a close advisor to Sharon, noted that the prime minister understood that as the Intifadah continued many Israelis were fed up with fighting the "war of the settlers."[241] Despite pouring money, manpower, material, and arms into the Gaza Strip, the army had not been able to protect the Gaza settlements. The withdrawal, Sharon reasoned, would also be welcomed by the Americans, as it suggested that Israel could comply with the

---

[237] Ibid., 181.   [238] Ibid., 185.
[239] Justice Minister Tzipi Livni told a meeting of legal experts that the separation fence was Israel's future border and that in practice the High Court was demarcating the border by its decisions in the fence cases. Cited in Norman G. Finkelstein, *Beyond Chutzpah: On the Misuse of Anti-Semitism and the Abuse of History* (Berkeley: University of California Press, 2005), 269.
[240] Ben-Eliezer, *Old Conflict, New War*, 198.   [241] Ibid., 163.

roadmap of 2002, a document put forward by the Quartet – the United States, Russia, the European Union, and the United Nations – to bring about a permanent settlement between Israel and the Palestinians.[242] For Sharon, the evacuation of settlements thus enabled him to garner crucial political support from the United States while redirecting international attention away from the ideologically more important expansion of unauthorized outposts and settlements in the West Bank.[243] As Weisglass stressed during a 2015 seminar: "With the "Gaza disengagement [we] came to a clear understanding with them [the United States]. Since the U.S. president saw that this territory was Israeli territory, we have built thousands of units in Gush Etzion and Ma'aleh Adumim."[244]

The extent of U.S. support for Sharon's disengagement plan – and its acceptance of the "new realities on the ground" – became clear in April 2004. In a letter to the Israeli leader, President Bush announced that in light of these "new realities [it] is unrealistic that the outcome of final status negotiations will be a full and complete return to the armistice lines of 1949."[245] At the same time, Bush argued in his exchange of letters with Sharon that large settlement blocs close to the Green Line should remain part of Israel.[246] Secretary of State Condoleezza Rice reaffirmed Bush' promise that a final-status agreement on borders would take into account the existence of "Israeli population centers" in the West Bank, because, as she noted, "We needed to get something in return from the Israelis if we were going to give them assurances; at a minimum, we needed to know that the Gaza withdrawal would be the beginning of the process […]."[247]

On February 16, 2005, the Knesset enacted into law the bill for implementing a withdrawal from the Gaza Strip. Despite initial strong

---

[242] Ibid., 198, 199.
[243] Another project, also taking place across the Green Line, showed equally clearly that the internal Israeli negotiation on the country's future borders were not yet concluded. The project in question was that of the settlers' "unauthorized outposts." Of 156 such sites, 112 were located east of the planned fence route. This was no coincidence: most of these outposts were created along roads and on dominant terrain in order to serve as connecting points between relatively isolated settlements remote from Israel. This would strengthen the Israeli hold in the territories and rob any future Palestinian state of territorial continuity. Sharon had promised to evacuate outposts but continued to allow their establishment. More than 50 outposts were added on his watch. In 2005 building continued in about 40 of them, and 33 of those had permanent structures. Ibid., 187/8.
[244] Tovah Lazaroff, "Former Chief of Staff: Ariel Sharon Designed Gaza Disengagement to Save West Bank Settlements," *The Jerusalem Post*, August 16, 2015, www.jpost.com/Arab-Israeli-Conflict/Former-chief-of-staff-Ariel-Sharon-designed-Gaza-disengagement-to-save-West-Bank-settlements-41221, accessed on August 16, 2017.
[245] Dennis Ross, *Doomed to Succeed: The U.S.–Israel Relationship from Truman to Obama* (New York: Farrar, Straus and Giroux, 2015), 324.
[246] Colin Shindler, *The Rise of the Israeli Right Door* (New York: Cambridge University Press, 2015), 353.
[247] Ross, *Doomed to Succeed*, 324.

opposition by the far Right and sections of Sharon's own party, Sharon managed to secure a majority in the cabinet for his plan: a total of fifty-nine Knesset members voted in favor, forty against, and five abstained.[248] The following August, in a complex logistical operation that excluded ideologically sensitive army units, the army evacuated 8,800 settlers and 5,000 of their supporters from the Gaza Strip. The settlers and their supporters did not go without a struggle; for them, settler existence in Gaza signified that every inch of the "Land of Israel" belonged to the Jews.[249] Holocaust symbols, including the Star of David, were used to stir up emotions and associate the withdrawal with the forcible expulsion of Jews in the Nazi era. Using similar rhetoric, Noam Livnat, a settler and the brother of the minister of education, claimed to have collected more than 10,000 signatures of individuals who declared that they would refuse an order to evacuate settlements, based on the ethnonational principle that had become a slogan of the settlers: "Jews do not expel Jews."[250]

Post-Oslo Negotiations: The Ongoing Multilateral Approach

Despite Sharon's adoption of an anti-Oslo position[251] and the persistence of violence, multilateral efforts to further a final peace accord between the Israelis and the Palestinians took place at the beginning of the twentieth century, creating the dual existence of military and political tracks to confront the conflict. During the height of the Second Intifadah, in February 2002, an all-Arab initiative was presented by the Saudi Crown Prince Abdullah. According to this "Beirut Initiative," first made public in a February interview with Thomas Friedman, a columnist for *The New York Times*, the Arab League agreed – for the first time – to recognize and normalize relations with the Israeli state in exchange for a withdrawal to the 1967 borders and a just and agreed-upon solution "to the refugee problem."[252]

---

[248] Shindler, *Rise*, 353.   [249] Zertal and Eldar, *Lords of the Land*, xi.

[250] Ben-Eliezer, *Old Conflict, New War*, 201/2; Nadav Shragal, "From Disengagement to Reengagement," *Haaretz*, August 17, 2005, www.haaretz.com/1.4932915.

[251] According to Weisglass, the significance of the disengagement plan was "the freezing of the peace process" in order to "prevent the establishment of a Palestinian state, (...) a discussion on the refugees, the borders and Jerusalem." Ari Shavit, "Top PM Aide: Gaza Plan Aims to Freeze the Peace Process," *Haaretz*, October 6, 2004, www.haaretz .com/1.4710372, accessed April 16, 2017.

[252] Thomas L. Friedman, "An Intriguing Signal from the Saudi Crown Prince," *The New York Times*, February 17, 2002, www.nytimes.com/2002/02/17/opinion/an-intriguing-signal-from-the-saudi-crown-prince.html. In September 2020, in an apparent departure from this principle, the United Arab Emirates and Bahrain agreed to establish formal diplomatic ties with Israel as part of the U.S.-brokered Abraham

Another multilateral initiative was presented in October 2002, when the above-mentioned Quartet presented its roadmap. Largely reflecting the policies outlined by President Bush in his speech of June 2002, the document – similarly to the 1993 Oslo Accords – aimed to bring about a permanent settlement to the Israeli-Palestinian conflict, albeit this time with clearly defined timetables and definitive goals. Published on April 30, 2003, the roadmap also involved a reform of the PA; it called for the appointment of a prime minister with executive powers alongside the president, a role first filled by the secretary of the PLO Executive Committee, Mahmoud Abbas.[253] Two further important multi-state attempts were made to make peace between Israel and the PA, including in Annapolis in November 2003 and in Sharm el-Sheikh in February 2005.[254] During the latter, the peace talks, which were supervised by the United States, Egypt and Jordan, led Israel and the PA to declare an end to the five-year-long Intifadah, which by then had claimed countless lives.[255] In the wake of the summit, Abbas, who had been elected president of the PA following the death of Arafat in November 2004, welcomed the implementation of the agreed-upon cease-fire and Sharon's withdrawal from Gaza as a signal that the war with Israel was effectively over, or as he stated in an interview, Israel was speaking a "different language."[256]

The Second Lebanon War

Even with the declared end to the Second Intifadah, the second half of the 2000s continued to be marked by violence, both in the Israeli–Palestinian domain and in the inter-Palestinian political domain. With the outbreak of the Second Lebanon War in the summer of 2006, civilians in Israel and Lebanon were subjected to bombings, air strikes, and missiles on a daily basis, obscuring the boundaries between the front lines and the home front as had been the case during the Second Intifadah. The thirty-three-day war, which lasted from July 12 to August 14, also once again challenged the defensive war strategy invoked

Accords in an effort to suspend Netanyahu's nascent plans to formally annex swaths of the West Bank.

[253] United Nations' Quartet, *Performance-Based Roadmap to a Permanent Two-State Solution to the Israeli Palestinian Conflict* (United Nations, April 2003), 4.

[254] Tanya Reinhart, *The Road Map to Nowhere: Israel/Palestine since 2003* (London; New York: Verso, 2006), 77, 78.

[255] Ben-Eliezer, *Old Conflict, New War*, 196.

[256] Steven Erlanger, "Abbas Declares War with Israel Effectively Over," *The New York Times*, February 14, 2005, www.nytimes.com/2005/02/14/world/middleeast/abbas-declares-war-with-israel-effectively-over.html?mtrref=www.google.com, accessed August 16, 2016.

by Israel since 1948, which had previously been disputed with the 1982 Israeli invasion of Lebanon.[257] Moreover, Israel's decision to go to war with Hezbollah in response to the killing and capture of two Israeli reserve soldiers along the southern Lebanese border proved to be an overreaction with important tactical consequences, namely the exposure of flaws in Israel's national security assumptions and defense strategy.[258]

The 2006 Israel–Hezbollah War revealed the IDF's failure to adequately respond to non-traditional war campaigns and effective counterinsurgency launched by Hezbollah forces.[259] Despite its superior air power and technology,[260] the IDF was not able to stop the bombing of its northern towns and villages and realize its goals, which included the removal of Hezbollah from the border.[261] The IDF's inability to shelter Israelis from constant attack – and the resulting exposure of vulnerability of Israel's home front – had far-reaching effects. Ehud Olmert, who had become prime minister in the wake of Sharon's stroke earlier in 2006, and his minister of defense, Amir Peretz, both of whom had no military record or involvement in security affairs, faced public mistrust and were condemned for their lack of military decisiveness. On the other side of the border, despite the heavy loss of lives – almost half of them civilians – and the increased internal ethnic division, the military Shi'a group Hezbollah was seen as having identified a successful strategy to withstand the Israeli war machine that had previously defeated combined Arab armies.[262]

The Gaza Wars

Two years after the Second Lebanon War, Israel once again found itself engaged in a military campaign, this time focusing on the Hamas-run Gaza Strip. The withdrawal from Gaza, Arnon Soffer, a geostrategic advisor to Sharon and successive governments, warned in 2004 would lead the Islamist organization Hamas to assume power, bringing about

---

[257] As Avi Shlaim notes, the Likud's ill-conceived and ill-fated invasion of Lebanon marked a watershed. Until then, Zionist leaders had been careful to cultivate the image of peace lovers who would stand up and fight only when war was forced upon them. Until then, the notion of *ein breira* (Hebrew: no alternative) was central to the explanation of why Israel went to war and a means of legitimizing its involvement in wars. Avi Shlaim, "The Debate about 1948," *International Journal of Middle East Studies* 27:3 (1995): 290.

[258] Brian J. Murphy, "No Heroic Battles: Lessons of the Second Lebanon War" (MA Diss., U.S. Army Command and General Staff College, 2010), iv.

[259] Ibid., 8.

[260] 17,000 air strikes were conducted in thirty-four days. At the same time, 100,000 tank and artillery shells were launched. Ben-Eliezer, *Old Conflict, New War*, 215.

[261] Amos Harel and Avi Issacharoff, *Thirty-Four Days: Israel, Hezbollah, and the War in Lebanon* (New York: Palgrave Macmillan, 2008), vii.

[262] Ben-Eliezer, *Old Conflict, New War*, 214.

the use of overwhelming violence by Israel as a means to enforce the unilateral separation. As he declared: "We will tell the Palestinians that if a single missile is fired over the fence, we will fire ten in response. And women and children will be killed and houses will be destroyed [...] it's going to be a human catastrophe [and] a terrible war."[263] Early in 2008, Israeli Minister of Defense Matan Vilnai offered a similar prophecy, warning the residents of Gaza that they "will bring upon themselves a bigger Holocaust because we will use all our might to defend ourselves."[264]

Soffer's predications materialized when in January 2006 Hamas won 56 percent of the votes – or seventy-four seats – in the Palestinian Legislative Council in an election designated "free and fair" by the United States Congressional Research Service.[265] The resulting emergence of a Fatah-Hamas unity government proved unsustainable; Fatah rejected the results of the election while Hamas refused to share power with Fatah, a dominant power in the West Bank.[266] Violent clashes between the U.S.-backed Fatah forces and Hamas' Al-Qassam Brigades led Hamas to take control of the Gaza Strip and establish a new government under Prime Minister Ismail Haniyeh on March 17, 2007.[267] In the eyes of the Israelis, Hamas' victory proved their fears of a radicalized Palestinian society; Hamas' military rule was – particularly in the aftermath of Operation Cast Lead – portrayed as primitive and barbaric, reinforcing Israeli national security concerns and challenging bilateral engagement.[268]

The outbreak of a Palestinian civil war had dire effects for those living in the tiny enclave. Israel placed Gaza under siege and enforced severe restrictions on its exports and imports. When missile attacks started to rain down on Israeli towns, Israel launched a devastating military campaign in December 2008, marking the official end of the cease-fire that had been in place since 2005. Abbas, who had been given advance notice of the campaign by the Israeli Defense Ministry, failed to inform the

---

[263] Max Blumenthal, *The Fifty-One Day War: Ruin and Resistance in Gaza* (New York: Nation Books, 2015), 5.
[264] Jo Roberts, *Contested Land, Contested Memory: Israel's Jews and Arabs and the Ghosts of Catastrophe* (Toronto: Dundurn Press, 2013), 255.
[265] Aaron D. Pina, *Palestinian Elections* (Washington, DC: CRS Report for Congress, February 2006), 10, 11.
[266] Ibid., 13.
[267] Nidal al-Mughrabi, "Palestinian Unity Government Takes Office," *Reuters*, March 17, 2007, www.reuters.com/article/us-palestinians/palestinian-unity-government-takes-office-idUSL1652735820070317, accessed October 15, 2018.
[268] See Palestinian Center for Policy and Survey Research, *Joint Palestinian-Israeli Poll 24 – June, 2007* (PSR, 2007); Baukhol, "Security and Fear," 39.

governors of Gaza of the coming onslaught.[269] Named "Operation Cast Lead," the three-week Gaza War led to the death of 1,387 Palestinians, most of them civilians. The Israeli side suffered a total of thirteen losses, which included three civilian deaths by rockets.[270]

In the aftermath of the destruction caused by a ground operation and airstrikes, the UN set out on a fact-finding mission that would decide on the question of blame and offer insight into the disproportionate loss of Palestinian lives. The inquest, led by South African judge Richard Goldstone, resulted in a 575-page report published in September 2009 which accused both sides of violating international laws and possible crimes of humanity.[271] The document charged Hamas with likely war crimes for firing rockets into southern Israel and targeting Israeli civilians. Simultaneously, the reports held the IDF responsible for attacking infrastructure, education, and health facilities, engaging in indiscriminate killing and wielding excessive force.[272] Despite Goldstone's retraction of the report in the Washington Post in 2011,[273] official support for the report's findings has remained steadfast. Shortly after the publication of his recantation, the three other members of the Goldstone Mission – Christine Chinkin, Hina Jilani, and Desmond Travers – issued a joint statement in the Guardian which unequivocally affirmed the report's findings, stating: "We concur in our view that there is no justification for any demand or expectation for reconsideration of the report as nothing of substance has appeared that would in any way change the context, findings or conclusions of that report."[274]

---

[269] Max Blumenthal, *Goliath: Life and Loathing in Greater Israel* (New York: Nation Books, 2013), 5.

[270] Ben-Eliezer, *Old Conflict, New War*, 217.

[271] Desmond Tutu, "Foreword: A Call to the Community of Conscience," in *The Goldstone Report: The Legacy of the Landmark Investigation of the Gaza Conflict*, ed. Adam Horowitz, Lizzy Ratner, and Philip Weiss (New York: Nation Books, 2011), viii.

[272] For these acts of aggression, the document, which relied on 188 interviews and 300 reports, called on Israel and Hamas to undertake a genuine and credible investigation into the accusations. While Israel did not cooperate with the UN's fact-finding mission, it did publish an official response to the report following investigations of the IDF of 150 events of breaches of the rules of war under international law committed during Operation Cast Lead. In thirty-six cases, the military advocate general decided to launch a criminal investigation. Ben-Eliezer, *Old Conflict, New War*, 218, 219.

[273] According to John Fonte this retraction was sought by Israeli leaders Netanyahu and President Shimon Peres. John Fonte, *Sovereignty or Submission: Will Americans Rule Themselves or Be Ruled by Others?* (New York: Encounter Books, 2011), 301.

[274] Hina Jilani, Christine Chinkin, and Desmond Travers, "Goldstone Report: Statement Issues by members of UN Mission on Gaza War," *The Guardian*, April 14, 2011, www.theguardian.com/commentisfree/2011/apr/14/goldstone-report-statement-un-gaza, accessed October 15, 2018.

Operation Pillar of Defense and Operation Protective Edge

In his epochal work, *On War*, Karl von Clausewitz astutely notes that war always includes the rational objective of protecting the state and its interest; as a result, war can be seen as "simply the continuation of policy by other means."[275] With the existence of ongoing tensions between Israel and Hamas in the aftermath of Operation Cast Lead,[276] the outbreak of military confrontations between both parties has largely been a question of decisive prompts rather than singular events. In 2012, another round of full-scale confrontation was triggered when hundreds of rockets and mortar rounds fell on Israeli communities surrounding Gaza. For Netanyahu, the attacks, which followed twenty months of internal political rivalries among smaller, extremist Palestinian factions, external pressure from the ongoing Arab Spring and looming Israeli elections, were the final straw, as he stated on November 13: "Whoever believes they can harm the daily lives of the residents of the south and not pay a heavy price is mistaken. I am responsible for choosing the right time to collect the highest price and so it shall be."[277]

The objectives outlined by Defense Minister Barak indicate that Operation Pillar of Defense offered a means to decrease the military capability of Hamas and restore the deterrence that had been eroded since 2011. At the same time, the 2012 operation was meant to re-establish the safety of the home front, both an ideological and politically sensitive concept, which had been eroded as rockets rained on Tel Aviv and other heavily populated areas in central Israel for the first time since the 1991 Gulf War.[278] However, while ostensibly seeking to challenge Hamas' military capability, a 2017 report by Rand Corporation, a think tank, found that Israel's defense strategy toward Hamas is aimed at "deliver[ing] enough punishment to render Hamas militarily ineffective for a substantial period but not so weak that it could be replaced by a worse foe."[279]

---

[275] Carl von Clausewitz, *On War*, trans. and ed. Michael Howard and Peter Paret (Princeton: Princeton University Press, 1967), 645.

[276] Raphael S. Cohen et al., *From Cast Lead to Protective Edge: Lessons from Israel's Wars in Gaza* (Santa Monica: Rand Corporation, 2017), xi.

[277] Aaron Kalman and Associated Press, "Netanyahu Says It's His Responsibility to Exact Price for Rockets on the South," *Times of Israel*, November 13, 2012, www.timesofisrael .com/im-responsible-states-netanyahu/?fb_comment_id=513426285335266_6329976, accessed October 15, 2018.

[278] Israeli Ministry of Foreign Affairs, "Pillar of Defense – Statement by DM Ehud Barak," http://mfa.gov.il/MFA/PressRoom/2012/Pages/Pillar_of_Defense-Statement_DM_Barak_ 14-Nov-2012.aspx, accessed October 15, 2018.

[279] Cohen et al., *From Cast Lead to Protective Edge*, xv.

As military campaigns without definitive military conclusions or long-lasting political resolutions, cease-fire agreements have often functioned as brief intermissions to a deadly sequel; the Egyptian-brokered cease-fire of 2012 followed this pattern. For Hamas, the violence that preceded Operation Protective Edge in the summer of 2014 was principally aimed at creating economic relief following the closure of dozens of smuggling tunnels by the Muslim Brotherhood-adverse Abdel Fattah el-Sisi regime and the decline in Iranian and Syrian support as a result of the ongoing Syrian civil war.[280] Armed opposition to Israel, Hamas envisioned, would extract important economic concessions, including the opening of the Rafah border. Indeed, in an interview on August 25, Hamas's exiled political leader, Khaled Mashaal, called on President Barack Obama to push Israel to stop a "holocaust" against the Palestinians and "call [on] Israel to stop its aggression on Gaza – and to lift the siege and open the cross borders and to rebuild Gaza [...] This is our demands [sic]."[281]

Similarly to Operation Case Lead, Operation Protective Edge, which lasted from July 8 to August 26, claimed a disproportionate amount of Palestinian lives and bore extensive damage on Gazan infrastructure. On the Israeli side, the operation claimed the lives of sixty-six soldiers; six civilians also died as a result of the 4,692 rockets and mortar shells fired by Hamas from the Gaza Strip.[282] B'Tselem, an Israeli human rights group, estimated that 2,202 Palestinians were killed, 63 percent of them – or 1,391 individuals – did not take part in the fighting.[283] In addition, the UN estimated that 500,000 people, or 28 percent of Gaza's population, were internally displaced, while some 108,000 people had their homes rendered uninhabitable.[284] In a September 2017 commemoration of the deadly campaign in Gaza, Sahd Abusalama, a Palestinian artist, noted that for him, Operation Protective Edge consisted a

---

[280] Harel Chorev and Yvette Shumacher, "The Road to Operation Protective Edge: Gaps in Strategic Perception," *Israel Journal of Foreign Affairs* 8:3 (2014): 11, 12.

[281] Michael Isikoff, "In Personal Plea, Top Hamas Leader Calls on Obama to Stop 'Holocaust' in Gaza," *Yahoo News*, August 25, 2014, www.yahoo.com/news/in-personal-plea–top-hamas-leader-calls-on-obama-to-stop–holocaust–in-gaza-180315615 .html, accessed October 15, 2018.

[282] The Israeli Tax Authority estimated that Protective Edge caused almost $55 million in direct damage to private and public infrastructure and another $443 million in indirect damage as a result of economic disruptions caused by the conflict. Cohen et al., *From Cast Lead to Protective Edge*, ixv.

[283] B'Tselem, *Whitewash Protocol: The So-Called Investigation of "Operation Protective Edge"* (B'Tselem, September 2016), 3.

[284] Cohen et al., *From Cast Lead to Protective Edge*, ixv, iv.

"remembrance of [the] ongoing Nakba which Palestinians have experienced since 1948."[285]

The violent ebbs and flows that characterize the post-Oslo period form a consistent reminder of the hitherto failure to effectuate a durable peace between the Israelis and the Palestinians. The accords' implied obligation to negotiate in good faith has been stymied by these recurrent outbreaks of violence – and in turn, as reflected in Abusalama's statement, have driven collective fears and narratives that justify the conflict's persistence. Indeed, throughout the years following the Oslo Accords, there has been a steady decline in Israeli and Palestinian belief in peace and negotiations and, simultaneously, an increase in adversarial sentiments. Polls conducted between 1995 and 2013 thus respectively reveal a 50 and 38[286] percentile point decline in Israeli and Palestinian confidence in the realization of a peace agreement.[287] These annual polls also note that both Israelis and Palestinians attribute negative objectives to each other, even in years of relative calm. In 2013, almost 40 percent of the surveyed Israelis believed that Palestinians aspirations involved conquering the State of Israel and destroying much of the Jewish population in Israel; similarly, almost 60 percent of Palestinians believed that "Israel's goals in the long run are to extend its borders to cover all the area between the Jordan River and the Mediterranean Sea and expel its Arab citizens."[288] The effective state

---

[285] Ramzy Baroud, "The 2014 War through the Eyes of Gaza's Youth," *Al Jazeera*, September 14, 2017, www.aljazeera.com/indepth/opinion/2017/09/2014-war-eyes-gaza-youth-170912143258604.html, accessed October 15, 2018.

[286] The Peace Index, *Peace Index* (Israel Democracy Institute, May 1995); Palestinian Center for Policy and Survey Research, *CPRS Public Opinion Poll 17* (CRS, 1995); Palestinian Center for Policy and Survey Research, *Joint Israeli Palestinian Poll 48, June 2013* (CRS, 2013).

[287] Excluding Peace Now's large-scale mobilization in 2005 in support of Sharon's withdrawal from Gaza, the decline in Israeli confidence in peace has coincided with a waning of the Israeli peace camp. As Samy Cohen points out, the Israeli peace movement has become less visible in the last two decades and has, on the whole, been unable to replicate the success of the 1970s and 1980s, when large street organization were able to effect policy changes. Cohen found that, beyond failed peace negotiations and a rise in deadly violence, feelings of fear inspired by the Palestinians and the lack of confidence in the "other" have led a great majority of Israelis to echo Barak's comments of July 2000 and refuse to consider the Palestinians a viable partner for peace. Samy Cohen, *Doves among Hawks: Struggles of the Israeli Peace Movements* (Oxford: Oxford University Press, 2019), 5, 6.

[288] Palestinian Center for Policy and Survey Research, *Joint Israeli Palestinian Poll 48, June 2013* (CRS, 2013). This finding was also found in subsequent polls. See Palestinian Center for Policy and Survey Research, *Joint Israeli Palestinian Poll – June 2014* (CRS, 2014); Palestinian Center for Policy and Survey Research, *Joint Israeli Palestinian Poll – 54* (CRS, December 2014); Palestinian Center for Policy and Survey Research, *Joint Israeli Palestinian Poll – 56* (CRS, June 2015).

of war and ongoing mutual distrust equally challenge the joint deliberation and de-threatenization[289] required to disabuse of the exclusive,
nationalist narratives that are the subject of this work. It is to the
collective transmission and contemporary political and cultural contextualization of these "collective catastrophe[s],"[290] that this work
now turns.

---

[289] Kamel and Huber, "De-Threatenization of the Other," 367.   [290] Ibid.

Part I

The Textbook of Memory

Following the 1993 Declaration of Principles, which maintained that Israel and the Palestinian Authority should seek to foster mutual understanding and tolerance and, accordingly, abstain from incitement, a series of studies was conducted to examine the Palestinian and Israeli education system.[1] On both sides, the Israeli curriculum and, following its inception in 1994, the Palestinian curriculum were deemed lacking. The curricula were criticized for their lack of recognition of the other, preservation of a culture of hatred, and the creation of historical narratives that overlook and exclude the other's perspective.[2] While the espoused critique at times was premature, unwarranted, and politically motivated, this first part reveals the existence of incompatible narratives in Israeli and Palestinian history textbooks based on a negation or minimization of the other's seminal history.

In the following two chapters, I am concerned with the exclusive and ethnocentric presentation of both societies' own history in the Israeli and Palestinian curriculum in the period 1994–2016. This primary analysis is supplemented by a secondary examination of the presentation of the other's historical narrative in Israeli and Palestinian history textbooks. Beyond an examination of the modern history curriculum, Chapter 5 includes an analysis of Palestinian national education textbooks, which were used between 1994 and 2000 as an interim measure to imbue a

---

[1] Ayman K. Agbaria, "On Enmity and Acceptance: The Case of the Israeli and Palestinian Civic Education," *Al-Majmuah* 2 (2010): 4, 6. It is worth noting that the 2019 Trump peace plan also called for an end to incitement and "hostile propaganda (in) textbooks, curriculum, and related materials, (as) well as an end to the glorification of violence, terrorism, and martyrdom." See The White House, *Peace to Prosperity: A Vision to Improve the Lives of the Palestinian and Israeli People* (The White House, January 2020), 34.

[2] For studies which have become subject to academic scrutiny based on perceived political agendas, see Arnon Groiss, "De-legitimization of Israel in Palestinian Authority Schoolbooks," *Israel Affairs* 18 (2012): 455–484; Arnon Groiss, *Jews, Israel and Peace in Palestinian School Textbooks: A Survey of the Textbooks Published by the Palestinian National Authority in the Years 2000–2001* (CMIP, 2001); Nurit Peled-Elhanan, "Legitimation of Massacres in Israeli School History Books," *Discourse & Society* 21 (2010): 377–404.

national consciousness during the creation of a Palestinian curriculum. Through the analyses of the presentation of the in-group's own history and (the existence of) the out-group's historical narrative in these various textbooks, this part identifies the ways in which schooling contributes to and justifies the above-mentioned conflict narratives and illuminates what Riad Nasser in Foucauldian terms referred to as "the mechanisms that stay hidden from those socialized and indoctrinated by it."[3]

The Post-Oslo Palestinian and Israeli Educational Systems

The focus in the ensuing section lies on state education, which forms the largest and most important sector in both societies under review. Nevertheless, it is important to note that both the Palestinian and Israeli educational systems encompass numerous educational sectors. The latter-mentioned – the Israeli education system – is divided into four sectors, which are subject to the authority of the Ministry of Education (MOE): a general state system, a religious state system, state schools for Israeli-Palestinian and Druze students – the so-called Arab sector – and independent state-funded schools of agricultural communities. Of these different sectors, the general state system constitutes the largest and accounts for approximately 56 percent of all Israeli pupils.[4] Beyond the MOE-regulated sectors, which all have separate curricula, ultra-orthodox schools, and, to some degree, private schools and Christian institutions have autonomous statuses and, consequently, they do not fall within the state educational framework.[5]

The Palestinian education system also incorporates different school systems despite having become more centralized since 1994.[6] In the

[3] Riad M. Nasser, *Palestinian Identity in Jordan and Israel: The Necessary other in Making a Nation* (New York/London: Routledge, 2005), 44; Michel Foucault, *Discipline and Punish: The Birth of the Prison* (London: Allan Lane, 1977), 100.

[4] In the 2011/2012 school year, around 56 percent of the pupils in the Hebrew education system attended state schools, about 19 percent attended state-religious schools, and some 25 percent were enrolled in ultra-Orthodox schools. State of Israel: Ministry of Education, "Facts and Figures in the Education System," http://meyda.education.gov.il/files/minhalcalcala/facts.pdf, accessed November 15, 2016.

[5] Sami Adwan and Ruth Firer, *The Israeli-Palestinian Conflict in History and Civics Textbooks of Both Nations* (Hannover: Verlag Hahnsche Buchhandlung, 2004), 22, 23.

[6] While the Palestinian Ministry of Education claims that it has had full control over the curriculum in East-Jerusalem since 1994, analyses of the East-Jerusalem educational system have found a diverging system with authority in many schools remaining with the Israelis. See Samira Alayan, "History Curricula and Textbooks in Palestine: Between Nation Building and Quality Education," in *The Politics of Education Reform in the Middle East: Self and Other in Textbooks and Curricula*, ed. Samira Alayan et al. (New York:

Gaza Strip and the West Bank, for instance, UNRWA schools are responsible for the education of about 22 percent of the Palestinian refugee population. Both public (governmental) and private schools can be found in the Gaza Strip, the West Bank and East Jerusalem and respectively account for 71 percent and 7 percent of Palestinian pupils. The same textbooks are used in the three types of schools, with only slight differences.[7] Unlike the examination in the other two societal realms, Palestinian society within the 1948 borders will not constitute a primary focus in this study. Education of Palestinian pupils living within the 1948 borders is included in the above-mentioned "Arab sector" and is controlled by the Israeli Ministry of Education. As such, this educational framework is not a solid representation of Palestinian society inside the 1948 borders due to a lack of Palestinian influence over the development of educational materials and discriminatory Israeli educational policies, which include insufficient teacher training and a lack of financial resources to replace outdated infrastructure and tackle high student drop-out rates.[8] As a result, Ismael Abu-Saad, a Palestinian professor of education at Ben-Gurion University, argues that despite attempts by Palestinian educators to create a more inclusive curriculum, the curriculum is designed to "'de-educate', or dispossess, indigenous Palestinian pupils of the knowledge of their own people and history. It gives them only carefully screened and censored exposure to their history, culture, and identity; and suppresses any aspects that challenge or contradict the Zionist narrative and mission."[9]

This work's emphasis on formal education as conveyed through the official curricula and in educational policies derives from the authoritative nature of the Palestinian and Israeli educational establishment and the educational content produced. Indeed, although one cannot assume "that what is in the text is actually taught [or] that what is taught is actually learned [as] teachers mediate classroom materials and students selectively accept, reinterpret, and reject what counts as legitimate

Berghahn Books, 2012); Shir Hever, *The Political Economy of Israel's Occupation: Repression beyond Exploitation* (London: Pluto Press, 2010).

[7] Adwan and Firer, *Israeli-Palestinian Conflict*, 101.

[8] Hever, *Political Economy of Israel's Occupation*, 7–15; Nurit Peled-Elhanan, *Palestine in Israeli School Books: Ideology and Propaganda in Education* (London: I.B. Tauris, 2012); Najah Al-Ramahi and Brian Davies, "Changing Primary Education in Palestine: Pulling in Several Directions at Once," *International Studies in Sociology of Education* 12 (2002): 59–76; Riad Nasser and Irene Nasser, "Textbooks as a Vehicle for Segregation and Domination: State Efforts to Shape Palestinian Israelis' Identities as Citizens," *Journal of Curriculum Studies* 40 (2008): 626–650.

[9] Ismael Abu-Saad, "Present Absentees: The Arab School Curriculum in Israel as a Tool for De-Educating Indigenous Palestinians," *Holy Land Studies* 7 (2009): 18, 19.

knowledge,"[10] previous studies conducted on Israeli and Palestinian textbook interpretation and dissemination testify to the transmission of "approved knowledge." With reference to the Palestinian curriculum, Fouad Moughrabi, a Palestinian educationalist and scholar, notes that educational adherence derives from the highly centralized system of education produced by the PA. Under this system, an army of supervisors and inspectors monitor the compliance with the textbooks' content, leaving "history teachers [with] little leeway to introduce additional material or to stray from the words of the textbook [while] students memorize a lousy text and answer questions on exams based on recall."[11] The results of classroom participant observation in Israeli-Jewish society similarly indicate a strong correlation between that which is presented in textbooks and the knowledge imparted by the teacher. Joyce Dalsheim, for instance, discovered an unwillingness among teachers to stray from questions directly pertaining to the subject under examination. Moreover, according to Dalsheim, individual student efforts to acquire extra-curricular knowledge are stymied through textbooks' lack of footnotes, leading students to be left "with the authoritative text, presumed to be speaking the only truth."[12] In spite of constant exposure to electronic media, official textbooks in Israel and the Palestinian Territories, "as the modern version of village storytellers," therefore constitute one of the primary ways in which the state – or a state-like apparatus – continue to shape attachment to the nation and individual's understanding of the past and the present.[13]

The History Curriculum: An Approved Version of History

While references to the Holocaust and the Nakba are made throughout, respectively, the Israeli and Palestinian curriculum, this section is principally concerned with history curricula, which provide both a mirror into a society's view of their own past and, through their conception of that past, present-day concerns. Ever since the rise of the nation-state in

---

[10] Michael W. Apple and Linda K. Christian-Smith, ed., *The Politics of the Textbook* (New York/London: Routledge, 1991), 9, 14.

[11] Fouad Moughrabi, "Palestine Now and Then: Notes on Oral History," *Journal of Educational Visions* 48, 49 (2015): 30 (in Arabic).

[12] Joyce Dalsheim, "Settler Nationalism, Collective Memories of Violence and the 'Uncanny Other'," *Social Identities: Journal for the Study of Race, Nation and Culture* 10:2 (2004): 158, 159, 164.

[13] Deborah S. Hutton and Howard D. Mehlinger, "International Textbooks Revision. Examples from the Unites States," in *Perceptions of History. International Textbook Research on Britain, Germany and the United States*, ed. Volker R. Berghahn and Hanna Schissler (Oxford: Berg, 1987), 141.

Europe, history textbooks have been used as an instrument for glorifying the nation, consolidating its national identity and justifying particular forms of social and political systems.[14] In his influential study on nations and nationalism in Europe, Eric Hobsbawm pointed out that "states ... use [their] increasingly powerful machinery for communicating with their inhabitants, above all in [...] schools, to spread the image and heritage of the nation and to inculcate attachment to it."[15] Although constituting the "approved, even official version [of history]," the knowledge included in textbooks cannot be considered neutral or unbiased.[16] Rather, textbooks must be treated as ideological tools to promote a certain belief system and legitimize an established political and social order.[17] Accordingly, textbooks play a dual role: on the one hand, they provide a sense of continuity between the past and the present by transmitting accepted historical narratives; on the other hand, they alter – or rewrite – the past to suit cultural or social contemporary needs.[18]

Previous studies on educational content in East Asia[19] and the former Yugoslav Republics[20] have also shown that the creation of a "useable past" to enable national identification affects historical writings on another group or society, particularly when constituting a (former) opponent. Part of the process of justifying a conflict, both past and

---

[14] Elie Podeh, *The Arab-Israeli Conflict in Israeli History Textbooks, 1948–2000* (Westport, CT: Bergin & Garvey, 2000), 3.

[15] Eric Hobsbawm, *Nations and Nationalism since 1780: Programme, Myth, Reality* (Cambridge: Cambridge University Press, 1990), 91.

[16] Howard D. Mehlinger, "International Textbook Revision: Examples from the United States," *Internationale Schulbuchforschung* 7 (1985): 287.

[17] Elie Podeh, "History and Memory in the Israeli Educational System: The Portrayal of the Arab-Israeli Conflict in History Textbooks (1948–2000)," *History and Memory* 12 (2000): 66.

[18] In his study of Russian history books, James Wertsch showed that following the dismantlement of the USSR, history books were rewritten to reflect the demands of the new Russian reality, thereby demonstrating that the "usable past" changes according to a society's present demands. James Wertsch, *Voices of Collective Remembering* (Cambridge: Cambridge University Press, 2002), 87–117.

[19] Studies conducted on the presentation of the other's narrative in the Asia-Pacific War include: Alexander Bukh, "Japan's History Textbooks Debate: National Identity in Narratives of Victimhood and Victimization," *Asian Survey* 47:5 (2007): 683–704; Zheng Wang, "Old Wounds, New Narratives: Joint History Textbook Writing and Peacebuilding in East Asia," *History and Memory* 21:1 (2009): 101–126.

[20] For an analysis of the curricula in Croatia, Serbia, and Bosnia and the minimization of the other's suffering during the Bosnian War, see Sirkka Ahonen, "Post-Conflict History Education in Finland, South Africa and Bosnia-Herzegovina," *Journal of Humanities and Social Science Education* 1 (2013): 90–103; Wolfgang Hoepken, "Between Civic Identity and Nationalism: History Textbooks in East-Central and Southeastern Europe," in *Democratic Transition in Croatia Value Transformation, Education, and Media Political Science*, ed. Sabrina P. Ramet and Davorka Matic (College Station: Texas A&M University Press, 2007), 163–192.

present, entails a negative characterization of the opponent while describing the in-group in positive terms.[21] The description of the self in positive terminology in conflicts, inadvertently, leads to ethnocentric views of the other. Michael Apple, therefore, concludes that most history textbooks present a biased and simplistic view of conflicts, which seeks to reinforce "our side is good; their side is bad. We are peace-loving and want an end to strife; they are warlike and aim to dominate."[22]

The Creation of a Useable Past: Delegitimizing the Other's Narrative

Delegitimization of the other in textbooks of societies in conflict does not solely rely on negative or stereotypical descriptions of historical encounters between the two societies in conflict. The other's history, religion, and culture, which are not directly related to the conflict, can also fall subject to negative descriptions or simply be omitted. Historical events that led to suffering or bereavement are among those narratives that might humanize and legitimize the other, potentially giving rise to a sense of "a common humanity" and, with this, political entitlement.[23] Thus, in times of conflict, students are usually commanded to forget what Paul Ricoeur called "the other drama" and, instead, "look ahead of catastrophes."[24] One of the ways in which this is achieved is by determining what knowledge is to be imparted in schoolbooks, i.e. what is to be included and excluded from the curriculum. It is in this context that Jacques Derrida's 1967 statement *Il n'y a pas dehors-texte* (French: There is no outside-text) finds relevance. While widely debated, the assertion has been interpreted to mean that conception, or "reality,"[25] and context cannot be divorced.[26] It follows that that which is *dehors* has been intentionally omitted in the attempt to shape the narrative of schoolbooks in line with the author's and/or society's views.

---

[21] Zvi Bekerman and Michalinos Zembylas, *Teaching Contested Narrative: Identity, Memory, and Reconciliation in Peace Education and Beyond* (Cambridge: Cambridge University Press, 2012), 111.

[22] Michael Apple, *Ideology and Curriculum* (New York: Routledge, 2004), 80.

[23] The utilization of victimhood to claim political entitlement has been termed *le capital victimaire* (French: victim capital) by Daniel Bensaid. Cited in Laleh Khalili, *Heroes and Martyrs of Palestine: The Politics of National Commemoration* (Cambridge: Cambridge University Press, 2007), 35.

[24] Cited in Peled-Elhanan, "Legitimation of Massacres," 400.

[25] James Tony Whitson, "Post-Structuralist Pedagogy as Counter-Hegemonic Praxis," in *Postmodernism, Postcolonialism and Pedagogy*, ed. Peter McLaren (Somerville: James Nicholas Publishers, 1995), 129, 130.

[26] Mark Dooley and Liam Kavanagh, *The Philosophy of Derrida* (London/New York: Routledge, 2007), 55, 56.

While the notion of *dehors* insinuates a lack of information, extra-textual information, at times, is implicitly present. Examples of implicit knowledge include the evaluation of events or concepts by the author by adding qualifying terminology or normative language, such as "unique" or "unprecedented." Conversely, hidden knowledge or the "missing text" can indicate a lack of factual accuracy, completeness, errors, and/or omissions. Beyond the qualitative analysis, I will also apply quantitative methods. This methodological category, which includes recording the usage of specific terms, individual references, illustrations, and amount of space devoted to a topic, further discloses the examined textbooks' goals in the ensuing chapters.

2   The Holocaust in Israeli Textbooks
Death and Deliverance

When Education Minister Shai Piron (2013–2014) decided to begin formally teaching the Holocaust as early as the first grade, the backlash was quick. "On the Paths of Memory," introduced in 2014, left many parents wondering whether their six-year-olds had the cognitive and emotional ability to comprehend and internalize human capacity for evil without a full grasp of the Hebrew language and basic everyday concepts. Israeli educators,[1] for their part, questioned the merits of raising a "generation imbued with the anxiety of victimhood,"[2] even if exposure to the horrors of the Holocaust only occurred in the context of Holocaust Memorial Day and sought to curb the utilization of external, age-inappropriate material.[3] "On the Paths of Memory," as such, primarily constituted a reactionary initiative, offering teachers an approved educational framework to cultivate and transmit the Holocaust to the youngest in Israeli society.

A constant presence in the contours of Israeli society, the Holocaust features prominently in its educational system in a quest to pass the legacy of the past to the younger generation; following the first grade, the Israeli path of memory continues to accompany Israeli students throughout their middle- and high-school education. Aided by memorial day ceremonies and week-long pilgrimages to Poland, the "land of the Shoah,"[4] Israeli

---

[1] Critics of the program included Holocaust researcher Nili Keren. Yarden Skop, "Israel Unveils New Holocaust Studies Program Starting in Kindergarten," *Haaretz*, April 24, 2014, www.haaretz.com/israel-news/.premium-1.587252, accessed April 25, 2014; Nili Keren, "The Answers Are Not in the Camps," *Haaretz*, October 10, 2013, www.haaretz .co.il/opinions/letters/1.2145706, accessed September 27, 2017.

[2] Daniel Ben-Simon, "Israel Debates Holocaust Education for First Graders," *Al-Monitor*, October 24, 2013, www.al-monitor.com/pulse/ar/originals/2013/10/holocaust-education-shai-piron-debate.html, accessed March 16, 2020.

[3] Orna Katz, the current superintendent of history, noted that in the absence of official guidance, teachers resorted to introducing materials that, at times, were unsuitable for young children. Interview conducted with Orna Katz on March 31, 2016.

[4] As Jackie Feldman writes,

Israeli teenagers perform an intensive, week-long pilgrimage, that performs the history of the Jewish people and the paradigm of *hurban* (destruction) to *guela* (redemption), as schematized in the Zionist master narrative. This pilgrimage is constructed as a ritual

77

teenagers are instructed to learn – and live – the Holocaust at a pivotal stage of their development and shortly prior to their mobilization into the army. Through an in-depth analysis of the Israeli history curriculum, this chapter seeks to reveal how the teaching of the Holocaust merges into "a powerful sense of identification"[5] and promotes a collective self-understanding in service of contemporary social and political values.

Using Jean-François Lyotard's postmodern moral philosophy, Ilan Gur Ze'ev argues that as a result of Palestinian denial of the Holocaust, Israelis understand and present the Holocaust solely from an ethnocentric point of view, leading to a refusal to acknowledge other genocides and the suffering of others.[6] While this work disputes the notion that Palestinian denial stands at the basis of an ethnocentric presentation of the Holocaust, the refusal to acknowledge others' suffering is evident in the Israeli educational system in the teaching of the Holocaust and the 1948 War. In the context of Holocaust education, this does not necessarily mean that other victims of the Second World War are completely neglected, but, rather, their fate and suffering are deemphasized. The extent of minimization in the Israeli curriculum takes on varying forms and degrees and depends on the textbook author(s) and the year of publication. Nevertheless, throughout the middle- and high-school textbooks examined, deemphasizing exists through a minimal discussion of the persecution of other, non-Jewish victims[7] by the Nazis during the Second World War.[8] Simultaneously, the unique nature of the Holocaust and its particularistic current meaning for Israeli-Jews are reinforced, generating the perpetuation of a "victimhood culture."[9]

reenactment of survival. The students leave the life world, the land of Israel for Poland, the land of the Shoah, where they witness the destruction of the Jews of the exile. But there, they survive to return with the witness on his triumphant ascent to Israel.

Jackie Feldman, *Above the Death Pits, Beneath the Flag: Youth Voyages to Poland and the Performance of Israeli National Identity* (New York/Oxford: Berghahn, 2008), 255.

[5] Education Minister Amnon Rubinstein cited in Ben-Simon, "Israel Debates Holocaust Education."

[6] Ilan Gur-Ze'ev, "The Morality of Acknowledging/Not-Acknowledging the Other's Holocaust/Genocide," *Journal of Moral Education* 27 (1998): 170.

[7] While it is recognized that a scholarly consensus concerning the likeness of the fate of non-Jewish victims to that of the Jews is lacking, this research will follow historical data offered by the United States Holocaust Memorial Museum on the numbers of non-Jewish victims. See Table 2.1.

[8] For discussions on the uniqueness of the Jewish Holocaust, see Yehuda Bauer, *Rethinking the Holocaust* (New Haven/London: Yale University Press, 2002), 45, 62, 63 78; Henry Friedlander, *The Origins of Nazi Genocide: From Euthanasia to the Final Solution* (Chapel Hill: University of North Carolina Press, 1995), xiii.

[9] Interview conducted with Rabbi Shai Piron on May 30, 2016.

Apart from revealing the narrative and presentational methods aimed at minimizing the fate of Palestinians during the 1948 War, the final paragraphs of this chapter stress political, historiographical, and societal developments as key frameworks to understanding the presented narrative of the 1948 War in ten Israeli textbooks. Differentiating between Zionist, Zionist-critical, and revisionist narratives of the war, I demonstrate that new historiographical writings have made their way into textbooks, albeit solely those by the self-proclaimed dean of the new historians – Benny Morris.[10] Nevertheless, under the influence of right-wing educational policies, particularly since the mid-2000s, any acknowledgment of individual instances of expulsion is downplayed; instead, the beneficial and practical effects of the mass Palestinian exodus are stressed. Consequently, formal and nonformal educational attempts to expose Israeli-Jews and Palestinians living inside the 1948 borders to the Palestinian narrative of the war – encompassed in the Arabic designation al-Nakba – have repeatedly been thwarted, forming the antithesis of Milḥemet ha-'Atsma'ut (Hebrew: the War of Independence) and its classification as a miraculous revival.

The Holocaust in Israeli Education:
A Historical Overview

Although the Holocaust is now taught intensively in Israel's Hebrew-language state school system, its textual presentation has undergone frequent changes, reflecting Israeli society and its collective memory of the Holocaust.[11] The developments in Holocaust education in Israel can broadly be divided into three distinct periods: an early "Zionist period," a second "foundational period," and a third "construction period."[12] The

---

[10] Morris coined the term "new historians" in an 1988 article in the American liberal Jewish magazine Tikkun entitled "The New Historiography: Israel Confronts Its Past" to describe himself and three other academics, Avi Shlaim, Ilan Pappé, and Simha Flapan, as the new historians who "have looked and are looking afresh at the Israeli historical experience, and their conclusions, by and large, are at odds with those of the Old Historians." Benny Morris, "The New Historiography: Israel Confronts Its Past," in Making Israel, ed. Benny Morris (Ann Arbor: The University of Michigan Press, 2007), 14.

[11] Erik H. Cohen, "Teacher Autonomy within a Flexible National Curriculum: Development of Shoah Education in Israeli State Schools," Journal of Curriculum Studies 48 (2016): 168.

[12] Dalia Ofer, "History, Memory and Identity: Perceptions of the Holocaust in Israel," in Jews in Israel: Contemporary Social and Cultural Patterns, ed. Uzi Rebhun and Chaim Isaac Waxman (Hanover; London: Brandeis University Press, 2004), 394–417; Ruth Firer, Agents of the Holocaust Lesson (Tel Aviv: Hakibbutz Hameuchad, 1989) (in Hebrew); Yuval Dror, "National Denial, Splitting, and Narcissism: Group Defence Mechanisms

first period is generally considered to have commenced with the establishment of the Israeli state or in the latter years of the British Mandate.[13]
History books in this early period tended to focus on Jewish resistance
and rebellion rather than victimhood and annihilation. This emphasis
reflected societal attitudes toward the Holocaust, which considered self-
defense in sharp contrast to passivity – those who went "as sheep to the
slaughter."[14] Accordingly, the passivity and consequential victimhood of
the Jews was regarded as shameful behavior, while instances of religious
self-sacrifice or armed resistance were considered honorable. While textbooks did mention the physical suffering of the Jews, these accounts
tended to be shorter, particularly when compared to the description of
armed resistance. Thus, in 1987, Ruth Firer pointed out that during the
Zionist period, nine out of fourteen textbooks on the Holocaust devoted
at least twice as much space to the description of armed resistance as to
"suffering and destruction" and the "maintenance of humanity."[15] More
recent research found that during this early stage, about two-thirds of the
textbooks were dedicated to the subject of revolt. In these textbooks,
revolt was not always carried out by European Jews but rather by
"Hebrews" and "Zionists" in order to link the exilic Jews and the recently
established Jewish state through the insinuation that Zionism had fought
against the Nazi regime and won by creating the Jewish state.[16] While it is
clear that the abovementioned educational framework echoes research
findings on early Israeli society, contrary to later periods, it is doubtful
that societal trends were heavily influenced by the educational system,

---

of Teachers and Students in Palestinian in Response to the Holocaust," *Mediterranean
Journal of Educational Studies* 1 (1996): 107–137; Chaim Schatzker, "Teaching the
Holocaust in Changing Times," *Moreshet* 52 (1992): 165–171.

[13] Idit Gil, "Teaching the Shoah in History Classes in Israeli High Schools," *Israel Studies*
14 (2009): 3; Zehavit Gross, "Holocaust Education in Jewish Schools in Israel: Goals,
Dilemmas, Challenges," *Prospects* 40 (2010): 94, 95.

[14] The term *Sabonim*, Hebrew slang for cowards, also became widely used after the
establishment of Israel. It pointed to the survivors of the Holocaust who had made
their way to the "Promised Land." The term, according to Elias Khoury, carries dual
meanings: a metaphoric allusion to cowardice and a literal meaning deriving from the
origin of the word sabon, meaning soap. This is a reference to one of the alleged barbaric
practices of the Nazis, which was to produce soap from the bodies of victims, an
unfounded claim which was held by many as true at that time. See Elias Khoury,
"Foreword," in Goldberg and Bashir, *A New Grammar of Trauma and History*, ix, x.

[15] Ruth Firer, "Israel: The Holocaust in History Textbooks," in *The Treatment of the
Holocaust in Textbooks: The Federal Republic of Germany, Israel, the United States of
America*, ed. Randolph L. Braham (Boulder/New York: Social Science Monographs
and the Institute for Holocaust Studies of the City University of New York, 1987),
180, 181.

[16] Segev also notes that Jewish resistance fighters were referred to as "Israelites, defenders
of Masada." Tom Segev, *The Seventh Million* (New York: Hill and Wang, 1993), 480.

because, as Erik Cohen points out, Holocaust education at this time was voluntary and sporadic.[17]

The stirrings of a new framework for Holocaust education are generally traced back to the late 1960s, becoming more noticeable in the following decade – the 1970s. In her analysis of 100 textbooks in the first forty years of the country's existence, Firer discovered a shift in the educational approach to the Holocaust in textbooks published in the early 1970s, namely a departure from the previous intentionalist approach to a more functionalist approach.[18] Similarly to the earlier Zionist period, educational changes were deemed to reflect societal developments. Two events in the 1960s are considered to have influenced the educational system in particular: the 1961 Eichmann trial and the tension-ridden three-week "waiting period" preceding the 1967 War. While the former revealed widespread ignorance of the Holocaust, the latter ominously reminded Israeli Jews of the fear of annihilation "here" in Israel, this time emanating from their Palestinian neighbors who, according to a *Haaretz* columnist, posed as "the new Hitler."[19] In the educational sector, these events spurred on the creation of special material and introductory programs for teachers and students.[20] Yet, despite attempts to further knowledge on the Holocaust, there were no remarkable changes in the official curriculum in the late 1960s.[21] In his epochal work, *The Seventh Million*, Tom Segev points out that in a sixty-hour unit dealing with the history of the struggle to establish the state, only ten hours were devoted to the Holocaust.[22] Moreover, as was the case in the early Zionist period, the emphasis in educational material did not lie on Jewish victims, as evidenced by the Ministry of Education's demand that teachers should avoid referring to victims numerically.[23]

It is during the 1970s that concrete educational policies were put into place that led to a formal educational framework in the 1980s. The effects of the two pivotal events of the 1960s in addition to the 1973

---

[17] Cohen, "Teacher Autonomy within a Flexible National Curriculum," 173.
[18] Whereas the intentionalist approach presented the Holocaust as a manifestation of Jewish exilic life and therefore considered an independent Israel as the only way to guarantee the future safety of all Jews, the functionalist approach attributed the extermination of the Jews to historical developments and societal and political circumstances over time. Segev, *Seventh Million*, 479, 480.
[19] Arad, "Shoah," 201.
[20] Dalia Ofer, "Israel," in *The World Reacts to the Holocaust*, ed. David Wyman (Baltimore: Johns Hopkins Press, 1996), 891.
[21] Nili Keren, "Ideologies: Attitudes and Holocaust Teaching in the State of Israel–History and Recent Development," in *Remembering for the Future*, ed. Yehuda Bauer (Oxford: Pergamon, 1989), 1031.
[22] Segev, *Seventh Million*, 479.   [23] Ibid.

War further contributed to the erosion of the dichotomy between "there" and "here,"[24] causing deep fear and anxiety and nullifying the disdain, alienation, and shame that some had felt toward Holocaust victims.[25] These experiences, coupled with the anachronistic content provided in former history books, led to appeals being made to the Ministry of Education to create changes in educational policy and the curriculum; following Menachem Begin's rise to power in 1977, these calls were answered.[26] Both for the Likud leader and the minister of education he nominated, Zevulun Hammer, the leader of the National Religious Party, the Holocaust was a defining event.

The Holocaust, according to Hammer, could serve to strengthen the Zionist cause:

How to bring the Jewish nation to immigrate to [the land of Israel], and how to convince Israeli students, those born here, raised here, and educated here, not to emigrate from here. I see this as a central topic of Israeli education ... [the Holocaust] has an important part in our physical struggle, and no less significant, in our spiritual struggle, the desire to live in the State of Israel.[27]

Under Hammer's leadership, the MOE announced in 1979 that the Holocaust would be a standard requirement for senior high-school students and that no less than thirty school hours should be dedicated to teaching the Holocaust.[28] A year later, on March 25, 1980, the Knesset's Committee of Education and Culture convened to discuss a modification of the 1953 Compulsory State Educational Law. This law stated that education should be based on "the cultural values of the people of Israel and their scientific achievements; love of the homeland and loyalty to the state and the Jewish people."[29] The bill under discussion demanded that, in addition to these educational principles, all students educated in Israeli schools should have "awareness of the Holocaust and heroism."[30] The initiator of the law was Member of Knesset (MK) Sarah Stern-Katan, a survivor of the Holocaust and a former member of a Zionist

[24] The Yom Kippur War or October War of 1973, with its thousands of casualties, created a manifest crisis in the national ethos of the *Sabra*. The surprise of the attack and initial success of the Egyptian and Syrian armies found many young soldiers in the position of having to beg for their lives from their captors, rather than dying heroically for the common cause. This, in retrospect, suggested that survival, in contrast to fighting, may have also been legitimate within the context of the Holocaust. Dan Bar-On, "The Israeli Society between the Culture of Death and the Culture of Life," *Israel Studies* 2 (1998): 94.
[25] Dan Porat, "From the Scandal to the Holocaust in Israeli Education," *Journal of Contemporary History* 39 (2004): 627.
[26] Ofer, "Israel," 891.   [27] Cited in Porat, "Scandal to the Holocaust," 632, 633.
[28] Gil, "Teaching the Shoah in History Classes," 4.   [29] Segev, *Seventh Million*, 482.
[30] Porat, "Scandal to the Holocaust," 630, 631.

underground group during the Second World War. She argued that the Holocaust was an event "in which our nation was the primary victim ... We the victims have a national testament, a holy obligation to learn, teach and transmit to future generations the events of the Holocaust of our nation."[31] The following day, the Holocaust joined the ranks of the history of the Jewish diaspora, Zionism, and the Israeli–Arab conflict as the only three mandatory topics (out of twenty-six) in the high-school curriculum.[32] Another change initiated by the MOE in the 1981–1982 school year was to incorporate the Holocaust in the matriculation exams to ensure that Israeli students would not graduate from high school without having been tested on their knowledge of the Holocaust.[33] The effects of this introduction on the content of examinations were palpable. In his review of high-school examinations from the early 1980s, Segev found that knowledge of the Holocaust and, in particular, the fate of the Jews was crucial to passing exams, as Holocaust-related questions accounted for 20 percent of the overall score in the final examination in history.[34]

Together with historian and Holocaust survivor Yisrael Gutman, Chaim Schatzker was responsible for the first MOE-approved textbook for all high schools, entitled *The Holocaust and Its Meaning* (1982).[35] The 200-page textbook, which would become a standard textbook on the Holocaust for over a decade in the state educational system, presented the Holocaust as a unique event in history, isolated from both world and Jewish history. Accordingly, the Holocaust was described as detached from the events of the Second World War, and Jewish history that preceded the Holocaust was almost completely disregarded.[36] In a 1979 interview, Schatzker explained the reasoning behind the need to present the Holocaust in this fashion: "I do not want to obscure the Holocaust by placing it within [the context of] Jewish history [as this] would dwarf the Holocaust and remove its unique value."[37] Similar statements can be found in his 1980 article, entitled "The Teaching of the Holocaust: Dilemmas and Considerations," in which Schatzker argued that while the Holocaust had a universal moral message "to coming generations," this universal human element should not detract from the Jewish uniqueness of the Holocaust in Israeli society. Furthermore, he noted that "an oversimplification of the term universal" by applying the term Holocaust to any other tragic event or by including

---

[31] Ibid., 631.   [32] Ibid., 630, 631; Segev, *Seventh Million*, 482.
[33] Porat, "Scandal to the Holocaust," 630.   [34] Segev, *Seventh Million*, 482.
[35] Firer, "Israel," 182, 183.   [36] Porat, "Scandal to the Holocaust," 633.
[37] Cited in Ibid., 634.

all the atrocities by the Nazi regime would lead "the real, historic Holocaust [to be] emptied of all its inherent, unique meaning."[38]

The uniqueness of the Holocaust was not only communicated by the structure of Schatzker and Gutman's textbook but also in the text itself. In a subchapter entitled "Holocaust Deniers and Those Who Reduce Its Image in Holocaust Literature," Schatzker and Gutman included a group of historians "who negate the uniqueness of the Holocaust by locating it within wider contexts of time and space and [compare it to the suffering of] other nations."[39] The book's first edition was severely criticized, especially by Firer (1983) and Nili Keren (1984) for, among other things, exclusion of the controversial topic of the *Judenrat*. In response, the second edition, published in 1987, added a chapter on the Jewish councils and a new chapter addressing the Final Solution for "the entire Jewish people."[40] This latter chapter explicitly noted that the Nazis applied the Final Solution to all Jews, including the Sephardic Jews of North Africa, in order to bolster identification with the Holocaust among Jews from Arab and African countries who, with the rise to power of Menachem Begin in 1977, had begun to demand legitimation of their non-Western culture and heritage, previously denied during the period of *mamlakhtiyut* (Hebrew: "statism").[41] The book's accomplishment in this regard was remarkable; two years after the publication of the second edition, Uri Farago found that Sephardic students identified more with the Holocaust than they had previously.[42] Moreover, as will become evident below, the relevance of the Holocaust for both Ashkenazi and Sephardic students was to become a central focus in history books in

[38] Chaim Schatzker, "The Teaching of the Holocaust: Dilemmas and Considerations," *The Annals of the American Academy of Political and Social Science* 450 (1980): 223.

[39] This statement hinted at neo-conservative German historians such as Ernst Nolte who from the early 1980s had attempted to contextualize the Holocaust by comparing it with other murderous acts such as Stalin's Gulag, leading to the infamous "Historikerstreit." Porat, "Scandal to the Holocaust," 634; Yisrael Gutman and Chaim Schatzker, *The Holocaust and Its Meaning* (Jerusalem: Zalman Shazar Center, 1987), 219.

[40] Gross, "Holocaust Education in Jewish Schools in Israel," 100, 101.

[41] See p. 239 for a discussion of "statism" and its role in Holocaust discourse. Hanna Yablonka, "Oriental Jewry and the Holocaust: A Tri-Generational Perspective," *Israeli Studies* 14:1 (2009): 95; Elizier Don-Yehiya, "Memory and Political Culture: Israeli Society and the Holocaust," *Studies in Contemporary Jewry* 9 (1993): 144.

[42] Twenty years later, Erik Cohen confirmed this result, finding no major difference between Ashkenazi and Sephardic students in their perceptions of the Holocaust. Cohen found that the Holocaust constituted a common denominator among students of various backgrounds with 77 percent of Israeli students responding that the Holocaust affected their worldview. Erik Cohen, *Shoah Education in Israeli State Schools: An Educational Research 2007–2009* (Ramat Gan: Bar Ilan University, 2009), 1; Uri Farago, "Jewish Identity of Israeli Youth 1965–1985," *Yahadut Zmaneinu* 5 (1989): 259–285 (in Hebrew).

subsequent years, forming a continual reminder of a communal fate despite diverging experiences.

The Holocaust in Contemporary Israeli Textbooks

In order to examine the discussion of Jewish and non-Jewish victimhood in contemporary Israeli history books and, consequently, their evolution from the first official textbook on the Holocaust, fifteen textbooks (see Table 2.2) were examined. Of these books, five solely discussed the Holocaust and the Second World War, seven focused on the Holocaust and the establishment of the Israeli state, and three dealt with the establishment of the Israeli state. All the reviewed books were written for students between the ages of thirteen and eighteen, with the vast majority being for students aged between sixteen and eighteen (thirteen books). Two of the books were specifically written for final-year students and, as such, are relied upon for the preparation of final examinations (the *Bagrut*). Save two, all of the books analyzed here received approval from the MOE and therefore were able to be taught in classrooms. While the MOE does not collect data on the popularity of approved textbooks, an inquiry among Israeli teachers found that Eli Bar-Navi's 1998 textbook and Eyal Naveh's 1999 textbook were among the most widely used, indicating that despite the publication of new textbooks, teachers may prefer to utilize textbooks they are familiar with.[43]

In the books that included the Second World War and the Holocaust, three different methods were identified that minimized the suffering and persecution of non-Jewish victims: the aggregation of non-Jewish victims, a dearth in historical information concerning the persecution of non-Jewish victims, and an absence of witness testimonies. The exposure to non-Jewish victims stands in direct opposition to the presentation of Jewish victimhood, which, in addition to being conceived of as a unique fate with a particularistic Zionist meaning, offers students an in-depth analysis of the effects of Nazi genocidal policies on individual Jewish communities, further bolstered by extensive witness testimonies and photographic evidence.

The Presentation of Non-Jewish Victims

Aggregation Aggregation, or the linguistic fusing of a "part-whole" or "part-of" into an object representing the components' relationship, is

---

[43] Adwan and Firer, *Israeli–Palestinian Conflict*, 37.

Table 2.1. *Non-Jewish victims of Nazi persecution*[a]

Victims of the Holocaust and Nazi persecution	Documented numbers
Soviet civilians	Around seven million (including 1.3 million Soviet Jewish civilians, who are included in the six million figure for Jews)
Soviet prisoners of war	Around three million (including about 50,000 Jewish soldiers)
Non-Jewish Polish civilians	Around 1.8 million (including between 50,000 and 100,000 members of the Polish elites)
Serb civilians (in the territories of Croatia, Bosnia, and Herzegovina)	312,000
People with disabilities living in institutions	Up to 250,000
Roma (Gypsies)	196,000–220,000
Jehovah's Witnesses	Around 1,900
Repeat criminal offenders and so-called a-socials	At least 70,000
Homosexuals	Hundreds, potentially thousands (possibly also counted in part under the 70,000 repeat criminal offenders and so-called a-socials)
German political opponents and resistance activists in Axis-occupied territory	Undetermined

[a] "Documenting Numbers of Victims of the Holocaust and Nazi Persecution," United States Holocaust Memorial Museum, www.ushmm.org/wlc/en/article.php?ModuleId=10008193, accessed October 16, 2016.

a regularly utilized device in speech; it allows for a facile rendering of key linkages and similarities between individual components. The unavoidable generalization that spurs from this semantic practice, however, does have ramifications for the understanding – and acknowledgment – of the original "parts" that make up the "whole," as is evidenced in the presentation of non-Jewish victims' across Israeli textbooks. In the earliest book examined in this study, Naveh's 1994 textbook *The Twentieth Century: The Century That Changed the World Order*, examples of this aggregation can be found.[44] In a paragraph under the heading "The Shoah Is a Unique

[44] Theo van Leeuwen, *Discourse and Practice: New Tools for Critical Discourse Analysis* (Oxford: Oxford University Press, 2008), 38.

Table 2.2. *Analyzed textbooks in the Israeli school system*

Title	Author	Year of publication	Grade	Content analyzed
The 20th Century: The Century That Changed the World Order	Eyal Naveh	1994	Bagrut (final year)	Second World War; 1948 War
Sensitivity to Human Suffering: Genocide in the 20th Century	Yair Auron	1994	High School	Second World War
The 20th Century: Contemporary History of the Jewish People	Eli Bar-Navi	1998	Bagrut	Second World War; 1948 War
The World and the Jews in Past Generations, Part 2, 1920–1970	Elizier Domke	1999	High School	Second World War; 1948 War
The 20th Century: On the Verge of Tomorrow	Eyal Naveh	1999	Middle School	Second World War; 1948 War
Modern Times, Part II 1920–2000	Eyal Naveh and Eli Bar-Navi	1999	High School	Second World War; 1948 War
Shoah and Memory	Israel Gutman	1999	High School	Second World War
Shoah: A Journey into Memory	Nili Keren	1999	High School	Second World War
World of Changes	Danny Ya'akovi	1999	Middle School	Second World War; 1948 War
Era of Fear and Hope 1870–1970	Ketzi'a Avieli-Tabibian	2001	High School	Second World War; 1948 War
Travel in Time: Building a State in the Middle East	Ketzi'a Avieli-Tabibian	2003	High School	1948 War
Travel in Time: From Peace to War and Shoah: Europe, the Mediterranean Sea and the Jews in the First Half of the 20th Century	Ketzi'a Avieli-Tabibian	2008	High School	Second World War
Totalitarianism and Shoah, Europe, the Mediterranean and the Jews in the First Half of the 20th Century	Eyal Naveh, Naomi Vered, and David Shachar	2009	High School	Second World War

Table 2.2. (*cont.*)

Title	Author	Year of publication	Grade	Content analyzed
Nationality: Building a State in the Middle East	Elizier Domke	2009	High School	1948 War
Creating a Democratic Jewish State in the Middle East – The Establishment of the State of Israel	Yigal Msaol	2014	High School	1948 War

Event in the History of Mankind,"[45] Naveh writes: "The Nazi killing machine did not only exterminate members of unwanted races; hundreds of thousands of government opponents, disabled and mentally ill, homosexuals and other people deemed 'unworthy of life' were killed too [...] also among some groups of Gypsies, sentenced to extermination as an inferior race, many were sent to Auschwitz, and similarly millions of communists from Russia, criminals, homosexuals, those refusing to work, prostitutes and political opponents from all over the Reich [were sentenced to death]."[46] Four years later, an almost identical statement can be found in Bar-Navi's *The Twentieth Century, Contemporary History of the Jewish People*, which states: "The industry of death did not only exterminate members of unwanted races, hundreds of thousands of government opponents, disabled and mentally ill, homosexuals and other people deemed 'unworthy of life' were killed too. This reached its peak in the death camps and gas chambers and incinerators."[47] Through grouping several persecuted groups together in one sentence, Naveh and Bar-Navi minimize the victimization of non-Jews in two distinct manners. Firstly, by grouping together various individuals, Naveh and Bar-Navi suggest that both the reasons for their persecution and their fates were similar; and,

[45] The biblical word Shoah, meaning destruction or ruin, is the standard word in Hebrew for the murder of European Jewry. While the English word Holocaust has sometimes raised objections due to its sacrificial connotation, it remains the most widely used term in the English-speaking word to denote the genocide of Europe's Jewish population.
[46] Eyal Naveh, *The Twentieth Century: The Century That Changed the World Order* (Tel Aviv: Tel Aviv Books, 1994), 134, 141.
[47] Eli Bar-Navi, *The Twentieth Century: Contemporary History of the Jewish People* (Tel Aviv: Tel Aviv Books, 1998), 133.

secondly, by specifying one number ("hundreds of thousands") the number of victims within the individual groups remains unclear, adding to the generalization of their fate.

In 1999, two important changes took place in the history curriculum, which led to revisions in the presentation of the Second World War and victims of Nazism. Firstly, the MOE recommended that of the eighty-five history teaching hours to 11th and 12th graders, forty-five should be assigned to the Holocaust, Nazism, and the Second World War, making them the most important subjects in the high-school curriculum. Secondly, Jewish history – in which the Holocaust was taught – was integrated with general history, which was meant to lead to the incorporation of others' fate in the Second World War.[48] As a result of the new curriculum, a departure from previous content can be identified in the textbook produced by the historian and educator Keren. *Shoah: A Journey into Memory* is the first among the textbooks examined to argue that a close reading of the Nuremberg Laws demonstrates that the race laws also applied to Gypsies.[49] Keren also offers a more detailed discussion of the systematic persecution of Gypsies and equally notes that a comprehensive plan of persecution "existed for members of the Roma tribe, just like it did for Jews," indicating that Jews were not the only group that was systematically targeted.[50] A further shift from previous textbooks can be noted in Keren's discussion of the euthanasia program, which was introduced in 1939–1940. In addition to mentioning the policy itself, Keren discusses its implementation in purpose-built centers and the execution of the program by doctors, midwives, and nurses.[51]

The above-mentioned curriculum changes did not lead content modifications to be adopted uniformly. Gutman's and Naveh's books, also published in 1999, echo the content of earlier textbooks concerning non-Jewish victims. Gutman, at times, does not even identify the various groups of non-Jewish victims. For instance, in his discussion of the treatment of Jews and non-Jews at Auschwitz, Gutman writes the following: "Most [of those that were] sent to Birkenau transported from all over Nazi-occupied Europe were Jews, and on their arrival, most [Jews] were directly exterminated [...] The fate of the Jews deported to the camp was different from the fate of non-Jews. Immediately upon their arrival in the camp, non-Jews became prisoners."[52] Through juxtaposing

---

[48] Gil, "Teaching the Shoah in History Classes," 5.
[49] Nili Keren, *Shoah: A Journey into Memory* (Tel Aviv: Tel Aviv Books, 1999), 72.
[50] Ibid., 73.   [51] Ibid., 56, 57.
[52] Israel Gutman, *Shoah and Memory* (Jerusalem: Zalman Shazar Center, 1999), 130.

the fate of Jews against that of all non-Jews, Gutman fails to differentiate between the various divisions and accompanying treatment of prisoners at a camp like Auschwitz-Birkenau.[53] Using a similar method of aggregation, Naveh refers to scores of non-Jewish victims as "other people" (Hebrew: *bnei adam nosafim*): "The Shoah, during which close to six million Jews were killed, is one of the most dreadful events in the history of mankind [...] during the war the Nazis also killed other people who they defined as 'unworthy of life' and among them were tens of thousands of Gypsies."[54] A few pages later, the same practice of aggregation is repeated in Naveh's discussion of death camps: "In some death camps, tens of thousands of Gypsies were also killed [along with] hundreds of thousands of Poles and other people."[55]

Although the amalgamation of non-Jewish victims has occurred less frequently since 1999, this does not mean that the practice has been completely forsaken. Ketzi'a Avieli-Tabibian's 2001 book *Era of Fear and Hope* notes that approximately "three quarters of a million people, a third of them Jews, died" on death marches while Naveh's 2009 book, entitled *Totalitarianism and the Holocaust*, points out that "about a 1.1 million people were killed in Auschwitz Birkenau of which about a million were Jews."[56] Here, it is evident that while both Naveh and Tabibian have accorded exact numbers to Jewish victims, the other victims remain nameless. On the whole, however, Tabibian's *Era of Fear and Hope* (2001) and *Travel in Time* (2008) do place more emphasis on the persecution of individual groups under the Nazi regime. This becomes clear from the fact that separate content is offered on the fate of Gypsies, homosexuals, and victims of religious and political persecution.[57] Similarly, Naveh's 2009 book allows for further differentiation among the groups of non-Jewish victims. Concerning Gypsies, Naveh thus notes

[53] Hermann Langbein notes that prisoners in Auschwitz were forced to wear a triangle that indicated the type of imprisonment and, in the case of non-Germans, nationality, which determined the type of work given in the camp and, consequently, the quality of life and survival chances in the camp, creating a "hierarchy among prisoners" and a "camp elite." Hermann Langbein, *People in Auschwitz* (Chapel Hill: University of North Carolina Press, 2004), 11–15; 63–240.

[54] Eyal Naveh, *The Twentieth Century on the Verge of Tomorrow* (Tel Aviv: Tel Aviv Books, 1999), 110.

[55] Ibid., 112.

[56] Ketzi'a Avieli-Tabibian, *Era of Fear and Hope 1870–1970* (Tel Aviv: Matach Publishing, 2001), 230; Eyal Naveh, Naomi Vered, and David Shachar, *Totalitarianism and Shoah, Europe, the Mediterranean and the Jews in the First Half of the Twentieth Century* (Tel Aviv: Reches, 2009), 272, 275.

[57] Avieli-Tabibian, *Era of Fear and Hope*, 215; Ketzi'a Avieli-Tabibian, *Travel in Time: From Peace to War and Shoah: Europe, the Mediterranean Sea and the Jews in the First Half of the Twentieth Century* (Ramat Aviv: Matach Publishing, 2008), 118, 134, 424.

that not all Gypsies were persecuted, but especially the Roma.[58] Nevertheless, similarly to his predecessor Keren, Naveh fails to explain to his readers why the Nazis differentiated between Gypsy tribes and, perhaps more crucially, whether this differentiation was upheld.[59]

Historical Paucity

Inadequate historical information resulting from inaccurate and ana-chronistic material has contributed to a minimized understanding of non-Jewish victimhood. An example of the first practice occurs in Naveh's 1994 book. In his analysis of the German invasion of the Soviet Union, Naveh notes that in addition to suffering great losses, "more than two million soldiers fell into captivity and were sent as forced laborers to German concentration camps." Beyond presenting an inaccurate number of Soviet prisoners of war (POWs), 3.5 million below existing estimates, the fate of these soldiers, of whom 3.3 million died from starvation, exposure, and mistreatment in German camps,[60] remains unclear and it is up to the reader to speculate whether the soldiers were freed after the war or died in these camps.[61] An almost identical statement appears in Naveh's 1999 book, where Naveh states: "More than two million [Russian] soldiers fell into captivity and were sent as forced laborers to German concentration camps. The Russian Air Force ceased to function. In the areas that were conquered by the Germans many massacres were committed on the population and the Nazis continued [undertaking] extermination policies against the Jews."[62] In this context, it remains ambiguous how "the massacres" were executed and how many Russians died as a result. Gutman's 1999 text-book *Shoah and Memory* also withholds crucial historical information. In his discussion of the fate of Gypsies Gutman relays to his readers that there was no systematic policy that led to the *Porrajmos*;[63] "[rather] most

---

[58] Naveh, *Totalitarianism*, 284.

[59] For historical works on Gypsy persecution, see Donald Kenrick and Grattan Puxon, *Gypsies under the Swastika* (Hatfield: University of Hertfordshire Press, 2009); Guenter Lewy, *The Nazi Persecution of the Gypsies* (Oxford: Oxford University Press, 2000); Ian Hancock, "Gypsy History in Germany and Neighboring Lands: A Chronology to the Holocaust and Beyond," *Nationalities Papers* 19 (1991): 395–412.

[60] Peter Calvocoressi, Guy Wint, and John Pritchard, *Total War: The Western Hemisphere* (New York: Pantheon Books, 1990), 278. For a later work confirming these numbers, see Tony Judt, *Postwar: A History of Europe since 1945* (London: Pimlico, 2007), 19.

[61] Naveh, *World Order*, 118.   [62] Naveh, *Verge of Tomorrow*, 103, 104.

[63] *Porrajmos* – Romani for devouring – is a term used to designate the Nazi genocide of the Roma which came into wide usage in the 1990s, including as a result of its scholarly use by the Romani scholar Ian Hancock. See Ian Hancock, "On the Interpretation of a Word: Porrajmos as Holocaust," *Radoc*, 2006, www.radoc.net/radoc.php?doc=art_e_holocaust_interpretation&lang=ry&articles=true, accessed August 30, 2017.

of them remained prisoners in the camp [Auschwitz-Birkenau], although many of them died of the living conditions that existed in the family camps from which they were deported."[64] However, without having mentioned the persecution process of Gypsies, which included concentrated incarceration in established Gypsy family camps, the notion of a family camp remains alien to Gutman's readers.[65]

While the failure to mention historical developments or concepts can be considered historically problematic, it does not constitute misinformation. Despite being rare, historically incorrect material has been identified, including pertaining to the Nazi's euthanasia program. Thus, on this topic, Naveh (1994) informs students of the following: "Furthermore, in the 1930s, they [German Nazis] conducted experiments [on the level of] industrialized extermination: more than 100,000[66] disabled and mentally ill Germans were suffocated in death trucks using gas in the engine exhaust. These experiments reduced in the wake of public protests, but the experience gained was used in the killing of Jews."[67] Crucially, the euthanasia program – known as the T4 Program – did not constitute experiments (Hebrew: *nisuyim*) that were used as a prequel[68] to the genocide of the Jews. Rather, the program was a self-contained policy installed in 1939–1945 to systematically rid German society of "undesired

---

[64] Gutman, *Shoah*, 130.

[65] On the subject of Gypsy family camps, see Michael Berenbaum, *The Holocaust and History: The Known, the Unknown, the Disputed, and the Reexamined* (Bloomington/Indianapolis: Indiana University Press, 1998), 394; Friedlander, *Origins of Nazi Genocide*, 292.

[66] In 2018, the German Federal Archives estimated that the number of estimated victims of the T4 program was much higher; according to historical documentation, the euthanasia program claimed the lives of 200,000 patients within the German Reich, in addition to almost 100,000 men, women, and children in other European countries. See Das Bundesarchiv, "Euthanasia im Dritten Reich," Deutschland: Das Bundesarchiv, August 30, 2018, www.bundesarchiv.de/DE/Content/Artikel/Ueber-uns/Aus-unserer-Arbeit/euthanasie-im-dritten-reich.html, accessed February 15, 2020 (in German).

[67] Naveh, *World Order*, 140.

[68] According to Dan Stone, there is a vital link between the euthanasia program, which additionally took place in occupied and annexed German territory, and the Holocaust, namely the development of a genocidal mindset and a willingness among the German people in general to accept such procedures. In that sense, as Stone notes, "there is no disagreement about the fact that the 'success' of the T4 programme helped to pave the way for the later, more far-reaching genocide of the Jews." Similarly, Götz Aly notes that "the significance of Operation T-4 as a prelude to the gas chambers of Belzec and Auschwitz lies not so much in its developments of techniques of camouflage and murder as in its undeniable political success – in the overt as well as tacit acceptance of the murder of marginalized, defenceless people [...]." Dan Stone, *Histories of the Holocaust* (Oxford: Oxford University Press, 2010), 191; Götz Aly, "Medicine against the Useless," in *Cleansing the Fatherland Nazi Medicine and Racial Hygiene*, ed. Götz Aly, Peter Chroust, and Christian Pross (Baltimore: The Johns Hopkins University Press, 1994), 92.

elements."[69] On the same subject, a further historical inaccuracy appears in several textbooks, including in Keren (1999), Tabibian (2001, 2008), and Naveh (2009). According to these authors, the euthanasia program was halted in 1941, as a result of protest by the Catholic Church and/or on Hitler's orders. Nevertheless, while both did exist, Henry Friedlander as early as 1995 pointed out that the belief that they led to the end of killings was based "on a post-war myth"; instead, the euthanasia program continued unabated until 1945.[70]

Witness Testimony

An analysis of the selection – and usage – of witness testimony offers important insight into the particulars of the authors' sought narrative. Oral sources, both contemporary and post-factum, provide historians and textbook authors alike with an important supplementation – and reinforcement – of archival documentation and the related discussion of historical events. The inclusion of source material in history books as such is not simply meant as a pedagogical incentive, but is also considered a means to authenticate the historical narrative through eyewitnesses' assumed adherence to veracity. As Rosanne Kennedy notes, following the Holocaust and especially after the Eichmann trial in Jerusalem, witness testimony became "a truth telling of the past."[71] In his 1999 textbook, Naveh equally claims that witness testimony can be effectively used to challenge Holocaust deniers. In a paragraph entitled "Survivors' Testimony Perpetuates the Memory of the Shoah," Naveh thus writes: "Their [survivors'] stories play an important role in the battle against Holocaust deniers who claim that the Holocaust did not happen and that the death camps and gas chambers were a Zionist Jewish invention."[72]

A further reasoning for the inclusion of testimony is pointed out by Kennedy and Meg McLagan who argue that identification with the victims is enforced through its usage because testimony shows that "pain is universal [as it] crosses social, economic, and geographic

---

[69] See Friedlander, *Origins of Nazi Genocide*, xii, xiii; Aly Götz, "Medicine against the Useless," in *Cleansing the Fatherland: Nazi Medicine and Racial Hygiene*, ed. Aly Götz et al. (Chapel Hill: University of North Carolina Press, 1995), 22–99.

[70] Friedlander, *Origins of Nazi Genocide*, 151; also see Michael Burleigh, *Death and Deliverance: 'Euthanasia' in Germany, C.1900 to 1945* (Wiltshire: Cambridge University Press, 1994), 111, 238.

[71] Rosanne Kennedy, "Moving Testimony: Human Rights, Palestinian Memory, and the Transnational Public Sphere," in *Transnational Memory: Circulation, Articulation, Scales*, ed. Chiara De Cesari and Ann Rigney (Berlin: De Gruyte, 2014), 51.

[72] Naveh, *Verge of Tomorrow*, 118, 119.

boundaries."[73] This specific utilization of Holocaust testimony in Israeli textbooks was confirmed in Segev's 1993 work, which demonstrated that testimony is used to describe the horrors of individuals in order to reinforce the credibility of the information and intensify the students' identification with the victims.[74] Indeed, Michael Yaron, the Superintendent of History at the MOE between 1993 and 2011, maintained that when students are exposed to stories by Holocaust survivors "it is only natural that they have empathy with the survivors. They identify with the victim's story."[75]

According to Firer, primary source analysis is one of the favorite methods of teaching in Israel, as it gives the class "the opportunity to act as the historian or political scientist."[76] In the twelve history textbooks treating the subject of the Second World War, extensive Jewish witness testimony is used in the discussion of, inter alia, the execution of medical experiments in Auschwitz, mass shootings in the Soviet Union, Kristallnacht, and the infamous death marches.

The above-mentioned battle for credibility and identification, however, does not appear to apply to the fate of non-Jewish victims; witness accounts throughout the analyzed textbooks are written exclusively by Jewish survivors and victims. While the use of extensive witness accounts to elucidate the fate of those named in a few sentences might appear superfluous, three books dedicate entire pages to the fate of the Gypsies: Keren (1999), Tabibian (2008), and Naveh (2009). Of these books, only Keren incorporates witness testimony. However, instead of using Gypsy testimony available at the time, including by Hans Braun and Ina Friedman, Keren uses testimony by five Israeli-Jews and an extract from Hermann Rauschning's *Hitler Speaks*, which had previously been debunked as a fraud.[77]

Textbook Censorship

Textbook writers in the period under examination were not necessarily encouraged to include the suffering of non-Jewish victims under the Nazi

---

[73] Ibid., 54; Meg McLagan, "Principles, Publicity, and Politics: Notes on Human Rights Media," *American Anthropologist* 105 (2003): 607.

[74] Segev, *Seventh Million*, 480.

[75] Interview conducted with Michael Yaron on April 14, 2016.

[76] Adwan and Firer, *Israeli–Palestinian Conflict*, 86.

[77] Keren, *Shoah*, 72, 72. Ian Kershaw wrote in his 1998 work on Hitler that he had not used Rauschning's book because it is "now regarded to have so little authenticity that it is best to disregard it all together." Ian Kershaw, *Hitler, 1889–1936: Hubris* (London: Penguin Press, 1998), xiv. For Gypsy testimony see Hans Braun, *"A Sinto Survivor Speaks,"* in *Papers from the Sixth and Seventh Annual Meetings, Gypsy Lore Society, North American Chapter*, ed. Joanne Grumet (New York: The Society, 1986), 165–171; Ina Friedman, *The Other Victims: First-Person Stories of Non-Jews Persecuted by the Nazis* (Boston: Houghton Mifflin, 1990), 7–24.

regime, as the fate of a book published by Yair Auron in 1994 demonstrates. Following the 1992 elections, Meretz, the Israeli leftist Zionist party, was given ministerial responsibility for education. Shulamit Aloni, the minister of education at the time, approached genocide scholar Auron to develop a new history course on the Holocaust and genocides that befell other people in the twentieth century since a 1993 study by the ministry had found that "young people are both ignorant of and indifferent to disasters and acts of genocide committed in the 20th century [....] Such ignorance has marked and long-term effects on the understanding and conclusions of the young Israeli regarding the Holocaust that the Jewish people suffered."[78] Subsequently, Auron developed a textbook entitled *Sensitivity to Human Suffering: Genocide in the 20th Century*, which, as the title indicates, discussed the phenomenon of genocide in the twentieth century and contained a partial list of genocides committed in the twentieth century, including the Armenian genocide, the Stalinist regime's murder of political opponents, the genocide of the Gypsies in the Second World War, and the Cambodian genocide.[79]

Auron's educational program was officially canceled some days before its formal introduction as a trial. The official statement was that "from a professional point of view" the program was unsuitable as it was based on literary rather than historical research.[80] In an interview conducted in May 2016, however, Auron argued that the book was rejected for political reasons, as it was deemed that a discussion of the Armenian genocide in textbooks would affect political relations with Turkey.[81] This argument was corroborated by Yaron who was in charge of the history curriculum at the time. According to Yaron, who prefers to refer to the Armenian genocide as an "issue," the ministry was asked by the government not to develop the textbook, because it was deemed harmful to the diplomatic relationship between Israel and Turkey.[82] Indeed, research by Eldad Ben Aharon found that Israel's stance toward the Armenian genocide derives from a pragmatic foreign policy that hinges on adopting Turkey's "denial narrative" to secure bilateral economic, military, and arms trading agreements.[83] At the same time, Ben Aharon notes, ethnic

---

[78] Gur-Ze'ev, "Morality," 167, 8; interview conducted with Yair Auron on May 29, 2016.
[79] Yair Auron, *Sensitivity to Human Suffering: Genocide in the Twentieth Century* (Tel Aviv: Teacher's College, 1994), 17.
[80] Gur-Ze'ev, "Morality," 168.
[81] Interview conducted with Yair Auron on May 29, 2016.
[82] Interview conducted with Michael Yaron on April 14, 2016.
[83] Eldad Ben Aharon, "Between Ankara and Jerusalem: The Armenian Genocide as a Zero-Sum Game in Israel's Foreign Policy (1980's–2010's)," *Journal of Balkan and Near Eastern Studies* 20:5 (2018): 472.

competition between Jews and Armenians as victims of genocide precludes
Israeli recognition, or as Israeli Foreign Minister Shimon Peres put it in
2001: "We reject attempts to create a similarity between the Holocaust
and the Armenian allegations. Nothing similar to the Holocaust occurred.
It is a tragedy what the Armenians went through, but not genocide."[84]

Further statements by Yaron indicate that Auron's in-depth discussion
of the systematic persecution of Gypsies prior to and during the Second
World War also did not fit Yaron's own historical views.[85] According to
Yaron, the suffering of non-Jewish victims should not be considered
equal to that of Jewish victims in the Holocaust: "Homosexuals and
communists also suffered, but they were not systematically persecuted.
At the Wannsee Conference it was decided that every Jew would be
persecuted. It is important to note that others did suffer, but it is not
the same. Russians did die, but as a result of the war [while] six million
[Jews] didn't die in battle."[86] As such, despite the fact that Auron had no
intention of questioning the uniqueness of the Holocaust or presenting
the Holocaust as simply one example of twentieth century genocide,
Gur-Ze'ev argued that the textbook's rejection occurred as a result of
its implicit questioning of the justification for the state of Israel or, in
Gur-Ze'ev's preferred post-modern discourse, "the hegemonic Zionist
metanarrative."[87]

Even though the rejection of Auron's textbook took place more than
twenty years ago, Or Kashti, a senior education reporter at *Haaretz*, notes
that the incorporation of genocide studies and non-Jewish victims has
largely failed in Israeli textbooks on the Second World War. As Kashti
states: "The only inclusive aspect in Holocaust teaching is that the
murder of Gypsies is acknowledged and, on a good day, leftists [political
opponents] and victims of euthanasia will also be mentioned."[88]
According to Naveh, the author of several of the aforementioned textbooks, the exclusion of non-Jewish victims does not necessarily represent
the authors' own historical views, but constitutes a compromise which
enables authors like himself to gain approval from the textbook approval
body: "If I were free to write what I wanted, I would take a much more
universal approach, because the Holocaust is a crisis of civilization in
which the Jews were victims just as the Gypsies and homosexuals [were].

---

[84] Cited in Eldad Ben Aharon, "A Unique Denial: Israel's Foreign Policy and the
Armenian Genocide," *British Journal of Middle Eastern Studies* 42:4 (2015): 638.
[85] Auron, *Sensitivity to Human Suffering*, 118–129.   [86] Ibid.
[87] Gur-Ze'ev, "Morality," 171.
[88] Interview conducted with Or Kashti on April 6, 2016.

I am critical of way the Holocaust is taught in Israel which represents the Holocaust as our victimhood [as if] the whole world is against us and [therefore] is very ethnocentric, Zionist, and simplistic. As a historian and educator, I am critical of this trend. It is ahistorical."[89]

The Uniqueness of the Holocaust

The exclusive nature of Jewish victimhood during the Second World War is not only emphasized through a minimization of non-Jewish victimhood, but equally through a concentration on the uniqueness of the Holocaust and its continued importance for Israeli-Jewish society. The singularity of the Holocaust is mentioned in all the books analyzed in this case study save three: Tabibian (2001, 2008) and Danny Ya'akovi (1999). For instance, Naveh in his 1994 book notes under the heading "The Shoah Is a Unique Event in the History of Mankind" that "The Shoah of the Jews that took place during the Second World War was a unique event and without historical precedent in human history in terms of its nature, scope, and intensity."[90] Naveh's conception and presentation of the Holocaust remains constant throughout his textbooks. In his 1999 book, Naveh reminds his readers that "The Shoah was a unique event in history, and was not executed by animals, but by human beings and the highest price for their crimes was paid by Jews."[91] Ten years later, despite placing more emphasis on non-Jewish victimhood in the Second World War, Naveh ends his chapter on the Final Solution in a summary of the chapter's most important content, which reads: "The Jewish genocide is unique in human history and there is no equal in the civilized world."[92] In the same year that Naveh's second book (1999) was published, a new trend can be identified in describing the uniqueness of the Holocaust in the books of Keren and Gutman. This trend, introduced in Bar-Navi's 1998 work, describes the Holocaust's singularity in comparison to other massacres and genocides, thereby reflecting the new history curriculum, which sought to situate Jewish history within world history. However, it is through noting the similarities between other acts of mass murder that authors such as Bar-Navi, Gutman and Keren argue that the Holocaust should be considered a singular event based on its unique characteristics. As Bar-Navi writes:

Massacres have accompanied the history of mankind forever. People have slaughtered each other for a piece of land, a water well, the right way to

---

[89] Interview conducted with Eyal Naveh on March 16 and May 15, 2016.
[90] Naveh, *World Order*, 134.   [91] Ibid., 111.   [92] Ibid., 287.

worship the creator and other reasons. With that, the systematic murder of the Jewish people in the Second World War was a unique event in the history of mankind, unprecedented in nature, scope and intensity. The Jews were not merely an enemy, but an inferior foe. He [the Jew] was perceived as a virus and his elimination [was considered] a way to purify the body of mankind [...].[93]

Similar statements appear in textbooks published the following year, including by Keren and Gutman who note that while "instances of hideous genocide have occurred,"[94] the Holocaust must be considered an "extraordinary event of genocide"[95] and "an unprecedented event."[96]

As mentioned above, three of the fifteen books did not mention the singularity of the Holocaust. Of these, Ya'akovi's 1999 book is of particular interest. While Ya'akovi, in similar fashion to Gutman, Keren, and Bar-Navi, mentions other genocides in the twentieth century, unlike his predecessors, Ya'akovi questions the uniqueness of the Holocaust. Under the heading "The Shoah Was Not the Only Genocide in the 20th Century," Ya'akovi writes the following:

The Shoah was not the only genocide that took place in the 20th century. Before it, there was the genocide of the Armenians at the hands of the Turks during the First World War. After the Second World War, there were other cases of genocide, many of them took place in the Third World, for instance in Biafra and Bangladesh and Cambodia and Rwanda. Also, during the war in former Yugoslavia there were instances of genocide. In this light, should we see the Holocaust of the Jews as a unique event in history?[97]

Ya'akovi's[98] explicit questioning of the uniqueness of the Holocaust meant that the book never made it to the classrooms. After its publication, the book aroused a huge public debate and it was even discussed in the Knesset. Eventually, the textbook was rejected "because it didn't draw the appropriate historical lessons from the Holocaust."[99]

The Holocaust and Its Meaning for the Entire Jewish Nation

While the Holocaust predominantly took place in mainland Europe, the unique nature of the Holocaust does not refer exclusively to the fate of Ashkenazi Jews. Gil notes that the educational aims set out in 1980,

---

[93] Bar-Navi, *The Twentieth Century*, 132.   [94] Keren, *Shoah*, Introduction.
[95] Ibid.   [96] Gutman, *Shoah*, 216.
[97] Danny Ya'akovi, *World of Changes* (Tel Aviv: Maalot Publishing, 1999), 140.
[98] Ya'akovi was a member of the history staff at the ministry's curriculum division until the book's publication. Yoram Hazony, Michael B. Oren, Daniel Polisar, *The Quiet Revolution in the Teaching of Zionist History: A Comparative Study of Education Ministry Textbooks on the Twentieth Century* (Shalem Press, 2000), 1.
[99] Gross, "Holocaust Education in Jewish Schools in Israel," 101.

which stipulated that "the student should identify with the victims of the Shoah," led to a textual inclusion of North African Jewry.[100] This research, however, found that whereas textbooks before 1999 stressed the extermination of the entire Jewish nation without regard for origin as one of the main goals of Nazi ideology, later textbooks made a concrete effort to describe the fate of Jews in North Africa in depth. Accordingly, Gutman and Keren devote several pages to North African countries affected by Nazi rule: Morocco, Algeria, Tunisia, and Libya.[101] Furthermore, both authors argue that while the fate of the Jews in North Africa differed from their brethren in Europe, this was a result of the war's evolution rather than Nazi policy. As Keren stipulates:

At the Wannsee Conference, [Reinhard] Heydrich was in control of the list of countries with Jews [...] Next to the name of France (the non-occupied part) appears the number 700,000, and there is no doubt that this number also referred to the areas under French rule in North Africa, which included Tunisia. The Jews of Tunisia were therefore included in the plan to murder the Jewish people.[102]

Under the heading "At a Geographical Distance [But] a Shared Fate," Gutman also emphasizes the need to consider the fate of the Jews of North Africa in the framework of the Holocaust and as Holocaust victims rather than in the context of World War II, as civilians caught between Allied and Axis armies.[103]

Therefore, he notes:

Despite their distance from the war in Europe and the centers of extermination, the Jews of North Africa were not spared persecution and death in the period of the Shoah. The political stance of indifference and the government structure meant that the fate of the Jews of the Maghreb was not the same as the fate of the Jews in Europe. And yet, despite differences [...] the events of the Holocaust did not pass over the Jews of North Africa altogether.[104]

The continuation of this trend in subsequent years can be seen in the presentation of North African Jewry's fate as part and parcel of the Holocaust. Tabibian (2008) explains that the suffering of the North African Jews was part of the Holocaust since "the racial Nazi ideology referred to all Jews," as indicated in "a telegram by ambassador [Joachim

---

[100] Gil, "Teaching the Shoah in History Classes," 4, 5.
[101] Gutman, *Shoah*, 151–157; Keren, *Shoah*, 50–51, 138.   [102] Keren, *Shoah*, 138.
[103] According to Hanna Yablonka, this latter interpretation had been dominant in the first decades following the war. Yablonka, "Oriental Jewry and the Holocaust," 98.
[104] The inclusion of North African Jews in the Holocaust is further reinforced by Gutman in the questions that follow this text, which ask the students to discuss the relationship between European rule and the fate of the Jews in North Africa during the Holocaust. Gutman, *Shoah*, 157.

von] Ribbentrop in Rome on 13 January 1943, [which] reiterated that the architects of German Nazi policies considered Jews in all places enemies."[105] Interestingly, it is Naveh's (2009) extensive discussion of the fate of Jews in North Africa in 2009 that shows the effect of other textbooks' content on textbook writers and the incorporation of endorsed historiography. In contrast to his 1994 book, Naveh dedicates five pages to Jewish life during the Second World War in North Africa. Furthermore, on the last two pages, Naveh not only presents his readers with a historiographical reasoning for its inclusion in this book, but also offers arguments for the incorporation of the events in North Africa in the framework of the Holocaust:

> For many years historians of the Shoah did not treat the fate of the Jews in North Africa in the period of the Second World War as part of the Shoah of the Jewish people. Today, most historians think that the events that were experienced by the Jews in North Africa are part of the Shoah because of the similarities [in the adopted policies]. In Chapter 16, you will find that the Germans included the Jews of North Africa in the comprehensive plan of the Final Solution, which was discussed at the Wannsee Conference, and therefore it is possible to surmise that if their control had continued, the fate of the Jews in Tunisia, Libya, Algeria, and Morocco would have been the same [as that] of the murdered Jews in Europe.[106]

While the content of the Naveh's text uses other historians' arguments as a basis for the inclusion of Sephardic Jews in the Holocaust, the justification for this practice is reinforced in the chapter summary in which Naveh resolutely concludes: "The fate of the Jews of Western Europe, Central Europe and Southern Europe and Northern Africa was no different in principle from the fate of the Eastern European Jews."[107]

The Holocaust and Israel

It is clear that an emphasis on the uniqueness of the Holocaust for the entire Jewish nation in an Israeli-Jewish classroom bolsters its relevance for that group; and a clear articulation of this particular pertinence exists in several of the examined textbooks. Various methods are used to discuss the central role of the Holocaust for all Israeli-Jews – indicated by the usage of "we" – and to draw a direct link between the Holocaust and the establishment of the state of Israel. The first method can be found in Naveh's 1994 book in which Naveh refers to the unique relation that Israeli-Jews have with the Holocaust and, at the same time,

[105] Avieli-Tabibian, *Travel in Time*, 238–240.   [106] Naveh, *Totalitarianism*, 240, 241.
[107] Ibid., 241.

reinforces the continuation of this connection by including himself: "As Jews, we have, of course, a unique connection to the Holocaust, and therefore it takes up extensive place in the curriculum and culture of the state of Israel [...] The following chapter tries to lay out central dilemmas of the Shoah – which continue – for us as human beings, as Jews and as Israelis, and examines the possibility of attributing meaning to it."[108] A similar practice can be discerned in textbooks written by Keren and Gutman who, like Naveh, situate themselves among the students in order to relay the importance of the Holocaust and its teaching. Keren thus argues: "For good or for bad, the Shoah is part of the human experience and it is up to us to learn it first and foremost as human beings. But not only in this manner, we learn it as Jews."[109] In this context, usage of "we" or "us" is meant to further legitimize the Holocaust's importance for Israeli-Jewish society, because, as Theo van Leeuwen explains, when the "I" is someone in whom authority is vested, such as a textbook writer or scholar, the content is deemed credible.[110] The relevance of the Holocaust is also underscored by referring to the students' own assumed (familial) dealings with the Holocaust. Based on his understanding of the students' preoccupations, Naveh therefore promises in his introduction that his book "will create an understanding among you of your parents and grandparents [in order] to shape your own world views and deal in a better way with that [which] is presented each day and each hour on television, on the radio, and in the newspapers."[111] Using similar argumentation, Keren intends that "the book that is in front of you will open paths up for you to deal with the events of the Shoah and will give you the means to understand, even if only partially, one of the unprecedented events that occurred in the 20th century and of which the Jews were the main victims."[112]

The connection between the Holocaust and the state of Israel is signaled in the books' structural makeup. Of the examined books, seven books discussed the Holocaust and, subsequently, the establishment of the state of Israel, thereby drawing a direct connection between the two (see Table 2.2). More explicit connections between the Holocaust and the establishment of Israel can be seen in the textbooks' content, including in Keren's 1999 book in which she maintains:

Between the years 1948 and 1949, close to 200,000 Jewish survivors of the Shoah came to Israel. The most substantial number of immigrants (75 percent) came in

---

[108] Naveh, *World Order*, 134.   [109] Keren, *Shoah*, Introduction.
[110] Theo van Leeuwen, "Legitimation in Discourse and Communication," *Discourse & Communication* 1 (2007): 94.
[111] Naveh, *Verge of Tomorrow*, Introduction.   [112] Ibid.

these years. More than 60 percent of them were of the age between 15 and 29 and 16 percent of them were between 30 and 44. This fact was crucial for the involvement of survivors of the Shoah in the battle for independence and the building of the new state. Many of them immediately became fighters in the War of Independence and were involved in the development of the state of Israel in the years that followed.[113]

A few pages further, Keren even notes, somewhat controversially, that without the Holocaust, it is doubtful that Zionism would have been realized: "As such, the Holocaust is, in the deepest sense, one of the reasons and justifications of the Zionist enterprise, as is reflected in the state of Israel."[114] The connection between the Holocaust and the establishment of Israel is not only emphasized in books that principally deal with the Holocaust. Elizier Domke's 2009 book *Nationality: Building a State in the Middle East* describes itself as "the successor to [the textbook] 'Totalitarianism and Shoah'" and Yigal Msaol's 2014 book *Creating a Democratic Jewish State in the Middle East* is introduced with the following sentence: "It is impossible to ignore the difference between the depth of the crisis and the extent of Zionist achievement and the rapid transition 'from Shoah to revival'."[115] The presentation of this battle for revival will be the subject of the remainder of this chapter.

The 1948 War in Israeli Textbooks

Influenced by the emergence of new historiography and its intellectual response, Israeli society has been forced to confront the legacy of the 1948 War and the elite establishment approach purported in the state's early years of a righteous and triumphant newborn people. Similar to textbooks dealing with the Holocaust, Israeli history books on the 1948 War and the mass displacement of Palestinians have been subject to historical periodization to reflect their content and, with that, existing societal approaches towards the war. Perhaps the most prolific historian to discuss the portrayal of the 1948 War and its aftermath is Elie Podeh. In two works published in 2000, Podeh examines the evolution of the presentation of the 1948 War in Israeli textbooks from the 1950s until the late 1990s based on the identification of three generations of textbooks.

---

[113] Ibid., 167.   [114] Ibid., 171.
[115] Elizier Domke, *Nationality: Building a State in the Middle East* (Jerusalem: Zalman Shazar Center, 2009), Introduction; Yigal Msaol, *Creating a Democratic Jewish State in the Middle East – The Establishment of the State of Israel* (Ma'ale Adumim: Hi-School Books, 2014), Introduction.

Podeh notes that the historical narrative in the first generation of textbooks was laden with pathos and incorporated simplistic, one-sided, and often blatantly distorted content. These distortions included a number of "Zionist myths," one of which was the depiction of the Arab-Israeli conflict as a battle of "the few against the many," a contemporary paradigm of the biblical David and Goliath, which was invoked to illustrate that the Jews, as throughout their history, were a persecuted minority.[116] Since early textbooks described the 1948 War exclusively from an Israeli-Jewish point of view, the fact that the Palestinians and other Arabs considered the war a catastrophe was not mentioned.[117] Rather, textbooks written in the 1950s and 1960s argued that Israel had played no part in creating "the refugee problem," and that Palestinians, in line with traditional Zionist scholarship,[118] had simply fled the country as a result of calls by their leaders despite Israeli attempts to persuade them to stay. As such, a textbook published in 1954 noted that "it was the Arab leadership's promise that the victorious Arab armies would return the refugees to their homes which, in fact, animated and fueled the mass flight."[119] While Podeh identifies a middle phase or a second generation of textbooks concerning the 1948 War, lasting from 1967 to 1984/5, the content appears very similar to the earlier phase as blame was firmly placed with the refugees themselves and the Arab leadership, indicated through the use of words such as "flight," "abandon," "exit," "desert," "vacate," and so on.[120] One notable departure that does occur in the content of second-generation textbooks is the inclusion of Plan D (Hebrew: *Tokhnit Dalet*),[121] albeit in a heavily censored format, as parts of the plan which

---

[116] Podeh, "History and Memory in the Israeli Educational System," 76, 77. Also see Rafi Nets-Zehngut, "Israeli Approved Textbooks and the 1948 Palestinian Exodus," *Israel Studies* 18 (2013): 49.

[117] Podeh, *Arab-Israeli Conflict*, 102.

[118] See, for instance, Netanel Lorch, *The Edge of the Sword: Israel's War of Independence, 1947-1949* (New York: Putnam, 1961), 286.

[119] Podeh, *Arab-Israeli Conflict*, 105, 106.   [120] Ibid., 105, 107.

[121] In March 1948, following several military failures, the Haganah recognized the need for a strategic plan to defend the Jewish state in the event of an Arab invasion once the British finally evacuated the country. The result was Plan D, which called for a series of offensive operations to establish a Jewish territorial continuum from Metullah in the north to Revivim in the south. It stipulated that Palestinian villages – principally those that could not be permanently controlled – were to be destroyed. The villages were to be encircled and searched for both weapons and irregular forces. In cases where opposition was encountered, the enemy forces were to be annihilated and the villagers expelled across the border. Plan D was put into operation much earlier than expected, as part of Operation Nachshon. One of its objectives was "to clear a whole area, permanently, of Arab villages and hostile or potentially hostile villagers." Benny Morris, *The Birth of the Palestinian Refugee Problem Revisited* (Cambridge: Cambridge University Press, 2004), 236; Podeh, "History and Memory in the Israeli Educational System," 99.

might evidence expulsion practices were omitted in a bid to not damage Israel's image.[122]

According to various Israeli scholars, including Podeh, Rafi Nets-Zehngut, and Firer, a more critical and informed historical narrative on the 1948 War has been presented in Israeli textbooks since the 1990s as a result of the changes in Israeli society, the peace process, and the emergence of a new historiography, which debunked earlier Zionist myths concerning the establishment of the Israeli state.[123] In the analysis below, however, I demonstrate that while a more critical narrative of the 1948 War is indeed present in textbooks since 1994, remnants of old myths and historiography remain. Ten history books, published between the period 1994 and 2014, were examined as part of this secondary case study. In these textbooks, "The War of Independence," as it is called in Israeli textbooks, is discussed at length across dozens of pages which note the various stages of the war (civil and international; Yishuv forces and state forces), the involvement of different armed (Jewish) factions, and the establishment of the Israeli state, among other themes. The ensuing paragraphs will focus primarily on the presentation of what Morris in 1987 termed "the birth of the refugee problem."[124] In order to determine whether the narrative in the textbooks has become more critical, two main topics will be examined. First, attention will center on the explanations given for the mass displacement of Palestinians. Textbooks stating that Palestinians left willingly for various reasons, e.g., due to fear, societal collapse, or as a result of calls by their own or other Arab leaders, will be considered to contain a Zionist narrative. Textbooks claiming that some Palestinians left voluntarily while a significant number were expelled are considered to be revisionist. A narrative will be labeled Zionist-critical if it maintains that most Palestinians left willingly while an insignificant number were expelled.[125] Second, this case study will examine whether the suffering of Palestinians and the war's effects on Palestinian society are included in the narrative. Here, emphasis will be placed on the incorporation of the Palestinian narrative of the war, including usage of the Palestinian designation of the war – al-Nakba – and recognition of the loss, both material and personal, that occurred as a consequence of mass displacement.

---

[122] Podeh, *Arab-Israeli Conflict*, 108.
[123] Podeh, "History and Memory in the Israeli Educational System," 84; Nets-Zehngut, "Israeli Approved Textbooks," 48–54.
[124] Benny Morris, *The Birth of the Palestinian Refugee Problem 1947–1949* (Cambridge: Cambridge University Press, 1987).
[125] Adopted from Nets-Zehngut, "Israeli Approved Textbooks," 47.

The Origins of Mass Displacement in the 1948 War

The new historians'[126] dispelling – and exposure – of several metanarratives and foundational "myths"[127] that had been formulated in the aftermath of the 1948 War was met with strident criticism[128]; as a result, the
incorporation of this revisionist scholarship, much of which was written
abroad, in official state-sanctioned textbooks was not easily reconciled. It
is, therefore, unsurprising that the first book examined as part of this case
study, Naveh's 1994 textbook, clearly embodies the old Zionist narrative
with regard to the description of Palestinian displacement in 1948,
because, as Naveh argues, "the Zionist narrative at that time was the
official narrative of the state of Israel."[129] In accordance with this narrative, Naveh writes: "the Arab inhabitants of *ha-aretz* (Hebrew: the land of
Israel) started to flee en masse and the Arab settlements in *Eretz* Israel
were defeated [and] more than 600,000 Arab inhabitants were uprooted
from their homes and settlements and fled the country, especially to
the Gaza Strip and the West Bank, which fell under the control of

---

[126] Some historians who have traditionally been associated with this group, such as Benny
Morris, advocate using the term new historians rather than revisionist historians.
However, as Avi Shlaim points out "Neither term is entirely satisfactory. The term
revisionists in the Zionist lexicon refers to the right-wing followers of Ze'ev Jabotinsky
who broke away from the mainstream Zionism in 1925 whereas the new historians are
located on the political map somewhere to the left of the mainstream. On the other hand
the term new historians is rather self-congratulatory and dismissive, by implication, of
everything written before the new historians appeared on the scene as old and
worthless." Shlaim, "Debate," 288.

[127] Simha Flapan, for instance, sought to challenge and debunk the "myths that Israel
forged during the formation of the state (...) not as an academic exercise but as a
contribution to a better understanding of the Palestinian problem and to a more
constructive approach to its solution." These myths included: that Zionists accepted
the UN partition and planned for peace; that Arabs rejected the UN partition plan and
launched war; that Palestinians fled voluntarily, intending reconquest; that all the Arab
states united to expel the Jews from Palestine; that the Arab invasion made war
inevitable; that defenseless Israel faced destruction by the Arab Goliath; and that
Israel has always sought peace, but no Arab leader has responded. Simha Flapan, *The
Birth of Israel: Myths and Realities* (New York: Pantheon, 1987), 8–10.

[128] One of the most strident critics of the new historians, Shabtai Teveth, argued in
1989 that the new historiography was politically motivated, pro-Palestinian and aimed
at delegitimizing Zionism and the state of Israel. In a similar vein, the late Israeli writer,
Aharon Megged, unleashed an attack on the new historians in a 1994 article in Haaretz.
In this article, he argued that "hundreds of (Israel's) leading writers, intellectuals,
academics, authors, and journalists ... have been unceasingly and diligently preaching
that (Israel's) case is not just," while participating in an "assault on Zionist legitimacy
(by) the denial of the historic link of our people with the land of our forefather." Shabtai
Teveth, "Charging Israel with Original Sin," *Commentary* 88 (1989): 24–33; Megged
cited in Hillel Halkin, "Israel against Itself," *Commentary*, November 1994, www
.commentarymagazine.com/articles/hillel-halkin/israel-against-itself/, accessed March
17, 2020.

[129] Ibid., 56.

the Jordanian Legion."[130] Emblematic of Education Minister Amnon
Rubinstein's anti-new historian stance,[131] any responsibility of the Jewish
forces in the displacement of these "Arab inhabitants" or the Plan Dalet
initiative is omitted. Rather, Naveh notes somewhat cryptically that
"when it became clear that the Arab initiative caused the great powers
to reconsider their support for the [UN] partition plan, the leaders of
the Yishuv decided to reach a decision in the battlefield and take
control [...]."[132]

In the years following the publication of Naveh's book, a new generation of textbooks was written in accordance with the history curriculum
adopted in 1995[133] and, at times, revisionist historiography. The books
published in this period indicate a transition point as both Zionist-critical
and revisionist narratives can be identified. The inclusion of a revisionist
narrative, however, does not necessarily imply that it has been adopted;
instead, two further books written in this period firmly reject the revisionist stance, creating a revisionist-critical narrative. The presence of
such a revisionist-critical account can be found in Bar-Navi's 1998
textbook, which asserts that "Both sides have conflicting accounts. The
Israelis accuse Arabs of propaganda, which, according to their claims,
encouraged the Arabs of Israel to temporarily leave their homeland until
the Arab armies had freed it from the hands of the Zionists. From their
side, the Arabs declare that Arab citizens were ousted from their land and
that the expulsion from *ha-aretz* was part of the Zionist plan – meaning
that they had planned it from the start."[134] According to Bar-Navi, both
these explanations are false and, instead, he points out that the reasons
for the flight are complex and can be summed up in one word: "war."[135]
Domke's 1999 book *The World and the Jews in Past Generations* also
acknowledges the existence of revisionist historiography by remarking
in the introduction that "The new historians caused – and still arouse –
controversy and are often accused of being extremely anti-Zionist."[136]

[130] Naveh, *World Order*, 203, 204.
[131] In 1995, Rubinstein, the minister of education, culture, and sport (1993–1996), attacked
the new historians, arguing that they aimed to "bury" Zionism by "presenting it as an
essentially colonialist and racist movement, attributing to it all the evils of darkened
nationalism, without displaying towards it the slightest sympathy that the left-wing
usually elicits towards national liberation movements; and above all, by considering the
very establishment of Israel as an act of villainy and plunder." Uri Ram, "Postnationalist
Pasts: The Case of Israel," *Social Science History* 22: 4 (1998): 536.
[132] Naveh, *World Order*, 203.
[133] Podeh, "History and Memory in the Israeli Educational System," 74.
[134] Bar-Navi, *The Twentieth Century*, 195.   [135] Ibid., 195.
[136] Elizier Domke, *The World and the Jews in Past Generations, Part 2, 1920–1970*
(Jerusalem: Zalman Shazar Center, 1999), 284.

Accordingly, Domke steers clear from new historiography and contends that following the war "there were Arab cities that had been occupied and those that had become empty [and] approximately 400 Arab villages [that] were abandoned." Usage of the words "abandoned" and "empty" clearly aim to place responsibility in the hands of the Palestinians. Nevertheless, it is in this book that a new trend can be identified which rejects the notion of an expulsion order or systematic expulsions, but which acknowledges individual cases of expulsion in line with a Zionist-critical narrative. Thus, Domke alleges in one sentence that "there were those who fled and those who were expelled."[137] A similar practice can be found in Tabibian's 2001 and 2003 textbook in which it is pointed out that although there were individual cases of expulsion that were authorized by the political echelon, they did not constitute "a premediated plan on behalf of the Jews or the Arabs [because] there was no consistent national policy."[138]

The inclusion of a revisionist narrative in Naveh's 1999 textbook reinforces the notion that historiography can influence textbook authors. In contrast to the Zionist narrative used in his 1994 textbook, Naveh argues that "during the battles many of the country's Arabs were expelled. Some ran away before the arrival of the Jews in the village or in the Arab neighborhood of the city and some were expelled by the occupying force."[139] The teacher's guide is even more explicit and instructs the teacher to emphasize that "in this war for a home and land, acts of expulsion were committed at the hand of the winners. When Yishuv forces conquered mixed cities and Arab communities, they expelled Arab Palestinian inhabitants on more than one occasion. Therefore, this period is called the Nakba (catastrophe or Shoah) by Arabs."[140] In a personal interview conducted in 2016, Naveh maintained that the inclusion of the word Nakba in the seldomly used teacher's guide was a calculated move. In his own words, the application of the Palestinian designation for the 1948 War in the teacher's guide was meant "to avoid scrutiny from the textbook approval body."[141]

Censoring the Revisionist Narrative

Naveh's above-mentioned trepidation to include the term Nakba in a textbook was not unfounded, as the fate of two textbooks published in

---

[137] Ibid., 284.
[138] Avieli-Tabibian, *Era of Fear and Hope*, 314; Ketzi'a Avieli-Tabibian, *Travel in Time: Building a State in the Middle East* (Ramat Aviv: Matach Publishing, 2003), 119.
[139] Naveh, *Verge of Tomorrow*, 138, 143, 146.
[140] Eyal Naveh, *The Twentieth Century on the Verge of Tomorrow, Teacher's Guide* (Tel Aviv: Tel Aviv Books, 1999), 108.
[141] Interviews conducted with Eyal Naveh on March 16 and May 15, 2016.

the following years shows.[142] *World of Changes*, a history textbook written
by Ya'akovi (1999), was rejected by the textbook approval committee
after initially having been attacked by the Shalem Center Research
Institute. In a report published in 2000 entitled *The Quiet Revolution in
the Teaching of Zionist History*, the institute found that Ya'akovi's book
had reduced coverage of the "classic Zionist narrative."[143] Indeed, on its
publication, Ya'akovi's book presented the most critical account of the
1948 War. While Ya'akovi, similarly to Domke and Tabibian, identified
"acts of expulsion," *World of Changes* was the only book that presented a
map depicting the departure routes Palestinians had taken in 1948
and, unlike its predecessors, provided exact numbers of those who settled
in surrounding Arab countries.[144] Moreover, Ya'akovi gave the names
of destroyed Palestinian villages; 1948 Eilat, for instance, is called
by its Arabic name (Um Rash-Rash). At the same time, Ya'akovi repeatedly uses the word "Palestinians" rather than "Arabs,"[145] thereby identifying those who suffered as a result of the war and challenging
what Zara Zimbardo terms "linguistic ethnocide" – or the erasure of
Palestinians' specific cultural and national identity through their designation as "Arabs."[146] *World of Changes* never made it to the classroom.[147]
Following its publication, the book was removed from the list of
approved textbooks by Likud's Minister of Education Limor Livnat at
the recommendation of the Knesset Education Committee.[148] While the
exact reasoning for the rejection of this textbook remains ambiguous,
Naveh argues that the decision was in line with existent political efforts,
particularly by politicians such as Ariel Sharon and Livnat, to rid educational textbooks and Israeli society of revisionist history, and instead
emphasize Zionist values.[149]

[142] Naveh's book did become subject to international and national criticism for its discussion of Jewish and Israeli history, particularly by an entity called the "Group of Professors for Political and Social Strength." Nets-Zehngut, "Israeli Approved Textbooks," 56, 57.
[143] Hazony, Oren, and Polisar, *Quiet Revolution in the Teaching of Zionist History*, 2.
[144] Ya'akovi, *World*, 162, 163.   [145] Ibid., 163.
[146] Zara Zimbardo, "Narrative Conflict: An Inquiry into the Histories of Israeli and Palestinian History Textbooks" (Paper, California Institute for Integral Studies, 2006), 14.
[147] Peled-Elhanan, *Palestine in Israeli School Books*, 57.
[148] Lisa Strömbom, "Identity Shifts and Conflict Transformation – Probing the Israeli History Debates," *Mediterranean Politics* 18 (2013): 90; Eva Etzioni-Halevy, *The Divided People: Can Israel's Breakup be Stopped?* (Lanham; Oxford: Lexington Books, 2002), 135.
[149] Eyal Naveh, *Travel into the Past: Disputes on Historical Issues in Israel* (forthcoming, 2016), 117 (in Hebrew).

The rejection of the original version of the second book, entitled *Nationality: Building a State in the Middle East* (2009), is less shrouded in ambiguity. The book, which was written by Domke in accordance with the Bartal Committee's curriculum plan, presented a Zionist-critical narrative of the 1948 War.[150] In coherence with this narrative, Domke notes that Palestinians were encouraged to leave "with the help of propaganda and psychological warfare and, in some cases, like Ramla and Lod, [the Jews] even expelled them."[151] The uproar that followed the publication of the book, however, did not focus on Domke's adherence to a Zionist-critical narrative; rather, Domke's book fell subject to scrutiny due to its exposure of the Palestinian narrative of the war. Domke's book initially included Palestinian and Israeli sources that discussed the reasons for Palestinians leaving their homes during the war under the heading "What caused the departure of the Palestinian refugees from the territory of Israel, flight or expulsion?." The first interpretation represented the stance of Yohanan Cohen in line with the arguments presented in his 1962 book *The Key Is in the Hands of the Arabs*. In this work Cohen asserts that Arab leaders already at the beginning of 1948 called on Arab civilians to temporarily move to neighboring countries in order to escape being hit by the war and in order to secure a fast victory.[152] Presenting a vastly different position to Cohen's, the Palestinian historian Walid Khalidi, echoing his 1959 article on the causes of the Palestinian exodus,[153] argued that ethnic cleansing by Jewish forces took place even before the establishment of the state, specifying that:

thirteen operations were carried out within the framework of Plan Dalet [...] it was a historic opportunity [for Jews] to cleanse *ha-aretz* Israel of Arabs [...] on the military level, the method [used] consisted of massive surprise attacks on Palestinian civilians [who were] weakened by ongoing shelling. On the psychological level, loudspeakers reran broadcasts and speeches, warning of diseases and punishments and offering escape routes from death. This was accompanied by calculated acts of cruelty against small villages, which encouraged flight from villages and [...] cities.[154]

---

[150] Between 1995 and 2003, Yisrael Bartal chaired the Israeli high-school curriculum committee which issued recommendations for pedagogical methodologies that would survey Zionist issues in the broad context of Jewish history and world history. Mark Avrum Ehrlich, *Encyclopedia of the Jewish Diaspora: Origins, Experiences, and Culture, Volume 1* (Santa Barbara/Denver/Oxford: ABC-CLIO, 2009), 348.

[151] Domke, *Nationality*, 107.   [152] Ibid., 107, 108; Naveh, *Travel into the Past*, 117.

[153] Walid Khalidi, "Why Did the Palestinians Leave, Revisited," *Journal of Palestine Studies* 34:2 (2005): 42–54.

[154] Domke, *Nationality*, 108–109.

Following its publication, the MOE received a complaint from a history teacher at Tel-Hay Teacher College regarding the inclusion of Khalidi's stance and his reference to "ethnic cleansing."[155] Subsequently, the MOE requested to remove all Palestinian sources and to substitute them either with Palestinian texts that were "more faithful to reality" or with Israeli sources.[156] The reason given was that the author had not considered the power of Khalidi's text and the effect if might have on students. Another argument, presented in a *Haaretz* article by a history teacher, opined that it was impossible to teach this book to students because they had no tools to differentiate between an Arab propagandist and an impartial researcher. In the teacher's view, presenting Israeli-held arguments as being equal to the claims of an Arab propagandist was similar to presenting the claims of the Nazis and the counter-claims of the Jews, as the teacher noted: "According to this logic, the next step will be to present the Protocols of the Elders of Zion or Holocaust denial and leave the students with the question: Did it happen or not?."[157] In order to have the book republished, the authors replaced the Palestinian source with the least controversial revisionist historian in Israel: Morris. Using Morris' influential book, *The Birth of the Palestinian Refugee Problem*, the new citation pointed out that there was no political decision by the Jews to expel the Arabs and there was also no evidence to suggest that Arabs leaders called [on] them to leave; rather, the flight was due to circumstances on the ground, the result of direct deportation by *Tzahal* (Hebrew: army) forces, and the psychological warfare that accompanied it.[158]

The treatment of Domke's book further highlights the influence ministers can have on the content of textbooks in Israel. At the beginning of 2009, the government was replaced, and Gideon Saar was appointed minister of education in Benjamin Netanyahu's government. According to the former superintendent for history, Saar was approached by the former head of the Mossad, Efraim Halevy, and asked to remove the Khalidi quote, because, as Yaron notes, "he [Khalidi] had done terrible things to us."[159] While Saar does not corroborate this story, in a personal interview he noted his criticism of the inclusion of Khalidi's position and the need to rectify the mistakes of his Labor predecessor, Yuli Tamir.[160] The current superintendent of history, Orna Katz, elaborated further on Saar's response to Domke's book. According to Katz, two different

---

[155] Peled-Elhanan, *Palestine in Israeli School Books*, 23.   [156] Ibid., 216.
[157] Naveh, *Travel into the Past*, 117, 118.   [158] Domke, *The World and the Jews*, 109.
[159] Interview conducted with Michael Yaron on April 14, 2016.
[160] Interview conducted with Gideon Saar on May 1, 2016.

arguments came up following the book's publication. First, she noted that Khalidi's reference to ethnic cleansing was deemed unacceptable in an Israeli book, as it constituted a "fundamentally false claim" and created an "unprofessional bias towards the Palestinian narrative."[161] Second, the fact that Khalidi is a professor meant that Israeli educators were fearful that students would believe him due to his authoritative position.[162]

Following the exclusion of Khalidi's stance, the Palestinian narrative of a systematic policy of expulsion in 1948 does not reappear. Instead, the final book analyzed in this case study, Msaol's 2014 book, concludes that "It is important to emphasize that these [expulsion] actions did not stem from a desire for ethnic cleansing [...] and did not stem from an order by the political echelon [...] Acts of expulsion were not consistent and were affected by the disorder that prevailed in the war."[163] Furthermore, the quotes included in this final work are solely those of Israeli political and army officials who reinforce Msaol's Zionist-critical work. Accordingly, former Foreign Minister Moshe Sharet is cited saying that Arabs left on their own accord: "The enemy attacker had created this [...] and he has to bear the consequences of this and all the remaining land and houses that remained [...] All this war booty, we deserved it as compensation for the bloodshed, for the destruction [...] it is a natural compensation [...]."[164] An almost identical stance is presented by former Minister of Agriculture Aharon Zisling, who notes that while hundreds of thousands of Arabs were expelled from *ha-aretz*, this was "due to their own fault" which will lead them to "cause the entire Middle East to wage war against us [and] they will carry in them an aspiration for revenge."[165]

The Nakba in Israeli Textbooks

In a historiographical – and societal – debate that centers, in part, on retrospective culpability, discussions concerning the number of Palestinian refugees, in addition to their post-war living conditions, take on a heightened role. Despite a continual emphasis on Palestinian culpability for the war and its outcome, Israeli textbooks do mention the vast number of Palestinian refugees, placing the number at between 540,000 and 750,000, which is slightly below the estimates offered by Morris in

[161] Orna Katz, "Response to Professor Nurit Peled-Elhanan," *Ministry of Education* (undated), 3.
[162] Interview conducted with Orna Katz on March 31, 2016.
[163] Msaol, *Creating a Democratic Jewish State*, 150.   [164] Ibid., 153.   [165] Ibid., 153.

his 2004 book *The Birth Revisited*.[166] Only one book, *Modern Times II* published in 1999 by Bar-Navi and Naveh, includes the higher number of Palestinian refugees (one million) purported by "the Arabs."[167] The establishment of refugee camps in the Gaza Strip, the West Bank, and other neighboring Arab countries to temporarily house these refugees is also referenced across the textbooks. Yet, the trying conditions in these camps as a result of poverty, disease, and hunger are only described in Msaol's 2014 book and Domke's edited 2009 textbook.[168] Still, it is unlikely that any discussion of the hardship refugees faced following the war will elicit empathetic identification by the students. While the books acknowledge that Israel refused to absorb the refugees after the war, leading to a de facto expulsion of all refugees regardless of earlier circumstances, this act is justified through presenting the refugees as a security issue and a demographic threat to the newly established Jewish state. Domke (1999), for example, notes that at the end of the war, Israel was faced with three main threats. One of these constituted the presence of "hundreds of thousands of refugees near the Israeli borders [whose return] Israel saw as a threat to its existence." On the following page, the author notes that this threat was due to the "infiltration of refugees into Israel which later became a war of terrorism."[169] The existence of a security threat also appears in Tabibian's 2003 textbook and Msaol's 2014 history book, as illustrated in the usage of normative language, including "infiltration" (Hebrew: *histan'nut*)[170] and "hostile refugees."[171]

Further minimization of the refugees' trials occurs in the discussion of the positive and practical effects of the mass Palestinian exodus. Ya'akovi (1999) writes that the housing problem that developed in the 1950s as a result of mass immigration from European and Arab countries to an extent was solved by housing new Jewish immigrants in former Palestinian villages and cities, as occurred in *Ayn Hawd*, which was later changed to *Ein Hod*.[172] In a similar vein, Naveh and Bar-Navi argue that while in Palestinian collective memory the 1948 War is a disaster, a

---

[166] My analysis found that whereas textbooks published between 1994 and 1999 offer broader ranges based on different Israeli estimates, textbooks published since 2003 stipulate a number of 650,000. Benny Morris concludes that the number of Palestinian refugees displaced was between 600,000 and 760,000. Morris, *Birth*, 602–604.
[167] Eli Bar-Navi and Eyal Naveh, *Modern Times, Part II 1920–2000* (Tel Aviv: Tel Aviv Books, 1999), 238.
[168] Msaol, *Creating a Democratic Jewish State*, 148, 151; Domke, *Nationality*, 107.
[169] Domke, *The World and the Jews*, 284, 285.
[170] Avieli-Tabibian, *Building a State*, 171; Msaol, *Creating a Democratic Jewish State*, 151.
[171] Bar-Navi, *The Twentieth Century*, 195.   [172] Ya'akovi, *World*, 175, 176.

Nakba, due to the "loss of land, and also [as a result of] becoming a nation of refugees [...] in the eyes of the Israelis, the fleeing of the Palestinians solved, in part, a formidable demographic problem. And even a moderate person like Chaim Weizmann spoke in this context of a miracle."[173]

The inclusion of the term "Nakba" and its current role in Palestinian identity represents an anomalous phenomenon in Israeli textbooks. In addition to Naveh and Bar-Navi's 1999 textbook, the term can only be found in Tabibian's 2001 and 2003 textbooks, which point out that "the Arabs call the 1948 War, what we call the War of Independence, al-Nakba, which in Arabic means catastrophe."[174] According to Nurit Peled-Elhanan, one of the staunchest critics of Israeli textbooks, the reason for the lack of a standard discussion of the Nakba in Israeli textbooks is due to fear of "empathic unsettlement." This term, coined by Dominick LaCapra in 2001, refers to the response of secondary witnesses – including historians – to traumatic events, which should involve empathic unsettlement, entailing, in LaCapra's words, "being responsive to the traumatic experience of others."[175] In the Israeli context, Peled-Elhanan notes, such empathic unsettlement regarding Palestinian victimhood during the Nakba or in the following years would risk de-legitimizing the Israeli-Zionist narrative.[176] The validity of this argument is evidenced by events that took place in the summer of 2007, when Education Minister Tamir approved adding the term Nakba to textbooks for the "Israeli-Arab" educational sector. In the wake of this decision, a political and media storm erupted. Tamir's approval of the term was described as propaganda, and calls were made for her removal by the opposition leader at the time: Netanyahu.[177] Particular focus lay on the Arabic version of one Hebrew textbook for primary school children, entitled "Living together in Israel." In this book, the 1948 War was elaborated on and included the term Nakba: "The Arabs call the war 'Nakba', which means war of disaster and loss [...] many Arabs and Jews

---

[173] Bar-Navi and Naveh, *Modern Times*, 239.

[174] Avieli-Tabibian, *Era of Fear and Hope*, 314. Also see Avieli-Tabibian, *Building a State*, 126, 127.

[175] Dominick LaCapra, *Writing History, Writing Trauma* (Baltimore/London: Johns Hopkins University Press, 2001), 41.

[176] Peled-Elhanan, *Palestine in Israeli School Books*, 64. Also see Ilan Gur-Ze'ev, *Philosophy, Politics and Education in Israel* (Haifa: Haifa University Press, 1999), 59 (in Hebrew).

[177] MK Ronit Tirosh (Kadima (Hebrew: forward)), the director general of the Ministry of Education, argued that the decision was similar to propaganda broadcasts by Hamas and that it would fuel hatred between people. On the other hand, Palestinian politicians welcomed the decision and saw it as the beginning of a process of reconciliation. Naveh, *Travel into the Past*, 12.

were killed in the war. Some Arab citizens were forced to leave their homes and others were expelled, and they became refugees in neighboring Arab states. Most of the Arabs who remained in *ha-aretz* continued to live in their communities, but some of them became refugees and were forced to live in other Arab communities in the Israeli state as their villages were destroyed in the war and after it."[178]

Following the publication of the book, the education committee of the Knesset, in which future Minister of Education Saar took part, convened and called for the excision of the Nakba from the textbook.[179] In a 2016 interview, Saar explained his stance at the time by arguing that any reference to the Nakba is unacceptable as it might give "Arab students the feeling that they are living in a state that was born out of sin [and] one cannot say that the establishment of Israel was a curse or disaster for them. They waged a war. They lost the war and that's it [...] When you translate the word Nakba, the word means Holocaust. You need to leave our Holocaust alone. The formation of this state is not a Holocaust to its Arab citizens. It is a blessing to our Arab citizens."[180] Upon assuming the role of minister of education in 2009, Saar's quest to erase the Nakba from the Israeli educational system was fueled by the introduction of the Nakba Law. This law did not exclude the mentioning of the Nakba, but it did bar governmental agencies and those that received governmental funding from organizing or financing activities concerning the Palestinian Nakba.[181] Although educational officials, such as Katz, are quick to point out that the Nakba Bill does not have any effect on textbooks, in reality, the law has made it more problematic to deal with the Nakba in any societal sphere. Kashti thus claims that any apprehension is further reinforced as a result of the bill's ambiguity, which has meant that teachers and textbook writers steer clear of any mention of the Nakba.[182]

While the above-mentioned initiatives to curb the discussion of the Nakba took place in a public sphere, a more implicit rejection of the Palestinian narrative occurred prior to the introduction of the Nakba Law and the 2007 textbook controversy. In 2000, two Israeli historians and educators, Naveh and Dan Bar-On, and a Palestinian professor of education, Sami Adwan, embarked on an educational project with the aim of enabling Palestinian and Israeli high-school pupils to

---

[178] Ibid., 111.
[179] The ministry rejected the committee's recommendations and the book was used in the Arab sector. Ibid., 112, 113.
[180] Interview conducted with Gideon Saar on May 1, 2016.
[181] Naveh, *Travel into the Past*, 114.
[182] Peled-Elhanan, *Palestine in Israeli School Books*, 15.

understand the other's historical perception.[183] By undertaking work-shops with Palestinians and Israeli teachers, Bar-On, Naveh, and Adwan put together a textbook entitled *Side by Side* which encompassed Israeli and Palestinian narratives of key historical milestones in the Israeli-Palestinian conflict, including the 1948 War. While the Israeli narrative largely follows the content of Naveh's 1999 textbook mentioned above, the Palestinian narrative is more descriptive, as several Palestinian eye-witness accounts are incorporated in the narrative. The narrative offers first-hand testimony of the Deir Yassin massacre and of the suffering that accompanied the years after the mass exodus, including in photographs of former Palestinian villages and houses which show the destruction and conversion of former Palestinian villages into Israeli-Jewish ones.[184] The aim of the project, according to Naveh and Adwan, was to provide an additional means for teachers in Palestinian and Israeli schools to educate their pupils on the other's narrative. Nevertheless, both in Palestinian and Israeli society, the project became subject to scrutiny.[185] In the Israeli context, this occurred at the state level. Following usage of the booklet in six schools, several teachers were summoned to the MOE and received letters from the former superintendent, Yaron, informing them that their jobs would be at risk if they continued with the project.[186] At the same time, Livnat, the minister of education at the time, forbade usage of the booklet in classrooms, making the project less interesting to donors who desired its practical applicability.[187]

According to Katz, who was involved in the evaluation of the *Side by Side* project for the MOE, the book's rejection did not occur on political grounds, but rather as a result of historical and pedagogical reasons. In direct contrast to research findings on adolescent pedagogy,[188] she contends that the presentation of two narratives is problematic, as "young pupils without the historical knowledge cannot decide who is right and who is wrong. You need to first teach them the story and what

---

[183] Sami Adwan, Dan Bar-On, and Eyal Naveh, *Side by Side: Parallel Histories of Israeli Palestine* (Prime, 2012), ix, x.

[184] Sami Adwan, Dan Bar-On, and Eyal Naveh, *Learning Each Other's Narrative: Palestinians and Israelis* (Beit Jallah: Prime, 2003), 20–36.

[185] Interview conducted with Eyal Naveh on March 16 and May 15, 2016; interview conducted with Sami Adwan on May 13, 2016.

[186] Naveh, *Travel into the Past*, 122.

[187] Interviews conducted with Eyal Naveh on March 16 and May 15, 2016.

[188] Conflict researchers have identified adolescence as an appropriate stage to create opportunities for open dialogue among representatives of conflicted groups, as adolescents have been found to be open to new attitudes and ideologies. See John Wallach and Michael Wallach, *The Enemy Has a Face: The Seeds of Peace Experience* (Washington, DC: Institute of Peace, 2000); Sagy, Kaplan, and Adwan, "Interpretations of the Past," 26–38.

happened." Moreover, Katz questioned the historical veracity of the content: "There were total lies in the content and it just was not good. When you are teaching that for the Palestinians the War of Independence was a Nakba, that for them it was a disaster, that is wrong." Echoing Golda Meir's infamous 1969 statement, Katz argues that the falsity of the project also lay in the usage of the word "Palestinians."[189] As she notes: "They weren't called Palestinians then. They didn't accept the UN Resolution, and they started the war, with killing and terror. When you read the Palestinian narrative, this is not mentioned at all. It is like Jews came out of nowhere and took their houses. This is not a narrative."[190] Despite these comments, Katz vehemently opposes any mention of censorship in Israeli textbooks. Instead, she maintains that attention should be rendered to the Palestinian education system, which, according to her, is guilty of indoctrination, stimulating hatred and the exclusion of others.[191]

Concluding Remarks

Reflecting on his tenure as minister of education, Piron noted that it was only when he retired from political life that he realized that the Holocaust was being manipulated into a "national message," which emphasizes the Holocaust's unique relevance to Jews and presents "the state as the answer to the Holocaust."[192] Piron's delayed recognition of an exclusive Israeli-Jewish victimhood narrative means that this chapter identified its manifestations, both implicitly and explicitly, throughout the period under review. Transmitted as "approved knowledge" to the descendants of the second and third generation, this narrative relies on the explicit portrayal of the Holocaust as a uniquely Jewish tragedy with universal relevance to the entire Jewish nation and, therefore, pertinent to every Israeli-Jewish youth. Simultaneously, the overt minimization of other groups' suffering as a result of Nazi (genocidal) policies is de-emphasized both qualitatively – indicated through the conveyance of incomplete and anachronistic historical information – and quantitatively – as illustrated in numerical aggregation practices. The existence of what Gur-Ze'ev

---

[189] In an interview with *The Sunday Times* published on the June 15, 1969, Meir stated that "There is no such thing as a Palestinian people … They did not exist." Cited in Charles Tripp, *The Power and the People: Paths of Resistance in the Middle East* (Cambridge: Cambridge University Press, 2013), 29.

[190] Interview conducted with Orna Katz on March 31, 2016.

[191] In her paper on Peled-Elhanan's work, Katz also mentions militarism and glorification of death as part of Palestinian education. Katz, "Response to Professor," 3.

[192] Interview conducted with Rabbi Shai Piron on May 30, 2016.

termed the "Zionist metanarrative,"[193] moreover, dictates that educational content deemed to challenge the uniqueness of the Holocaust or the singular fate of the Jews has been discredited, as demonstrated by the fate of Auron's 1994 work with the telling title *Sensitivity to Human Suffering*.

Beyond informing the de-emphasizing of non-Jewish victims in Israeli textbooks, the identified Zionist metanarrative lays the foundations for further exclusionary manifestations, namely the minimization of the Palestinians' fate in the 1948 War. Textbooks that illustrate a teleological movement from the center(s) of Jewish destruction, "there" in the *galut* (Hebrew: exile), to revival, "here" in Israel – as conveyed implicitly through the narrative structure of seven analyzed textbooks – advocate a post-Holocaust justification for the Zionist enterprise and, consequently, necessitate an untainted recovery from the preceding crisis. Indeed, despite the textual incorporation of new historiography from the late 1990s onwards, the sole emphasis on Morris' work has facilitated the creation of a Zionist-critical narrative in which a systematic policy of expulsion is firmly cast aside; instead, overt reminders of traditional Zionist historiography formulating a miraculous rebirth remain. Yet, official attempts to erase the Palestinian narrative of the war, including its designation as a catastrophe, from the Israeli curriculum should not only be viewed as an outcome of its incompatibility with a Zionist redemption. Rather, as the following chapters will illustrate, post-Oslo Palestinian mnemonics conceive of the Nakba as "ongoing present" and, as a result, dictate that Israeli recognition of the Palestinian watershed entails an awareness of its contemporary usage as a public confrontation by the downtrodden.

---

[193] Gur-Ze'ev, "Morality," 171.

3   Teaching the Nakba
Old Wounds, New Textbooks

The inauguration of the Palestinian Ministry of Education in 1994 represented a watershed moment for Palestinians in the West Bank and
the Gaza Strip. For the first time in history, Palestinians became in
charge of their own educational system. This chapter aims to examine
the educational changes pertaining to the representation of the Nakba
that followed this historic moment. Through an extensive examination of
the various curriculum plans put forward by the Ministry of Education in
the wake of the 1994 Gaza–Jericho Agreement and personal interviews
conducted with former ministers and educational officials involved in
the curriculum's creation, it becomes apparent that Palestinian history
and culture were deemed an integral component of the new Palestinian
curriculum. Furthermore, a close reading of the plans' content and the
elucidation provided by educational officials reveals that the incorporation of the 1948 War and its catastrophic effects on Palestinian society –
highlighted in the continual usage of the term *al-Nakba* – were considered crucial to furthering national identification and a historical
consciousness.

Facilitated by the educational self-determination attained through the
Oslo Accords, inclusion of the ramifications of the 1948 War should
also be viewed as a rectification of the hitherto exclusion of the Nakba
and, to a large extent, the 1948 War in Palestinian education under the
Jordanian regime (1948–1967) and, following the occupation of the
West Bank, under Israeli rule (1967–1994). Yet, while the incorporation
of *al-Nakba* formed a historical and political milestone, I demonstrate
that the conservative educational outlooks favored by the Palestinian
Ministry of Education coupled with the influence of Israeli lobbying
efforts led to the production of educational content that lacks a rigorous
and in-depth historical analysis of the 1948 War and the mass displacement that ensued, leaving a more formative inter- and transgenerational
transmission of *al-Nakba* to the extracurricular realms discussed in subsequent sections.

Notwithstanding the existence of a tepid Nakba narrative, the latter part of this chapter argues that its significance can be found implicitly in the overt omission of the Holocaust in the Palestinian curriculum. Thus, reactionary educational policies in the domestic sphere are considered a materialization of a quid pro quo, which, as a result of Israeli educational and societal treatment of the Nakba, bring about a retributive omission of "their narrative." The application of Zygmunt Bauman's theoretical understanding of a victimhood competition among groups in conflict together with the conflation of Jews and Israelis underlies this analysis, which, in the Palestinian educational context, dictates that the ethnical epithets used in referencing Israeli – i.e., Jewish – participation in the 1948 War legitimize the silencing of Nazi racial policies and their culmination in the Holocaust.

A Brief History of the Palestinian Educational System

From the days of the Ottoman Empire, when formal schooling first emerged, foreigners administered the education system in the areas now commonly referred to as the Palestinian Territories.[1] According to Denise Asaad, neither the Turks nor their successors, the British, had any interest in developing a genuine Palestinian curriculum and instead designed an educational system that was intended to serve colonial rule.[2] Following the 1948 War, for the first time, Palestinian education came under the control of Arab states: the Gaza Strip fell under the Egyptian Administration and Jordan – at the time Transjordan – administratively governed the West Bank, a realization of King Abdullah's long-held wish to unify both banks of the Jordan.[3]

Within the West Bank and Gaza, the United Nations set up its Relief and Works Agency (UNRWA) in 1950 to, among other things, provide education to Palestinian refugees of the 1948 War. The curriculum in these refugee camps followed the national curriculum of the host countries. Accordingly, the West Bank followed the Jordanian curriculum and

---

[1] Susan Nicolai, *Fragmented Foundations: Education and Chronic Crisis in the Occupied Palestinian Territory* (London; Paris: UNESCO International Institute for Educational Planning and Save the Children UK, 2007), 311.
[2] Denise Assad, "Palestinian Educational Philosophy between Past and Present," *Studies in Philosophy and Education* 19 (2000): 390.
[3] The passage of a Palestinian unification motion on April 25, 1950 in the new Jordanian parliament, according to Philip Robbins, was accepted by the majority of West Bankers. Under the terms of the union, West Bankers were immediately offered Jordanian citizenship. Philip Robins, *A History of Jordan* (Cornwall: Cambridge University Press, 2019), 76, 77.

Gazan schools adhered to the Egyptian education system.[4] Brown notes
that as these education systems focused on developing Egyptian and
Jordanian children and building their national identities, Palestinian
identity, culture, and history were largely absent from the curriculum.
Rather, Palestinian students devoted attention to "pharaonic Egypt and
the Hashemite leadership."[5] The Jordanian education system in particular was seen to do nothing to enhance Palestinian identity.[6] Iris Fruchter-
Ronen, who performed an analysis of Jordanian history and civics
textbooks between 1964 and 1994, demonstrates that Jordanian
textbooks up to 1967 made use of three techniques to impede identification with Palestine and, in turn, stimulate integration into Jordanian
society.[7] First, the presence of Palestinians was almost completely
ignored; second, attempts were made to assimilate Palestinians into the
Jordanian state through "Jordanization"; and, third, Palestinians were
excluded or perceived as an external factor.[8] A clear example of the first
method can be found in the 1966 textbook *My Little Homeland* (Arabic:
Waṭanī al-Saghīr). In this book, the nation is divided and defined
according to the various groups of residents that comprise it, namely,
"urban residents, villagers, and Bedouins," while ignoring the inhabitants of Palestinian refugee camps, constituting almost a quarter of the
total population.[9]

Education in the Wake of the 1967 War

The shortcomings of the Jordanian curriculum were recognized at the
time by Palestinians. A study by the planning office of the Palestinian
Liberation Organization conducted in 1972, entitled "The Palestinian
Liberation Organization: An Analysis of the (Social) Educational
Curriculum in Jordan, Lebanon and Syria," was particularly critical of

[4] Agustín Velloso de Santisteban, "Palestinian," *International Journal of Educational Development* 22 (2002): 148.
[5] Brown, *Palestinian Politics after the Oslo Accords*, 198.
[6] Nicolai, *Fragmented Foundations*, 33, 34.
[7] According to Eugene Rogan, this trend in schoolbooks mirrors Jordanian historiography after the 1948 War which attempted to write a narrative that would build consensus between Palestinians and Jordanians around a common national project of the Hashemite Kingdom of Jordan. Eugene L. Rogan, "Jordan and 1948: The Persistence of an Official History," in *The War for Palestine: Rewriting the History of 1948*, ed. Eugene L. Rogan and Avi Shlaim (Cambridge: Cambridge University Press, 2001), 120.
[8] Iris Fruchter-Ronen, "The Palestinian Issue as Constructed in Jordanian School Textbooks, 1964–1994: Changes in the National Narrative," *Middle Eastern Studies* 49 (2013): 285.
[9] Y'aqub al-Dajani et al., *My Little Country* (Amman: Ministry of Education, 1966), 21.

Jordanian education.[10] The study showed that only 1.3 percent of all geography books and about 1.9 percent of all history books in Jordan referred to Palestine/Palestinian. Furthermore, according to the study, textbooks also failed to mention the 1948 exodus of Palestinians from their homes, their suffering as a result of *al-Nakba,* and their aspirations.[11] In his 1973 analysis of the study, the Palestinian academic Ibrahim Abu-Lughod therefore concluded that both the social and science curriculum would leave the Palestinian student:

... in no position to identify the major outlines of Palestinian history prior to or during the Mandate Period; he would not be able to identify the specific importance of Palestine to Palestinians or to the Arab people in general; he would remain ignorant of the social and economic life of the Palestinians prior to 1948; and he would remain unaware of the type and nature of the struggle which the Palestinian people waged to prevent the usurpation of Palestine.[12]

Abu-Lughod's damning appraisal of the Jordanian curriculum was not only a result of disinterest on the Jordanians' part in developing a Palestinian educational system.[13] Rather, the possibility of creating an affinity for Palestinian land and history was further thwarted following the 1967 War, with the Israeli occupation of the West Bank. For the first twelve years of the occupation, the education system fell under the direct authority of the Israeli military governor; after the 1979 Camp David Accords between Egypt and Israel, a separate administration was established: "The Office of Education for Judea and Samaria."[14] Although considered a civil administration in nature, the office continued to report to the military and was staffed entirely by military personnel in uniform.[15] Under the control of this office, the quality of the Palestinian education system further declined due to a lack of funding designated by the Israeli government, insufficient educational supplies and facilities, and restricted access to schools.[16] Restrictions imposed on freedom of movement were particularly aimed at the West

---

[10] Centre for Planning, *The Palestinian Liberation Organisation, An Analysis of the Educational Curriculum in Jordan, Lebanon and Syria* (Beirut, 1972), 14–26, 55–56 (in Arabic).

[11] Ghassan Shabaneh, "Education and Identity: The Role of UNRWA's Education Programmes in the Reconstruction of Palestinian Nationalism," *Journal of Refugee Studies* 25 (2012): 506.

[12] Ibrahim Abu-Lughod, "Educating a Community in Exile: The Palestinian Experience," *Journal of Palestine Studies* 11 (1973): 96.

[13] Shabaneh, "Education and Identity," 506.

[14] Alayan, "History Curricula and Textbooks in Palestine," 3.

[15] Nicolai, *Fragmented Foundations*, 34, 35.

[16] Ismael Abu-Saad, "Introduction: A Historical Context of Palestinian Arab Education," *The American Behavioral Scientist* 8 (2006): 1043.

Bank and, in the latter part of the 1978/1979 academic year, nearly paralyzed the educational system there, as village students were forbidden to attend schools in the cities and numerous schools were shut shown.[17]

The decline in educational quality was reinforced as a result of what Ismael Abu-Saad terms "an inappropriate curriculum."[18] While the previous Egyptian and Jordanian curricula were kept in place, the Israeli administration censored textbooks with the aim of removing information it considered to be against its interests.[19] As a result of this censorship, the word Palestine was removed, maps were changed to show Israel and its borders inclusive of occupied territory, and anything Israeli censors deemed nationalist was excised and replaced.[20] In addition to changing the content of textbooks, Military Order 107 from August 27, 1967 listed fifty-five textbooks, including Arabic language books, history, geography, sociology, and philosophy books, which were prohibited outright based on their content.[21] Israeli censorship did not only manifest itself in the content of the curriculum, but also in interference in the conveyance of the material. Nicolai notes that the Israeli government paid teachers' salaries and, consequently, was able to select teachers with "acceptable" political views, and those that were deemed controversial "were dismissed and transferred to distant locations."[22] Still, several studies have confirmed that despite the fact that the curriculum was unrelated to students' reality and aspirations, Palestinian teachers were

[17] Muhammad Hallaj, "The Mission of Palestinian Higher Education," *Journal of Palestine Studies* 9 (1980): 94. In February 1988, all schools and universities in the West Bank were closed by the authorities to curb the Intifadah. The closure affected 1,174 educational institutions, 303,000 primary and secondary school pupils, and 22,000 university and college students. The authorities justified the closures on security ground, describing the schools as "centers of unrest" and "centers of violent protest" and higher education institutions as "traditionally a hotbed of anti-Israeli protest." Jacqueline Sfeir and Susan Bertoni assert that the disruptions of the First Intifadah "led to a long-lasting drop in academic standards at all levels of education." Article 19, *Cry for Change: Israeli Censorship in the Occupied Territories* (London: Library Association Publishing, 1992), 18, 19; Jacqueline Sfeir and Susan Bertoni, *The Challenge of Education in Palestine: The Second Intifada* (Bethlehem: Bethlehem University, Faculty of Education, 2003), 11.
[18] Abu-Saad, "Introduction," 1043.
[19] Alayan, "History Curricula and Textbooks in Palestine," 3; Sami Adwan, "A Curriculum for Peace and Coexistence," in *The Psychology of Peace and Conflict: The Israeli–Palestinian Experience* (Jerusalem: Harry S. Truman Research Institute for the Advancement of Peace, 1996), 86.
[20] Salah Alzaroo and Gillian Hunt, "Education in the Context of Conflict and Instability: The Palestinian Case." *Social Policy & Administration* 37 (2003): 170.
[21] Nicolai, *Fragmented Foundations*, 55; Neve Gordan, *Israel's Occupation* (Berkeley: University of California Press, 2008), 253.
[22] Nicolai, *Fragmented Foundations*, 25, 35.

able to transmit a national consciousness. Velloso de Santisteban, for instance, argues that behind closed doors teachers put forth their own messages, which were different and even opposite to the official messages, making them "significant socializing agents," including on the topic of *al-Nakba*.[23] The history of the 1948 War was taught in an extracurricular fashion, as indicated by one UNRWA teacher who noted: "We strived to give our students elements of their history, so that they would not forget about their homes. We explained to them where they came from, why they were there, and what the right of return meant. All of that technically was prohibited. But that could not be prevented [as] nobody could control what the teacher could tell the student inside the classroom."[24]

The Stirrings of a New Educational System

Following the 1993 Oslo Accords, on May 4, 1994, the Gaza–Jericho Autonomy Agreement was signed. While this agreement did not create a Palestinian state, it did produce the PA, which for the purposes of administration and services acts as a government. The next step in the process, the Agreement on the Preparatory Transfer of Powers and Responsibilities, which was signed on August 29, 1994, led to the transfer of power from Israel to the PA in primary social services.[25] In the same month that the agreement was signed, the transfer of authority in the sphere of education from the Israeli Civil Administration to the PA led to the establishment of the first Palestinian Ministry of Education under the direction of the education minister, Yasser Amr, the deputy minister, Naim Abu-Hummos, and just four other people.[26] As the PA took control of education, the educational system in place was seen as "an outdated, second-hand amalgam from other cultures";[27] therefore,

[23] Velloso de Santisteban, "Palestinian," 148, 149.
[24] Shabaneh, "Education and Identity," 509.
[25] Nicolai, *Fragmented Foundations*, 24, 40.
[26] Naim Abu-Hummos was considered a strong educationalist with a PhD in Education from San Francisco State University. Interview conducted with Naim Abu-Hummos on July 19, 2016; Nicolai, *Fragmented Foundations*, 44.
[27] In 1994, when the MOE was established, it catered to the whole education sector from preprimary to higher education. In 1996, the MOE was divided into two separate ministries: The Ministry of Education and the Ministry of Higher Education. In 2002, these two ministries merged again. According to Abu-Hummos, the division in 1996 was a political decision: "Arafat wanted to add certain people to the cabinet, in this case Hanan Daoud Khalil Ashrawi. The consolidation in 2002 might have had something to do with the fact that I had been in charge of higher education and general education before. So it was clear I would be able to do so as minister." Nicolai, *Fragmented Foundations*, 41; interview conducted with Naim Abu-Hummos on July 19, 2016.

as Abu-Hummos stated in a 2016 interview, the first aim of the ministry
was to develop a new curriculum.[28]

The First Curriculum Development Plan

With the financial aid and support from UNESCO and the Italian Ministry
of International Cooperation, the Palestinian Curriculum Development
Center (PCDC)[29] began its work in 1995.[30] Under the leadership of the
contemporary vice-president of Birzeit University, Ibrahim Abu-Lughod, a
team of educational specialists and intellectuals set out to analyze the
previous Jordanian and Egyptian curricula and offer educational principles
that would be incorporated in a unified Palestinian curriculum.[31] The
results of these analyses and educational recommendations were offered
to the Ministry of Education and UNESCO in September 1996 in two
volumes entitled *The Comprehensive Plan for the Development of the First
Palestinian Curriculum for General Education*.[32] The former curricula's failure to adequately address the culture and history of Palestinian people is
one of the most consistent themes in the entire report, which constituted
"perhaps the most stinging and detailed indictment of existing education in
Arab countries and the most radical reform proposed by an official body
since universal education was introduced."[33] The report repeatedly notes
that the Egyptian and Jordanian curricula "are not sufficiently attuned to
the national identity, do not promote national and patriotic affiliation, and
do not reflect Palestinian history and reality or Palestinian culture and
heritage."[34] Furthermore, the report, similarly to the PLO's 1972 report,
concludes that "the curriculum in the Gaza strip is focused on Egyptian
identity and on the history and geography of Egypt ... and in the West
Bank, the curriculum is focused on Jordanian identity and on Jordanian

---

[28] Interview conducted with Naim Abu-Hummos on July 19, 2016.
[29] A symposium convened by the PLO and UNESCO on the future of Palestinian
education held in August 1990 in Jerusalem recommended the establishment of an
institution charged with the creation of a new educational system. In 1993, this led to
the founding of the PCDC. Ibrahim Abu-Lughod et al., *The Comprehensive Plan for
the Development of the First Palestinian Curriculum for General Education* (Ramallah:
Curriculum Development Center, 1996), 5 (in Arabic).
[30] Ibid., 3.   [31] Ibid., 5.   [32] Abu-Lughod et al., *Comprehensive Plan*, 3.
[33] Brown argues that one of the most radical aspects of the committee's work lay in the fact
that it stimulated creative and critical thinking among students. Nathan Brown,
Democracy, History, and the Contest over the Palestinian Curriculum (London: Adam
Institute, 2001), 21; Nathan Brown, "Contesting National Identity in Palestinian
Education," in *Israeli and Palestinian Narratives of Conflict: History's Double Helix*, ed.
Robert Rotberg (Bloomington: Indiana University Press, 2006), 238.
[34] Abu-Lughod et al., *Comprehensive Plan*, 413, 444, 447, 449.

history and geography."[35] Consequently, the basic philosophy of the pro-posed curriculum, according to the committee, had to be "rooted in a Palestinian consciousness of its national heritage, its long and significant history, and its national affiliation with the land of Palestine and with Arab national culture."[36]

While no concrete method is offered on how national affiliation and Palestinian consciousness could be attained, Ali Jarbawi (2012–2013; 2009–2012), the future education minister and minister of planning who was in charge of analyzing past history curricula, formulated some fundamental questions that related to the general philosophy of a future history curriculum.[37] The last question that needed to be addressed prior to the creation of the curriculum concerned the teaching of Palestine and was appropriately entitled: "What Palestine Do We Teach?." According to Jarbawi, this question "was of extreme importance, sensitivity and pain." Yet, in the attempt to determine the answer, Jarbawi points out that further questions needed to be addressed first: "Is it the historical Palestine with all its geography or the Palestine that is a product of the signed political agreements with Israel? And how should Israel be dealt with? Is it merely a neighbor or a state that is founded on the destruction of most of Palestine?."[38] Jarbawi concluded that the curriculum "must acknowledge the realities of the situation without falsifying historical truths and their repercussions in various dimensions in the context of social science instruction."[39] In an interview, Jarbawi reflected on this rather ambiguous conclusion. First, he noted the importance of the geographical representation of Palestine at the time of the report, as its publication coincided with a phase of transition during ongoing peace talks, which were supposed to lead to the creation of a Palestinian state in 1999 and, consequently, a final border agreement. In the absence of such an agreement, however, the Abu-Lughod committee was faced with the difficult task of determining what type of maps to use, which, according to Jarbawi, led to the decision to use historic pre-1948 maps in the interim.[40] Furthermore, Jarbawi stated that acknowledgment of the his-torical truth meant the incorporation of the realities of the 1948 War and

---

[35] Ibid., 447.   [36] Ibid., 7. For similar statements, see 6, 55, 454.

[37] Other questions included: "Will the new Palestinian curriculum, similarly to the Jordanian one, focus on teaching social studies only (history and geography)? Or will it follow the Egyptian curriculum and be more general, which means teaching different subjects that are part of the field of social science, such as economy, sociology, and philosophy?" Ibid., 451, 452.

[38] Ibid., 454–455.   [39] Ibid.

[40] Interview conducted with Ali Jarbawi on May 16, 2016. For evidence of the adoption of this practice, see *Principles of Human Geography for the 6th Grade* (Al-Bireh; Ramallah: Palestinian Authority, Ministry of Education, 2000), 53.

its effects on the Palestinian people: "We should tell the historical narrative as it is. I have to write that in 1948 we lost 80 percent of our homeland and in 1967 the remaining 20 percent was lost, and we have continued to be under occupation since then."[41] The importance of including the 1948 War in the new curriculum was not only meant to lead to historical accuracy, but also to create a Palestinian consciousness, as Jarbawi explained: "The Nakba is part of who we are, it is part of Palestinian nationalism. There are also other important historical moments in Palestinian history, including 1917, 1936, and the British Mandate period. But of these events, the Nakba is most important in Palestinian history. By putting this in the curriculum, it will shape people as Palestinians."[42]

The report's explicit and implicit recommendations were met with apprehension by the Ministry of Education, and the report was not offered to the government for approval.[43] Members of the Abu-Lughod committee point to the report's progressive nature as the primary reason for its rejection. Moughrabi, a member of the Abu-Lughod Committee, contends that the report's recommendations were considered too radical and ambitious.[44] Similar comments were made by Jarbawi, who also notes that some of the committee's recommendations were deemed too costly by the ministry.[45] On the other side, Abu-Hummos, who reviewed the report on behalf of the ministry, argued that the report was too esoteric in nature due to the fact that the committee was mainly made up of professors rather than policy makers. As such, Abu-Hummos notes that while the report proved a good starting point, it needed more work; subsequently, another committee was appointed, made up of ministry employees and led by a more conservative figure: Saleh Yassin.[46]

The Second Curriculum Plan

Under the direction of Yassin, another curriculum plan was drafted and approved by the cabinet and the Palestinian Legislative Council in 1998. As such, this plan can be considered to be the official statement of the foundations and aims of the Palestinian educational system.[47] The plan, entitled "The First Palestinian Curriculum Plan," similar to the plan put forward by the Abu-Lughod committee, was funded by the Italian

---

[41] Interview conducted with Ali Jarbawi on May 16, 2016.   [42] Ibid.
[43] Interview conducted with Naim Abu-Hummos on July 19, 2016.
[44] Interview conducted with Fouad Moughrabi on April 26, 2016.
[45] Interview conducted with Ali Jarbawi on May 16, 2016.
[46] Interview conducted with Naim Abu-Hummos on July 19, 2016; interview conducted with Fouad Moughrabi on April 26, 2016.
[47] Velloso de Santisteban, "Palestinian," 150.

Table 3.1. *The Palestinian textbook production plan*[a]

Phase	Target grade	Number of books	Planned introduction	Actual introduction
Phase 1	Grades 1 and 6	Fifteen books for Grade 1; seventeen books for Grade 6	2000	2000
Phase 2	Grades 2 and 7	Fifteen books for Grade 2; twenty-five books for Grade 7	2001	2001
Phase 3	Grades 3, 8, and 10	Fifteen books for Grade 3; twenty-five books for Grade 8; thirty-seven books for Grade 10	2002	2002: Grades 3 and 8 2004: Grade 10
Phase 4	Grades 4, 9, and 11	Fifteen books for Grade 4; twenty-five books for Grade 9; twenty-three books for Grade 11	2003	2003: Grades 4 and 9 2005: Grade 11
Phase 5	Grades 5 and 12	Seventeen books for Grade 5; twenty-one books for Grade 12	2004	2004: Grades 5 and 10 2006: Grade 12

[a] Adopted from Ministry of Education, *First*, 48, 51.

Ministry of Education and supported in its execution by UNESCO.[48] In addition to using the 1996 educational plan, the new curriculum plan was based on PLO documents, including the 1988 National Independence Document, and analyses of different educational models in the Arab world and elsewhere.[49] In contrast to the plan presented by the Abu-Lughod committee, the new plan focused more on practical administrative matters relating to the future educational system, which included creating a blueprint for the introduction of 250 textbooks to different grades between 2000 and 2004.[50]

---

[48] For further information on the funding of the Palestinian MOE and the new curriculum, see Fouad Moughrabi, "Palestinian Education for the Twenty-First Century," paper presented at 2016 Hisham Sharabi Memorial Lecture, May 6, 2016; Nicolai, *Fragmented Foundations*, 67.

[49] Ministry of Education, General Administration of Curricula (Palestinian Curriculum Development Center), *First Palestinian Curriculum Plan* (Jerusalem: al-Maʿārif, 1998), 2 (in Arabic).

[50] The total estimated cost for the new education system was $9,927,929. Ministry of Education, *First*, 52.

While several of the Abu-Lughod committee's recommendations were unambiguously rejected by the ministry, including the committee's intention to do away with the matriculation exam – the *Tawjīhī* – and to seek a more subdued role for Islam in education, the committee's influence can be perceived in the new plan. Thus, the 1998 plan emphasized the importance of the curriculum for the creation of a Palestinian consciousness and the introduction of a Palestinian perspective on Palestinian history and society.[51] In an attempt to create a Palestinian curriculum that met the aspirations of the community, various educational foundations were introduced. The writers noted that the intellectual and national foundations of the curriculum, in addition to strengthening faith in Allah, were meant to reinforce belonging to the Palestinian homeland.[52] These foundations, according to the authors of the plan, were to be applied across the four dimensions of the curriculum: the domestic (Arabic: *waṭanī*), the religious, the national (Arabic: *qawmī*), and the international dimension. It is in the national and domestic dimension that Palestinian heritage, culture, and history find the most expression.[53] The bolstering of a Palestinian identity was not only meant to create more unity among the Palestinian people in the face of a fragmented reality, but also intended to serve future political goals of the PA, namely, the establishment of a Palestinian state. The centrality of this goal is highlighted in the preface to the plan, which states: "And we – we the Ministry of Education – must create a new curriculum, which is to be characterized by inclusiveness, clear definitions, and [which must prepare] the Palestinian people to restore all their national rights on their national soil and establish their independent state with its capital in Jerusalem under the leadership of our brother, Yasser Arafat."[54]

The importance of the creation of a Palestinian societal, political, and historical consciousness was emphasized throughout the creation of the curriculum.[55] In a position paper written by the Ministry of Education in 2002, it was noted that "Besides portraying a national identity and legitimatizing its National Authority, the curriculum traces the cultural development of the Palestinian people throughout history and celebrates its livelihood, aiming at empowering a people who missed developmental

---

[51] Ibid., 5, 6, 9, 10, 17, 32.   [52] Ibid., 6.   [53] Ibid., 32.
[54] Ministry of Education, *First*, Introduction.
[55] The plan does not provide a solid overview of the amount of time spent on history and national education. Thus, while stipulating that national and civic education should make up between 5.6 and 8.43 percent of the curriculum, history education, according to the plan, only takes place in grades 11 and 12 (5.7 percent), while in reality the subject is taught in grades 5–12. Ibid., 22–29.

opportunities as a result of occupation." The paper further contended that both in textbooks already produced and future textbooks, the content aims to "account for the political complexities," which included the presentation of crucial historic events.[56] One of the events that according to the ministry would receive due notice was the 1948 War, as specified in a policy update in 2001. In this publication, entitled "The Palestinian Curriculum and Textbooks: A Clarification," the ministry argued that "the Palestinian problem" did not start with the Israeli occupation of the West Bank and Gaza in 1967, but with the dispossession and eviction of the Palestinians from their homeland in historic Palestine and the establishment of the State of Israel in 1948. Since, according to the ministry, this fact is alive in the individual and collective memories of the Palestinians, textbooks would not be credible if they did not address this fact, as the authors noted: "We will not brainwash our children and miseducate them about the past."[57]

The Jordanian Curriculum and the 1948 War

While the PCDC was working on the new curriculum, as an interim measure, the Palestinian MOE made an agreement with the Jordanian and the Egyptian ministries in 1996. This agreement enabled the MOE to reprint both curricula in their entirety and use these textbooks in Palestinian classrooms.[58] In her analysis of the contemporary Jordanian history and civics textbooks, Fruchter-Ronen argues that from 1990 onwards, in contrast to previous periods, Palestinians received detailed recognition in Jordanian textbooks. The temporary introduction of these non-censored works, she argues, therefore offered students a more coherent understanding of Palestinian society and history. In an attempt to reinforce her argument, Fruchter-Ronen points to a 1994 national and civic textbook, which states that Palestinian refugees were banished from Palestine by force.[59] The Jordanian books that were examined as part of this case study, similarly to Fruchter-Ronen's findings, did not ignore the uprooting of Palestinians as a result of the 1948 War. Nonetheless, solely noting that Palestinians were uprooted in the 1948 War does not

---

[56] Israel-Palestine Center for Research and Information, *Report I: Analysis and Evaluation of the New Palestinian Curriculum Reviewing Palestinian Textbooks and Tolerance Education Program* (IPCRI, 2003), 15; Ministry of Education, *Palestinian Curriculum: Position Paper* (Ramallah: Ministry of Education, 2002).
[57] "The Palestinian Curriculum and Textbooks: A Clarification," Palestinian Authority, Ministry of Education, www.pac-usa.org/palestinian_curriculum_and_text.htm, accessed April 14, 2016.
[58] Adwan and Firer, *Israeli–Palestinian Conflict*, 103.
[59] Fruchter-Ronen, "Palestinian Issue," 291, 292; S. I. Al-Hababa, *National and Civic Education* (Amman: Ministry of Education, 1994), 17.

Table 3.2. *Examined Palestinian textbooks in the Palestinian school system*

Jordanian history textbooks	Year of publication	Grade	Content analyzed
History of the Modern World, Part II	1994 (edition 1999)	8th grade	1948 War
Teacher's guide, History of the Modern World, Part II	1995	8th grade	1948 War
The History of the Arabs and the Modern World	1994 (edition 2003)	12th grade	1948 War; Second World War
The History of the Arabs and the Modern World	1996	12th grade	1948 War
The History of the Arabs and the Modern World	1998	12th grade	1948 War; Second World War
Contemporary World History, Part II	1994 (edition 1999)	8th grade	Second World War
Teacher's Guide: Contemporary World History, Part II	1995	8th grade	Second World War
History of Western Civilization and the Modern World	1994 (edition 2001/2002)	11th grade	1948 War; Second World War

National education textbooks	Year of publication	Grade	Content analyzed
National and Civic Education	1994	5th grade	1948 War
Palestinian National Education	1996	4th grade	1948 War
Palestinian National Education	1996	5th grade	1948 War
Palestinian National Education	1996	8th grade	1948 War
Palestinian National Education	1998	5th grade	1948 War
National Education	2001	7th grade	1948 War
National Education	2001/2002 (edition 2008)	2nd grade	1948 War
National Education	2004/2005 (edition 2004)	5th grade	1948 War
National Education	2003/2004 (edition 2004)	4th grade	1948 War
National Education	2011	4th grade	1948 War

Palestinian history textbooks	Year of publication	Grade	Content analyzed
The Modern and Contemporary History of the Arabs	2002/2003 (edition 2003)	9th grade	1948 War

Table 3.2. (*cont.*)

Palestinian history textbooks	Year of publication	Grade	Content analyzed
The Modern and Contemporary History of the Arabs	2003/2004 (edition 2010)	9th grade	1948 War
History of the Modern World	2004/2005 (edition 2010)	10th grade	Second World War; 1948 War
Contemporary and Modern Palestinian History, Part II	2005/2006 (edition 2011)	11th grade	1948 War
History of the Arabs and the World in the 20th Century	2006/2007 (edition 2012)	12th grade	Second World War; 1948 War

constitute a detailed discussion or recognition of the significance of this event. Rather, this research found that Jordanian history textbooks that were used in the West Bank failed to offer any detailed description of the mass displacement in 1948 and its immediate and long-term effects on Palestinian society.

In the execution of my analysis of Jordanian textbooks between 1994 and 2000, two textual methods led to a reduced discussion and recognition of the effects of the 1948 War on Palestinian society. First, it was found that the 1948 War, if mentioned at all, was given as a fill-in type of bracketed information; and, second, the analysis of the textbooks' content revealed that the causes, development, and outcome of the war were introduced without providing the necessary contextual framework. A clear example of the first practice can be discovered in two textbooks: *History of the Modern World* for the 8th grade and *History of Western Civilization and the Modern World* for the 11th grade. In the former textbook, students were informed of the 1948 War in a total of three sentences: "The UN decided on 29 October 1947 to divide Palestine into two states: one Jewish and one Palestinian. The Arabs rejected the partition plan, and a war occurred between the Jews and the Arabs, and Britain withdrew from Palestine. The war between the two parties led to the Jewish occupation of most of Palestine, except for the West Bank and Gaza."[60] In the questions to the chapter, the lack of emphasis on the 1948 War was further reinforced. In the only question that referred to

[60] *History of the Modern World, Part II for the 8th Grade* (Ramallah: Palestinian Authority, Ministry of Education, 1999), 60, 61.

Palestine, students were asked to describe the reasons behind the national revolt among Palestinians. While not explicitly stated, the question alluded to the 1936–1939 Palestinian revolt discussed earlier in the chapter rather than the protests that erupted in wake of the adoption of the UN Partition Plan.[61] In the second textbook for the 11th grade, bearing the title *History of Western Civilization and the Modern World*, even less attention was rendered to the 1948 War, and the war was framed in the context of a consolidation of Hashemite dominion and national objectives. In the sixth chapter, which explored the rise of various political independence movements in the twentieth century, Palestinian students were told that: "As for Palestine and the east of Jordan, the presence of the British Mandate continued to exist until Abdallah bin al-Hussein was able to pave the way for independence, which was achieved on 25 May 1946. Concerning Palestine, its land was taken over by Israel in 1948. The remainder of the land was incorporated in the Hashemite Kingdom in 1950."[62]

The cited passages clearly indicate a lack of sufficient historical context regarding the outbreak of the war and its development. Thus, *History of Western Civilization and the Modern World* used the discussion of the war as means of furthering identification with Jordanian history, leading to factual inaccuracies and omissions. In the passage above, the end of the British Mandate was described as a sole result of the Jordanian struggle for independence, thereby failing to mention the effects of the strife and the subsequent civil war between the Palestinians and the inhabitants of the Yishuv or the UN Partition Plan. An incomplete historical narrative was also presented in the 1994 history textbook, entitled *The History of the Arabs and the Modern World* for the 12th grade. Here, Zionism, considered "a racist doctrine equal to Nazism," was presented as an immediate nuclear threat to the entire Arab world.[63] This threat, according to the book, characterized Zionism from its establishment and spurred on a pan-Arab military involvement in the 1948 War. As a result, this textbook forwent any critical examination of the disparate war aims and the (inadequate) military preparation among the various Arab states.[64]

---

[61] Ibid., 62.

[62] *History of Western Civilization and the Modern World for the 11th Grade* (Ramallah: Palestinian Authority, Ministry of Education, 2001/2), 178, 179, 180.

[63] To this day, Israel has not acknowledged possession of nuclear weapons. Nevertheless, scholars argue that since 1966, Israel has had nuclear-weapons capability. See Avner Cohen, "And Then There Was One," *Bulletin of the Atomic Scientists* 54:5 (1998): 51–55; Ari Shavit, *My Promised Land* (Melbourne: Scribe, 2014), 188.

[64] See Ilan Pappé, *The Making of the Arab–Israeli Conflict, 1947–1951* (London: I.B. Tauris, 1992); Avi Shlaim, *Collusion across the Jordan: King Abdullah, the Zionist Movement and the Partition of Palestine* (Oxford: Clarendon Press, 1988).

Moreover, rather than discussing the consequences of this war with attention to the Palestinians' plight, emphasis lay on the economic effects of military participation on the internal development of Arab countries as a result of "the establishment of the Zionist entity." As such, while "the aggressive [Zionist] expansionist spirit [threatened] the land of Palestine and the Arab communities in various Arab countries," *The History of the Arabs and the Modern World* (1994) contends that the "confrontation of the aggression [...] exhausted the budget of some Arab countries, and the money came from development projects and investment accounts, which caused a delay in the revival [Ar. *al-nahḍah*] of the Arabs and their progress."[65]

The New Palestinian Textbooks: The 1948 War in National Education Textbooks between 1995 and 2000

Although it had been decided to restore the Jordanian and Egyptian curricula in full until the introduction of the new textbooks, the MOE was conscious of the fact that the Egyptian and Jordanian textbooks failed to deal with issues concerning Palestinian identity and society in a comprehensive manner. As Andre Mazawi contended: "In spite of their differences, both [the Jordanian curriculum and the Egyptian curriculum were] similar in terms of their conceptual fragmentation and lack of systematic and Palestinian-oriented approach."[66] Similarly, Abu-Hummos noted that "particularly for geographic and history books, the content did not match our history or identity. But I was a firm believer that if we wanted change, we needed to do this ourselves."[67] In order to make the interim curriculum more Palestinian in nature, national education textbooks were added to the curriculum so that, as Abu-Hummos put it, "students could learn about Palestinian history and society since the whole curriculum was Jordanian [and Egyptian]."[68] It is in these books, which were published from 1995 onwards, that an initial departure can be seen from the content of the Jordanian textbooks through a more substantial discussion of the Palestinian experience of the 1948 War and its effects on Palestinian society. The primary goals of the national education textbooks were to further identification among students with Palestinian history and society and to prepare the students

---

[65] *The History of the Arabs and the Modern World for the 12th Grade* (Ramallah: Palestinian Authority, Ministry of Education, 1994), 123, 124.
[66] Andre Elias Mazawi, "The Reconstruction of Palestinian Education: Between History, Policy Politics and Policy-Making," *Journal of Education Policy* 15 (2000): 373.
[67] Interview conducted with Naim Abu-Hummos on July 19, 2016; Brown, *Democracy*, 2.
[68] Interview conducted with Naim Abu-Hummos on July 19, 2016; Brown, *Democracy*, 2.

to contribute to their society. These objectives are further indicated in the introductions to the books, which address the students as follows: "Dear student, the chief goal of national education is to raise an upright citizen and to strengthen one's sense of belonging to the *ummah* [Ar. nation] and the homeland."[69] One of the ways in which these goals are meant to be achieved is through an emphasis on the events of the 1948 War.

References to the 1948 War can be found in the Palestinian national education textbooks for grades 2, 4, 5, 7, and 8. The content presented in these books differs in two important ways from the narrative in the above-mentioned Jordanian textbooks. First, even though the events of the war are not discussed in any detail, the textbooks do point out that as a result of the war large numbers of Palestinians became refugees. The national education textbook for grade 5, for instance, speaks of "large numbers of Palestinians [refugees]," while the textbook for grade 8 specifies "millions of refugees."[70] Blame for this mass displacement is defined with reference to the religious ethnicity of those held responsible. Thus, rather than invoking the Yishuv community prior to May 1948 and the Israeli state or army in the wake of the establishment of Israel, the examined textbooks uniformly place responsibility in the hands of "the Jews [who] took control of most of the Palestinian land" without elucidating how this led "most Palestinian people [to] leave cities and towns."[71] Moreover, even when the concept of a Zionist transfer policy[72] is invoked, as occurs in the 1996 *Palestinian National Education* textbook for grade 8, the ethnical characteristics of the movement stand central, leading the book to unambiguously conclude that "Zionism's goal is the transformation of Palestine into a Jewish state by throwing out its Arab inhabitants and bringing Jews from all over the world to settle in Palestine."[73] A further departure from the content on the 1948 War in Jordanian books can be identified in the discussion of both the immediate and long-term effects of the displacement and "Jewish rule over most of Palestine's land."[74]

[69] *Palestinian National Education for the 5th Grade* (Ramallah: Palestinian Authority, Ministry of Education, 1998), Introduction.
[70] *Palestinian National Education for the 5th Grade* (Ramallah: Palestinian Authority, Ministry of Education, 1996), 36; *Palestinian National Education for the 8th Grade* (Ramallah: Palestinian Authority, Ministry of Education, 1996), 20, 21.
[71] *Fifth Grade* (1996), 36.
[72] According to historians such as Pappé and Nur Masalha, a Zionist consensus had come into existence during the late 1930s under the leadership of David Ben-Gurion which sought the transfer of the Palestinian population from Palestine to establish a Jewish homeland. See Nur Masalha, *Expulsion of the Palestinians: The Concept of "Transfer" in Zionist Political Thought, 1882–1948* (Washington, DC: Institute for Palestine Studies, 1992); Ilan Pappé, ed., *The Israel/Palestine Question* (London/New York: Routledge, 1999), 190.
[73] *Eigth Grade* (1996), 20, 48.   [74] *Fifth Grade* (1998), 34.

Several national education books make references to the establishment of refugee camps following the 1948 War. The aforementioned textbook *Palestinian National Education* for grade 8, for example, states that "Palestinian refugees settled in Europe and North and South America and large numbers of them settled in Jordan, Lebanon, and Syria," considered the "diaspora."[75]

The most extensive discussion of the effects of the 1948 War on Palestinian society can be found in the 1998 national education textbook for the fifth grade. Through discussing the period following the 1948 War in a separate chapter entitled "Palestine after the Year 1948," this book not only indicates the importance of the event, but also presents the 1948 War as a watershed moment for Palestinian society.[76] Accordingly, the book points out that the era following the 1948 War was characterized by the geographical, political, and societal effects of the war, including the displacement of many Palestinians and their emigration to surrounding Arab nations, the loss of Palestinian land and the need to learn new trades, the desire to preserve Palestinian heritage by building popular institutions, and the founding of the PLO.[77] While presenting the 1948 War as having had a unique effect on Palestinian society, the latter textbook argues that the mass uprooting of Palestinians was not a one-time event; rather, in the discussion on the 1967 War, the book proclaims that as a result of "the 1967 June War between Israel and surrounding Arab nations [...] thousands of Palestinians were displaced to different countries abroad, as occurred in 1948."[78]

The 1948 War in National Education Textbooks since 2000

The theme of "ongoing displacement" has taken on a more central role in national education books published from 2000 onwards as a means of emphasizing the continuous effects of the Nakba on Palestinian society.[79] In the 5th grade national education textbook published in 2004, the authors point out that "Palestinian society suffered a Nakba in 1948 at the hands of the Zionist movement. This led many Palestinians to flee from the land and an Israeli state to be established on part of Palestine. Palestinian society befell a *naksah* (Arabic: Setback) in 1967, which led the Israelis to occupy the rest of Palestine, that is the West Bank and

---

[75] *Eighth Grade* (1996), 20. Also see *Fifth Grade* (1996), 36; *Palestinian National Education for the Fourth Grade* (Ramallah: Palestinian Authority, Ministry of Education, 1996), 39.
[76] *Fifth Grade* (1998), 36.   [77] Ibid., 34–36.   [78] Ibid., 37.
[79] For displacement prior to 1948 at the hands of the "Zionists" and the British, see *Palestinian National Education for the 7th Grade* (Ramallah: Palestinian Authority, Ministry of Education, 2001), 20, 21.

Gaza, in addition to occupying the Egyptian Sinai and the Golan Heights from Syria."[80] Although the new textbook is similar to the 1998 textbook in its assertion that displacement for Palestinians was not a one-off occurrence, the new content shows an important change in the discussion of the 1948 War, namely usage of the term *al-Nakba*. In addition to the 2004 book, where the word is used throughout as a reference to the 1948 War, the term can be found in the national education textbook for grade 6 in which Israel is blamed "for the Nakba of the Palestinian people."[81] A further difference that can be identified in the national education books published after 2000 is the explicit conveyance of the significance of the 1948 War. In the 2004 textbook for the fifth grade, for instance, the Nakba is presented as one of the defining moments for Palestinian society, alongside the British occupation, the Israeli occupation, the emergence of the PA, and the two Intifadas.[82]

Refugee Life and the Effects of the 1948 War

Two further important deviations from the interim national education books and the Jordanian curriculum are the inclusion of Palestinian refugees as part of the internal makeup of Palestinian society and, relatedly, an emphasis on the birth of the refugee problem and its contemporary effects on Palestinian life. With regard to the former, national education textbooks published since 2000, for the first time, consider Palestinian refugees and refugee camps part of the internal makeup of Palestinian society. Consequently, although camps are described as being "[a] place[s] where Palestinian refugees live who were forced to leave their towns and villages in Palestine and to which they are determined to return,"[83] the camp has become one of four standard ways of living (the others being city life, Bedouin life, and village life).[84] Similar statements appear in the 2004 national education textbook for the 4th grade in which, apart from referring to Palestinian refugees in the

---

[80] *Palestinian National Education for the 5th Grade* (Al-Bireh; Ramallah: Palestinian Authority, Ministry of Education, 2004), 30.

[81] *Fifth Grade* (2004), 29, 30, 31; *Palestinian National Education for the 6th Grade* (Ramallah: Palestinian Authority, Ministry of Education, 2000), 16.

[82] *Fifth Grade* (2004), 29.

[83] Camps are also described as "emergency clusters of living where Palestinian citizens fled to from their cities and villages in 1948." *Palestinian National Education for the 2nd Grade* (Al-Bireh; Ramallah: Palestinian Authority, Ministry of Education, 2008), 36. For further references to the desire to return see *Seventh Grade* (2001), 7; *Palestinian National Education for the 4th Grade* (Al-Bireh; Ramallah: Palestinian Authority, Ministry of Education, 2004), 43.

[84] *Fifth Grade* (2004), 35.

diaspora, the authors note that "the inhabitants of Palestine" live in a variety of places and consist of "city residents, residents of villages and the countryside, and residents of refugee camps."[85]

The new national education textbooks also emphasize the effects of the 1948 War on Palestinian society and probe the exodus itself through questions and student activities. Questions focus both on the circumstances of the exodus itself and its short- and long-term effects on society. Questions relating to the former include "Was emigration optional or did it occur under force?" and "How did UNRWA support Palestinian refugees?" Examples of the latter include "What is the name of the group of people who live as Palestinian refugees and who were expelled from their villages?" and "Show the effects of the Nakba that befell Palestinian society in 1948."[86] The majority of the activities that students are asked to partake in center on engaging them in the realities of present-day refugee life. In the fourth grade textbook, students are therefore instructed to consider "the existence of the hundreds of thousands of people that live in Palestinian camps" and "to memorize the names of the Arab countries to which many Palestinians fled after they were expelled from their Palestinian homeland."[87] An activity that can be found in all the books aims to familiarize the students with the names, places, and workings of refugee camps. For this purpose, in *Palestinian National Education* for the 2nd grade, students are asked "to collect pictures from various Palestinians camps and put them on the walls inside the classroom."[88] Students in the fifth grade are requested to "search for and write down the names of three camps in Palestine, Syria, Lebanon, and Jordan" and "write on the activities of UNRWA in your area and discuss your work on the school radio."[89]

The Creation of the Curriculum and the Al-Aqsa Intifadah

Even though the exact reasoning for the novel concentration on the 1948 War and its present-day ramifications is not mentioned in the books examined, the introductions written by the Ministry of Education do offer insight into the motives behind the change in content. In the introduction to the national education textbooks for the fourth and fifth grade, the ministry notes that it "saw a necessity to develop a curriculum that takes into account particular Palestinian characteristics in order to

---

[85] *Fourth Grade* (2004), 42. For similar statements see *Second Grade* (2008), 36–40.
[86] *Fifth Grade* (2004), 31, 36, 48; *Fourth Grade* (2004), 42, 43.
[87] *Fourth Grade* (2004), 43, 44.   [88] *Second Grade* (2008), 39.
[89] *Fifth Grade* (2004), 36, 49.

achieve the ambitions of the Palestinian people [because] the creation of
a Palestinian curriculum is an important basis for the creation of well-
being among the Palestinian people and for the consolidation of a democracy [...]."[90] A further ambition of the national education textbooks is
laid out in the second introduction to the fourth grade textbook in which
the ministry points out that these national education textbooks constitute
"an opportunity to raise awareness among students of their homeland."[91]

A more detailed description of how the introduction of Palestinian
history can achieve the above-mentioned goals can be found in the
2008 national education textbook. Here, in contrast to former textbooks,
a link is drawn between the usage of Palestinian history and the creation
of a Palestinian identity: "The [ministry is] keen to plant a sense of
belonging to the land and the heritage in the hearts of the youths [...]
by supplying them with the history of their grandfathers. [Therefore,] in
this book [...] students are given an overview of Palestinian history."[92]
According to Goetz Nordbruch, the reflection of these statements in the
content of the textbooks shows an increased emphasis on nationalism by
the ministry.[93] However, as the desire to raise Palestinian consciousness
was also identified in the earlier national education textbooks, attention
should be rendered to the stormy political atmosphere in the early 2000s.
Adel El Sayed sees a direct connection between the ministry's increased
emphasis on a sense of belonging and the homeland in the new textbooks
and the effects of the Second Intifadah, also referred to as the Al-Aqsa
Intifadah. According to El Sayed, the Intifadah, which lasted from
September 2000 to February 2005, led to a re-examination of the notion
of belonging and homeland. "The Palestinian National Authority and the
teachers," in El Sayed's words, "would not give away one inch of their
'dream', as long as Israel was 'expanding' its territory."[94] Indeed, the
potential effect of the 2000–2005 Al-Aqsa Intifadah on the new textbooks' production and content cannot be neglected, as noted in an
interview with the former minister of education, Abu-Hummos. The
former minister contended that the Intifadah impacted the textbook
production process in two important ways. First, Abu-Hummos pointed
out that the damage caused to the recently erected educational

[90] *Fifth Grade* (2004), Introduction; *Fourth Grade* (2004), Introduction.
[91] *Fourth Grade* (2004), Second Introduction.   [92] *Second Grade* (2008), Introduction.
[93] "The New Palestinian Textbooks for National Education – A Review," Goetz
Nordbruch, www.gei.de/fileadmin/gei.de/pdf/abteilungen/schulbuch_und_gesellschaft/
israel_palaestina/palest02.pdf, accessed February 2, 2016.
[94] "Palestinian Geography Textbooks," Adel El Sayed, www.gei.de/fileadmin/gei.de/pdf/
abteilungen/schulbuch_und_gesellschaft/israel_palaestina/palest05.pdf, accessed February
29, 2016.

infrastructure – totaling more than five million dollars – impeded the curriculum's development.[95] Second, the former minister revealed that due to restrictions on freedom of movement, the individuals involved in the textbook writing and checking committees were hampered in their work, thereby hinting at the possibility that textbook writers' individual experiences during the Intifadah influenced the content.[96]

The Accusation of Incitement

The development of the new Palestinian books was also affected by heavy Israeli scrutiny and international lobbying efforts, especially by the Israeli Center for Monitoring the Impact of Peace (CMIP), which continues to impact (former) education officials' willingness to speak to foreign researchers.[97] In 1998, CMIP, at the time headed by Itamar Marcus, an Israeli political activist from the West Bank settlement of Efrat,[98] produced a report entitled "The Palestinian Authority Schoolbooks" in which the center claimed to have found several incendiary statements about Israel and Jews in the new curriculum, including a call for "the liberation of Palestine from its thieving conquerors, an expression used to name Israel and the Jews."[99] Even though Brown pointed out that the cited statements were part of the previous Jordanian and Egyptian textbooks, the findings were used to influence international funding bodies.[100] CMIP encouraged European Union parliament members to pressurize the European Commission on the matter. Despite the fact that

[95] Abu-Hummos notes that with the acceleration of violence in the early 2000s, a decision was made to store the new educational material in a safe. Nevertheless, while the educational content was kept safe, the damage caused by the IDF to the ministry, its facilities, and individual schools was vast. According to the MOE and UNESCO, the destruction totaled more than $5 million. Interview conducted with Naim Abu-Hummos on July 19, 2016.

[96] Nicolai, *Fragmented Foundations*, 190.

[97] Yassin, the current director of the Palestinian Development Centre, refused to speak to the author of this work because, as he said, "the curriculum is too sensitive an issue," while former Minister of Education Abu-Hummos was suspicious of the author's interest in the curriculum and queried as to whether the author might have a hidden political agenda.

[98] In 1996, Marcus also founded an organization called Palestinian Media Watch (PMW), which conducts analyses of Palestinian media in order to relay "the messages that the Palestinian leaders, from the Palestinian Authority, Fatah and Hamas, send to the population through the broad range of institutions and infrastructures they control." In reality, most of the work by PMW seeks to bring to light incitement in Palestinian media against Israel and Jews, as indicated by the research center's focus on the "PA's indoctrination of adults and children to seek Shahada (Martyrdom)." "About Us," Palestinian Media Watch, www.palwatch.org/pages/aboutus.aspx, accessed December 22, 2016.

[99] CMIP, *Newsletter September 1998*, 2.

[100] Brown, *Palestinian Politics after the Oslo Accords*, 237, 299, 301.

the EU had not provided funding for the Palestinian books from the outset, a condition was added to the EU budget insisting that support would only be given for textbooks that were in compliance with basic European values.[101]

A second report published by CMIP in 2001 caused similar reactions. The report, entitled "Jews, Israel, and Peace in Palestinian School Textbooks," found that Palestinian textbooks "foster a multi-faceted rejection of its [Israel's] existence [and the tendency] to reject and delegitimize Israel [has] gained impetus through instilling animosity and the implicit aspiration to replace the State of Israel with the State of Palestine."[102] This time, Hillary Clinton, who was running for the U.S. Senate, criticized the content of Palestinian textbooks and warned that "All future aid to the Palestinian Authority must be contingent on strict compliance with their obligation to change all the textbooks in all grades [...]."[103] CMIP's international lobbying also had more immediate effects. In December 2000, the Italian government, one of the main funders of the new Palestinian curriculum, informed the PA that due to the report's findings it could no longer finance the development of the new Palestinian school curriculum. Simultaneously, the World Bank notified the Palestinian Ministry of Education that the money allocated for the development of schoolbooks and teacher training would have to be diverted to other projects.[104] According to Moughrabi, the continued reliance on foreign donors for further development of the Palestinian curriculum meant that the ministry refrained from any content that might create further incitement. With reference to the 1948 War, Moughrabi stated in an interview that this has resulted "in a watered-down version of Palestinian history and an incomplete picture of the events that unfolded."[105]

The New History Textbooks

Despite Moughrabi's appraisal of the effects of self-censorship, references to the 1948 War can be found throughout the new curriculum in Arabic language textbooks, geography books, and Islamic education

[101] Herb Keinon, "EU Money to be Denied for PA Schoolbooks," *Jerusalem Post*, November 2, 2001.
[102] The report also sought to argue that Palestinian textbooks glorified martyrdom and terror. Groiss, *Jews, Israel and Peace*, 3, 4, 6, 50–51.
[103] Brown, *Democracy*, 8.
[104] Fouad Moughrabi, "The Politics of Palestinian Textbooks," *Journal of Palestine Studies* 31 (2001): 9.
[105] Interview conducted with Fouad Moughrabi on April 26, 2016.

textbooks, indicating that the importance of a (diluted) inclusion of the events in times of political upheaval outweighed the threat of incitement.[106] Similarly, a more detailed account of the 1948 War and its effects on Palestinian society can be found in history textbooks published since 2000. In contrast to the new national education textbooks discussed above, the new history curriculum places more emphasis on the role of Zionism as a foundational policy that led to the takeover of Palestinian land and the displacement of Palestinians in 1948, post-1948 measures to "Judaize" (Arabic: *tahwīd*) the land, and Palestinian suffering during and following the 1948 War. With regard to the first-mentioned theme, in three of the books published after 2000 for grades 9 and 10, Zionism is presented as a settler-colonial movement that from its beginning had its eyes set on Palestine and the displacement of its inhabitants. In *The Modern and Contemporary History of the Arabs* for the 9th grade, Zionism is thus considered "a political settler movement, established by European Jews [at the end] of the 19th century with the goal of having Jews from different nationalities all over the world gather in Palestine [to] displace the Palestinian people in Palestine from their land [to] establish Israel."[107] Nevertheless, this book notes that Zionism alone did not lead to the displacement of Palestinians, but instead was the result of the synergy of "colonial British interests and the goals of the Zionist movement."[108] A similar argument is made in the 2003 and the 2010 history textbooks, both entitled *The Modern and Contemporary History of the Arabs*. These books point out that British and American support for the Zionist movement facilitated Jewish emigration to Palestine and removed restrictions that prevented Jews from acquiring Palestinian lands.[109] Furthermore, the 2010 textbook argues that the

---

[106] See *Reading and Texts, Part I for the 8th Grade* (Ramallah: Palestinian Authority, Ministry of Education, 2009), 67; *The Geography of Palestine for the 7th Grade* (Ramallah: Palestinian Authority, Ministry of Education, 2002), 36; *Islamic Education for the 6th Grade* (Ramallah: Palestinian Authority, Ministry of Education, 2000), 6. For content on the right and desire to return in the new textbooks, see *Islamic Education, Part I for the 6th Grade* (Ramallah: Palestinian Authority, Ministry of Education, 2011), 69; *History of the Ancient Civilizations for the 5th Grade* (Ramallah: Palestinian Authority, Ministry of Education, 2005), 7; *Our Beautiful Language, Part I for the 5th Grade* (Ramallah: Palestinian Authority, Ministry of Education, 2011), 50; 91; *Reading and Texts, Part I for the 9th Grade* (Ramallah: Palestinian Authority, Ministry of Education, 2011), 120; *Our Beautiful Language, Part I for the 7th Grade* (Ramallah: Palestinian Authority, Ministry of Education, 2002), 34.

[107] *The Modern and Contemporary History of the Arabs for the 9th Grade* (Al-Bireh; Ramallah: Palestinian Authority, Ministry of Education, 2003), 72.

[108] *History of the Modern World for the 10th Grade* (Ramallah: Palestinian Authority, Ministry of Education, 2010), 53.

[109] *9th Grade* (2003), 74; *The Modern and Contemporary History of the Arabs for the 9th Grade* (Ramallah: Palestinian Authority, Ministry of Education, 2010), 56.

Zionist movement received support from European nations, which, without qualifying the support received, according to the book, was bent on "spreading the ideas of Zionism among Jews themselves in order to accelerate the establishment of a Jewish state in Palestine [...] and, on the other hand, was meant to rid themselves of the Jews."[110]

Ongoing Dispossession of Palestinian Land and the 1948 Exodus

The history books analyzed as part of this case study maintain that the ambitions of the Zionist movement were not fulfilled with the establishment of the state of Israel in 1948. Instead, the textbooks seek to demonstrate that Israel resorted to the Judaization of Palestinian land and continued dispossession of Palestinian land. The 11th grade textbook *Contemporary and Modern Palestinian History* (2011) dedicates an entire chapter to these activities. In this chapter, entitled "Israeli Politics after 1948," the authors note that following the 1948 War attempts were made to create a Jewish demographic majority and reject the Arab-Palestinian nature of the land and its people, including through the 1950 Law of Return and the 1952 Nationality Law, which "granted Israeli nationality to all Jews immigrating to Palestine."[111] Both this book and the 12th grade history book (2012) also argue that continued displacement and dispossession took place after 1948 at the hands of the Israelis. Political efforts aimed at a further dislodging of Palestinians included the transfer of ownership to the Jewish National Fund (JNF), the seizure of land for army and security purposes, and the building of settlements and the separation wall, which "did not stop at the borders of the annexed territories but continued beyond in order to disrupt Arab communities."[112] For the first time, these books include the fate of internally displaced refugees, namely those displaced within the 1948 territories, and Palestinians who were able to remain in their homes and localities. Thus, the 11th grade textbook notes that even though Palestinians inside the 1948 borders were given Israeli nationality, they do not enjoy the same rights and privileges as Israeli-Jews due to "restrictions on their rights of ownership, freedom of expression, freedom of organization, freedom of movement and [...] schooling."[113] While similar statements appear in the 12th grade textbook, more attention

---

[110] Ibid., 54.

[111] *Contemporary and Modern Palestinian History, Part II for the 11th Grade* (Ramallah: Palestinian Authority, Ministry of Education, 2011), 36.

[112] *History of the Arabs and the World in the Twentieth Century for the 12th Grade* (Ramallah: Palestinian Authority, Ministry of Education, 2012), 96; *11th Grade* (2011), 37.

[113] *Eleventh Grade* (2011), 36.

is rendered to the denial of Palestinian national identity inside the 1948 borders emanating from usage of "racist terminology [such as] 'Arab-Israelis' or the 'Arab Sector in Israel'."[114]

The new history books introduce Palestinian students to two further themes, namely the circumstances that accompanied the mass exodus in 1948 and the living conditions in refugee camps. With regard to the former, the 2011 textbook *Contemporary and Modern Palestinian History* stipulates that "various methods were used to empty Palestinian land of its native inhabitants, including psychological warfare, which [involved] the Haganah radio spreading rumors, and [the execution of] killing operations [in] cities and villages [such as] Deir Yassin, Tantura, and Lud."[115] Moreover, both the 12th grade textbooks *History of the Arabs and the World in the Twentieth Century* (2012) and the 11th grade *Contemporary and Modern Palestinian History* (2011) note that despite the fact that the UN specified "the right of return" and compensation for displaced Palestinians, this decision was not recognized by Israel.[116] As a result of this, the 2011 textbook maintains that refugees live in "difficult political, economic, and social circumstances."[117] These trying living conditions are further highlighted by the use of photographs. Under the heading "Pictures of Refugee Suffering in 1948," the departure of Palestinians from their homes is shown next to their subsequent life in refugee camps.[118] Although the textbook does not offer any further details pertaining to these difficult circumstances, the accompanying questions ask students to explain Palestinian refugees' living conditions after the 1948 War.[119] As such, the activity that follows this new information is likely to create a more extensive discussion, albeit one that relies on the teacher and students' own knowledge of refugee life.

An Exclusive Victimhood Narrative: The Holocaust and the Palestinian Curriculum

Despite the increased emphasis on the Nakba in the new Palestinian curriculum, the analysis above demonstrates that the 1948 War still lacks an in-depth historical analysis. The development of the mass exodus, which incorporates the usage of the Plan D offensive and the stages and effects of departure among various Palestinian societal groups, thus remains wholly elusive.[120] Furthermore, though it can be assumed that classroom

---

[114] *Twelfth Grade* (2012), 95.   [115] *Eleventh Grade* (2011), 32.
[116] *Twelfth Grade* (2012), 95; *Eleventh Grade* (2011), 33.   [117] *Eleventh Grade* (2011), 33.
[118] Ibid.   [119] Ibid., 35.
[120] For an analysis of the various stages of departure among "elite" Palestinians and villagers, see Noga Kadman, *Erased from Space and Consciousness: Israel and the*

discussions and activities that accompany the material on the 1948 War will touch on the societal effects of the war through familial stories, identification methods, such as first-hand witness accounts and photographs, were found lacking across all the examined textbooks save one.[121] The existence of a superficial Nakba narrative, however, should not be considered a statement on its perceived educational significance, since the Nakba's prominence in educational plans and the ensuing curriculum is manifest. At the same time, the dearth in historical information pertaining to the war reflects the meager length of the new Palestinian history and national education textbooks – encompassing between 60 and 80 pages on average. As the final part of this chapter will argue, the historic and contemporary relevance of the Nakba can be found implicitly in Palestinian textbooks' minimization of Nazism and the omission of the Holocaust, deemed an acknowledgment of the other's victimhood.

The Palestinian History Curriculum and the Holocaust

It is evident that a retaliatory exclusion of the Holocaust is – somewhat ironically – underwritten by a tacit acknowledgment of the events; yet, the new Palestinian history books seek to prevent a transgenerational conveyance through a complete excision of the Holocaust. Of the new history textbooks, only two discuss the Second World War: the 12th grade textbook *History of the Arabs and the World in the Twentieth Century* and the 10th grade book *History of the Modern World*. While both books provide detailed information on the various fronts and battles during the Second World War, the authors expend great efforts to avoid any meaningful discussion of the full extent and effects of Nazi ideology. For instance, although the 10th grade textbook *History of the Modern World* notes that one of the goals of the Nazi party was "the preservation of the Aryan race and blood and forbidding weak people from mixing with them," it remains unclear who these "weak people" were and how the goal was realized.[122] A similar practice can be found in the discussion on the consequences of the Second World War. Among the five outcomes, the authors note that "millions of people were displaced and mass devastation [occurred] as a result of the war." Nevertheless, as the chapter has failed to note the systematic persecution of the Jews by the

Depopulated Palestinian Villages of 1948 (Bloomington: Indiana University Press, 2015), 8–13.
[121] Gunther Kress, *Literacy in the New Media Age* (London: Routledge, 2003), 69.
[122] *Tenth Grade* (2010), 62.

Nazis, the student is left with the conclusion that displacement and mass devastation solely refers to those lost in battle.[123] An ahistorical narrative of the Second World War and Nazism can also be found in the 12th grade textbook *History of the Arabs and the World in the Twentieth Century*. Despite contending that Nazi ideology was "inconsistent with democratic rule and general freedom," this book, like its predecessor, fails to offer any insight into the application of Nazi ideology and its targets prior to and during the war.[124] Instead, Nazi racial theory is presented as an esoteric philosophy which occurred in a vacuum against "those who were backwards."[125] Consequently, the book's discussion of post-war international tribunals trying Nazi leaders as war criminals loses its relevance as their only crime appears to be their alliance with the losing party.[126]

The content on Nazi ideology and its role in the Second World War in the new Palestinian textbooks largely constitutes a continuation of the narrative presented in Jordanian history books, which were used from 1994 until 2003. Yet, the Jordanian textbooks differed from the Palestinian history books in two ways. First, without explicitly mentioning the Holocaust, the Jordanian history books did place more emphasis on Nazi discrimination against the Jews; second, this racial persecution was perceived in a positive, constructive light. Accordingly, Adolf Hitler was presented as an exemplary leader who attempted to rescue his people from misery and defeat.[127]

A greater emphasis on Jewish discrimination was found in three of the Jordanian textbooks examined as part of this case study: the 11th grade textbook *History of Western Civilization and the Modern World* and the 12th grade book *The History of the Arabs and the Modern World* (the 1994 and 1998 edition). In these books, references were made to Nazi ideology and policies concerning Jews. In the 1998 textbook, the authors noted that the Nuremberg Laws "banned all Jewish employees from public office and prohibited Jewish lawyers, reporters, doctors, pharmacists, and publishers from practicing their professions and did not allow

---

[123] Ibid., 67.   [124] *Twelfth Grade* (2012), 94.   [125] Ibid.

[126] Ibid., 40. A study conducted by Samira Alayan in 2015 similarly found that the Holocaust was omitted from Palestinian textbooks; the presented narrative does not show its unique meaning for the Jewish people. In her analysis of the 2006 edition of this 12th grade textbook, Alayan found that the textbook also sought to provide a nexus between Nazi race theory and Apartheid. In this first edition, the section on race theory and the Nazi regime was immediately followed by a new paragraph in which racism and Apartheid were compared with the treatment of Palestinians at the hands of Zionists. See Alayan, "Holocaust in Palestinian Textbooks," 90, 95

[127] As evidence of this trend, Robert Satloff in his work *Among Righteous* noted that *Mein Kampf* is a best-seller in many parts of the Arab world. Robert Satloff, *Among the Righteous* (New York: PublicAffairs, 2006), 162, 163.

Jews to inherit property."[128] The 1994 edition of the same book hinted at the genocidal policies of the regime toward the "subversives" by noting that Hitler sought to "cleanse Germany of decadent elements and especially [of] the Jews" and "eliminate any element that might thwart Germany's rule in the world."[129] However, similarly to the new books, there was no mention of Jewish victims; instead, the only textbook that dealt with victims of the war was the 8th grade textbook *Contemporary World History* (1999). Here, students were presented with a table that showed the number of killed and injured civilians of several of the countries involved in the war and were asked to explain the large amount of deaths in Germany and the Soviet Union.[130] Nevertheless, without having offered the students any concrete insight into the mass murder committed in and by these countries, the answers would likely have lacked any historical grounding.

The aforementioned ahistorical narrative was reinforced through the presentation of Nazi and Fascist ideology. In the 11th grade textbook *History of Western Civilization and the Modern World* Nazism and Fascism were presented under the heading "Contemporary Intellectual Movements," alongside the philosophical and scientific work of Martin Heidegger, Henri Bergson, and Albert Einstein.[131] An even more warped understanding of Nazism was conveyed in one of the questions in the 12th grade history book *The History of the Arabs and the Modern World*; here, students were asked to "write about the achievements of the German Nazi government."[132] Similar glorifying content could be found in the 8th grade textbook *Modern World History* and its teaching guide. In this textbook, Hitler was portrayed as the man who "changed the economic crisis and attempted to rescue the German people from repeated misery and defeat." Furthermore, in the teaching guide to this book, the teacher was told that the answer to the question "Did the Nazis' rise to power contribute to [the outbreak] of the Second World War" was: "No, the Nazis attempted to restore German power, the German army, and the economy. They also wanted to restore control of German land and provinces that had been stripped from Germany in the First World War. This led to fear and

---

[128] *The History of the Arabs and the Modern World for the 12th Grade* (Ramallah: Palestinian Authority, Ministry of Education, 1998), 107.
[129] *The History of the Arabs and the Modern World for the 12th Grade* (Ramallah: Palestinian Authority, Ministry of Education, 2003), 107.
[130] *Contemporary World History, Part II for the 8th Grade* (Ramallah: Palestinian Authority, Ministry of Education, 1998), 46.
[131] *History of Western Civilization and the Modern World for the 11th Grade* (Ramallah: Palestinian Authority, Ministry of Education, 2001/2), 186, 188.
[132] *Twelfth Grade* (2003), 112.

discent from other European countries, like France and Britain, which led to the Second World War."[133] Accordingly, the expansionist aims of Nazi Germany were also considered in a positive light, and the teacher was informed to relay to the students that "Hitler thought that the occupation of the Soviet Union would lead to peace in Europe."[134] Building on Bishara's 1995 analysis of Arabs' understanding of the Holocaust, Samira Alayan provides insight into this distorted historical interpretation of Nazism and Fascism. Alayan demonstrates that empathy felt in the Palestinian context toward Germany is both motivated by an attempt to deal with the "Zionist instrumentalization of the Holocaust" and an ongoing anti-colonial discourse.[135] Interviews conducted with participants of Dajani's Auschwitz trip equally reveal that a veneration of Hitler remains in existence; the ongoing purchase and study of Hitler's autobiography *Mein Kampf*, as such, was explained as providing valuable insights into effective leadership and organization of marginalized groups.[136]

Conversations held with educational officials involved in the development of the new curriculum reveal that the inclusion of the Holocaust in the new curriculum was not considered a priority "between and betwixt," or between conflict and peace. When questioned about the absence of the Holocaust, Jarbawi testified to what David Shipler in 1987 described as a "screen[ing out of] the suffering of your enemy [when] you are being [or have been] victimized by them."[137] Demonstrative of a riposte based on conflation, former Education Minister Jarbawi argued that since Palestinian history is not presented adequately in the Israeli curriculum, the Palestinian curriculum does not need to deal with the Holocaust: "If I want to be factually correct, I need to say that the Zionists expelled Palestinians from their country, and I might add that because of the rise of Hitler in 1933, 65,000 emigrants came here [...] These are established facts. But if I mention this, I have to say that Israel took our land and ripped us from our country. But at the same time, Israel is not asked how this history is presented there."[138] The theoretical framework behind this politicization of victimhood was highlighted by Bauman in his 2004 work "Categorical Murder, or: How to Remember the Holocaust."

---

[133] *Eighth Grade* (1998), 35; *Teacher's Guide: Contemporary World History, Part II for the 8th Grade* (Amman: Ministry of Education, 1995), 81.
[134] *Eighth Grade* (1995), 81.
[135] Bishara, "The Arabs and the Holocaust," 54; Alayan, "Holocaust in Palestinian Textbooks," 85.
[136] Interview conducted with Saleem Sowidan and Hanan Emseeh on April 25, 2016.
[137] Cited in Gilbert Achcar, *Arabs and the Holocaust* (London: Saqi Books, 2010), 221.
[138] Interview conducted with Ali Jarbawi on May 16, 2016.

In this work, Bauman maintained that when dealing with the memory of a catastrophe, it is typical for one group to highlight its own victimhood and suffering and set it against another group, particularly against those who perpetrated the catastrophe.[139]

Other officials, including former Education Minister Abu-Hummos and the current assistant to the minister of education, Tharwat Zaid Keilani, argued that the Holocaust was part of the curriculum. Keilani even contended that the current curriculum does not just focus on Jewish victims, but on all the Nazis' victims.[140] Yet, these statements and the above-mentioned findings do not match.[141] Moreover, excerpts from a symposium held in Cyprus in April 2000 indicate that members of the Palestinian Legislative Council (PLC) firmly rejected a textual inclusion of the Holocaust, as suggested by Anis Al-Qaq, the contemporary PA undersecretary of planning and international cooperation.[142] For Musa Al-Zu'but, chairman of the education committee of the Palestinian Legislative Council, this rejection was based on the "exaggeration [of the Holocaust] in order to present the Jews as victims of a great crime, to justify [the claim] that Palestine is necessary as a homeland for them, and to give them the right to demand compensation." Making a similar argument, Hatem Abd Al-Qader, a PLC member and Fatah leader, said that teaching the Holocaust in the Palestinian schools would constitute "a great danger to the [development of a] Palestinian mentality. It would be dangerous to change the Palestinian curriculum in such a direction." First, Abd Al-Qader claimed, "the Jews should learn about our disaster, the massacres, the murder and the exile, because this disaster is still alive."[143]

---

[139]   Zygmunt Bauman, "Categorical Murder, or: How to Remember the Holocaust," in *Representing the Shoah for the Twenty-first Century*, ed. Ronit Lentin (Oxford/New York: Berghahn Books, 2004), 24–40; Litvak and Webman, *From Empathy to Denial*, 14.

[140]   Interview conducted with Tharwat Zaid Keilani on May 26, 2016; Interview conducted with Naim Abu-Hummos on July 19, 2016.

[141]   For Hamas' opposition to the inclusion of the Holocaust in the Palestinian (UNRWA) curriculum in Gaza, see Howard Schneider, "Hamas Objects to Possible Lessons About Holocaust in U.N.-Run Schools in Gaza," *The Washington Post*, September 2, 2009, www.washingtonpost.com/wp-dyn/content/article/2009/09/01/AR200909010249 6.html?hpid=sec-world, accessed July 26, 2017.

[142]   Al-Qaq stated at the symposium that he was "interested in teaching the history of the Holocaust in Arab and Palestinian schools … I believe that Palestine and the entire Arab world need to learn about the Holocaust, and therefore this subject should be included in the school curriculum." MEMRI, "Palestinians Debate Including the Holocaust in the Curriculum," *Special Dispatch* 187 (2000), www.memri.org/reports/palestinians-debate-including-holocaust-curriculum, accessed July 26, 2017.

[143]   Ibid.

The firm opposition against the inclusion of the Holocaust was further reflected in the hostile political and societal reactions to the *Side by Side* project, which took place during the disintegration of the Oslo Peace Accords and the subsequent outbreak of the Second Intifadah. As mentioned in the previous chapter, *Side by Side* aimed to expose Palestinian and Israeli high-school students to the other's narrative, including the Holocaust. In an interview, Adwan, who was responsible for the Palestinian narrative, stated that the teaching of the Holocaust was met with extreme hostility. In contrast to the official rejection that occurred on the Israeli side, Adwan maintains that pressure came from the community and political parties who in letters accused him and teachers involved in the project of collaboration and teaching the "enemy's narrative." With reference to these reactions, Adwan contends that the absence of the Holocaust in the curriculum does not only derive from the lack of Israeli recognition of the Nakba, but also, as indicated in Abd Al-Qader's statements, due to ongoing Palestinian suffering as a result of the occupation, being the "victims of the victims."[144] As he stated in a personal interview: "If you talk about the trauma of your oppressor does that justify their actions? Does it excuse what they are doing? Does it minimize your own suffering? I think that it can."[145] Moreover, as Adwan points out, within the context of a daily life characterized by the Israeli occupation, even the most exemplary textbooks would not be able to "dupe [...] children into believing the opposite of what they see and experience."[146] Indeed, when further pressed, Jarbawi similarly noted that the ongoing occupation constitutes the main obstacle to recognition of the Holocaust and the implementation of projects such as *Side by Side*: "You can't convince any Palestinian under occupation or in the diaspora who comes to Ramallah that we need to talk about the Holocaust and recognize the emergence of state of Israel due to the Holocaust. Why should we learn about the Holocaust? It is not a priority while Palestinians remain under occupation."[147]

Concluding Remarks

In the wake of the 1994 Gaza–Jericho Autonomy Agreement, the Palestinian Ministry of Education was able to convey the Palestinian past

---

[144] Raja Shehadeh, *The Third Way: A Journal of Life of the West Bank* (London: Quartet Books, 1982), 64.
[145] Interview conducted with Sami Adwan on May 13, 2016.
[146] Cited in Zimbardo, "Narrative Conflict," 30.
[147] Interview conducted with Ali Jarbawi on May 16, 2016.

and contemporary grievances spurring from former events with the production of the first Palestinian curriculum. Previously denied the educational imbuing of a national consciousness under Jordanian and, subsequently, Israeli rule, the ministry sought – as indicated both in educational plans and subsequent ministerial clarifications – to foster a collective Palestinian identity, with as its principal watershed: *al-Nakba*. As such, the identified historical dearth in content on the 1948 War in national education and history books published since 1994 should not be considered emblematic of a societal disregard concerning *al-Nakba*; instead, it is representative of the general brevity and superficiality of the new textbooks, produced in a matter of years during the tumult of the Second Intifadah. In spite of reliance on foreign donors and the effects of the Al-Aqsa Intifadah, the final inclusion of the Nakba as a formative past event and, through its perceived contemporary manifestations, a present continuous therefore can be deemed a testament to the role of the Nakba in Palestinian consciousness.

Beyond the novel textual incorporation of the Nakba in new Palestinian textbooks, the latter part of this chapter illustrated that the collective importance ascribed to *al-Nakba* can also be found in the glaring disregard of the Holocaust in the curriculum. A conflation of Jews and Israelis – as evidenced in textbook content pertaining to the 1948 War – forms the foundation for the materialization of Bauman's retaliatory theory, which formulates that any official acknowledgment of the Holocaust is perceived as a justification for the establishment of the Israeli state and, consequently, a minimization of all ensuing Palestinian suffering. The firm rejection of Al-Qaq's proposal at the April 2000 Cyprus conference to include the Holocaust in the Palestinian curriculum testifies to the very quid pro quo principle that lies at the heart of Bauman's theory, as the marginalization of the Nakba in Israeli-Jewish society is invoked to justify the omission of the Holocaust. In addition to textbooks' identification of ongoing dispossession of Palestinian land and, inside the 1948 borders, the denial of a Palestinian national identity, awareness of continual Israeli cultural and political palimpsest practices also derives from Nakba commemorative activities in the post-Oslo era. The following chapter thus demonstrates that Nakba mnemonics have been instrumentalized on both sides of the Green Line to present an ongoing Nakba emanating from Israeli legal and cultural restrictions on its invocation by the Palestinian community.

Part II

The Landscape of Memory

In his lecture entitled "What is a nation?," delivered at the Sorbonne in 1882, Renan argued that the most crucial trait of a nation is its members' identification with the collective without actually being acquainted with the members of that collective.[1] This collective identification, according to Renan, could be achieved through conveying and sustaining the memory of social groups in public commemorations. While Renan's observations were made over a hundred years ago, the creation of an "imagined community" through mnemonic practices remains relevant today.[2] Indeed, despite post-modern criticism of notions of "collectivity" and an increased interest in – and acknowledgment of – subaltern memory and identity, Hobsbawm notes that there is no indication of the weakening of the usage of neo-traditional symbolic practices associated with enhancing citizenship membership and group belonging.[3]

The continued significance of commemoration practices, in part, derives from contemporary and future political and social purposes, which are embedded in the re-enactment of historical moments in the present.[4] With reference to the political goals, Paul Connerton contends that social invocation of a shared past can legitimate a present social order, thereby also indicating that collective mnemonic acts are contemporary educational mediums for transmitting hegemonic narratives or "master commemorative narratives" to a broader public – and from one

---

[1] Paul Connerton, *How Modernity Forgets* (Cambridge: Cambridge University Press, 2009), 48.
[2] Benedict Anderson, *Imagined Communities: Reflections on the Origin and Spread of Nationalism* (London: Verso, 2006), 6.
[3] Eric Hobsbawm and Terence Ranger, ed., *The Invention of Tradition* (Cambridge: Cambridge University Press, 2012), 12.
[4] Brendan Browne, "Commemoration in Conflict," *Journal of Comparative Research in Anthropology and Sociology* 2 (2013): 145; Judith Tydor Baumel, "In Everlasting Memory: Individual and Communal Holocaust Commemoration in Israel," *Israel Affairs* 1 (1995): 146.

generation to the next.[5] It follows that this politically motivated invocation of a shared past does not necessarily seek to counter collective
amnesia of the historic past, but rather revives and modifies the past to
achieve the desired transmission in the present.[6] Yet, as indicated above,
commemorative acts do not only serve the interests of groups seeking
political legitimization, but also the individuals that together form active
participants within the commemorative group.[7] In other words, public
acts of remembrance that involve recalling moments in a group's shared
history are at once individual and collective.[8] In this context, Simone
Weil's Durkheimian-style phrase "a collective has its roots in the past"
finds relevance as it indicates that the collective memory acts that stimulate awareness of a group's history enhance communal identity, legitimating individuals in their own eyes and creating social cohesion.[9] The
stimulation of social cohesion and the legitimating nature of collective
mnemonic acts – both for individual and collective purposes – do not
only rely on the invocation of a shared past. Rather, a ritual collective
performance, which can include singing the same anthem, defines the
boundaries of the group and ensures that the collective act of commemoration "becomes an event in itself that is to be shared and remembered."[10] The fusion of an individual's biography with that of the
group also forms an indispensable part in the consolidation of group
solidarity.[11] Expanding on the Gramscian top-down analysis, Carol
Kidron and Geoffrey White's ethnographic bottom-up analysis of individual and family memory at memory sites showed that individuals and

---

[5] Connerton, *How Modernity Forgets*, 3. On the concept of "master narratives," see Yael
Zerubavel, *Recovered Roots: Collective Memory and the Making of Israeli National Tradition*
(Chicago/London: University of Chicago Press, 1995), 10–12.
[6] It is because of this legitimizing nature of public commemoration that John Jackson notes
that every new social order anxious to establish its image and acquire public support
produces many commemorative monuments, symbols, and public celebrations. John
B. Jackson, *The Necessity for Ruins and Other Topics* (Amherst: University of
Massachusetts Press, 1980), 92.
[7] Émile Durkheim, *Critical Assessments of Leading Sociologists*, ed. W. S. F. Pickering
(London/New York: Routledge, 2001), 96.
[8] Emile Durkheim, *Suicide: A Study in Sociology*, trans. John A. Spaulding and George
Simpson (New York: Free Press, 1951), 297–325. Also see Halbwachs, *On Collective*,
chapter six.
[9] Connerton, *How Modernity Forgets*, 3. 48; James Young, "When a Day Remembers:
A Performative History of 'Yom ha-Shoah'," *History and Memory* 2 (1990): 71.
[10] James Young, *The Texture of Memory: Holocaust Memorials and Meaning* (New Haven/
London: Yale University Press, 1993), 6, 7; Feldman, *Above the Death Pits*, 12.
[11] Eviatar Zerubavel, "Calendars and History: A Comparative Study of the Social
Organization of National Memory," in *States of Memory: Continuities, Conflicts and
Transformations in National Retrospection*, ed. Jeffrey K. Olick (Durham, NC: Duke
University Press, 2003), 316.

families negotiate the hegemonically imposed group discourse and weave it into their personal memories.[12] Consequently, the existence of a pure hegemonic metanarrative or master narrative must be questioned, as the performative nature of commemoration – that it fundamentally requires an audience – means that a commemoration needs to draw on an audience's specific values, experiences, memories, sympathies, and beliefs. In short, for commemoration to resonate with the audience, it must say something about their past, make some meaning of their present lives, and offer something about their future, thereby necessitating the incorporation of a bottom-up narrative.[13]

The Commemoration of Watersheds

While the term commemoration refers to all those devices and acts through which a nation or group recalls its past, it is evident that not all historical events are commemorated. Renan, in his lecture, maintained that commemorations of grief are of particular importance to societies, as he argued: "where national memories are concerned, griefs are of more value than triumphs, for they impose duties, and require a common effort."[14] Exploring the instrumentalization of national griefs, scholars such as George Mosse and Avner Ben-Amos have argued that the commemoration of national deaths – cast as a form of a national sacrifice – has been particularly prevalent in numerous states in the modern era in the attempt to mold a holistic collective memory and identity.[15] The existence of grief, however, is not imperative to a commemoration of a past. Instead, as Meir Litvak contends, events that are commemorated need to be "invested with extraordinary significance and assigned a qualitatively distinct past in our conception of the past [thus lifting] from an ordinary historical sequence those extraordinary events that embody

---

[12] Carol Kidron, "Survivor Family Memory Work at Sites of Holocaust Remembrance: Institutional Enlistment or Family Agency?," *History & Memory* 1 (2015): 40, 49; Geoffrey M. White, "Emotional Remembering: The Pragmatics of National Memory," *Ethos* 27 (1999): 505–529.

[13] Khalili, *Heroes and Martyrs of Palestine*, 222.

[14] Cited in Homi K. Bhabha, ed., *Nation & Narration* (London/New York: Routledge, 1990), 19.

[15] George L. Mosse, *Fallen Soldiers: Reshaping the Memory of the World Wars* (New York: Oxford University Press, 1990); Avner Ben-Amos, "War Commemoration and the Formation of Israeli National Identity," *Journal of Political and Military Sociology* 31 (2003): 171–195; Don Handelman and Lea Shamgar-Handelman, "The Presence of Absence: The Memorialism of National Death in Israel," in *Grasping Land*, ed. Eyal Ben-Ari and Yoram Bilu (Albany: State University of New York Press, 1997), 85–128.

our deepest and most fundamental values."[16] It is because of this "lifting" of extraordinary events that Claude Lévi-Strauss noted that history contains "hot chronologies," which are those periods that appear replete with historical action and significance for the present.[17] Although hot chronologies or seminal events can occur throughout a society's history, the "hottest" part of any group or society's past tends to be the beginning, because, as Mircea Eliade wrote in 1963, a beginning gives rise to the notion that "it is the first manifestation of a thing that is significant and valid."[18] More recently, Eviatar Zerubavel, building on Eliade's theory, argued that founding moments, as watersheds, are prime examples of historical punctuation marks observed by mnemonic communities.[19] The particular significance of origins or founding moments, importantly, does not solely depend on the existence of a historical break or a new beginning, but on the conception of an "origin [as a] proto-typical event [setting] a pattern which affects subsequent developments."[20]

The Nakba and the Holocaust as Watersheds

The Nakba and the Holocaust, respectively, constitute watersheds in the collective consciousness of Palestinians and Israeli-Jews. As such, they are not merely formative past events, but equally seminal moments that continue to affect and guide contemporary life, including through their invocation in commemorative practices. The following two chapters are principally concerned with the rituals and performances that accompany the conveyance of these watersheds in the respective societies. Using Hobsbawm and Terence Ranger's seminal work on invented traditions as a key theoretical framework, this section emphasizes the constructed nature of mnemonic acts by discussing the evolution, formalization, and ritualization of the commemorative acts under review.[21] Part and parcel of this ritualization entails a discussion of the narrative(s) and symbols put forward in commemorative acts, as every commemoration

---

[16] Meir Litvak, ed., *Palestinian Collective Memory and National Identity* (Basingstoke: Palgrave Macmillan, 2009), 15.
[17] These "hot chronologies" contrast with "cold chronologies," when it appears nothing of major significance happened. Claude Lévi-Strauss, *The Savage Mind* (Chicago: University of Chicago Press, 1966), 259.
[18] Eliade Mircea, *Myth and Reality* (New York: Harper & Row, 1963), 34.
[19] Zerubavel, "Calendars and History," 321.
[20] Schwartz, "Social Context of Communication," 376.
[21] Hobsbawm and Ranger, *Invention*, 4.

explicitly or implicitly contains a narrative used as a vehicle of transmission. Yet, as commemorative rituals and narratives are not static, but rather develop and are modified according to the contemporary needs of the commemorating group, this section also seeks to reveal the differences found in the mnemonic acts in the time period under review and expound on any political and social motives behind changing practices.

The acts and devices used to invoke a group's past are vast and include monuments, holidays, cemeteries, archives, memorial books, memorial days, memorial festivals, memorial sculptures, re-enactments of events, iconization of places and people, and memorial institutions.[22] The majority of these acts and devices, which can be both mournful and celebratory in nature, fall beyond the scope of this research. Instead, the focus will lie on national memorial days – *Yawm al-Nakbah* (Arabic: Nakba day) and *Yom ha-Shoah* (Hebrew: Holocaust day) – and on places of commemoration, thereby differentiating between non-physical and physical acts of commemoration, or abstract and non-abstract mnemonics.[23] Physical mnemonic acts, in contrast to non-physical acts, are site-specific and in this research, in addition to physical memorials and institutes, include (former) landscape as "signposts of memory."[24] Crucially, landscape in the context of this study cannot be viewed as an agent of power independent of human intentions in which, in the words of William Mitchell, "we [as] passive figures find – or lose – ourselves."[25] Instead, it is clear that when dealing with contested territory, the commemorative event itself and those partaking in the act can become subject to scrutiny and interference, particularly when the commemorative landscape falls under the control of the non-commemorating hegemonic group. Consequently, as will be discussed in Chapter 4, commemorative return visits to former Palestinian villages inside the 1948 borders are deemed confrontational mnemonic acts because of their inherent challenge of post-1948 physical erasure policies and the failure to implement the right of return by the dominant Israeli state.

---

[22] Young, *Texture of Memory*, 4; John R. Gillis, ed., *Commemorations: The Politics of National Identity* (Princeton: Princeton University Press, 1994), 14.

[23] While this work recognizes that since 2005 International Holocaust Remembrance Day is also commemorated annually on the 27th of January in Israel, the mnemonics of this holiday fall beyond the scope of this research as a result of its late materialization within the time period under review.

[24] Benvenisti, *Sacred Landscape*, 8.

[25] William John Thomas Mitchell, ed., *Landscape and Power* (Chicago/London: University of Chicago Press, 1994), 2.

Commemorating the Past in Physical and Non-Physical Mnemonic Acts

Scholars have repeatedly utilized Pierre Nora's work on French post-revolutionary memory sites as a theoretical framework to discuss the role of physical memory sites in Israeli and Palestinian commemoration.[26] Nora's "lieux de mémoire" theory, however, will not be applied in this research for two main reasons. First, while Nora's *lieux* denote both non-physical commemorations and physical sites of memory "as anything having to do with [...] the presence of the past," Nora's "lieux de mémoire" have come into existence as a result of a lack of "milieux de mémoire," settings in which memory is part of everyday experiences.[27] In other words, "lieux de mémoire," as consecrated memory sites, would not exist if the memories of the past had not been "swept away by history."[28] Yet, the Nakba and Holocaust feature distinctly in the Palestinian and Israeli "milieux de mémoire"; and they are not fundamental vestiges of a "historical nation" that has ceased to transmit its memory.[29] Second, inherent in Nora's argument is the notion of a creation of both physical and non-physical sites of memory whereby creation denotes falsification.[30] Crucially, in the case of Palestinian sites of memory, the construction of a former Palestinian landscape is neither intentional nor does it seek to allude to a pre-existing "milieux de mémoire."

As a result of mass Palestinian displacement and the Israeli control over territory that followed the 1948 War and the 1967 War, the analysis of physical sites and non-physical mnemonic acts in Israeli and Palestinian society will vary substantially. In the Israeli context, physical and non-physical mnemonic acts will be examined at three main Holocaust memorial institutes in Israel: Yad Vashem, Lohamei Hagetaot (known as the Ghetto Fighters' House in English), and Yad Mordechai, which were established in the 1950s and 1960s. Conversely, Palestinian society – both inside the 1948 borders and the West Bank – has not yet been able to dedicate an official institute to the

---

[26] See, for instance, Amos Goldberg, "The 'Jewish Narrative' in the Yad Vashem Global Holocaust Museum," *Journal of Genocide Research* 14 (2012): 187–213; Dalia Ofer, "We Israelis Remember, But How? The Memory of the Holocaust and the Israeli Experience," *Israel Studies* 18 (2013): 70–85; Lentin, *Co-Memory and Melancholia*; Sa'di and Abu-Lughod, *Nakba*.

[27] Pierre Nora, *Realms of Memory: Rethinking the French Past*, trans. Lawrence D. Kritzman (New York: Columbia University Press, 1996–1998), 1, 14, 16.

[28] Ibid., 2.   [29] Ibid., 1, 6–7.

[30] Anderson, *Imagined Communities*, 6; Ernest Gellner, *Thought and Change* (London: Weidenfeld and Nicolson, 1964), 169.

commemoration of the Nakba. As a consequence, following the 1993 Oslo Accords, organizations independent from the Israeli and Palestinian governments have played a pivotal role in mnemonic acts dedicated to the Nakba.[31] The fragmented political reality since 1948 and, in particular, the various states of military rule applied by Israel inside the 1948 borders until 1966 and in the West Bank since 1967 have determined that both the execution and organization of Nakba commemoration differ immensely on both sides of the 1948 borders. Within the 1948 borders, since 1966, the access to former Palestinian villages has meant that Nakba commemorations – particularly following the Oslo Accords – have centered on physical mnemonic acts, incorporating traditional village commemorations in the collective realm. However, in the West Bank, restrictions on Palestinian movement into Israel and, since the Second Intifadah, inside the West Bank, have meant that non-site-specific commemorative acts dominate. Crucially, these non-physical commemorative acts do not denote a lack of "physicality" in the traditional sense. Thus, under the leadership of the human rights organization Badil (Arabic: alternative), "return marches" constitute a primary form of commemoration on *Yawm al-Nakbah* and are conducted in cities and refugee camps in the West Bank.

The diverging political reality has created a further disparity in the official nature of the Israeli and Palestinian institutes and organizations involved in commemoration.[32] In the Israeli context, all three Holocaust institutes under examination can be deemed to conform with the official state narrative. As such, while Yad Vashem is the only Holocaust institute whose maintenance is legally fixed in the state budget,[33] the state's involvement in – and (financial) endorsement of – commemorative acts at Yad Mordechai and Lohamei Hagetaot indicate that mnemonic practices at these institutes are sanctioned by the state and therefore are representative of the official master narrative. Conversely, the absence of Palestinian governance in Palestinian society inside the 1948 borders and post-Oslo hostility toward the PA has meant that an overt state-sanctioned narrative has largely remained absent in Nakba

---

[31] In 2005, the Palestinian writer and academic Masalha pointed out that memory sites dedicated to the Nakba do not exist: "There is no Nakba museum, no Nakba Hall of Names [...] no tombstones or monuments for the hundreds of Palestinian villages and towns ethnically cleansed and destroyed in 1948." Nur Masalha, "Remembering the Palestinian Nakba: Commemoration, Oral History and Narratives of Memory," *Holy Land Studies* 7:2 (2008): 139.

[32] Nora, *Realms of Memory*, 19.

[33] See "Knesset, Martyrs' and Heroes Commemoration (Yad Vashem) Law, 5713–1953," Knesset, https://knesset.gov.il/review/data/eng/law/kns2_yadvashem_eng.pdf, accessed February 2, 2020.

commemorations. Nevertheless, since both official and unofficial commemorations require an agent or agents, the notion of commemorative agency pertains to both Israeli and Palestinian society. Moreover, in both contexts, state and non-state actors' involvement in commemorative acts has meant that the forms, contents, and referents of commemoration have been those which the actors have considered relevant and legitimate for their target audience. Therefore, in addition to examining the commemorative acts and devices themselves through utilizing historical documents published by the mnemonic institutes and organizations, the following two chapters rely on interviews conducted with the organizational actors to highlight the existence and transformation of commemorative motives.

4   Recreating and Reclaiming the Lost Homeland

In March 1998, a Nakba and Steadfastness Committee (NSC) was set up by Palestinian citizens of Israel. Among the committee's initiatives, one gained front-page headlines in the media: a call for Palestinian municipalities in Israel to establish memorial monuments for the Palestinian martyrs (Arabic: *shuhadā'*) of 1948.[1] The NSC's initiative was emblematic of a change in Nakba commemoration among Palestinians living inside the 1948 borders and those living in the West Bank in the lead-up to the fiftieth anniversary of the 1948 War. In addition to calls for memorial monuments and the creation of a museum dedicated to the Nakba, a vast proliferation of Palestinian memoirs, oral history projects, films, and academic studies concerning the Nakba occurred across the West Bank and inside the 1948 borders from the early 1990s onwards.[2] This increased interest in the Nakba should not merely be ascribed to the temporal significance of the year 1998. Rather, both in the West Bank and inside Israel, following the 1993 Oslo Accords, preoccupation with the marginalized refugee community coupled with the rise in civil society organizations created an atmosphere in which Nakba commemoration

---

[1] Tamir Sorek, "Cautious Commemoration: Localism, Communalism, and Nationalism in Palestinian Memorial Monuments in Israel," *Comparative Studies in Society and History* 50 (2008): 377; Alexander Bligh, ed., *The Israeli Palestinians: An Arab Minority in the Jewish State* (London: Frank Cass, 2003), 170.

[2] In 1997, the Taawon-Welfare organization, whose members include(d) Ibrahim Abu-Lughod and Abdel Al-Qattan, determined that a museum should be created in dedication to the memory of the Nakba on the fiftieth anniversary of the 1948 War. In the end, the second generation – to which the current chairman Omar Al-Qattan belongs – decided that the museum should celebrate Palestine's culture more broadly. Interview conducted with Omar Al-Qattan on March 11, 2016. Films included: Edward Said's "In Search of Palestine" and Muhammad Bakri's "1948." Academic works included: Masalha, *Expulsion of the Palestinians*; Pappé, *The Making of the Arab-Israeli Conflict*; Walid Khalidi, *All That Remains: The Palestinian Villages Occupied and Depopulated by Israel in 1948* (Washington, DC: Institute for Palestine Studies, 1992); Elias Sanbar, *Les Palestiniens dans le siècle* (Paris: Gallimard, 1994); Elias Sanbar, *Palestine, le pays à venir* (Paris: L'Olivier, 1996); and Salman Abu Sitta, *The Palestinian Nakba 1948: The Register of Depopulated Localities in Palestine* (London: Palestinian Return Centre, 1998).

became at once more organized and cohesive. Moving from the traditional local sphere to the collective realm, new forms of Nakba commemoration also articulated the urgent desire to further awareness of the Nakba among younger generations with the specific aim of encouraging the continuing political struggle for the right of return (Arabic: *haq al-'awdah*) and, more generally, resisting ongoing marginalization of the Palestinian community inside Israel and the West Bank.

The emphasis on the confrontational nature of Nakba mnemonic practices in the following chapter, in addition to reflecting the dynamics of mnemonic community-making which designate clear group lines,[3] is based on the theoretical concept that the subject driving the confrontation propels the emergence of an exclusive victimhood. The framework behind this notion derives from a combination of theoretical foundations discussed previously. The convergence of Bauman's general exclusivity theory and comments made by Adwan inferring blindness to Jewish suffering experienced in the Holocaust in light of current Palestinian suffering leads to the creation of a "defensive denial theory." Here, it is not necessarily the experienced discursive denial of the Nakba by Israeli-Jews but rather the physical and political ramifications of this denial that are key to understanding unfolding trends of exclusivity on the part of their neighbors. The exclusionary narrative is not one that unfolds overtly; the analyzed commemorative acts are not "sites" of a narrative collision. Nevertheless, the societal invocation of the Nakba as a "present continuous" does shed light on existing trends of marginalization discussed throughout this work, which hinge on a retaliatory screening out of any past suffering of the out-group, as it is deemed responsible for both the original and continuing suffering.

Through an analysis of the activities of three leading civil society organizations – namely Baladna, ADRID, and Badil – the chapter below examines two collective mnemonic Nakba practices established in the wake of the Oslo Accords: annual Nakba Day commemoration and collective returns to former Palestinian villages. With reference to the organizations' varying social and geographical focuses, this chapter will attest to the fact that, while similar in narrative and political goals, the execution of Nakba mnemonic practices in the West Bank and inside Israel differs, reflecting historic commemoration practices and the fragmented political reality. Furthermore, the inclusion of Badil, which focuses on the ongoing marginalization of all Palestinian youth in Israeli society rather than solely that of refugees, allows insight to be

---

[3] Chiara De Cesari and Ann Rigney, *Transnational Memory, Circulation, Articulation, Scales* (Berlin: De Gruyter, 2014), 9.

gained into commemorative Nakba practices among the nonrefugee community inside the 1948 borders, thereby revealing the practical usage of Nakba commemoration as a means of political confrontation.

The Capitulation of Oslo

The rise in civil organizations dedicated to commemorating the Nakba in the 1990s cannot be understood without reference to the 1993 Oslo Peace Accords for which the groundwork had been laid two years earlier, during the 1991 Madrid Conference. The Oslo Accords had far-reaching effects for the self-understanding and political engagement of Palestinians living inside the 1948 borders and Palestinian refugees living inside the West Bank. Since the birth of the Palestinian Liberation Organization in 1964, the right of return and the associated refugee issue had been seen as the organization's mainstays, as indicated by the inclusion of the right of return in the Palestinian Declaration of Independence in 1988.[4] The PLO's commitment to the right of return was deemed such that in 1978 dozens of Palestinians inside Israel demanded recognition of the PLO based on the notion that acceptance of the PLO as the true legitimate representative of the Palestinian people would lead to "the solution of the refugee problem according to the repeated resolutions of the United Nations Organization."[5] Yet, under the leadership of the PLO, the Oslo Accords relegated one of the most central points of the Israeli-Palestinian conflict – the question of Palestinian refugees – to later final-status negotiations.[6] The acceptance of the accords by the PLO meant that, in the words of the Palestinian writer Ghada Karmi, "it apparently became acceptable to settle someone else's country, expel its inhabitants and ensure by all means that they never return. By the same token, it became unacceptable – in bad taste even – to mention that these things had actually happened."[7] In the eyes of the Palestinian refugee community, however, "the capitulation of Oslo" demanded a response.[8]

---

[4] The Declaration of Independence was accepted by the Palestinian National Council in Algeria on November 15, 1988. Oren Yiftachel, "Territory as the Kernel of the Nation: Space, Time and Nationalism in Israel/Palestine," *Geopolitics* 7 (2002): 216.

[5] Pamela Ann Smith and Mohammed Kiwan, "'Sons of the Village' Assert Palestinian Identity in Israel," *MERIP Reports* 68 (1978): 18.

[6] Benvenisti, *Sacred Landscape*, 266; Ghada Karmi and Eugene Cotran, eds., *The Palestinian Exodus 1948–1998* (Reading: Ithaca Press, 1999), 3; Browne, "Commemoration," 153.

[7] Cited in Fouad Ajami, *The Dream Place of the Arabs* (New York: Pantheon, 1998), 268.

[8] Ibid.

Somewhat paradoxically, the 1993 Oslo Accords facilitated the very political and social framework in which criticism against Oslo could be articulated. Under the control of the Jordanians (1948–1967) and, subsequently, the Israelis (1967–1994), Palestinians in the West Bank had been subject to measures preventing Palestinians from commemorating the Nakba in an attempt to quash the formation of Palestinian nationalism.[9] Yet, with the establishment of the PNA as a semiautonomous entity, an environment was created in which the invocation of the Nakba could take place more freely, as indicated by its inclusion in textbooks.

From the early 1990s, a new political framework had also come into existence among Palestinians inside Israel, characterized by a heightened national and political consciousness. In addition to the failure of the Oslo Accords to address the plight of the internal refugees, three interconnected motives can be identified for the increased politicization: the erosion of Palestinian civil rights, a rise in Israeli right-wing politics, and attempts to thwart Nakba commemoration. A convergence of these three motives took place in December 1992, when Gonen Segev, the right-wing Knesset Member of the Tzomet (Hebrew: crossroads) party, sought to outlaw a student association at the University of Haifa for referencing the Nakba in a calendar marking key dates in the Palestinian national narrative.[10] While Segev's demand to "bash the head of the snake while it is still young" was rejected, it laid the groundwork for future legislative attempts in 2001, 2009, and 2010 to clip the wings of Palestinian commemoration inside the 1948 borders, which eventually culminated in the 2011 Nakba Law.[11] It is in the context of these political developments and the PNA's evasion of any meaningful discussion on the right of return that Palestinian civil society organizations took advantage of the emergence of the new post-Oslo framework and thrust themselves into the forefront by addressing the political marginalization

---

[9] Rosemary Sayigh, *Palestinians: From Peasants to Revolutionaries: A People's History* (London: Zed Press, 1979), 111; Masalha, *Palestine Nakba*, 6.

[10] Masalha, *Palestine Nakba*, 244, 245.

[11] The Nakba bill bars groups financed by the state from sponsoring remembrance activities for the Nakba on "Israel's Independence Day or the day of its establishment as a day of mourning." Note that the law is phrased in such a way that even the commemoration of Nakba day on the 15th of May (rather than Independence Day) would justify punishment. Sorek, *Palestinian Commemoration in Israel*, 159. See this work's Introduction and Chapter 2 for a further discussion of the evolution of the 2011 Nakba Bill.

of the refugee community and – in the process – reconstructing Nakba mnemonic practices.[12]

The Return Visit: A Negation of the Nakba

In her 1999 article "After the Nakba," Karmi reflects on her parents' mysterious habit of questioning Palestinians visiting them in London on their exact place of origin. According to Karmi, this ritual of establishing a person's origin "became for Palestinians a kind of mapping, a surrogate repopulation of Palestine in negation of the Nakba. It was their way of recreating the lost homeland, as if the families and the villages and the relations they had once known were all still there, waiting to be reclaimed."[13] The recreation and reclaiming of the lost homeland did not only take place among exilic Palestinians. Following displacement, the village of origin became a major symbol for displaced Palestinians living within the 1948 borders (known in Arabic as the internal refugees, al-muhajjarīn fī al-dākhil),[14] providing them with a legitimate identity within the host village and shaping their perception of the past and the future.[15] A survey conducted in 1996 by Mustafa Cabaha and Ronit Brazilai showed that the affiliation with the village of origin had

---

[12] During the 1990s, an extraordinary large number of new Palestinian civil society associations were established. Some 656 associations were officially registered inside Israel, including Ittijah (Arabic: direction) (1995), which represents fifty-five Israeli-Palestinians associations and offers services to more than 150 Palestinian associations. Palestinian associations inside the Green Line, such as Adalah (Arabic: justice) and the Arab Centre for Alternative Planning, support the internally displaced. Nihad Boqai' and Terry Rempel, "Patterns of Internal Displacement, Social Adjustment and the Challenge of Return," in Catastrophe Remembered: Palestine, Israel and the Internal Refugees: Essays in Memory of Edward W. Said (1935–2003), ed. Nur Masalha (London: Zed Books, 2005), 101.

[13] Ghada Karmi, "After the Nakba: An Experience of Exile in England," Journal of Palestine Studies 28 (1999): 55.

[14] Estimates of the total number of internally displaced inside Israel vary. According to ADRID, of the approximately 250,000 Palestinians that remained inside the 1948 borders after the 1948 War, 25 percent were displaced from their homes and became internal refugees. Today, some 250,000 internal refugees live inside Israel in eighty towns and villages. This number, however, does not include those displaced and forcibly relocated after the 1948 War, conservatively estimated at 75,000 persons. Nur Masalha, "Introduction," in Masalha, Catastrophe Remembered, 9; ADRID, The Internally Displaced and the Right of Return (ADRID, undated), 1.

[15] Internal refugees' sense of belonging is also dictated by the geographical segregation and rejection by the inhabitants of the host village based on religious discrimination. In addition to family ties, religion was a very important sociocultural element in choosing places of refuge, especially for the displaced Christian minority. Despite greater interaction with the host village in the past few decades, social differences, geographical segregation, and rejection by local people continue to engender a sense of estrangement beyond the first generation. Boqai' and Rempel, "Patterns," 77, 89.

continued to be transmitted across generations; in fact, the survey's results revealed that this bond was strongest among members of the third generation of whom 70 percent stated that they belonged to the village of origin.[16] The explicit sense of belonging among internal refugees, in contrast to many Palestinian refugees in the diaspora, has been substantiated through the physical proximity to the villages of origin and the ability to return and experience these villages, albeit under varying restrictions imposed by the Israeli state.

In the wake of the 1948 War, return visits to former Palestinians villages inside the 1948 borders were heavily restricted due to the existence of a military administration. Under this administration imposed on Palestinians living inside Israel, temporary residence cards were made compulsory not only to obtain work permits but also to secure one's place of residence, and travel passes were made necessary to leave that place[17] – a system that equally enabled Israeli surveillance bodies to acquire and store personal data on Palestinians.[18] As a consequence of this intricate bureaucratic system, return visits were traditionally conducted on the one day of the year that freedom of movement existed: Israel's Independence Day.[19] Upon the lifting of military rule in 1966, return visits by families and individuals became more frequent, marking holidays, religious feasts, and, following 1976 Land Day, as an annual observance of *Yawm al-Arḍ* (Arabic: Land Day) protests.[20] In the same decade that return visits became a form of protest, "returns" were also performed as an educational ritual. Summer camps were organized for the children of the original inhabitants of a displaced village, aimed at transmitting communal memories in a bid to strengthen local Palestinian identity.[21] The first of these "Roots and Belonging Camps" took place in the 1970s in Kafr Bir'im, and, from the mid-1980s, groups of internally displaced Palestinians (IDPs) from other villages followed suit.[22] During these summer camps, individuals belonging to the first generation were often invited to talk about the village before the 1948 Nakba and village

---

[16] Masalha, *Catastrophe Remembered*, 88.   [17] Khalili, *Time in the Shadows*, 200.

[18] Ahmad H. Sa'di, "Stifling Surveillance: Israel's Surveillance and Control of the Palestinians during the Military Government Era," *Jerusalem Quarterly* 68 (2016): 43.

[19] Eitan Bronstein, "The Nakba in Hebrew: Israeli-Jewish Awareness of the Palestinian Catastrophe and Internal Refugees," in Masalha, *Catastrophe Remembered*, 217.

[20] After Israeli authorities killed six Palestinians in the Galilee protesting land confiscations on March 30, 1976, Palestinians inside Israel began annual observances of Land Day. Alain Epp Weaver, "Remembering the Nakba in Hebrew: Return Visits as the Performance of a Binational Future," *Holy Land Studies* 6 (2008): 134.

[21] Alain Epp Weaver, *Mapping Exile and Return: Palestinian Dispossession and a Political Theology for a Shared Future* (Minneapolis: Fortress Press, 2014), 102.

[22] Ibid., 102.

traditions were once again performed in order to "live [...] the village 24 hours a day."[23]

Implementing a Temporary Return

The National Committee for the Rights of the Internally Displaced in Israel, since 2000 known as the Association for the Defense of the Rights of the Internally Displaced (ADRID or *jam'iyyah al-difā' 'an huqūq al-muhajjarīn*), was founded on March 11, 1995 in response to the failure to address the Palestinian community in Israel and, more specifically, the internal refugees in any accord or compromise.[24] Internal documents charting the establishment and goals of ADRID note that neither the PA, recognized as the legitimate representative of the Palestinian people, nor the Israeli government, which considered IDPs to be Israeli citizens, managed to comprehensively address the fate of the internally displaced and that of the Palestinian minority in the Madrid Conference of 1991 or the 1993 Oslo Accords.[25] As the document on the first popular meeting of the committee explains: "The 1991 Madrid Conference excluded references to UN Resolution 194, which emphasizes our right of return and neglected the existence of the Palestinian Arab minority in the homeland."[26] In order to "gather and unify our struggle for the right of return to our villages and towns of origin," on its foundation in Qasr al-Salam/Tamra, the committee presented itself as "the only legitimate representative of the internally displaced in Israel."[27]

Following its establishment in 1995, ADRID focused its attention on four main goals: (I) increasing awareness among the public and various groups of the plight of the internally displaced; (II) demanding and obtaining full legal rights for internal refugees; (III) gaining access to abandoned and/or destroyed towns and villages; and (IV) realizing the right of return for IDPs to their towns and villages.[28] Mohammed Kaial, one of the founders of the original committee and a descendant from the displaced village of al-Birweh, notes that in the attempt to increase awareness among both IDPs and the nonrefugee population inside Israel, activities have centered on depopulated or destroyed

---

[23] Badil Resource Center for Palestinian Residency and Refugee Rights, *Returning to Kafr Bir'im* (Badil, 2006), 95, 96; Masalha, *Palestine Nakba*, 249.

[24] ADRID operated as a public committee for many years and in May 2000 obtained official registration as an NGO and nonprofit organization in Israel. ADRID, *The First Meeting of the Internally Displaced, March 11, 1995* (The National Committee for the Rights of the Internally Displaced in Israel, 2000); ADRID, *General Organizational Profile* (ADRID, undated).

[25] ADRID, *First Meeting*, 5.   [26] Ibid., 5.   [27] Ibid., 2.   [28] ADRID, *General*, 2.

Palestinian villages.[29] In collaboration with village committees,[30] which formerly represented the inhabitants of specific destroyed or depopulated villages, ADRID has conducted restorations of historic and religious sites, such as mosques and cemeteries, collected archival material on villages, and run summer camps for children and youth in their villages of origin. Through these return visits, awareness is raised among the second, third, and fourth generation of IDPs, because, as Kaial points out, "they hear about the history of the village and how people lived and they see their land, where their houses were and trees that still exist, it's their history, it's not too distant, it's recent history."[31] During the seventeenth annual summer camp held on August 5, 2005, hundreds of children of Kafr Bir'im spending a week in the razed village were visited by the first generation who came to talk to the youth about their lives in the villages before 1948, thereby making the village a fully-fledged educational project. One of these visitors was Sami Zahra, an IDP from Bir'im, who "told them [the participants] about our lives before the Nakba, our habits and traditions, and about the occupation of the village. I also walk with these groups among the houses, half of which still exist, and explain about them and about [sic] the names of their owners."[32]

Since 2001, another organization, Baladna (Arabic: our country), has been active in bringing youth to former Palestinian villages in a bid to expose the Nakba to them. Baladna, the largest independent Palestinian youth organization group working in the 1948 area, presents itself as a "development and capacity-building agency for Arab-Palestinian youth in Israel" and aims to engage Palestinian youth in discussions and debates concerning "the history, grievances and culture of Palestinians in Israel, the Occupied Territories and [the] diaspora," which are currently not provided in the Israeli education system.[33] The Nakba constitutes one of the main historical grievances that have been addressed in the organization's educational, cultural, and leadership programs, which, according to internal reports, reach "tens of thousands of youths."[34] These programs consist of visitations to refugee camps in the West Bank and Lebanon, return visits to depopulated Palestinian villages within Israel, and discussions and lectures concerning the Nakba and

[29] Ibid.; Interview conducted with Mohammed Kaial on April 18, 2016.
[30] For an example of how this collaboration is conducted, see Wakim Wakim, "The 'Internally Displaced': Seeking Return within One's Own Land," *Journal of Palestine Studies* 31 (2001): 35, 36.
[31] ADRID, *General*, 2. Interview conducted with Mohammed Kaial on April 18, 2016.
[32] Badil, *Returning*, 97.
[33] Baladna, *2009 Annual Activities Report* (Association for Arab Youth, Baladna, 2010), 6.
[34] Baladna, *2013–2014 Annual Activities Report* (Association for Arab Youth, Baladna, 2014), 3.

its marginalization in Israeli-Jewish society.[35] According to one of the founders of the organization, Nadim Nashif, the aim of these activities is "to instill a basic narrative and information concerning the Nakba as 25 percent of us [Palestinians inside Israel] are internally displaced, but not all parents tell children the family story [...] we think it is important that they [Palestinian youth] have the chance to learn the facts."[36] '*Udnā*[37] (Arabic: we returned), launched in 2013, is one of Baladna's educational programs dealing with the Nakba.[38] During the program, which takes place over a period of one year, third-generation descendants from depopulated villages return to their village of origin and learn about the specific events surrounding their families and the community's displacement.[39] Crucially, the third generation's return to the former village is not solely meant as an educational experience; instead, the project revolves around the returnees' practical visualization of a return, including by creating 3D models of their rebuilt villages.[40] As such, the project's coordinator, Jomama Ashqar, argues that the project "is about moving from theory to action [and implementation of] the right of return."[41] The comments of the group leader in the Qubti project reflect the realization of Ashqar's vision, as the '*Udnā* participant noted: "Like many of Maa'lool's youth, I was not born in the village of my ancestors and I was deprived of my right to return. However, [now] I believe that return is not only a dream, it is a possible reality."[42]

The Return Visit as an Act of Confrontation

While the return visits conducted by ADRID do not necessarily engage in a concrete visualization of a collective future return, the secretary of the organization, Wakim Wakim, contends that return visits to destroyed or depopulated villages emphasize "that the place still exists to which a

---

[35] Baladna, *2010–2011 Activities Report* (Association for Arab Youth, Baladna, 2011), 32; Baladna, *2014–2015 Annual Activities Report* (Association for Arab Youth, Baladna, 2015), 16.

[36] Interview conducted with Nadim Nashif on March 29, 2016.

[37] In Arabic, the project's name (عدنا) indicates a past tense verb form (we returned). However, the organization uses a possessive noun (our return) in their English publications on the project.

[38] According to Baladna's annual activities reports, the number of participants vary. Thus, in 2013, seventy participants were trained to conceptualize a return to their village, 1,600 people attended local events concerning the project, and 50,000 people received online information about the project. Baladna, *2013–2014*, 29.

[39] The project is conducted in coordination with ADRID, Badil, Zochrot, and the Arab Association for Human Rights. Baladna, *Biennial Activities Report 2011–2013* (Association for Arab Youth, Baladna, 2013), 32, 33.

[40] Ibid.   [41] Interview conducted with Jomama Ashqar on April 18, 2016.

[42] Baladna, *2013–2014*, 29.

return is possible."[43] In a booklet published by ADRID on the displaced village of Miske, the ability for a future return is further highlighted: "The committee's objective in the long run is to return to the land. Not only through demands, slogans, and struggles, but also through actual implementation of these slogans in the field. Simply to go back to the village. To go back to the future."[44] As indicated in the earlier statement, while permanent collective return remains the key political goal, the very practice of returning to a former Palestinian site of residence in the present can be considered a temporary realization of a return and a reimagining of the contemporary village through the congregation of the village's descendants.[45] It is because of this realization of a return in the present that the return visits conducted by ADRID and Baladna centering on the village of origin can also be considered a direct confrontation of Israeli policies aimed at thwarting return through disregarding UN Resolution 194.[46] Indeed, a report published by Baladna in 2013–2014 pointed out that the return by the displaced youth can be considered an act aimed at "actualizing their right of return despite political obstacles imposed by Israel."[47] Similarly, a decade earlier, in 2001, Wakim maintained that ADRID's activities seek "to confront the grandsons of Zionism on the issue of displacement."[48]

The confrontational nature of return visits is evidenced in past responses, both by the Israeli authorities and Israeli-Jewish inhabitants. In April 2005, for instance, a group of Palestinian descendants returned to the destroyed village of Miske to plant olive trees and figs, which in the Israeli-Zionist narrative remains highly symbolically being "freighted with the statist meaning [of] resettling the land."[49] In response, the Israeli authorities uprooted the seedlings, closed the roads leading to the remaining village buildings, and blocked their doors. A year later, following the rendition of the play *Uncle Matta*, which tells the story of the Nakba to small children, the authorities used bulldozers to destroy the remains of the buildings and planted citrus trees in their place.[50] The destruction of the remains of a Palestinian village, as occurred in Miske

---

[43] Wakim, "The 'Internally Displaced'," 38.

[44] ADRID, *Miske, The Displaced Village, the 13th March of Return* (ADRID, 2010), 18.

[45] For a different conception of the return visit, namely as a pilgrimage that constitutes "a journey to a sacred place [with] the pilgrim, disengaging from daily tasks [to go] through a rite of passage," see Efrat Ben-Ze'ev, *Remembering Palestine in 1948: Beyond National Narratives* (New York/Cambridge: Cambridge University Press, 2011), 102–104.

[46] UN General Assembly Resolution 194, adopted on December 11, 1948, proclaimed that all refugees wishing to return to their homes and live at peace with their neighbors should be permitted to do so at the earliest practical date and that compensation should be paid for loss or damage to property. Pappé and Hilal, *Across the Wall*, 101.

[47] Baladna, *2013–2014*, 28.   [48] Wakim, "The 'Internally Displaced'," 248.

[49] Young, *Texture of Memory*, 219, 220.   [50] ADRID, *Miske*, 19.

in 2006, was not a novel phenomenon. In 1951, following a ruling by the Israeli Supreme Court that they did have the right to return to the village, Palestinians from El-Ghabsiya headed back to their homes. On arrival, they were met by Israeli forces who blocked their way and refused to recognize the decision of the court. Moreover, with the aim of dissuading any future return, government bulldozers destroyed all the houses in the village between 1955 and 1956.[51] Similar practices took place in the village of Bir'im and Iqrit, both located near the Lebanese border. Following rulings from the Israeli High Court in, respectively, 1953 and 1951 that the state must allow the internal refugees to return, the army ignored the rulings and razed the villages.[52]

According to Eitan Bronstein, the founder of the Israeli organization Zochrot, widespread ongoing denial and ignorance of the Nakba can lead to overt displays of hostility by Israeli-Jewish citizens when confronted with return visits, as they become unknowing and unwilling participants in a remembrance practice.[53] Founded in 2002, Zochrot conducts return visits to depopulated or destroyed Palestinian towns to further awareness of the Nakba.[54] In an interview, Umar al-Ghubari, an IDP working as a guide for Zochrot, further explained the reasoning behind the hostile responses to Palestinian return visits, which range from rude remarks to physical attacks. al-Ghubari contends that the concept of a temporary return by Palestinians supported by an Israeli-Jewish group indicates to current inhabitants of former Palestinian villages that they "are not allowed to sleep comfortably the whole year feeling that nothing was there and no one cares what happens [and as such] the return forces people living in the area to see more than what the state wants them to see."[55] Moreover, the return[56] and the physical retracement of the past, aided by placing signs, remind people that, in al-Ghubari's words, "they are living in a place where a trauma took place,"[57] thereby evoking,

---

[51] Dahoud Bader, *El-Ghabsiya, We Still Have the Keys: The Story of an Uprooted Palestinian Village* (ADRID, 2002), 17.
[52] Kafr Bir'im was largely flattened by aerial bombardment and artillery shelling after the Supreme Court upheld the appeal of its residents against the prohibition on their return. Despite awareness of the Supreme Court's decision, the army destroyed the previously Christian village on Christmas Day 1951. Kadman, *Erased from Space and Consciousness*, 26; Masalha, *Palestine Nakba*, 108.
[53] Interview conducted with Eitan Bronstein on May 3, 2016. See Bronstein, "Nakba in Hebrew," 214–241; Ben-Ze'ev, *Remembering Palestine in 1948*, 5.
[54] While Zochrot's activities are principally aimed at Israeli-Jews, in practice, Palestinians also partake in activities as participants, historical eyewitnesses, and guides.
[55] Interview conducted with Umar al-Ghubari on April 12, 2016.
[56] For a fictional imagination of a return, see the 1969 novella *The Return to Haifa* by Ghassan Kanafani.
[57] Ibid.

Figure 4.1 Zochrot's return to al-Ruways
Credit: Ryan Rodrick Beiler

in Freudian terminology, the uncanny: something "once well-known
[which] had long been familiar [and now] concealed, kept from sight,
so that others do not get to know about it."[58]

---

[58] Ibid.; Sigmund Freud, *The Uncanny*, ed. David McLintock (London: Penguin Books,
2003), 124, 129.

Challenging Israeli Palimpsest Practices

Al-Ghubari's statements indicate that return visits to depopulated or destroyed Palestinian villages also seek to expose the erasure practices of the Israeli state, which sought to create a spatial realization of what the Israeli geographer and former mayor of Jerusalem Meron Benvenisti called "white patches."[59] Some ethnographers, as the sociologist Oz Almog demonstrated, dealt with this human presence and the conflicts it generated by describing the Palestinian landscape as barren and virgin-like[60]; nevertheless, following the 1948 War, this mental map also became an empirical fact with the eradication of the Palestinian community from the actual landscape.[61] As the prominent military leader and politician Moshe Dayan noted during a lecture at the Technion Institute in March 1969:

> The Jewish villages have replaced the Arab villages, and today you would not be able to know even the names of those Arab villages, and I wouldn't blame you, for the geography books do not exist anymore. The entirety of Arab villages themselves have no more existence. Nahlal has replaced Ma'aloul, Givat replaced Jabaa', Sarid replaced Khanfis, and Kfar Yeshoshua replaced Tal al-Shammam.[62]

In her recently published book, entitled *Erased from Space and Consciousness: Israel and the Depopulated Palestinian Villages of 1948*, the Israeli writer Noga Kadman notes that the erasure of Palestinian landscape following the 1948 War was achieved in phases, through a combination of military and legislative steps. These steps entailed setting up

---

[59] Benvenisti, *Sacred Landscape*, 69, 70.   [60] Almog cited in Ibid., 67.

[61] An article published in July 2019 by Haaretz found that the Israeli state has also engaged in a systematic documentary eradication of the Nakba through the removal of historical documents pertaining to the Nakba. The article notes that Malmab, the Defense Ministry's secretive security department, has, since the mid-2000s or early 2010s, been scouring Israel's archives to remove documents, as "uncovering them could generate unrest among the country's Arab population." The efforts include documents that have already been published to "undermine the credibility of studies about the history of the refugee problem." Hagar Shezaf, "Burying the Nakba: How Israel Systematically Hides Evidence of 1948 Expulsion of Arabs," *Haaretz*, July 5, 2019, www.haaretz.com/israel-news/.premium.MAGAZINE-how-israel-systematically-hides-evidence-of-1948-expulsion-of-arabs-1.7435103, accessed February 23, 2019. For information on the resealing of previously available documents, see Benny Morris, "Israel's Concealing of Nakba Documents Is Totalitarian," *Haaretz*, July 15, 2019, www.haaretz.com/opinion/.premium-israel-s-concealing-of-documents-on-the-nakba-is-totalitarian-1.7495203, accessed February 23, 2020.

[62] Cited in Honaida Ghanim, "When Yaffa Met (J)Yaffa: Intersections between the Holocaust and the Nakba in the Shadow of Zionism," in *The Holocaust and the Nakba: A New Grammar of Trauma and History*, ed. Amos Goldberg and Bashir Bashir (New York: Columbia University Press, 2018), 103.

new Jewish communities on Palestinian land and populating refugee homes with (immigrant) Jews; installing temporary emergency regulations that allowed the state to take hold of any private property without legal or administrative due process; applying laws that retroactively legitimized expropriation of Palestinian property by military units during the war and enabled further expropriations; using British Defense Emergency Regulations that allowed the declaration of closed military zones for security needs; and the enactment of the Absentee Property Law of 1950, which transferred ownership rights of refugee property to the custodian of absentee property.[63] Part and parcel of the execution of these policies was the demolition of former Palestinian landscape, aiming to make the absence of refugees permanent.[64] Thus, of the 418 depopulated villages discussed by Walid Khalidi in his ethnographic study "All That Remains," 293 (70 percent) were totally destroyed and 90 (22 percent) were largely destroyed.[65] The mass destruction of Palestinian landscape, which continued in the decades after the war, led the Palestinian scholar Nur Masalha to conclude that the Nakba was followed by a "memoricide," meaning "the systematic erasure of the expelled Palestinians[66] [and] the excision of their history and deeply rooted heritage in the land [...]."[67]

The occurrence of a physical palimpsest in the "Holy Land's landscape" following the 1948 War was, of course, by no means a unique phenomenon. In 1994, William Mitchell contended that the face "of the Holy Landscape" had been so scarred "by war, excavation and

---

[63] Kadman, *Erased from Space and Consciousness*, 16. Also see Baruch Kimmerling, *Zionism and Territory: The Socio-Territorial Dimensions of Zionist Politics* (Berkeley: Institute of International Studies, University of California, 1983), 136.

[64] In August 1957, the Ministry of Labor was asked by then Foreign Minister Golda Meir to ensure the clearing of ruins of Palestinian neighborhoods and villages. Priority was given in the request to "getting rid of ruins" in villages whose inhabitants remained in the country, such as al-Birweh in the western Galilee and Saffuriyya in the lower Galilee. At times, the remains of these villages became subject to forestation efforts by the Jewish National Fund in order to "conceal" Palestinian existence. Kadman, *Erased from Space and Consciousness*, 26; Boqai' and Rempel, "Patterns," 73.

[65] Khalidi, *All That Remains*.

[66] Documents declassified in 2019 describe the ways Israel prevented Palestinians from returning to villages they had left in 1948, even after military restrictions on them had been lifted. The main method involved dense planting of trees within and surrounding these towns; to ensure the villages would not be repopulated, the state had the Jewish National Fund plant trees around and in them. See Yotam Berger, "Declassified: Israel Made Sure Arabs Couldn't Return to Their Villages," *Haaretz*, May 27, 2019, www.haaretz.com/.premium-israel-lifted-military-rule-over-arabs-in-1966-only-after-ensuring-they-couldn-t-ret-1.7297983, accessed February 23, 2019.

[67] Nur Masalha, "Remembering the Palestinian Nakba: Commemoration, Oral History and Narratives of Memory," *Holy Land Studies* 7 (2008): 130; Masalha, *Palestine Nakba*, 10.

displacement that no illusion of innocent, original nature can be sustained for a moment."[68] A similar observation had been made fifty years prior by Halbwachs during his study of Christian pilgrimage sites. Halbwachs noted that various groups had attempted to transform the space to yield and adapt the physical surroundings to their wishes.[69] Yet, as, according to Halbwachs, the group "becomes enclosed within the framework it has built,"[70] by returning to the remains of the depopulated sites, organizations such as ADRID and Baladna seek to counter a mental conversion of the Palestinian landscape into an Israeli one. Moreover, despite the absence caused as a result of demolition and destruction, the return negates the notion that the ruins can only belong to the past and instead indicates that they can be foundations for a future, as Wakim maintained: "the tradition we started of visiting the destroyed villages [...] emphasizes that the sites of these villages, however ruined, are still there [and] a return is possible."[71]

In a similar fashion, booklets published by ADRID on the history of depopulated villages and what remains today aim to lay claim to former Palestinian places of residence through conveying memories of a time that no longer exists, but that is not forgotten. As such, while these booklets introduce the reader to the history of the depopulated village, they should not be considered merely a medium that seeks to expose the past or "a kind of 'in memoriam'."[72] Rather, as one booklet on the depopulated village of Miske notes: "[this is] not a commemoration of a past event [...] but a desire to return."[73] Following in the tradition of memorial books published immediately after the 1948 War, which included encyclopedic works by Arif al-Arif[74] and Mustapha Murad al-Dabbagh,[75] the booklets written by ADRID since the early 1990s contain interviews with former inhabitants of depopulated villages in an attempt to recreate and reclaim the village imaginatively, through knowing it and, as such, "breathe life into a name."[76] For instance, in a booklet published

---

[68] Mitchell, *Landscape*, 27.   [69] Halbwachs, *Collective*, 54.   [70] Ibid.
[71] Wakim, "The 'Internally Displaced'," 38.   [72] Khalidi, *All That Remains*, xvii.
[73] ADRID, *Miske*, 2.
[74] El-Arif wanted "to tell people what had happened, and therefore I have sworn to recount only what I have seen with my own eyes [so that] when the day comes that history is made right, future historians will be able to rely on [these] writings, [which are] supported by facts, names, places, and figures." Arif el-Arif, *The Nakba: The Nakba of Jerusalem and the Lost Paradise, 1947–1952. Part One: From the Partition Resolution 29/11/1947 to the Beginning of the First Truce 11/6/1948* (Beirut: Institute for Palestine Studies, 2012), lix (in Arabic).
[75] Mustapha Murad al-Dabbagh, *Our Country Palestine* (Beirut: Dar al-Tali'a, 1956) (in Arabic).
[76] Khalidi, *All That Remains*, xvii. Another physical memorial project was conducted from 1979 by two Birzeit University scholars, Sharif Kanaana and Kamal Abdel Fattah. In

on the village of Khubeizy, former resident Ahmad Khalil Moustafa
Muhammed Salit, in addition to recounting memories of idyllic village
life pre-1948, visually describes Khubeizy to his readers: "I remember
the mosque building that was in the east side of the village, north of
the cemetery, and a bit to the south there was the house of the *mukhtār*
[Ar. village head] Abdel Kader al-Haj Gasson. The mosque was built of
limestone and composed of one room 8x7 wide [and] the mosque had a
wooden staircase from its northern side."[77] Whereas Salit's visual
recounting of Khubeizy invokes buildings that no longer exist in a landscape reclaimed by nature, the consequences of physical palimpsest
practices are exposed in booklets produced on the repurposed villages
of Amqa and Kuwaykat/Kweikat. Here, buildings are recalled by
former residents that have been reclaimed for other purposes, including
two former schools that currently function as a night club and an animal
feed center.[78]

The March of Return

The March of Return, held annually since 1998, is the largest commemoration dedicated to the Nakba with tens of thousands of Palestinians
participating every year. According to research conducted by Tamir
Sorek, the number of "Arab citizens who reported participation" has
been steadily rising since the beginning of the twenty-first century.
Thus, whereas only 12.9 percent took part in the annual march in
2003, this number rose to 47.9 percent in 2012,[79] meaning that over
half of those who commemorated Nakba Day in 2012 (90.9 percent of
Palestinians inside the 1948 borders) partook in the march.[80] The first

1985, the university's documentation center launched a series of monographs on the
destroyed villages. Since 1993, this work has been overseen by Saleh Abdel Jawad.
Sherna Berger Gluck, "Oral History and al-Nakbah," *Oral History Review* 35 (2008):
69; Masalha, *Palestine Nakba*, 135; Rochelle Davis, "Mapping the Past, Recreating the
Homeland: Palestinian Memories of Pre-1948 Village Life," in *Nakba: Palestine, 1948,
and the Claims of Memory*, ed. Ahmad Sa'di and Lila Abu-Lughod (New York: Columbia
University Press, 2007), 53, 72.

[77] ADRID, Khubeizy, *The Eyes of al-Rawda* (ADRID and the Public Committee for the
Preparation of the 16th March of Return, 2013), 6.

[78] ADRID, *Fifteenth Return Rally to Kweikat and Amqa Villages: No Going Back on the Right
of Return* (ADRID and The People Committee of Kweikat and Amqa, 2012), 18–21.

[79] 14.7 percent of those who participated in the 2012 Nakba commemoration reported that
they were harassed by Israeli authorities. Sorek, *Palestinian Commemoration in Israel*,
7, 271.

[80] Anonymous, "Result of a Survey by the Site al-Arab: 90.9% Commemorate the Nakba
and Do Not Recognize Israel's Independence [Day]," *Kul al-Arab*, April 28, 2012, www
.alarab.com/Article/453971, accessed September 6, 2017.

Figure 4.2 Lifta – the "long-abandoned village"[81]
Following an attack on Lifta's coffeehouse on December 28, 1947, the
Palestinian historian al-Arif notes that most residents felt compelled to
leave. Although Lifta remains one of the best-preserved Palestinian
villages, no signs exist to indicate the village's recent history.[82]

March of Return, organized by ADRID in coordination with local committees of IDPs and Palestinian NGOs, was held on March 28, 1998 –
marking the annual commemoration of Land Day – with a march from

[81] In 1987, the Israeli Nature Reserves Authority planned to restore the "long-abandoned
   village" and to turn it into an open-air natural history and study center that would "stress
   the Jewish roots of the site." This project had an estimated cost of $10 million. To this
   day, the project has not been realized. Khalidi, *All That Remains*, 303.
[82] Ibid.

the host town of Nazareth to the depopulated village of El-Ghabsiya.[83] While 1998, with the Israeli state's jubilee serving as a catalyst, constituted the first time that the return march to El-Ghabsiya was organized as the major annual commemorative event to the Nakba, a historic tradition of villagers marching to their depopulated village to commemorate their expulsion was already in existence. Commencing in September 1954, the displaced of Kafr Bir'im staged an annual march from Jish to the "hill of tears," where they had witnessed the destruction of Bir'im the preceding year.[84] The march to El-Ghabsiya conducted in 1998 was also not a novel phenomenon. Upon the establishment of the El-Ghabsiya village committee in 1995, an annual rally was organized in the village during which the names of dozens of other depopulated villages were hung on the wall of the village's mosques and banners demanded "the implementation of the Supreme Court's decision" and "[restoration of] lands to the internal refugees."[85]

Following the first March of Return in 1998, it was decided that the march would be held on Israeli Independence Day – following the Hebrew calendar – because, as Kaial put it, "we wanted to show that Israel's day of independence is our day of catastrophe [and] to attract the attention of Palestinians, Israelis, and the international community.[86] Indeed, one of the key slogans of the March of Return, *yawm istiqlālikum – yawm nakbatinā* (Arabic: your independence day – our day of catastrophe), is indicative of this approach. Yet, a more practical reasoning behind the decision to conduct the annual March of Return on Israel's Independence Day can also be deduced. Land Day, in contrast to Independence Day, is a working day in Israel. Consequently, Kaial explains, any activities organized on Land Day would typically attract fewer participants.[87]

Under the leadership of ADRID, the March of Return inside the 1948 borders has turned into an orderly and family-friendly event that exhibits a predominantly secular nature, with ice cream trucks, free supplies of water, and a book-selling booth.[88] The composed nature of the event largely derives from the organization's desire to avoid any

---

[83] Interview conducted with Mohammed Kaial on April 18, 2016; Masalha, *Palestine Nakba*, 249, 250.

[84] Weaver, *Mapping Exile and Return*, 99.

[85] Boqai' and Rempel, "Patterns," 98; Sorek, *Palestinian Commemoration in Israel*, 74; Elie Rekhess, "The Arab Minority in Israel: Reconsidering the '1948 Paradigm'," *Israel Studies* 19 (2014): 198.

[86] Interview conducted with Mohammed Kaial on April 18, 2016.   [87] Ibid.

[88] For a discussion of the Islamist movement's lack of influence in this event, see Sorek, *Palestinian Commemoration in Israel*, 78.

potential conflict with local Jewish residents, which has meant that the organizers invest great effort in disciplining expressions to ensure the slogans and signs will not put the march in danger of it being interpreted as a violation of any law. In addition, the mapping of the exact path of every march is partly dictated by the desire to avoid clashes with Jewish residents of the existing locality built on the former village's land.[89] Nevertheless, at times, the march does lead to direct confrontation. In 2008, for instance, a group of Israeli-Jewish citizens sought to hamper the march by organizing a counter demonstration. At the invitation of the recently established Israeli organization Hashomer Hachadash (Hebrew: the new guard)[90] hundreds of people came to a picnic in Tsipori, which had been established on the land of the depopulated village of Safuriye. The route of the march was thereby obstructed because on its way to Safuriye the march was meant to go through Tsipori.[91]

The desire for rigid oversight of the event is further fueled by the political aims of the march, which might be jeopardized as a result of any violent action. The main goals of the march, as expressed by Kaial, are "to demonstrate the desire and right to return and to challenge the notion that we are absentees, as we are designated under Israeli law."[92] Consequently, similar to the return visits described earlier, the March of Return[93] seeks to challenge the lack of implementation of UN Resolution 194 by the Israeli state through embodying a reversal of the event that is commemorated: expulsion. In addition to chanting slogans on the implementation of the right of return, such as baqāʿ wa-ʿawdah (Arabic: remain and return) and lā ʿawdah ʿan haq al-ʿawdah (Arabic: there is no return on the right of return), the most important manifestation of this challenge occurs in the reciting of the oath of return and the unofficial

---

[89] Ibid., 155.

[90] Hashomer Hachadash, established in 2007 by Yoel Zilberman, describes itself as a "Zionist movement that connects the Nation, the Land and the People of Israel" and is partly funded by the Jewish National Fund. Its main mission is to "protect state-administered land from thieves and raiders in the Negev and the Galilee," because, according to the organization, "the legal landowners, who have worked tirelessly to maintain the land over the years, are facing a daily struggle of protecting their farms and ranches from criminals who want to oust them and illegally obtain their land." Hashomer Hachadash, *Five-Year Strategic Plan 2013–2018* (Hashomer Hachadash, undated), 1.

[91] Sorek, *Palestinian Commemoration in Israel*, 153.

[92] Interview conducted with Mohammed Kaial on April 18, 2016.

[93] The march has also been attended by Israeli-Jewish citizens who choose not to celebrate Israel's Independence Day and instead choose to "stand in solidarity with the Palestinian people." See Muhasin Nasser, "Arab Leaders Are Absent from the March of Return, and Jews Participate to Affirm the Nakba," *Kul al-Arab Online*, May 13, 2011, www.alarab.com/Article/372066, accessed March 12, 2020.

Figure 4.3 The March of Return to Safuriye
Credit: Jonathan Cook

Palestinian anthem, which in 2016 were recited one after the other.[94]
Reminiscent of the tradition of *ṣumūd* – literally steadfastness in hanging
on to the land, the place, and the homeland – the oath to return (Arabic:
qasam al-'awdah) witnesses a collective swearing "by god almighty" of
the participants to "refuse both personally and publicly any compensation or settlement" for "the land of the homeland, the land of my

---

[94] Participant observation conducted on March 12, 2016.

fathers and ancestors."[95] Implicit in this statement is a renunciation of the Acquisition for Public Purposes Ordinance, which was enacted by the British in 1943 and later used by the Israeli state to provide compensation for Palestinian land in exchange for the rights to the land. The importance of *ṣumūd* is further emphasized during the singing of *Mawṭanī* (Arabic: my homeland).[96] Originally written in the 1930s by the Palestinian poet Ibrahim Abd al-Fattah Touqan as a symbol of the Palestinian struggle against the British, the poem has been considered the unofficial Palestinian national anthem since then.[97] Despite transferring the main cause of the struggle from one actor to another, the answer remains the same: eternal loyalty and faithfulness to the homeland, "an honorable cause [for which] until your independence [...] our youth will not tire."[98]

Nakba Commemoration in the West Bank

In his 2007 book, entitled *Son of the Cypresses: Memories, Reflections, and Regrets from a Political Life*, Benvenisti claims that it was "the Israeli Arabs who taught the residents of the territories to commemorate Nakba Day."[99] While the concept of a mnemonic imitation cannot be fully disregarded, this statement fails to acknowledge the deeply rooted historic tradition of Nakba commemoration that took place in the territories. As early as 1949, the 15th of May was marked in several West Bank cities by demonstrations, strikes, and visits to the graves of those fallen in the 1948 War. These commemorative events were organized by worker and student associations, cultural and sport clubs, committees of refugees, and the Muslim Brotherhood.[100] Nakba commemoration was also adopted by the Palestinian national movement of the late 1950s, and every year on the 15th of May, the Fatah bulletin, *Filasṭinunā* (Arabic:

---

[95] ADRID, *Oath to Return* (ADRID, 2016).
[96] Another campaign invoking the tradition of *ṣumūd* was held by ADRID in 2015. The campaign, entitled "Do Not Give Up the Land of [Your] Ancestors," challenged an Israeli Supreme Court ruling in 2013, which, in coherence with the Acquisition for Public Purposes Ordinance of 1943, allowed for financial compensation claims to be made up until a certain date "otherwise they [the displaced Palestinians] will lose or waive their rights to the land." According to the campaign, by claiming and potentially being granted compensation, Israel sought to "involve the displaced in [Israel's] crimes and deny the right of return." ADRID, *Do Not Surrender the Land of [Your] Parents and Grandparents* (ADRID, 2015) (in Arabic).
[97] Sorek, *Palestinian Commemoration in Israel*, 78.
[98] ADRID, *National Anthem by the Poet Ibrahim Touqan* (ADRID, 2016) (in Arabic).
[99] Meron Benvenisti, *Son of the Cypresses: Memories, Reflections, and Regrets from a Political Life* (Berkeley/London: University of California Press, 2007), 164.
[100] Sorek, *Palestinian Commemoration in Israel*, 68.

our Palestine), dedicated analytical texts dealing with the meaning of the day and the lessons of the Nakba. Following the emergence of the PLO in 1964 and the rise of other commemorations dedicated to the armed struggle and the revolutionary spirit, the 15th of May did become somewhat marginalized.[101] This marginalization, however, did not mean that the Nakba was absent from the PLO's political agenda. Rather, as Brendan Browne points out, since for much of its existence the PLO conducted operations from exiled bases in Lebanon, Syria, and Jordan, the events of the Nakba significantly shaped the political and national aspirations of the Palestinian leadership. As a result, official or state-sponsored commemorations were deemed unnecessary given the fact that "the entire Palestinian struggle for statehood and liberation was premised on a reversal of events that took place in 1948."[102]

The continued political preoccupation of the PLO with the Nakba can be seen in two different documents published in the late 1980s. In a communiqué issued during the First Intifadah by the PLO and the United National Command of the Uprising on May 13, 1988, the Nakba constitutes the very first line in a document that highlights the "achievements of the Palestinian revolution, the glory of the magnificent uprising."[103] The document reminds its readers that "forty years have passed since the expulsion of our people from its homeland and the attempt to liquidate its existence and its national existence" and calls on Palestinians to commemorate "May 15, which denotes the Nakba, [as] a day of national mourning and a general strike."[104] In addition to commemorating the Nakba, the right of return for Palestinian refugees was also declared one of the mainstays of the PLO's agenda, as indicated by its inclusion in the 1988 Declaration of Independence, which proclaimed: "[Their] willed dispossession and expulsion was achieved by organized terror [...] In Palestine and in exile, the Palestinian Arab people never faltered and never abandoned its conviction in its rights of Return and Independence."[105]

Despite the official commitment to the right of return by the PLO, the marginalization of the refugee issue in the 1993 Oslo Accords dictated future political involvement in Nakba mnemonic practices in the West Bank. The political parties' marginal role in commemoration practices, however, cannot solely be attributed to the 1993 peace accords or

[101] Ibid.   [102] Browne, "Commemoration," 152.
[103] Shaul Mishal and Re'uven Aharoni, *Speaking Stones: Communiqués from the Intifada Underground* (Syracuse: Syracuse University Press, 1994), 93–97.
[104] Ibid.
[105] Institute for Palestine Studies, *The Palestinian-Israeli Peace Agreement: A Documentary Record* (Washington, DC: Institute for Palestine Studies, 1994), 268.

the subsequent failure to include the refugee issue in the political narrative. In 1998, for instance, Yasser Arafat, as president of the PNA and chairman of the PLO, publicly endorsed the right of return by invoking the concept of *ṣumūd* (Arabic: steadfastness), cautioning that "Palestinians selling Palestinian land deserve death."[106] Governmental support to conduct Nakba commemorations in the West Bank came in 2007 when the High National Committee for Commemoration of the Nakba was set up, which is affiliated with the PLO's Refugee Affairs Department.[107] Officially, this committee was established to ensure a more coordinated and structured commemoration of the Nakba. More important, however, was the committee's implicit aim to ensure political involvement and support for the rights of the refugees, which many had considered absent in prior years.[108] The appearance of political support for the right of return was particularly vital following the publication of secret documents concerning Palestinian-Israeli peace negotiations by the newspaper *Al Jazeera* in 2011.[109] These documents, which became known as the "Palestine Papers," revealed the extent to which Palestinian negotiators had been willing to give up on the right of return to merely "a handful … symbolic number of returnees" of 10,000 to satisfy Palestinian public demand.[110] The publication of these documents was deemed further proof of the PA's lack of true engagement with the refugee issue and, according to Khalid Al-Saifi, head of the cultural center *Ibdāʿ* (Arabic: creation) in Bethlehem's Dheisheh refugee camp and a former leader of the Popular Front for the Liberation of Palestine, meant that political parties became further disenfranchised.[111] As a result, the committee's involvement in Nakba commemoration over the years appears marginal, further indicated by Khaldun Bshara's comment

[106] Yiftachel, "Territory as the Kernel," 216.
[107] Khaldun A. M. Bshara, "Space and Memory: The Poetics and Politics of Home in the Palestinian Diaspora" (PhD diss., University of California, Irvine, 2012), 146, 147.
[108] Browne, "Commemoration," 153, 160.
[109] For articles published by *Al Jazeera* on this topic, see Anonymous, "PA Selling Sort the Refugees," *Al Jazeera*, January 25, 2011, www.aljazeera.com/palestinepapers/2011/01/2011124123324887267.html, accessed August 1, 2017; Amira Howeidy, "PA Relinquished Right of Return," *Al Jazeera*, January 24, 2011, www.aljazeera.com/palestinepapers/2011/01/2011124121923486877.html, accessed August 1, 2017.
[110] These accusations, which the former Palestinian chief negotiator Saeb Erekat refuted as "foundationless," came in the wake of further incendiary reports on the PNA. In 2010, WikiLeaks revealed cooperation between Arab leaders (including the PNA) and Israel during the wars in Gaza (2008), Lebanon (2006), and Iraq (2003), in addition to what Khaldun Bshara refers to as "other 'scandalous' economic and military relations," Bshara, "Space and Memory," 162.
[111] Interview conducted with Khalid Al-Saifi on April 3, 2016.

that they only show up "occasionally [...] to coordinate and carry out commemorative events."[112]

The Badil Resource Center for Palestinian Residency and Refugee Rights is one civil society organization that has assumed a key organizational role in planning annual Nakba events as a result of ongoing political wariness concerning the refugee issue.[113] Badil, established in January 1998 in response to the marginalization of the Palestinian refugees in the peace process, is an "independent, human rights, non-profit organization mandated to defend and promote the rights of Palestinian refugees and internally-displaced persons."[114] In coherence with its mandate, Ahmad Hammash, the current coordinator of Badil's outreach events, notes that Badil's work primarily focuses on advancing the rights of Palestinian refugees.[115] Since its founding, Badil has organized educational and cultural activities on the Nakba throughout the year that seek to engage both (descendants of) refugees and nonrefugees, including through holding public debates on the future of the Palestinian refugee question and implementation of the right of return, setting up youth camps dedicated to mobilizing participation in refugee issues, broadcasting videos on refugee life in camps across the West Bank, and organizing Nakba poster competitions and annual Nakba Day commemorations.[116]

Under the leadership of Badil, Nakba Day commemorations in the West Bank have been marked by collective return marches on the 15th of May.[117] Since the first "March of the Millions" in May 1998, annual marches have taken place all over the West Bank, departing both from refugee camps, such as Balata Camp (Nablus), Nur-Shams, Jenin, Tulkarem, al-Far'ah, al-'Ain, the two 'Askar camps, and from major West Bank cities.[118] The symbolism behind the marches conducted in

[112] Bshara, "Space and Memory," 146, 147.   [113] Browne, "Commemoration," 135.
[114] "About Badil," Badil Resource Center for Palestinian Residency and Refugee Rights, www.badil.org/en/about-badil, accessed July 19, 2016.
[115] Interview conducted with Ahmad Hammash on March 28 and April 13, 2016.
[116] Badil, *Fifty Years of Palestinian Exile and Dispossession: 1998 Campaign for the Defense of Palestinian Refugee Rights & Development* (Badil, 1998), Badil, *Press Release May 15, 2012* (Badil, 2012); Badil, *Nakba Memorial in Palestine* (Badil, 2001), Badil, *Major Nakba Memorial Events in Palestine* (Badil, 2003); Badil, *10 Days of Successful Badil Summer School Program* (Badil, 2011).
[117] In 1998, the PNA set up May 15 as the official Nakba Day to mark the date on which the establishment of the state of Israel was proclaimed (it was May 14). Michael Milshtein, "The Memory That Never Dies: The Nakba Memory and the Palestinian National Movement," in *Palestinian Collective Memory and National Identity*, ed. Meir Litvak (Basingstoke: Palgrave Macmillan, 2009), 54, 55.
[118] Badil, *Fifty-second Anniversary of the Palestinian Expulsion (al-Nakba): Violent Clashes with Israeli Occupation Army Public Marches and Rallies for Refugees' Right of return* (Badil, 2000); Badil, *Major Nakba Memorial Events in Palestine* (Badil, 2003).

Figure 4.4 Nakba commemoration at 'Aida refugee camp's
"Return Gate".
Image by MUSA AL-SHAER/AFP via Getty Images

the West Bank is the same as that which underpins those conducted inside the 1948 borders, namely a physical testimony of the desire to return to the villages of origin. This symbolism is evidenced in several Badil reports discussing Nakba marches in the West Bank. In 2000, for instance, a report, entitled *Fifty-second Anniversary of Palestinian Eviction: Symbolic Return Today – A Step Toward Real Return in the Future*, discussed a "symbolic return visit" conducted by some 150 Palestinian "eyewitnesses of the 1948 expulsion" and their grandchildren from Dheisheh, 'Aida, and 'Azza refugee camps to their villages of origin in present-day Israel. Divided into several stations, including the destroyed village of Bayt Nattif and the converted villages of Zakaryya and Bayt Jibrin – now known as the Israeli moshav of Zekharay and Kibbutz Beit Guvrin – the march sought to challenge the effectiveness of palimpsest by relying on eyewitnesses of 1948 and their descendants in order to bear "witness of [sic] the [historical] presence of this Palestinian community."[119] A more direct confrontation of the attempted erasure

---

[119] Badil, *Fifty-second Anniversary of Palestinian Eviction: Symbolic Return Today – A Step Toward Real Return in the Future* (Badil, 2000).

of a Palestinian presence also constituted part of the march. Thus, in Zakaryya/Zekharya, former residents of Zakaryya confronted current Israeli residents of Zekharya, claiming to be the rightful occupants of the homes and properties and declaring their right of return.[120] The importance of the right of return was reiterated in marches organized by Badil in various districts of the West Bank in 2000, 2001, 2003, and 2008, which were meant to "affirm the demand for the right of return, self-determination and the Palestinian state with Jerusalem as its capital."[121]

Nakba Commemoration as an Act of Protest

Ever since Yasser Arafat inaugurated Nakba Day on May 15, 1998, the line between Nakba commemoration and protest has become blurred,[122] leading Browne to conclude that the event is as much about the ongoing conflict with Israel as it is about the 1948 Nakba itself.[123] His argument is substantiated by the recurrent physical confrontations between those commemorating and the Israeli army, oftentimes leading to Palestinian deaths.[124] In 1998, for instance, during the aforementioned "March of the Millions," Palestinian press reported 8 killed and over 400 wounded as a result of the violence that accompanied the march.[125] Two years after the symbolic fiftieth anniversary of the Nakba, on May 15, 2000, large protests and violent confrontations with the Israeli army resulted in five Palestinian deaths and hundreds of injuries. More recently, in 2011, violent confrontations led to the death of twelve Palestinians on Nakba Day; and in 2014, an IDF sniper killed two Palestinians partaking in violent demonstrations.[126] At times, these physical confrontations occur when participants in the commemoration march approach the separation

---

[120] Ibid.

[121] Badil, *Our Displacement – Our Return: Palestinians Commemorate the 53rd Anniversary of Their Massive Displacement by Israel in 1948* (Badil, 2001).

[122] Michael Milshtein puts forward a different interpretation. Milshtein argues that the violent nature of Nakba mnemonics in the West Bank can be considered a result of the shrewd politics practiced by Arafat who "exploited changes in Nakba memory in 1998 to mobilize the Palestinian public and incite it to violent confrontations with Israel," Milshtein, "Memory That Never Dies," 53.

[123] Browne, "Commemoration," 156.

[124] Barry Rubin and Judith Rubin, *Yasir Arafat: A Political Biography* (New York: Oxford University Press, 2003), 187.

[125] Hillel Frisch, "Ethnicity or Nationalism? Comparing the Nakba Narrative amongst Israeli Arabs and Palestinians in the West Bank and Gaza," *Israel Affairs* 9 (2002): 170.

[126] Anne Barker, "Violence Erupts on Israel's Borders," *ABC*, May 16, 2011, www.abc.net.au/news/2011-05-15/violence-erupts-on-israels-borders/2694524l, accessed February 28, 2016; Sorek, *Palestinian Commemoration in Israel*, 77, 78.

Figure 4.5 Israeli soldiers stand guard during Hebron's 2010 Nakba Day Rally.
Image by HAZEM BADER/AFP via Getty Images

wall or checkpoints to throw stones or burn tires, usually with dire consequences as Palestinian protesters are regularly met by a violent and militarily dominant Israeli bombardment of tear gas and associated crowd dispersal methods, including rubber-coated steel pellets and, on occasion, live ammunition.[127] Thus, on Nakba Day 2008, when over 1,000 protestors broke off from the main Nakba commemoration in Ramallah and tried to enter Jerusalem through the Qalandia checkpoint, Israeli forces fired teargas and rubber bullets injuring more than 100. On the same day, Palestinian refugees attempting to enter the part of the West Bank town of Al-Walaja that was displaced in 1948 were forcibly dispersed by Israeli soldiers, leading to the arrest of eight Palestinians.[128] Interestingly, Al-Saifi notes that the tradition of violent confrontation precedes official Nakba Day commemoration and can be dated back to the pre-Intifadah years when violent clashes between Palestinians and the Israeli army were meant to instill confidence in the Palestinian people and to give them the feeling that "they were standing up for their

---

[127] Sorek, *Palestinian Commemoration in Israel*, 159.
[128] Badil, *Nakba Commemoration – 13 May 2008* (Badil, 2008).

rights."[129] These identified pre-Intifadah motives remain present today. In an interview, Hammash contended that despite the fact that Badil does not consider violent confrontation a part of Nakba Day commemoration, violence has been and will continue to be a part of mnemonic Nakba activities as many Palestinians in the West Bank deem it "important to remind Israelis that they have displaced us and violated our rights."[130]

The Nakba as an Eternal Present

These above-mentioned "rights" do not solely refer to the right of return; rather, in the West Bank, similarly to inside the 1948 borders, the Nakba is considered a continuous event, an ongoing Nakba. As Hammash explains: "We don't consider the Nakba a historic event that ended, but rather view it as ongoing [since] civilian displacement started before 1948 and has continued until today based on the Zionist desire 'maximum land, minimum Palestinian people'. [As such], we do not only want to commemorate Nakba on the 15th of May, but throughout the entire year."[131] Implicit in these comments is also the notion that the Nakba does not only belong to the refugees and their descendants, but, through its contemporary manifestations, in the words of Ahmad Sa'di, "connects all Palestinians to a specific point in time."[132] Indeed, speeches by Arafat and other official spokesmen, including the poet Darwish,[133] have invoked the ongoing ramifications of the Nakba for all Palestinians – both (descendants of) refugees and nonrefugees – in public speeches by framing the Nakba in the context of contemporary Palestinian political aspirations. In a radio interview conducted on the

[129] Interview conducted with Khalid Al-Saifi on April 3, 2016.
[130] Interview conducted with Ahmad Hammash on March 28 and April 13, 2016.
[131] Ibid.   [132] Sa'di, "Catastrophe, Memory and Identity," 177.
[133] The official Palestinian People's Appeal issued on May 14, 1998 and read by Darwish contended that "the past [Nakba] has not entirely departed [for Israel has continued to pursue] a policy of colonization and land confiscation, reneging on signed agreements, negating the terms of reference of the peace process, violating the timetable and denying the agenda of permanent status talks, while continuing the imposition of collective punitive measures on the Palestinian people." In his second speech in May 2003, delivered during the height of the Second Intifadah, Darwish reaffirmed the importance of reversing the ongoing Nakba based on "the right of return, complete withdrawal from Palestinian land occupied in 1967, and the right to self-determination and an independent sovereign state with Jerusalem as its capital." Mahmoud Darwish, "Not to Begin at the End," *Al-Ahram Online* 533, May 2001, http://weekly.ahram.org/Archive/2001/533/op1.htm, accessed September 21, 2017; "The Palestinian People's Appeal on the 50th Anniversary of the Catastrophe 'Al-Nakba,'" Palestinian Ministry of Information, www.pna.org/mininfo/nakba, accessed July 10, 2016.

fiftieth anniversary of the Nakba, Arafat, faced with the stagnation of peace agreements and ever-mounting tension, tied the continuous suffering as a result of the Nakba to the ongoing national struggle for a Palestinian state by proclaiming that the only way "the page of the Nakba could be turned over forever" was through "the return of the emigrant to his homeland and the building of our Palestinian state on our land … just like other peoples […] we want to celebrate in our capital, holy Jerusalem."[134]

As indicated in Arafat's comments, invocation of present-day Nakba manifestations in mnemonic discourse, while always emphasizing the Nakba as the original watershed, mirrors the perceived contemporary political and social marginalization as a result of the ongoing occupation – a theme that will be touched on extensively in the final chapter of this work. In 2006, a Badil report published on Nakba Day, for instance, conceptualized the ongoing Nakba in the framework of the construction of the separation wall, which had commenced six years earlier "in the occupied West Bank, including Eastern Jerusalem [and created a] continued forced displacement of Palestinians caused by land confiscation and de facto annexation."[135] In addition to continued land dispossession, the ongoing Nakba is also inferred to demonstrate that the difficult living conditions in the West Bank cannot be separated from the events of 1948. Implicitly invoking the negative economic effects of the Israeli blockade on Gaza imposed in 2007, which placed serious constraints on economic activity in the West Bank and spiked the consumer price index by 7 percent,[136] a 2008 report published by Badil argued that one of the ways in which Palestinians were suffering from the Nakba manifested itself in the rising prices of basic food staples. In order to exhibit "hunger and anger," Badil therefore called on Palestinians to participate in a Nakba march to the government center in Hebron "bringing along empty cooking pots, forks and spoons in a symbolic gesture."[137]

---

[134] Cited in Bligh, *The Israeli Palestinians*, 181.
[135] Badil, *The Palestinian Nakba at 58 – The Nakba Continues* (Badil, 2006). A similar statement appears in a 2012 report, which states: "The 64th anniversary of the Nakba signals 64 years of ongoing, systematic, forced displacement of the Palestinian people which began ruthlessly in 1948," Badil, *The Nakba-64 Commemoration May 15, 2012* (Badil, 2012). In 2006, 42 percent of the wall had already been completed. Alina Korn, "The Ghettoization of Palestinians," in *Thinking Palestine*, ed. Ronit Lentin (London: Zed Books, 2008), 117.
[136] This constituted a rise of 6 percent since mid-2007. Economic Monitoring Report to the Ad Hoc Liaison Committee, *Palestinian Economic Prospects: Gaza Recovery and West Bank Revival* (World Bank, June 2009), 9.
[137] Badil, *Nakba Commemoration – 10 May 2008* (Badil, 2008).

The execution of military actions and policies resulting from what Eyal Weizman terms "[Israel's] erratic occupation" are also considered emblematic of an ongoing Nakba.[138] During the height of the Second Intifadah, when Israel – for the first time since the 1967 War – used F-16 warplanes to bomb various cities in the West Bank,[139] a Badil report stated that commemorations of the ongoing Nakba that year both sought to symbolize Palestinian steadfastness and to challenge the "racist legislation and policies [...] and bombing and shelling from F-16 fighters and Apache helicopters in the 1967 Occupied Territories."[140] It is because of the manifestations of the Nakba in the present – both in times of extreme violence and in times of relative calm – that mnemonic Nakba practices can be considered an opportunity for the downtrodden to (violently) challenge the hegemony. These displays of dissent are common to commemorative rituals that take place in hostile environments, because, as Browne demonstrates with reference to 1916 Easter Rising Commemorations in Belfast, they create opportunities for marginalized factions to voice and demonstrate their grievances and reaffirm their position in society.[141] Part and parcel of these ritual performances is the creation of group solidarity as a means of differentiating between the groups in conflict while presenting a unified force in the face of ongoing conflict.[142] Indeed, the public outrage that accompanied the fifty-second anniversary of al-Nakba sought to do just that. According to a report published by Badil, the commemoration aimed to challenge Israeli policies in the Palestinian territories occupied in 1967, including "land confiscation, settlement expansion, house demolitions," and simultaneously expressed concern for the lives of the approximately 2,000 Palestinian political prisoners in Israeli jails on hunger strike for more than two weeks.[143] A similar demonstration of solidarity occurred during the earlier discussed return march to Zakarrya. Upon their return, participants in the march ended their trip by joining the Palestinian hunger

[138] Eyal Weizman, *Hollow Land: Israel's Architecture of Occupation* (London: Verso, 2007), 11.
[139] These attacks were often conducted in the wake of Palestinian suicide bomb attacks on Israeli civilians; in turn, creating a cycle of violence. Human Rights Watch, *Israel, the Occupied West Bank and Gaza Strip, and Palestinian Authority Territories* (Human Rights Watch, 2002), 441; John Wright, *The New York Times Almanac* (New York: Penguin Books, 2002), 51. Also see Tristan Dunning, *Hamas, Jihad and Popular Legitimacy: Reinterpreting Resistance in Palestine* (London: Routledge, 2016), 82.
[140] Badil, *Fifty-fourth Anniversary of the Palestinian Nakba (15 May 2002): Naka Memorial Events Organized by Internally Displaced Palestinians in Israel. Dispossession and Displacement 1948–2002: The Root Cause of the Israeli–Palestinian Conflict* (Badil, 2002).
[141] Browne, "Commemoration," 143.   [142] Ibid., 144, 146.
[143] Badil, *Fifty-Second Anniversary of the Palestinian Expulsion Nakba Day Activities* (Badil, 2000).

strikers at the Bethlehem Red Cross Center in order to express their demand for the immediate release of all Palestinian prisoners in Israeli jails. With this act, the participants offered a deliberate reminder that all contemporary strife must inherently be linked to the Nakba as an "eternal present."[144]

Concluding Remarks

Building on traditional forms of commemoration established in the years following *al-Nakba*, Palestinian mnemonics in the post-Oslo era underwent a distinct shift from the local to the collective sphere, as illustrated by the transformation of individual communities' return visits into the annual March of Return organized by ADRID. While bolstered by the symbolic fiftieth anniversary of the Nakba, the rise of civil society organizations dedicated to bringing the Nakba into the public realm were primarily driven by the political outcome of the Oslo Accords, which, under the leadership of the PLO, postponed the Palestinians refugee issue to permanent status negotiations.

Simultaneously, the post-Oslo political landscape – both in the Palestinian Territories and inside the 1948 borders – galvanized the very emergence of these civil organizations. Thus, whereas the establishment of the PA as a semiautonomous entity created an environment in which the Nakba could be publicly recalled, within the 1948 borders, the heightened Palestinian national consciousness largely arose as a result of political marginalization by the Israeli-Jewish majority, which from 1992 onwards included legislative attempts to thwart Nakba commemoration. As such, beyond raising awareness of the plight of the internal refugees and demanding recognition of UN Resolution 194, mnemonic activities organized by ADRID and Baladna seek to address the perceived contemporary manifestations of the Nakba, which pertain to refugees and nonrefugees – and their descendants – alike. While constituting a typical form of commemoration through their "re-enactment of the past" and through their simulacrum of a former scene or situation,[145] return visits conducted to former Palestinian communities primarily symbolize a direct challenge to ongoing physical and cultural palimpsest

---

[144] Badil, *Fifty-second Anniversary of Palestinian Eviction: Symbolic Return Today – A Step Toward Real Return in the Future Activities* (Badil, 2000); Sa'di, "Catastrophe, Memory and Identity," 177.

[145] Paul Connerton, *How Societies Remember* (Cambridge: Cambridge University Press, 1989), 72.

practices and, at the same time, affirm the persistence of the Palestinian minority's national identity within a converted landscape.

Inside the West Bank, the Palestinian leadership's forsaking of the refugee issue, further demonstrated by the 2011 publication of the Palestine Papers, equally informed the emergence of a nongovernmental organization: Badil and, more importantly, its ensuing mnemonic influence. Rather than emphasizing the Nakba as a historic watershed, commemorative activities organized by Badil conceive of the Nakba as a paradigm for the ongoing occupation and its effects on Palestinian life, encompassed in the phrase "ongoing Nakba." Importantly, through the conception of a continuous Nakba, mnemonic Nakba activities in the West Bank not only implicate the refugee community, but equally form a collective act for the nonrefugee community to (violently) protest the Israeli occupation and, instead, call for the establishment of an independent Palestinian state. Invocation of these so-called fixed national goals, as will become evident in the final chapter, can also be identified in "anniversarial" Nakba media. A prime medium to convey indignation over the perceived enemy's thwarting of national independence and the right of return, mass Palestinian media allow the political elite to express its unconditional adherence to the "national cause," while omitting any past willingness to relinquish these goals. Moreover, it is in this book's final chapter that the exclusionary manifestations of the defensive Nakba narrative come to light. Perceived as an Israeli justification for the establishment of the state, the Holocaust, as I will demonstrate, is not only overtly questioned, but also seized as an analogy for all ensuing Palestinian suffering.

5   A Past That Does Not Pass

In 1971, the Israeli author Amos Elon observed that all over Israel countless private and public monuments to the grimmest phase of European history perpetuate a traumatic memory that has become part of the rhythm and ritual of public life.[1] Since Elon's observations, the emphasis on the memory of the Holocaust, which lies "in all morbidity at the center of Israel's historical self-image," has remained pronounced through a continual engagement in public commemorations dedicated to the Holocaust.[2] A 2013 survey found that 86 percent of Israelis observe the two-minute siren on Holocaust Memorial Day by turning into "standing monuments."[3] While the collective observance of "the most impressive moment of the day"[4] has been observed since the early 1980s, the 200 percent rise in annual visitations to Israel's official Holocaust memorial in Jerusalem, Yad Vashem, between 1995 and 2000 is indicative of a heightened preoccupation with the past.[5] A further increase in Holocaust mnemonic practices can be observed in the strong surge in participation of Israeli youngsters in journeys – often referred to as pilgrimages – to death camps and former Jewish localities in Poland.[6]

---

[1] Amos Elon, *The Israelis: Founders and Sons* (New York: Holt, Rinehart, and Winston, 1971), 199.

[2] Ibid.; Feldman, *Above the Death Pits, beneath the Flag*, 61, 62.

[3] This number indicates that almost all non-ultra-orthodox Israelis partake in this ceremony. Young, *Texture of Memory*, 277; Kobi Isaiah, "Survey: Young People Respect Holocaust Day but Avoid Exposure," *NRG/Maariv*, April 8, 2013, www.nrg.co.il/online/16/ART2/458/624.html, accessed August 8, 2017.

[4] Charles S. Liebman and Elizer Don-Yehiya, *Civil Religion in Israel* (Berkeley: University of California Press, 1983), 152.

[5] Between the years 1995 and 2000, the number of visitors to Yad Vashem doubled, from one million to two. Yad Vashem, "Yad Vashem Masterplan 2001," *Yad Vashem Magazine*, Fall 1997, 10; Avner Shalev, "Recalling the Past, Realizing the Future," *Yad Vashem Magazine*, Winter 2001, 4, 5.

[6] Alon Lazar et al., "Jewish Israeli Teenagers, National Identity, and the Lessons of the Holocaust," *Holocaust and Genocide Studies* 18 (2004): 190. Also see Shlomo Romi and Michal Lev, "Experiential Learning of History through Youth Journeys to Poland: Israeli Jewish Youth and the Holocaust," *Israel Research in Education* 78 (2007): 88–102.

The first two Ministry of Education-organized tours left in October and November of 1988 with 190 participants. Seventeen years later, in 2005, more than 28,000 Israeli high-school students took part in these journeys, revealingly entitled "It Is My Brother Whom I Am Seeking."[7]

The heightened engagement with the Holocaust reflects conscious efforts made on the part of custodians of the second generation at Holocaust memorial institutes in Israel to further engage the Israeli public with the events of the past. Highly evocative commemoration ceremonies on Holocaust Remembrance Day, modern interactive exhibits and educational workshops, and programs for educators, army staff, and students underline the continued importance of the Holocaust for Israeli society. Through a study of the most prominent Holocaust institutes in Israel – Yad Vashem, Lohamei Hagetaot, and Yad Mordechai – the chapter below will demonstrate that these mnemonic rituals serve a defined political purpose, namely the justification of the need for a strong and independent Israeli state as the only viable way to hinder a recurrence of the Holocaust.

The need for a strong Jewish state is evidenced in commemorative practices through the transmission of two master narratives. The first master narrative relies on the presentation of the Jewish fighting experience during the Holocaust as a battle for Zionism, thereby not only creating a direct link between the Holocaust and the establishment of the Jewish state in 1948 but also portraying the Holocaust as the first battle aimed to secure a Jewish homeland. Second, the particularistic presentation of the Holocaust as a uniquely and exclusively Jewish experience seeks to convey a justification of Zionist efforts, indicated by the telescopic visitor experience at memorial museums, such as Yad Vashem and Yad Mordechai, where one moves from the darkness and catastrophe of Europe to the light and rebirth in Israel, the former destroyed; the latter victorious.[8]

Crucially, while the state-building efforts were realized, the presentation of the Holocaust as an exclusively Jewish experience evokes a continual need for the protection of the Jewish state as a haven from diasporic persecution and uncertainty, forming a metaphorical testimony to what Martin Jaffee described as "the victim-community" in which "the victim is always both victim and victor."[9] In this context, the overt

---

[7] This latter number equates to approximately 20 percent of all 11th graders. Feldman, *Above the Death Pits, beneath the Flag*, 2, 58.

[8] Handelman and Shamgar-Handelman, "The Presence of Absence," 103.

[9] Martin Jaffee, "The Victim-Community in Myth and History: Holocaust Ritual, the Question of Palestine, and the Rhetoric of Christian Witness," *Journal of Ecumenical Studies* 28:2 (1991): 231.

linkage between the Israeli state and the Holocaust is pertinent, as it indicates the notion that because the Holocaust belongs to the state, the millions of victims – as "potential Israelis" – represent a national death, leading to what Gulie Ne'eman Arad terms a postmortem "Zionization" of all victims.[10] It is because of this Zionist representation of Holocaust victims as a national death with the Israelis being the offspring of the survivors that, in the words of Omer Bartov, "all Israelis are potential victims, in the past, the present and the future [creating] a bond that ties all Israelis to each other as survivors of a catastrophe still living on the brink of an abyss."[11]

It is evident that the conveyance of an ongoing existential threat and victimhood identity can create a viable framework in which the suffering of others is overlooked or minimized based on a justified attempt to prevent a recurrence of the Holocaust, as Bartov asserts: "We [Israelis] are the sons and daughters of the murdered, and it is their image that must always shine darkly in our minds as we contemplate our existence, fight our wars [...]."[12] With this statement, Bartov also alludes to the incompatibility between the victim and the victimizer, for, as indicated in the introductory chapter, the existence of a defensive Israeli-Jewish victimhood can impede the negative self-acknowledgement as a culprit in political and military actions. Moreover, with reference to the denial of past and present effects of the 1948 War on Palestinian life, Bar-On explains that constantly reliving the role of the victim can form a scapegoat mechanism necessitating a subversion of the Palestinian narrative.[13] Indeed, the final paragraphs of this chapter make clear that the fate of the Palestinians in the 1948 War has not only been physically ignored but actively erased in favor of a transplantation of the Holocaust from Europe to the Middle East, searing the Holocaust into the Israeli landscape as a continual reminder of *le'olam lo 'od* (Hebrew: never again).

Incorporating the Holocaust in Israel's Physical and Mental Consciousness

The current Israeli landscape contains approximately 400 monuments dedicated to the remembrance of Holocaust, including public memorials, such as the Warsaw Ghetto Square at Yad Vashem and the Holocaust memorial flame near the Knesset, and private or communal Holocaust

---

[10] Arad, "Shoah," 198, 199.
[11] Omer Bartov, "Chambers of Horror: Holocaust Museums in Israel and the United States," *Israel Studies* 2 (1997): 66, 67.
[12] Ibid., 67.   [13] Bar-On, "Israeli Society," 106.

memorials in cemeteries.[14] The construction of these public and private memorials can be dated back to the end of the Second World War. Private memorials, established in memory of members of specific Jewish communities, were set up through the physical erection of tombstones and the production of *Yizkor* (Hebrew: may (God) remember) memorial books. At the initiative of the *Landsmannschaften* – organizations composed of former Jewish members of a European community – Yizkor books were written as a figurative memorial to the dead.[15] According to Judith Tydor Baumel, hundreds of Yizkor books were published until 1974, when their numbers began to decline drastically and a rise in survivor memoirs indicated a new interest in individuals' fate during the Holocaust.[16] An additional form of post-war communal commemoration constituted the erection of tombstones in memory of Holocaust victims, which were first erected in Tel-Aviv in 1947 by members of the former Polish-Jewish community of Zdonska-Wolla.[17] While a few memorial stones were unveiled in 1950 – two in the Nahalat Yitzhak cemetery in Tel-Aviv and one in the old Tel-Aviv cemetery – the height of this type of commemoration occurred between the mid-1960s and late 1980s. During this period, long boulevards were created in Tel-Aviv cemeteries, lined with all shapes and sizes of communal memorial stones.[18]

In addition to communal memorial acts, collective memorial sites dedicated to the entire Jewish community lost in the Holocaust were established in post-war years. These memorial sites, which sought to embed the Holocaust in the Israeli landscape, constituted the paradigms for the Holocaust institutes that form the crux of this chapter. One of the earliest memorials in Israel, the Holocaust Cellar (Hebrew: *Martef ha-Shoah*), which stands on Mount Zion near King David's Tomb, was inaugurated on the fast day of Tisha B'av. As part of the cellar's inauguration, Torah scrolls from a number of destroyed European Jewish communities, along with other ritual objects, such as Hanukkah candelabra and Torah crowns, were brought to Jerusalem and placed in the renovated cellar. Apart from these ritual objects, Holocaust victims' ashes

[14] Mooli Brog, "Victims and Victors: Holocaust and Military Commemoration in Israel Collective Memory," *Israel Studies* 8:3 (2003): 69.
[15] The books, which were edited by a professional author, historian, or editor, typically described the community's pre-war history, its existence in the Second World War, and, finally, its destruction at the hands of the Nazis. Most of the *Yizkor* books were written in Yiddish, the mother tongue of the survivors and *Landsmannschaft* members. Baumel, "Everlasting Memory," 146–170.
[16] Ibid., 152.   [17] Ibid., 155.   [18] Ibid.

were also brought from abroad.[19] The transplantation of Holocaust victims' ashes and objects from "the sites of horrors to the homeland of the people for whom it is most relevant" formed a model for the future official Holocaust institute, Yad Vashem.[20] Thus, in 1957, following a decision that the site should contain a symbolic tomb for the Holocaust, the ashes of tens of thousands of victims were buried in Yad Vashem's *Ohel Yizkor* (Hebrew: memorial tent) marked by an eternal fire.[21] A further form of the physical insertion of the Holocaust occurred five years after the dedication of the Holocaust Cellar. B'nai B'rith,[22] in cooperation with the Jewish National Fund, started planting the Martyrs' Forest in the Judean Hills outside Jerusalem as "a living memorial to the six million Jews who perished in the Holocaust."[23] The planting of six million trees was highly symbolic, as it not only literally incorporated the Holocaust in the natural landscape of Israel but also invoked Israeli's traditional reverence for *yedi'at ha-aretz* (Hebrew: knowledge of the land), creating a landmark by which Israelis continue to know their relationship to the land and – by extension – to the history of the Holocaust.[24]

Yom ha-Shoah

The incorporation of the Holocaust as part of the natural landscape was soon followed by the inclusion of the Holocaust in the temporal consciousness of Israeli-Jews by its placement on the commemorative calendar as an official memorial day. When the Knesset declared the 27th of Nissan as the official Holocaust and Ghetto Uprising Remembrance Day in 1951, the memorial day had already been the subject of many

---

[19] The cellar was established as part of the Sukkot festival and was inaugurated on the annual fast day of Tisha B'Av in 1949, which marks the destruction of the First and Second Temples, as well as other tragedies of Jewish history, such as the expulsion of the Jews from Spain in 1492. As such, the cellar can be deemed to commemorate the Holocaust in the framework of other Jewish tragedies. Jennifer Hansen-Glucklich, *Holocaust Memory Reframed: Museums and the Challenges of Representation* (New Brunswick: Rutgers University Press, 2014), 156.

[20] Shaul Krakover, "Attitudes of Israeli Visitors towards the Holocaust Remembrance Site of Yad Vashem," in *Horror and Human Tragedy Revisited: The Management of Sites of Atrocities for Tourism*, ed. Gregory Ashworth and Rudi Hartmann (New York: Cognizant, 2005), 109.

[21] Brog, "Victims and Victors," 76, 77; Mooli Brog, "Yad Vashem," in *The Holocaust Encyclopaedia*, ed. Walter Laquer and Judith Tydor Baumal (New Haven/London: Yale University Press, 2001), 697–700.

[22] B'nai B'rith, established in 1843, is one of the world's oldest and largest fraternal organizations. "About Us," B'nai B'rith International, www.bnaibrith.org/about-us .html, accessed August 7, 2017.

[23] Young, *Texture of Memory*, 220.   [24] Ibid.

discussions that primarily focused on its location in the Jewish calendar.[25] In the end, the 27th of Nissan prevailed as it was considered a compromise between the desire to establish a specific date for Holocaust remembrance and the need to separate it from other days of Jewish mourning. During the Knesset debate on the memorial day, Rabbi Mordechai Nurock, who headed the committee dealing with the commemorative day, further declared that the date was chosen to commemorate the redemptive moment of Israel's birth. As Nurock proclaimed: "We have seen a graveyard in front of us, a graveyard for six million of our brothers and sisters, and maybe because of their blood, shed like water, we have been privileged to have our state."[26] With this statement, the first official commemorative practice linking the destruction of European Jewry to the birth of Israel was borne.

The unidirectional narrative proclaimed by Nurock was reinforced through the temporal arrangement of Holocaust Remembrance Day in the Israeli-Jewish calendar, creating a distinct "before" and "after" in national time and manifesting a cycle of creation, death, and regeneration.[27] The commemoration of the destruction of European Jewry is followed a week later – a deliberate choice that stems from the traditional Jewish seven days of mourning – by Memorial Day for the Fallen Soldiers, which is immediately followed by the celebration of Independence Day.[28] The sequencing of the three days replicates and magnifies the cultural code of climactic pulsation, encoding a metanarrative commonly referred to as *me-Shoah le-tḵuma* (Hebrew: from Holocaust to resurrection): a movement from the catastrophe of the Holocaust (and Jewish exile in general) through the sacrifices of life made in the struggles for rebuilding and liberating the nation and peaking with

[25] For an extensive discussion of the evolution of *Yom ha-Shoah*, see Amos Ben-Amos and Ilana Bet-El, "Holocaust Day and Memorial Day in Israeli Schools: Ceremonies, Education and History," *Israel Studies* 4 (1999): 258–284; Dalia Ofer, "The Strength of Remembrance: Commemorating the Holocaust during the First Decade of Israel," *Jewish Social Studies* 6:2 (2000): 24–55.
[26] James Young, ed., *The Art of Memory: Holocaust Memorials in History* (New York: Jewish Museum; Prestel-Verlag, 1994), 152.
[27] Don Handelman, ed., *Nationalism and the Israeli State* (Oxford: Berg, 2004), 95.
[28] In January 1951, then Minister of Defense Ben-Gurion established the Public Council for Soldiers' Commemoration, which was made a partner in discussions concerning the commemoration of the fallen. The council recommended that the 4th of Iyar – a day prior to Independence Day – would become the "General Memorial Day for the Heroes of the War of Independence." This suggestion was approved by the Knesset on March 27, 1963. "Memorial Day for Israel's Fallen Soldiers," Knesset, www.knesset.gov.il/holidays/eng/memorial_day_eng.htm, accessed January 19, 2017.

the establishment of the state of Israel.[29] As such, the compromise of the 17th of Nissan also reflected the desire to uphold what Don Handelman has referred to as the "Zionist master narrative,"[30] which projects a sequential procession from suffering and loss to triumph and redemption.[31]

While Holocaust Memorial Day was fixed as a national day of mourning in 1951, the lack of any commemorative prescriptions meant that it failed to turn into an event of public importance.[32] Indeed, Segev argues that the ceremonies mainly interested the survivor activists themselves; "for the rest of the country, the 27th of Nissan was a day like any other."[33] Observing this phenomenon with disappointment, eight years later Nurock asked the Knesset to define in detail how the day was to be nationally observed. In response, on April 8, 1959, the Knesset enacted the Holocaust and Heroism Memorial Day Law. The law stated that the memorial day would be devoted to the memory of the Holocaust, acts of heroism, and acts of rebellion.[34] In honor of this memory, it was decided that two minutes of silence would be observed, memorial services would be held in army camps and educational institutes, and flags on public buildings would be flown at half-mast. Furthermore, a national ceremony was to be held on the eve of Holocaust Day during which the president of Israel or the chairman of the Knesset would open the formal commemoration, which was to be broadcast on radio and, after 1967, television.[35]

Commemorative ceremonies, in contrast to collective observations of Holocaust Day, had taken place since 1951 at numerous locations, including at Kibbutz Beit Lohamei Hagetaot, Kibbutz Yad Mordechai, and, from 1954, the official state ceremony was held in the Martyrs'

[29] Danny Kaplan, "The Songs of the Siren: Engineering National Time on Israeli Radio," *Cultural Anthropology* 24:2 (2009): 324, 325.
[30] Zerubavel, *Recovered Roots*, 12.
[31] According to James Young, this metanarrative can also be seen to start with Passover (the day of the Warsaw Ghetto Uprising) as God's deliverance of the Jews and concluding with the Jews' deliverance of themselves in Israel. Young, "When a Day Remembers," 6; Don Handelman and Elihu Katz, "Sequencing the National: Opening Remembrance Day and Independence Day," in *Nationalism and the Israeli State: Bureaucratic Logic in Public Events*, ed. Don Handelman (Oxford: Berg, 2004), 138.
[32] In 1953, it was decided to enhance the law and give it a more Jewish character. From then on, observance would begin at sundown the previous day – as is the case for Jewish holy days – and all places of entertainment would be closed. Segev, *Seventh Million*, 437, 438.
[33] Ibid., 437.   [34] Ibid.
[35] The law also mandated the broadcasting of special radio programs and, in 1967, when TV came to Israel, special TV programs. Ofer, "Israel," 863; Feldman, *Above the Death Pits, beneath the Flag*, 49; Yad Vashem, "Day of Memorial for Victims of the European Jewish Disaster and Heroism – 27 Nissan, 5719," *Yad Vashem Bulletin* 4/5 (1959): 27.

Forest. Four years later, in 1958, the first Holocaust Day Ceremony took place on the Mount of Remembrance in Jerusalem, the official site of Yad Vashem. During this ceremony, Nahum Goldmann, president of the World Jewish Congress, reaffirmed the importance of Holocaust remembrance for Israeli society by stating: "We must forbid forgetfulness and renew the feeling amongst the youth that they can be proud of the period of the Holocaust no less than they are proud of the victories and accomplishments of the IDF."[36] The overt linkage between Israel's military accomplishments and the Holocaust was not limited to the 1958 inaugural ceremony. Rather, commemorative ceremonies on *Yom ha-Shoah* in the period under review have attempted – both in form and in content – to incorporate the military in the commemorative rituals, reinforcing the redemptive nature of the state and, simultaneously, the continual need for a strong Jewish state.

The IDF and Holocaust Commemoration

In addition to educational institutions, military camps, and workplaces, collective Holocaust commemoration ceremonies take place annually at Yad Vashem, Lohamei Hagetaot,[37] and Yad Mordechai.[38] In accordance with the 1959 law, the official opening of *Yom ha-Shoah* occurs on the eve of the memorial day in a ceremony at Yad Vashem in the presence of the prime minister, the president, and the official rabbi of Israel. On the day of *Yom ha-Shoah* further official ceremonies take place at the above-mentioned institutes, which, since the mid-1990s, have been dedicated to annual themes. In recent years, these themes, which principally manifest themselves in the stories of those lighting the memorial candles and the texts recited during the ceremony, have included "Their Last Voice: Letters and Testaments from Jews in the Holocaust" (2002), "The Anguish of Liberation and the Return to Life" (2005), "Holocaust Survivors in Israel: 60 Years since the Establishment of the State" (2008), and "Jewish Solidarity during the Holocaust"

---

[36] Ben-Amos and Bet-El, "Holocaust Day and Memorial Day," 258–284.

[37] It is worth noting that in 2016 museum director Avnat Livne publicly criticized the ceremonies held at Lohamei Hagetaot, stating that "the overly ceremonious nature in recent years has created a feeling that we're not allowed to think critically about the Holocaust and its lessons." See Karni Am-Ad, "Top Holocaust Educator Slams Israeli Way of Remembrance," *Haaretz*, April 26, 2016, www.haaretz.com/israel-news/ .premium-top-holocaust-educator-slams-remembrance-1.5441419, accessed February 15, 2020.

[38] Memorial ceremonies are also conducted at the Holocaust institute at Tel Yitzhak and in the Knesset.

(2012).[39] Apart from the incorporation of these annual themes, the commemorative rituals at the three institutes tend to be interchangeable and consist of speeches given by politicians and Holocaust survivors, laying wreaths for the Righteous Among the Nations, lighting six memorial candles by (descendants of) Holocaust survivors in memory of "the six million martyrs,"[40] reciting the Yizkor prayer, and, since the late 1990s, making use of multimedia and artistic performances.[41]

The Israeli Defense Forces have also taken an active role in the execution of Holocaust Day ceremonies over the last two decades; they have participated in the performance of the commemoration and, through speeches given by high-ranking army officials, they feature extensively in the ceremony's content.[42] On the surface, the presence of armed soldiers and the incorporation of army commands and drills in Holocaust ceremonies can be considered an overt demonstration of the army's physical power and ability to protect the Jewish people, creating a demonstrative juxtaposition between Jewish life in the Israeli state and during the Second World War in Europe. Indeed, the descent of soldiers to the memorial site at Lohamei Hagetaot from two sides, forming a protective blanket enveloping the participants, is a prime example of this symbolic protection.[43] Nevertheless, more implicitly, the army's presence and participation in commemorate ceremonies in Israel seek to convey the presence of a continuous threat and, consequently, the ever-present need for a strong army to secure the survival of the Jewish state. At Yad Vashem, this message is conveyed through what Handelman terms "bureaucratic aesthetics."[44] Under the army's watch, prior to the commencement of the ceremony, the complex is sealed off as a closed military zone under Emergency Defense Regulations, and all access and movement within the area is controlled by soldiers, creating a "ghettoization" of Yad Vashem. Through this ghettoization, Handelman notes that as the participants commemorate the Holocaust,

---

[39] See Mirit Fischler et al., "Holocaust Remembrance Day," *Yad Vashem Magazine*, July 2012, 14; Yad Vashem, "Editor's Remarks," *Yad Vashem Magazine*, Spring 2002, 2; "Holocaust Martyrs' and Heroes' Remembrance Day," Yad Vashem, www.yadvashem .org/yv/en/remembrance/2017/previous_years.asp, accessed November 16, 2017.

[40] Don-Yehiya, "Memory and Political Culture," 154.

[41] Daphna Galili, "Marking the Days," *Yad Vashem Magazine*, Fall 2003, 28, 29.

[42] For the mnemonic (Zionist) symbolism used during the IDF's annual commemorative delegation to Auschwitz, see Arad, "Shoah," 192–196.

[43] GFH, *Development of the Memorial Ceremony on 16 April 1996* (Museum Lohamei Hagetaot, undated), 1 (in Hebrew); GFH, *Development of the Memorial Ceremony on 5 May 1997* (Museum Lohamei Hagetaot, undated), 1 (in Hebrew); GFH, *Development of the Memorial Ceremony on 23 April 1998* (Museum Lohamei Hagetaot, undated), 1 (in Hebrew).

[44] Handelman, *Nationalism*, 105.

200 The Landscape of Memory

they themselves are set apart as the potential victims of another looming Holocaust, thereby encouraging their self-classification as such and the need for army protection.[45] This necessity is further affirmed in speeches made by army officials during Holocaust Day ceremonies.[46] In his speech at Yad Vashem on April 13, 1999, Chief of Staff Shaul Mofaz told the audience that only a strong IDF would be able to ensure that a repeat of the Shoah would not occur: "As we stand here as officers of the IDF, we ask you to give expression to independence, integrity and security of the State of Israel and say publicly that the Shoah cannot occur again."[47] The next day, at Lohamei Hagetaot, the lieutenant general reiterated his message, stating that "the Jewish people are united today with one shared goal: to live a secure and peaceful life in the Israeli state and to ensure that a disaster like this will not befall us again. In order to do this, we need strength and power, which will ensure our withstanding any threat and enemy. This power rests on an independent state and a good and strong army, which can enable a proper life in the Israeli state and [its] continuation [...]."[48]

The importance of military strength is not only conveyed through emphasizing the current and future role of the IDF in Israeli society in commemorative ceremonies. Additionally, speeches and readings glorify Jewish resistance during the Holocaust, focusing in particular on the Warsaw Ghetto Uprising and the participation of Jewish fighters from the Yishuv as a source of inspiration for the IDF. In 2013, in his address to the Youth Movement Ceremony on Holocaust Remembrance Day, then Minister of Education Rabbi Piron pointed to the Warsaw Ghetto Uprising as "a source of inspiration for the younger generations."[49] Echoing his statements, one delegate from the socialist-Zionist youth group *Hashomer Hatzair* (Hebrew: the young guard), Eitan Cohen,

---

[45] Ibid.
[46] A similar comment was made during an IDF visit to Yad Vashem in preparation of *Yom ha-Shoah*. In 1998, Chief of Staff Amnon Kipkin-Shahak explained that the message conveyed through the army's visits was aimed to "remember, to see again and to understand [...] our task, here in this country, as the descendants of those who all but perished. To understand how important it is to have a secure Jewish national home and to understand the enormous responsibility shouldered by us [...]." Anonymous, "Members of the IDF General Staff Visit Yad Vashem," *Yad Vashem Magazine*, Summer 1998, 4.
[47] Michael Grayevski and Nurit Peltar, "A Strong IDF Is the Assurance That the Holocaust Won't Return," *Yedioth Ahronot*, April 13, 1999, 9.
[48] GFH, *Address by Chief of Staff during the Holocaust Day Memorial Ceremony at Kibbutz Lohamei Hagetaot 13 April 1999* (Museum Lohamei Hagetaot, April 15, 1999) (in Hebrew).
[49] Leah Goldstein et al., "Holocaust Remembrance Day," *Yad Vashem Magazine*, July 2013, 10.

pledged to "take responsibility for the society in which we live ... to act as
we learned from the ghetto fighters and others, who battled for their
humanity, for their faith and for their culture."[50] In this context, the
location of the IDF during the ceremony at Yad Vashem can be deemed
highly symbolic. At Yad Vashem, the memorial gathering is set at the
Warsaw Ghetto Plaza, dominated by a high brick wall that is divided into
two parts. On the right side of the wall, a typical portrayal of ghetto Jews
is depicted who sorrowfully "as sheep to the slaughter" are treading

Figure 5.1 Guarding the ghetto fighters' legacy
Yad Vashem, Holocaust Remembrance Day 2011
Credit: Image by GALI TIBBON/AFP via Getty Images.

[50] Ibid.

towards their death. On the left side, there is a sculpture of the fighters of the Warsaw Ghetto Uprising, showing tall and proud men confidently looking towards the horizon.[51] Framed by the Israeli state flag, the ceremony at Yad Vashem sees IDF soldiers standing on the left side of the wall, guarding the tradition of the ghetto fighters.

The Israeli appropriation of the ghetto fighters' legacy further rests on the attribution of Zionist efforts to "partisans and underground fighters" in an attempt to portray the Jewish fight against the Nazis as the antecedent to the establishment of a Jewish state.[52] The convergence of these conceptions can be seen at readings conducted in 1997 at Lohamei Hagetaot, where participants were instructed to "remember, people of Israel, the millions of our brothers and sisters who were slaughtered and burned [...] remember our soldiers who fell in Hebrew units in the Second World War [...] in order to free our country and to establish our state and in their sacrifice paved the way for the revival of Israel. Remember, remember the[se] people."[53] Two years later, during a reciting of the Yizkor prayer, participants were once again commanded to "remember [the] ghetto fighters [and] the hundreds of dear souls and the nameless of the Jewish underground who rose up in despair and became heroes [...] remember the soldiers who fell in the Jewish units in World War II, the messengers behind enemy lines, the pioneers, the qualified, the youth of Israel, dreamers and fighters, the people who fell in the liberation of our country and the establishment of our state and through their sacrifice paved the way for the restoration of Israel. Remember, remember the[se] people!"[54]

The Holocaust as a National Death

The above-cited invocation of Holocaust victims as "the youth of Israel" and "our brothers and sisters who were slaughtered and burned" further denotes that the Holocaust is considered a national Israeli tragedy and, consequently, that all victims belong to the state.[55] Indeed, during a speech given by Prime Minister Netanyahu on Holocaust Memorial Day in 1998, Holocaust victims were referred to "as our sons and

---

[51] Handelman, *Nationalism*, 108, 109.   [52] Segev, *Seventh Million*, 435.

[53] GFH, *Development*, 4.

[54] GFH, *Ceremony in Dedication of the Memory of the Shoah and Heroism on 13 April 1999* (Museum Lohamei Hagetaot, undated), 2 (in Hebrew).

[55] Jackie Feldman, "Between Yad Vashem and Mt. Herzl: Changing Inscriptions of Sacrifice on Jerusalem's Mountain of Memory," *Anthropological Quarterly* 80:4 (2007): 1169; Handelman, *Nationalism*, 160.

brothers" from whom "new life" was generated.[56] The portrayal of Holocaust victims as a collective national loss was by no means a novel occurrence. While presenting the Yad Vashem Law before the Knesset, Ben-Zion Dinur, the minister of education and culture (1951–1955) and the first chairman of Yad Vashem, explained that the goal of the Nazis had been "to obliterate the name of Israel."[57] Echoing this belief, President Chaim Herzog in his address at the Yad Vashem's children monument's dedication ceremony in 1987 reminded the audience that "these potential citizens of Israel were taken from us and it is our duty to turn their memory into a powerful demand, that the world pledge not to repeat such a crime."[58] Moreover, during the annual memorial day that same year, in recognition of all "potential citizens," Herzog bestowed collective "remembrance citizenship" on the Holocaust dead.[59] It is because of the interpretation of the Holocaust as a national tragedy and a national death that the Israeli state is presented as the only viable answer to the Holocaust itself. As such, practices during Holocaust Day intend to contrast sharply with – or oppose – diasporic existence since "state and diaspora were to go their separate ways, the former victorious, the latter destroyed."[60]

An examination conducted of the Holocaust survivors involved in Holocaust Day ceremonies and the content of speeches given on this day further evidences the desired affirmation of the righteousness of Zionism. At Yad Vashem, the Holocaust survivors selected as annual torchbearers between 1994 and 2016 had all made *Aliyah* (Hebrew: immigrate [literally to rise up]) to Palestine/Israel following the Holocaust, suggesting that Aliyah was the only and permanent choice made by post-Holocaust European Jewry.[61] Moreover, between 2006 and 2012, nine torchbearers

---

[56] Feldman, "Between Yad Vashem and Mt. Herzl," 1154.

[57] Orna Kenan, *Between Memory and History: The Evolution of Israeli Historiography of the Holocaust, 1945–1961* (New York: Peter Lang, 2003), 44.

[58] Segev, *Seventh Million*, 434; Young, *Texture of Memory*, 258.

[59] Yad Vashem, on its founding, was charged with the responsibility of "confer[ring] upon the members of the Jewish people who perished in the days of the Disaster and the resistance the commemorative citizenship of the state of Israel, as a token of their having been gathered to their people." In the course of negotiations, the American Jewish committee managed to obtain an undertaking from Yad Vashem that citizenship would only be granted to victims of the Holocaust when a relative or close friend had specifically requested it in writing. Ronald W. Zweig, "Politics of Commemoration," *Jewish Social Studies* 49:2 (1987): 161–162; Handelman and Shamgar-Handelman, "The Presence of Absence," 107.

[60] Handelman and Shamgar-Handelman, "The Presence of Absence," 103.

[61] This implication not only forgoes the "social silencing" of Holocaust victims on their arrival in Palestine/Israel but also fails to point to other mass emigration destinations for Holocaust victims – principally the United States which received approximately 137,450 Jewish refugees between 1945 and 1952 – and the large subsequent migration from Israel between 1945 and 1956, when Holocaust survivors made up 55.6 percent of all

were picked who had fought in the 1948 War, creating the semblance of what Handelman called "a single protracted battle," as if "the War of Independence" was a mere extension of "the Jewish fight [for survival] against the Nazis."[62] In his address at the youth movement ceremony on Holocaust Day in 2007, the current chairman of Yad Vashem, Avner Shalev, presented the outcome of this battle – the founding of the Israeli state – as a personal revival for survivors by honoring all those "who chose to start their lives over in *Eretz Yisra'el*. Those who took part in the founding of the state, who fought in Israel's wars and [...] who went through hell and emerged victorious."[63] These statements, echoing the traditional Zionist mantra "from catastrophe to redemption," had also been expressed ten years earlier in 1996 when Premier Shimon Peres stressed the necessity of the establishment of a Jewish homeland as a place of permanent refuge for victims of anti-Semitism and argued that "Zionism [had] restored [the] dignity and national status to the Jewish people. The nation took responsibility for its own destiny, and returned flourishing to [the] stage of history."[64] A year later, the restoration accorded by the realization of Zionism was once again invoked when Zevulun Hammer, the deputy prime minister of education, culture and sport, said: "You, our children, cannot imagine how survivors, as young as yourselves, raised themselves from the cataclysmic abyss, and planted the foundations of faith within the wilderness."[65]

Holocaust Memory Sites: Invoking the Holocaust, Living the Holocaust

While Holocaust Memorial Day is an official day of remembrance in Israel, Holocaust memorial practices take place throughout the year, including through individual and collective visits to Holocaust memorial

---

emigrants (totaling 77,267 individuals). In addition to racial discrimination and unemployment, according to Hanna Yablonka, this emigration resulted from the fact that Israel "was considered a stopover." Hanna Yablonka, *Survivors of the Holocaust: Israel after the War*, trans. Ora Cummings (Basingstoke: Macmillan, 1999), 15, 16; "United States Policy toward Jewish Refugees, 1941–1952," United States Holocaust Memorial Museum, www.ushmm.org/wlc/en/article.php?ModuleId=10007094, accessed August 8, 2017.

[62] Handelman, *Nationalism*, 99.
[63] Leah Goldstein, "Fulfil Obligation to Survivors," *Yad Vashem Magazine*, Summer 2007, 3.
[64] Anonymous, "24 Hours on the Mount of Remembrance: Yom ha-Shoah," *Yad Vashem Magazine*, June 1996, 2.
[65] Michael Morris Kamil, "Yizkor," *Yad Vashem Magazine*, Summer 1997, 3.

institutes and educational programs offered at memory sites. Through an analysis of Yad Mordechai, Lohamei Hagetaot, and Yad Vashem, the remainder of this chapter will evidence that these memorial sites, similarly to Holocaust Day commemorations, portray the Israeli state as the only viable response to the Holocaust, generating a linkage between the catastrophe of the Holocaust and the redemptive nature of the Israeli state. The conveyance of this distinctly Zionist message will be demonstrated with reference to the usage of teleological architecture and its reflection in the institutes' narratives as well as the content of the educational programs offered at the institutes. By invoking the "framing" of the Holocaust, the analysis also indicates that memory sites – as official agencies – seek to shape the experience – and consequently the memory – of visitors by encouraging them to engage in certain ritual behaviors and to emerge from their experiences with a transformed identity or consciousness. Accordingly, Holocaust mnemonic practices are principally regarded not as illustrations or interpretations of the story being told but rather as the stories themselves.

Yad Mordechai

Kibbutz Yad Mordechai, situated near the border with Gaza, is home to five major memorial spaces: a recreated battlefield on the site of Yad Mordechai's stand against the Egyptians during the 1948 War, a large statue of Mordechai Anielewicz, the leader of the Warsaw Ghetto Uprising, a cemetery for those fallen in the 1948 War, a site demonstrating the evacuation of children during the war, and a museum that links the narrative of the Holocaust to the 1948 War and the establishment of the Israeli state.[66] The kibbutz was initially founded in the 1930s by the *Hashomer Hatzair* movement in the north of Israel, in the vicinity of the city of Netanya. In 1943, the community moved to its current site near Ashkelon. The founders of the kibbutz, who had been members of the same youth movement as Mordechai Anielewicz, decided to name the kibbutz after him as "they knew he wanted to come here and they felt they had fulfilled his dream."[67] The museum, which was opened in 1968, is housed in a building that is best described as a bunker or fortress and, according to the current director of the museum, Vered Bar-Semech, is an expression of the Brutalist Bauhaus style that was used

---

[66] Yad Mordechai, *Museum Yad Mordechai "From Shoah to Revival". Background Material for the Visit of the Museum Council Committee* (Museum Yad Mordechai, 2013), 2 (in Hebrew).

[67] Interview conducted with Vered Bar-Semech on April 21, 2016.

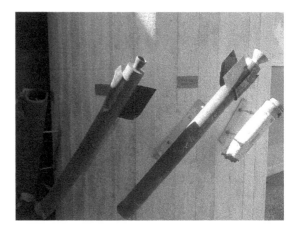

Figure 5.2 The entrance to Yad Mordechai

by the architect, Arieh Sharon.[68] In the contemporary context, however, the bunker takes on a more sinister meaning, particularly as a result of the placement of several rockets at its entrance, which were fired towards the kibbutz in recent years from the nearby Gaza Strip.

[68] Ibid.

Bearing the explicit name "Yad Mordechai: From Shoah to Revival," both the narrative presented in the building's architecture and the museum's exhibit are an overt testimony to the concept of destruction and redemption.[69] Upon entering the building, the 25,000 visitors that the museum attracts every year embark on a physical experience of this message with the immediate descent into the bunker, which leads visitors to a dark room where Jewish life before the Holocaust is depicted. Here, in the words of the writer Abba Kovner, one "is requested to see what no longer can be seen, to hear what no longer can be heard, to understand that which can never be understood."[70] Following exposure to the seven pillars of pre-Holocaust Jewish existence, the visitor begins a slow ascent to a large hall dedicated, on one side, to the extermination process and, on the other side, to Jewish resistance, where a window overlooking the statue of Mordechai Anielewicz and the kibbutz' landscape floods the room with light.[71] The intended message is clear: death lies in the dark artificially lit European *galut* (Hebrew: diaspora); natural light, life, and freedom lie in the Jewish state or, as pointed out in a document written in 1999, "the current message in the museum represents the Zionist [notion that] the state of Israel was the best solution for Jews in the diaspora."[72] The connection between Holocaust and rebirth in one room testifies to the presentation of the establishment of the Jewish state as a direct result of the Holocaust, as indicated in an internal document written by museum staff, which notes that "this approach emphasizes the relationship and the chronological sequence of events that Jews experienced during the first half of the 20th century. It connects the heroism of Mordechai Anielewicz and the resistance fighters in Europe with the fighters of the War of Independence whose heroism has its origins in the Jewish world that existed for many years in exile and was destroyed."[73] Kovner, who was one of the chief designers of the exhibits in the museum, was the main proponent of this approach. A Jewish partisan fighter during the Second World War, Kovner later joined the Givati Brigade as an Information Officer during the 1948 War, where he sought to raise troops' morale and confidence, including through cathartic

---

[69] Yad Mordechai, *Program to Change the Character of the Museum "From Shoah to Revival"* at *Kibbutz Yad Mordechai* (Museum Yad Mordechai, 1999), 2 (in Hebrew).

[70] Yad Mordechai, *Museum "From Shoah to Revival" at Kibbutz Yad Mordechai* (Museum Yad Mordechai, 1996), 1–6 (in Hebrew).

[71] Ibid., 3.   [72] Young, *Texture of Memory*, 231, 233.

[73] Yad Mordechai, *Program to Change the Character of the Museum "From Shoah to Revival"* at *Kibbutz Yad Mordechai* (Museum Yad Mordechai, 1999), 2 (in Hebrew); Yad Mordechai, *Summary of Museum Staff Meeting* (Museum Yad Mordechai, June 1999), 1 (in Hebrew).

entertainment and writing "battle pages" that served as important – if at times controversial – motivation and instigation tools for soldiers of the Givati Brigade on the Egyptian front.[74] According to Kovner, the museum should be "one open book," and therefore he objected to any segregation of exhibits on the 1948 War and the Holocaust.[75] A curatorship document written in 1996 confirms the continuance of Kovner's vision for the museum's narrative by noting: "The route that starts in the Shoah and the dark period for the Jewish people moves gradually and seemingly unnoticeable [...] from the museum of the Shoah to the war and victory museum. All this occurs in the same building."[76]

Yad Vashem

While the architecture employed at Yad Mordechai constitutes the most overt linkage between the Holocaust and the establishment of the Israeli state following the 1948 War, the concept of revival is equally illustrated in the location of Yad Vashem on *Har ha-Zikaron* (Hebrew: the Mount of Remembrance). Yad Vashem, meaning "a place and a name" taken from Isaiah (56:5), was legislated as the official State Memorial Authority on August 28, 1953 when the Knesset passed the Martyrs' and Heroes' Remembrance Law, also known as the Yad Vashem Law.[77] According to this law, Yad Vashem was mandated to commemorate "the valor and heroism of the soldiers, the fighters of the underground and the prisoners in the ghettos, as well as the sons and daughters of the Jewish people who struggled for their human dignity" and to "gather, study and publish the entire testimony concerning Holocaust and heroism and endow the nation with its lessons [to] ... foster an atmosphere of unanimity in memory."[78]

---

[74] See Dina Porat, *The Fall of a Sparrow: The Life and Times of Abba Kovner* (Stanford: Stanford University Press, 2010), 239, 240, 244, 250, 373.

[75] Yad Mordechai, *Museum Yad Mordechai: History of the Museum from the Book "Beyond the Physical" by Dina Porat* (Museum Yad Mordechai, undated), 2–4 (in Hebrew).

[76] Yad Mordechai, *Museum "From Shoah to Revival" at Kibbutz Yad Mordechai* (Museum Yad Mordechai, 1996), 5 (in Hebrew).

[77] The idea for a memorial institute first emerged in 1942. Mordechai Shenhavi, a member of Kibbutz Mishmar Ha'emek, suggested at a board meeting of the Jewish National Fund that a monument be established called Yad Vashem and which would be dedicated to the destroyed diaspora. Yehudit Shendar and Orly Ohana, "In the Footsteps of Heroes Monuments to Jewish Rebellion and Heroism at Yad Vashem," *Yad Vashem Magazine*, March 2013, 12, 13.

[78] The law also empowered Yad Vashem to set up a memorial project, to gather testimony and to "pass its lesson on to the people," to "implant among the nation ... the day determined by the Knesset as Memorial Day for the Holocaust and Heroism," to foster

Today, the forty-five-acre site on which Yad Vashem lies contains a Holocaust museum and several memorials, which comprise, inter alia, the Valley of Communities and the Children's Memorial.[79] At the top of *Har ha-Zikaron*, the founder of modern Zionism, Theodor Herzl, and the leaders and founders of the Jewish nation are buried on Mount Herzl and, nearby, the Israeli Military Cemetery commemorates those fallen in the service of the Jewish state.[80] In 2003, a new path, entitled "The Connecting Path," was built linking Mount Herzl and Yad Vashem. Constructed by members of youth movements, the path was first opened on April 22, 2003 to mark the sixtieth anniversary of the Warsaw Ghetto Uprising. During the path's festive inauguration, Holocaust survivors, soldiers, high-school students, and members of youth movements undertook a march from the valley of the communities, marking the destruction of European Jewry, to the entrance of the Mount Herzl cemetery.[81] The physical ascent up the hill accompanying this march, which is repeated annually, is indicative of the symbolic physical proximity of Yad Vashem to Mount Herzl and, more generally, the Zionist redemptive narrative, as the sign at the entrance of the path notes: "passage along it [the path] is a symbolic voyage in time from catastrophe to rebirth. It represents the journey from the Diaspora to the homeland of the Jewish people, from exile and destruction to a life of endeavor and hope in the State of Israel."[82] The physical bodily struggle of the climb from the valley of death (Yad Vashem) by those partaking in the march recreates the notion of a unified effort, a single body overcoming the tragedy of the Holocaust through national sacrifice, which eventually leads to the establishment of the Jewish state as envisioned by the founder of modern political Zionism, Herzl. As such, Yad Vashem is not "a foreign land within the Israeli landscape," as contended by Handelman and Lea Shamgar-Handelman,[83] but rather embedded in its depths as a watershed consciously reminiscent of the ongoing sacrifice paid in the name of – and for the sake of – the state.

According to Yitzhak Arad, former chairman of Yad Vashem (1972–1993), Yad Vashem's first permanent historical exhibit on the

"an experience of united memory of its heroes and victims," and to represent Israel in international projects commemorating the victims. Handelman and Shamgar-Handelman, "The Presence of Absence," 103.

[79] All visiting foreign dignitaries are taken to Yad Vashem along with school children, soldiers, policemen, and trade union members. Hansen-Glucklich, *Holocaust Memory Reframed*, 200; Bartov, "Chambers of Horror," 66.

[80] Feldman, "Between Yad Vashem and Mt. Herzl," 1154.   [81] Ibid., 1156.

[82] Observation conducted at Yad Vashem on May 7, 2016.

[83] Handelman and Shamgar-Handelman, "The Presence of Absence," 109.

Holocaust intended to reinforce the museum's physical setting by creating an overt link between the Holocaust and the establishment of the Israeli state.[84] The chronological narrative first presented in the exhibit of 1973 was divided into three main sections that focused on the Jewish world before the Holocaust and anti-Jewish Nazi policies between 1933 and 1939, the annihilation process between 1941 and 1945, and, finally, the liberation, illegal immigration to Israel, and redemption in the form of the establishment of the Israeli state.[85] In an interview, Arad, who oversaw the establishment of the first main exhibit, noted that the content of the museum largely followed his own life experiences, as he said: "My life's two major events were shown in the museum, the Holocaust and the establishment of the State of Israel. In both I was a first-hand witness and an active participant."[86] Consequently, Segev's observation that resistance of Nazism at Yad Vashem's former museum was described in such a way that the visitor gained the impression that "Jews fought a war with the Nazis" was not necessarily only representative of "the Israeli culture of memory" but, in fact, can be related to Arad's own partisan experience during the war.[87]

Similarly, the presentation of "the state of Israel as both the consequence and the panacea"[88] matched Arad's own development over the course of the Holocaust, as he states that "the aim of his life in the forest was to fight for a Jewish state [as] I saw my Jewish people without a state during the war and I saw what it means to be people without a state, we were on the fringes of society [...] As a historian it is hard to speak in hypotheticals, but I can imagine that if Israel had existed many Jews would have survived."[89] The notion that Zionism constituted the only appropriate answer to Nazism, as it had been for Arad, was further illustrated in the former museum's choreographed passage.[90] Arad, who continues to serve as an advisor to the institute, points out that the museum was built in such a way that there was only one way to go through it, thereby evidencing Bartov's observation that "in the museum, we walk through an exhibition of photographs and artifacts put together by those who had toured that country and wish to tell us about it."[91] The success of the conveyance of Arad's own Zionistic message was

---

[84] Interview conducted with Yitzhak Arad on June 1, 2016.   [85] Ibid.
[86] Arad, who hails from a Shtetl close to Vilna, organized a group of ghetto youths into an underground cell. Two years later, in 1943, together with a band of Soviet partisans Arad fought against the Germans from the Naroch Forest until the end of the war when he joined the Palmach. Interview conducted with Yitzhak Arad on June 1, 2016.
[87] Segev, *Seventh Million*, 424, 442.   [88] Bartov, "Chambers of Horror," 66.
[89] Interview conducted with Yitzhak Arad on June 1, 2016.
[90] Bartov, "Chambers of Horror," 66.   [91] Ibid., 71.

demonstrated in a survey published in 1998, which showed that 74 percent of visitors found that the historical museum helped them "understand the need for the state of Israel."[92]

The New Yad Vashem and the Zionist Rebirth

Under Arad's direction, it was decided to build a new museum exhibit in
the 1990s to, in Arad's words, "accommodate the large amount of
visitors and incorporate modern technology using similar methods as
the United States Holocaust Memorial Museum, which had opened in
1993."[93] The reconstruction of the museum complex, which according
to Yehudit Inbar, the director of the museum's division at Yad Vashem,
bears the influence of the Holocaust exhibit at the Imperial War
Museum,[94] was used to further a teleological understanding of the
Holocaust through the museum's exterior and interior design, creating
both a "landscape of memory" and a "landscape as memory."[95] Plans for
the new historical museum were announced in the "Yad Vashem 2001
Masterplan," which noted that "with the younger generation's increasing
desire to have direct, up-to-date access to information on the Holocaust,
[...] special sensitivity was given to the establishment of the new museum
complex."[96] Shalev, who became chairman of Yad Vashem in 1994,
maintains that it was decided in advance that the new museum "would

---

[92] A total of 281 high-school students from 27 groups participated in this study. Leonard
Bickman and Karl Hamner, "An Evaluation of the Yad Vashem Holocaust Museum,"
Evaluation Review 22:4 (1998): 443.

[93] Interview conducted with Yitzhak Arad on June 1, 2016.

[94] Felicity Heywood, "Giving Voice," *Museums Journal* 12 (December 2006): 21–23. For
an analysis of the Imperial War Museum's Holocaust exhibit, see Tony Kushner, "The
Holocaust and the Museum World in Britain: A Study in Ethnography," *Immigrants &
Minorities* 21 (2002): 12–40.

[95] Susanne Kuchler (1993) makes the distinction between landscapes of memory and
landscapes as memory. The landscape of memory is a picture of landscape, a static,
inscribed surface on which memories are fixed and labeled, and from which the social
and cultural referents of these memories can be read off. Landscape as memory indexes
the practice of landscape as memory-work that unceasingly reforms the shaping
and shapes of its own significance. The landscape as memory produces the landscape
of memory and perhaps their relationship is dialectical. Handelman and Shamgar-
Handelman, "The Presence of Absence," 88, 89.

[96] The Yad Vashem 2001 Masterplan, which was projected to cost 82 million dollars,
comprised six central elements: the construction of the archives and library building, the
computerization of Holocaust victims' names, documentation, and photographs; the
establishment of an international school for Holocaust studies; the establishment of a
new museum complex; the expansion of scholarly research carried out under the
auspices of the International Institute for Holocaust Research and its relocation to a
newly renovated premises; and the construction of a new visitors center on *Har ha-
Zikaron* to accommodate the millions of visitors. Shalev, "Recalling the Past."

not attempt to convey messages, or teach lessons advocating a particular worldview, but would present the events objectively, based on the accrued research findings, testimonies and the Jewish perspective."[97] Nevertheless, both the architecture employed in the construction of the museum's complex and the content offered in the museum's exhibit demonstrate what Erik Cohen calls "a classic Zionist theme regarding the Shoah of 'destruction to redemption',," as exemplified by "perennial persecution in exile rectified by the survival of the Jewish people in an independent state in Israel."[98]

The new museum, which was designed by the architect Moshe Safdie, opened to the public in 2005. Occupying a space of 4,445 square meters, the museum is divided into seven thematic exhibits beginning with "The world that was destroyed 1900–1933" and ending with the post-Holocaust period shown through the usage of authentic photographs, artefacts, and documents.[99] The complex consists of a linear pyramid, which, according to the architect, cuts into the hillside, "penetrating it from the south, extending under, emerging, indeed exploding, to the north."[100] From the outside, the cut across the hilltop appears to slit open the ground, leaving an "archaeological scar" aimed to symbolize the chasm created by the Holocaust, which is symbolically healed by the landscape of the Jewish state.[101] At Yad Vashem, similarly to Yad Mordechai, the redemptive nature of the Jewish state is demonstrated through a full visual bodily experience, namely a teleological journey "from darkness to light, from descent to elevation."[102] Upon leaving the entrance plaza and the visitors' center, providing the "conceptual corridor [...] between the mundane and familiar world and the sanctity of the memorial complex," the visitor descends into the darkness of the pyramid.[103] During the exposure to "the story of the destruction of European Jewry" rays of light from the opposite end of the building –

[97] Avner Shalev, "The New Holocaust History Museum," *Yad Vashem Magazine*, Fall 2003, 23, 24; Anonymous, "Yad Vashem Masterplan 2001," *Yad Vashem Magazine*, Fall 1997, 10; Avner Shalev, "Recalling the Past."
[98] Erik H. Cohen, "Educational Dark Tourism at an in Populo Site: The Holocaust Museum in Jerusalem," *Annals of Tourism Research* 38:1 (2011): 197.
[99] Yvette Nahmia-Messinas, "The New Museum Complex," *Yad Vashem Magazine*, Summer 2000, 10, 11.
[100] Hansen-Glucklich, *Holocaust Memory Reframed*, 37, 69; Ruth Eglas, "The Holocaust from the Inside Out," *Jerusalem Post Online*, January 12, 2009, www.jpost.com/Features/In-Thespotlight/The-Holocaust-from-the-inside-out, accessed August 9, 2017.
[101] Hansen-Glucklich, *Holocaust Memory Reframed*, 37, 69; "Yad Vashem Masterplan 2001," *Yad Vashem Magazine*, Fall 1997, 10, 11.
[102] Hansen-Glucklich, *Holocaust Memory Reframed*, 191.
[103] Anonymous, "Masterplan," 10.

literally the light at the end of the tunnel – accompany the visitor as he or she zigzags through the museum's exhibits, forming a constant reminder of the redemption that awaits. This redemption or rebirth, as noted previously, is reinforced through the physical experience that accompanies the conclusion of the museum. Leaving the darkness and death of the *galut* (Hebrew: exile) behind, basking in light, the visitor emerges onto a terrace overlooking the Jerusalem landscape sparking a metamorphotic rebirth and the integration of "a new Zionist identity."[104] The redemptive symbolism behind the dichotomic usage of light in the complex was affirmed in a publication on the Yad Vashem Masterplan in which it was noted that "upon leaving the partially underground museum complex, the visitor will walk out into the light and green hills of Jerusalem, the symbol of life and continuity, and the capital of the Jewish people."[105]

In addition to the choreographed passage, symbolic narratives within Yad Vashem's exhibit also contribute to the redemptive enactment. Thus, in pre-Holocaust Jewish Europe, *Hatikvah* (Hebrew: the hope) is played. *Hatikvah*, today the national anthem of Israel, is based on a text written by the poet Naftali Herz Imbed in 1877 and is considered a reflection of the desire to establish a Jewish state in the land of Israel.[106] While Zionism undoubtedly was part of pre-Holocaust Jewish life, through the rendition of *Hatikvah*, the museum visitors are both reminded of the fulfillment of the victims' dream and asked to reflect on what was lost due to the lack of an earlier realization of a Jewish state. As a result of this catastrophic loss in Europe, the museum presents the Jewish state as the only viable and secure place for Jews, indicated through usage of survivor testimonies and the emphasis on the reestablishment of survivors' lives in Israel. Survivor testimonies are used throughout the museum to, in the words of Shalev, "elicit visitors' empathy, understanding, and compassion for victims of the Shoah."[107] Yet, save three, Yad Vashem exclusively reserves witness testimony for Holocaust survivors who emigrated to Israel, thereby not only declaring the Holocaust a solely Israeli phenomenon but also seeking to indicate that there was a consensus that Zionism presented the only legitimate response to the Holocaust.[108] The link between the Holocaust and the establishment of the state of Israel is further reinforced in the final gallery of the permanent exhibition, which – in the context of Holocaust

---

[104] Hansen-Glucklich, *Holocaust Memory Reframed*, 191.
[105] Anonymous, "Masterplan," 11.
[106] Martin Gilbert, *Israel: A History* (London: Black Swan, 2008), 7.
[107] Shalev, "Holocaust," 23, 24.
[108] There are two testimonies in German and one in English; the remainder is in Hebrew. Observation conducted on May 7, 2016.

Figure 5.3 The architecture of redemption

survivors reestablishing their lives after the Second World War – focuses on the United Nations' resolution that led to the founding of Israel, the country's Declaration of Independence, the immigration of survivors to Israel, and the history of Zionism.[109] Following the reopening of the museum, in an interview conducted with the Israeli newspaper *Yedioth*

---

[109] Hansen-Glucklich, *Holocaust Memory Reframed*, 191.

Ahronot (Hebrew: latest news), Shalev affirmed the importance of this Zionist message, as he stated that the purpose of the museum could not be disentangled from the beliefs of "the people of Yad Vashem, for whom Zionism flows through our veins and is etched in our consciousness [and the belief] that the establishment of a sovereign Jewish state of Israel after the Shoah is the basis for a continued Jewish existence. This existence is a condition for continuing the creative and spiritual development of the Jewish people [...] to prevent another attack against them."[110]

The Holocaust as a Pedagogical Tool

Visits to Holocaust institutes in Israel often coincide with specialized pedagogic activities for teachers, students, and soldiers at "schools" set up as part of the institutions in the 1990s. While participation in teacher training at these institutes is mostly voluntary, visits by soldiers and security personnel have become a standard practice, in particular at Yad Vashem following the establishment of the Army Education Unit in 2000.[111] Three years prior to this, in June 1997, the Ministry of Education had already decided that the educational benefits of visits to Yad Vashem were of such importance that all Israeli pupils should visit the institute at least once over the course of their schooling. As a result, the number of Israeli participants in study seminars and programs at Yad Vashem has risen immensely over the years, from 60,000 in 1996 to 306,000 in 2013.[112]

While the content varies according to the institute and the needs of the participants, an analysis of the pedagogical activities offered at the three institutes demonstrates that throughout the programs offered the emphasis lies on strengthening identification with the Holocaust past. At Yad Mordechai, where educational activities commenced in the late 1980s,[113] the same time that high-school trips to Poland were first organized, these objectives are plainly stated in the curriculum material

---

[110] Avner Shalev, "The Purpose of the New Museum," *Yedioth Ahronot*, March 15, 2005, 24.
[111] Adi Loya, "The Army Education Unit," *Yad Vashem Magazine*, Summer 2000, 7.
[112] "Highlights of Yad Vashem's Activities in 2013," Yad Vashem, www.yadvashem.org/pressroom/highlights/2013, accessed December 5, 2016; Anonymous, "Highlights of Yad Vashem Activity in 2001," *Yad Vashem Magazine*, Spring 2002, 16; Avner Shalev, "Introducing 'Masterplan 2001' Yad Vashem's Development Project in the Age of the Communications Revolution," *Yad Vashem Magazine*, April 1996, 4, 5.
[113] In 1988, with the thaw in diplomatic relations between the Polish government and Israel, Oded Cohen, head of the Ministry of Education and Youth Division, was invited as part of an official Israeli Ministry of Education group to visit Poland, after which an itinerary was developed. Feldman, *Above the Death Pits, beneath the Flag*, 58.

offered to workshop organizers. Documentation on workshops for high-school students traveling to Poland indicates that one of the aims of these workshops is to "strengthen the relationship of young Israeli-Jews with their kibbutz past in order to deepen their identification with the fate of the Jewish people [and the] doom of the Jews in the Holocaust."[114] Similar rhetoric can be found in the espoused objectives of educational practices at Yad Vashem's International School for Holocaust Studies, which was established in 1994. In 2001, Inbal Kvity, the director of the Study Seminar Department at the International School, noted that the two main educational philosophies at the school center on exposing participants to Jewish life before and during the Holocaust, because, as Kvity explained, "to become acquainted with the victims and thereby properly mourn and commemorate them, they [participants] must first recognize them as individuals who had names, faces, human emotions and reactions."[115]

Educational programs do not solely seek identification as a means of encouraging proper commemoration but also stimulate forging a personal commitment to safeguard the continuity of the Jewish state. In fact, in an article written in 1999, Shalev contended that one of the general objectives of the educational efforts at the International School is "to strengthen each individual's personal commitment to a meaningful Jewish continuity, in view of his/her Jewish worldview and perception of the Jewish destiny."[116] At Lohamei Hagetaot, the importance of identification is particularly present in educational activities aimed at those tasked with this objective: IDF soldiers, who have been offered educational workshops at the institute since the 1980s. An internal document on educational activities for soldiers and commanders at the house states that the activities include "learning about the relationship between the experiences that Jews went through in the Shoah and the struggle for the existence of the state of Israel [to] deepen the understanding of the uniqueness of the IDF [...]."[117] Furthermore, the document stipulates that one of the main goals of this learning experience is "understanding the importance of establishing a strong and moral army [...] and the

---

[114] Yad Mordechai, *The Journey to Poland* (Museum Yad Mordechai, undated), 1 (in Hebrew).

[115] Inbal Kvity, "Not Just a Number, an Educational Approach to the Holocaust Victims," *Yad Vashem Magazine*, Fall 2001, 6,7.

[116] Avner Shalev, "Different School," *Yad Vashem Magazine*, Winter 1999, 3.

[117] GFH, *Returning with Soldiers. A Study Day for Officers al the Ghetto Fighters House following the Journey to Poland as "Witnesses in Uniform"* (Museum Lohamei Hagetaot, undated), 1 (in Hebrew).

personal commitment of every soldier to strengthening the state [of Israel]."[118]

A continued emphasis on the need for a strong state in the wake of the Holocaust, however, does not necessarily encourage the creation of a "moral army" or "an army based on institutional principles and universal Jewish values," as promised in workshop brochures.[119] While not acknowledged by the current educational director at Lohamei Hagetaot, a report published by *Haaretz* in July 1989, entitled "In the Battalion They Knew That We Were a Killer Company," found that educational programs for the army had been temporarily suspended at Lohamei Hagetaot.[120] Officially, the suspension took place because the army contended that the educational programs were not functioning properly, as the guides meant to accompany the soldiers were not sufficiently trained. Unofficially, however, the article argued that the suspension occurred as a result of the extreme violence used by soldiers, referring to themselves as the Mengele Unit, in the Occupied Territories in response to the Nazi brutality they had seen in the museum.[121] Further evidence that the content of Holocaust museums could encourage dubious military action was offered in a report published in 1998, which found that following a visit to the original museum at Yad Vashem students showed significantly greater agreement with the statement "one of the lessons of the Holocaust is that every action that the Jewish people undertake to ensure their existence is justified."[122] Despite the publication of these findings, which showed the nefarious consequences of the image of Israel "as the defender of the Jewish people" and a continuing "need to prevent another Holocaust," the espousal of these educational messages has continued throughout the years, including in times of extreme violence.[123] In the fall of 2002, during the height of the Al-Aqsa Intifadah, an article was published in Yad Vashem's magazine, which noted that even though "the IDF has had to channel the greater part of its energies into defending Israeli citizens, [...] data shows an increase of visiting soldiers [from] all military units and all army ranks."[124] While not definitively explaining the rise in visits during the Second Intifadah, Colonel Elazar Stern maintained that the

[118] Ibid.   [119] Ibid.   [120] Interview conducted with Rotem Korblitt on April 17, 2016.
[121] Dan Sagir, "In the Battalion They Knew That We Were a Killer Company," *Haaretz*, July 31, 1989, 11.
[122] Bickman and Hamner, "Evaluation of the Yad Vashem," 442.
[123] Interview conducted with Rotem Korblitt on April 17, 2016.
[124] Anonymous, "Yad Vashem in the Frontlines of IDF Education," *Yad Vashem Magazine*, Fall 2002, 2,3.

aim of studying the Holocaust at Yad Vashem during these times would
not only strengthen the soldiers' connection to the citizens of Israel but
additionally would enable IDF soldiers and commanders to apply the
moral lessons from the Holocaust to their own conduct and the ways in
which "they treat their enemies."[125]

Keeping the Holocaust in a Narrow Jewish Ghetto

During interviews conducted with high-level employees at the Holocaust
institutes under review, consistent importance was placed on the conveyance of the so-called universal and moral lessons of the Holocaust in the
institutes' exhibits and educational programs. Yet, the unequivocal
emphasis on the need for a strong Israeli state and the understanding
of the Holocaust as a national tragedy, which stands at the heart of the
mnemonic practices at these institutes, questions the very transmission
and internalization of "humanitarian values of tolerance and moral
courage."[126] Moreover, while the desired conveyance of "humanistic
and democratic values" would indicate that the presentation of the
Holocaust is "relevant from a human, a universal and a Jewish point of
view," the actual presentation of the Holocaust as a uniquely Jewish
experience at Lohamei Hagetaot,[127] Yad Mordechai, and Yad Vashem
demonstrates that the Holocaust is, in fact, solely relevant from a Jewish
perspective.[128] Consequently, these museums are a physical testament
to Charles Maier's 1993 work, which opines that despite the "ostensible
purpose of Holocaust museums to teach the [universal] lessons of
the Holocaust," the real lesson of these museums is that "the group

---

[125] Ibid.
[126] Yad Vashem, *Achievements and Challenges: Annual Report 2002* (Yad Vashem, 2011), 14.
[127] It is worth pointing out that in January 2015, Lohamei Hagetaot started carrying the
temporary exhibit "Deadly Medicine: Creating the Master Race," on loan from the
United States Holocaust Memorial Museum, which discussed Nazi racial health
policies. Somewhat problematically, however, the exhibit's introductory plaque failed
to specify the ethnicity and number of people who were targeted by these policies,
instead noting: "Guided by claims of biological superiority, the Nazis strived ruthlessly
not to perfect mankind, but to create a 'superior, Aryan race.' In this drive, they
implemented the 'Final Solution' that resulted in the murder of six million Jews and
persecuted or killed many others viewed as threats to the 'health' of the nation." Email
exchange with Anat Bratman-Elhalel, Archives Director Lohamei Hagetaot on
February 16, 2020.
[128] See Lohamei Hagetaot's statement on the Holocaust which notes that the Holocaust is
examined as a historical and universal crisis. Furthermore, the institute claims that
dealing with the Holocaust can "lead to understanding the importance of humanistic
and democratic values." "The Center for Humanistic Education," Lohamei Hagetaot,
www.gfh.org.il/?CategoryID=222&ArticleID, accessed January 15, 2016 (in Hebrew).

sponsoring the museum has suffered incredibly and wants recognition of the fact."[129]

At Yad Vashem, "the Jewish people's living memorial to the Holocaust," the creation of a "uniquely Jewish narrative" is sought through what Shalev termed "an experiential dimension."[130] This dimension includes "emphasizing the tragically unique Jewish experience of the Holocaust" through the usage of testimony, which, as noted previously, seeks to elicits visitors' compassion for victims of the Shoah.[131] Here, it is worth pointing out that the only three plaques in Yad Vashem on non-Jewish victims of the Nazis do not contain any witness testimony. Moreover, the historical information contained on the plaques is emblematic of minimization efforts found in schoolbooks (see Chapter 2). A combination of these aforementioned marginalization efforts can be seen on the first small plaque dedicated to non-Jewish victims in the new museum. Entitled "Non-Jewish Victims of Persecution and Oppression," the plaque discusses the fate of Roma, Sinti, homosexuals, and Jehovah's Witnesses during the Second World War in seven sentences without providing any insight into their fate at the hands of the Nazis and failing to offer precise numbers on deaths suffered by each group.[132] Explicit minimization of the number of non-Jewish victims was also found in Yad Vashem's exhibit. Thus, despite the fact that a symposium held at Yad Vashem in 2001 declared that the "continued euthanasia program" claimed some 250,000 victims by 1945, the plaque used in the new museum four years later, entitled "The Murder of Mentally Ill and Handicapped," asserts that only "some 70,000 German and Austrian children and adults were murdered" as a result of Hitler's euthanasia program.[133]

[129] Charles S. Maier, "A Surfeit of Memory? Reflections on History, Melancholy and Denial," *History and Memory* 5:2 (1993): 143, 144.
[130] Shalev, "Holocaust," 23, 24; Leah Goldstein, "Not Just a History Lesson," *Yad Vashem Magazine*, December 2013, 2–5.
[131] Leah Goldstein, "The Museum Complex: A Source of Inspiration," *Yad Vashem Magazine*, December 2013, 24, 25.
[132] The plaque reads: "The Nazi regime persecuted and victimized members of various groups that it considered enemies of the Reich. The Roma and Sinti were defined as racially inferior and antisocial due to their way of life. Thousands of the 44,000 who lived in the Reich were sent to concentration camps. Others were sent to ghettos and extermination camps. Homosexuals were outlawed because the Nazis considered them detrimental to the goal of natural procreation and wholesome family life. Some 15,000 homosexuals were interned in camps where several thousand of them perished due to conditions. Another small minority, Jehovah's [W]itnesses were persecuted because of their pacifist beliefs." Observation conducted on May 7, 2016.
[133] Anonymous, "The Nazi Euthanasia Program: A Symposium," *Yad Vashem Magazine*, Summer 2001, 16. See Table 2.1.

While precise insight into individual organizational decisions behind the contemporary exhibit are lacking, research and publications by high-level Yad Vashem employees do reveal a wider tendency to keep the Holocaust, in the words of Holocaust researcher Daniel Blatman, in "its traditional historiographical ghetto."[134] In a 2014 essay, Dan Michman, head of Yad Vashem's International Institute for Holocaust Research, criticized historians such as Donald Bloxham who try to conceptualize the Holocaust within a multidisciplinary historical and social framework while "'antisemitism' is understood simplistically as another group hatred, and the sheer intensity of the effort to eradicate the Jews is not explained."[135] Another example is Robert Rozett, also a Yad Vashem historian, who in 2012 criticized Lizzie Collingham's book on food rationing in Nazi Germany, the Soviet Union, China, and Japan during the Second World War for failing to single out the uniqueness of the Nazis' policy towards the Jews.[136]

Invoking Elkana's controversial 1988 article, Blatman argues that the exclusivity of the Holocaust, which disregards the destruction of other populations by the Nazi regime and keeps "the Holocaust in a narrow Jewish ghetto," creates a "readiness to believe that the whole world is against us, and that we are the eternal victims."[137] Livnat, the minister of education between 2001 and 2006, reinforced Blatman's thesis by claiming that especially for the children and descendants of the Holocaust Yad Vashem bears the heavy task of conveying the message that "in every generation, each person must see himself as though he were a Holocaust survivor."[138] Yet, this "melancholic exclusive narra-tive" at Yad Vashem is not only used to perpetuate "a profound existen-tial angst."[139] Rather, Blatman notes that a "victim-centered discourse" is used as a powerful political tool to "whitewash the ongoing crime

---

[134] Blatman, "Holocaust," 39.

[135] Michman goes on to argue that those who proclaim an anti-uniqueness approach "are irritated by the notion of the 'uniqueness' of one case, sometimes owing to political attitudes regarding the Israeli-Palestinian conflict." Dan Michman, "The Jewish Dimension of the Holocaust in Dire Straits? Current Challenges of Interpretation and Scope," in *Jewish Histories of the Holocaust: New Transnational Approaches*, ed. Norman J. W. Goda (New York: Berghahn Books, 2014), 20, 22.

[136] It is worth noting that Rozett's criticism of Donald Bloxham's scholarship coincides with denouncing the latter's rendering of responsibility for the Palestinian refugee issue on Israeli shoulders. Robert Rozett, "Diminishing the Holocaust: Scholarly Fodder for a Discourse of Distortion," *Israel Journal of Foreign Affairs* 6:1 (2012): 56, 58.

[137] Elkana called for an end to the "death cult" of Holocaust commemoration and called on his readers to not send kids to Yad Vashem. Elkana, "Plea," 13.

[138] Limor Livnat, "Greetings from Israeli Heads of State," *Yad Vashem Magazine*, Fall 2003, 5.

[139] Goldberg, "Jewish," 201.

against the Palestinians" and "maintain the occupation in Palestine."[140] Explaining this phenomenon, the historian Peter Novick contended that while the principal lesson of the Holocaust is that it sensitizes us to oppression and atrocity, making it "*the* benchmark of oppression and atrocity works in precisely the opposite direction" and leads to a trivialization of events deemed of lesser magnitude.[141]

The most apparent physical manifestation of this trifling lies in the fact that displacement of Palestinians on the very land where Holocaust institutes currently lie – creating a physical connection between the Holocaust and the Nakba – is wholly ignored. Kibbutz Lohamei Hagetaot, established on the ruined village of Samaria, for instance, fails to make any reference to the former Palestinian inhabitants of the settlement of Samaria.[142] At Yad Mordechai, which following the 1948 War expanded on the land of the Palestinian village of Hiribya, the displacement of Palestinians is similarly overlooked, creating an ironic reversal of the museum's concept, namely from (Israeli) revival to (Palestinian) catastrophe.[143] The most overt dissonance between remembrance and forgetting can be found at Yad Vashem, which like Yad Mordechai and Lohamei Hagetaot lies on the vestiges of a Palestinian village. Beyond the disregard of the Palestinian foundations upon which Yad Vashem was built, the redemptive landscape viewed upon exiting the museum does not symbolize a pure rebirth.[144] The current Israeli localities of Givat

[140] Daniel Blatman, "Yad Vashem Is Derelict in Its Duty to Free the Shoah from Its Jewish Ghetto," *Haaretz*, May 19, 2016.
[141] Emphasis added. Peter Novick, *The Holocaust in American Life* (Boston/New York: First Mariner Books, 2000), 14.
[142] The first settlers wanted to preserve the name of the ruined Palestinian village and decided to call the kibbutz Lohamei Hagetaot "Samaria." The JNF told them that the conjoining of ghetto fighters and the memory of Samaria was unthinkable and ruled that the kibbutz be named Asher, after the Israelite tribe that had inhabited the area in ancient times. Segev, *Seventh Million*, 451.
[143] Interestingly, the minutes of a staff meeting in June 1999 on the ideological nature of the museum do indicate awareness of the historical occurrence of a physical palimpsest. Thus, during the meeting, one museum staff member stated: "We also must introduce the topic of the Arabs who were expelled from their land during the War of Independence to the museum." Yad Mordechai, *Summary of Museum Staff Meeting* (Museum Yad Mordechai, June 1999), 1 (in Hebrew); Khalidi, *All*, 102.
[144] In the case of Yad Vashem, Khirbet Hamama, the Palestinian hamlet destroyed during the 1948 War, upon which Yad Vashem was built, is also ignored and remains unheard of by most Israelis. Further excluded from the narrative at Yad Vashem is the former Palestinian village of Ein Karem, visible directly below the Connecting Path. Ein Karem used to be one of the biggest villages in the Jerusalem district in terms of space and population and included 2,510 Muslims and 670 Christians. The village was occupied in July 1948, and in 1949, the Israelis established the colonies of Beit Zayit and Even Sapir on the village grounds. Feldman, "Between Yad Vashem and Mt. Herzl," 1161; Honaida Ghanim, "When Yaffa Met (J)Yaffa: Intersections between the Holocaust and

Shaul Beth and Har Nof, within sight of Yad Vashem and less than two miles away, are situated on the remains of the former Palestinian village of Deir Yassin, where on April 9, 1948 between 100 and 120 Palestinians were killed by Irgun and Lehi units.[145] Honaida Ghanim notes that the physical "obliteration" that was involved in the construction and location of Yad Vashem – upon the Palestinian lands of Khirbet al Hamama – can impact Palestinians' experience of the institute and its educational efforts. Palestinians passing by or visiting Yad Vashem, as Ghanim argues, would not intersect with the "purportedly objective role of the compound [and rather] he or she would intersect with its context in terms of its relationship with him or her and its theft of his or her own landscape, one that stretches out between Deir Yassin and Ein Karem, with all their implications in the catastrophe-stricken Palestinian history."[146] Indeed, in an empirical self-study, Ghassan Abdallah found that upon his visit to the memorial, he could not "help looking with a Palestinian's eyes and heart. And my reactions could not be isolated from the recent history of our country, invaded and taken over by force, money, intrigue, and alliances with the powerful of the day [...] how do you explain engraving Jewish communities in solid rock, in the Valley of Jewish Communities, while destroying Palestinian communities and erasing to the ground more than 400 of their villages?"[147]

Attempts to expose visitors at Yad Vashem to "look to the north and remember Deir Yassin" have fallen subject to scrutiny by the institute itself.[148] In 2009, Itamar Shapira, a guide at Yad Vashem, was fired after talking to a group "about the massacre at Deir Yassin [in order to indicate] that [while] we talk about the establishment of a refuge for world Jewry here after the Shoah, [there] were people already on this land and there are other traumas that drive other people."[149] Following the tour, complaints were made by a participant claiming that the guide

the Nakba in the Shadow of Zionism," in *The Holocaust and the Nakba: A New Grammar of Trauma and History*, ed. Amos Goldberg and Bashir Bashir (New York: Columbia University Press, 2018), 104.

[145] Benny Morris, *1948: A History of the First Arab–Israeli War* (New Haven: Yale University Press, 2008), 127. According to Pappé, the number of victims at Deir Yassin stands at 93, which does not include those killed in actual battle. Pappé, *Ethnic Cleansing*, 90–91.

[146] Ghanim, "When Yaffa Met (J)Yaffa," 104.

[147] Ghassan Abdallah, "A Palestinian at Yad Vashem," *Jerusalem Quarterly* 15 (2002): 43.

[148] Masalha, "Remembering the Palestinian Nakba," 145; Marc H. Ellis and Daniel A. McGowan, eds., *Remembering Deir Yassin: The Future of Israel and Palestine* (New York: Interlink Publishing Group, 1998), 6, 7.

[149] Yoav Stern, "A Guide at Yad Vashem Is Fired after Comparing the Suffering of the Jews to the Suffering of the Palestinians," *Haaretz*, April 23, 2009, www.haaretz.co.il/news/education/1.1257108, accessed April 25, 2014.

"is not allowed to use his position to transfer personal views […] especially not interpretations that have far-reaching current political implications." Despite dedicating itself to "building bridges of understanding
and tolerance," Yad Vashem saw itself compelled to let Shapira go,
because, as a spokesperson stated, "the institute is strict in keeping the
Holocaust out of any political agenda in its professional work – be it right
or left."[150]

Concluding Remarks

Although presented as the ultimate form of revival, the establishment of
Israel following the destruction of the Holocaust did not constitute a
complete rehabilitation in Israeli-Jewish consciousness. While maintaining a continual need for a strong Israeli state, the emphasis on a Jewish
rebirth in the wake of the Holocaust thus prompts the merging of the
dissonant categories of victim and victor. Identified both at Israeli
Holocaust institutes and in annual Holocaust commemorative ceremonies, the representation of each category in mnemonic form and in
content conceives of an eternal cycle of destruction and resurrection,
albeit one in which the latter – a metaphor for the existence of a strong
Israeli state and army – is merely a safeguard against the reoccurrence of
the former. Consequently, the conscious searing of the Holocaust into
the Israeli national calendar and landscape – itself emblematic of a
(figurative) "landscape as memory" – indexes the Holocaust as a constant reminder of a national tragedy through which all contemporary
actions must be contemplated.

The Zionization of the Holocaust, importantly, challenges the achievement of the universal pedagogic goals and democratic lessons espoused
by mnemonic agents at the three Holocaust institutes reviewed in this
chapter: Yad Vashem, Yad Mordechai, and Lohamei Hagetaot. The
accentuation of a commitment to ensuring the strength of the Israeli
state, as revealed in internal documents, highlights the particularistic
messages conveyed through educational workshops, which center on
securing Jewish continuity and the need to prevent another Holocaust.
The identification of a uniquely Jewish-Zionist narrative in the new
museum of Israel's most important memory site, Yad Vashem, moreover
suggests that in the process of appropriating the Holocaust as an Israeli-
Jewish tragedy, narratives that do not conform have become marginalized. Beyond the overt minimization of the fate of non-Jewish victims and

---

[150] Ibid.

post-Holocaust diasporic Jewry, the Zionist panacea channeled at the memory sites also demands a foregoing of the physical Palestinian history of the three sites themselves. Rebuked as a political act by Yad Vashem in 2009, visitors to the historic exhibits and participants in annual mnemonic rituals thus continue to (un)consciously take part in a cultural palimpsest as they are propelled to remember the superimposed Jewish watershed rather than the Nakba.

The following chapter illustrates, however, that it is not solely the physical insertion of the Holocaust in the landscape that drives the cultural palimpsest. In contrast to the implicit allusions in Holocaust mnemonics to the actor driving an incessant danger in the wake of resurrection, mass media output on the Holocaust articulates this threat explicitly in the context of the ongoing regional conflict. The effects of mediated equations between Palestinians and Nazis are twofold, namely undermining Israeli peace negotiations and, simultaneously, impeding any recognition of the Nakba, repeatedly castigated as a false myth propagated by those who seek to eradicate Israel.

Part III

Scoop on the Past

"Journalism," argued the American journalist Alan Barth in 1943, "is the first rough draft of history."[1] While Barth, with this statement, sought to demonstrate the media's importance in determining what in the future should be considered as having mattered today, for much if not most of the public, journalism also constitutes a primary source of information about a more distant past and shared understandings of that past.[2] While media's usage of distant historical events is somewhat counterintuitive due to the importance of temporal proximity in news, the prevalence of the present in the work of media professionals has been conclusively challenged by revealing the ongoing presence of the past in daily reporting, leading media scholar Carolyn Kitch to conclude that journalism is "full of the past."[3] The application of the past in media, what José van Dijk terms "mediated memories,"[4] is varied and includes the dissemination of public and private histories, historical contextualization of present-day events, and anniversary journalism.[5] Of particular importance here are the latter two applications of the past in which the past is narrated in service of "the beliefs and spiritual needs of the present" and through narration of the present, creating the concept of a "reversed memory."[6]

---

[1] Cited in Martin Conboy, ed., *How Journalism Uses History* (New York: Routledge, 2012), 33.
[2] Carolyn Kitch, "Placing Journalism inside Memory – and Memory Studies," *Memory Studies* 1 (2008): 311.
[3] Ibid., 311, 312.
[4] José van Dijck, *Mediated Memories in the Digital Age* (Stanford: Stanford University Press, 2007), 21.
[5] Media's preoccupation with the past stands as evidence against Barbie Zelizer's contention that journalists "neither explicitly speak of the past nor consider the past as part of their obvious purview." Barbie Zelizer, "Why Memory's Work on Journalism Does Not Reflect Journalism's Work on Memory," *Memory Studies* 1 (2008): 80.
[6] Motti Neiger, Eyal Zandberg, and Oren Meyers, "On Media Memory: Collective Memory in the New Media Age," in *Journalism and Memory*, ed. Barbie Zelizer and Keren Tenenboim-Weinblatt (Houndmills/Basingstoke/Hampshire: Palgrave Macmillan, 2014), 115.

Mediated pasts' contemporary objectives can take the form of a curriculum. Thus, the historical contextualization of the present not only presupposes news consumers as constant students, whose previous consumption of the past creates usable knowledge of the present, but also seeks to provide meaningful context to the present through importation of the past.[7] A more mission-oriented purpose can equally underlie the invocation of the past. In contrast to the "retrospective memory" characteristic of past usage for analogical purposes, the past – as a "prospective memory" – can be instrumentalized as a lesson to spur on a to-do list and to encourage the execution of an intended action.[8]

The concept of prospective memory constitutes a useful distinction in media's coverage of commemorative rituals, succinctly termed anniversary journalism.[9] Like holidays that halt everyday routines, anniversary journalism is guided by a series of special announcements and preludes that transform daily coverage into something special, which upon the conclusion of the event is guided back to regular "mediation." According to Jill Edy, anniversary journalism does not typically attempt to connect the past to the present in any meaningful way.[10] Yet, while media coverage of commemorative rituals can solely center on invoking the historical event(s) being commemorated, an emphasis on the commemorative act and the commemorative motives involved in restoring the past to the present can shape consumers' prospective concerns and actions. Indeed, ceremonial media events, particularly when enacted and depicted by the same hegemonic group, remind audiences what is worth remembering and simultaneously encourage participation in the mediated commemoration, enabling the members of the group – both the audience and the journalists alike – to manifest and perform their sense of belonging.[11] Kitch's research on anniversary journalism in American magazines in this context can be considered a useful framework, as it revealed that the construction of an orderly mediated American past encouraged a retrospective collective meaning and a communal belonging among both the magazine's staff and its audience.[12]

---

[7] Ibid., 11; James Carey, *Communications as Culture* (London: Routledge, 1989), 151–152.

[8] Keren Tenenboim-Weinblatt, "Journalism as an Agent of Prospective Memory," in Zelizer and Tenenboim-Weinblatt, ed., *Journalism and Memory*, 213.

[9] Carolyn Kitch, "Anniversary Journalism, Collective Memory, and the Cultural Authority to Tell the Story of the American Past," *Journal of Popular Culture* 36 (2002): 44–67.

[10] Jill A. Edy, "Journalistic Uses of Collective Memory," *Journal of Communication* 49 (1999): 76.

[11] Daniel Dayan and Elihu Katz, *Media Events: The Live Broadcasting of History* (Cambridge, MA/London: Harvard University Press, 1992), 16.

[12] This study focused on magazines' anniversaries of their own founding. Kitch, "Anniversary Journalism, Collective Memory, and the Cultural Authority," 44–67.

The Mediation of a National Identity

Memory scholars have found that through the creation and recreation of a nation's past, media are pivotal to the construction of individual and collective memory.[13] The media's role in the formation of a national consciousness is twofold. First, media shape a common social belonging through the collective and uniform act of media participation, creating what the political scientist Benedict Anderson termed an "imagined community."[14] The emergence of a shared national understanding, according to Anderson, principally manifests through a collective engagement, whereby the reading of a paper can take on the form and meaning of a "state ritual," "performed in silent privacy, in the lair of the skull [with] each communicant [being] well aware that the ceremony he performs is being replicated simultaneously by thousands (or millions) of others of whose existence he is confident, yet of whose identity he has not the slightest notion."[15] In addition to enforcing belonging through an imagined connectivity, the media also play a formative role in the construction of a collective history by transmitting "mediated pasts." Indeed, because few in a mainstream audience experience the past through a personal connection, media not only constitute one of the primary venues through which the past is exposed but, through their ability to reach huge communities, are equally able to dictate what – and how – histories need to be conserved.[16]

Far from being external instruments that hold versions of the past, media – like all mnemonic realms – construct a sense of the past. Addressing the role of American journalists in shaping the memory of John F. Kennedy's assassination, Barbie Zelizer found that the story of America's past "will remain in part a story of what the media have chosen to remember, a story of how the media's memories have in turn become America's own."[17] It follows that despite the documentary style of journalists' work, media's memories should not be considered an objective or innocent reflection of the past; instead, the media shape the past based

---

[13] Van Dijck, *Mediated Memories*, xiv.   [14] Anderson, *Imagined Communities*, 6.
[15] Ibid., 35, 36.   [16] Edy, "Journalistic Uses," 71.
[17] Edy's 2006 study further revealed the effects of news coverage on the public's interpretation of historic events. Contrasting news coverage of two events spawned by social unrest – the 1968 Democratic National Convention and the 1965 riots in Watts – Edy found that the media's varied interpretations of the causes and outcomes of the events were reflected in the public's mind. Jill Edy, *Troubled Pasts: News and the Collective Memory of Social Unrest* (Philadelphia: Temple University Press, 2006), 191; Barbie Zelizer, *Covering the Body: The Kennedy Assassination, the Media, and the Shaping of Collective Memory* (Chicago/London: University of Chicago Press, 1992), 214.

on contemporary needs and concerns.[18] One of the most influential and widely used frameworks for understanding the ways in which the press shape present concerns and future actions has been the notion of agenda setting. The media's agenda, which in turn influences the public agenda and – at times – the policy agenda, is conceptualized based on the amount and prominence of coverage given to particular issues within the media. While the concept of a media agenda has typically referred to contemporary political and societal events, it can also be applied to present-day exposure to historical events. Accordingly, an emphasis on historical events can infer a desire to bring these topics to the center of public attention, as topics targeted and focused on by the mass media will be perceived as important by media consumers.[19] Evidence that journalists' depictions of the past have repercussions for the ways in which a community relates to its past was given in a study conducted by Ingrid Volkmer in 2006. Applying Karl Mannheim's theory of "generational knowledge," Volkmer found that across three different generations individual's memories of major public events varied according to contemporary mass media images and texts relating to those events.[20]

The Media as an Interpretative Memory Community

Although the media, similarly to other "interpretative memory communities," are responsible for the creation and dissemination of public and private histories, these mediated memories fall within a larger cultural context. As such, media frames are best understood as organizing themes that are used to place events into an existing package that resonates with the audience. The necessity of the dialogical nature of media is, again, twofold. First, it is clear that in the field of cultural production – both public and commercial – all media are influenced by common themes, such as financial considerations and ratings, or simply put "they need to keep their customers, readers, audiences and users happy."[21] In order to

---

[18] Andreas Huyssen, "Present Pasts: Media, Politics, Amnesia," *Public Culture* 12:1 (2000): 30.

[19] Keren Tenenboim-Weinblatt, "Journalism as an Agent," 213–225; Donald McCombs and David Shaw, "The Agenda Setting Function of Mass Media," *Public Opinion Quarterly* 36:2 (1972): 176–187.

[20] "Generational knowledge" defines each generation's "identity location" within a given society. According to Mannheim, individuals who belong to the same generation are "endowed, to an extent, with a common location in the historical dimension of the social process." Karl Mannheim, *Essays on the Sociology of Knowledge* (London: Routledge & Kegan Paul, 1952), 290, 292; Ingrid Volkmer, ed., *News in Public Memory: An International Study of Media Memories across Generations* (New York: Peter Lang, 2006), 307.

[21] Joanne Garde-Hansen, *Media and Memory* (Edinburgh: Edinburgh University Press, 2011), 50.

fulfill the needs of both media consumers and patrons, the media typically create output that reflects and maintains the cultural hegemony of
the societies which they serve.[22] Consequently, in the words of Gadi
Wolfsfeld, "news stories are almost always about us about what is happening
or could happen to us. When there is news about 'others,' it centers on how
they affect [sic] us," creating what Wolfsfeld termed a mediated "ethnocentric view of the world."[23] As such, even though (individual) media producers
are responsible for the creation of culturally resonant narratives as "creators of
meaning,"[24] the necessary dialogic interaction between journalists and audiences blurs the line between the media producer and the consumer. Indeed,
the maintenance of a society and the creation, representation, and celebration
of shared, even if illusory, beliefs infer an awareness and reception of
(changing) communal narratives and traditions and, simultaneously, through
the reproduction of these shared narratives and symbols, testifies to an active
engagement in the communal and communitive ritual, creating what can be
termed a "producing consumer." Based on this understanding, mediated
pasts are a reciprocal creation of the media and their audiences who based on
past and contemporary exposure together construct a collective and shared
memory – what David Lowenthal calls "a unifying web of retrospection."[25]

The media's reproduction of shared myths, symbols, and traditions means
that an analysis of media provides valuable insight into a society's self-
understanding and the construction of this self-image. Moreover, any historical picture constructed without taking the media into consideration
would be distorted, as an analysis of media along a time axis can reveal
how a society shapes its ideological framing and worldview over time,
illuminating "the politics of identity, community, [and] nation as well as
the workings of media."[26] With regard to Israeli society, Segev therefore
stresses the importance of the press as a historical source by claiming that any
historian relying on the Israeli press would know almost everything about the

---

[22] In the case of commercial media, the assumption is that mediated messages reach a mass
audience or at least are intended to appeal to a mass audience in order to maximize profit
and influence. Public service media similarly can be assumed to represent broadly shared
social values and understandings, albeit potentially somewhat more elite driven than in
commercial systems, and to seek a mass audience as a requirement of their funding with
taxpayer or ratepayer support. Jill A. Edy, "Collective Memory in a Post-Broadcast
World," in Zelizer and Tenenboim-Weinblatt, ed., *Journalism and Memory*, 67.
[23] Gadi Wolfsfeld, *Media and the Path to Peace* (Cambridge: Cambridge University Press,
2004), 22.
[24] Joseph Turow, "The Challenge of Inference in Interinstitutional Research on Mass
Communication," *Communication Research* 18:2 (1991): 224.
[25] David Lowenthal, *The Past Is a Foreign Country* (Cambridge: Cambridge University
Press, 1985), 198.
[26] Kitch, "Placing Journalism," 313; Marita Sturken, "Memory, Consumerism and Media:
Reflections on the Emergence of the Field," *Memory Studies* 1 (2008): 73.

society at any given point in time.[27] In coherence with the conception of the media as a mirror into – and a reflection of – a society's workings and self-perception, the final part of this work will analyze Israeli-Jewish and Palestinian media exposure on, respectively, the Holocaust and the Nakba.

Mass Traditional Mediation as a Monument of Historical Consciousness

The emphasis in this section will lie on one form of traditional mass media: print newspapers. Yet, modern media forms[28] will not be neglected. Instead, taking into account the rapid rise of online journalism in Israeli and Palestinian society over the last decade, this work's focus on traditional forms of mass media will be extended to include an analysis of the online representation of printed media content, thereby also laying bare the reconstruction of "traditional" content on electronic platforms. Both in Israeli-Jewish society and in Palestinian society, (online) newspapers are analyzed that in the period under analysis have enjoyed the largest readership and circulation and, through forming the most important *cadres sociaux*, offer insight into the dissemination of historical discourses that have been subject to mass exposure.

As such, Chapter 6 will provide an examination of the two dominant Israeli daily newspapers throughout the time period under review: *Yedioth Ahronot* and *Maariv*.[29] Similarly, Chapter 7 will concentrate on Palestinian newspapers with the highest circulation: *Kul al-Arab* and *Al-Quds*. Through the inclusion of these papers, the final chapter of this work differentiates between media production in Palestinian society within the 1948 borders and Palestinian society outside of the Green

---

[27] Akiba A. Cohen et al., *The Holocaust and the Press: Nazi War Crimes Trials in Germany and Israel* (Cresskill, NJ: Hampton Press, 2002), 4.

[28] With the rise of electronic forms of communication in the twenty-first century, the terms "media" or "mass media" have been applied to invoke both the dissemination of public and private information and narratives through "traditional" media channels and "modern" or "mass social" platforms. While the application of the term "media," both in media scholarship and everyday life, often converges with a failure to acknowledge a clear differentiation between traditional and modern forms of mass media, the invocation and study of print media, including newspapers and magazines and (early) broadcast media (such as photography, radio, film, and television), typically concerns traditional media forms. Conversely, electronic media, including mass communication platforms on the internet and electronic communication devices, can be defined as contemporary forms of modern mass communication. Garde-Hansen, *Media*, 1; Van Dijck, *Mediated Memories*, xiv, xv.

[29] It should be noted that since 2010, *Israel Hayom* (Hebrew: Israel today), a free daily national newspaper founded in 2007 with financial backing from Sheldon Adelson, has enjoyed more exposure on weekdays than *Yedioth Ahronot*. Margret Müller, *The World According to Israeli Newspapers* (Berlin: Frank & Timme GmbH Verlag, 2017), 97–100.

Line, namely the West Bank and East Jerusalem.[30] Moreover, the incorporation of an analysis of *al-Hayat al-Jadida*, the official daily newspaper of the Palestinian National Authority established in 1995, will provide an understanding of officially endorsed and sanctioned media content relating to *al-Nakba* by the PA.[31]

The concentration on mass mediation means that this section does not constitute an exhaustive representation of either the Palestinian or the Israeli media landscape. The emphasis on *Yedioth Ahronot* and *Maariv*, through their respective centrist and centrist/right-of-center political leanings,[32] thus forgoes the inclusion of the elite, liberal progressive newspaper *Haaretz*, the only Israeli newspaper that consistently calls for a critical self-examination of the Israeli Holocaust discourse.[33] Similarly, Chapter 7's concentration on the most important Fatah-affiliated newspapers, i.e., *al-Hayat al-Jadida* and *Al-Quds*, has implications for the presented research findings, which reveal a curious lack of criticism of the PA and its handling of the refugee issue. While not offering an in-depth examination of the purge of PA-critical newspapers,[34] this work does reveal the PA's carrot and stick approach to Palestinian publications, which has encouraged realm-wide self-censorship.[35]

The content put forward in the following two chapters derived from archival research conducted during the summer of 2016 at the National Library of Israel, where physical newspapers, digitalized newspapers, and newspapers on microfilm were consulted, and subsequent online

---

[30] Readership across these borders does exist. According to a 2002 PCBS report, *Kul al-Arab* is also read frequently in the West Bank, with 68.8 percent of respondents maintaining to read it. Moreover, findings revealed that in Gaza 44.6 percent aged 18 and over read *Al-Quds*, while only 1.9 percent read *Kul al-Arab*. 25.4 percent of Gazan inhabitants claimed to read *al-Hayat al-Jadida*; nevertheless, these numbers cannot be considered indicative of trends following Hamas' takeover of Gaza in 2007. PCBS, *Mass Media Survey 2000 – Main Findings* (PCBS, 2002), 75.
[31] Sariel Birnbaum, "Historical Discourse in the Media of the Palestinian National Authority," in *Palestinian Collective Memory and National Identity*, ed. Meir Litvak (Basingstoke: Palgrave Macmillan, 2009), 140.
[32] Yoel Cohen, *God, Jews and the Media: Religion and Israel's Media* (London/New York: Routledge, 2012), 35, 74.
[33] Oren Meyers, Motti Neiger, and Eyal Zandberg, *Communicating Awe: Media Memory and Holocaust Commemoration* (Basingstoke: Palgrave Macmillan, 2014), 42.
[34] Two newspapers in particular have paid a heavy price for criticism directed at the PA: *al-Nahār* (Arabic: the afternoon) and *al-Ummah* (Arabic: the Muslim nation). Amal Jamal, *Media Politics and Democracy in Palestine: Political Culture, Pluralism, and the Palestinian Authority* (Brighton: Sussex Academic Press, 2005), 74, 75, 89.
[35] Hillel Nossek and Khalil Rinnawi, "Censorship and Freedom of the Press Under Changing Political Regimes: Palestinian Media from Israeli Occupation to the Palestinian Authority," *Gazette* 65 (2003): 199.

research. Prioritizing media content on the role of the respective pasts in each society and the motives of their invocation, the research yielded a body of approximately 600 and 800 articles for the Palestinian and Israeli case study, respectively. In consideration of this work's primary focus, the examination of mediated memories of the Holocaust and the Nakba concentrates on anniversary journalism, which through its repetition provides a prime framework to illuminate the contemporary preoccupations of a society and the construction of "new images [which] overlay the old."[36] Thus, both in Israeli and Palestinian newspapers, a historical analysis of media content produced on memorial days – *Yom ha-Shoah* and *Yawm al-Nakbah*, respectively – as "monuments of a historical consciousness"[37] will highlight the construction and maintenance of a national collective memory vis-à-vis these historical events. Indeed, Holocaust Memorial Day[38] and Nakba Day editions of Israeli and Palestinian newspapers provide a systematic research corpus through their dealings with the same subject every year on exactly the same day. Each of the examined articles fits into one of three categories: news reporting, editorial, or column.[39] In addition to analyzing the textual content in these various writing modes, the visual framing of media content will also be taken into account by examining the placement of content within physical newspapers and discussing the existence of culturally resonant symbols in cartoons and graphics that accompany or reinforce printed and online textual content.

The primary focus in this final section on anniversary journalism will be accompanied by a secondary analysis on the construction of daily Nakba and Holocaust memories. Indeed, although anniversaries or annual commemorations form prime ritual occasions to remind societies of a need to mark "its story, its constitutive narrative,"[40] the incorporation of the past into routine media indicates an ongoing pertinence of the past to the present. As such, while anniversary journalism can be

---

[36] Maurice Halbwachs, *The Collective Memory*, trans. Francis J. Ditter, Jr. and Vida Yazdi Ditter (New York: Harper & Row, 1952), 72.

[37] Walter Benjamin cited in Khalili, *Heroes and Martyrs of Palestine*, 81.

[38] As Holocaust Memorial Day, similar to religious Jewish holidays, commences at sundown, newspaper content will be analyzed on both the day preceding the memorial day and on Holocaust Memorial Day itself.

[39] Research on readership response has suggested that editorials are of particular influence on news consumers. See, for instance, a 1998 study that found that newspapers' editorial content was significantly related to candidate preferences in the 1992 elections in the United States. Russell J. Dalton, Paul A. Beck, and Robert Huckfeldt, "Partisan Cues and the Media: Information Flows in the 1992 Presidential Election," *The American Political Science Review* 92:1 (1998): 111.

[40] Robert Neelly Bellah et al., *Habits of the Heart: Individualism and Commitment in American Life* (Berkeley: University of California Press, 1985), 153.

considered a "realm of memory" in Norian terminology, the existence of daily mediated memories evidences that the media are not a memory site encompassing remnants of a past "swept away by history."[41] It is in this context that semi-structured interviews conducted with Palestinian and Israeli journalists on their role as memory agents will be illuminating as they testify to the desire and need to include their societies' respective pasts in routine media so as to continually evoke the past and its contemporary meaning. Crucially, however, in line with the dialogical understanding of media set out previously, media professionals, as "the people behind the text," will not be considered creators of novel mnemonic interpretations, but rather as constructors of cultural-interpretive media frames.[42] Consequently, the media mnemonic output presented in the following two chapters is considered a reflection of the respective societies' *Zeitgeist* and the cultural and political environment that dictate a resounding application of their foundational pasts.

[41] Nora, *Realms of Memory*, 2.   [42] Zandberg, "The Right to Tell the (Right) Story," 6.

6   Never Forget and Never Again

In his seminal book *Zakhor* (1982) (Hebrew: remember), Yosef Hayim Yerushalmi argued that the traditional response to disaster is collectivization and ritualization – processes that give collective meaning to personal experiences through a collective narrative.[1] In Israel, mass printed and, since the mid-2000s, online media not only reflect and contribute to a collective ongoing engagement with the Holocaust but also engage in its ritualization by inscribing the past into the present. Nevertheless, few studies have been conducted on the presentation of Holocaust memory in the Israeli press and, to date, none have concentrated on the systematic existence of exclusive narratives in daily mass media and in media output on Memorial Day to the Holocaust and Heroism (MDHH).[2]

Among the few collective spheres of Holocaust transmission in Israel, including those previously discussed in this work, media, through their daily presence, can be considered a major realm of mnemonic transmission. Indeed, despite financial constraints and gloomy forecasts as a result of intensifying competition with various other media, Israel's press (print and online) has remained a formative platform to convey collective narratives and to frame the past with contemporary meaning.[3] The influence of the press in the public domain is demonstrated by the sheer numbers of media consumers in Israel.[4] According to research conducted in the mid-2000s, more than 71 percent of the Israeli population read at least one daily paper and nearly 84 percent read a weekend paper. Of those reading a daily paper, more than one quarter spend over an hour

---

[1] Yosef Hayim Yerushalmi, *Zakhor: Jewish History and Jewish Memory* (Seattle: University of Washington Press, 1989), 15, 44.
[2] Systematic studies conducted on the Holocaust in the Israeli press exist in works by Moshe Zuckermann (1993), Akiva Cohen et al. (2002), Hillel Nossek (1994), and Zandberg, Neiger, and Meyers (2008; 2014).
[3] Dan Caspi, "A Revised Look at Online Journalism in Israel: Entrenching the Old Hegemony," *Israel Affairs* 17:3 (2011): 344.
[4] Yoram Peri, *Telepopulism. Media and Politics in Israel* (Stanford: Stanford University Press, 2004), 25.

reading the daily news.[5] In their daily readings, consumers of printed media in Israel rely on approximately twenty-two popular commercial daily newspapers of which *Yedioth Ahronot* and *Maariv* are the most influential. Since the founding of *Maariv* in February 1948 by dissidents of *Yedioth Ahronot*, the two newspapers have constantly competed for the largest readership. While *Maariv* took the helm in the first two decades following the establishment of the Israeli state, in the mid-1970s, *Yedioth Ahronot* took over the lead, maintaining its position there ever since.[6] In the period under examination in this study, *Yedioth Ahronot* was read by about two-thirds of the Israeli population and enjoyed a circulation of approximately 300,000 on weekdays and 600,000 on the weekend.[7] Targeting a similar mainstream audience through its combination of hard news and softer, tabloidlike coverage, *Maariv* is considered the second most popular newspaper in Israel, with a circulation of about 160,000 on weekdays and 270,000 on weekends.[8] The traditional dominance of *Yedioth Ahronot* and *Maariv* in the Israeli media landscape is also reflected in online usage of their corresponding news websites, titled *ynet.co.il* and *nrg.co.il*, which were set up in 2000 and 2004, respectively.[9] Research published in 2011 by the Israeli media researcher Dan Caspi on the percentage of hits by Israeli internet users showed that 59.6 percent of Israel's online media consumers, constituting two-and-a-quarter million Jewish citizens of Israel, consulted the *Ynet* page, whereas 23.5 percent or about 900,000 people consumed news through *Maariv's* website.[10]

Israel's above-mentioned two leading newspapers will stand central in the exploration of mass-mediated Holocaust memories in Israel's press. Through providing a systematic "cultural seismograph" of annual media content on MDHH and, subsequently, daily Holocaust output, this chapter not only evidences a heightened centrality of the Holocaust in

---

[5] Ibid., 3, 18, 19.
[6] Yoel Cohen, "Yedioth Aharonoth," in *Encyclopaedia Judaica*, ed. Michael Berenbaum and Fred Skolnik (The University of Michigan: Macmillan Reference USA, 2007), 293.
[7] Cohen et al., *The Holocaust and the Press*, 49, 50.   [8] Ibid., 49, 50.
[9] In addition to producing their own online content, in order not to threaten the interests of the printed papers, these websites rely on the papers for content. Caspi, "Revised Look at Online Journalism," 351, 353; Cohen, "Yedioth," 293.
[10] According to Caspi, *Walla* is the only Hebrew website that attracts more surfers than *Ynet*, largely because the portal offers abundant services, including web-based e-mail. Caspi, "Revised Look at Online Journalism," 328, 352, 353. Research conducted three years earlier, in 2008, conversely, named *Ynet* the most popular portal in Israel, with about 800,000 unique visitors a day. Nathan Lipson and Maayan Cohen, "Ynet Is the Leading Internet Portal," *Haaretz*, June 23, 2008, www.haaretz.com/print-edition/business/ynet-is-the-leading-israeli-internet-portal-1.248301, accessed September 11, 2017.

the wake of the Oslo Peace Accords but also reveals an increased contextualization of the Holocaust in line with contemporary societal and
political concerns, including those emanating from the ongoing Israeli-
Palestinian crisis. Consequently, even outside of MDHH's ritual media
event, the Holocaust remains a newsworthy narrative, constituting a
historical framework in which to view the present. It is because of this
analogical practice of "Holocaust framing" and the semblance of a never-
ceasing diasporic and domestic threat that this chapter testifies to the
mediated existence of a persistent Jewish suffering. The final paragraphs
of this chapter illustrate the effects of the presentation of an incessant
genocidal threat, including at the hands of the Palestinians, by charting
the mediated articulation of a superior Israeli-Jewish victimhood narrative in which the Holocaust is presented as a "constructionist narrative."
Castigated as a historical myth, the Palestinians' foundational history,
conversely, is portrayed as a form of propaganda used to spread vengeance and ensure that the Holocaust forms a perpetual reminder of, in
the words of a 2002 *Maariv* supplement, "Pain which has no end."[11]

The Israeli Media Landscape and the Holocaust: A Brief Overview

Chapter 2 of this work noted that the trial in Jerusalem in 1961 of
Adolf Eichmann has often been considered the beginning of a public
Israeli consciousness of the Holocaust. The increased awareness of the
Holocaust and the horrors of Nazism, according to scholars who uphold
the notion of a turning point in 1961, emanated from the mass media
exposure that accompanied the trial, exposing many Israelis for the first
time to a multitude of survivors' accounts, including those who did not
bear arms during the war.[12] Amit Pinchevski, Tamar Liebes, and Ora
Herman noted in their 2007 study "Eichmann on the Air" that the
complete and continuous recording of the proceedings, daily reports,
and live broadcasts by Israel's public radio station, *Kol Yisrael* (Hebrew:
voice of Israel), made the trial a formative event in Israeli history, as "it
was through the radio that most Israelis [...] encountered personal
testimonies of Holocaust survivors for the first time," creating a national

---

[11] *Maariv*, April 9, 2002, 1, 2 (supplement).
[12] In his 1993 work, Segev also pointed to the collective didactic nature of the event by
noting that "much of the trial was carried live on the radio; everywhere, people listened –
in houses and offices, in cafes and stores and buses and factories," Segev, *Seventh
Million*, 350–351.

affiliation with the pain and stories of the Holocaust victims.[13] The trial
did not only take place "on the air" but also in the newspapers.[14] Noah
Klinger, a veteran journalist at *Yedioth Ahronot* and a Holocaust survivor,
recalls that content written on the trial had a visible effect on his surroundings through triggering a willingness to believe the survivors: "I
started writing about the Holocaust in the 1950s, but people simply did
not trust survivors' stories in Israel. After the trial that changed. Aviezer
Golan, a famous journalist, told me after the Eichmann trial that he
didn't believe me before the trial, but following the trial, he said it was
even worse than I had made out."[15]

While the Eichmann trial might have been the first collective media
event dedicated to the Holocaust, as indicated by Klinger's comments, it
by no means constituted the first discussion of the Holocaust in Israeli
media. Anita Shapira's analysis of the fifteen-year period between the
end of the Second World War and the capture of Eichmann shows that
the Holocaust was constantly at the heart of the public media debate,
thereby effectively challenging the notion of a public marginalization of
the Holocaust.[16] Shapira identified Holocaust rhetoric in the media's
coverage of speeches by David Ben-Gurion,[17] particularly those on the
1952 Reparations Agreement with West Germany, and Menachem

---

[13] Amit Pinchevsk, Tamar Liebes, and Ora Herman, "Eichmann on the Air: Radio and the
Making of an Historic Trial," *Historical Journal of Film, Radio and Television* 27:1 (2007):
10, 13.

[14] Daniel Levy and Natan Sznaider, *The Holocaust and Memory in the Global Age*
(Philadelphia: Temple University Press, 2006), 105–108.

[15] Interview conducted with Noah Klinger on July 24, 2016. Aviezer Golan, together with
David Karasik, can be considered the founders of *Yedioth Ahronot* through their
inauguration of a journalistic weekly forum with the same name in 1939. Golan is also
known for his 1978 book *Operation Susannah*, which concerns the ill-fated attempt by the
then nascent Israeli Mossad to destabilize Nasser's Egypt in the early 1950s using
Egyptian-born and other non-Israeli Jews. Oren Soffer, *Mass Communication in Israel:
Nationalism, Globalization, and Segmentation* (New York/London: Berghahn Books,
2015), 33; Aviezer Golan, *Operation Susannah* (New York: Harper & Row, 1978).

[16] Anita Shapira, "The Holocaust: Private Memories, Public Memory," *Jewish Social
Studies* 4:2 (1998): 43.

[17] For a further discussion on Ben-Gurion's attitude toward the Holocaust and Holocaust
commemoration, see Roni Stauber, *The Holocaust in Israeli Public Debate in the 1950s*
(Edgware, UK: Vallentine Mitchell, 2007), 52; Roni Stauber, "The Jewish Response
during the Holocaust: The Educational Debate in Israel in the 1950s," *Shofar* 22:4
(2004): 61. Stauber argues that Ben-Gurion spoke little of Jewish victimhood; rather,
the figure of the Jewish victim in the Diaspora – or Galut – had been supplanted by that
of the youthful heroes, and their active heroism, during the 1948 War. According to
Stauber, Ben-Gurion's distinction between "here" and "there" – the stress on the battle
within Israel, which stressed life and state-building over Diaspora martyrdom – was
generally accepted by the Mapai leadership in the early 1950s, as it emphasized new life
in Israel – regeneration and the construction of Israel, as opposed to *hurban*, or death in
the ghetto.

Begin, with the latter turning to the memory of the Holocaust to renew
the popularity of his Herut (Hebrew: freedom) party. Further coverage of
the Holocaust appeared during what became known as the "Kastner
trial," which was the first time the Israeli public at large was exposed to
stories of wartime rescue attempts and the moral dilemmas involved in
negotiating with the Nazis through widespread coverage of the trial's
proceedings by the recently founded daily *Maariv*.[18]

The inclusion of Holocaust survivor stories in the media in the 1950s
should not infer an unpoliticized coverage of the Holocaust. Indeed,
while *Maariv* was not owned by a political party, through its association
with Ze'ev Jabotinsky's Revisionist movement, it nevertheless had a
distinctly political character and, consequently, published Holocaust
stories that served its nationalist ideology.[19] For *Maariv*, this meant the
production and publication of media output that fit the Zionist idea,
because as Arie Dissenchik, *Maariv's* editor between 1956 and 1974,
argued: "journalism [is] the main carrier of the Zionist idea. Newspapers
built the land of Israel with letters before the JNF acquired and
developed the land."[20] Underlying these efforts, to a considerable extent,
was also the ideology of *mamlakhtiyut* (Hebrew: "statism"). Those
espousing *mamlakhtiyut* not only tended to disregard and reject the
diaspora as a hallmark of passivity and defeat but also, in line with Ben-
Gurion's conception of statism, envisaged Israel as a focus of active
allegiance and identification for all members of the Jewish people.[21] In
this context, Eyal Zandberg's study into which survivors had the "right to
tell the right story" is highly relevant, as it reveals the political Zionist
nature of the Holocaust during the first decades of Israel's existence.
Zandberg notes that party-affiliated and political newspapers only
involved Holocaust survivors who could integrate their own private story
with the collective, ideological one. In practice, this led to an emphasis
on personal stories of members of the underground movement who
played an active role in the ghetto uprisings or fought with the partisans
against the Nazis, since, as Zandberg maintains, "They fitted in with the

---

[18] Shapira, "Holocaust," 44, 45.
[19] The evening tabloid *Maariv* was established by a group of journalists associated with
Revisionist Zionism, some of whom had worked with the founder, Jabotinsky, and
supported the right-wing nationalist camp. Peri, *Telepopulism*, 75.
[20] Cited in ibid., 2.
[21] For an analysis of the role of *mamlakhtiyut* in Israeli Holocaust discourse, see Eliezer
Don-Yehiya, "Memory and Political Culture: Israeli Society and the Holocaust," in
Modern Jews and Their Musical Agendas, ed. Ezra Mendelsohn (New York: Oxford
University Press, 1993), 139–162.

Zionist narrative" and therefore were deemed the most appropriate group of survivors.[22]

In adherence with the Zionist narrative, interpretations both in party-affiliated and nonaffiliated newspapers were put forward that positioned the state of Israel as the dominant factor, which, in line with the formulation *me-Shoah le-tkuma* (Hebrew: from Holocaust to resurrection), viewed the victims of the Holocaust as convinced Zionists and, as a result, potential Israelis. Golda Meir's commemorative speech during the 1976 Holocaust assembly – cited extensively in *Maariv* – clearly embodied this dominant Zionist narrative. In her speech, Meir maintained that the Holocaust had not only been "aimed at the individual Jew" but "[as] a collective Holocaust [had been] directed against the state of Israel."[23] An editorial published in April 1980 in *Davar*, the official journal of the state's General Federation of Labor, the Histadrut, similarly invoked the effects of the Holocaust on Israeli state-building efforts by ascribing Zionist beliefs to those who perished, with the writer claiming that "for us in Israel, who are thirsty for new immigrants, every day presents us with the fateful loss of millions, most of whom would undoubtedly have wanted to take part in building the Jewish state."[24] Five years later, an editorial in the same outlet reinforced the connection between the Holocaust and the resurrection of the state of Israel, this time declaring that the establishment of "the Jewish state [was] due to the sacrifice of six million of its members." Moreover, the article argued that with the founding of the Jewish state "it [the Jewish people] can defend itself and protect itself. The situation has undergone a revolutionary shift."[25]

The emphasis on a distinct shift resulting from the state's establishment and the citizens' ability to defend themselves was also highlighted in publications by the socialist newspaper *'Al ha-Mishmar* (Hebrew: the guard). The headline of an editorial on Holocaust Memorial Day in 1987 reminded readers "to remember the magnitude of our victory [over Nazism]" because, as the article explained, while the Third Reich was utterly defeated, "the Jewish people is alive and kicking, has established its own national state, protects itself and is stronger today than ever before ... the annihilators lost and the annihilated were victorious."[26] A similar message was presented in *Yedioth Ahronot* in an editorial written

[22] Zandberg, "The Right to Tell the (Right) Story," 13.
[23] *Maariv*, April 27, 1976. Cited in Don-Yehiya, "Memory," 151, 2.
[24] Cited in Meyers, Neiger and Zandberg, *Communicating Awe*, 45.
[25] *Davar*, April 18, 1985. Meyers, Neiger, and Zandberg, *Communicating Awe*, 45.
[26] *'Al Hamishmar*, April 26, 1987. Cited in ibid., 53.

as if it were addressed to the victims of the Holocaust: "The furnaces are silent and yet they have a voice, the voice of historical justice ... look, brothers and sisters: the Third Reich was defeated, eradicated; the word Nazi is a curse in almost every language, and the people of Israel lives and blossoms in its country [...] Victory is ours, and yours."[27]

The Holocaust as a Past Continuous

Despite the declaration of the Jewish people's victory through the establishment of a state and an army, other publications produced in the mid-1980s did not present the Holocaust as a finite event; rather, the memory of the Holocaust was continually evoked as a formative memory for future generations. Editorials written during this time noted that the Holocaust no longer "belonged" solely to the survivors alone, but constituted "an open wound [for] every Israeli," leading one writer from 'Al ha-Mishmar to conclude that the Holocaust "does not only belong to the history of our people [but hovers above] the present and future of our people."[28] As such, the "armed camp," which President Ronald Reagan[29] argued had been established by Israel in response to the threat by the PLO, was justified by Maariv's Schmuel Schnitzer who claimed that it was part of a national lesson and "a necessity of life" for Israel since the Holocaust had demonstrated that Jews could not trust other nations' decency and integrity.[30] Commenting on the ramifications of the conveyance of the Holocaust as a "past continuous," a Haaretz editorial aptly concluded in April 1982 that "those of us who were not there ... also see ourselves as if we had been saved from the valley of death."[31]

The corresponding representation of the Holocaust in both party and privately owned commercial newspapers demonstrates that the 1977 takeover of the Likud party did not necessarily impact the content of mediated Holocaust memories. The change in the political landscape has typically been conceived as heralding in a new epoch in Israel's media landscape, resulting from the alienation of Israeli journalists from the political establishment and, concurrently, an increased preference

---

[27] Yedioth Ahronot, April 22, 1990. Cited in ibid., 54.
[28] 'Al Hamishmar, April 10, 1983. Cited in ibid., 53.
[29] These comments were made by Reagan with reference to the threat posed by the PLO to Israel from Lebanon. James Reston, "Washington; Reagan and Begin," The New York Times, June 23, 1982, www.nytimes.com/1982/06/23/opinion/washington-reagan-and-begin.html, accessed August 14, 2017.
[30] Cited in Don-Yehiya, "Memory," 151, 2.
[31] Haaretz, April 20, 1982. Cited in Meyers, Neiger, and Zandberg, Communicating Awe, 52.

among media consumers for privately owned commercial newspapers that adhered to the rhetoric of (ideological) objectivity in simple, direct language. With regard to the topic at hand, however, it appears that the privately owned commercial newspapers exhibited little change. As such, while writers discussing the Holocaust no longer have to identify with and underwrite the newspapers' political leanings, a teleological Zionist understanding of the Holocaust continues to stand central, including through the presentation of a dichotomic interpretation of Israel and the diaspora, the former a necessary safe haven from the continued bulwark of anti-Semitism existent in the latter. Yet, as will become evident below, when coupled with the domestic contextualization of the Holocaust, the ongoing perception of Israel as the panacea in both commemorative and daily journalism creates a paradoxical meaning, albeit with one clear message: Jewish existence is never secure.

Holocaust Memorial Day: A Ritualized Media Event

In addition to the numerous commemorative ceremonies outlined in Chapter 5, Israeli media partake in their own commemorative ritual on Holocaust Memorial Day. In coherence with the 1959 Holocaust Memorial Law, which stipulates that media "will express the uniqueness of the day," the majority of Israeli media outlets dedicate their resources to the construction of Holocaust media output and to conveying the state bereavement ritual.[32] Consequently, MDHH has created a unique situation in which on one day a year media are not guided by financial gain, but by "symbolic profit" through collectively turning their attention to the same past.

According to a study conducted in 2014, the creation of a Holocaust consciousness on MDHH relies on commemorative newspaper supplements, which, Oren Meyers maintains, constitute "an Israeli national ritual through breaking the linear continuity of time to recollect the nation's history."[33] An analysis of publications on MDHH between 1994 and 2016 by *Maariv* and *Yedioth Ahronot*, however, indicates that the annual ritualization of the Holocaust also relies on prospective mediation by means of commemorative reminders and through the usage

[32] The law stipulated that on "Remembrance Day [...] wireless programmes [radio] shall express the special character of the day." Knesset, *Martyrs' and Heroes' Remembrance Day Law, 5719–1959* (Sefer ha-Chukim 280, 1959), 112 (in Hebrew).

[33] These supplements are *Maariv's ha-Yom* (Hebrew: today) and *Yedioth Ahronot's 24 Sha'ot* (Hebrew: 24 hours). Oren Meyers, "Still Photographs, Dynamic Memories: A Study of the Visual Presentation of Israel's Past in Commemorative Newspaper Supplements," *The Communication Review* 5:3 (2002): 181, 182.

of Holocaust symbolism throughout the newspapers. With regard to the former, in the years under examination, both *Maariv* and *Yedioth Ahronot* provided prescriptive reminders of the Holocaust and its commemoration. On several of its front pages on MDHH, *Maariv* prompted its readers "To Remember the Six Million" (1995), "[To Remember] Today Are Ceremonies to Remember the Six Million" (2002), "To Bow [Your] Heads to the Six Million Killed in the Holocaust" (2012), and "To Never Forget" (2015). *Yedioth Ahronot's* front page on Holocaust Memorial Day also sought to encourage readers to partake in the commemorative ritual, as demonstrated in phrases such as "[We] Remember the Six Million" (2002), "Do Not Forget" (2003; 2005; 2006), "Remember" (2004; 2012; 2013), and "Never Forget" (2007).

In addition to textual reminders of the commemorative nature of the day, from the mid-2000s, *Maariv* and *Yedioth Ahronot* increasingly have employed powerful Holocaust symbolism in their publications on MDHH, which further attests to the existence of a media ritualization. In these MDHH publications, the usage of barbed wire and a Jewish Star with Dutch and German text throughout the newspapers not only testifies to a radical divergence from "normal" media but also, through the invocation of *Jood/Jude* (Dutch/German: Jew), seeks to impart the collective meaning of the event for Israeli-Jewish society. This symbolism has been adopted online. On Holocaust Memorial Day in 2012, 2013, 2014, 2015, and 2016, articles on *Maariv's* and *Yedioth Ahronot's* websites were accompanied by Yizkor candles, barbed wire, and Jewish badges, evidencing the adoption of visual print mechanisms in order to convey a continuity of commemorative meaning despite the change of media platform.[34]

"Our Holocaust": The Holocaust as a Common Destiny

The concretizing of Durkheimian notions of social cohesiveness or "an imagined community" is further realized through content that highlights the Holocaust's relevance for all Israelis, including through Holocaust

---

[34] For examples, see Brit Peretz, "Ganz during the March of the Living: Every Survivor and Soldier Is Part of the Victory," *Ynet/Yedioth Ahronot*, April 8, 2013, www.ynet.co.il/articles/0,7340,L-4365327,00.html, accessed May 6, 2017; Noam Dvir, "Remember and Do Not Forget: Israel Is One with the Six Million," *Ynet/Yedioth Ahronot*, April 28, 2014, www.ynet.co.il/articles/0,7340,L-4513981,00.html, accessed May 6, 2017; Elkana Shor, "The Last Generation: Holocaust Remembrance Must Come from Home," *NRG/Maariv*, April 28, 2014, www.nrg.co.il/online/1/ART2/575/582.html, accessed April 28, 2017.

Maariv, April 27, 1995, "In Memory of the Six Million"

Maariv, April 9, 2002, "Today: Memorial Ceremonies for the Six Million"

Yedioth Ahronot, April 16, 2007, "[We] Will Never Forget"

Yedioth Ahronot, April 15, 2015, "This Morning at 10:00am: A Siren in Memory of Those Who Perished in the Shoah"

Figure 6.1 Prospective mediation

"Jude" *Maariv*, May 2, 2000   "Jude." *Maariv*, April 18, 2003   "Jude." *Maariv*, April 16, 2015

"Jude." *Yedioth Ahronot*, April 9, 2002   "Jood." *Yedioth Ahronot*, April 21, 2009   "Jood." *Yedioth Ahronot*, April 8, 2013

Figure 6.2 Holocaust media symbolism

"appropriation," as indicated in phrases such as "our Holocaust,"[35] "against us,"[36] and "our common destiny."[37] In a 2006 article revealingly entitled "History Chose Us," Eshel Gan, for instance, cites an interviewee who notes that the central message conveyed to Israeli youth in order to remember the Holocaust should be "we are all Jews and we

[35] Meir Turjeman and Noah Klinger, "Our Holocaust," *Yedioth Ahronot*, April 28, 2016, 5.
[36] Noah Klinger, "Not [on] Another Planet," *Yedioth Ahronot*, April 28, 2014, 2. Also see Assaf Chaim and Avi Shilon, "The Shoah Is Present in Our Blood Cycle," *Maariv*, April 9, 2002, 10, 11; Meir Lau, "Also Today, Precisely Today," *Yedioth Ahronot*, April 9, 2002, 2.
[37] Eshel Gan, "History Chose Us," *Nrg/Maariv*, April 24, 2006, www.nrg.co.il/online/1/ART1/076/987.html, accessed April 28, 2017.

have a common destiny, whether we like it or not."[38] In 2016, *Maariv* was even more explicit in "claiming" the Holocaust, as the entire commemorative supplement was dedicated to *Shoah shelanu* (Hebrew: our Holocaust).[39] The pertinence of the Holocaust to Israeli-Jews is equally expressed by highlighting the uniquely Jewish nature of the Nazi genocide and, at times, a simultaneous minimization of the "uniqueness" of other genocides.[40] A convergence of these themes materialized twice in 1995, in a news article and a column by *Maariv's* columnist Ben-Dror Yemini. Yemini, in his column on MDHH, argued that "the uniqueness of the Holocaust" meant that Holocaust commemorative ceremonies should be held separately from ceremonies dedicated to the murder of the Gypsies.[41] A similar message was imparted in a *Yedioth Ahronot* article citing M. K. Livnat who sought to forbid holding a joint ceremony for the Shoah and the "tragedy" of the Armenians, as "the joint ceremony would deform Jewish history and compare the murder of six million Jews in the Holocaust to the tragedy of other people [...] when such a comparison cannot be made."[42] In 2007, *Yedioth Ahronot's* front page also maintained the uniqueness of the Holocaust in comparison to other "war crimes." In an article entitled "Not a Genocide, Murder of the Jews" the author Sever Plocker argued: "There is no other tragedy in the history of mankind or war crime that is similar to the Holocaust of the Jewish people."[43]

In an interview conducted with Klinger, a recurring presence in *Yedioth Ahronot* on MDHH, the focus on Jewish victimhood and the uniqueness of the Holocaust were presented as both a moral and historical responsibility, as he noted: "In Auschwitz there were 1,300,000 people. 1,200,000 were Jews, 75,000 Poles, and 23,000 were Gypsies. What is there to compare? I have nothing to say about the Gypsies."[44]

---

[38]   Ibid.   [39]   "Our Shoah," *Maariv*, May 5, 2016, supplement.

[40]   Amos Carmel, "About the Sin That Was Not Committed," *Yedioth Ahronot*, May 5, 1997, 5; Meir Stiglitz, "To Death There Was Government," *Maariv*, May 5, 1997, 5; Klinger, "Not [on] Another Planet," 2.

[41]   Ben-Dror Yemini, "Between Judaism and Universalism," *Maariv*, April 27, 1995, 3.

[42]   Gabi Baron, "MK Livnat: Forbid Holding a Joint Ceremony for the Shoah and Armenians," *Yedioth Ahronot*, April 24, 1995, 14. Also see Nurit Pelter and Michael Grayevski, "We Have an Obligation to Remember and Forget," *Yedioth Ahronot*, April 13, 1999, 9.

[43]   Sever Plocker, "Not Genocide, [but] Murder of Jews," *Yedioth Ahronot*, April 16, 2007, front page. Also see a 2014 article by Efraim Zuroff in which he criticized the comparison between the crimes of the Nazis against the Jews and the "imagined genocide" of the Soviets because, as Zuroff maintained, it led to an inclusive commemoration of all victims of totalitarian regimes "as if they [...] had committed similar crimes on the same scale." Efraim Zuroff, "Europe Is Rewriting History and Minimizing the Holocaust," *NRG/Maariv*, April 27, 2014, www.nrg.co.il/online/1/ART2/574/844.html, accessed April 19, 2016.

[44]   According to data published by the United States Holocaust Memorial Museum (USHMM), Klinger's figures miss the mark, as around 200,000 non-Jewish victims were deported to Auschwitz, including 140,000–150,000 non-Jewish Poles, 23,000

Moreover, invoking the Armenian "killing" as an example, Klinger noted that, unlike the Turks who exploited the war to perpetrate "the killing," the Germans "had a plan, it was predetermined."[45] Yet, media content projecting an exclusive Jewish victimhood and the Holocaust's uniqueness should not merely be considered a reflection of journalists' own historical understandings; instead, based on the dialogical relation between journalists and media consumers, the media's formulation of a unique Jewish victimhood is indicative of its cultural ubiquity and resonance in Israeli society. Indeed, Motti Neiger, an Israeli media scholar and a long-time media observer, explained that a "focus on other victims of Nazism would lead to less interest among readers. It does not fit the framework people are used to consuming regarding the Holocaust [and] on *Yom ha-Shoah* there is no tolerance for other narratives that do not fit with the narrative of Jewish victimhood."[46]

A Prescriptive and Prospective Holocaust Memory

In coherence with this "accepted narrative" of an "unprecedented evilness and brutality,"[47] several articles on MDHH claim that the Holocaust "is inevitable for youth"[48] and "will pass from one generation to another"[49] as "a burden of memory"[50] that is part of "our [Israeli] blood cycle."[51] Nevertheless, on the whole, MDHH publications stress the need for an active transmission to the next Israeli-Jewish generation, thereby creating a "prescriptive memory" or a "prospective memory." Implicit transmission of a prospective memory is most conclusively demonstrated through the publication of letters written by first-generation Holocaust survivors to their (great-)(grand)children and through the inclusion of their offspring in commemorative ceremonies in Israel and journeys to death camps in

---

Roma and Sinti (Gypsies), 15,000 Soviet prisoners of war, and 25,000 others (Soviet civilians, Lithuanians, Czechs, French, Yugoslavs, Germans, Austrians, and Italians). The majority of these victims were killed: 74,000 Poles, 21,000 Roma (Gypsies), and 15,000 Soviet prisoners of war; and 10,000–15,000 members of other nationalities (Soviet civilians, Czechs, Yugoslavs, French, Germans, and Austrians). At least 960,000 Jews were killed in Auschwitz. "Auschwitz," United States Holocaust Memorial Museum, www.ushmm.org/wlc/en/article.php?ModuleId=10005189, accessed September 11, 2017.

[45] Interview conducted with Noah Klinger on July 24, 2016.
[46] Interview conducted with Motti Neiger on April 11, 2016.
[47] Amnon Danker, "Memory," *Maariv*, May 5, 2006, 3.
[48] Sarah Blau, "The Shoah Is Present," *Maariv*, April 9, 2002, 11.
[49] Sever Plocker, "The Memory That Does Not Cease," *Yedioth Ahronot*, May 2, 2000, 2.
[50] Tal Bashan, "A Healthier Mind," *Maariv*, April 16, 2015, 3.
[51] Chaim and Shilon, "The Shoah Is Present in Our Blood Cycle," 10, 11. Also see Sharon Machat, "Effect of the Third Generation," *Maariv*, April 29, 2003, 6, 7.

Figure 6.3 "Our Holocaust"
Maariv, May 5, 2016

Poland.[52] The concept of an "active" or explicit obligation and duty toward generational transmission has also been identified, albeit almost exclusively from 2000 onwards.[53] *Maariv's* 2000 MDHH edition included a "commemorative ad" for its special MDHH edition aimed at children, which sought to present the Holocaust through the eyes of the Holocaust's youngest victims in "excerpts from diaries written by children during that awful war."[54] The "responsibility of members of the [second and] third generation" is further laid out in other initiatives that seek to "inspire the youth to take responsibility for Holocaust remembrance," often referring to the ever-diminishing number of survivors.[55] In light of an absence of direct contact with the first generation, an editorial published in 2012, entitled "Children of the Next Generation," stipulated the need to shape the image of future generations through the educational system "in the language in which the children speak today,"[56] while another editorial published in 2014 emphasized the preservation of Holocaust Remembrance Day to pass on the Holocaust "to the children, grandchildren, and their offspring [...] as a battle for memory."[57]

In addition to pointing to extra-media modes of transmission, on MDHH, *Maariv* and *Yedioth Ahronot* have sought to contribute to the transmission of mediated Holocaust memories. Principally, these media outlets have engaged in Holocaust exposure by sharing Holocaust

---

[52] Anonymous, "Ceremony at Tel Yizhak: The Grandchildren Will Accompany the Torchlighters," *Yedioth Ahronot*, May 5, 2005, 3 (supplement); Itamar Eichner, "The Third Generation of Holocaust Survivors and Their Grandchildren Will Accompany Sharon," *Yedioth Ahronot*, May 5, 2005, 4; Dubi Eichenwald, "In the Name of the Father," *Yedioth Ahronot*, April 29, 2003, 16; Nechama Doek, "Flight A986," *Yedioth Ahronot*, April 21, 2009, 12,13; Yiftat Menaharedt, "Touching Pain," *Yedioth Ahronot*, April 12, 1999, 9; Anonymous, "Personal Testimony: Holocaust Survivors and Members of the Second Generation Write Their Memories," *Yedioth Ahronot*, April 29, 2003, supplement; Abigail Uzi, "When You Grow Up," *Yedioth Ahronot*, April 19, 2012, supplement; Anonymous, "Recounting," *Yedioth Ahronot*, April 4, 2012, 8–15.

[53] The pre-2000 exception is *Yedioth Ahronot's* 1997 article by Ilyah Avnat. See Ilyah Avnat, "Mother and Daughter in Torch Race," *Yedioth Ahronot*, May 5, 1997, 17 (supplement). For post-2000 articles conveying an active obligation toward generational transmission, see Anonymous, "A Second Generation of Pain," *Yedioth Ahronot*, April 19, 2004, 4 (supplement); Yair Lapid et al., "Sons of Holocaust Survivors Write About the Nightmares, Hopes and Lessons," *Yedioth Ahronot*, April 19, 2004, 4 (supplement); David Regev, Zvi Singer, and Tamar Trabelsi Hadad, "Saving the Memory," *Yedioth Ahronot*, May 1, 2011, 2; Aya Ben Naftali, "Witnesses to the Last Witness," *Yedioth Ahronot*, April 12, 2012.

[54] Anonymous, "Maariv for Kids," *Maariv*, May 2, 2000, advertisement; Miriam Kotz, "How to Tell Them about This?," *Yedioth Ahronot*, April 28, 2014, 7.

[55] Gan, "History Chose Us." For a further article invoking the diminishing number of the survivors and the need to collect their testimonies, see Regev, Singer, and Hadad, "Saving the Memory," 2.

[56] Yaez Paz-Melamed, "Children of the Next Generation," *NRG/Maariv*, April 19, 2012, www.nrg.co.il/online/1/ART2/359/511.html, accessed April 28, 2017.

[57] Shor, "The Last Generation."

survivors' experiences, thereby reflecting their emergence as the dominant storytellers of the Holocaust "as direct witnesses" in Israeli society.[58] While survivors' stories are no longer only selected for their representation of the "ghetto fighter spirit," the metaphoric Zionist narrative of "catastrophe and redemption" remains, through the creation of a liminal sphere, juxtaposing the "there" (Europe) and "then" (1939–1945) with the "here" (Israel) and the "now" (present). Consequently, MDHH output stresses the survivors' personal "victory over Nazi Germany"[59] and their contribution to the establishment of a strong Israeli state as "a triumph of light over darkness,"[60] an "overcoming of evil"[61] and a "personal revenge."[62]

The Diasporic Threat

The transmission of survivors' past to future generations, crucially, is not solely intended as a means of illuminating the past in a teleological fashion. Speeches cited in 2007 and 2015 by then Prime Minister Ehud Olmert and Knesset President Reuven Rivlin highlight that "transferring the torch of life" to the younger generation is meant to impart an awareness "of the dangers [and] vigilance against threats."[63] Principally, this threat constitutes the perseverance of anti-Semitism, Nazism, and Fascism in the diaspora and, accordingly, affirms the need for a strong Jewish state. Since 1994, media output on MDHH has reported an annual growth in anti-Semitism in the diaspora[64] with reference to the annual reports

---

[58] Zandberg, "The Right to Tell the (Right) Story," 11.

[59] Urah Arif, "Postal Service Issues a Special Commemoration Kit," *Yedioth Ahronot*, April 25, 1995, 17.

[60] Golan Yusifon and Rivka Freilich, "Weitzman: There Will Not Be Another Auschwitz," *Maariv*, May 2, 2000, 4.

[61] Anonymous, "We Are Here," *Yedioth Ahronot*, April 8, 2013, 10.

[62] Meir Lau, "From Generation to Generation," *Yedioth Ahronot*, April 8, 2013, 1. For further articles describing Holocaust survivors' victory as individuals and a society, see Dov Eichwald, "We Stood on the Cursed Land of Auschwitz and Knew We Had Won," *Yedioth Ahronot*, April 9, 2000, 22; Rivka Freilich, "We Are Here: The Soldiers of Yehuda," *Maariv*, May 2, 2000, 13; Orna Barbibai, "We Return to the Camp as Victors," *Maariv*, April 9, 2013, 2; Danny Adino Abebe, "We Won: They Survived the Horrors of the Holocaust, Established Glorious Families and Chose Life," *Yedioth Ahronot*, April 15, 2015, 2, 3.

[63] Anonymous, "Carry the Torch of Life," *Maariv*, April 16, 2015, front page; Danny Adino Abebe, Natasha Mozgovia, and Yossi Bar, "The Pain and the Memory," *Yedioth Ahronot*, April 16, 2007, 2.

[64] Reports provided to the United States Congress also note that since the beginning of the twenty-first century there has been an "increasing frequency and severity of anti-Semitic incidents [which] have disrupted the sense of safety and well-being of Jewish communities [abroad]." Department of State to the Committee on Foreign Relations and the Committee on International Relations, *Anti-Semitism in the United States: Report on Global Anti-Semitism* (Washington DC, January 2005).

conducted by the Stephen Roth Institute for the Study of Contemporary Antisemitism and Racism at the University of Tel Aviv.[65] These studies, which concentrate on contemporary manifestations of anti-Semitism and anti-Israeli policies abroad, are released on the eve of MDHH and are widely cited in Holocaust day media, hinting that the attitudes and behaviors that characterized the Nazi regime are still existing phenomena and, therefore, "that the Holocaust is not over yet."[66]

From 1998 onwards, reports conducted by the Stephen Roth Institute have consistently presented a "sharp increase" in violent anti-Semitic incidents in the world executed by "Muslim Arabs [and] extreme right-wingers," with a primary focus on Europe and the United States.[67] An article published on the annual study in 2010 with the telling title "[They] Hate Us More," for instance, noted that ever since the early 1990s, the report's authors have documented an increase in anti-Semitic incidents worldwide executed by "the extreme right wing [although] in most cases the events' perpetrators were identified as Arabs or Muslims."[68] Interestingly, an analysis of these reports shows that even when "there has been a decline in the total number of [anti-Semitic] incidents," the "seriousness" of the incidents means that, in the media, the evidence is presented so as to indicate that there is a "worrying escalation [in anti-Semitism]."[69] In addition to the annual report on anti-Semitism, other news items published on MDHH seek to evidence diasporic anti-Semitic virulence. A news article published on MDHH 2008 thus discussed the desecration of dozens of Jewish graves in Germany as "an awful reminder" of "hateful anti-Semitism."[70] In 2014,

---

[65] The studies examine both violent and nonviolent forms of anti-Semitism in the diaspora, in addition to the existence of anti-Israeli sentiments, which include imposing "boycott[s] on Israeli academic institutions and those associated with them, as part of the denial of Israel's right to exist as a Jewish state." Tamar Triblisi-Chadad, "Less Anti-Semitic Incidents in the World," *Yedioth Ahronot*, April 25, 2006, 9.

[66] Motti Neiger, Eyal Zandberg, and Oren Meyers, "Reversed Memory: Commemorating the Past through Coverage of the Present," in *Journalism and Memory*, ed. Barbie Zelizer and Keren Tenenboim-Weinblatt (Houndmills/Basingstoke/Hampshire: Palgrave Macmillan, 2014), 123.

[67] Tamar Triblisi-Chadad, "A Sharp Increase in the Number of Attacks on Jews," *Yedioth Ahronot*, April 9, 2002, 14. For examples of further articles, see Anonymous, "Hate Is Increasing. 2004: Sharp Increase in Anti-Semitism," *Maariv*, May 5, 2006, 3; Michael Shapira, "Maariv Report: More Serious Anti-Semitic Attacks in 2007," *NRG/Maariv*, April 30, 2008, www.nrg.co.il/online/1/ART1/727/972.html, accessed April 17, 2017; Chaim Asrovitz, "A Rise of 40% in Violent Anti-Semitic Incidents in the World," *Maariv*, April 16, 2015, 3.

[68] Tamar Triblisi-Chadad and Itamar Eichner, "[They] Hate Us More," *Yedioth Ahronot*, April 12, 2010, 4, 5.

[69] Triblisi-Chadad, "Less Anti-Semitic Incidents in the World," 9. Also see Shapira, "Maariv Report."

[70] Anonymous, "Berlin Mayor: This Is Hateful Anti-Semitism," *Yedioth Ahronot*, April 30, 2008, 4; Anonymous, "Dozens of Graves Desecrated in Germany on the Eve of Holocaust Day," *Maariv*, April 30, 2008, front page; AP, "More Than 30 Graves Desecrated in Berlin," *NRG/*

readers were offered a more thorough introduction into the tenets of anti-Semitism across Europe or, as the article put it, "A journey through the strongholds of anti-Semitism on the continent."[71] The findings of the reports and other news items are reinforced through reciting commemorative speeches conducted on MDHH by politicians and in editorials published on MDHH. Materializations of the first occurred in the coverage of speeches conducted by Ezar Weizman, Ariel Sharon, Moshe Katsav, Benjamin Netanyahu, and Shimon Peres. In 2004, an article entitled "We Won't Forget" referred to President Katsav's speech at Yad Vashem's commemorative opening ceremony. Katsav noted that a "wave of anti-Semitism [is] sweeping through Europe today [...] We are witnessing the burning of synagogues, the desecration of Jewish orphanages, and hate speech. Again, Jews are afraid to wear a skullcap and wear a Star of David when walking in the street. Once again [...] Jewish children are being beaten and cursed."[72] Editorials written on MDHH further evoke the threat of anti-Semitism abroad by expressing the inherent nature of diasporic anti-Semitism, thereby presenting anti-Semitism as something endemic to gentiles in line with Eastern European Zionist thinkers like Leon Pinsker, Moses Lilienblum, and Nachum Sokolow.[73] Accordingly, an editorial published in 1994 by Plocker in *Yedioth Ahronot* noted that the rise of neo-Fascism indicated that "the immunity against the virus is starting to weaken and possibly will stop working."[74] Editorials written by Klinger and the late author Aharon Megged also point to the intrinsic existence of anti-Semitism, with Megged discussing "the disease of hatred of Jews spreading from country to country at a much faster rate than AIDS or SARS" and Klinger identifying anti-Semitism as "a disease and a tradition that has been handed down from generation to generation, to this very day [resulting] in abysmal and irrational hatred against us."[75]

Maariv, April 29, 2008, www.nrg.co.il/online/1/ART1/727/764.html, accessed April 18, 2017; Yarden Michaeli, "An Awful Reminder," *Maariv*, April 30, 2008, 2.

[71] Nissan Tzur, "An Extreme Right-Wing View: Anti-Semitism Is Once Again Conquering Europe," *NRG/Maariv*, April 20, 2014, www.nrg.co.il/online/1/ART2/573/804.html, accessed April 18, 2017.

[72] Zvi Singer and Natasha Mozgovia, "We Won't Forget," *Yedioth Ahronot*, April 19, 2004, 12, 13. See also Ora Ariv, "It Is Up to Israel to Spearhead the Fight against Followers of Nazism," *Yedioth Ahronot*, April 27, 1995, 14; Edna Adato and Zvi Singer, "Remember," *Maariv*, April 29, 2003, 2.

[73] Shulamit Volkov, *Germans, Jews, and Antisemites: Trials in Emancipation* (Cambridge: Cambridge University Press, 2006), 17; Robert Wistrich, *Between Redemption and Perdition: Modern Anti-Semitism and Jewish Identity* (London: Routledge, 1990), 190–195.

[74] Sever Plocker, "If This Is Man," *Yedioth Ahronot*, April 7, 1994, 6.

[75] Aharon Megged, "A New Incarnation of Old Hatred," *Yedioth Ahronot*, April 29, 2003, 11 (supplement); Klinger, "Not [on] Another Planet," 2. For further examples, see Meir Lau, "What Will Be When We Are No Longer Here," *Yedioth Ahronot*, May 5, 2016, 2

Maariv and *Yedioth Ahronot's* emphasis on anti-Semitic manifestations on the same day as Holocaust commemoration ceremonies aims to evidence the need to "learn a lesson from the Holocaust,"[76] since, as one article put it, "there is a chance of another Holocaust."[77] Moreover, as the late President Weizman proclaimed in 1995, the perseverance of Nazism "in the middle of Western culture" should "ring a warning bell to the diaspora Jews and force them to have a serious discussion concerning Jewish existence in the diaspora."[78] It is against this ongoing threat of a second Holocaust that the Israeli state is presented as a refuge through the existence of a strong IDF, reinforcing the dichotomy between Israel as a safe haven and the diaspora as a universal "land of the evil."[79] In articles and cartoons published on MDHH, "the state of Israel and a strong and secure IDF"[80] are thus not only conceived "as a triumph of light over darkness and righteousness over evil"[81] but also as "the only guarantee to our safety and to ensure a Holocaust won't happen a second time."[82] As *Maariv's* front page promised in 2006 "Never Will They Find Us Not Ready, Never."[83]

(supplement), in which Israel's former Ashkenazi Chief Rabbi (1993–2003) noted that "anti-Semitism exists from generation to generation."

[76] Noah Klinger and Zvi Singer, "Don't Forget," *Yedioth Ahronot*, May 5, 2005, 4.

[77] Tamar Trabelsi Hadad, Zvi Singer, Joel Beno, and Oron Meiri, "A Third of the Youth: It Is Possible That a Second Shoah Will Happen," *Yedioth Ahronot*, April 13, 2015, 4.

[78] Ariv, "It Is Up to Israel to Spearhead the Fight," 14. A similar argument was put forward in 2002 in an editorial published by Lau who noted that the fact that "the whole world is against us" and the existence of "a national home, a state and an army with power and ability" means that diaspora Jews' "way must be one and only, in one direction and now – to the Land of Israel." Lau, "Also Today, Precisely Today," 2.

[79] Ami Ben David, "Unprecedented Heavy Security during the March of the Living," *Maariv*, April 9, 2002, 11.

[80] Nurit Pelter and Michael Grayevski, "A Strong IDF Is the Assurance That the Holocaust Won't Return," *Yedioth Ahronot*, April 13, 1999, 9.

[81] Yusifon and Freilich, "Weitzman," 4.

[82] Michael Grayevski, "Israel Is the Assurance That the Holocaust Will Not Return," *Yedioth Ahronot*, April 23, 1998, 3.

[83] Anonymous, "The Prime Minister Is Going to Lead the March of the Living Today in Auschwitz. 'Never Will They Find Us Not Ready, Never,' Sharon Promised," *Maariv*, May 5, 2006, front page. For further examples of articles on the existence of the IDF and the Israeli state as an insurance against another Holocaust, see Yehuda Golan and Uri Arzi, "Oy to a People That Doesn't Have a National Home and Oy to a People That Doesn't Have a Defensive Force, Said Prime Minister Shimon Peres Yesterday during the Ceremony at Yad Vashem," *Maariv*, April 25, 1996, 2; Anonymous, "A Safe Haven for Future Generations," *Maariv*, April 9, 2002, 10; Dalia Mazori, "Netanyahu: We Will Never Reach the Situation Where It Is Too Late," *Maariv*, April 9, 2013, 2; Anonymous, "Netanyahu: The West Has Not Learned a Lesson, but This Time We Will Defend Ourselves," *NRG/Maariv*, April 27, 2014, www.nrg.co.il/online/1/ART2/575/352.html, accessed May 8, 2017.

"Dad, we beat them." *Yedioth Ahronot*, April 8, 2013

"Sixty [years] of Israel. From Shoah to Resurrection." *Yedioth Ahronot*, April 30, 2008

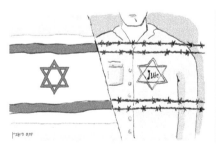

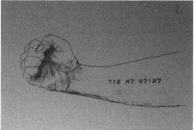

Yedioth Ahronot, April 4, 2010

"Never Again." *Maariv*, April 8, 2013

Figure 6.4 Israel as the redemptive answer to the Holocaust

The Domestic Threat

Despite the presentation of Israel as a bulwark against diasporic anti-Semitism, somewhat paradoxically, Jewish life in Israel is not perceived as free from similar threats. Studies conducted among the Israeli public in 2007 found that a third of Israelis feared a second Holocaust.[84] By 2015, these numbers had risen, with 47 percent of the second and third generation and 46 percent of the general public being fearful of another Holocaust.[85] While the reports do not indicate the source of this fear, an examination of media output on MDHH demonstrates that in addition to the invocation of a diasporic threat, the possibility of a reoccurrence of a Holocaust against the Jewish people in Israel is represented as a consequence of the ongoing Israeli-Palestinian conflict and, since the mid-2000s, "the Iranian threat." The threat of further extermination is conveyed both implicitly, through the framing of the Holocaust, and explicitly in news items and editorials. An editorial published by Geula Cohen in *Maariv* in 2000, for instance, maintained that "we should not fall asleep on duty [as] what happened there can happen here." According to Cohen, the threat of a Holocaust occurring "tomorrow, [here] in the land of Israel" was compounded by the ongoing negotiations between Ehud Barak and Arafat, which, Cohen argued, "deprived us from the sources of our strength."[86] With reference to the PA's "true intentions" of "a map of the world in which Israel does not exist," Uri Elizier on MDHH 2006 also noted in an article with the telling name "It's Still Possible" that the "main lesson [is] that the Holocaust can take place [again]."[87]

The suggestion of an ongoing threat is further imbued by framing Holocaust commemoration on MDHH in the context of the ongoing Israeli-Palestinian conflict. *Yedioth Ahronot's* and *Maariv's* front pages on MDHH in 1999 and 2002 were, for example, dominated by the death of soldiers in, respectively, Jenin and Lebanon, as well as Holocaust commemorative acts in Israel. The placement of the announcements of the soldiers' death directly next to images of soldiers at commemoration

---

[84] Hadad, et al., "A Third of the Youth," 4.
[85] Dalia Mazori, "About Half of the Israeli Public Fears a Second Shoah," *NRG/Maariv*, April 13, 2015, www.nrg.co.il/online/1/ART2/688/669.html, accessed May 8, 2017. For a non-MDHH article on this, see Mohammed S. Watad, "The Duty to Scream," *NRG/ Maariv*, April 15, 2015, www.nrg.co.il/online/1/ART2/689/240.html, accessed May 8, 2017.
[86] Geula Cohen, "My Holocaust Syndrome," *Maariv*, May 2, 2000, 5 (supplement).
[87] Uri Elizier, "It's Still Possible," *Yedioth Ahronot*, April 21, 2006, 22. Also see Gabi Keshler, "Palestinian Suicide Bombers Are Just as Bad as the Nazis," *Maariv*, April 9, 2002, 11.

ceremonies at Yad Vashem not only creates a direct link between the Holocaust and ongoing Jewish suffering but also blurs the line between Jewish victims of Nazism and victims of the conflict as, in the words of *Maariv's* 2002 special supplement, "pain which doesn't have an end."[88] The insinuation of a direct interconnection between the Holocaust and the continual suffering as a result of regional and domestic political strife is reinforced through survivors' stories. In 2002, *Maariv* readers were introduced to David Polanski, known as Jork, who smuggled arms to the Warsaw Ghetto during the Second World War. After having "survived those horrible years," Jork presents what he calls "his personal [second] Holocaust," namely the loss of his son Eitan in the Yom Kippur War.[89] In 2014, Holocaust survivor Judith Shilo also recounted the occurrence of "another Holocaust in Israel," this time alluding to the death of her granddaughter and her son in attacks perpetrated by Palestinians, leading the author to conclude that "even here disasters [after the Holocaust] continue to follow her."[90]

The most explicit and consistent conveyance of an ongoing threat to Israeli-Jews on MDHH has taken place since 2006, following Mahmoud Ahmadinejad's ascendance to the presidency in Iran in 2005 and subsequent calls by him to "wipe Israel off the map."[91] As such, in the same article that Elizier discussed the PA's intention to rid itself of Israel, Ahmadinejad is compared to Hitler who "also first spoke only [meaning that] anyone who talks about destroying Israel intends to do so."[92] As a result of this intention by "one of the most extreme leaders since Hitler," an article published in *Yedioth Ahronot* on the same day went so far as to argue that "the threat posed by Iran today is even more serious than the threat posed by the Nazis because the Iranians are closer to nuclear weapons than Hitler was."[93] In the wake of Netanyahu's re-ascendance to power in 2009, the mention of the Iranian threat has largely moved from editorials and news articles citing the Iranian leadership to articles

---

[88] *Yedioth Ahronot*, April 13, 1999, front page; *Yedioth Ahronot*, April 9, 2002, front page. Also see *Yedioth Ahronot*, April 7, 1994, front page; Eliel Sachar, "She Survived the Shoah [but] Was Killed in an Attack," *Maariv*, April 9, 2002, 9.

[89] Amir Gilat, "This Is Me, Jork, at the Square of the Three Crosses," *Maariv*, April 9, 2002, 1, 2 (supplement).

[90] Smadar Shir, "I Didn't Think That in Israel Another Shoah Would Happen to Me," *Yedioth Ahronot*, April 28, 2014, 4.

[91] Fathi Nazeela, "Iran's New President Says Israel 'Must Be Wiped Off the Map'," *The New York Times*, October 27, 2005, www.nytimes.com/2005/10/27/world/middleeast/irans-new-president-says-israel-must-be-wiped-off-the-map.html?_r=0, accessed April 18, 2017.

[92] Elizier, "It's Still Possible," 22.

[93] Smadar Perry and Itamar Eichner, "Denying the Shoah on Holocaust Memorial Day," *Yedioth Ahronot*, April 25, 2006, 6.

"A Soldier is Killed in Lebanon
During the Dismantling of a Bomb."
Yedioth Ahronot, April 13, 1999

"Killed Yesterday in Jenin,"
Yedioth Ahronot, April 9, 2002

Figure 6.5 Pain which has no end

recounting speeches conducted by the prime minister and, until 2014, President Shimon Peres.[94] Thus, on MDHH 2010, 2011, 2013, 2014, and 2015 speeches by Netanyahu and Peres were cited to stress "the

[94] Anonymous, "Never Again: The Lesson of the Holocaust Is to Fight Evil, the Prime Minister Said Last Night at Yad Vashem. However, Facing the Iranian Threat, the World Acts as It Always Had," *Maariv*, April 12, 2010, front page; Zvi Singer and Noah Klinger, "Six Million Tears," *Yedioth Ahronot*, April 12, 2010, 2.

possibility of another Holocaust against the Jewish people," as Iranian leaders "are rushing to develop nuclear weapons and openly declare their desire to destroy Israel."[95] At the opening ceremony for Holocaust Memorial Day at Yad Vashem in 2015, Netanyahu even compared the 2015 Iranian nuclear agreement – or Joint Comprehensive Plan of Action – between world powers to curb Iran's nuclear weapons program to the 1938 Munich Agreement between Adolf Hitler and European powers allowing Germany to annex parts of Czechoslovak. Warning of indifference in the face of this renewed threat to Jews, Netanyahu pledged "that an independent State of Israel will know how to protect them against their bitter Iranian foe." The tragic lesson of the Holocaust, according to Netanyahu, was clear: "We must be able to defend our-selves by ourselves against all threats and any enemy [...] day-in, day-out, every morning and every evening."[96]

Addressing the Holocaust at Every Chance: Daily Holocaust Mediation

Interviews conducted with Israeli journalists responsible for Holocaust media output indicate that the production of Holocaust-related content is considered vital throughout the year. As such, even without a legal requirement, media discourse is saturated with direct and indirect references to the Holocaust because, as Neiger argued, Israeli journal-ists address the Holocaust "every time they have a chance."[97] When asked about the reasoning for the daily allusions to the Holocaust, media professionals showed awareness of their role as media agents by claiming a responsibility in transmitting the Holocaust to the next generation. Eldad Beck, a correspondent for *Yedioth Ahronot* based in Germany, pointed out that as a representative of the second-generation he considers it his task to keep the memory of the Holocaust alive in Israel, since, as he noted, "My generation might become the missing link in the chain of memory. We are between those who experienced the Holocaust and those who won't know those who experienced it.

---

[95] Dalia Mazori, "Netanyahu: We Must Not Remain Silent in the Face of Iran's Threats," *Maariv*, April 11, 2010, Akiva Novick, "Never Again," *Yedioth Ahronot*, May 2, 2011, 2. Also see Danny Adino Abebe and Geul Banu, "Remember the Dead," *Yedioth Ahronot*, April 8, 2013, 4; Dalia Mazori, "Netanyahu: We Will Never Reach the Situation Where It Will Be Too Late," *Maariv*, April 9, 2013, 2.

[96] Cited in Akiva Eldar, "Netanyahu Invokes Holocaust to Sow Fear, Hate," *Al-Monitor*, April 12, 2018, www.al-monitor.com/pulse/originals/2018/04/israel-syria-iran-benjamin-netanyahu-bashar-al-assad-shoah.html, accessed March 13, 2020.

[97] Interview conducted with Motti Neiger on April 11, 2016.

So, my generation has been given the mission to keep the memory of the Holocaust alive."[98]

Unlike MDHH, daily news content on the Holocaust cannot solely depend on its commemorative relevance and, instead, news articles need to fulfill standards of "newsworthiness."[99] While producing content of contemporary cultural significance or, in Joan Galtung and Mari Holmboe Ruge's news value terminology, "meaningfulness" and "cultural proximity," mediated day-to-day Holocaust output largely mirrors themes discussed on MDHH, including through the portrayal of the Holocaust as an ongoing threat emanating from domestic and international conflict and diasporic anti-Semitism. Consequently, similar to MDHH output, daily Holocaust content renders a paradox, as an emphasis on diasporic anti-Semitism presents "the state of Israel as the sole answer."[100]

A Daily Reliving of the National Trauma

In contrast to MDHH output on anti-Semitism, daily invocation of anti-Semitism has mainly taken place since the early 2000s, following the outbreak of the Al-Aqsa Intifadah. In publications concerning (violent) anti-Semitic acts, anti-Semitic political manifestations, and Holocaust denial, the image of a wholly anti-Semitic and unsafe diaspora is reinforced.[101] Thus, a 2014 article on anti-Semitic incidents in Germany claimed that "as Germans are no longer afraid to hate Jews, in the streets you can hear things like 'Jews should be put in the gas chambers' or 'the Jews should be burned' [making] these the worst times since the Nazi era."[102] A similarly dismal

---

[98] Interview conducted with Eldad Beck on August 8, 2016.

[99] Joan Galtung and Mari Holmboe Ruge (1965) provided a comprehensive systematic definition of newsworthiness or "news values" based on twelve dimensions of events that make them likely to be represented in news media: frequency; threshold; unambiguity; cultural proximity or meaningfulness; consonance; unexpectedness; continuity; composition; reference to elite nations; actions of the elite; personification; and negativity. John Galtung and Mari Holmboe Ruge, "The Structure of Foreign News: The Presentation of the Congo, Cuba and Cyprus Crises in Four Norwegian Newspapers," *Journal of International Peace Research* 1 (1965): 64–91. For a (more) contemporary interpretation of what "makes news," including the contemporary interest in celebrity news, see Tony Harcup and Deirdre O'Neill, "What Is News? Galtung and Ruge Revisited," *Journalism Studies* 2:2 (2001): 261–280.

[100] Interview conducted with Motti Neiger on April 11, 2016.

[101] Aran Tipenbron, "Five Hundred New Members in the Neo-Nazi Party," *Yedioth Ahronot*, August 14, 2000, 2, 3; Maya Mahler, "Holocaust Denial? In Spain It's Okay," *Yedioth Ahronot*, January 27, 2008, 10; Eldad Beck, Natasha Mozgovia, and Itamar Eichner, "Munich: Carnival on International Holocaust Day," *Yedioth Ahronot*, January 27, 2008, 10.

[102] Channel 2 News, "Government Report States: 40% of European Residents Is Anti-Semitic," *NRG/Maariv*, January 24, 2016, www.nrg.co.il/online/16/ART2/750/278

picture of Jewish life in Europe was presented in an article published two years prior, this time pertaining to France, which claimed that "just a little over five hours away, 400,000 Jews [are] forced to deal almost daily with an atmosphere of hatred, attacks and expressions of extreme hostility on the part of their neighbors. The authorities, for their own reasons, close their eyes and the media contributes their share to the intensification of hatred."[103] A report published by *Maariv* in 2016, accompanied by the symbolic Yizkor candle, indicated that these anti-Semitic manifestations should not be considered an aberration; the article claimed that almost half of European residents, 40 percent, are anti-Semitic. While the report was not published on MDHH, the Yizkor candle placed the report in the traditional framework of MDHH media output, forming an overt reminder to readers to remember the continuation of anti-Semitism as a perpetual threat and an inherent phenomenon in the diaspora.[104]

During interviews, both first- and second-generation Israeli journalists expressed a desire to discuss anti-Semitic trends in the diaspora as a means of continually reaffirming the relevance of the past for the present. Beck, who has published work on the heightened level of anti-Semitism in Europe, including by discussing the desecration of German Jewish cemeteries and revealing Holocaust denial, maintained that it is was his "duty to discuss new manifestations of anti-Semitism."[105] According to Beck, this responsibility spurred from a detection of a desire among Israelis and Germans "to put the past behind them [which] is extremely dangerous."[106] Similarly, Klinger noted that he has an obligation to "warn future generations [as] anti-Semitism is a tradition that is alive and growing from day to day."[107] Moreover,

.html, accessed April 18, 2017; Benjamin Weinthal, "German Citizens Are No Longer Afraid to Hate Jews," *NRG/Maariv*, October 8, 2014, www.nrg.co.il/online/1/ART2/631/117.html, accessed April 18, 2017.

[103] Alex Doron, "Is Paris Burning? The Plague of Anti-Semitism in France," *NRG/Maariv*, January 8, 2012, www.nrg.co.il/online/1/ART2/324/215.html, accessed April 18, 2017. Also see Michael Tuchfeld, "In Australia, There Are Fears: Anti-Semitism Is Coming Here as Well," *NRG/Maariv*, October 27, 2014, www.nrg.co.il/online/1/ART2/651/001.html, accessed April 18, 2017; Asaf Golan, "Expert: There Is a Clear Rise in Anti-Semitism in Turkey," *NRG/Maariv*, January 8, 2014, www.nrg.co.il/online/1/ART2/538/183.html, accessed April 18, 2017.

[104] Channel 2 News, "Government Report States"; Zvika Klein, "Escaping from France: A Peak in the Immigration of Jews from Western Europe in 2015," *NRG/Maariv*, www.nrg.co.il/online/1/ART2/748/600.html, accessed April 18, 2017.

[105] Beck, Mozgovia, and Eichner, "Munich," 10; Eldad Beck, "The Righteous in Sodom," *Yedioth Ahronot*, April 21, 2009, 4; Eldad Beck, "Ten% of Jewish Cemeteries in Germany Were Desecrated in 5 Years," *Yedioth Ahronot*, January 27, 2008, 10.

[106] Interview conducted with Eldad Beck on August 8, 2016.

[107] Interview conducted with Noah Klinger on July 24, 2016

coverage of anti-Semitism, Klinger said, is meant to inform his readers of "the need for a strong Jewish state [as] the Holocaust is a reason to have a strong army."[108]

The Holocaust as a National Trauma: Evoking the Ongoing Threat

In coherence with the conception of the Israeli state as a deterrent to a second Holocaust, a June 2013 article written by Beck cited Netanyahu as saying "we will do everything we can to prevent another Holocaust."[109] When asked about the reasoning behind the uncritical inclusion[110] of this statement and its potential effects on readership, Beck indicated that he, like Netanyahu, believed that the potential of another Holocaust should not be disregarded in light of the current situation in the Middle East: "When you live in Israel you cannot ignore this threat [and] the thought that another Holocaust might happen to the Jewish people is not something you can exclude."[111] An analysis of references to the Holocaust in daily media content in the time period under review indicates that, particularly in times of violence and political tension, the Holocaust has been utilized as a frame of reference, because, as Neiger notes, it is understood as a "national trauma" and a "collective fear [as] it is not just something that occurred, but something that will occur again."[112]

---

[108] Ibid.

[109] Eldad Beck, "Netanyahu at Auschwitz: We Will Do Everything to Prevent Another Holocaust," *Ynet/Yedioth Ahronot*, June 13, 2013, www.ynet.co.il/articles/0,7340,L-4392024,00.html, accessed April 18, 2017.

[110] It is worth noting that there are other potential reasons for the media's uncritical approach toward Netanyahu. A report by *The Economist* found that reporters have, at times, been censored when their reports were critical of the prime minister. Simultaneously, Netanyahu has sought to change the media landscape by pushing for laws and rules that would "undercut his critics and boost his allies." In November 2019, the prime minister was officially indicted in cases 2000 and 4000. Case 4000 saw Netanyahu being accused of negotiating illicit deals with Shaul Elovitch – in return for favorable coverage in Bezeq's Walla News site. Case 2000 centers on Netanyahu's deal with Arnon Mozes, the publisher of *Yedioth Ahronot*. Mozes was to provide favorable coverage of the prime minister in exchange for legislation to damage its competitor, the free daily newspaper Israel Hayom. See Anonymous, "Binyamin Netanyahu and the Press: 'My own media'," *The Economist*, January 26, 2019, 39, 40.

[111] Interview conducted with Eldad Beck on August 8, 2016. Also see Noah Klinger, "Eighty-two%: The Shoah Will Return," *Yedioth Ahronot*, January 25, 2008, 8.

[112] Interview conducted with Motti Neiger on April 11, 2016. Research executed by Moshe Zuckermann also demonstrated that the Holocaust infiltrated media coverage during the First Gulf War. See Moshe Zuckermann, *Shoah in the Sealed Room: The Holocaust in Israeli Press during the Gulf War* (Tel Aviv: Author's Publication, 1992).

The identified mediated instrumentalization of the Holocaust as an analogy and, simultaneously, as a warning, spurring on the need of preventative action, indicates that retrospective and prospective memory need not constitute separate analytical categories. During the 2005 military disengagement from Gaza, in addition to the destruction of the Second Temple, the Holocaust was therefore instrumentalized as an interpretive framework for the events by Israeli settlers and, at times, the media.[113] An editorial published by Elihu Schultz in *Maariv* argued that forcible eviction of settlers from their homes was reminiscent of the expulsion of German Jews. Consequently, Schulz maintained "no one should delude him/herself [of the fact that] after the disengagement [with] the help of the government and all parties, the Arabs will win and establish concentration camps in the Negev or Sinai. I already know the list of names of the 'Kapos' that will serve them. You have been warned!"[114]

An examination of media during the peace negotiations in the 1990s reveals that the Holocaust was also used as a prospective memory to appeal to political leaders and demand preventative action. Vehemently and unconditionally opposing the 1993 Oslo Peace Accords, former MK Elyakim Haetzni, a fervent ideologue in favor of Israeli settlement of the Occupied Territories, conjured up the Holocaust to convey his objection to the "land for peace" doctrine.[115] In his 1999 *Yedioth Ahronot* article published on the commemoration of the massacre of Hebron's Jews during the 1929 Palestine riots, Haetzni not only described the "horrible cruelty" and the "flaming hatred" of the Palestinians toward the Jews in Hebron but also noted that the 1929 "pogrom [in] the Land of Israel" is

---

[113] Keren Tenenboim-Weinblatt, "We Will Get through This Together': Journalism, Trauma and the Israeli Disengagement from the Gaza Strip," *Media, Culture & Society* 30:4 (2008): 505.

[114] Elihu Schultz, "The Holocaust Is Here," *NRG/Maariv*, August 3, 2005, www.nrg.co.il/online/1/ART/966/578.html, accessed April 19, 2017.

[115] This doctrine was first successfully executed in the 1979 Egypt–Israel peace treaty, which saw a complete withdrawal by Israel of its armed forces and civilians from the Sinai Peninsula. The land for peace formula was also ostensibly adopted by Israel when it embarked on peace talks with the PLO in 1993. The article cited here follows the Protocol Concerning the Redeployment in Hebron (1997), which called for an Israeli withdrawal from 80 percent of Hebron, and the Wye River Memorandum, signed on October 23, 1998 by Arafat and Netanyahu, which called for the transfer of land to Palestinians and the shifting of parts of Area B to Area A. A few months after the Wye River agreement, Netanyahu withdrew from further implementation of the agreement, ostensibly because of the failure of the PA to fulfil its security-related obligations toward Israel. Christine Bell, *Peace Agreements and Human Rights* (Oxford: Oxford University Press, 2000), 90.

sufficient "proof that a Holocaust is also possible."[116] From the same end of the political spectrum, a political appeal was launched against Prime Minister Ehud Barak in 1998 following his intention to negotiate land for a peace agreement, this time by Yehuda Ariel. Ariel, who was not a Holocaust survivor but "lived with the Holocaust through marriage," argued that the Holocaust meant that "all the people, and especially Holocaust survivors and their children, should object to any attempt to give up our fathers' land."[117] Presenting the most radical form of ideological opposition to the Oslo Accords, *Yedioth Ahronot* offered a platform to the assassin of Prime Minister Yitzhak Rabin, Yigal Amir. In a letter published two years after the murder, Amir, using the popular discourse emblematic of right-wing opposition to Rabin and the 1993 Oslo Accords,[118] compared the assassination of Rabin with the possible killing of Hitler that might have prevented the Holocaust. "Had someone killed Hitler before the Holocaust," Amir argued, "he probably would have been cursed, jailed and tortured by the Jews, for they would not have wanted to know what he had prevented."[119]

The Holocaust and the Nakba: Two Parallel Lines That Will Never Meet

The conscious coupling of anti-Israeli sentiments and Holocaust denial has equally led the Holocaust to be introduced into daily media content, fulfilling various criteria of newsworthiness simultaneously, as a topic of cultural meaningfulness, continuity, and negativity. Directing attention to the Iranian threat, an article published by *Yedioth Ahronot* in 2006 cited Israel's representative to the UN, Dan Gillerman, as saying that while Iran was denying the Holocaust, it was preparing a second one.[120] In addition to Iran, which has been presented as a bastion of anti-Semitism and Holocaust denial particularly following the organization of an

---

[116] Elyakim Haetzni, "Who Is a Good Jew," *Yedioth Ahronot*, August 3, 1999. Cited in Arye Naor, "Lessons of the Holocaust versus Territories for Peace, 1967–2001," *Israel Studies* 8:1 (2003): 131, 2.

[117] Yehuda Ariel cited in Zandberg, "The Right to Tell the (Right) Story," 15.

[118] According to Dan Ephron, it became standard to compare Rabin to Hitler or his government to the Judenrat, including by his political opponents. Ariel Sharon, for instance, stated after the signing of Oslo: "What's the difference between the Jewish leadership in the ghetto and this government. There, they were forced to collaborate. Here they do it willingly." Dan Ephron, *Killing a King: The Assassination of Yitzhak Rabin and the Remaking of Israel* (New York: W.W. Norton, 2016), 143.

[119] Cited in Naor, "Lessons," 143, 144.

[120] Israel News, "Gillerman at the UN Ceremony: Iran Is Preparing the Next Holocaust," *Ynet/Yedioth Ahronot*, January 2, 2006, www.ynet.co.il/articles/0,7340,L-3207235,00.html, accessed April 19, 2017.

"International Holocaust Cartoon Competition" in 2016, Holocaust denial or its minimization by Palestinians has also been considered emblematic of anti-Zionism and, therefore, a threat to the existence of Israel.[121] Relying on polls conducted at the University of Haifa, articles written in *Maariv* have presented Holocaust denial among the approximately 40 percent of "Israeli Arabs" and "Arabs" in the same sentence as Palestinians' rejection of "Israel's right to exist as a Jewish and democratic state."[122] It is in this context that the Nakba has also been branded a myth that is used by Palestinians to counter or minimize the historical truth of the Holocaust.[123] For instance, a 1998 article entitled "Nakba, Shoah and More" noted that "myths are myths and historical truths are historical truths and these are two parallel lines that will never meet." Relying on traditional Zionist-Israeli historiography of the 1948 War, Amos Kinan reminded his readers in this article that "the Palestinians of *Eretz* Israel" rejected the partition plan and that the Arab world was uniform in its desire to "attack it [Israel] and to destroy it." Moreover, according to the author, any comparison between the Holocaust and the Nakba, as had been attempted by "Arab-Israeli demagogues," constitutes a danger to their people, leading Kinan to conclude that "until the Arabs deal themselves courageously with their own history, until they hold a dialogue with themselves, a true dialogue with people like myself will not take place."[124]

Additional articles denouncing the "inconceivable comparison" between the Nakba "as a fruit of historical writing of Palestinian propaganda" and the

---

[121] Itamar Eichner, "Holocaust Denial Competition: 50,000 Dollars to the Winner," *Ynet/Yedioth Ahronot*, January 12, 2016, www.ynet.co.il/articles/0,7340,L-4752001,00.html, accessed April 19, 2017; Itamar Eichner, "Khomeini's Holocaust Denial Video: Zionists Kill Children," *Ynet/Yedioth Ahronot*, January 28, 2016, www.ynet.co.il/articles/0,7340,L-4759216,00.html, accessed April 19, 2017; AP, "They Do Not Deny, but Just Compare the [Holocaust] to the [Plight of the] Palestinians: Holocaust Painting Competition in Iran," *Ynet/Yedioth Ahronot*, May 14, 2016, www.ynet.co.il/articles/0,7340,L-4802860,00.html, accessed April 19, 2017; News Agencies, "Iran Presents: An Exhibition of Caricatures on the Holocaust," *NRG/Maariv*, May 13, 2016, www.nrg.co.il/online/1/ART2/777/717.html, accessed April 19, 2017.

[122] Jonathan Halley, "More than 40% of the Arabs in Israel Are Holocaust Deniers," *NRG/Maariv*, May 18, 2009, www.nrg.co.il/online/1/ART1/892/038.html, accessed April 21, 2017.

[123] Jonathan Halley, "Survey: 66% of Israeli Arabs Reject Its Existence," *NRG/Maariv*, May 18, 2011, www.nrg.co.il/online/1/ART2/242/096.html.2011, accessed April 21, 2017. This article noted "that almost 30 percent of Israeli Arabs reject the existence of the Jewish state and almost 38 percent do not believe that a Holocaust was committed" while also pointing out that 71 percent believe that "the Jews are the main culprits for the Nakba that befell the Palestinians in 1948."

[124] Amos Kinan, "Nakba, Shoah and More," *Yedioth Ahronot*, April 3, 1998, 25.

Holocaust aim to reveal the Palestinians' formative role in designing and executing the Holocaust with reference to the Palestinian leader and Grand Mufti of Jerusalem at the time, al-Haj Amin al-Husseini, a theory previously espoused in Netanyahu's 1993 book *A Place among the Nations*.[125] According to one article published in 2011 and written by a director of Im Tirtzu[126] at Bar-Ilan University, al-Husseini not only prevented Jews from finding refuge from the Nazis in Palestine as a result of the 1936–1939 Palestinian revolt but also "tried to organize the extermination of Jews in Palestine [...] and did not conceal his desire to establish a concentration camp in Jenin."[127]

It is because of the failure to acknowledge the Mufti's encouragement of the extermination of the Jews and an unwillingness among Palestinians to recognize "their responsibility [for the Nakba]" that Yemini posits that the Nakba, like the Holocaust, served to build a national memory. Yet, in contrast to the Jews, for whom the memory of the Holocaust was "used for construction," Yemini argues, for the Arabs, the Nakba encouraged "a victimhood discourse" and strengthened "feelings of hatred and vengeance, remaining the main engine of the terror industry and [fueling] the perpetuation of the refugee status."[128]

---

[125] In this book, Netanyahu, similarly to his predecessor, Ben-Gurion, argued that the former Mufti of Jerusalem had been at least a catalyst in persuading Hitler to carry out the extermination of the Jews. Moreover, Netanyahu claimed that relations between the Arabs and Nazis continued after World War II and were most recently resumed by the PLO. Benjamin Netanyahu, *A Place among the Nations: Israel and the World* (London: Bantam Books, 1993), 193, 194. Also see Eldad Beck and Itamar Eichner, "In Germany too, Netanyahu again Blamed Mufti for His Responsibility," *Ynet*, October 21, 2015, www.ynet.co.il/articles/0,7340,L-4714608,00.html, accessed August 16, 2017.

[126] Im Tirtzu (Hebrew: if you will), invoking Herzl's famous statement "If you will, it is not a dream," indicates in its mission statement that it works "on behalf of Zionism and Jewish democratic values" while seeking to unmask and expose "various threats to Zionism and Israel." In May 2011, Im Tirtzu launched a campaign entitled "Nakba Nonsense" which conceived of the Nakba as a "lie that threatens to drown us like a tsunami." Ben Hartman and Lahav Harkov, "Im Tirtzu Launches Campaign against 'Myths' of the Nakba," *Jerusalem Post*, May 13, 2011, www.jpost.com/National-News/Im-Tirtzu-launches-campaign-against-myths-of-the-Nakba, accessed July 10, 2017; "About Us," Im Tirtzu, https://imti.org.il/en/about-us/movement/, accessed July 10, 2017.

[127] Nati Avnery, "About the Holocaust and the Nakba," *NRG/Maariv*, May 16, 2011, www.nrg.co.il/online/1/ART2/241/319.html, accessed April 21, 2017. For historical articles in *Maariv* making a similar argument, see Idith Zertal, *Israel's Holocaust and the Politics of Nationhood*, trans. Chaya Galai (Cambridge: Cambridge University Press, 2005), 101.

[128] Ben-Dror Yemini, "The Disgrace of the Shoah and the Nakba," *Yedioth Ahronot*, August 28, 2015. Also see Ben-Dror Yemini, "The Holocaust and the Nakba: The Jews Turned to Construction; the Palestinians Turned to Incitement," *NRG/Maariv*, April 27, 2014, www.nrg.co.il/online/1/ART2/575/324.html, accessed June 1, 2017.

The Mufti's support of Nazi Germany[129] has also been invoked to downplay the Palestinian Nakba.[130] In his 2009 article titled "The Jewish Nakba: Expulsions, Massacres and Forced Conversations," Yemini notes that the Mufti's desire to "slaughter the Jews" materialized with the "mini-Holocaust of the Jews in Arab countries." In Yemini's view, the Jewish Nakba, which refers to the exodus of some 850,000 Jews[131] from Arab countries following the establishment of the state of Israel,[132] "was worse than the Palestinian Nakba. The only difference is that the Jews did not turn that Nakba into their founding ethos."[133] The Palestinian Nakba, he goes on to argue in a 2014 op-ed on the same topic, thus both "ignor[es] the broad picture," and is – as the Jewish Nakba[134] indicates – merely symptomatic of the "huge population

---

[129] It is worth noting that in a 2015 speech at the World Zionist Congress, Netanyahu erron, eously claimed that the Mufti of Jerusalem had "a central role in fomenting the Final Solution" in an attempt to characterize Palestinian hostility toward Israel as a product of "innate, ancient Arab hatred of Jews." Dina Porat, the chief historian of Yad Vashem, deemed the Israeli leader's revisionism "completely erroneous, on all counts." Ishaan Tharoor, "The Real Reason a Palestinian Mufti Allied with Hitler? It's Not So Shocking," *The Washington Post*, October 22, 2015, www.washingtonpost.com/news/worldviews/wp/2015/10/22/the-real-reason-a-palestinian-mufti-allied-with-hitler-its-not-so-shocking/, accessed April 3, 2020.

[130] According to the United States Holocaust Memorial Museum, the Mufti's meeting with – and support of – Hitler was mostly about his desire to secure national status for his people and be recognized as a future Arab leader. Nevertheless, even after he realized the Germans would not give him what he sought, al-Husseini continued to work with both Fascist Italy and Nazi Germany until 1945, broadcasting anti-Allied and anti-Jewish propaganda by radio to the Arab world and indoctrinating Muslim men to serve in Axis military and auxiliary units. See "Hajj Amin Al-Husayni: Wartime Propagandist," United States Holocaust Memorial Museum, https://encyclopedia.ushmm.org/content/en/article/hajj-amin-al-husayni-wartime-propagandist, accessed April 3, 2020.

[131] Push factors included persecution, antisemitism, political and economic instability, and a desire to fulfill Zionist yearnings, indicating a multitude of (voluntary) reasons for Jewish emigration. As Tom Segev notes: "Deciding to emigrate to Israel from one of the Arab countries was often a very personal decision. [...] It was based on the particular circumstances of the individual's life. They were not all poor, or 'dwellers in dark caves and smoking pits'. [...] Nor were they always subject to persecution, repression or discrimination in their native lands. They emigrated for a variety of reasons, depending on the country, the time, the community, and the person." Tom Segev, *1949 The First Israelis* (New York: Simon and Schuster, 1986), 161.

[132] Warren Hoge, "Groups Seeks Justice for 'Forgotten' Jews," *The New York Times*, November 5, 2007, www.nytimes.com/2007/11/04/world/americas/04iht-nations.4.8182206.html, accessed February 8, 2020.

[133] Ben-Dror Yemini, "The Jewish Nakba: Expulsions, Massacres and Forced Conversions," *Ynet*, May 16, 2009, www.makorrishon.co.il/nrg/online/1/ART1/891/209.html, accessed February 8, 2020.

[134] In 2014, the Knesset designated November 30 as the official date of the annual commemoration for the 850,000 Jewish refugees who were displaced from Arab countries and Iran in the twentieth century.

exchanges" that took place in the last century. The implication of this argument, which ignores the discrepancy in national rights for Jewish immigrants – both past and present – in Israel and the ongoing statelessness for Palestinians, is clear: "millions of Jews are not going to return to Arab states [and] millions of Palestinians are not coming back to Israel."[135]

Concluding Remarks

The temporal inclusion[136] of the Holocaust in Israeli mass media highlights its location at the core of the nation's cultural activity and awareness.[137] The explicit conveyance of the Holocaust to future generations on MDHH, as sought through mnemonic prompts in printed mass media and, since 2012, online media, therefore does not solely aim to demonstrate an explicit duty to remember an appropriated Holocaust as a historical event but also seeks to impart a prospective or a prescriptive memory. Characterized by the reiteration of the "never again" slogan, the significance of this prospective memory lies in its antithetical message, which dictates it *can* happen again.

While the mediated portrayal of the diaspora as a continual bastion of anti-Semitism can be interpreted as a reinforcement of the Zionist dichotomy between the "here" and the "there," the discussion of a domestic threat paradoxically demonstrates that Jewish continuity is never guaranteed. Analogical usage of the Holocaust in the post-Oslo era on mass media platforms reveals that, both on MDHH and in daily mediation, the Holocaust is continually evoked as an impending threat to oppose the perceived political complacence and compromise and demand preventative action.

Bolstered by the framing of the Israeli-Palestinian conflict in the context of an ongoing threat and an ascribed historical – and contemporary – desire to eradicate Jewry, part and parcel of this prescriptive memory constitutes a mediated marginalization of the Palestinian Nakba. Portrayed as a historical myth used to spur on a false victimhood narrative among the perceived enemy, the Nakba is denounced as a symptom

---

[135] Ben-Dror Yemini, "What About the Jewish Nakba," *Ynet*, November 28, 2014, www
.ynetnews.com/articles/0,7340,L-4597344,00.html, accessed February 8, 2020.

[136] Temporal here follows the term's usage by Robert Wistrich, as a means of indicating the past's contemporary application. Robert S. Wistrich, "Israel and the Holocaust Trauma," *Jewish History* 11:2 (1997): 18.

[137] Dina Porat, *Israeli Society, the Holocaust and Its Survivors* (London: Vallentine Mitchell, 2008), 5.

of a general unwillingness among Palestinians to take historical responsibility, including for their participation in the Final Solution.

Crucially, the explicit allusion to the Nakba within Holocaust media output testifies to an awareness of its formative role within contemporary Palestinian consciousness and reveals that a minimization of the other's history is not solely based on its active physical erasure. Usage of the Arabic term, including in article titles, instead, illustrates a practice of social repression that hinges on debunking the credibility of those adhering to the narrative and, thereby, pouring scorn on the term's usage. The final chapter of this work, in a similar fashion, demonstrates that Holocaust minimization does not solely rely on its societal preclusion. In addition to the overt questioning of the historical veracity of the Jewish genocide, the Holocaust, somewhat incongruously, has thus been conjured within Nakba media output as a means of highlighting the depths of Palestinian suffering at the hands of the Israelis.

7   Preserving the Past, Mobilizing the Past

The 1993 Oslo Accords not only had far-reaching effects for Palestinian education and commemoration but in 1995 also led to the establishment of an official Palestinian press sanctioned by the newly established authority and free from Israeli censorship, with the telling name *al-Hayat al-Jadida* (Arabic: the new life). In the same year, following the establishment of the Ministry of Information, the Palestinian Authority issued the Palestinian Press Law, which replaced Israeli military regulations in the Occupied Territories and cancelled all Israeli military orders.[1] Consequently, for the first time, articles on Palestinian displacement in 1948 and its implications for Palestinian self-understanding, including word usage such as *'awdah* (Arabic: return) and *ṣumūd* (Arabic: steadfastness), were able to appear freely in Palestinian news content.[2]

In contrast to the West Bank, the accords did not provide a new political or legislative framework for media inside the 1948 borders and East Jerusalem; nevertheless, the Oslo Accords did have a direct impact on media content concerning the 1948 displacement. Notwithstanding the continued formal existence of Israeli censorship in East Jerusalem, in coherence with the 1993 Declaration of Principles, which called for "co-ordination and co-operation in the field of communications and

---

[1] The Press Law was adopted by the Palestinian Council of Ministries on July 17 and signed by Arafat on July 25, 1995. The Press Law contains fifty-one articles that most closely resemble many of the articles in the 1993 Jordanian Press Law. The Palestinian law sets conditions for licensing, publishing, running printing presses or research centers, and printing books and describes the role of the authority and the legal system. The law also regulates advertising and the distribution and importation of publications. Orayb Najjar, "The 1995 Palestinian Press Law: A Comparative Study," *Communication Law and Policy* 2:1 (1997): 46; Amal Jamal, "The Palestinian Media: An Obedient Servant or a Vanguard of Democracy?," *Journal of Palestine Studies* 29:3 (2000): 50.

[2] Robert I. Friedman, "Israeli Censorship of the Palestinian Press," *Journal of Palestine Studies* 13:1 (1983): 98.

media,"[3] East Jerusalem media, as the chapter below will testify, were able to address the Nakba as a collective historical grievance with contemporary relevance following the peace negotiations. Inside the 1948 borders, privately owned Arabic daily and weekly newspapers had already started appearing in Nazareth in the 1980s, including *Kul al-Arab* (Arabic: all the Arabs) in 1987 and *al-Sinnārah* (Arabic: the fishing hook) in 1983 and, consequently, were able to address the minority's concerns.[4] Yet, the Oslo Accords, termed "a Palestinian Versailles,"[5] did constitute an important break in media production, as the marginalization of (internal) refugees in the peace process and the lead-up to the symbolic fiftieth anniversary of the Nakba prompted recurring media production on the Nakba in the years following the accords.

The ensuing chapter offers an examination of mediated Nakba output in two Palestinian newspapers that in the time period under review have enjoyed the largest readership and circulation – *Kul al-Arab* and *Al-Quds* (Arabic: Jerusalem) – and in one newspaper that represents the official stance of the PA, the abovementioned *al-Hayat al-Jadida*.[6] Although few academic studies have been conducted on reading habits and consumption patterns of (online) Arabic newspapers, readership surveys have been held by various polling institutes, including the I'lam Centre for Research of Arabic Media and the Palestinian Central Bureau for Statics (PCBS), which evidence the centrality of the abovementioned news

---

[3] See *Declaration of Principles on Interim Self-Government Arrangements*, September 13, 1993. The text can be found on the Israeli Ministry of Foreign Affairs' website. "Declaration of Principles on Interim Self-Government Arrangements," September 13, 1993, http://mfa .gov.il/MFA/ForeignPolicy/Peace/Guide/Pages/Declaration%20of%20Principles.aspx, accessed June 20, 2017.

[4] Hanna Adoni, Dan Caspi, and Akiva Cohen, *Media, Minorities and Hybrid Identities: The Arab and Russian communities in Israel* (Cresskill, NJ: Hampton Press, 2006), 61, 63.

[5] Edward Said, "The Morning After," *London Review of Books* 15:20 (1993): 3–5.

[6] There is a lack of reliable figures on online news consumption by the Palestinian community inside the 1948 borders, East Jerusalem, and the West Bank and electronic media consumption's evolvement in the period under review. Nevertheless, an article published by *Haaretz* in 2008 noted that 45,000 people a day visit the *Kul al-Arab* website, making it the second most popular site after panet.com, which is linked to the Arabic newspaper *Panorama*. While concrete insight into electronic media consumption in the Palestinian Territories and East Jerusalem does not exist, statistics published by the Palestinian Central Bureau of Statistics in 2014 indicate that 35.7 percent of persons (10 years and over) use the internet (54.5 percent in the West Bank) to read online newspapers, magazines, or electronic books. Nathan Lipson and Maayan Cohen, "Google Trends Presents a Very Different Picture of the Popularity of Israeli Websites," *Haaretz*, June 23, 2008, www.haaretz.com/print-edition/business/ynet-is-the-leading-israeli-internet-portal-1.248301, accessed August 16, 2017; PCBS, *Percentage Distribution of Persons (10 Years and Over) Who Use Computer by Internet Use and Selected Background Characteristics* (PCBS, 2014); PCBS, *Percentage of Persons (10 Years and Over) in the Palestine Who Use the Internet by Purpose of Use* (PCBS, 2014).

outlets and testify to media consumption patterns among Palestinians living in Israel, East Jerusalem, and the West Bank. Studies conducted inside the 1948 borders indicate that members of the Palestinian community are avid media consumers, albeit on an irregular basis. A survey conducted in 2005 by the I'lam Centre revealed that 80 percent read Arabic newspapers infrequently, with 45 percent consuming newspapers on the weekends and sometimes during the week and only 9 percent of the respondents reading Arabic news on a daily basis.[7] A year later, however, a study found that the number of media consumers was higher, with 72.7 percent reading weekly Arabic publications.[8] Emblematic of this latter-mentioned trend, polls conducted inside Israel consistently have found that the commercial weekly newspaper *Kul al-Arab* has remained the most popular newspapers since its founding, with 29.5 percent of the respondents in a 2011 survey preferring it over the other two major weekly newspapers, *al-Sinnārah* and *Panorama*.[9]

Surveys conducted on readership habits in the West Bank (inclusive of East Jerusalem) reveal similar consumer patterns to those existing inside the 1948 borders. According to the last major survey published by PCBS in 2002, only 12.5 percent read newspapers on a daily basis and 39.7 "sometimes" read daily publications.[10] Figures on newspaper circulation in East Jerusalem and Ramallah are more difficult to verify, as polling among media consumers is infrequent and estimates by newspaper staff are notoriously high. Thus, *Al-Quds*, founded in 1951, according to its publishers distributes 50,000 copies daily; however, media observers and polls conducted by the Palestinian Central Bureau for Statistics have called this figure into question, claiming that the level does not exceed 30,000 copies. Despite this discrepancy, since the late 1980s, *Al-Quds*, which is distributed widely in Jerusalem, Ramallah, and Bethlehem, has been the paper with the highest circulation in the West Bank and East

---

[7] Dan Caspi and Mustafa Kabaha, *The Palestinian Arab In/Outsiders: Media and Conflict in Israel* (London/Portland: Vallentine Mitchell, 2011), 202.

[8] According to a survey conducted by Hanna Adoni, Dan Caspi, and Akiva Cohen, members of the Palestinian community in Israel also consume Hebrew media outlets and, according to their research, 54.4 percent read Hebrew newspapers. Adoni, Caspi, and Cohen, *Media, Minorities and Hybrid Identities*, 79, 82.

[9] *al-Sinnārah* ranked second with 26.1 percent, while *Panorama* occupied a third place with 13.5 percent. One in six interviewees, 15.8 percent, ranked *al-Ittiḥād* (Arabic: the union) as the most important newspaper. Caspi and Kabaha, *Palestinian*, 64, 202; Amal Jamal, *The Arab Public Sphere in Israel: Media Space and Cultural Resistance* (Bloomington: Indiana University Press, 2009), 83.

[10] PCBS, *Mass Media Survey 2000 – Main Findings* (PCBS, 2002), 66.

Jerusalem.[11] The aforementioned 2002 survey held in the Palestinian Territories found that 81.1 percent of respondents preferred *Al-Quds*, far outnumbering *al-Hayat al-Jadida* (4.8 percent).[12] Indeed, *al-Hayat al-Jadida*, which is wholly owned and funded by the PA and since 1997 has kept most of the staff on its payroll, is the least popular "major" newspaper.[13] Research conducted by Nibal Thawabteh puts the circulation number at approximately 7,000 copies, 3,000 less than the publishers claim. Despite these low numbers, *al-Hayat al-Jadida* does enjoy a remarkable reception in certain areas of the West Bank, including in the governorates of Hebron, Jenin, and Tulkarem and in the ministries and government organizations in Ramallah.[14]

Similarly to Chapter 6, the analysis that follows forms a systematic examination of anniversary journalism, i.e., annual mediation on Nakba Day. Yet, reflecting historical commemoration practices discussed in Chapter 4, in the years under examination, anniversarial Nakba invocation has occurred on various important historical dates. Prior to the official inauguration of Nakba Day on the 15th of May by the chairman of the PLO, Arafat, mediated Nakba output – like annual Nakba commemorations – mainly took place on the 14th of May in *Al-Quds* and *al-Hayat al-Jadida*, marking the establishment of the Israeli state in 1948. Moreover, in coherence with local commemorative practices representative of the pre-1994 era, massacres and displacements of individual communities, such as Deir Yassin, are mentioned in Palestinian newspapers on their respective historical dates, forming a reminder of a shared fate despite diverging communal experiences. Consequently, the term "anniversary journalism" will be applied in this chapter in a broad sense, as a means of referring to both anniversarial and daily media Nakba output that seeks to highlight the historical events that have collectively become known as *al-Nakba*. The broad application of anniversary journalism should not infer the amalgamation of commemorative and daily mediated Nakba memories. Rather, this chapter will illustrate that the Nakba, as a persistent symbol of daily Palestinian marginalization, particularly in the West Bank and East Jerusalem, has transformed the media into a "counterhegemonic public space," which propagates

[11] Nibal Thawabteh, "Palestinian Media Map: Production Congestion and Consumption Dispersion," in *Journalism Education in Countries with Limited Media*, ed. Beate Josephi (New York: Peter Lang, 2010), 74; PCBS, *Mass Media Survey 2000*, 22.
[12] PCBS, *Mass Media Survey 2000*, 74.
[13] Nossek and Rinnawi, "Censorship and Freedom of the Press," 188; Layla al-Zubaidi, *Walking a Tightrope. News Media and Freedom Expression in the Arab Middle East* (Ramallah: Heinrich Böll Foundation, 2004), 70.
[14] Thawabteh, "Palestinian Media Map," 75.

a Palestinian national awareness and active mobilization against the Israeli presence.

Indeed, although the Oslo Accords on both sides of the Green Line transformed Nakba mediated output, the divergent historic media land-scapes in these areas meant that the creation of a media *for* and *by* Palestinians constituted different degrees of change.[15] Reflecting the disparate historical and political circumstances, the emergence of an independent Palestinian media in the West Bank and East Jerusalem has meant that the Palestinian press, in coherence with what Denis McQuail defines as the developmental media model, has become a means of expressing "national problems" and "nationalist goals."[16] While Nakba media output primarily constitutes an interpretative frame-work for contemporary grievances held by the Palestinian minority inside the 1948 borders, which include a failure to teach the Palestinian narrative of the 1948 War in schoolbooks and, since 2011, legalized efforts by the Israeli majority to thwart Nakba commemoration, it is in the West Bank and East Jerusalem that the Nakba has become an all-encompassing metaphor. Mediated Nakba output here urges for the undoing of the Nakba by calling for the implementation of the right of return and, simultaneously, demanding the establishment of a Palestinian state with East Jerusalem as its capital. Emblematic of a collective watershed, the Nakba has also been instrumentalized as a rallying point in times of interterritorial political tensions between Hamas and Fatah in order to demonstrate societal and political unity, all the while pointing at the same common culprit: Israel.

The concentration on the mediated presentation of an ongoing Nakba as a direct result of Israeli actions rests on the theoretical concept of a defensive victimhood narrative, previously laid out in Chapter 4. As such, rather than simply being symptomatic of a retaliatory quid pro quo based on Israeli attempts to prevent invocation of the Nakba, the subversion of the Holocaust – identified in the mediated convergence of the Holocaust and the Nakba – occurs as a result of its discursive incompatibility with the Palestinian narrative. Portrayed as the enemy's foundational past that has been continuously instrumentalized to drive the Zionist project and,

---

[15] Dan Caspi and Nelly Elias, "Don't Patronize Me: Media-*by* and Media *for* Minorities," *Ethnic and Racial Studies* 34:1 (2011): 62–82.

[16] The developmental model is chiefly found in developing countries, particularly in new states in Africa, South America, and Southeast Asia created after the Second World War. According to this model, the media are expected to facilitate the advancement of declared national goals, with most emphasis being placed on unifying the nation and promoting social integration. Denis McQuail, *Mass Communication Theory* (London: Sage Publications, 2000), 155.

in the process, inflict persistent Palestinian suffering, any full acknowledgment of the Holocaust is thus repudiated as it is deemed to inherently entail a negation of the Palestinian watershed and its contemporary
manifestations.[17]

The Historic Palestinian Media Landscape

Palestinian press' development following the 1948 War, to a large extent,
has been dictated by the vicissitudes of the Israeli-Palestinian conflict,
shifting from a wholly repressed medium under the various ruling
authorities to a mobilized mode of expression for – and on behalf of –
the Palestinians in the wake of the First Intifadah and the Oslo Accords.
The liberation of the Palestinian press "from the shackles of the [Israeli]
establishment"[18] came forth from vastly different media environments
on both sides of the Green Line, reflecting the disparate political circumstances and the dynamics of the relationship between the Israeli state and
the respective Palestinian communities. As this chapter will elucidate, the
media models installed by the Israeli state and the Israeli military government subsequent to the 1948 War inside Israel and the Six-Day War
in the West Bank were to be formative frameworks for post-1994
Palestinian media, this time, however, mirroring Palestinian communities' own engagement with the Israeli hegemony.

Demonstrative of the societal and political aftermath of the 1948 War,
inside the 1948 borders an integrationist media model was developed by
the Israeli victorious majority for the Palestinian vanquished minority of
approximately 156,000, creating what Dan Caspi and Mustafa Kabaha
succinctly term a "media-for" model. The production of Arabic media
by the Israeli establishment, which included the Israeli government,
various Zionist political parties, and the Israeli communist party in its
various reincarnations, was meant to serve as a medium through which
the Jewish majority could communicate with the minority while simultaneously reducing the objections of the minority to the national goals of
the majority and diminishing the realization of Palestinian national
ambitions.[19] In al-Yawm (Arabic: the day) (1948–1966), a newspaper
affiliated with the ruling party Mapai and its satellites in return for

---

[17] Rotberg, "Building Legitimacy," 3.   [18] Caspi and Kabaha, *Palestinian*, 15.
[19] These publications were also designed for Jewish immigrants from Muslim
countries. Thus, al-Waṭan (Arabic: the homeland) appeared on behalf of Mapai
(1952–1953) and was directed mainly at new immigrants from Arabic-speaking
countries. Arabic newspapers such as al-Waṭan, suffered from a short lifespan if
only because they were perceived as an exigency, stemming from the need to
communicate with new immigrants from Arabic-speaking countries in their own

generous (financial) support, the Israeli state was therefore presented in a positive light, as indicated in the writings of Wafi'a Iqdays. In June 1950, Iqdays informed his readers that "the benefits and the fruits of Israeli democracy" meant that "anyone who claims that the situation has not taken a turn for the good since the end of the fighting probably suffers from the 'malady of exaggeration'."[20]

Although the termination of the military government in 1966 led to increased freedom of movement among Palestinian journalists and, consequently, access to their target population, the amalgamation of previously installed legalized modes of censorship and the incorporation of the newly Occupied Territories meant that a media *for* and *by* Palestinians remained elusive. Fueled by a heightened climate of suspicion resulting from exposure to East Jerusalem and West Bank newspapers, previous adoption of the British Ordinance of 1933 and the Defense (Emergency) Regulations of 1945 by the Ministry of Interior in 1948 enabled close surveillance of Arabic press produced by Palestinians.[21] Content related to the conflict, the coverage of settlements, land expropriation, and discrimination toward the Palestinian population, both in the Occupied Territories and inside Israel, were particularly subject to scrutiny by censors, leading Palestinian journalists to engage in self-censorship to avoid attracting warnings or suspensions. Moreover, notwithstanding the emergence of a (censored) Palestinian media-by model, including in communist outlets such as *al-Jadīd* (Arabic: the new), the continued dependence on political funding and the partisan nature of Arabic newspapers led to a dearth in Palestinian readership. As a result, between 1967 and 1983, circulation numbers remained largely similar to the first period, with the most popular daily newspaper, *al-Ānbā'* (Arabic: the news), a mouthpiece for Israeli government policies, only reaching a circulation of approximately 4–6,000 despite distribution on both sides of the Green Line and a rising literacy rate.[22]

---

language, "the language of the enemy." Adoni, Caspi, and Cohen, *Media, Minorities and Hybrid Identities*, 60.

[20] Caspi and Kabaha, *Palestinian*, 79, 80.

[21] The 1933 Ordinance empowered the Israeli government to shut down a newspaper if it was deemed detrimental to public interest, while Regulation 95 of the Defense Regulations enabled the administration to refuse to grant a license for the publication of a newspaper without giving any reason for its decision. Soffer, *Mass Communication in Israel*, 40, 41.

[22] Amal Jamal, "Mechanisms of Governmentality and Constructing Hollow Citizenship: Arab Palestinians in Israel," in *Israel and Its Palestinian Citizens: Ethnic Privileges in the Jewish State*, ed. Nadim N. Rouhana and Sahar S. Huneidi (Cambridge: Cambridge University Press, 2017), 176, 177; Caspi and Kabaha, *Palestinian*, 145.

In contrast to the media landscape inside the 1948 borders, a popular Palestinian press did emerge in East Jerusalem and the West Bank in the wake of the 1967 War, albeit under heavy restrictions imposed by the Israeli state. In addition to the media-for model, namely a media wholly owned and managed by the Israeli military regime, a Palestinian press came forth out of the merger of West Bank newspapers and the forced move to Amman in March 1967 under King Hussein bin Talal. *Al-Quds*, representing the fusion of *al-Difā'* (Arabic: the defense) and *al-Jihād* (Arabic: the [inner] struggle or holy war), became the first "independent" daily to obtain publication rights from the Israeli military government and, despite its initial pro-Jordanian stance, became the most popular publication in the territories.[23] Yet, as was the case for Palestinian media in Israel, a fully independent press in the newly Occupied Territories remained absent. Similarly to their predecessors, the Jordanians and the British, the Israelis applied legal means to subdue any mediated Palestinian (and Arab) nationalism in annexed East Jerusalem and the occupied West Bank, including by censoring any criticism of the Israeli occupation and thwarting usage of the media as a medium for political mobilization. The issuing of military orders together with the adoption of the above-mentioned British press regulations meant that Palestinian publications in the territories operated under more severe constraints than those published inside the 1948 borders.[24] As such, the system of external prior censorship in coherence with the 1945 Emergency Regulations was bolstered by military orders issued from 1967 onwards, which forbid the publication of anything that according to the military court was deemed of "political significance" and "prejudicial to the defense of [the state] or to the public safety or to public order."[25]

[23] Orayb Najjar, "Power and the Palestinian Press: Israeli Censorship on the West Bank, 1967–1991" (PhD Diss., Indiana University, 1992), 95, 96; Article 19, *Journalism under Occupation Israel's Regulation of the Palestinian Press* (New York: Committee to Protect Journalists, 1988), 24, 25.
[24] Wael Abdelal, *Hamas and the Media: Politics and Strategy* (London: Routledge, 2016), 34; Najjar, "Power and the Palestinian Press," 87.
[25] Khalil Rinnawi and Hillel Nossek differentiate between three different modes of censorship: (I) the external mode, which refers to censorship implemented through written laws, regulations, or other legal and formal tools; (II) the consensual mode, which concerns various permanent or ad hoc agreements and arrangements between government or other bodies and the media, and whose aim is to prevent the publication of damaging material without needing to resort to legal means and without imposing the burden of responsibility solely on the media, and (III) the self-internal mode, referring to the form of voluntarily applied censorship that the media impose on themselves. It is clear that in this case the external mode was applied. Nossek and Rinnawi, "Censorship and Freedom of the Press," 184.

News items of political significance were not limited to material that incited violence or hatred or civil disorder, as claimed by the Israeli authorities. Rather, in his 1983 study of Israeli censorship, Robert E. Friedman demonstrated that the "campaign to silence the Palestinian press" intensified in tense periods. In the aftermath of Israel's 1982 invasion of Lebanon, Palestinian editors complained that Israeli censorship had become so severe that the Arabic dailies in East Jerusalem, including Al-Quds, had been forced to fill their pages "with innocuous social items and non-controversial stories translated from the Hebrew press."[26] The "careful monitoring and occasional [...] censoring [of] the Palestinian press,"[27] also meant a systematic undermining of Palestinian consciousness and nationalism. In his 1983 work, Benvenisti noted that censors' primary concern was "to eradicate expression that could foster Palestinian nationalist feelings, or that suggest[ed] that Palestinians are a nation with a national heritage," including by excluding text containing the word "Palestine."[28] Moreover, it was because of Israeli authorities' tendency to view Palestinian publications as propaganda organs "inciting masses to violence"[29] rather than vehicles of news that one Palestinian journalist concluded in 1986 that Israel's censorship measures were designed to "censor our heritage, our history, and our culture, in order to deprive us of our Palestinian consciousness."[30] Contemporary reports on censored content by human rights organizations indicate that, in addition to words such as suffering, colonialism, and Zionism, words that had taken on a symbolically loaded meaning were targeted for censorship, such as *kifāḥ* (Arabic: struggle), *ṣumūd* (Arabic: steadfastness), and *'awdah* (Arabic: return).[31]

The Emergence of a Mobilized Palestinian Press

The existence of censorship practices in the post-1967 era in East Jerusalem and the West Bank proved formative for the conception of

[26] Friedman, "Israeli Censorship," 100.   [27] Ibid., 98.
[28] After the 1967 War, the Israeli military government in Nablus informed all printers in the city that it was forbidden to print any text containing the word "Palestine," regardless of the text's content. Najjar, "Power and the Palestinian Press," 274/5; Meron Benvenisti, *Israeli Censorship on Arab Publication* (New York: Fund for Free Expression, 1983), 1.
[29] Friedman, "Israel Censorship," 101.
[30] Benvenisti, *Israeli Censorship*, 44; Radwan Abu Ayyash, Head of the Arab Journalists' Association in the Occupied Territories, quoted by Ori Nir in *Haaretz*, August 29, 1986.
[31] Najjar, "Power and the Palestinian Press," 170. For further information on censorship in action, see Article 19, *Cry for Change*; B'Tselem, *Censorship of the Palestinian Press in East Jerusalem* (B'Tselem, 1990), 17–26; Article 19, *Journalism*.

media as a potential mobilization medium on behalf of the Palestinians, which was to be practically realized following the Oslo Accords. Palestinian journalists living under previous Israeli censorship noted that, in theory, it was the task of journalists "to mobilize the masses against the occupation and the escalation of national activities in that struggle."[32] Yet it was not merely the systematic prevention of a mediated resistance under Israel's military government that informed the emergence of a mobilized media under the PA. With the 1980 amendment of the Tamir Law, any material deemed to support terrorist organizations[33] was made punishable by a prison term of up to three years or a fine or both; consequently, any mediated mention of the PLO, considered a terrorist organization under Israeli law until 1993, was curtailed.[34] For *Al-Quds*, a newspaper located in annexed East Jerusalem and therefore jurisdictionally part of the state of Israel, the Tamir Law meant that the publication's pro-PLO stance became subject to increased scrutiny. The cessation of talks between Arafat and King Hussein in February 1986 and Israeli officials' accusation of *Al-Quds* accepting money from the PLO thus went hand in hand with a mass clampdown on the newspaper.[35] *Al-Quds'* suppression was further aggravated during the First Intifadah, when any material that could be interpreted as implicitly supporting the PLO became subject to censorship. As such, the newspaper's explicit support of the PA following the Oslo Accords,[36] part and parcel of Nakba media output, formed the realization of a

---

[32] Amahl Bishara, "New Media and Political Change in the Occupied Palestinian Territories: Assembling Media Worlds and Cultivating Networks of Care," *Middle East Journal of Culture and Communication* 3:1 (2010): 67; Benvenisti, *Israeli Censorship*, 38–39.
[33] Reporting conducted by Reporters Without Borders found that in the 1980s and 1990s "alleged links with a terrorist organisation" led to the closure of "at least six Arab papers in the Galilee and Jerusalem." See Reporters Without Borders, *Government Orders Closure of Arab Weekly* (Reporters Without Borders, December 2002).
[34] The 1980 amendment of the 1948 "Prevention of Terrorism Act," known as the Tamir Law, made it a criminal offense for anyone to "publish, in writing or orally, words of praise or sympathy for, or an appeal for aid or support of, a terrorist organization." While not explicitly defined, the amendment, Orayb Najjar contends, was aimed at the PLO and any publication using PLO discourse. In 1986, the Israeli government passed another amendment, making it illegal to contact officials of "terrorist organizations." Najjar, "Power and the Palestinian Press," 146; Friedman, "Israel Censorship," 98, 99.
[35] In addition to censoring texts written by authority figures and the periodical suspension of distribution permits, *Al-Quds'* editors were placed under administrative detention or given deportation orders. Najjar, "Power and the Palestinian Press," 163.
[36] It is worth noting that the late Saeb Erekat, a key Fatah leader and deputy head of the Palestinian delegation to the Madrid conference, served on the editorial board of *Al-Quds* from 1982–1994.

collective political engagement and consciousness that had previously been thwarted.

Research conducted on the emergence of an independent Palestinian press inside the 1948 borders in the mid-1980s suggests that financial motivations proved decisive in the development of a media *for* and *by* the Palestinian minority. Hanna Adoni, Dan Caspi, and Akiva Cohen argue that the rise of privately owned newspapers resulted from the uncovering of substantial advertising potential among Palestinians, thereby immunizing newspapers from the effects of political subsidies and pressure.[37] Although the discovery of new economic opportunities might have enabled the establishment of Palestinian commercial newspapers, including *Kul al-Arab* in 1987, their resonance among readers should be considered in the contemporary political climate and in the context of what Margaret Gibson and John Ogbu term "an involuntary minority."[38] The Palestinian public's withdrawal from the Israeli public sphere in the late 1980s, resulting from the experienced marginalization of Palestinian affairs, in particular bolstered cultural autonomy, because as the poet Samih al-Qasim and editor of *Kul al-Arab* stated in 1993: "We don't want a Berlin wall between Arabs and Jews. But it is natural that we would want to feel more comfortable with our language, with our culture, with our spiritual needs. We want our own theater, which doesn't exist now. We need to rebuild ourselves. We have been in a siege since 1948. We are unknown. For decades, nobody has heard about us."[39] The need for a creation of what Amal Jamal describes as "a counterhegemonic public space" was reinforced in the wake of the outbreak of the First Intifadah, a period which brought about a surge in Palestinian identity at the expense of a hybrid identity, in part, Jamal claims, as a result of new Arabic publications demonstrating unsurprising empathy with the Palestinian side.[40] Despite a continued dependence on (Israeli-Jewish) advertising firms, for the first time, Palestinian media, located in the eye of the storm of the Arab-Israeli conflict, could express

---

[37] Readers' appreciation of the newly founded commercial press was clearly articulated. Thus, while the organ of the communist party al-Ittiḥād retained its four-digit circulation, weekly circulation of *Kul al-Arab* in the late 1980s ranged from 30,000 to 35,000 copies. Adoni, Caspi, and Cohen, *Media, Minorities and Hybrid Identities*, 62.

[38] Margaret Gibson and John U. Ogbu, *Minority Status and Schooling: A Comparative Study of Immigrant and Involuntary Minorities* (New York/London: Garland Publishing, 1991).

[39] Samih al-Qasim cited in the *New York Times*. Clyde Haberman, "Israeli Arabs Say P.L.O. Pact Is a Path to First-Class Status," *The New York Times*, November 24, 1993, www .nytimes.com/1993/11/24/world/israeli-arabs-say-plo-pact-is-a-path-to-first-class-status .html?sec=&spon=&pagewanted=1, accessed August 16, 2016.

[40] Jamal, *The Arab Public Sphere in Israel*, 1, 4, 5; Adoni, Caspi, and Cohen, *Media, Minorities and Hybrid Identities*, 62, 163.

the unique circumstances of the Palestinian population in Israel and respond to cultural and political events in relation to their past, including by portraying the Nakba as an ongoing event that contextualizes relations with the dominant majority.[41]

Exposing the Nakba as a Historical Event:
A Land with a People

Five years after the Declaration of Principles and two years prior to the outbreak of the Al-Aqsa Intifadah, Palestinians in the West Bank, East Jerusalem, and Israel commemorated the fiftieth anniversary of the Nakba. Mirroring the collective preoccupation with the past, Palestinian media partook in what can be identified as the first mediated Nakba "anniversarial event," with Nakba output surfacing in the weeks and months preceding what was to become Nakba Day.

Wadiah Awadah, a former journalist at *Kul al-Arab* responsible for the consistent publication of refugees' narratives in the lead-up to the fiftieth anniversary, maintains that the increased media output prior to the anniversary was indicative of the heightened interest among readers in the Nakba on its upcoming fiftieth anniversary.[42] Nevertheless, the absence of a formal Nakba Memorial Day prior to Arafat's inauguration of Nakba Day on May 15, 1998, discussed in Chapter 4, should not be discounted, both in the mediated run-up to the anniversary and on the designated anniversary itself. As such, while "official" coverage of Nakba Day took place in *Al-Quds* and *Kul al-Arab* on May 15 in line with historic commemoration practices, *al-Hayat al-Jadida*, in anticipation of Arafat's decision, offered Nakba Day mediation on May 14, the anniversary of Israel's founding in 1948.

The novelty of Nakba media output on the occasion of the fiftieth anniversary is evidenced by both the placement of Nakba media output and the sheer amount of articles dedicated to the topic. In contrast to previous years, the examined newspapers' front pages on Nakba Day reminded readers of the momentous commemorative events taking place, creating, in the words of Daniel Dayan and Elihu Katz, a "suspended mediation."[43] Moreover, in weeks preceding the 1998 anniversary and on the anniversary itself, Palestinian media on both sides of the

[41] Jamal, *The Arab Public Sphere in Israel*, 1.
[42] Interview conducted with Wadiah Awadah on July 13 and 15, 2016. The collection of these narratives was published in the following book: Wadiah Awadah, *Memory That Does Not Die: Eyewitness Open Their Hearts to Talk about What Happened to Them in 1948 – The Year of the Nakba* (Haifa: ADRID, 2000) (in Arabic).
[43] Dayan and Katz, *Media Events*, 5.

Green Line provided readers with a historical overview of the displacement that took place in 1948 with the aim of revealing Israel's "complete web of lies and rumors and historical falsities of a land without a people for a people without a land"[44] and, perhaps most importantly, exposing "the forgery of the Zionist claim that the Palestinian refugees left willingly following calls by their own leaders."[45] Individual refugee stories deemed representative of the expulsion of the "more than 750,000"[46] Palestinians and of the 40,000 internally displaced "present absentees" at the hands of the "Zionist gangs" thus not only laid claim to the pre-1948 cultural and physical landscape but also testified to the ongoing ramifications of a forced displacement in line with the political landscape created in the aftermath of the 1948 War.[47] Demonstrative of the readership's *cadres sociaux*, *Kul al-Arab* disclosed internal refugees' stories, while *Al-Quds* concentrated on the plight of those living in refugee camps in the West Bank.[48]

The fiftieth anniversary of the Nakba in 1998, as the first mass mediated anniversarial event, constituted a formative framework for Nakba Day mediation in subsequent years, during which newspapers have simultaneously acted as active participants in Nakba mnemonics and as "commemorative mobilization agents."[49] In addition to giving prominence to the anniversary of the Nakba on their front pages, since 1998, the newspapers under review have offered what can be termed "commemorative prompts," reminding their readers in content and in graphics of

---

[44] Ahmad Qariya, "Lessons of the 50th Anniversary and Options for the Future," *al-Hayat al-Jadida*, May 12, 1998, 5.

[45] Hussein Suweitee, "The Expellees," *Kul al-Arab*, May 15, 1998, 2, 3.

[46] Mohammed al-Rahmihi, "The Main Challenges after 50 Years of Nakba," *Al-Quds*, May 2, 1998, 15.

[47] Suweitee, "Expellees," 2, 3.

[48] For the adoption of this model in ensuing years, see Samih al-Qasim, "1948 ... The Storm Talks ... Basil Hushes," Kul al-Arab, May 15, 1998, 4, 5; Wadiah Awadah, "Jaffa That Was," *Kul al-Arab*, May 15, 1998, 10, 11 (on internal refugees' fate). For examples of stories invoking West Bank refugees, see Anonymous, "The March and the Meaning," *Al-Quds*, May 14, 1998, 13; Rumur Sharur, "Abu al-Adeen al-Damouni Refuses [Giving Up] the Name of [His Original] Village," *al-Hayat al-Jadida*, May 15, 2000, 7; AFP, "Dheisheh Refugees Commemorate the Nakba in the Villages from Which They Were Expelled," *Al-Quds*, May 18, 2000, 7; Anonymous, "The 66th Anniversary of the Nakba and the Bitterness of Genocide and Displacement," *al-Hayat al-Jadida*, May 14, 2014, 14; Abdul Rahman Yunis, "The Refugee Mrs. al-Lahham: If We Had Known We Would Become Refugees, We Would Not Have Left Our Villages," *Al-Quds Online*, May 18, 2016, www.alquds.com/articles/ 146355753444634 /0200/, accessed April 19, 2017.

[49] The pre-1998 commemorative mediated exceptions include: Anonymous, "Today the Anniversary of the 15th of May," *Al-Quds*, May 15, 1996, front page; Hafez al-Barghouti, "Our Life," *Al-Hayat al-Jadida*, May 14, 1997, 20; Hassan al-Kashif, "Remembering," *al-Hayat al-Jadida*, May 14, 1997, 20.

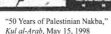

"50 Years of Palestinian Nakba,"   *Al-Quds*, May 15, 1998
Kul al-Arab, May 15, 1998

"Let's Participate in the March of the Millions." *Al-Hayat al-Jadida*, May 13, 1998

Figure 7.1 The Nakba as a mediated commemoration

the year of the anniversary and calling upon them to participate in commemorative marches and festivals or, as *Kul al-Arab* put it in 1998, to "answer the call of the national and humanistic obligation to commemorate the Nakba memory and to revive the national memory and to assure the continuation of the struggle in a popular rally."[50]

A further textual commemorative reminder that finds its origin in 1998 is the placement of official political statements in Nakba anniversary issues, revealing both the politics of commemoration and the "institutional manifestation of Palestinian nation-statism."[51] In 1998, an announcement by the legislative council thus not only set out the roadmap for the reversal of the Nakba "in spite of entering the peace process" but also called on the "masses to commemorate the anniversary of the

---

[50] See Anonymous, "On the 50th Anniversary of the Nakba," *al-Hayat al-Jadida*, May 14, 1998, front page; Hussein Suweitee, "Fifty Years since the Nakba, Fifty Years of Struggle," *Kul al-Arab*, May 15, 1998, front page; Wafa, "In Order for Our People and the World Not to Forget the Palestinian Nakba," *Al-Quds*, May 15, 1998, front page.
[51] Khalili, *Heroes and Martyrs of Palestine*, 192.

"On the 60ᵗʰ Anniversary of the Nakba. General Strikes Among Arab Student Groups Create High Tensions in the Country's Universities." *Kul-al-Aarb*, May 16, 2008

"68 Years of the Nakba." *Al-Quds Online*, May 15, 2016

"Citizens Gather Around the '64 Years' Candles in Ramallah in Preparation for the Commemoration of the Nakba." *al-Hayat al-Jadida*, May 15, 2012

Figure 7.1 (*cont.*)

Nakba extensively and [...] to participate in the Palestinian March of the Millions."[52] In coherence with the political landscape in the West Bank (and indeed Gaza), these official statements, typically only published in *Al-Quds* and *al-Hayat al-Jadida*,[53] have moved from representing the legislative council, virtually defunct since 2006, to incorporating the announcements of various political parties and semipolitical commemorative agencies.[54] Following the split between Hamas and Fatah, official announcements by the Fatah-backed PLO, the Higher Committee for Nakba Commemoration, and the PLO's Refugee Department were firmly situated within the political framework approved by the Fatah-led Palestinian Authority in the West Bank.[55] Juxtaposing Hamas' "prolonging of division and preservation of partisan interests [at] the expense of the supreme interests of our people and their national cause" with the PLO's commitment to "national unity," the anniversary of the Nakba thus became a political opportunity to garner support among those who believed in "the rights of our Palestinian people."[56]

---

[52] Anonymous, "Announcement by the Legislative Council on the 50th Anniversary of the Nakba," *al-Hayat al-Jadida*, May 13, 1998, 2.

[53] It is worth noting that *Kul al-Arab* has placed commemorative reminders by the High Follow-Up Committee, an extra-parliamentary organization that represents Palestinian citizens of Israel. For an example, see Anonymous, "The High Follow-up Committee Calls for Wide Participation in Nakba Commemoration Activities and the March of Return," *Kul al-Arab Online*, May 10, 2016, www.alarab.com/Article/746379, accessed August 17, 2017.

[54] These include political parties that are part of the PLO's umbrella organization, such as the Popular Democratic Front for the Liberation of Palestine (PDFLP), the Popular Front for the Liberation of Palestine (PFLP), and the Palestinian People's Party (PPP), in addition to the Palestinian Prisoners Club, the Union of Farmers and Agricultural Collectives, and the National Committee for the Commemoration of the Nakba. For examples, see Anonymous, "Call upon Our People to Commemorate the 52nd Nakba Anniversary," *al-Hayat al-Jadida*, May 13, 2000, front page; Lama Qandeel, "The National Commemoration Committee for the Commemoration of the Nakba of 60th Anniversary Announces Its Program in the Country and the Diaspora," *al-Hayat al-Jadida*, April 14, 2008, 9; Anonymous, "On the 62nd Anniversary of the Nakba We Stick to the Land and There Is No Alternative to Return. Announcement by the PLO, the Higher Committee for Nakba Commemoration, Refugee Affairs Department," *al-Hayat al-Jadida*, May 14, 2010, 12; Anonymous, "The President on the Anniversary of the Nakba: Palestinians Do Not Forget ... and Will Not Forget," *al-Hayat al-Jadida*, May 15, 2016, front page. Anonymous, "The National Committee for the Commemoration of the Nakba Calls for Broad Participation in Nakba Activities," *Al-Quds Online*, May 14, 2016, www.alquds.com/articles/1463231183412484000/, accessed April 19, 2017.

[55] Jonathan Schanzer, *Hamas vs. Fatah: The Struggle for Palestine* (New York: Palgrave Macmillan, 2008), 26.

[56] Anonymous, "The PLO on the Anniversary of the Nakba: The Struggle for Freedom and Independence Continues," *al-Hayat al-Jadida*, May 15, 2012, 6.

Preserving the Past for Future Generations: The Media as a Prospective Memory Realm

Although the above-mentioned commemorative prompts might point to a contemporary mnemonic preoccupation, media exposure to the anniversarial events of the Nakba is equally considered a means of conveying the past to present and future generations in order to ensure knowledge of the past. Calls to transmit the Nakba to future generations have been identified from 1995 onwards and emphasize external familial transmission alongside the media as a "prospective" memory realm. The earliest materialization of the first can be found in *Al-Quds'* issue of April 10, 1995. Here, readers are not only exposed to a reportage of the commemorative festival conducted on the forty-eighth anniversary of the Deir Yassin massacre (April 9) but also to an explicit call by the contemporary governor of Ramallah and al-Bireh, Mustafa Aysha Abu Firaz, addressed to a "group of Deir Yassin scouts," the "grandchildren of the strugglers," to become "the soldiers of the homeland [and] to remember with utmost emotion several of the homeland's martyrs who with their blood gave water to the soil."[57] Two years later, in 1997, *al-Hayat al-Jadida* dedicated two editorials to the media's role as a formative realm of transmission. Criticizing the media's own previous neglect of the Nakba and its anniversary, editorials by Hassan al-Kashif and Hafez al-Barghouti stressed the media's responsibility to address the Nakba in the public sphere to "commemorate it and educate the youth on what happened and its significance,"[58] even if "the burden of memories abolishes the pleasures of life."[59] When questioned about the timing of these editorials in the PA's mouthpiece, Omar Hilmi al-Ghoul, a columnist for *al-Hayat al-Jadida* and former chief political advisor to the prime minister of Palestine, Salam Fayyad (2007–2013), emphasized the political transition in the wake of the Oslo Accords. Al-Ghoul contended that following

---

[57] Khalid Amar, "A Festival in Ramallah Commemorates the Anniversary of the Deir Yassin Massacre," *Al-Quds*, April 10, 1995, 2.

[58] al-Kashif, "Remembering," 20.

[59] al-Barghouti, "Our Life," 20. For calls on the media to expose the public to the Nakba, see Nanal Musa, "The Committee for Commemoration of the Nakba Calls on the International Community to Take Responsibility," *Al-Hayat al-Jadida*, May 14, 2005, 4; Ibrahim Alama, "The Memory of the Pride of the Past ... Celebration of the Future: A Conversation with Samih al-Qasim," *Al-Hayat al-Jadida*, May 15, 2008, 8 (supplement on the Nakba); Nufud al-Bakri, "Sticking to the Right of Return Based on International Resolutions and Activating Diplomatic, Media and Academic Works to Address the Refugee Issue," *Al-Hayat al-Jadida*, May 15, 2012, 6; Anonymous, "Extensive Preparations in All of the Governorates of the Homeland for the Commemoration of the Nakba Tomorrow," *Al-Quds*, May 14, 2001, 5.

the establishment of an independent Palestinian media, the duty to transmit the Nakba was amplified, because, as Al-Ghoul stated, "I, like other officials, am responsible for expressing the interests of my people [...] our heritage, culture and national identity cannot be forgotten."[60]

Beyond the effects of the Oslo Accords on media's role as a "prospective memory agent," the lingering mortality of first-generation Nakba eyewitnesses, inferred in al-Kashif's article, should not be neglected.[61] Indeed, for Awadah, the increased attention given to the Nakba from the mid-1990s onwards also spurred from the realization that transferring stories of the Nakba to future generations was pertinent, as "eyewitnesses of the Nakba might die without sharing their stories."[62] In order to "forge a Palestinian identity and record history," Awadah "started collecting stories about the Nakba and the time before the Nakba so that our narrative will remain alive [and] so that the new generation would know what happened during the Nakba."[63] While the media's self-proclaimed role as an agent of Nakba transmission can be found explicitly in editorials in the lead-up to the fiftieth anniversary and implicitly in reportages on the fiftieth anniversary itself, calls for Nakba generational transmission have most consistently appeared from the mid-2000s onwards, in editorials calling for extra-media educational and commemorative initiatives and through the collection and transmission of refugees' testimonies.[64]

[60] Interview conducted with Omar Hilmi al-Ghoul on August 15 and 16, 2016, via email.

[61] Al-Kashif wrote that the passing of "grandparents [as] the best, most honest and most convincing storytellers [who] etched the entire story in the memory of the descendants" meant that "it is the duty of all media devices [including] newspapers" to "evoke [the Nakba] until its memory becomes a collective and unified one of the people." al-Kashif, "Remembering," 20.

[62] Interview conducted with Wadiah Awadah on July 13 and 15, 2016. Awadah noted that the Nakba had a profound impact on his family as his grandfather was displaced to Jordan.

[63] The ability to focus on the Nakba extensively, as Awadah admits, also resulted from the interests of the contemporary editor, al-Qasim, for whom the Nakba constituted his "first images," and, perhaps most importantly, the positive feedback from readers "who seemed to really appreciate writings on the Nakba, as until then they had only encountered the Israeli narrative of the 1948 War in public settings." Interview conducted with Wadiah Awadah on July 13 and 15, 2016; Mahmoud Darwish, Samih al-Qasim, and Abdullah Udhari, *Victims of a Map: A Bilingual Anthology of Arabic Poetry* (London: Saqi, 2005), 50; Caspi and Kabaha, *Palestinian*, 119.

[64] For editorials calling for educational transmission of the Nakba, see Anonymous, "Towards a Better Awareness on the Anniversary of the Nakba," *Al-Quds Online*, April 21, 2015, www.alquds.com/articles/1429595927270852900/, accessed April 19, 2017. For commemorative activities for children, see Anonymous, "The Cultural Forum Center in Bidu Village Organizes a Massive Rally in Commemoration of the Nakba," *Al-Hayat al-Jadida*, May 10, 2008, 5. For calls on Arab and international media sources to participate in efforts to collect testimonies of Palestinian refugees, see Al-Quds Online, "Ministry of Information: The Suffering of Our Refugees Gives Evidence of the Biggest Political Crime by Britain and the Occupation [Israel]," *Al-Quds Online*, May 15, 2016, www.alquds.com/articles/1463302629997788600/, accessed April 19, 2017.

Figure 7.2 Preserving the Nakba for future generations
"The Nakba … the Old Ones Dig Up [Remember] and the Young Ones
Preserve." *Al-Hayat al-Jadida*, May 15, 2016

Indicative of the decreased life expectancy of the remaining first-generation Nakba eyewitnesses,[65] refugees representing the *jīl al-Nakbah* (Arabic: the Nakba generation)[66] have been commanded to pass on the stories to "the grandchildren," the *jīl Awslū* (Arabic: the Oslo generation), "[to] refute the statement made by the founders of the Jewish state that the adults will die and the children will forget."[67]

The Nakba as a Present Continuous: Nakba Mediation inside the 1948 Borders

Mediated calls for engagement with Nakba mnemonics reflect the Palestinian communities' particularistic relation with the Israeli state, thereby testifying to the notion that mass media do not function in a vacuum. Rather, mass media interact with the historical, cultural, and political circumstances of each society, as well as its contemporary interactions with other (dominant) groups.[68] Inside the 1948 borders, Nakba mediated output has consequently simultaneously constituted an interpretative framework, reflecting the Palestinians' minority status, and an analogical tool, exposing the ongoing manifestations of the Nakba resulting from their minority status. Israel's marginalization of the Palestinian narrative in the educational system and attempts to prevent Palestinian commemoration of the Nakba are clear examples of the former, albeit with different temporal manifestations. Whereas the failure to convey the Palestinian conception of the 1948 War to Israeli and Palestinian students can first be identified in 1998, right-wing organizational thwarting of Nakba commemoration on Israel's Independence Day surfaced ten years later, in 2008.[69] Following the

---

[65] Life expectancy at birth for Palestinians born between 1939 and 1941 was approximately forty-seven years. Jacob Metzer, *The Divided Economy for Mandatory Palestine* (Cambridge: Cambridge University Press, 1998), 45.

[66] Ben-Ze'ev, *Remembering*, 2.

[67] Nader al-Qasir, "Generations That Lived through the Nakba Are Departing and the New Generations Are Holding More Firmly to the Right of Return and the National Principles," *Al-Hayat al-Jadida*, May 15, 2012, 7. For other refugees calling for transgenerational transmission, see Supplement, *Al-Hayat al-Jadida*, May 15, 2007, 16; Yunis, "The Refugee Mrs. al-Lahham"; Muhasin Nassar, Mohammed Wattad, and Rallib Qiwan, "General Strikes among Student Groups Create High Tensions in the Country's Universities," *Kul al-Arab*, May 16, 2008, 8; Supplement, *Al-Hayat al-Jadida*, 16.

[68] Adoni, Caspi, and Cohen, *Media, Minorities and Hybrid Identities*, 5.

[69] Suweitee, "Expellees," 2, 3. Articles were found to (implicitly) infer the contemporary Zionist-critical content of textbooks, which largely failed to convey the Palestinian conception of the 1948 War. More explicit criticism of the education in the so-called Israeli-Arab sector followed the removal of the word Nakba from textbooks in 2009, which, according to one editorial, was indicative of the "discrimination" suffered by "Israeli Arabs." Anonymous, "Nakba Removed from Textbooks," *Kul al-Arab*, July 23, 2009, www.alarab.com/Article/154553, accessed July 10, 2017.

sixtieth anniversary of the Nakba, *Kul al-Arab*'s front page informed its readers of clashes that had taken place the previous day at Haifa University when Palestinian students seeking to commemorate the Nakba were confronted by members of Hatikvah (Hebrew: the hope). Hatikvah, a far-right political party, had been established the previous year under the leadership of Ayre Eldad in order to counter Likud's implementation of "the policies of Peace Now" and to expose the Palestinian narrative as "a lie."[70] In addition to exposing attempts by recently established far-right groups, such as Hatikvah and Im Tirtzu (2006), to prevent commemoration, in the wake of the Knesset's 2009 approval of a preliminary Nakba Bill and the subsequent ratification of its amendment in 2011, Nakba mediated output has emphasized collective mnemonics in spite of the "racist and dangerous law,"[71] which seeks to "ban the commemoration of the Nakba,"[72] leading to "a worsening of [Israeli] denial of the Palestinian Nakba."[73]

Contemporary marginalization is not solely deemed emblematic of Palestinians' present-day status in Israel; rather, it is the foundational event creating this involuntary minority that spawns the conception of the Nakba as an analogy for subsequent marginalization, or a present continuous Nakba. Indeed, anniversarial Nakba mediation in *Kul al-Arab* does not conceive of the Nakba as a past event, but rather as "an ongoing Nakba." As one article put it in 2010, *al-Nakbah mā zālāt mustamirah* (Arabic: the Nakba does not stop continuing).[74] Apart from emphasizing "racist

---

[70] Gil Stern Hoffman, "Ayre Eldad to Head New Secular Right Party," *Jerusalem Post*, November 20, 2007, www.jpost.com/Israel/Arye-Eldad-to-head-new-secular-Right-party, accessed July 10, 2017; Shay Fogelman, "Port in a Storm," *Haaretz*, June 3, 2011, www.haaretz.com/israel-news/port-in-a-storm-1.365729, accessed July 10, 2017.

[71] Anonymous, "El-Sanah: Knesset's Decision on the First Reading of the Nakba Law Reflects the Failure of the Zionist Movement," *Kul al-Arab*, March 18, 2010, www .alarab.com/Article/265751, accessed March 7, 2017.

[72] Anonymous, "Lieberman Proposes to Prevent Nakba Commemoration," *Kul al-Arab*, May 15, 2009, www.alarab.com/Article/137997, accessed March 7, 2017.

[73] Anonymous, "Netanyahu: The Revival of What They Call the Nakba Leads to Incitement against Israel," *Kul al-Arab Online*, May 18, 2014, www.alarab.com/Article/ 612265, accessed July 11, 2017.

[74] Anonymous, "Zahalka in a Protest Rally in Occupied Jerusalem: The Judaization of Jerusalem Is the Biggest Nakba," *Kul al-Arab Online*, May 16, 2010, www.alarab.com/ Article/300474, accessed July 11, 2017. It should be noted that *Kul al-Arab* also mentions the ongoing hardship of refugee life in Gaza and the West Bank. For recent examples, see Anonymous, "Archbishop Hanna in Ramallah: The Nakba Is the Reality in Which We Live and We Will Not Give Up a Grain of Soil of Palestinian Soil," *Kul al-Arab Online*, May 14, 2013, www.alarab.com/Article/534462, accessed March 6, 2017; Mustafa Ibrahim, "The Children of al-Shati and the Palestinian Nakba," *Kul al-Arab Online*, May 12, 2016, www.alarab.com/Article/746643, accessed March 6, 2017.

discrimination and apartheid,"[75] and "the [geopolitical] division of the Palestinian people into five groups,"[76] materialization of the continuous Nakba is principally found in Israeli land confiscation policies and contemporary Palestinian displacement inside the 1948 borders. Although media dedicated to present-day Palestinian displacement at the hands of the Israelis can be identified from the late 1990s onwards,[77] it is only a decade later that it is explicitly placed in the context of an ongoing Nakba, itself an outcome of what is termed the "ongoing Zionist project."[78] This project, which is equated with the "Judaization of the land" and "the ethnic cleansing [of Palestinians]," is deemed perceivable in contemporaneous house demolitions "under the pretext of illegal construction," the Judaization of East Jerusalem, and the failure to implement UN resolution 194.[79] Indicative of the historical implementation of policies that enable these practices, including the designation of "open landscape areas"[80] in East Jerusalem following the adoption of the 1980 Basic Law,[81] materializations of the ongoing Nakba are identified year-on-year, albeit in a contemporary context.[82] In 2012, a *Kul al-Arab* article invoking a speech

[75] Walid Thahir, "The Nakba and the Dream of Return," *Kul al-Arab Online*, May 26, 2013, www.alarab.com/Article/537058, accessed August 16, 2017.

[76] These five groups are: The Palestinians of Jerusalem, the Palestinians inside Israel, the Palestinians in the West Bank, the Palestinians in Gaza, and the Palestinians in the diaspora. Ali Heidar, "Ongoing Nakba," *Kul al-Arab Online*, May 14, 2013, www.alarab.com/Article/534410, accessed July 11, 2017.

[77] Suweitee, "Expellees."

[78] Abdul Anbatawi, "On the Anniversary of the Nakba: The Disaster Continues in [Our] Existence and Awareness," *Kul al-Arab Online*, May 18, 2013, www.alarab.com/Article/535363, accessed March 6, 2017. Also see Farid Hassan, "Sixty-seven Years of the Nakba," *Kul al-Arab Online*, May 16, 2015, www.alarab.com/Article/680650, accessed July 11, 2017.

[79] Ahmed Natour, "The Nakba Continues," *Kul al-Arab Online*, May 2, 2015, www.alarab.com/Article/677910, accessed March 6, 2017.

[80] In these open landscape areas, which constitute 40 percent of East Jerusalem, building is forbidden. According to B'Tselem, a human rights organization, the Jerusalem Municipality enforces the building laws on Palestinians much more stringently than on the Jewish population, even though the number of violations is much higher in the Jewish neighborhoods. B'Tselem, *Discrimination in Planning, Building, and Land Expropriation* (B'Tselem, 2011); Eyal Benvenisti, *The International Law of Occupation* (Oxford: Oxford University Press, 2012), 205.

[81] In 1980, the Knesset adopted the Basic Law, declaring Jerusalem the capital of Israel and merged East Jerusalem with West Jerusalem. The UN Security Council declared the law a violation of international law. John B. Quigley, *The Case for Palestine: An International Law Perspective* (Durham/London: Duke University Press, 2005), 172.

[82] For examples of articles discussing contemporary Nakba manifestations, see Abu Wahib, "The Nakba Continues," *Kul al-Arab Online*, April 18, 2013, www.alarab.com/Article/528196, accessed July 11, 2017; Anonymous, "The Naqab Foundation: The Crime of Demolition in Atir, a New Nakba on the Anniversary of the Nakba," *Kul al-Arab Online*, May 16, 2013, www.alarab.com/Article/534910, accessed July 11, 2017 (on Palestinian Bedouin displacement in the Negev); Hassan, "Sixty-seven Years of the Nakba"; Sami

by the party leader of Balad (Arabic: country or land), MK Jamal Zahalka, noted that "Israel continues the war it began in 1948 [which sought] to plunder the land of the homeland" with reference to a "series of racist confiscation laws [recently] passed by the Knesset under the Netanyahu government."[83] A year later, a report on the displacement of 14,000 (Bedouin) Palestinians and the destruction of 2,000 homes in the Negev was considered an indication of "ongoing Israeli policies [aimed] at uprooting Palestinians from their land to this day."[84]

Mobilizing the Past: Nakba Mediation in East Jerusalem and the West Bank

Beyond conceiving of the Nakba as an interpretative framework, Nakba anniversarial mediation in the West Bank and East Jerusalem has taken on a retrospective analogical role to illustrate the occupied/annexed fate of the Palestinian majority in the West Bank and East Jerusalem.[85] Analogies in the West Bank and East Jerusalem concerning contemporary manifestations of the Nakba pertain both to the present and the past. With regard to the latter, this means that, at times, the other's past has been employed as a comparative means to denote the depths of Palestinian suffering and to reveal the Israeli state as the contemporary

---

Meaari, "The Nakba Is Not a Memory ... It Is a Continuous State," *Kul al-Arab Online*, May 15, 2018, www.alarab.com/Article/857648, accessed March 12, 2020.

[83] Anonymous, "Zahalka: During the Nakba Israel Occupied the Land with Weapons and Today [Israel Does It] by Legal Measures," *Kul al-Arab Online*, May 27, 2012, www.alarab.com/Article/461097, accessed March 6, 2017. These laws include the Admissions Committee Law (2011) and the Israel Land Administration Law (2009). The latter allows land owned by the Palestinian refugees and internally displaced persons to be sold off to private investors and placed beyond future restitution claims. The former requires anyone seeking to move to any community in the Negev and Galilee regions with fewer than 400 families to obtain approval from committees consisting of town residents, a member of the Jewish Agency or the World Zionist Organization, and several others. The law empowers these committees to reject candidates who, among other things, "are not suitable to the community's way of life" or "might harm the community's fabric." Adalah, *New Discriminatory Laws and Bills in Israel* (June 2011), 3–5.

[84] Anonymous, "From al-Araqib to Susiya: A Short Documentary on the Anniversary of the Nakba Calls for Justice," *Kul al-Arab Online*, May 15, 2013, www.alarab.com/Article/534646, accessed March 7, 2017.

[85] In 2009, the Palestinian population was estimated to be 275,900; the Israeli settler population of East Jerusalem was approximately 198,000. A year earlier, the West Bank settler population stood at 285,800 settlers, making up 14 percent of the Palestinian population (2,016,786 in 2008 in the West Bank). Michael Dumper, *Jerusalem Unbound: Geography, History, and the Future of the Holy City* (New York: Columbia University Press, 2014),143; PCBS, *Estimated Population in the Palestinian Territory Mid-Year by Governorate,1997–2016* (PCBS, 2016); PCBS, *Localities in Jerusalem Governorate by Type of Locality and Population Estimates, 2007–2016* (PCBS, 2016).

embodiment of evil.[86] Al-Ghoul, who continually writes on the "racist Nazism in Israel"[87] and the "fascist existence on Israeli streets"[88] in his columns, has argued that the "Hebrew state regrettably conjures the Holocaust [to install] a more brutal and scummy Holocaust, through occupation, racism and Fascism"[89] that "surpasses Italian Fascism and German Nazism."[90] When questioned about the content of these publications, Al-Ghoul reaffirmed his belief in these statements, maintaining that not only has "the Holocaust been one of the most important levers of the Zionist colonial project, [which] was the motive or cover for the creation of an Israeli state [at] the expense of the Arab Palestinians," but Israel has since its establishment been "practicing the Holocaust and the methods of Nazi Germany [as] is reflected in the long series of massacres, killings, wars and murder." Moreover, according to al-Ghoul, "the continued ethnic cleansing of Palestinians and the looting and confiscation of their land [and] the lack of freedom of movement to and from the West Bank" are all "manifestations of the Holocaust."[91]

Although this type of inflammatory material does exist, which through the equation of Nazi crimes and Israeli actions is aimed at undermining the Holocaust,[92] the Nakba has most often been instrumentalized as a

---

[86] Faisal Abu Khadra, "The Palestinian People Will Not Kneel," *Al-Quds Online*, December 18, 2015, www.alquds.com/articles/1450420728492938700/, accessed April 19, 2017.

[87] Omar Hilmi al-Ghoul, "No Change to the Initiative," *al-Hayat al-Jadida Online*, May 29, 2016, www.alhaya.ps/ar_page.php?id=15bcd60y22793568Y15bcd60, accessed April 20, 2017.

[88] Omar Hilmi al-Ghoul, "The Circle of Fascism Is Complete," *al-Hayat al-Jadida Online*, March 31, 2016, www.alhaya.ps/ar_page.php?id=125e4bby19260603Y125e4bb, accessed April 21, 2017.

[89] Omar Hilmi al-Ghoul, "Evoking the Lessons of the Holocaust," *al-Hayat al-Jadida Online*, May 8, 2015, www.alhaya.ps/ar_page.php?id=1496aaby21588651Y1496aab, accessed April 19, 2017.

[90] Omar Hilmi al-Ghoul, "Dancing to the Drums of Racism," *al-Hayat al-Jadida Online*. December 26, 2015, www.alhaya.ps/ar_page.php?id=c87891y13138065Yc87891, accessed April 19, 2017.

[91] Interview conducted with Omar Hilmi al-Ghoul on August 15 and 16, 2016 via email.

[92] Holocaust denial does exist in Palestinian media and was identified in several articles. Chari Mansour, in a 2001 editorial, questioned "the myth of the Holocaust and its exaggeration" by arguing that the number six million "is a deceitful number and a sensational number because the widest of the [gas] chambers would not have been able to process even one percent of these numbers." In 1998, various articles denying the Holocaust appeared, including one citing the former Mufti of Jerusalem, Sheikh Ekrima Sa'id Sabri, who maintained that the Holocaust had been exaggerated by Israel to gain international support. In another article, Seif Ali al-Jarwan noted that "The persecution of the Jews is a deceitful myth [which] they still use and still benefit from." The equation of Zionism and Nazism, as undertaken by al-Ghoul, also was not a novel theme. In 1997, *al-Hayat al-Jadida* claimed that the emergence of Zionism "encouraged the rise of terrorist and racist ideologies such as Nazism," and then pointed to the "great

mobilization medium. Nakba mediation has, effectively, become a primary means of expressing Palestinian national concerns and goals. Chief among these nationalist aims are implementing the right of return, challenging the ongoing Israeli occupation and the illegal dispossession of land earmarked for the Palestinian state in the Oslo Accords, and advancing the establishment of a Palestinian state with East Jerusalem as its capital.[93] Contemporary politics seek to contextualize the need for these nationalist objectives – a necessity which is further exemplified by recurrent employment of the symbolically charged terminology of *tamassuk* (Arabic: holding on) and *ṣumūd* (Arabic: steadfastness). As such, amid the Oslo Accords, adherence to the right of return is stressed by opposition parties, as seen in an April 1994 *Al-Quds* interview with the general director of the DFLP, Nayef Hawatmeh. In line with the party's perception of the Oslo Accords as a surrendering of Palestinian rights, the article criticizes the absence of any meaningful discussion concerning the "sacred right of return [which] is fixed according to UN Resolution 194 [1948] and in Resolution 237 [1967]." In order to "restart negotiations and rebuild the [peace] process," Hawatmeh therefore calls for a safeguarding of "the return of the displaced without pre-conditions."[94]

While what the Palestinian historian Abdul Latif Tibawi termed an "Arab Zionism"[95] can be identified in subsequent years, including in pictures of keys as an ever-present reminder of *sana'ūd* (Arabic: we will

---

similarity" between the two movements as both espouse a belief in their racial superiority. For references to a "Gaza Strip Holocaust", inferring the 2008 Cast Lead Operation, see Anonymous, "On the 62nd Nakba, Declarations of the Factions Assure Determination on the Right of Return," *Al-Quds*, May 15, 2010, 3. Seif Ali al-Jarwan, "The Jews and [Their] Control of the Media," *Al-Hayat al-Jadida*, July 2, 1998; Sheikh Ekrima Sa'id Sabri, *Al-Hayat al-Jadida*, July 2, 1998; Chari Mansour, "Marketing Ashes," *Al-Hayat al-Jadida*, April, 13, 2001, 10; Ahmad Dachbur, "Jew against Jew," *Al-Hayat al-Jadida*, June 24, 2003 (page number unknown). Litvak and Webman, "Perceptions of the Holocaust," 129, 131, 136.

[93] For examples, see Wafa, "In Order for Our People," 1, 14; Anonymous, "Extensive Preparations in All of the Governorates of the Homeland," 5; Anonymous, "On the 62nd Anniversary of the Nakba," 12; Anonymous, "The National Committee for the Commemoration of the Nakba," *Al-Quds Online*, May 14, 2016, www.alquds.com/articles/1463231183412484000/, accessed April 19, 2017.

[94] Rashid Hilal, "Nayif Hawatmeh: We move toward holding a national popular conference, return is a sacred right to Palestinians, we reject inter-Palestinian fighting," *Al-Quds*, April 8, 1994, 4. For the DFLP's conception of Oslo, see Michael Bröning, *Political Parties in Palestine: Leadership and Thought* (New York/Basingstoke: Palgrave Macmillan, 2013), 177.

[95] Tibawi realized that there is "a striking similarity between present Arab [Palestinian] aspirations and emotions concerning 'the return' and those from which Zionism was born." He called this feeling "New Zionism" that is, "Arab Zionism with the aim of returning to the [Palestinian] homeland." Abdul Latif Tibawi, "The Palestine Arab Refugees in Arabic Poetry and Art," *Middle East Journal* 17:5 (1963): 508, 509.

return),[96] explicit criticism of the PLO and, subsequently, the PA's handling of the refugee problem is practically nonexistent.[97] Studies conducted on freedom of expression in Palestinian press, including (semi-)independent and wholly owned outlets by the PA, demonstrate that despite the absence of censorship regulations as existed until 1994, the PA has exercised its own form of control over media institutions.[98] In line with the 1993 Press and Publication Law, journalists are required to follow burdensome administrative regulations and produce content that reinforces "national unity." Content that is deemed to undermine "the general system" or that is "inconsistent with morals" is banned. At the same time, defamation is a criminal offense and journalists have been prosecuted for publishing criticism of Palestinian officials.[99] The encouragement of self-censorship through a carrot and stick policy and the existence of overt, external censorship through detaining journalists and withdrawing publication licenses even led a 2000 Committee to Protect Journalists (CPJ) report to claim that the "censorship, intimidation, and arbitrary arrests of Palestinian journalists that marked full-fledged Israeli occupation are now practiced by Palestinian President Yasser Arafat and his coterie."[100] The existence of censorship practices is evident in Nakba meditation on the right of return. Although articles published in the aftermath of the Oslo Accords firmly reject "all solutions

---

[96] Sa'di noted that the house key is also considered the last symbol of home and a reminder that before *al-Nakba*, Palestinians had a different life. Sa'di, "Catastrophe, Memory and Identity," 181.

[97] For an exception, see Tahir Taseer al-Masri, "The Refugees and the Right of Return," *Al-Quds*, April 10, 1996, 13. Al-Masri argues that the PA should introduce a "Right of Return" law, which would allow refugees to return to a future Palestinian state.

[98] Bishara, "New Media and Political Change," 63–81; Najjar, "The 1995 Palestinian Press Law," 41–103.

[99] A 2015 report by MADA found that between 2008 and 2015, violations of Palestinian freedom of press by the PA and Palestinian security services increased by 75 percent, with the five most common violations being: summoning and interrogation processes, arrests, physical assaults, detentions, and denial of coverage. MADA, Palestinian Center for Development and Media Freedoms, *The Violations of Media Freedoms: Annual Report 2015* (Ramallah, 2015), 26–28.

[100] Cited in CPJ, *Attacks on the Press 1999: Israel and the Occupied Territories* (CPJ, 2000). In the aftermath of the PA's closing of the PA-critical daily *al-Nahār* (Arabic: the afternoon), known for its pro-Jordanian sympathies, on July 28, 1994, just three months after the authority was established, other newspapers, including *Al-Quds*, reduced coverage of opposition parties and dissenting viewpoints in its op-ed pages, leading Nigel Parsons to claim that it "was intimidated into taking a very pro-Arafat, if not pro-Fatah view." When self-censorship has not been successfully implemented, as occurred in 1995, when Mahir al-Alami, an *Al-Quds* editor, failed to comply with a PA request to publish a flattering story and photo of Arafat, the PA resorted to externally imposed censorship, by detaining al-Alami and temporarily withdrawing *Al-Quds'* publishing license. Nigel Parsons, *The Politics of the Palestinian Authority: From Oslo to Al-Aqsa* (New York/London: Routledge, 2005), 174, 175.

Al-Quds, May 14, 2001   *al-Hayat al-Jadida*, May 14, 2005

al-Hayat al-Jadida, May 16, 2008

Figure 7.3 The key and the dream of a return

that do not provide the right of return to four million refugees"[101] and
any negotiations and wavering of this "sacred right"[102] based on any
"statute of limitations,"[103] the PA's own negotiations on this right are not
mentioned. Even in the wake of Al Jazeera's publication of the Palestine
Papers (see Chapter 4), responsibility for "the perpetuating of the

---

[101] Wafa, "In Order for Our People," 1, 14.   [102] Hilal, "Nayif Hawatmeh," 4.
[103] Atif Abu al-Rab, "Jenin, Activities and Marches Stress the Right of Return," *Hayat al-*
Jadida, May 16, 2001, 6. Also see Anonymous, "Announcement by the Legislative
Council."

(تصوير: عصام الريماوي)   الحاج احمد صافي وزوجته يحملان مفاتيح منزلهما في قرية بيت نبالا التي هجروا منها الى مخيم الجلزون قرب رام الله.

al-Hayat al-Jadida, May 15, 2012

"Returning to Haifa." *Al-Quds Online*, May 15, 2016

Figure 7.3 (*cont.*)

"We Will Return." *Al-Quds Online,* May 14, 2016.

Figure 7.3 (*cont.*)

Nakba,"[104] according to the late PA chief negotiator Erekat, needed to be firmly placed with Israel and the international community, and his claim of a sole "solution to the refugee issue based on UN resolution 194"[105] goes wholly unchallenged.

The allusion to the international community alongside Israel, as afore-mentioned, should not infer that the international community is deemed equally accountable for the existence and perpetuation of Palestinians' national problems. Indeed, while articles published on Nakba Day note that the anniversary is welcomed as a means of reminding the world "of the historical injustice inflicted upon our people"[106] and to demand "the world's commitment to international law,"[107] it is Israel that is chiefly

---

[104] Anonymous, "The Masses Commemorate the 62nd Anniversary of the Nakba," *al-Hayat al-Jadida,* May 15, 2010, front page.

[105] Anonymous, "On the 62nd Nakba, Declarations of the Factions Assure Determination on the Right of Return," 3.

[106] Wafa, "A Torchlit March to Commemorate the 66th Anniversary of the Nakba in Ramallah," *al-Hayat al-Jadida,* May 15, 2014, 11.

[107] Anonymous, "On the 62nd Nakba [Anniversary], Declaration of the Factions Assures Determination on the Right of Return," *Al-Quds,* May 15, 2010, 3; Anonymous, "The Masses Commemorate the 62nd Anniversary of the Nakba," front page.

held responsible for "challenging international laws, regulations, treaties and the will of the international community."[108] Beyond the "continuous occupation," which, according to President Abbas, characterizes "the permanent Nakba,"[109] land confiscation is deemed the principal defiance of international law and of "individual and collective [Palestinian] rights."[110] In response to the maintenance of settlement activity in the West Bank[111] and East Jerusalem in line with Netanyahu's 1997 "Allon Plus Plan,"[112] annual Nakba mediation since the mid-1990s has consistently proclaimed "the destruction of the two-state solution."[113] A result of "Zionist colonial aggression,"[114] the dismantling of the peace process is the culmination of a "continuation of the settlement policy,"[115] "the Judaization of East Jerusalem,"[116] and, since 2003, "the racist separation wall."[117]

In order to confront "these serious challenges [to] our national project and the goals of people [to live] in freedom and independence,"[118] Nakba mediated output has sought reinforcement of – and adherence to – the so-called fixed national principles,[119] which dictate "no peace or

---

[108] Qandeel, "The National Commemoration Committee," 9.

[109] Anonymous, "The President: It Is Time for the Calamity Called the Nakba of the Palestinian People to End," *al-Hayat al-Jadida*, May 18, 2008, front page.

[110] al-Rab, "Jenin, Activities and Marches Stress," 6.

[111] A secret plan by the Israeli Civil Administration to dedicate 10 percent of the West Bank to further settlements was uncovered in 2012. In the plan, a total of 569 parcels of land were marked out, encompassing around 155,000 acres. Since the late 1990s, twenty-three unauthorized outposts had been built on land included on the maps. The maps also mark eighty-one sites in areas A and B – under Palestinian civil control – which indicates that the Civil Administration began identifying available land before the Oslo Accords. Akiva Eldar, "Israel Defense Ministry Plan Earmarks 10 Percent of West Bank for Settlement Expansion," *Haaretz*, March 30, 2012, www.haaretz.com/israel-news/israel-defense-ministry-plan-earmarks-10-percent-of-west-bank-for-settlement-expansion-1.421589, accessed August 21, 2017.

[112] Netanyahu's plan, bearing a similar title to the 1967 Allon Plan proposed by former Labor politician Yigal Allon, sought the annexation of 60 percent of the West Bank to Israel "for security reasons" and offered to hand over the remaining 40 percent to the PA. It should be noted that some scholars, such as Dov Waxman, considered this plan evidence of Netanyahu's continuation of the peace process, as "he became the first Likud leader to publicly present a plan that called for an Israeli withdrawal from over half of the West Bank." Dov Waxman, *The Pursuit of Peace and the Crisis of Israeli Identity: Defending/Defining the Nation* (New York: Palgrave Macmillan, 2006), 131.

[113] Anonymous, "The President on the Anniversary of the Nakba," front page.

[114] Natif Hawatmeh, "Nakba, Intifadah and Resistance," *al-Hayat al-Jadida*, May 16, 2001, 8.

[115] Anonymous, "The President on the Anniversary of the Nakba," front page.

[116] Anonymous, "The PLO on the Anniversary of the Nakba," 6.

[117] Anonymous, "The Director of the Palestinian Bureau of Statistics," *Al-Quds*, May 15, 2005, 12.

[118] Anonymous, "The PLO on the Anniversary of the Nakba," 6.

[119] Anonymous, "The President," front page.

security or stability unless the Palestinian refugee issue is resolved based on resolution 194; return, self-determination and establishment of the [Palestinian] state."[120] In addition to participation in mnemonic activities to "show national anger,"[121] loyalty to these principles is advocated through *tamassuk* (Arabic: holding on) to the land in spite of "incursions into Palestinian territories"[122] and, at times, hailing violent confrontations with "occupation forces."[123] In the latter context, it is worth noting that in *al-Hayat al-Jadida*'s 2000 Nakba Day black and white edition, the blood of a "martyr who died in [Nakba Day] clashes at Qalqilya" did appear in color on the front page, thereby suggesting that the "confrontation with occupation soldiers to stress their commitment to the right of return and refuse nationalization projects" validates an interruption in the commemorative mediation.[124] Importantly, glorification of violent confrontations prior and subsequent to the Al-Aqsa Intifadah – deemed a renewal of the "people's allegiance [to the land] with blood"[125] – also indicates that mobilization efforts in Nakba meditation do not necessarily only coincide with times of increased violence or heightened political strife.[126]

The achievement of the "fixed national interests" is not solely dependent on demonstrating social mobilization on Nakba Day but also on the existence of national political unity.[127] Repeated calls in Nakba media output seeking "unity among all political factions" can be traced to two

[120] Anonymous, "The Masses in Our Homeland and the Diaspora Commemorate the 57th Anniversary of the Nakba," *al-Hayat al-Jadida*, May 15, 2005, front page.
[121] Anonymous, "The Two Committees, the National and the Subcommittee Affirm the Final Program for the 60th Nakba [Anniversary]," *al-Hayat al-Jadida*, April 5, 2008, 9.
[122] Staff Editorial, "After 53 Years, the Features of the Nakba Are Present Once Again," *Al-Quds*, May 15, 2001, 13; Anonymous, "Between the Nakba and the Dawn of a New Birth," *Al-Quds*, May 14, 2001, 13.
[123] Anonymous, "National Forces Call to Commemorate the Nakba with a Large Participation," *Al-Quds Online*, April 23, 2016, www.alquds.com/articles/146142750087623/5500, accessed March 16, 2017.
[124] Anonymous, "A Martyr in Qalqilya and Hundreds Injured in a Fire in Magidu [Prison] and Dozens of Civilians Injured in Confrontations with Occupation Soldiers in Gaza, Qalqilya, Nablus and Ramallah," *al-Hayat al-Jadida*, May 15, 2000, front page.
[125] For Munir Abu Razaq, "The People Renew Their Allegiance with Blood and the Leader Confirms the Inevitability of Victory," *al-Hayat al-Jadida*, May 16, 2001, 6.
[126] Anonymous, "Our People Commemorating the Nakba [Led to] Three Martyrs and Hundreds of Injured," *al-Hayat al-Jadida*, May 16, 2000, front page; Anonymous, "More than Seventy Injured in Clashes in Bethlehem," *al-Hayat al-Jadida*, May 16, 2000, 5; Anonymous, "Dozens Injured in Clashes in Qalqilya," *al-Hayat al-Jadida*, May 16, 2000, 5; Anonymous, "Confrontations in Hebron and Dozens of Injured," *al-Hayat al-Jadida*, May 16, 2000, 5; Anonymous, "260 Protesters Were Injured in Confrontations in the Palestinian Territories during Nakba Marches," *Kul al-Arab Online*, May 15, 2012, www.alarab.com/Article/458419, accessed May 5, 2017.
[127] Nufud al-Bakri, "The DFLP Calls for Social Mobilization on the Anniversary of the Nakba to Defend the Land," *al-Hayat al-Jadida*, May 14, 2000, 5.

"The remaining Palestinian people [held captive by] settlements." *al-Hayat al-Jadida*, May 14, 1998

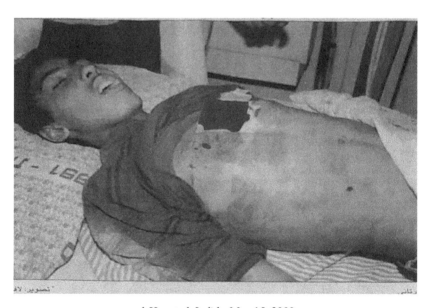

al-Hayat al-Jadida, May 15, 2000

Figure 7.4 Holding on to the national goals

distinct periods: in the wake of the 1993 Oslo I Accord and, more consistently, following the outbreak of what Joel S. Migdal termed "a Palestinian civil war" between Hamas and Fatah in 2006/7.[128] Indeed, in the period under examination, the advancement of a "national unity" and "true solidarity" in Nakba mediation forms a mirror into the domestic Palestinian political landscape.[129] As such, while in the period following the 1993 Oslo Accords, editorials and news articles stress the creation of "unity among all Palestinian factions [in] the ongoing negotiations"[130] and the "solidification of the work of the PLO to strengthen the unity of our people,"[131] the rift between Fatah and Hamas prompted calls for "national unity [through] political reconciliation."[132] Yet, despite the difference in timing and in political objectives, both in the aftermath of Oslo and subsequent to the various reconciliatory attempts between Hamas and Fatah,[133] advancement of domestic political unity within Nakba mediation must be understood as a clear engagement with its neighbors. Moving from the political consolidation of the PLO in the 1990s to the pursuit of a new Palestinian unity government from the late 2000s onwards, Nakba mediation in East Jerusalem and the West Bank forms a continual explicit negation of Israel's "no partner for peace narrative,"[134] all the while holding on to "the supreme interests of our people and their national cause."[135]

---

[128] Joel S. Migdal, *Shifting Sands: The United States in the Middle East* (New York: Columbia University Press, 2014), 351.

[129] Anonymous, "Announcement by the Legislative Council," 2.

[130] Mustafa al-Rimawi, "Return Is a Sacred Right to Every Expellee, There Is a Need for a Palestinian Initiative to Regain Unity," *Al-Quds*, April 6, 1994, 6. Also see Hilaal, "Nayif Hawatmeh," 4.

[131] Anonymous, "General National Body Calls for Broad Participation in Nakba Commemoration Activities," *al-Hayat al-Jadida*, May 13, 2000, 8.

[132] Anonymous, "The President," front page.

[133] Instrumentalization of the Nakba's anniversary to endow recent reconciliatory attempts, including the March 2008 Sana'a Declaration, the February 2012 Doha Agreement, and the April 2014 Gaza Agreement, are principally voiced in *al-Hayat al-Jadida* by Fatah affiliates, including President Abbas and, from prison, by the political figure Marwan al-Barghouti. For examples, see Anonymous, "The PLO on the Anniversary of the Nakba," 6; Anonymous, "In a statement on the occasion of the Nakba anniversary the captive leader Al-Barghouti [says]: We bless the reconciliation agreement and there is no partner in Israel," *al-Hayat al-Jadida*, May 15, 2014, 6; Nufud al-Bakri, "A Meeting in Gaza Demanding Support for the Right of Return and the Speedy Completion of the Reconciliation Agreement," *al-Hayat al-Jadida*, May 15, 2014, 4.

[134] Raffaella A. Del Sarto, *Israel under Siege: The Politics of Insecurity and the Rise of the Israeli Neo-Revisionist Right* (Washington DC: Georgetown University Press, 2017), 2, 35.

[135] Anonymous, "The PLO on the Anniversary of the Nakba," 6.

Concluding Remarks

In the build-up to the fiftieth anniversary to the Nakba, Palestinian media on both sides of the Green Line collectively turned their attention to the past. Bolstered by the post-Oslo media landscape in the West Bank and East Jerusalem and, inside the 1948 borders, the perceived capitulation of Oslo, Nakba anniversarial mediation became a means of expressing the communities' concerns in coherence with the readerships' *cadres sociaux*. The commemorative prompts identified within Palestinian media, which originated during the 1998 anniversary, moreover, both testify to the media's heightened role as an agent of transgenerational transmission and equally reveal usage of Nakba mediation as a form of "commemorative mobilization."

Forming the inverse of Israeli-dictated mediation in the wake of the 1948 and 1967 War, post-Oslo media *for* and *by* Palestinians reflects the communities' relations with the Israeli hegemony. Demonstrative of its readership's principal concerns, *Kul al-Arab* has presented the Nakba as an interpretative framework for contemporary grievances resulting from Palestinians' status as an involuntary minority in Israel. As such, within anniversarial mediation, the Nakba as a present continuous does not simply signify the historical fate of internal refugees but furthermore is considered the foundational event that generated the marginalization experienced at the hands of the majority. In addition to legislative attempts by far-right Israeli groups to thwart Nakba commemoration, which culminated in the 2011 Nakba Bill, the ongoing Nakba is presented in the framework of a continuous Judaization of Palestinian land. Considered symptomatic of the Zionist transfer policy, Nakba media output thus presents "the ethnic cleansing"[136] of Palestine both as an outcome of the continued implementation of pre-Oslo legislation and the introduction of new laws, including the 2009 Land Administration Law, which allows refugees' land to be sold off to private investors and placed beyond future restitution claims.

Nakba anniversarial mediation in the West Bank and East Jerusalem, similarly to inside the 1948 borders, illustrates the Palestinians' particularistic relations with the Israeli hegemony, shedding light on the majority's occupied/annexed fate. Application of the Nakba as an interpretative framework and, simultaneously, an analogical tool testifies to the mediated expression of what McQuail defined as national goals. Through repeated usage of previously censored symbolic terminology, the

---

[136] Natour, "The Nakba Continues."

readership of the semi-independent *Al-Quds* and the PA's mouthpiece, *Al-Hayat al-Jadida*, is admonished to adhere to these national objectives, which call for an end to "the permanent Nakba"[137] through a resolution to the refugee problem, the right of self-determination, and the establishment of a Palestinian state.

Yet, invocation of the so-called fixed national principles, as expressed in the publication of (semi-)political mnemonic reminders, is not only meant to advance collective adherence to national objectives but, importantly, seeks to challenge the main actor deemed responsible for their suspension: Israel. Charged with the destruction of the two-state solution through repeated and, as revealed in 2012, clandestine settlement incursion into the Palestinian state to-be, Nakba mediated output has consequently become a realm of collective social mobilization against "the Zionist entity," albeit one that does not deviate from the politically accepted discourse of the PA. A comprehensive metaphor for the effects of "Zionist colonial aggression" and its ongoing implications for daily Palestinian life, Nakba media output has come to embody all Palestinian suffering – by refugees and non-refugees alike – at the hands of the Israelis, which at times makes use of the most tendentious charge to debunk the contemporary opponent: the execution of a Palestinian Holocaust.

---

[137] Anonymous, "The President," front page.

Conclusion

"The nation's biography," writes Anderson at the closure of *Imagined Communities*, "snatches wars and holocausts." But, to serve the narrative purpose, Anderson continues, "these events must be remembered/forgotten as 'our own'."[1] This work's examination of societal transmission of Nakba and Holocaust narratives in, respectively, Palestinian and Israeli-Jewish society has not only testified to the mnemonic plasticity engrained in this statement but also exposed the societal usages of exclusionary narratives. Through charting the interdependence between mnemonic agents and the intended recipients, this study has highlighted the formation and preservation – what Anderson implies with remembering – of these narratives, which like all collective narratives illustrate contemporary concerns and societal understandings and, consequently, are characterized by their malleability.

The Ongoing Nakba

The ability to articulate collective needs and attitudes in official mnemonic realms, which determines the scope and validity of the conveyed narrative, is, as this work has demonstrated, closely interlinked with the existing political landscape. In East Jerusalem and the West Bank, the post-Oslo political landscape proved formative to the transformation of commemorative traditions and previously thwarted educational and media content into group narratives that, under the auspices of the PA, could be voiced outside the local and familial sphere. Yet, while the PA's authority in social realms allowed for mass exposure to the historical events of *al-Nakba* in the wake of the Oslo Peace Accords, it was to a large extent the PA's own "capitulation at Oslo"[2] that dictated the

---

[1] Anderson, *Imagined Communities*, 206.
[2] Moshé Machover, *Israelis and Palestinians: Conflict and Resolution* (Chicago, IL: Haymarket Books, 2012), 178.

Nakba's contemporary relevance, albeit significantly bolstered by the temporal importance of the Nakba's fiftieth anniversary in 1998.

The PA's postponement of the refugee problem to final status negoti-ations was also integral to Nakba mnemonics and mediation inside the 1948 borders. Although Oslo did not provide a new political order for the Palestinian minority in Israel, the collective response to the Oslo Accords spurred from the emergence of an (semi-)independent cultural realm in the mid-1980s, which, after the First Intifadah, became a political plat-form to express the social concerns of "the Palestinians inside" – *Filasṭiniu al-dākhil*. Emboldened by continued Israeli attempts to remove their narrative from public consciousness and the PA's negligence of their fate, the Palestinian minority used its cultural autonomy to address grievances resulting from its post-Nakba status as an involun-tary minority.

Indeed, across the three mnemonic realms explored in the Palestinian case study, the pervasive concept of an ongoing Nakba has largely depended on relations with – and conceptions of – the Israeli majority and, in the case of the West Bank and East Jerusalem, the ongoing Israeli occupation/annexation. Notwithstanding the differences that have arisen as a result of the PA's influence in the mnemonic realm and, in the educational sphere, its reliance on international donors, the narratives demonstrate the perceived marginalization suffered at the hands of the Israeli hegemony. For the Palestinians living inside the 1948 borders, the Nakba as a present continuous is principally characterized by contem-porary political marginalization and as an outcome of what Ilan Pappé succinctly termed a cultural memoricide.[3] Consequently, the Nakba, as the watershed from which the vanquished minority spawned, has been conceived of as both an interpretative historical framework and, simul-taneously, through its perceived continuity, a retrospective analogy. Public demonstrations aimed at exposing cultural and physical palimp-sest practices deemed emblematic of the ongoing Nakba therefore not only seek a transmission of the past but also constitute a demand for social equality.

Analogical usage of the Nakba in the West Bank and East Jerusalem, principally identified in mnemonic activities and Palestinian media, con-versely, is not meant to further civil rights, a paradoxical undertaking in view of Palestinians' current demographic majority status in these areas. Rather, the Nakba has been instrumentalized as a common rallying point for all Palestinians – refugees and non-refugees alike – to bolster

---

[3] Pappé, *Ethnic Cleansing*, 225–234.

mobilization in favor of the so-called fixed national principles, including through violent means. Providing a coherent response to all perceived Israeli trespasses, these national aims have continuously demanded the return of refugees alongside the establishment of an independent Palestinian state both during the implementation of the Oslo Accords and in the wake of the political deadlock created with the failure of Oslo at the dawn of the twenty-first century. Importantly, while the articulation of national goals in Nakba mnemonics is first and foremost directed at Israel, it also allows the PA to show its ostensible support for their realization and, perhaps most importantly, prevent criticism against the authority's own role in the perpetuation of the refugee problem. Successful implementation of the carrot and stick policy meant that in the wake of the Oslo Accords and the 2011 publication of the Palestine Papers, the PA could prevent exposure of a political willingness to negotiate a refugee settlement in the PA's political mouthpiece, *al-Hayat al-Jadida*, and the semi-independent *Al-Quds* and, instead, claim an uncompromising dedication to the "national cause."

The "Never Again" State of Israel

In contrast to Palestinian mnemonics, the post-Oslo era in Israeli-Jewish society was not characterized by the dissemination of a novel Holocaust consciousness resulting from a new-found mnemonic agency. Still, the particularistic Holocaust narrative discerned in the post-Oslo era cannot be considered disconnected from the existing political landscape. The mediated identification of contemporary manifestations of Nazism and Fascism, including among the Palestinian leadership, itself a decade-old phenomenon,[4] thus suggests a continual threat and, accordingly, the need for a strong Jewish state to assure commitment to the idiom "never again"; that is, never again to be a Jewish victim in Israel.

Indeed, the redemptive nature of the Israeli state, as the antithesis of exilic destruction and death, did not constitute an immaculate rebirth. Instead, the onset of an interminable conflict spurred on the conception of the Holocaust as a present continuous; with that, the condition of victimization and persecution is deemed permanent and unchangeable.[5] Crucially, this understanding of the Holocaust is not founded on the contemporary execution of genocidal policies, but rather, as indicated in

---

[4] See Amir Eshel, *Futurity: Contemporary Literature and the Quest for the Past* (Chicago/London: University of Chicago Press, 2013), 141; Zertal, *Israel's Holocaust and the Politics*, 173.
[5] Peleg, *Victimhood Discourse*, 3.

Chapters 5 and 6, the persistence of a threat against Jewry. In Israel, this threat is perceived in the continued suffering of Jews, including at the hands of their neighbors. Although explicitly conveyed in Israeli mass media and the ritual commemorative performance of the security apparatus, implicit invocation of an incessant danger to Jewish existence also relies on the transmission of what this study has described as an ethnocentric Holocaust narrative. Across the three collective realms under examination, I identified a specific inclusive victimhood which proscribes that regardless of the familial background, all Israeli-Jews must perceive of themselves as Holocaust survivors and, as such, the singled-out victims of Nazism. The unique nature of Jews' fate in the Second World War is further stressed through the de-emphasis of non-Jewish victims of Nazism, which not only relies on a minimization of their fate but also, at times, conveyance of ahistorical and anachronistic information.

The Victims of the Victims

Remembering and forgetting are, as Anderson's formulation illustrates, two sides of the same coin. The act of collective remembering requires (individual) experiences that do not fit the group's contemporary aims or an easily-digestible schema to fall to the wayside of history, destined to become a counter-narrative. It follows that, with reference to Nazi persecution, a complete acknowledgment of the racially inspired suffering of non-Jewish ethnic groups, which, among other devastation to human life, culminated in the *Porrajmos* of Roma gypsies, questions the singular fate of the Jews. A universally defined conception of suffering under Nazism also proves incompatible with the articulation of a continued threat against Jewry based on a metaphoric instrumentalization of the Holocaust and exemplified by the slogan *ha-'olam kulo negdenu* (Hebrew: the entire world is against us).[6] In other words, in the socially constructed paradigm or prism through which Israeli-Jews define their collective victimhood, the condition of victimhood is highly particularistic, unique, and definitely not universal.[7] Moreover, just as recognition of non-Jewish victimhood would question the singularity of Jewish suffering, admission of Palestinian suffering resulting from mass displacement in what Israelis call the "War of Independence" would shed doubt on the purity of the revival that followed the destruction and the related military concepts of *tohar ha-neshek* (Hebrew: purity of arms)

---

[6] Auron, *Israeli Identities*, xviii; Sagy, Kaplan, and Adwan, "Interpretations of the Past and Expectations," 28.
[7] Peleg, *Victimhood Discourse*, 3.

and *ein brira* (Hebrew: no choice/alternative).[8] An awareness of the
Palestinian conception of the Nakba, which draws a vertical line from
the European Holocaust to the Palestinian catastrophe and, in the words
of the Palestinian writer Raja Shehadeh, portrays the Palestinians as "the
victims of the victims of the Nazis,"[9] therefore can be considered foundational to Israeli minimization of the Nakba. Crucially, full recognition
of the Palestinian narrative, which perceives of the Nakba as "a
Palestinian Shoah,"[10] would also entail engagement with the discourse's
contemporary usage, as both an interpretative framework and an analogy
for ongoing Israeli marginalization of "the other." Israeli-Jewish memory
agents responsible for pitting the Holocaust as a constructionist memory
against a vengeful subversive Palestinian victimhood consequently would
be forced to reevaluate the source of the other's trauma and "[embark
on] the most terrifying ghost train."[11]

A Hidden Memory

Through examining the emergence and perpetuation of exclusionary
narratives, this work has sought to shed light on the origins of existing
trends of denial. While denial can imply a complete rebuttal of the
occurrence of an event, the previous invocation of "awareness" – similarly to the consistent usage of "minimization" and "de-emphasizing"
throughout this work – illustrates that inherent to the Israeli practice of
the social silencing of the Palestinian Nakba is the Freudian notion of
repression, creating a "hidden memory." Application of the individual
psychic processes of remembering, repression, and forgetting to the
public phenomenon demonstrates that marginalization of the
Palestinian narrative does not testify to a historical lacuna of knowledge
of the out-group's narrative, but rather the existence of an uncanny
memory, in need of repression or forgetting.[12] Indeed, Israeli police's
prevention of the 2017 Palestinian March of Return for the first time in
its history is a recent example of an organized suppression based on a
cognizance of Palestinians' political usage of the Nakba to "express their

---

[8] The concepts of "no alternative" and a "purity of arms" were not only meant to present
the 1948 War (and indeed subsequent wars) as a just cause but also as an Israeli act of
defense against annihilation, whereby any violence against adversaries was justified as a
last resort and necessity. Mira M. Sucahrov, *The International Self: Psychoanalysis and the
Search for Israeli–Palestinian Peace* (Albany: State University of New York Press, 2005),
45, 46.
[9] Shehadeh, *Third Way*, 64.
[10] Eli Senyor, "Nakba Day: 'It is as important to us as the Holocaust is to Jews'," *Ynet*, May
16, 2016, www.ynet.co.il/articles/0,7340,L-3251361,00.html, accessed May 18, 2016.
[11] Pappé, "Fear, Victimhood, Self and Other," 159.   [12] Huyssen, "Present Pasts," 27.

collective identity as a national minority."[13] Rather than spawning from
an unfamiliarity or *unheimlichkeit*,[14] the social silencing of the Nakba "as
a threat"[15] results precisely from its familiarity and the knowledge of its
radical incompatibility with that which is deemed *heimlich* for Israeli-
Jews. In this context, *heimlich* not only denotes a mental state of comfort
but, through denying or minimizing a historical Palestinian presence and
the mass displacement in 1948, bolsters the notion of an original Jewish
heim (German: home) in present-day Israel.

The uncanny, as something familiar and simultaneously irreconcil-
able, also finds relevance in the interpretation of Palestinian repudiation of the Holocaust. Thus, the high percentage of Palestinians inside
Israel who deny the Holocaust, as noted in the introduction, should not
be equated to a lack of knowledge of the Jewish genocide based on a
historical deficiency. Israeli-Jewish collective rituals dedicated to the
Holocaust and the increased educational exposure to the genocide
in the Palestinian educational sector[16] dictate that the rejection of
the majority's narrative is premised on the concept of a tit-for-tat,
whereby the increased Israeli (legal) thwarting of the Nakba prompts
a similar response in Palestinian public consciousness. Echoing
Smooha's 2009 findings,[17] this study found that the relegation of the
Nakba to a subversive narrative has spawned the minority's invocation
of their foundational history as a form of opposition or protest against
the Israeli-Jewish majority and the Zionist "settler-colonial project" it
sustains, and one that allows for the ongoing dispossession and marginalization of Palestinians while maintaining the image of the eternal
powerless – and victim – for itself.[18] The ideological instrumentalization of the Holocaust has consequently created a further obstacle to the
recognition of the Jewish tragedy since the duality – or package deal –

[13] Pappé cited in Jonathan Cook, "Why Is Israel Afraid of the Nakba's March of Return?," *Al Jazeera*, April 10, 2017, www.aljazeera.com/indepth/features/2017/04/israeli-police-block-palestinian-march-return-170409055747446.html, accessed August 29, 2017.
[14] Freud, *Uncanny*, 124, 125.   [15] Pappé cited in Cook, "Why."
[16] In 2015, under the direction of then Education Minister Piron, a program entitled "In Memory's Lanes" was launched. The program, which highlights Jewish suffering in the Holocaust, for the first time, was also included in the curricula of "the Arab sector," because, as Piron noted, "The Holocaust is a fundamental issue for Israeli society, they need to learn about this country. And if it's not mandatory, they might not learn about it." Interview conducted with Shai Piron on May 30, 2016.
[17] Smooha does not interpret the survey responses as "overt Holocaust denial" in the western sense of the phenomenon but rather as a form of opposition or protest. Auron, *Israeli Identities*, 139. Also see Fadi Eyadat, "Survey Finds Nearly Half of Israeli Arabs Deny Holocaust," *Haaretz*, May 18, 2009, www.haaretz.com/survey-finds-nearly-half-of-israeli-arabs-deny-holocaust-1.276206, accessed August 30, 2017.
[18] Zreik, "Settler Become a Native," 358, 359.

poses a deep challenge to perceptions of Zionism as solely a criminal colonial movement.[19]

Substantiated by the increase in Holocaust denial practices following the eruption of the Second Intifadah, the existence of a contemporary "protest narrative" forms the theoretical framework for the emergence of a context-specific exclusive Palestinian victimhood.[20] Rather than proclaiming a universally exclusive victimhood from the outset, the ensuing exclusionary narrative does not materialize in Nakba mnemonics inside the 1948 borders but solely manifests in direct confrontation with the Holocaust, based on an understanding of its importance among those held responsible for ongoing Palestinian suffering. A similar retaliatory silencing of Israeli-Jews' foundational past was found to be the source of the glaring absence of Jewish suffering at the hands of the Nazis from the new Palestinian curriculum and, in contrast to Nakba mnemonics inside the 1948 borders, the overt minimization of the Jewish genocide in mass Palestinian media output dedicated to the Nakba. Implicitly and, to a lesser extent, explicitly, mnemonic agents revealed that an acknowledgement of Jewish suffering, deemed representative of the trauma of the Israeli "enemy," not only equated to a justification of Israel's establishment in 1948 and its repercussions for Palestinians but also would minimize all ensuing Palestinian suffering. With the outbreak of the violence of the Second Intifadah, attempts to include the Holocaust in Palestinian textbooks – characteristic of the so-called people-to-people initiatives in post-Oslo years[21] – were thus met with extreme hostility, as they signified advancement of the enemy's narrative. Yet, as this work relayed in its final chapter, Holocaust minimization does not solely rely on its absence. Instead, the perception of successful Israeli political instrumentalization of the Holocaust means that part and parcel of the marginalization of the Holocaust is also, somewhat ironically, its conjuring by Palestinians as the ultimate yardstick of evil, measuring the gravity of Israeli actions.

The Research Findings and Their Application

Consistent omission of the out-group's narrative in collective realms can, both among Palestinians and Israelis, boost denial practices among

---

[19] Omar Kamil, *Der Holocaust im arabischen Gedächtnis. Eine Diskursgeschichte 1945–1967* (Göttingen: Vandenhoeck & Ruprecht, 2012), 141 (in German).

[20] Shipler, *Arab and Jew*, 344; Litvak and Webman, "Perceptions of the Holocaust," 137.

[21] Iftat Maoz, "Peace Building in Violent Conflict: Israeli–Palestinian Post-Oslo People-to-People Activities," *International Journal of Politics, Culture, and Society* 17:3 (2004): 563–574.

future generations. This work, as such, is both about the long shadow of the past and the even longer shadow of the present and the future.[22] An unsettling narrative no longer, the out-group's foundational narrative would, with the continued collision and incompatibility of meta-historical belief systems, become an uncanny memory resulting from a dearth of historical exposure, albeit one based on unfamiliarity. While recognizing the possibility of a relentless continuation and exacerbation of the refutation of the other's past, this work does not propose a method of fusing the two foundational narratives; nor does this work suggest ways in which the identified exclusionary narratives can be challenged and modified. These people-to-people initiatives depend not only on a mutual willingness but – as indicated by the fate of the *Side by Side* project discussed extensively in Part I of this work – the existing political atmosphere within and between the two societies.

Determining the degree to which contemporary conceptions of past events should be modified if they are not to become the "gravedigger of the present"[23] is a task to be undertaken under the supervision of committed experts and, eventually, if deemed (politically) worthy of dissemination across official societal realms, the mnemonic elite. Nevertheless, it is evident that in the execution of the initial "people-to-people diplomacy,"[24] this work finds practical applicability through its comprehensive review of the instrumentalization of the past in both Israeli-Jewish and Palestinian society and, concurrently, its exposure of the mnemonic motives that inform the denial of the out-group's foundational history. Moreover, this study's reinforcement of the notion that conceptions of the past are equally determined by that which is textually present or (ritually) portrayed and consciously excluded dictates that any transformation of officially ratified narratives will depend on "forgetting"[25] that which "demonstrates the justness of today's cause" and "the perfidy of today's opponent."[26]

Victimhood is, as Ilan Peleg notes, a "rather universal theme among human beings, both individuals and groups"; collective victimhood has been a particularly prevalent theme in societies embroiled in intergroup conflict.[27] The universality of collective narratives and their societal instrumentalization, including as tales of empowerment in times of

---

[22] Peleg, *Victimhood Discourse*, 1.
[23] Friedrich Nietzsche, *Nietzsche: Untimely Mediations*, ed. Daniel Breazale (Cambridge: Cambridge University Press, 1997), 62.
[24] Sapir Handelman, ed., *People-to-People Diplomacy in Israel and Palestine: The Minds of Peace Experiment* (London/New York: Routledge, 2014), 2.
[25] Renan, "What Is a Nation?" 80.   [26] Rotberg, "Building Legitimacy," 1.
[27] Peleg, *Victimhood Discourse*, 1, 2.

(low-level) conflict, means that this work's findings allow for a global applicability beyond the Israeli–Palestinian arena. This study's usage of theoretical concepts can equally be used for the analysis of any society, polity, or culture, particularly those involved in continuous conflict with other societies.[28] As noted in Part I, studies conducted on official textbooks used in (post-conflict) nations indicate that foregoing a former opponent's suffering or collective narrative pertaining to the outbreak of conflict while highlighting the in-group's mnemonic discourse are not unique to Israel-Palestine. The identification of a retaliatory minimization of the out-group's foundational narrative study, as discovered in the Palestinian case study, can be applied as a theoretical framework in future studies on the societal materialization of exclusive narratives in, for example, Bosnia-Herzegovina, where past studies have observed that Muslims, Croats, and Serbs "each attribute victimhood to oneself and guilt to the two others."[29] Similarly, the minimization of Palestinian suffering in the 1948 War in Israeli textbooks and the societal objection it has aroused in Palestinian society can be comparatively administered in examinations of Japanese educational content on the Asia-Pacific War, which has been found to downplay the suffering inflicted by the Japanese on the Chinese and Koreans and, according to a recent study, contributes to the existence of continued negative perceptions of Japan among the Chinese population.[30]

In addition to offering a practical applicability to non-regional scholarship and cross-cultural initiatives, it is the intent of this work to provide fertile ground for future scholarship on Israeli-Jewish and Palestinian mnemonic discourse that challenges the idealization of the past's invocation and, instead, exposes its neurasthenic and disabling effects in "service of the nation."[31] Constrictions on personal movement and a sharpened concentration within the three societal realms ensure that the last word has not yet been written on the inter- and transgenerational transmission of the respective foundational narratives. A scholarly void in need of future consideration is the lack of an extensive analysis of Nakba mnemonic discourse in Gaza in the post-Oslo era resulting from the fragile political situation and its effects on Gazan citizens and foreign researchers' freedom and safety of movement. While the dissemination of PNA-authorized Nakba narratives, including in textbooks and in the PA's official newspaper, will have been those identified in this study in

---

[28] Ibid., 9.   [29] Ahonen, "Post-Conflict History Education," 95.
[30] Daniel Sneider, "Textbooks and Patriotic Education: Wartime Memory Formation in China and Japan," *Asia-Pacific Review* 20:1 (2013): 49.
[31] Zertal, *Israel's Holocaust and the Politics of Nationhood*, 9; Maier, "A Surfeit of Memory," 141.

the decade following the Oslo accords, in the wake of the 2006 Hamas-Fatah rift, Nakba discourse in Gaza cannot be assumed to mirror the mnemonics found in the territories under the authority of the Fatah-controlled Palestinian Authority. Chapter 7's exposure of the instrumentalization of Nakba mnemonics as a powerful political tool to boost the credibility of Fatah officials and, simultaneously, cast doubt on Hamas' dedication to the "national cause" begs further study into popular usage of Nakba mnemonics inside the Gaza Strip and its reflection of the most recent Palestinian civil war.[32] The diverging legal status of East Jerusalemites and their post-Oslo transformation into "others" among the rest of the Palestinian people similarly demands further analysis into the usage and application of Nakba mnemonics. Beyond examining participation in established mnemonics on both sides of the Green Line and its reflection of identity politics,[33] in line with this research's findings, the concept of a singular East Jerusalemite Nakba mnemonic narrative that characterizes a separate Jerusalem-based identity[34] and reflects current societal and political grievances should not be disregarded. Recent revelations of ongoing, albeit offhand, Israeli censorship of history textbooks in East Jerusalem equally require close examination of the material taught to students across East Jerusalem schools. In her 2018 study of fourteen history textbooks, Samira Alayan noted that the required Israeli approval of PNA textbooks had led to the increased censoring of "anti-Israeli materials," primarily pertaining to Palestinian national identity symbols and aimed at "undermining the formation of a collective memory."[35] While Alayan found that Israeli censorship did not affect the PA's critical content on the 1948 War, her case study did highlight a continuous power struggle between the PNA and Israeli authorities and the growing pressure to add the Israeli curricula to schools centering on the Israeli narrative.[36]

Finally, it is envisaged that forthcoming academic works on mnemonic discourse in Palestinian and Israeli media realm, particularly those concentrating on the post-2010 era, will be able to take a more comprehensive approach to the role of Nakba and Holocaust mnemonics in mass

---

[32] Schanzer, *Hamas vs. Fatah*, 9.
[33] According to a 2012 study, approximately 82 percent of Palestinian youth in East Jerusalem deemed it "important" or "extremely important" to foster ties with West Bank residents, whereas only approximately 52 percent gave similar responses when questioned about forging ties with Palestinians inside Israel. Badil, *One People United: A Deterritorialized Palestinian Identity* (Badil, 2012), 24, 25.
[34] Dumper, *Jerusalem Unbound*, 78.
[35] Samira Alayan, "White Pages: Israeli Censorship of Palestinian Textbooks in East Jerusalem," *Social Semiotics* 28:4 (2018): 516, 528.
[36] Ibid., 527.

digital media. As such, beyond the online conversion of traditional media discussed in this work's final section, mass online social platforms, including Facebook and Twitter – both extensively used in the respective communities over the last decade[37] – will also need to be probed to determine the digital mnemonic narrative and, in the process, establish its theoretical resemblance to more traditional collective realms of memory.[38] Offered here, therefore, is a first attempt to develop an interpretive perspective of the hermeneutical centrality that permits one voice to nurture "its own torment"[39] to overcome or drown out the other and, as a result, sentences Palestinians and Israeli-Jews to remain "wounded spirits in a promised land."[40]

---

[37] According to a survey by the PCBS, internet usage among Palestinians above the age of 10 increased by 27.5 percent between 2004 and 2011 to 39.4 percent. A further survey indicated that at the end of the first decade of the twenty-first century, social network usage among Palestinians was high, with 21 percent using Facebook and Twitter extensively, predominantly those aged between 18 and 24. Israel, according to a study conducted in 2012, has one of the highest household internet penetration rates in the world; internet usage was estimated at 82 percent among the adult Jewish population (constituting a 23percent increase from 2005) and 70 percent of internet users claim to have at least one social network account. Sharon Haleva-Amir, "Online Israeli Politics: The Current State of the Art," *Israel Affairs* 17:3 (2011): 467; Philip Seib, ed., *New Media and the New Middle East* (New York: Palgrave Macmillan, 2007), 163; Near East Consulting, *Survey of Palestinian Media* (Ramallah: Near East Consulting for Fondation Hirondelle, 2010); PCBS, *Access and Use of ICT by Households and Individuals by Year* (PCBS, undated), www.pcbs.gov.ps/Portals/_Rainbow/Documents/ICT2_E.htm, accessed September 2, 2017.

[38] The potential of memory transmission through digital media was acknowledged in 2011 by media theorists Andrew Hoskins and Jose van Dijck. Nevertheless, Hoskins argues that digital memory is not collective, but rather connective. Andrew Hoskins, "7/7 and Connective Memory: Interactional Trajectories of Remembering in Post-Scarcity Culture," *Memory Studies* 4:3 (2011): 272; José van Dijck, "Flickr and the Culture of Connectivity: Sharing Views, Experiences, Memories," *Memory Studies* 4:4 (2011): 401–415.

[39] Jaffee, "Victim-Community in Myth and History," 225, 238.

[40] Shipler, *Arab and Jew.*

Bibliography

Secondary Literature

Abbas, Mahmoud. *Through Secret Channels*. Reading: Garnet, 1995.

Abdallah, Ghassan. "A Palestinian at Yad Vashem." *Jerusalem Quarterly* 15 (2002): 42–45.

Abdelal, Wael. *Hamas and the Media: Politics and Strategy*. London: Routledge, 2016.

Abraham, Nicholas and Maria Torok. *The Shell and the Kernel: Renewals of Psychoanalysis*. Edited and translated by Nicholas Rand. Chicago/London: University of Chicago Press, 1994.

Abu-Lughod, Ibrahim. "Educating a Community in Exile: The Palestinian Experience." *Journal of Palestine Studies* 11 (1973): 94–111.

Abu-Lughod, Lila and Ahmad H. Sa'di. "Introduction: The Claims of Memory." In *Nakba: Palestine, 1948, and the Claims of Memory*, edited by Lila Abu-Lughod and Ahmad H. Sa'di, 1–27. New York: Columbia University Press, 2007.

Abu-Saad, Ismael. "Introduction: A Historical Context of Palestinian Arab Education." *The American Behavioral Scientist* 8 (2006): 1035–1051.

"Present Absentees: The Arab School Curriculum in Israel as a Tool for De-Educating Indigenous Palestinians." *Holy Land Studies* 7 (2009): 17–43.

Achcar, Gilbert. *The Arabs and the Holocaust*. New York: Metropolitan Books, 2009.

The Arabs and the Holocaust. London: Saqi Books, 2010.

Adoni, Hanna, Dan Caspi, and Akiva Cohen. *Media, Minorities and Hybrid Identities: The Arab and Russian Communities in Israel*. Cresskill, NJ: Hampton Press, 2006.

Adwan, Sami. "A Curriculum for Peace and Coexistence." In *The Psychology of Peace and Conflict: The Israeli–Palestinian Experience*, edited by the Harry S. Truman Research Institute, 86–93. Jerusalem: Harry S. Truman Research Institute for the Advancement of Peace, 1996.

Adwan, Sami, Dan Bar-On, and Eyal Naveh. *Learning Each Other's Narrative: Palestinians and Israelis*. Beit Jallah: Prime, 2003.

Adwan, Sami and Ruth Firer. *The Israeli–Palestinian Conflict in History and Civics Textbooks of Both Nations*. Hannover: Verlag Hahnsche Buchhandlung, 2004.

Agbaria, Ayman K. "On Enmity and Acceptance: The Case of the Israeli and Palestinian Civic Education." *Al-Majmuah* 2 (2010): 1–25.

Aharon, Eldad Ben. "A Unique Denial: Israel's Foreign Policy and the Armenian Genocide." *British Journal of Middle Eastern Studies* 42:4 (2015): 638–654.

"Between Ankara and Jerusalem: The Armenian Genocide as a Zero-Sum Game in Israel's Foreign Policy (1980's–2010's)." *Journal of Balkan and Near Eastern Studies* 20:5 (2018): 459–476.

Ahonen, Sirkka. "Post-Conflict History Education in Finland, South Africa and Bosnia-Herzegovina." *Journal of Humanities and Social Science Education* 1 (2013): 90–103.

Ajami, Fouad. *The Dream Place of the Arabs.* New York: Pantheon Books, 1998.

Alayan, Samira. "History Curricula and Textbooks in Palestine: Between Nation Building and Quality Education." In *The Politics of Education Reform in the Middle East: Self and Other in Textbooks and Curricula*, edited by Samira Alayan, Achim Rohde, and Sarhan Dhouib, 209–236. New York: Berghahn Books, 2012.

"The Holocaust in Palestinian Textbooks: Differences and Similarities in Israel and Palestine." *Comparative Education Review* 60:1 (2015): 80–104.

"White Pages: Israeli Censorship of Palestinian Textbooks in East Jerusalem." *Social Semiotics* 28:4 (2018): 512–532.

Al-Dabbagh, Mustapha Murad. *Our Country Palestine*, 10 vols. Beirut: Dar al-Tali'a, 1956. (In Arabic)

Allen, Lori. "Martyr Bodies in the Media: Human Rights, Aesthetics and the Politics of Immediation in the Palestinian Intifada." *American Ethnologist* 36 (2009): 161–180.

Altbach, Philip G. "Textbooks in Comparative Context." In *Educational Technology – Its Creation, Development and Cross-cultural Transfer*, edited by R. Murray Thomas and Victor N. Kobayashi, 159–176. Oxford: Pergamon, 1987.

Aly, Götz. "Medicine against the Useless." In *Cleansing the Fatherland: Nazi Medicine and Racial Hygiene*, edited by Götz Aly, Peter Chroust, and Christian Pross, 22–99. Baltimore: The Johns Hopkins University Press, 1994.

Alzaroo, Salah and Gillian Hunt. "Education in the Context of Conflict and Instability: The Palestinian Case." *Social Policy and Administration* 37 (2003): 165–180.

Anderson, Benedict. *Imagined Communities: Reflections on the Origin and Spread of Nationalism.* London: Verso, 2006.

Anziska, Seth. *Preventing Palestine: A Political History from Camp David to Oslo.* Princeton: Princeton University Press, 2018.

Apple, Michael. *Ideology and Curriculum.* New York: Routledge, 2004.

Official Knowledge: Democratic Education in a Conservative Age. New York: Routledge, 2014.

Apple, Michael and Linda Christian-Smith, eds. *The Politics of the Textbook.* New York/London: Routledge, 1991.

Arad, Julie Ne'eman. "The Shoah as Israel's Political Trope." In *Divergent Jewish Cultures: Israel and America*, edited by Deborah Dash Moore and S. Ilan Troen, 192–216. New Haven: Yale University Press, 2001.

Armbrust, Walter. *Mass Mediations: New Approaches to Popular Culture in the Middle East and Beyond.* Berkeley/London: University of California Press, 2000.

Aronoff, Myron J. "The Origins of Israeli Political Culture." In *Israeli Democracy under Stress*, edited by Ehud Sprinzak and Larry Diamond, 47–63. Boulder, CO: Lynne Rienner, 1993.

Ashrawi, Hanan. *This Side of Peace.* New York: Touchstone, 1995.

Assad, Denise. "Palestinian Educational Philosophy between Past and Present." *Studies in Philosophy and Education* 19 (2000): 387–403.

Assaf, Omar. *The Palestinian Public School Teachers Movement in the West Bank, 1967–2000.* Ramallah: Muwatin – The Palestinian Institute for the Study of Democracy, 2004. (In Arabic)

Assaf, Said. "Educational Disruption and Recovery in Palestine." In *Educational Destruction and Reconstruction in Disrupted Societies*, edited by Sobhi Tawil, 51–61. Geneva: International Bureau of Education and the University of Geneva, 1997.

Assman, Aleida and Sebastian Conrad. "Introduction." In *Memory in a Global Age: Discourses, Practices and Trajectories*, edited by Aleida Assman and Sebastian Conrad, 1–16. New York: Palgrave Macmillan, 2010.

Assmann, Jan. *Das kulturelle Gedächtnis.* München: Verlag C. H. Beck, 1992. (In German)

Auron, Yair. *The Holocaust, the Resurrection and the Nakba.* Ramallah: Madar Press, 2013.

Israeli Identities: Jews and Arabs Facing the Self and the Other. New York/Oxford: Berghahn Books, 2012.

Awadah, Wadiah. *Memory That Does Not Die: Eyewitness Open Their Hearts to Talk about What Happened to Them in 1948 – The Year of the Nakba.* Haifa: ADRID, 2000. (In Arabic)

Ayalon, Ami, ed. *Middle East Contemporary Survey, Volume XVI 1992.* Boulder, CO/Oxford: Westview Press, 1995.

Ayres, William. "Mediating International Conflicts: Is Image Change Necessary?" *Journal of Peace Research* 34:4 (1997): 431–447.

Bagnall, Gaynor. "Performance and Performativity at Heritage Sites." *Museum and Society* 1 (1993): 87–103.

Bar-On, Dan. "Cultural Identity and Demonization of the Relevant Other: Lessons from the Palestinian–Israeli Conflict." In *International Handbook of Human Response to Trauma*, edited by Arieh Y. Shalev, Rachel Yehuda, and Alexander C. McFarlane, 115–125. New York/London: Kluwer Academic/Plenum, 2000.

"Israeli Society between the Culture of Death and the Culture of Life." *Israel Studies* 2:2 (1997): 88–112.

Barry, Randall K. *ALA-LX Romanization Tables: Transliteration Schemes for Non-Roman Scripts.* Washington, DC: U.S. Library of Congress, 1991.

Bar-Tal, Daniel. "Delegitimizing Relations between Israeli-Jews and Palestinians: A Social Psychological Analysis." In *Arab–Jewish Relations in Israel: A Quest in Human Understanding*, edited by John Hofman, 217–248. Bristol/Indiana: Wyndham Hall Press, 1988.

Intergroup Conflicts and Their Resolution: A Social Psychological Perspective. New York/London: Psychology Press, 2011.

Bar-Tal, Daniel and Gavriel Salomon. "Israeli-Jewish Narratives of the Israeli–Palestinian Conflict: Evolvement, Contents, Functions, and Consequences." In *Israeli and Palestinian Narratives of Conflict: History's Double Helix*, edited by Robert Rotberg, 19–46. Bloomington: Indiana University Press, 2006.

Bartov, Omer. "Chambers of Horror: Holocaust Museums in Israel and the United States." *Israel Studies* 2 (1997): 66–87.

Bashir, Bashir. "Neutralizing History and Memory in Divided Societies: The Case of Making Peace in Palestine/Israel." In *The Goodness Regime*, edited by Jamana Manna and Sille Storihle, 20–27. New York, Berlin: Strenberg Press, 2016.

Bashir, Bashir and Amos Goldberg. "Introduction: The Holocaust and the Nakba: A New Syntax of History Memory and Political Thought." In *The Holocaust and the Nakba: A New Grammar of Trauma and History*, edited by Amos Goldberg and Bashir Bashir, 1–42. New York: Columbia University Press, 2018.

Bauer, Yehuda. *Rethinking the Holocaust*. New Haven/London: Yale University Press, 2002.

Baukhol, Ingrid. "Security and Fear in Israeli and Palestinian Conflict Narratives: A Social-Psychological Study." MA thesis, University of Gothenburg, 2015.

Bauman, Zygmunt. "Categorical Murder, or: How to Remember the Holocaust." In *Re-presenting the Shoah for the Twenty-first Century*, edited by Ronit Lentin, 24–40. Oxford/New York: Berghahn Books, 2004.

Baumel, Judith Tydor. "In Everlasting Memory: Individual and Communal Holocaust Commemoration in Israel." *Israel Affairs* 1 (1995): 146–170.

Becker, Jonathan. "A Disappearing Enemy: The Image of the United States in Soviet Political Cartoons." *Journalism and Mass Communication Quarterly* 73:3 (1996): 609–619.

Beilin, Yossi. *The Path to Geneva: The Quest for a Permanent Solution, 1996–2003*. New York: RDV Books, 2004.

Touching Peace: From the Oslo Accord to a Final Agreement. London: George Weidenfeld & Nicholson, 1999.

Bekerman, Zvi and Michalinos Zembylas. *Teaching Contested Narrative: Identity, Memory, and Reconciliation in Peace Education and Beyond*. Cambridge: Cambridge University Press, 2012.

Bell, Christine. *Peace Agreements and Human Rights*. Oxford: Oxford University Press, 2000.

Bellah, Robert Neelly, Richard Madsen, William M. Sullivan, Ann Swidler, Steven M. Tipton. *Habits of the Heart: Individualism and Commitment in American Life*. Berkeley: University of California Press, 1985.

Ben-Amos, Amos and Ilana Bet-El. "Holocaust Day and Memorial Day in Israeli Schools: Ceremonies, Education and History." *Israel Studies* 4 (1999): 258–284.

Ben-Amos, Avner. "War Commemoration and the Formation of Israeli National Identity." *Journal of Political and Military Sociology* 31 (2003): 171–195.

Ben-Eliezer, Uri, *Old Conflict, New War: Israel's Politics toward the Palestinians.* New York: Palgrave Macmillan, 2012.

Ben-Israel, Galit M. and Marina Shorer-Zeltser."Telling a Story by Dry Statistics: Suicide Terror Attacks in Israel: (1993–2008)." In *Contemporary Suicide Terrorism: Origins, Trends and Ways of Tackling It,* edited by Tatiāña Dronzina and Rachid El Houdaïgui, 52–67. Amsterdam: IOS Press BV, 2012.

Benvenisti, Eyal. *The International Law of Occupation.* Oxford: Oxford University Press, 2012.

Benvenisti, Meron. *Israeli Censorship on Arab Publication.* New York: Fund for Free Expression, 1983.

Sacred Landscape: The Buried History of the Holy Land since 1948. Berkeley: University of California Press, 2000.

Son of the Cypresses: Memories, Reflections, and Regrets from a Political Life. Berkeley/London: University of California Press, 2007.

Ben-Ze'ev, Efrat. *Remembering Palestine in 1948: Beyond National Narratives.* New York/Cambridge: Cambridge University Press, 2011.

"Social Silence: Transference, De-sensitization and De-focusing among Israeli Students." In *Zoom In: Palestinian Refugees of 1948, Remembrances,* edited by Sami Adwan, Efrat Ben-Ze'ev, Menachem Klein, Ihab Saloul, Tamir Sorek, and Mahmoud Yazbak, 165–175. Dordrecht: Institute of Historical Justice and Reconciliation and Republic of Letters Publishers, 2011.

Berenbaum, Michael. *The Holocaust and History: The Known, the Unknown, the Disputed, and the Reexamined.* Bloomington/Indianapolis: Indiana University Press, 1998.

Bhabha, Homi K., ed. *Nation & Narration.* London/New York: Routledge, 1990.

Bickman, Leonard and Karl Hamner. "An Evaluation of the Yad Vashem Holocaust Museum." *Evaluation Review* 22:4 (1998): 435–446.

Bilu, Yoram. "The Image of the Enemy: Cracks in the Wall of Hatred." *Palestine-Israeli Journal* 4 (1994): 24–28.

Birnbaum, Sariel. "Historical Discourse in the Media of the Palestinian National Authority." In *Palestinian Collective Memory and National Identity,* edited by Meir Litvak, 135–168. Basingstoke: Palgrave Macmillan, 2009.

Bishara, Amahl. "New Media and Political Change in the Occupied Palestinian Territories: Assembling Media Worlds and Cultivating Networks of Care." *Middle East Journal of Culture and Communication* 3:1 (2010): 63–81.

Bishara, Azmi. "The Arabs and the Holocaust. The Analysis of a Problematic Conjunctive Letter." *Zmanim* 53 (1995): 54–71. (In Hebrew)

"Reflections on the Realities of the Oslo Accords." In *After Oslo: New Realities, Old Problems,* edited by George Giacaman and Dag Jørund Lønning, 212–226. London: Pluto Press, 1998.

Blatman, Daniel. "Holocaust Scholarship: Towards a Post-Uniqueness Era." *Journal of Genocide Research* 17:1 (2015): 21–43.

Bligh, Alexander, ed. *The Israeli Palestinians: An Arab Minority in the Jewish State.* London: Frank Cass, 2003.

Blumenthal, Max. *The 51 Day War: Ruin and Resistance in Gaza.* New York: Nation Books, 2015.

Goliath: Life and Loathing in Greater Israel. New York: Nation Books, 2013.

Boqai', Nihad and Terry Rempel. "Patterns of Internal Displacement, Social Adjustment and the Challenge of Return." In *Catastrophe Remembered: Palestine, Israel and the Internal Refugees: Essays in Memory of Edward W. Said, (1935–2003)*, edited by Nur Masalha, 73–113. London: Zed Books, 2005.

Bowers, Chet A. *The Promise of Theory: Education and the Politics of Cultural Change.* New York: Teachers College Press, 1987.

Braun, Hans. "A Sinto Survivor Speaks." In *Papers from the Sixth and Seventh Annual Meetings, Gypsy Lore Society, North American Chapter*, edited by Joanne Grumet, 165–171. New York: The Society, 1986.

Broder, Hendryk. *Die Irren von Zion.* Hamburg: Hoffmann u. Campe, 1998.

Brog, Mooli. "Victims and Victors: Holocaust and Military Commemoration in Israel Collective Memory." *Israel Studies* 8:3 (2003): 65–99.

"Yad Vashem." In *The Holocaust Encyclopaedia*, edited by Walter Laquer and Judith Tydor Baumal, 697–700. New Haven/London: Yale University Press, 2001.

Bröning, Michael. *Political Parties in Palestine: Leadership and Thought.* New York/ Basingstoke: Palgrave Macmillan, 2013.

Bronstein, Eitan. "The Nakba in Hebrew: Israeli-Jewish Awareness of the Palestinian Catastrophe and Internal Refugees." In *On Catastrophe Remembered: Palestine, Israel and the Internal Refugees*, edited by Nur Masalha, 214–241. London: Zed Books, 2005.

Browne, Brendan C. "Commemoration in Conflict." *Journal of Comparative Research in Anthropology and Sociology* 2 (2013): 143–163.

"Transitional Justice and the Case of Palestine." In *Research Handbook on Transitional Justice*, edited by Cheryl Lawther, Luke Moffett, and Dov Jacobs, 488–507. Cheltenham/Northampton: Edward Elgar, 2010.

Brown, Nathan. "Contesting National Identity in Palestinian Education." In *Israeli and Palestinian Narratives of Conflict: History's Double Helix*, edited by Robert Rotberg, 225–243. Bloomington: Indiana University Press, 2006.

Democracy, History, and the Contest over the Palestinian Curriculum. London: Adam Institute, 2001.

Palestinian Politics after the Oslo Accords: Resuming Arab Palestine. Berkeley: University of California Press, 2003.

Bshara, Khaldun A. M. "Space and Memory: The Poetics and Politics of Home in the Palestinian Diaspora." PhD diss., University of California, Irvine, 2012.

Bukh, Alexander. "Japan's History Textbooks Debate: National Identity in Narratives of Victimhood and Victimization." *Asian Survey* 47:5 (2007): 683–704.

Burke, Peter. "History as Social Memory." In *The Collective Memory Reader*, edited by Jeffrey K. Olick, Vered Vinitzky-Seroussi, and Daniel Levy, 188–193. New York/Oxford: Oxford University Press, 2011.

Burleigh, Michael. *Death and Deliverance: "Euthanasia" in Germany, C.1900 to 1945.* Wiltshire: Cambridge University Press, 1994.

Cabaha, Mustafa and Ronit Brazilai. "Refugees in Their Homeland: The Internal Refugees in the State of Israel 1948–1996." Givat Haviva: Institute for Peace Studies, 1996. (In Hebrew)

Calvocoressi, Peter, Guy Wint, and John Pritchard. *Total War: The Western Hemisphere*. New York: Pantheon Books, 1990.

Carey, James. *Communications as Culture*. London: Routledge, 1989.

Caspi, Dan. "A Revised Look at Online Journalism in Israel: Entrenching the Old Hegemony." *Israel Affairs* 17:3 (2011): 341–363.

Caspi, Dan and Nelly Elias. "Don't Patronize Me: Media-*by* and Media- *for* Minorities." *Ethnic and Racial Studies* 34:1 (2011): 62–82.

Caspi, Dan and Mustafa Kabaha. "From Al-Quds al-Sharif to al-'Ein: On the Arab Press in Israel." *Panim* 16 (2001): 44–56. (In Hebrew)

    The Palestinian Arab In/Outsiders: Media and Conflict in Israel. London/Portland: Vallentine Mitchell, 2011.

Caspi, Dan and Yehiel Limor. *The In/Outsiders: The Media in Israel*. Cresskill, NJ: Hampton Press, 1999.

Caspit, Ben. *The Netanyahu Years*. Translated by Ora Cummings. New York: Thomas Dunne Books, 2012.

Cesarani, David. "Does the Singularity of the Holocaust Make It Incomparable and Inoperative for Commemorating, Studying and Preventing Genocide? Britain's Holocaust Memorial Day as a Case Study." *The Journal of Holocaust Education* 10:2 (2001): 40–56.

Chaitin, Julia and Shoshana Steinberg. "You Should Know Better: Expressions of Empathy and Disregard among Victims of Massive Social Trauma." *Journal of Aggression, Maltreatment, and Trauma* 17:2 (2008): 197–226.

Chaumont, Jean-Michel. *La concurrence des victimes: Génocide, identité, reconnaissance*. La Découverte: Paris, 2010. (In French)

Chomsky, Noam. "The Oslo Accords: Their Context, Their Consequences." In *The Oslo Accords: A Critical Assessment*, edited by Petter Bauck and Mohammed Omer, 1–12. Cairo: The American University in Cairo Press, 2017.

Chorev, Harel and Yvette Shumacher. "The Road to Operation Protective Edge: Gaps in Strategic Perception." *Israel Journal of Foreign Affairs* 8:3 (2014): 9–24.

Clifford, Rebecca. *Commemorating the Holocaust: The Dilemmas of Remembrance in France and Italy*. Oxford: Oxford University Press, 2013.

Cohen, Akiba A., Tamar Zemach-Marom, Jurgen Wilke, and Birgit Schenk. *The Holocaust and the Press: Nazi War Crimes Trials in Germany and Israel*. Cresskill, NJ: Hampton Press, 2002.

Cohen, Avner. "And Then There Was One." *Bulletin of the Atomic Scientists* 54:5 (1998): 51–55.

Cohen, Erik H. "Educational Dark Tourism at an in Populo Site: The Holocaust Museum in Jerusalem." *Annals of Tourism Research* 38:1 (2011): 193–209.

Cohen, Erik H. *Shoah Education in Israeli State Schools: An Educational Research 2007–2009*. Ramat Gan: Bar Ilan University, 2009.

    "Teacher Autonomy within a Flexible National Curriculum: Development of Shoah Education in Israeli State Schools." *Journal of Curriculum Studies* 48 (2016): 167–191.

Cohen, Samy. *Doves among Hawks: Struggles of the Israeli Peace Movements*. Oxford: Oxford University Press, 2019.

Cohen, Yoel. *God, Jews and the Media: Religion and Israel's Media.* London/New York: Routledge, 2012.

"Yedioth Aharonoth." In *Encyclopaedia Judaica,* edited by Michael Berenbaum and Fred Skolnik, 293. The University of Michigan: Macmillan Reference USA, 2007.

Conboy, Martin, ed. *How Journalism Uses History.* New York: Routledge, 2012.

Connerton, Paul. *How Modernity Forgets.* Cambridge: Cambridge University Press, 2009.

How Societies Remember. Cambridge: Cambridge University Press, 1989.

Corbin, Jane, *Gaza First: The Secret Norway Channel to Peace between Israel and the PLO.* London: Bloomsbury, 1994.

Cordesman, Anthony H. *The Israeli–Palestinian War: Escalating to Nowhere.* Westport, CT/London: Praeger Security International, 2005.

Dalsheim, Joyce. "Settler Nationalism, Collective Memories of Violence and the 'Uncanny Other'." *Social Identities: Journal for the Study of Race, Nation and Culture* 10:2 (2004): 151–170.

Dalton, Russell J., Paul A. Beck, and Robert Huckfeldt. "Partisan Cues and the Media: Information Flows in the 1992 Presidential Election." *The American Political Science Review* 92:1 (1998): 111–126.

Darwish, Mahmoud. "Resigning from the PLO Executive Committee." In *The Israel-Arab Reader: A Documentary History of the Middle East Conflict,* edited by Walter Laqueur and Dan Schueftan, 373–374. New York: Penguin Books, 2016.

Darwish, Mahmoud, Samih al-Qasim, and Abdullah Udhari. *Victims of a Map: A Bilingual Anthology of Arabic Poetry.* London: Saqi, 2005.

Davis, Rochelle. "Mapping the Past, Recreating the Homeland: Palestinian Memories of pre-1948 Village Life." In *Nakba: Palestine, 1948, and the Claims of Memory,* edited by Ahmad Sa'di and Lila Abu-Lughod, 53–76. New York: Columbia University Press, 2007.

Davis, Susan. "'Set Your Mood to Patriotic': History as Televised Special Event." *Radical History Review* 42 (1988): 122–143.

Dayan, Daniel and Elihu Katz. *Media Events: The Live Broadcasting of History.* Cambridge, MA/London: Harvard University Press, 1992.

Deeb, Dennis J. *Israel, Palestine, and the Quest for Middle East Peace.* Lanham: University Press of American, 2013.

Del Sarto, Raffaella. *Israel under Siege: The Politics of Insecurity and the Rise of the Israeli Neo-Revisionist Right.* Washington, DC: Georgetown University Press, 2017.

Don-Yehiya, Elizier. "Memory and Political Culture: Israeli Society and the Holocaust." In *Modern Jews and Their Musical Agendas,* edited by Ezra Mendelsohn, 139–162. New York: Oxford University Press, 1993.

"Memory and Political Culture: Israeli Society and the Holocaust." *Studies in Contemporary Jewry* 9 (1993): 139–162.

Dooley, Mark and Liam Kavanagh. *The Philosophy of Derrida.* London/New York: Routledge, 2007.

Dror, Yuval. "National Denial, Splitting, and Narcissism: Group Defense Mechanisms of Teachers and Students in Palestinian in Response to the Holocaust." *Mediterranean Journal of Educational Studies* 1 (1996): 107–137.

Dumper, Michael. *Jerusalem Unbound: Geography, History, and the Future of the Holy City*. New York: Columbia University Press, 2014.

Dunning, Tristan. *Hamas, Jihad and Popular Legitimacy: Reinterpreting Resistance in Palestine*. London: Routledge, 2016.

Durkheim, Émile. *Critical Assessments of Leading Sociologists*. Edited by W. S. F. Pickering. London/New York: Routledge, 2001.

"The Elementary Forms of Religious Life." In *The Collective Memory Reader*, edited by Jeffrey K. Olick, Vered Vinitzky-Seroussi, and Daniel Levy, 136–138. New York/Oxford: Oxford University Press, 2011.

Suicide: A Study in Sociology. Translated by John A. Spaulding and George Simpson. New York: Free Press, 1951.

Eckmann, Monique. "History and Memory of the Other: An Experimental Encounter-Programme with Israeli-Jews and Palestinians from Israel." In *Perceptions of the Holocaust in Europe and Muslim Communities*, edited by Günther Jikeli and Joëlle Allouche-Benayoun, 133–153. Dordrecht: Springer, 2013.

Edy, Jill A. "Collective Memory in a Post-Broadcast World." In *Journalism and Memory*, edited by Barbie Zelizer and Keren Tenenboim-Weinblatt, 66–79. Houndmills/Basingstoke/Hampshire: Palgrave Macmillan, 2014.

"Journalistic Uses of Collective Memory." *Journal of Communication* 49 (1999): 71–85.

Edy, Jill A. *Troubled Pasts: News and the Collective Memory of Social Unrest*. Philadelphia: Temple University Press, 2006.

Ehrlich, Mark Avrum. *Encyclopedia of the Jewish Diaspora: Origins, Experiences, and Culture, Volume 1*. Santa Barbara/Denver/Oxford: ABC-CLIO, 2009.

El Sayed, Adel. "Palestinian Geography Textbooks." www.gei.de/fileadmin/gei .de/pdf/abteilungen/schulbuch_und_gesellschaft/israel_palaestina/palest05 .pdf. Accessed February 29, 2016.

El-Arif, Arif. *The Nakba: The Nakba of Jerusalem and the Lost Paradise, 1947–1952. Part One: From the Partition Resolution 29/11/1947 to the Beginning of the First Truce 11/6/1948*. Beirut: Institute for Palestine Studies, 2012. (In Arabic)

Ellis, Marc H. and Daniel A. McGowan, eds. *Remembering Deir Yassin: The Future of Israel and Palestine*. New York: Interlink Publishing Group, 1998.

Elon, Amos. *The Israelis: Founders and Sons*. New York: Holt, Rinehart, and Winston, 1971.

Ephron, Dan. *Killing a King: The Assassination of Yitzhak Rabin and the Remaking of Israel*. New York: W.W. Norton, 2016.

Eshel, Amir. *Futurity: Contemporary Literature and the Quest for the Past*. Chicago/London: University of Chicago Press, 2013.

Etzioni-Halevy, Eva. *The Divided People: Can Israel's Breakup Be Stopped?*. Lanham/Oxford: Lexington Books, 2002.

Farago, Uri. "Jewish Identity of Israeli Youth 1965–1985." *Yahadut Zmaneinu* 5 (1989): 259–285. (In Hebrew)

Feldman, Jackie. *Above the Death Pits, Beneath the Flag: Youth Voyages to Poland and the Performance of Israeli National Identity*. New York/Oxford: Berghahn Books, 2008.

"Between Yad Vashem and Mt. Herzl: Changing Inscriptions of Sacrifice on Jerusalem's Mountain of Memory." *Anthropological Quarterly* 80:4 (2007): 1147–1174.

Finkelstein, Norman G. *Beyond Chutzpah: On the Misuse of Anti-Semitism and the Abuse of History*. Berkeley: University of California Press, 2005

Firer, Ruth. *Agents of the Holocaust Lesson*. Tel Aviv: Hakibbutz Hameuchad, 1989. (In Hebrew)

"Israel: The Holocaust in History Textbooks." In *The Treatment of the Holocaust in Textbooks: The Federal Republic of Germany, Israel, The United States of America*, edited by Randolph L. Braham, 177–192. Boulder/New York: Social Science Monographs and the Institute for Holocaust Studies of the City University of New York, 1987.

Flapan, Simha. *The Birth of Israel: Myths and Realities*. New York: Pantheon Books, 1987.

Fonte, John. *Sovereignty or Submission: Will Americans Rule Themselves or be Ruled by Others?*. New York: Encounter Books, 2011.

Foucault, Michel. *Discipline and Punish: The Birth of the Prison*. London: Allan Lane, 1977.

"The Subject and Power." *Critical Inquiry* 8 (1982): 777–795.

Fourie, Pieter Jacobus, ed. *Media Studies: Content, Audiences, and Production*. Lansdowne: Juta, 2001.

Freedman, Robert O. "Netanyahu and Peace: From Sound Bites to Sound Policies?" In *The Middle East and the Peace Process: The impact of the Oslo Accords*, edited by Robert O. Freedman, 1–8. Gainesville: University Press of Florida, 1998.

Friedlander, Henry. *The Origins of Nazi Genocide: From Euthanasia to the Final Solution*. Chapel Hill: University of North Carolina Press, 1995.

Friedländer, Saul "Die Shoah als Element in der Konstruktion israelischer Erinnerung." *Babylon* 2 (1987): 10–22. (In German)

"The Shoah between Memory and History." *Jerusalem Quarterly* 37 (1990): 5–11.

Friedland, Roger and Richard Hecht. *To Rule Jerusalem*. London: University of California Press, 2000.

Friedman, Ina. *The Other Victims: First-Person Stories of Non-Jews Persecuted by the Nazis*. Boston: Houghton Mifflin, 1990.

Friedman, Robert I. "Israeli Censorship of the Palestinian Press." *Journal of Palestine Studies* 13:1 (1983): 93–101.

Frisch, Hillel. "Ethnicity or Nationalism? Comparing the Nakba Narrative amongst Israeli Arabs and Palestinians in the West Bank and Gaza." *Israel Affairs* 9 (2002): 165–184.

Fruchter-Ronen, Iris. "The Palestinian Issue as Constructed in Jordanian School Textbooks, 1964–94: Changes in the National Narrative." *Middle Eastern Studies* 49 (2013): 280 295.

Gable, Eric and Richard Handlers. "Pubic History, Private Memory: Notes from the Ethnography of Colonial Williamsburg, Virginia, USA." *Ethnos* 65 (2000): 237–252.

Galtung, John and Mari Holmboe Ruge. "The Structure of Foreign News: The Presentation of the Congo, Cuba and Cyprus Crises in Four Norwegian Newspapers." *Journal of International Peace Research* 1 (1965): 64–91.

Garde-Hansen, Joanne. *Media and Memory*. Edinburgh: Edinburgh University Press, 2011.

Gellner, Ernest. *Thought and Change*. London: Weidenfeld and Nicolson, 1964.

Ghanim, Honaida. "When Yaffa Met (J)Yaffa: Intersections between the Holocaust and the Nakba in the Shadow of Zionism." In *The Holocaust and the Nakba: A New Grammar of Trauma and History*, edited by Amos Goldberg and Bashir Bashir, 92–113. New York: Columbia University Press, 2018.

Ghazi-Bouillon, Asima. *Understanding the Middle East Peace Process: Israeli Academia and the Struggle for Identity*. Abingdon: Routledge, 2009.

Giacaman, George. "In the Throes of Oslo: Palestinian Society, Civil Society and the Future." In *After Oslo: New Realities, Old Problems*, edited by George Giacaman and Dag Jørund Lønning, 1–15. London: Pluto Press, 1998.

Gibson, Margaret and John U. Ogbu. *Minority Status and Schooling: A Comparative Study of Immigrant and Involuntary Minorities*. New York/London: Garland Publishing, 1991.

Gilbert, Martin. *Israel: A History*. London: Black Swan, 2008.

Gil, Idit. "Teaching the Shoah in History Classes in Israeli High Schools." *Israel Studies* 14 (2009): 1–25.

Gillis, John R., ed. *Commemorations: The Politics of National Identity*. Princeton: Princeton University Press, 1994.

Gluck, Sherna Berger. "Oral History and al-Nakbah." *Oral History Review* 35 (2008): 68–80.

Golan, Aviezer. *Operation Susannah*. New York: Harper & Row, 1978.

Goldberg, Amos. "The 'Jewish Narrative' in the Yad Vashem Global Holocaust Museum." *Journal of Genocide Research* 14: (2012): 187–213.

Goldberg, Amos and Bashir Bashir. *The Holocaust and the Nakba:* Memory, National Identity *and Jewish-Arab* Partnership. Jerusalem: The Van Leer Jerusalem Institute and Hakibbutz Hameuchad, 2015. (In Hebrew)

Gordan, Neve. *Israel's Occupation*. Berkeley: University of California Press, 2008.

Groiss, Arnon. "De-Legitimization of Israel in Palestinian Authority Schoolbooks." *Israel Affairs* 18 (2012): 455–484.

Gross, Zehavit. "Holocaust Education in Jewish Schools in Israel: Goals, Dilemmas, Challenges." *Prospects* 40 (2010): 93–113.

Gur-Ze'ev, Ilan. *Destroying the Other's Collective Memory*. New York: Peter Lang, 2003. "The Morality of Acknowledging/Not-Acknowledging the Other's Holocaust/Genocide." *Journal of Moral Education* 27 (1998): 161–177. *Philosophy, Politics and Education in Israel*. Haifa: Haifa University Press, 1999. (In Hebrew)

Habibi, Emile. "Your Holocaust, Our Catastrophe." *Politica* 8 (1986): 26–27. (In Hebrew)

Haklai, Oded. "The Decisive Path of State Indecisiveness: Israel in the West Bank in Comparative Perspective." In *Settlers in Contested Lands: Territorial*

Disputes and Ethnic Conflicts, edited by Oded Haklai and Neophytos Loizides, 17–39. Stanford: Stanford University Press, 2015.

Halbwachs, Maurice. *On Collective Memory*. Edited and translated by Lewis Coser. Chicago: Chicago University Press, 1992.

"The Collective Memory." In *The Collective Memory Reader*, edited by Jeffrey K. Olick, Vered Vinitzky-Seroussi, and Daniel Levy, 139–142. New York/ Oxford: Oxford University Press, 2011.

The Collective Memory. Translated by Francis J. Ditter, Jr. and Vida Yazdi Ditter. New York: Harper & Row, 1952.

Haleva-Amir, Sharon. "Online Israeli Politics: The Current State of the Art." *Israel Affairs* 17:3 (2011): 467–485.

Halkin, Hillel. "Israel against Itself." *Commentary*, November 1994. www .commentarymagazine.com/articles/hillel-halkin/israel-against-itself/. Accessed March 17, 2020.

Hallaj, Muhammad. "The Mission of Palestinian Higher Education." *Journal of Palestine Studies* 9 (1980): 75–95.

Hammer, Juliane. *Palestinians Born in Exile: Diaspora and the Search for a Homeland*. Austin: University of Texas Press, 2005.

Hanafi, Sari. "Spacio-Cide: Colonial Politics, Invisibility and Rezoning in Palestinian Territory." *Contemporary Arab Affairs* 2:1 (2009): 106–121.

Hancock, Ian. "Gypsy History in Germany and Neighboring Lands: A Chronology to the Holocaust and Beyond." *Nationalities Papers* 19 (1991): 395–412.

"On the Interpretation of a Word: Porrajmos as Holocaust." *Radoc*, 2006. www.radoc.net/radoc.php?doc=art_e_holocaust_interpretation&lang=ry& articles=true. Accessed August 30, 2017.

Handelman, Don, ed. *Nationalism and the Israeli State*. Oxford: Berg, 2004.

Handelman, Don and Elihu Katz. "Sequencing the National: Opening Remembrance Day and Independence Day." In *Nationalism and the Israeli State: Bureaucratic Logic in Public Events*, edited by Don Handelman, 119–142. Oxford: Berg, 2004.

Handelman, Don and Lea Shamgar-Handelman. "The Presence of Absence: The Memorialism of National Death in Israel." In *Grasping Land*, edited by Eyal Ben-Ari and Yoram Bilu, 85–128. Albany: State University of New York Press, 1997.

Handelman, Sapir, ed. *People-to-People Diplomacy in Israel and Palestine: The Minds of Peace Experiment*. London/New York: Routledge, 2014.

Hansen-Glucklich, Jennifer. *Holocaust Memory Reframed: Museums and the Challenges of Representation*. New Brunswick: Rutgers University Press, 2014.

Harcup, Tony and Deirdre O'Neill. "What Is News? Galtung and Ruge Revisited." *Journalism Studies* 2:2 (2001): 261–280.

Harel, Amos and Avi Issacharoff. *34 Days: Israel, Hezbollah, and the War in Lebanon*. New York: Palgrave Macmillan, 2008.

Hassan, Shamir. "Oslo Accords: The Genesis and Consequences for Palestine." *Social Scientist* 39: 7/8 (2011): 65–72.

Hever, Shir. *The Political Economy of Israel's Occupation: Repression beyond Exploitation*. London: Pluto Press, 2010.

Heywood, Felicity. "Giving Voice." *Museums Journal* 12 (2006): 21–23.

Hirsch, Marianne. "The Generation of Post-Memory." *Poetics Today* 29:1 (2008): 103–128.

Hobsbawm, Eric. *Nations and Nationalism since 1780: Programme, Myth, Reality.* Cambridge: Cambridge University Press, 1990.

Hobsbawm, Eric and Terence Ranger, eds. *The Invention of Tradition.* Cambridge: Cambridge University Press, 2012.

Hochberg, Gil. *In Spite of Partition: Jews, Arabs, and the Limits of Separatist Imagination.* Princeton: Princeton University Press, 2007.

Hoepken, Wolfgang. "Between Civic Identity and Nationalism: History Textbooks in East-Central and Southeastern Europe." In *Democratic Transition in Croatia Value Transformation, Education, and Media Political Science*, edited by Sabrina P. Ramet and Davorka Matic, 163–192. College Station Texas A&M University Press, 2007.

Hoffman, Eva. *After Such Knowledge: Memory, History, and the Legacy of the Holocaust.* New York: Public Affairs, 2004.

Honig-Parnass, Tikva. "Zionism's Fixation: War without End." In *Readings on Israel, the Palestinians, and the U.S. War on Terror*, edited by Tikva Honig-Parnass and Toufic Haddad, 128–132. Chicago: Haymarket Books, 2007.

Hoskins, Andrew. "7/7 and Connective Memory: Interactional Trajectories of Remembering in Post-scarcity Culture." *Memory Studies* 4:3 (2011): 269–280.

Hutton, Deborah S. and Howard D. Mehlinger. "International Textbooks Revision. Examples from the Unites States." In *Perceptions of History. International Textbook Research on Britain, Germany and the United States*, edited by Volker R. Berghahn and Hanna Schissler, 141–156. Oxford: Berg, 1987.

Huyssen, Andreas. "Present Pasts: Media, Politics, Amnesia." *Public Culture* 12:1 (2000): 21–38.

Present Pasts: Urban Palimpsests and the Politics of Memory. Stanford: Stanford University Press, 2003.

Ihab, Saloul. *Catastrophe and Exile in the Modern Palestinian Imagination: Telling Memories.* New York/Basingstoke: Palgrave Macmillan, 2012.

Jackson, John B. *The Necessity for Ruins and Other Topics.* Amherst: University of Massachusetts Press, 1980.

Jacobowitz, Florence and Shelley Hornstein, eds. *Image and Remembrance: Representation and the Holocaust.* Bloomington: Indiana University Press, 2003.

Jaffee, Martin S. "The Victim-Community in Myth and History: Holocaust Ritual, the Question of Palestine and the Rhetoric of Christina Witness." *Journal of Ecumenical Studies* 28:2 (1991): 223–238.

Jamal, Amal. *The Arab Public Sphere in Israel: Media Space and Cultural Resistance.* Bloomington: Indiana University Press, 2009.

"Mechanisms of Governmentality and Constructing Hollow Citizenship: Arab Palestinians in Israel." In *Israel and Its Palestinian Citizens: Ethnic Privileges in the Jewish State*, edited by Nadim N. Rouhana and Sahar S. Huneidi, 159–190. Cambridge: Cambridge University Press, 2017.

Media Politics and Democracy in Palestine: Political Culture, Pluralism, and the Palestinian Authority. Brighton: Sussex Academic Press, 2005.

"The Palestinian Media: An Obedient Servant or a Vanguard of Democracy?." *Journal of Palestine Studies* 29:3 (2000): 45–59.

Judt, Tony. *Postwar: A History of Europe since 1945.* London: Pimlico, 2007.

Kadman, Noga. *Erased from Space and Consciousness: Israel and the Depopulated Palestinian Villages of 1948.* Bloomington: Indiana University Press, 2015.

Kamel, Lorenzo and Daniela Huber. "The De-Threatenization of the Other: An Israeli and a Palestinian Case of Understanding the Other's Suffering." *Peace & Change* 37:3 (2012): 366–388.

Kamil, Omar. *Der Holocaust im arabischen Gedächtnis. Eine Diskursgeschichte 1945–1967.* Göttingen: Vandenhoeck & Ruprecht, 2012. (In German)

Kaplan, Danny. "The Songs of the Siren: Engineering National Time on Israeli Radio." *Cultural Anthropology* 24:2 (2009): 313–345.

Kapralski, Slawomir. "Identity Building and the Holocaust: Roma Political Nationalism." *Nationalities Papers* 25 (1997): 269–283.

Karmi, Ghada. "After the Nakba: An Experience of Exile in England." *Journal of Palestine Studies* 28 (1999): 52–63.

Karmi, Ghada and Eugene Cotran, eds. *The Palestinian Exodus 1948–1998.* Reading: Ithaca Press, 1999.

Karpin, Michael I. *Imperfect Compromise: A New Consensus among Israelis and Palestinians.* Washington, DC: Potomac Books, 2013.

Kelman, Herbert C. "The Interdependence of Israeli and Palestinian National Identities." *Journal of Social Issues* 55:3 (1999): 581–600.

Kenan, Orna. *Between Memory and History: The Evolution of Israeli Historiography of the Holocaust, 1945–1961.* New York: Peter Lang, 2003.

Kennedy, Rosanne. "Moving Testimony: Human Rights, Palestinian Memory, and the Transnational Public Sphere." In *Transnational Memory: Circulation, Articulation, Scales,* edited by Chiara De Cesari and Ann Rigney, 51–78. Berlin: De Gruyte, 2014.

Kenrick, Donald and Grattan Puxon. *Gypsies under the Swastika.* Hatfield: University of Hertfordshire Press, 2009.

Keren, Nili. "Ideologies: Attitudes and Holocaust Teaching in the State of Israel-History and Recent Development." In *Remembering for the Future,* edited by Yehuda Bauer, 1029–1037. Oxford: Pergamon, 1989.

Kershaw, Ian. *Hitler, 1889–1936: Hubris.* London: Penguin Press, 1998.

Khalidi, Rashid. "A Universal Jubilee? Palestinians 50 Years after 1948." *Tikkun* 13:1 (1998): 54–56.

The Iron Cage: The Story of the Palestinian Struggle for Statehood. Oxford: Oneworld, 2007.

Palestinian Identity: The Construction of Modern National Consciousness. New York: Columbia University Press, 2010.

"The Palestinians and 1948: The Underlying Causes of Failure." In *The War for Palestine: Rewriting the History of 1948,* edited by Eugene L. Rogan and Avi Shlaim, 12–36. Cambridge: Cambridge University Press, 2001.

Khalidi, Walid. *All That Remains: The Palestinian Villages Occupied and Depopulated by Israel in 1948.* Washington, DC: Institute for Palestine Studies, 1992.

"Why Did the Palestinians Leave, Revisited." *Journal of Palestine Studies* 34:2 (2005): 42–54.

Khalili, Laleh. *Heroes and Martyrs of Palestine: The Politics of National Commemoration*. Cambridge: Cambridge University Press, 2006.

Time in the Shadows: Confinement in Counterinsurgencies. Stanford: Stanford University Press, 2013.

Khatib, Ghassan. *Palestinian Politics and the Middle East Peace Process*. London/ New York: Routledge, 2010.

Khoury, Elias. "Foreword." In *The Holocaust and the Nakba: A New Grammar of Trauma and History*, edited by Amos Goldberg and Bashir Bashir, ix–xvi. New York: Columbia University Press, 2018.

Khoury, Nadim. "Holocaust/Nakba and the Counterpublic of Memory." In *The Holocaust and the Nakba: A New Grammar of Trauma and History*, edited by Amos Goldberg and Bashir Bashir, 114–132. New York: Columbia University Press, 2018.

"Postnational Memory: Narrating the Holocaust and the Nakba." *Philosophy and Social Criticism* 46 (2019): 1–20.

Kidron, Carol. "Survivor Family Memory Work at Sites of Holocaust Remembrance: Institutional Enlistment or Family Agency?." *History and Memory* 1 (2015): 45–73.

Kimmerling, Baruch. *Zionism and Territory: The Socio-Territorial Dimensions of Zionist Politics*. Berkeley: Institute of International Studies, University of California, 1983.

Kitch, Carolyn. "Anniversary Journalism, Collective Memory, and the Cultural Authority to Tell the Story of the American Past." *Journal of Popular Culture* 36 (2002): 44–67.

"Placing Journalism inside Memory – and Memory Studies." *Memory Studies* 1 (2008): 311–320.

Klamper, Elisabeth. "Persecution and Annihilation of Roma and Sinti in Austria, 1938–1945." *Journal of the Gypsy Lore Society* 3 (1993): 55–65.

Klar, Yechiel, Noa Schori-Eyal, and Yonat Klar. "The 'Never Again' State of Israel: The Emergence of the Holocaust as a Core Feature of Israeli Identity and Its Four Incongruent Voices." *Journal of Social Issues* 69 (2013): 125–143.

Klein, Menachem. *The Shift: Israel-Palestine from Border Struggle to Ethnic Conflict*. London: Hurst & Company, 2010.

Klieman, Aaron S. *Constructive Ambiguity in Middle East Peace-Making*. Tel Aviv: Tel Aviv University, Tami Steinmetz Center for Peace Research, 1999.

Kokkola, Lydia. *Representing the Holocaust in Children's Literature*. New York: Routledge, 2009.

Koldas, Umut. "The Nakba in Palestinian Memory in Israel." *Middle Eastern Studies* 47 (2011): 947–959.

Korn, Alina. "The Ghettoization of Palestinians." In *Thinking Palestine*, edited by Ronit Lentin, 116–130. London: Zed Books, 2008.

Krakover, Shaul. "Attitudes of Israeli Visitors towards the Holocaust Remembrance Site of Yad Vashem." In *Horror and Human Tragedy Revisited: The Management of Sites of Atrocities for Tourism*, edited by Gregory Ashworth and Rudi Hartmann, 108–117. New York: Cognizant, 2005.

Kress, Gunther. *Literacy in the New Media Age*. London: Routledge, 2003.

Kushner, Tony. "The Holocaust and the Museum World in Britain: A Study in Ethnography." *Immigrants & Minorities* 21 (2002): 12–40.

LaCapra, Dominick. *Representing the Holocaust: History, Theory, Trauma*. Ithaca/London: Cornell University Press, 1994.

    Writing History, Writing Trauma. Baltimore/London: Johns Hopkins University Press, 2001.

Langbein, Hermann. *People in Auschwitz*. Chapel Hill: University of North Carolina Press, 2004.

Lazar, Alon, Julia Chaitin, Tamar Gross, and Dan Bar-On. "Jewish Israeli Teenagers, National Identity, and the Lessons of the Holocaust." *Holocaust and Genocide Studies* 18 (2004): 188–204.

Lazar, Alon and Tal Litvak Hirsch. "Cultural Trauma as a Potential Symbolic Boundary." *International Journal of Politics, Culture, and Society IJPS* 22:2 (2009): 183–190.

Lentin, Ronit. *Co-memory and Melancholia: Israelis Memorialising the Palestinian Nakba*. Manchester: Manchester University Press, 2010.

Lévi-Strauss, Claude. *The Savage Mind*. Chicago: University of Chicago Press, 1966.

Levy, Daniel and Natan Sznaider. *The Holocaust and Memory in the Global Age*. Philadelphia: Temple University Press, 2006.

Lewy, Guenter. *The Nazi Persecution of the Gypsies*. Oxford: Oxford University Press, 2000.

Liebes, Tamar. "Acoustic Space: The Role of Radio in Israeli Collective History." *Jewish History* 20 (2006): 60–90.

Liebman, Charles S. and Elizer Don-Yehiya. *Civil Religion in Israel: Traditional Judaism and Political Culture in the Jewish State*. Berkeley: University of California Press, 1983.

Linenthal, Edward. *Preserving Memory: The Struggle to Create America's Holocaust Museum*. New York: Viking, 1995.

Litvak, Meir, ed. *Palestinian Collective Memory and National Identity*. Basingstoke: Palgrave Macmillan, 2009.

Litvak, Meir and Esther Webman. *From Empathy to Denial: Arab Responses to the Holocaust*. London: Hurst, 2011.

    "Perceptions of the Holocaust in Palestinian Public Discourse." *Israel Studies* 8:3 (2003): 123–140.

Litvak-Hirsch, Tal, Julia Chaitin, and Eizis Zaher. "Perceptions of the Holocaust of Palestinian Young Adults, Citizens of Israel." *Peace and Conflict: Journal of Peace Psychology* 16:3 (2010): 231–252.

Lorch, Netanel. *The Edge of the Sword: Israel's War of Independence, 1947–1949*. New York: Putnam, 1961.

Lowenthal, David. *The Past Is a Foreign Country*. Cambridge: Cambridge University Press, 1985.

Lukacs, Yehuda, ed. *The Israeli–Palestinian Conflict: A Documentary Record 1967–1990*. Cambridge: Cambridge University Press, 1992.

Machover, Moshé. *Israelis and Palestinians: Conflict and Resolution*. Chicago: Haymarket Books, 2012.

Maier, Charles S. "A Surfeit of Memory? Reflections on History, Melancholy and Denial." *History and Memory* 5:2 (1993): 136–151.

Maiola, Giovanna and David Ward. "Democracy and the Media in Palestine: A Comparison of Election Coverage by Local and Pan-Arab Media." In *Arab Media and Political Renewal: Community, Legitimacy, and Public Life*, edited by Naomi Sakr, 96–117. London: I.B. Tauris, 2007.

Makovsky, David. *Making Peace with the PLO: The Rabin Government's Road to the Oslo Accord*. Boulder, CO/San Francisco/Oxford: Westview Press, 1995.

Manna, Adil and Moti Golani. *Two Sides of the Coin: Independence and Nakba 1948*. Dordrecht: Republic of Letters, 2011.

Mannheim, Karl. *Essays on the Sociology of Knowledge*. London: Routledge & Kegan Paul, 1952.

Mansour, Atallah. "The Arab Press in Israel." *Kesher* 7 (1990): 71–77. (In Hebrew)

Maoz, Iftat. "Peace Building in Violent Conflict: Israeli-Palestinian Post-Oslo People-to-People Activities." *International Journal of Politics, Culture, and Society* 17:3 (2004): 563–574.

Masalha, Nur. "Sixty Years after the Nakba: Historical Truth, Collective Memory and Ethical Obligations." *Kyoto Bulletin of Islamic Area Studies* 3:1 (2009): 37–88.

Expulsion of the Palestinians: The Concept of "Transfer" in Zionist Political Thought, 1882–1948. Washington, DC: Institute for Palestine studies, 1992.

"Remembering the Palestinian Nakba: Commemoration, Oral History and Narratives of Memory." *Holy Land Studies* 7:2 (2008): 123–156.

The Palestine Nakba: Decolonising History, Narrating the Subaltern, Reclaiming Memory. London: Zed Books, 2012.

Massad, Joseph. "Palestinians and Jewish History: Recognition or Submission?." *Journal of Palestine Studies* 30 (2000): 52–67.

Mazawi, Andre Elias. "The Reconstruction of Palestinian Education: Between History, Policy Politics and Policy-Making." *Journal of Education Policy* 15 (2000): 371–375.

McCombs, Donald and David Shaw. "The Agenda Setting Function of Mass Media." *Public Opinion Quarterly* 36:2 (1972): 176–187.

McLagan, Meg. "Principles, Publicity, and Politics: Notes on Human Rights Media." *American Anthropologist* 105 (2003): 605–612.

McMahon, Sean F. *The Discourse of Palestinian–Israeli Relations: Persistent Analytics and Practices*. New York/London: Routledge Taylor & Francis Group, 2010.

McQuail, Denis. *Mass Communication Theory*. London: Sage, 2000.

Mass Communication Theory: An Introduction. Beverly Hills: Sage, 1984.

Mehlinger, Howard D. "International Textbook Revision: Examples from the United States." *Internationale Schulbuchforschung* 7 (1985): 287–298.

Metzer, Jacob. *The Divided Economy for Mandatory Palestine*. Cambridge: Cambridge University Press, 1998.

Meyers, Oren. "Still Photographs, Dynamic Memories: A Study of the Visual Presentation of Israel's Past in Commemorative Newspaper Supplements." *The Communication Review* 5:3 (2002): 179–205.

Meyers, Oren, Motti Neiger, and Eyal Zandberg. *Communicating Awe: Media Memory and Holocaust Commemoration*. Basingstoke: Palgrave Macmillan, 2014.

Michman, Dan. "The Jewish Dimension of the Holocaust in Dire Straits? Current Challenges of Interpretation and Scope." In *Jewish Histories of the Holocaust: New Transnational Approaches*, edited by Norman J. W. Goda, 17–38. New York: Berghahn Books, 2014.

Migdal, Joel S. *Shifting Sands: The United States in the Middle East*. New York: Columbia University Press, 2014.

Miller, Anita, Jordan Miller, and Sigalit Zetouni. *Sharon: Israel's Warrior-Politician*. Chicago: Academy Chicago Publishers and Olive Publishing, 2004.

Milshtein, Michael. "The Memory That Never Dies: The Nakba Memory and the Palestinian National Movement." In *Palestinian Collective Memory and National Identity*, edited by Meir Litvak, 47–69. Basingstoke: Palgrave Macmillan, 2009.

Milton-Edwards, Beverley. *The Israeli–Palestinian Conflict: A People's War*. New York: Routledge, 2009.

Mircea, Eliade. *Myth and Reality*. New York: Harper & Row, 1963.

Mishal, Shaul and Re¤uven Aharoni. *Speaking Stones: Communiqués from the Intifada Underground*. Syracuse: Syracuse University Press, 1994.

Mitchell, Thomas G. *Likud Leaders: The Lives and Careers of Menahem Begin, Yitzhak Shamir, Benjamin Netanyahu and Ariel Sharon*. Jefferson: McFarland & Company, 2015.

Mitchell, William John Thomas, ed. *Landscape and Power*. Chicago/London: University of Chicago Press, 1994.

Mofaz, Shaul. "Operation Defensive Shield: Lessons and Aftermath." *The Washington Institute for Near East Policy*, June 18, 2002. www.washingtoninstitute.org/policy-analysis/view/operation-defensive-shield-lessons-and-aftermath. Accessed January 19, 2020.

Morris, Benny. *1948: A History of the First Arab–Israeli War*. New Haven: Yale University Press, 2008.

The Birth of the Palestinian Refugee Problem 1947–1949*. Cambridge: Cambridge University Press, 1987.

The Birth of the Palestinian Refugee Problem Revisited. Cambridge: Cambridge University Press, 2004.

"The New Historiography: Israel Confronts Its Past." In *Making Israel*, edited by Benny Morris, 11–28. Ann Arbor: The University of Michigan Press, 2007.

Moses, Rafael. *Persistent Shadows of the Holocaust: The Meaning to Those Not Directly Affected*. Madison, CT: International Universities Press, 1993.

Mosse, George L. *Fallen Soldiers: Reshaping the Memory of the World Wars*. New York: Oxford University Press, 1990.

Moughrabi, Fouad. "Palestine Now and Then: Notes on Oral History." *Journal of Educational Visions* 48/49 (2015): 21–32. (In Arabic)

"Palestinian Education for the Twenty-First Century." Paper presented at the 2016 Hisham Sharabi Memorial Lecture, Washington DC, May 6, 2016.

"The Politics of Palestinian Textbooks." *Journal of Palestine Studies* 31 (2001): 5–19.

Müller, Margret. *The World According to Israeli Newspapers.* Berlin: Frank & Timme GmbH Verlag, 2017.

Murphy, Brian J. "No Heroic Battles: Lessons of the Second Lebanon War." MA diss., U.S. Army Command and General Staff College, 2010.

Najjar, Orayb. "Power and the Palestinian Press: Israeli Censorship on the West Bank, 1967–1991." PhD diss., Indiana University, 1992.

"The 1995 Palestinian Press Law: A Comparative Study." *Communication Law and Policy* 2:1 (1997): 41–103.

Naor, Arye. "Lessons of the Holocaust versus Territories for Peace, 1967–2001." *Israel Studies* 8:1 (2003): 130–152.

Nasser, Riad. *Palestinian Identity in Jordan and Israel: The Necessary Other in Making a Nation.* New York/London: Routledge, 2005.

Nasser, Riad and Irene Nasser. "Textbooks as a Vehicle for Segregation and Domination: State Efforts to Shape Palestinian Israelis' Identities as Citizens." *Journal of Curriculum Studies* 40 (2008): 626–650.

Naveh, Eyal. *Travel into the Past: Disputes on Historical Issues in Israel.* Unpublished manuscript, 2016. (In Hebrew)

Nazzal, Nafez and Laila Nazzal. "The Politicization of Palestinian Children: An Analysis of Nursery Rhymes." *Palestine-Israel Journal of Politics, Economics and Culture* 3 (1996): 26–36.

Neiger, Motti, Eyal Zandberg, and Oren Meyers. "On Media Memory: Collective Memory in the New Media Age." In *Journalism and Memory*, edited by Barbie Zelizer and Keren Tenenboim-Weinblatt, 113–128. Houndmills/Basingstoke/Hampshire: Palgrave Macmillan, 2014.

Netanyahu, Benjamin. *A Place among the Nations: Israel and the World.* London: Bantam Books, 1993.

Nets-Zehngut, Rafi. "Israeli Approved Textbooks and the 1948 Palestinian Exodus." *Israel Studies* 18 (2013): 41–68.

Nets-Zehngut, Rafi and Daniel Bar-Tal. *The Israeli-Jewish Collective Memory of the Israeli–Arab/Palestinian Conflict.* Rep. N.p.: International Peace Research Association, 2008.

Neubach, Keren. *Campaign 96.* Tel Aviv: Yediot Ahronot, 1996. (In Hebrew)

Nietzsche, Friedrich. *Nietzsche: Untimely Mediations.* Edited by Daniel Breazale. Cambridge: Cambridge University Press, 1997.

Nora, Pierre. *Realms of Memory: Rethinking the French Past.* Translated by Lawrence D. Kritzman. New York: Columbia University Press, 1996–1998.

Nordbruch, Goetz. "The New Palestinian Textbooks for National Education – A Review." www.gei.de/fileadmin/gei.de/pdf/abteilungen/schulbuch_und_gesellschaft/israel_palaestina/palest02.pdf. Accessed February 2, 2016.

Nossek, Hillel. "The Holocaust and the Revival of Israel in the Coverage of Salient Terrorist Events in the Israeli Press." *Journal of Narrative and Life History* 4 (1994): 119–134.

Nossek, Hillel and Khalil Rinnawi. "Censorship and Freedom of the Press under Changing Political Regimes: Palestinian Media from Israeli Occupation to the Palestinian Authority." *Gazette* 65 (2003): 183–202.

Novick, Peter. *The Holocaust in American Life*. Boston/New York: First Mariner Books, 2000.

"The Holocaust Is Not—and Is Not Likely to Become—a Global Memory." In *Marking Evil: Holocaust Memory in the Global Age*, edited by Amos Goldberg and Haim Hazan, 47–55. Oxford/New York: Berghahn Books, 2015.

Ofer, Dalia. "History, Memory and Identity: Perceptions of the Holocaust in Israel." In *Jews in Israel: Contemporary Social and Cultural Patterns*, edited by Uzi Rebhun and Chaim Waxman, 394–417. Hanover/London: Brandeis University Press, 2004.

"Israel." In *The World Reacts to the Holocaust*, edited by Wyman David, 836–923. Baltimore: Johns Hopkins University Press, 1996.

"The Past That Does Not Pass: Israelis and Holocaust." *Israel Studies* 14 (2009): 1–35.

"The Strength of Remembrance: Commemorating the Holocaust during the First Decade of Israel." *Jewish Social Studies* 6:2 (2000): 24–55.

"We Israelis Remember, But How? The Memory of the Holocaust and the Israeli Experience." *Israel Studies* 18 (2013): 70–85.

Olick, Jeffrey. "Collective Memory: The Two Cultures." *Sociological Theory*, 17:3 (1999): 333–348.

Osborne, Peter, ed. *Walter Benjamin: Critical Evaluations in Cultural Theory*. London: Routledge, 2005.

Otsuki, Tomoe. "A Point of Connection through Transnational History Textbooks? An Examination of History That Opens to the Future, the Joint History Textbook Initiative of Dean, Japan, and South Korea." In *Educational Conflict and Development*, edited by Julia Paulson, 145–165. Oxford: Symposium Books, 2011.

Oz, Amos. *A Tale of Love and Darkness*. London: Vintage Books, 2005.

Pappé, Ilan. *The Ethnic Cleansing of Palestine*. Oxford: Oneworld, 2006.

"Fear, Victimhood, Self and Other: On the Road to Reconciliation." In *Across the Wall: Narratives of Israeli– Palestinian History*, edited by Ilan Pappé and Jamil Hilal, 155–176. London: I.B. Tauris, 2010.

Pappé, Ilan, ed. *The Israel/Palestine Question*. London/New York: Routledge, 1999.

The Making of the Arab–Israeli Conflict 1947–1951. London: I.B. Tauris, 1992.

Pappé, Ilan and Jamil Hilal, eds. *Across the Wall: Narratives of Israeli-Palestinian History*. London: I.B. Tauris, 2010.

Parsons, Nigel. *The Politics of the Palestinian Authority: From Oslo to Al-Aqsa*. New York/London: Routledge, 2005.

Pedahzur, Ami. *The Triumph of Israel's Radical Right*. New York: Oxford University Press, 2012.

Peled-Elhanan, Nurit. "Legitimation of Massacres in Israeli School History Books." *Discourse & Society* 21 (2010): 377–404.

Palestine in Israeli School Books: Ideology and Propaganda in Education. London: I.B. Tauris, 2012.

Peleg, Ilan, ed. *Victimhood Discourse in Contemporary Israel*. Lanham: Lexington Books, 2019.

Peleg, Ilan and Dov Waxman. *Israel's Palestinians: The Conflict Within*. Cambridge: Cambridge University Press, 2011.

Penslar, Derek Jonathan. "Transmitting Culture: Radio in Israel." *Jewish Social Studies* 10:1 (2003): 1–29.

Peres, Shimon. *Battling for Peace*. London: George Weidenfeld & Nicholson, 1995.

Peretz, Don and Gideon Doron. "Israel's 1996 Elections: A Second Political Earthquake?." *The Middle East Journal* 50:4 (Autumn 1996): 529–546.

Peri, Yoram. *Telepopulism. Media and Politics in Israel*. Stanford: Stanford University Press, 2004.

Pinchevski, Amit, Tamar Liebes, and Ora Herman. "Eichmann on the Air: Radio and the Making of an Historic Trial." *Historical Journal of Film, Radio and Television* 27:1 (2007): 1–25.

Pingel, Falk. "Can Truths Be Negotiated: History Textbook Revision as a Means to Reconciliation." *The Annals of the American Academy of Political and Social Science* 617:1 (2008): 181–198.

Podeh, Elie. *The Arab-Israeli Conflict in Israeli History Textbooks, 1948–2000*. Westport, CT: Bergin & Garvey, 2000.

"History and Memory in the Israeli Educational System: The Portrayal of the Arab–Israeli Conflict in History Textbooks (1948– 2000)." *History and Memory* 12 (2000): 65–100.

Pollefeyt, Didier. "Between a Dangerous Memory and a Memory in Danger: The Israeli–Palestinian Struggle from a Christian Post-Holocaust Perspective." In *Anguished Hope: Holocaust Scholars Confront the Palestinian–Israeli Conflict*, edited by Leonard Grob and John Roth, 135–146. Grand Rapids, MI/ Cambridge: William B. Eerdmans, 2008.

Porat, Dan. "From the Scandal to the Holocaust in Israeli Education." *Journal of Contemporary History* 39 (2004): 619–636.

Porat, Dina. *The Fall of a Sparrow: The Life and Times of Abba Kovner*. Stanford: Stanford University Press, 2010.

Israeli Society, the Holocaust and Its Survivors. London: Vallentine Mitchell, 2008.

Pressman, Jeremy. "Visions in Collision: What Happened at Camp David and Taba?." *International Security* 28:2 (2003): 5–43.

Quigley, John. *The Case for Palestine: An International Law Perspective*. Durham, NC/London: Duke University Press, 2005.

Rabinowitz, Dan and Khawla Abu-Baker. *Coffins on Our Shoulders: The Experience of the Palestinian Citizens of Israel*. Berkeley: University of California Press, 2005.

Ram, Uri. "Postnationalist Pasts: The Case of Israel." *Social Science History* 22: 4 (1998): 513–545.

Reinhart, Tanya. *The Road Map to Nowhere: Israel/Palestine since 2003*. London/ New York: Verso, 2006.

Rekhess, Elie. "The Arab Minority in Israel: Reconsidering the '1948 Paradigm'." *Israel Studies* 19 (2014): 187–217.

Renan, Ernest. "What Is a Nation?" In *The Collective Memory Reader*, edited by Jeffrey K. Olick, Vered Vinitzky-Seroussi, and Daniel Levy, 80–83. New York/Oxford: Oxford University Press, 2011.

Ricoeur, Paul, trans. *Time and Narrative*. Chicago: The University of Chicago Press, 1984.

Roberts, Jo. *Contested Land, Contested Memory: Israel's Jews and Arabs and the Ghosts of Catastrophe*. Toronto: Dundurn Press, 2013.

Robins, Philip. *A History of Jordan*. Cornwall: Cambridge University Press, 2019.

Rogan, Eugene L. "Jordan and 1948: The Persistence of an Official History." In *The War for Palestine: Rewriting the History of 1948*, edited by Eugene L. Rogan and Avi Shlaim, 104–124. Cambridge: Cambridge University Press, 2001.

Romi, Shlomo and Michal Lev. "Experiential Learning of History through Youth Journeys to Poland: Israeli Jewish Youth and the Holocaust." *Israel Research in Education* 78 (2007): 88–102.

Rose, Caroline. "Going Global? National versus Post-national Citizenship Education in Contemporary Chinese and Japanese Social Studies Curricula." In *Constructing Modern Asian Citizenship*, edited by Edward Vickers and Krishna Kumar, 83–104. New York: Routledge, 2015.

Rosenbaum, Alan S. "Introduction to the First Edition." In *Is the Holocaust Unique? Perspectives on Comparative Genocide*, edited by Alan S. Rosenbaum, 1–8. New York: Routledge, 2009.

Rosenbaum, Alan S., ed. *Is the Holocaust Unique? Perspectives on Comparative Genocide*. Boulder: Westview Press, 1996.

Rosenblum, Mark. "Netanyahu and Peace: From Sound Bites to Sound Policies?" In *The Middle East and the Peace Process*, edited by Robert O. Freedman, 35–80. Gainesville: University Press of Florida, 1998.

Rosenfeld, Gavriel D. "The Politics of Uniqueness: Reflections on the Recent Polemical Turn in Holocaust and Genocide Scholarship." *Holocaust and Genocide Studies* 13 (1999): 28–61.

Rosler, Nimrod. "Leadership and Peacemaking: Yitzhak Rabin and the Oslo Accords." *International Journal of Intercultural Relations* 54 (2016): 55–67.

Ross, Dennis. *Doomed to Succeed: The U.S.–Israel Relationship from Truman to Obama*. New York: Farrar, Straus and Giroux, 2015.

Rotberg, Robert. "Building Legitimacy through Narrative." In *Israeli and Palestinian Narratives of Conflict: History's Double Helix*, edited by Robert Rotberg, 1–18. Bloomington: Indiana University Press, 2006.

Rozett, Robert. "Diminishing the Holocaust: Scholarly Fodder for a Discourse of Distortion." *Israel Journal of Foreign Affairs* 6:1 (2012): 53–64.

Rubin, Barry and Judith Rubin, *Yasir Arafat: A Political Biography*. New York: Oxford University Press, 2003.

Rynhold, Jonathan. "Cultural Shift and Foreign Policy Change: Israel and the Making of the Oslo Accords." *Cooperation and Conflict* 42:4 (December 2007): 419–440.

Sa'di, Ahmad H. "Catastrophe, Memory and Identity: Al-Nakbah as a Component of Palestinian Identity." *Israel Studies* 7:2 (2002): 175–198.

Sa'di, Ahmad H. "Stifling Surveillance: Israel's Surveillance and Control of the Palestinians during the Military Government Era." *Jerusalem Quarterly* 68 (2016): 36–55.

Sa'di, Ahmad H. and Lila Abu-Lughod, eds. *Nakba: Palestine, 1948, and the Claims of Memory*. New York: Columbia University Press, 2007.

Sagy, Shifra, Avi Kaplan, and Sami Adwan. "Interpretations of the Past and Expectations for the Future among Israeli and Palestinian Youth." *American Journal of Orthopsychiatry* 72:1 (2002): 26–38.

Said, Edward. *After the Last Sky: Palestinian Lives.* New York: Columbia University Press, 1999.

The End of the Peace Process: Oslo and After. London: Granta, 2000.

The End of the Peace Process: Oslo and After. New York: Vintage Book, 2001.

"Invention, Memory, and Place." *Critical Inquiry* 26 (2000): 175–192.

"The Morning After." *London Review of Books* 15:20 (1993): 3–5.

The Politics of Dispossession: The Struggle for Palestinian Self-Determination, 1969–1994. London: Vintage Books, 1994.

Sanbar, Elias. *Les Palestiniens dans le siècle.* Paris: Gallimard, Paris, 1994.

"Out of Place, Out of Time." *Mediterranean Historical Review* 16:1 (2001): 87–94.

Palestine, le pays à venir. Paris: L'Olivier, 1996.

Satloff, Robert. *Among Righteous.* New York: Public Affairs, 2006.

Sayigh, Rosemary. *Palestinians: From Peasants to Revolutionaries: A People's History.* London: Zed Press, 1979.

Schanzer, Jonathan. *Hamas vs. Fatah: The Struggle for Palestine.* New York: Palgrave Macmillan, 2008.

Schatzker, Chaim. "Teaching the Holocaust in Changing Times." *Moreshet* 52 (1992): 165–171.

"The Teaching of the Holocaust: Dilemmas and Considerations." *The Annals of the American Academy of Political and Social Science* 450 (1980): 218–226.

Schindler, Colin. *The Rise of the Israeli Right: From Odessa to Hebron.* London: Cambridge University Press, 2015.

Schwab, Gabriele. *Haunting Legacies: Violent Histories and Transgenerational Trauma.* New York: Columbia University Press, 2010.

Schwartz, Barry. "The Social Context of Commemoration: A Study in Collective Memory." *Social Forces* 61 (1982): 374–402.

Segev, Tom. *1949 The First Israelis.* New York: Simon and Schuster, 1986.

The Seventh Million: The Israelis and the Holocaust. New York: Hill and Wang, 1993.

Seib, Philip, ed. *New Media and the New Middle East.* New York: Palgrave Macmillan, 2007.

Shabaneh, Ghassan. "Education and Identity: The Role of UNRWA's Education Programmes in the Reconstruction of Palestinian Nationalism." *Journal of Refugee Studies* 25 (2012): 491–513.

Shapira, Anita. "The Holocaust: Private Memories, Public Memory." *Jewish Social Studies* 4:2 (1998): 40–58.

Shavit, Ari. *My Promised Land: The Triumph and Tragedy of Israel.* Melbourne: Scribe, 2014.

Shay, Shaul. "Ebb and Flow versus The Al-Aqsa Intifadah: The Israeli-Palestinian Conflict, 2000–2003." In *Never-Ending Conflict: Israeli Military History,* edited by Mordechai Bar-On, 230–250. Mechanicsburg: Stackpole Books, 2004.

Shehadeh, Raja. *The Third Way: A Journal of Life of the West Bank.* London: Quartet Books, 1982.

Shenhav, Yehouda. *Beyond the Two-State Solution: A Jewish Political Essay.* Cambridge: Polity Press, 2012.

Sher, Gilad. *Within Reach: The Israeli–Palestinian Peace* Negotiations, *1999–2001.* Tel Aviv: Miskal-Yedioth Ahronoth Books and Chemed Books, 2001. (In Hebrew)

Shindler, Colin. *The Rise of the Israeli Right Door.* New York: Cambridge University Press, 2015.

Shipler, David K. *Arab and Jew: Wounded Spirits in a Promised Land.* London: Bloomsbury, 1989.

Shlaim, Avi. *Collusion across the Jordan: King Abdullah, the Zionist Movement and the Partition of Palestine.* Oxford: Clarendon Press, 1988.

"The Debate about 1948." *International journal of Middle East Studies* 27:3 (1995): 287–304.

Shoham, Edna, Neomi Shiloah, and Raya Kalisman. "Arab Teachers and Holocaust Education: Arab Teachers Study Holocaust Education in Israel." *Teaching and Teacher Education* 19:6 (2003): 609–625.

Sitta, Salman Abu. *The Palestinian Nakba 1948: The Register of Depopulated Localities in Palestine.* London: Palestinian Return Centre, 1998.

Smith, Pamela Ann and Mohammed Kiwan. "'Sons of the Village' Assert Palestinian Identity in Israel." *MERIP Reports* 68 (1978): 15–18.

Sneider, Daniel. "Textbooks and Patriotic Education: Wartime Memory Formation in China and Japan." *Asia-Pacific Review* 20:1 (2013): 35–54.

Soffer, Oren. *Mass Communication in Israel: Nationalism, Globalization, and Segmentation.* New York/London: Berghahn Books, 2015.

Sorek, Tamir. "Commemoration: Localism, Communalism, and Nationalism in Palestinian Memorial Monuments in Israel." *Comparative Studies in Society and History* 50 (2008): 337–368.

Palestinian Commemoration in Israel: Calendars, Monuments, and Martyrs. Stanford: Stanford University Press, 2015.

"The Victimhood Trap." In *Zoom In: Palestinian Refugees of 1948, Remembrances,* edited by Sami Adwan, Efrat Ben-Ze'ev, Menachem Klein, Ihab Saloul, Tamir Sorek, and Mahmoud Yazbak, 191–196. Dordrecht: Institute of Historical Justice and Reconciliation and Republic of Letters Publishers, 2011.

Stauber, Roni. *The Holocaust in Israeli Public Debate in the 1950s.* Edgware: Vallentine Mitchell, 2007.

"The Jewish Response during the Holocaust: The Educational Debate in Israel in the 1950s." *Shofar* 22:4 (2004): 57–66.

Stevenson, Jonathan. "Irreversible Peace in Northern Ireland?." *Survival* 42:3 (2002): 5–26

Strömbom, Lisa. "Identity Shifts and Conflict Transformation – Probing the Israeli History Debates." *Mediterranean Politics* 18 (2013): 78–96.

Stone, Dan. *Histories of the Holocaust.* Oxford: Oxford University Press, 2010.

"Memory, Memorials and Museums." In *The Historiography of the Holocaust,* edited by Dan Stone, 508–532. Houndmills/New York: Palgrave Macmillan, 2004.

Sturken, Marita. "Memory, Consumerism and Media: Reflections on the Emergence of the Field." *Memory Studies* 1 (2008): 73–78.

Subotic, Jelena. "Political Memory as an Obstacle to Justice in Serbia, Croatia and Bosnia-Herzegovina" In *Transitional Justice and Reconciliation: Lessons from the Balkans*, edited by Martina Fischer and Olivera Simic, 121–137. London: Routledge, 2016.

Sucahrov, Mira M. *The International Self: Psychoanalysis and the Search for Israeli–Palestinian Peace*. Albany: State University of New York Press, 2005.

Tawil-Souri, Helga. "Qalandia Checkpoint: The Historical Geography of a Non-Place." *Jerusalem Quarterly* 42 (2010): 26–48.

Telhami, Shibley. *The World through Arab Eyes: Arab Public Opinion and the Reshaping of the Middle East*. New York: Basic Books, 2013.

Tenenboim-Weinblatt, Keren. "Journalism as an Agent of Prospective Memory." In *Journalism and Memory*, edited by Barbie Zelizer and Keren Tenenboim-Weinblatt, 213–225. Houndmills/Basingstoke/Hampshire: Palgrave Macmillan, 2014.

"'We Will Get through This Together': Journalism, Trauma and the Israeli Disengagement from the Gaza Strip." *Media, Culture & Society* 30:4 (2008): 495–513.

Tessler, Mark A. *A History of the Israeli-Palestinian Conflict*. Bloomington: Indiana University Press, 1994.

Teveth, Shabtai. "Charging Israel with Original Sin." *Commentary* 88 (1989): 24–33.

Thawabteh, Nibal. "Palestinian Media Map: Production Congestion and Consumption Dispersion." In *Journalism Education in Countries with Limited Media*, edited by Beate Josephi, 73–93. New York: Peter Lang, 2010.

Tibawi, Abdul Latif. "The Palestine Arab Refugees in Arabic Poetry and Art." *Middle East Journal* 17:5 (1963): 507–526.

Tripp, Charles. *The Power and the People: Paths of Resistance in the Middle East*. Cambridge: Cambridge University Press, 2013.

Turow, Joseph. "The Challenge of Inference in Interinstitutional Research on Mass Communication." *Communication Research* 18:2 (1991): 222–239.

Tutu, Desmond. "Foreword: A Call to the Community of Conscience." In *The Goldstone Report: The Legacy of the Landmark Investigation of the Gaza Conflict*, edited by Adam Horowitz, Lizzy Ratner, and Philip Weiss, vii–ix. New York: Nation Books, 2011.

Van Alphen, Ernst. "Second-Generation Testimony, Transmission of Trauma, and Postmemory." *Poetics Today* 27:2: (2006): 473–488.

Van Dijck, José. "Flickr and the Culture of Connectivity: Sharing Views, Experiences, Memories." *Memory Studies* 4:4 (2011): 401–415.

Mediated Memories in the Digital Age. Stanford: Stanford University Press, 2007.

Van Leeuwen, Theo. *Discourse and Practice: New Tools for Critical Discourse Analysis*. Oxford: Oxford University Press, 2008.

"Legitimation in Discourse and Communication." *Discourse & Communication* 1 (2007): 91–112.

Velloso de Santisteban, Agustín. "Palestinian Education: A National Curriculum against All Odds." *International Journal of Educational Development* 22 (2002): 145–154.

Volkmer, Ingrid, ed. *News in Public Memory: An International Study of Media Memories across Generations*. New York: Peter Lang, 2006.

Volkov, Shulamit. *Germans, Jews, and Antisemites: Trials in Emancipation.* Cambridge: Cambridge University Press, 2006.

Vollhardt, Johanna Ray. "'Crime against Humanity' or 'Crime against Jews'? Acknowledgment in Construals of the Holocaust and Its Importance for Intergroup Relations." *Journal of Social Issues* 69:1 (2013): 144–161.

Von Clausewitz, Carl. *On War.* Translated and edited by Michael Howard and Peter Paret. Princeton: Princeton University Press, 1967.

Waage, Hilde Henriksen. "Norway's Role in the Middle East Peace Talks: Between a Strong State and a Weak Belligerent." *Journal of Palestine Studies* 24:4 (Summer 2005): 6–24.

"Postscript to Oslo: The Mystery of Norway's Missing Files." *Journal of Palestine Studies* 38:1 (2008): 54–65.

Wakim, Wakim. "The 'Internally Displaced': Seeking Return within One's Own Land." *Journal of Palestine Studies* 31 (2001): 32–38.

Wallach, John and Michael Wallach. *The Enemy Has a Face: The Seeds of Peace Experience.* Washington, DC: Institute of Peace, 2000.

Wang, Zheng. "Old Wounds, New Narratives: Joint History Textbook Writing and Peacebuilding in East Asia." *History and Memory* 21:1 (2009): 101–126.

Warner, Michael. *Publics and Counterpublics.* New York: Zone Books, 2002.

Watson, Geoffrey R. *The Oslo Accords: International Law and the Israeli–Palestinian Peace Agreements.* Oxford/New York: Oxford University Press, 2000.

Waxman, Dov. *The Pursuit of Peace and the Crisis of Israeli Identity: Defending/Defining the Nation.* New York: Palgrave Macmillan, 2006.

Weaver, Alain Epp. *Mapping Exile and Return: Palestinian Dispossession and a Political Theology for a Shared Future.* Minneapolis: Fortress Press, 2014.

"Remembering the Nakba in Hebrew: Return Visits as the Performance of a Binational Future." *Holy Land Studies* 6 (2008): 125–144.

Weinberger, Peter Ezra. "Co-opting the PLO: A Critical Reconstruction of the Oslo Accords, 1993–1995." PhD diss., London School of Economics, 2002.

Weiss, Meira. "Bereavement, Commemoration, and Collective Identity in Contemporary Israeli Society." *Anthropological Quarterly* 70:2 (1997): 91–101.

Weiss-Wendt, Anton. *The Nazi Genocide of the Roma: Reassessment and Commemoration.* New York: Berghahn Books, 2013.

Weizman, Eyal. *Hollow Land: Israel's Architecture of Occupation.* London: Verso, 2007.

Wermenbol, Grace. "The Ongoing Political Divide." *The Middle East Institute,* September 16, 2019. www.mei.edu/publications/ongoing-divide-palestin ian-participation-israeli-elections. Accessed January 19, 2020.

Wertsch, James. *Voices of Collective Remembering.* Cambridge: Cambridge University Press, 2002.

White, Geoffrey M. "Emotional Remembering: The Pragmatics of National Memory." *Ethos* 27 (1999): 505–529.

Whitson, James Tony. "Post-Structuralist Pedagogy as Counter-Hegemonic Praxis." In *Modernism, Post-colonialism and Pedagogy,* edited by Peter McLaren, 121–144. Australia: James Nicolas Publishers, 1995.

Wistrich, Robert. *Between Redemption and Perdition: Modern Anti-Semitism and Jewish Identity.* London: Routledge, 1990.

"Israel and the Holocaust Trauma." *Jewish History* 11:2 (1997): 13–20.

Wolfsfeld, Gadi. *Media and the Path to Peace*. Cambridge: Cambridge University Press, 2004.

Wright, John. *The New York Times Almanac*. New York: Penguin Books, 2002.

Yablonka, Hanna. "Oriental Jewry and the Holocaust: A Tri-Generational Perspective." *Israel Studies* 14:1 (2009): 94–122.

Survivors of the Holocaust: Israel after the War. Translated by Ora Cummings. Basingstoke: Macmillan, 1999.

Yerushalmi, Yosef Hayim. *Zakhor: Jewish History and Jewish Memory*. Seattle: University of Washington Press, 1989.

Yiftachel, Oren. "Territory as the Kernel of the Nation: Space, Time and Nationalism in Israel/Palestine." *Geopolitics* 7 (2002): 215–248.

Young, James, ed. *The Art of Memory: Holocaust Memorials in History*. New York: Jewish Museum/Prestel-Verlag, 1994.

Young, James. *The Texture of Memory: Holocaust Memorials and Meaning*. New Haven/London: Yale University Press, 1993.

"When a Day Remembers: A Performative History of 'Yom ha-Shoah'." *History and Memory* 2 (1990): 54–75.

Zandberg, Eyal. "Between Destruction and Victory: Holocaust Memory in Israeli Press 1948–2000." In *Coverage as Storytelling – Reflections on Media Discourse*, edited by Motti Neiger, Menahem Blondheim, and Tamar Liebes, 191–215. Jerusalem: The Hebrew University Magnes Press and Smart Institute of Communication, 2008.

"The Right to Tell the (Right) Story: Journalism, Authority and Memory." *Media, Culture & Society* 32:1 (2010): 5–24.

Zelizer, Barbie. *Covering the Body: The Kennedy Assassination, the Media, and the Shaping of Collective Memory*. Chicago/London: University of Chicago Press, 1992.

"Journalists as Interpretative Communities." *Critical Studies in Mass Communication* 10:3 (1993): 219–237.

"Why Memory's Work on Journalism Does Not Reflect Journalism's Work on Memory." *Memory Studies* 1 (2008): 79–87.

Zertal, Idith. *Israel's Holocaust and the Politics of Nationhood*. Translated by Chaya Galai. Cambridge: Cambridge University Press, 2005.

Zertal, Idith and Akiva Eldar. *Lords of the Land: The War over Israel's Settlements in the Occupied Territories, 1967–2007*. New York: Nation Books, 2007.

Zerubavel, Eviatar. "Calendars and History: A Comparative Study of the Social Organization of National Memory." In *States of Memory: Continuities, Conflicts and Transformations in National Retrospection*, edited by Jeffrey K. Olick, 315–337. Durham, NC: Duke University Press, 2003.

Zerubavel, Yael. *Recovered Roots: Collective Memory and the Making of Israeli National Tradition*. Chicago/London: University of Chicago Press, 1995.

Zimbardo, Zara. "Narrative Conflict: An Inquiry into the Histories of Israeli and Palestinian History Textbooks." Paper, California Institute for Integral Studies, 2006.

Zreik, Raef. "When Does a Settler Become a Native? (With Apologies to Mamdani)." *Constellations* 23 (2016): 351–364.

Zuckermann, Moshe. "The Curse of Forgetting: Israel and the Holocaust." *Telos: A Quarterly Journal of Critical Thought* 78 (Winter 1988–1989): 43–54.
   Shoah in the Sealed Room: The Holocaust in Israeli Press during the Gulf War. Tel Aviv: Author's Publication, 1992.
Zweig, Ronald W. "Politics of Commemoration." *Jewish Social Studies* 49:2 (1987): 155–166.

Administrative and Historical Documentation

Abu-Lughod, Ibrahim, Ali Jarbawi, Waleed Deeb, Khalil Nakhleh, Ya'coub Nashwan, Sanaa Abu-Daggo, Rana Barakat, Wasseem Kurdi, Jaber Shaqalaih, Dina Abou El-Haj, Jihad Shwaikh, Mousa Barhoum, Eliah Dabeet, and Kamal Shamshoum. *The Comprehensive Plan for the Development of the First Palestinian Curriculum for General Education.* Ramallah: Curriculum Development Center, 1996. (In Arabic)
ADRID. *Fifteenth Return Rally to Kweikat and Amqa Villages: No Going Back on the Right of Return.* ADRID and The People Committee of Kweikat and Amqa, 2012.
   Do Not Surrender the Land of [Your] Parents and Grandparents. ADRID, 2015. (In Arabic)
   The First Meeting of the Internally Displaced, March 11, 1995. The National Committee for the Rights of the Internally Displaced in Israel, 2000.
   General Organizational Profile. ADRID, undated.
   The Internally Displaced and the Right of Return. ADRID, undated.
   Khubeizy, *The Eyes of al-Rawda.* ADRID and the Public Committee for the Preparation of the 16th March of Return, 2013.
   Miske, The Displaced Village, the 13th March of Return. ADRID, 2010.
   National Anthem *[by] the* Poet *Ibrahim Touqan.* ADRID, 2016. (In Arabic)
   Oath to Return. ADRID, 2016. (In Arabic)
Adwan, Sami, Dan Bar-On, and Eyal Naveh. *Side by Side: Parallel Histories of Israeli Palestine.* Prime, 2012.
Anonymous. "Twenty-Four Hours on the Mount of Remembrance: Yom ha-Shoah." *Yad Vashem Magazine*, June 1996.
   "Highlights of Yad Vashem Activity in 2001." Yad Vashem Magazine, Spring 2002.
   "Members of the IDF General Staff Visit Yad Vashem." *Yad Vashem Magazine*, Summer 1998.
   "New Director of the International School for Holocaust Studies." *Yad Vashem Magazine*, January 2007.
   "The Nazi Euthanasia Program: A Symposium." *Yad Vashem Magazine*, Summer 2001.
   "Yad Vashem in the Frontlines of IDF Education." *Yad Vashem Magazine*, Fall 2002.
   "Yad Vashem Masterplan 2001." *Yad Vashem Magazine*, Fall 1997.
Bader, Dahoud. *El-Ghabsiya. We Still Have the Keys: The Story of an Uprooted Palestinian Village.* ADRID, 2002.
Badil. *Ten Days of Successful Badil Summer School Program.* Badil, 2011.

Fifty Years of Palestinian Exile and Dispossession 1998 Campaign for the Defense of Palestinian Refugee Rights & Development. Badil, 1998.

Fifty-second Anniversary of Palestinian Eviction: Symbolic Return Today – A Step toward Real Return in the Future. Badil, 2000.

Fifty-second Anniversary of the Palestinian Expulsion (al-Nakba): Violent Clashes with Israeli Occupation Army Public Marches and Rallies for Refugees' Right of Return. Badil, 2000.

Fifty-second Anniversary of the Palestinian Expulsion Nakba Day Activities. Badil, 2000.

Fifty-fourth Anniversary of the Palestinian Nakba (15 May 2002): Naka Memorial Events Organized by Internally Displaced Palestinians in Israel. Dispossession and Displacement 1948–2002: The Root Cause of the Israeli–Palestinian Conflict. Badil, 2002.

Major Nakba Memorial Events in Palestine. Badil, 2003.

Nakba Commemoration – 13 May 2008. Badil, 2008.

Nakba Memorial in Palestine. Badil, 2001.

The Nakba-64 Commemoration May 15, 2012. Badil, 2012.

One People United: A Deterritorialized Palestinian Identity. Badil, 2012.

Our Displacement – Our Return: Palestinians Commemorate the 53rd Anniversary of Their Massive Displacement by Israel in 1948. Badil, 2001.

Badi. *The Palestinian Nakba at 58 – The Nakba Continues*. Badil, 2006.

Palestinians Remember the Nakba (8–15 May: "No Alternative but Return"). Badil, 2008.

Press Release May 15, 2012. Badil, 2012.

Badil Resource Center for Palestinian Residency and Refugee Rights. "About Badil." www.badil.org/en/about-badil. Accessed July 19, 2016.

Returning to Kafr Bir'im. Badil, 2006.

Baladna. *2009 Annual Activities Report*. Association for Arab Youth, Baladna, 2010.

2010–2011 Activities Report. Association for Arab Youth, Baladna, 2011.

2013–2014 Annual Activities Report. Association for Arab Youth, Baladna, 2014.

2014–2015 Annual Activities Report. Association for Arab Youth, Baladna, 2015.

Biennial Activities Report 2011–2013. Association for Arab Youth, Baladna, 2013.

Berman, Rochel. "Committed to Remembrance." *Yad Vashem Magazine*, Fall 2001.

Das Bundesarchiv. "Euthanasia im Dritten Reich." Deutschland: Das Bundesarchiv, August 30, 2018. www.bundesarchiv.de/DE/Content/ Artikel/Ueber-uns/Aus-unserer-Arbeit/euthanasie-im-dritten-reich.html. Accessed February 15, 2020. (In German)

Fischler, Mirit, Naama Galil, Uri Kalt, Inbal Kvity Ben Dov, and Yochi Nissani. "Holocaust Remembrance Day." *Yad Vashem Magazine*, July 2012.

Galili, Daphna. "Marking the Days." *Yad Vashem Magazine*, Fall 2003.

GFH. *Address by Chief of Staff during the Holocaust Day Memorial Ceremony at Kibbutz Lohamei Hagetaot 13 April 1999*. Museum Lohamei Hagetaot, April 15, 1999. (In Hebrew)

Ceremony in Dedication of the Memory of the Shoah and Heroism on 13 April 1999. Museum Lohamei Hagetaot, undated. (In Hebrew)

Development of the Memorial Ceremony on 16 April 1996. Museum Lohamei Hagetaot, undated. (In Hebrew)

Development of the Memorial Ceremony on 23 April 1998. Museum Lohamei Hagetaot, undated. (In Hebrew)

Development of the Memorial Ceremony on 5 May 1997. Museum Lohamei Hagetaot, undated. (In Hebrew)

Returning with Soldiers. A Study Day for Officers al the Ghetto Fighters House Following the Journey to Poland as "Witnesses in Uniform". Museum Lohamei Hagetaot, undated. (In Hebrew)

Goldstein, Leah. "Fulfil Obligation to Survivors." *Yad Vashem Magazine,* Summer 2007.

"The Museum Complex: A Source of Inspiration." *Yad Vashem Magazine,* December 2013.

"Not Just a History Lesson." *Yad Vashem Magazine,* December 2013.

Kamil, Michael Morris. "Learn to Remember." *Yad Vashem Magazine,* September 1996.

"Yizkor." *Yad Vashem Magazine,* Summer 1997.

Katz, Orna. "Response to Professor Nurit Peled-Elhanan." *Ministry of Education,* undated.

Kvity, Inbal. "Not Just a Number, an Educational Approach to the Holocaust Victims." *Yad Vashem Magazine,* Fall 2001.

Livnat, Limor. "Greetings from Israeli Heads of State." *Yad Vashem Magazine,* Fall 2003.

Lohamei Hagetaot. "The Center for Humanistic Education." 2016, www.gfh .org.il/?CategoryID=222&ArticleID. Accessed January 15. (In Hebrew)

Loya, Adi. "The Army Education Unit." *Yad Vashem Magazine,* Summer 2000.

Mada al-Carmel. *The Haifa Declaration.* Haifa: Mada al-Carmel, 2007.

Ministry of Education. *Palestinian Curriculum: Position Paper.* Ramallah: Ministry of Education, 2002.

Ministry of Education, General Administration of Curricula (Palestinian Curriculum Development Center). *First Palestinian Curriculum Plan.* Jerusalem: al-Maʿārif, 1998. (In Arabic)

Nahmia-Messinas, Yvette. "The New Museum Complex." *Yad Vashem Magazine,* Summer 2000.

Nicolai, Susan. *Fragmented Foundations: Education and Chronic Crisis in the Occupied Palestinian Territory.* London; Paris: UNESCO, International Institute for Educational Planning & Save the Children UK, 2007.

Shalev, Avner. "Different School." *Yad Vashem Magazine,* Winter 1999.

"Introducing Masterplan 2001 Yad Vashem's Development Project in the Age of the communications revolution." *Yad Vashem Magazine,* April 1996.

"The New Holocaust History Museum." *Yad Vashem Magazine,* Fall 2003.

"Recalling the Past, Realizing the Future." *Yad Vashem Magazine,* Winter 2001.

Shendar, Yehudit and Orly Ohana. "In the Footsteps of Heroes Monuments to Jewish Rebellion and Heroism at Yad Vashem." *Yad Vashem Magazine,* March 2013.

Yad Mordechai. *The Journey to Poland*. Museum Yad Mordechai, undated. (In Hebrew)

Museum "From Shoah to Revival" at Kibbutz Yad Mordechai. Museum Yad Mordechai, 1996. (In Hebrew)

Museum Yad Mordechai "From Shoah to Revival". Background Material for the Visit of the Museum Council Committee. Museum Yad Mordechai, 2013. (In Hebrew)

Museum Yad Mordechai: History of the Museum from the Book "Beyond the Physical" by Dina Porat. Museum Yad Mordechai, undated. (In Hebrew)

Program to Change the Character of the Museum "From Shoah to Revival" at Kibbutz Yad Mordechai. Museum Yad Mordechai, 1999. (In Hebrew)

Summary of Museum Staff Meeting. Museum Yad Mordechai, June 1999. (In Hebrew)

Yad Vashem. *Achievements and Challenges: Annual Report 2002*. Yad Vashem, 2011.

"Day of Memorial for Victims of the European Jewish Disaster and Heroism – 27 Nissan, 5719." *Yad Vashem Bulletin* 4/5, 1959.

"Editor's Remarks." *Yad Vashem Magazine*, Spring 2002.

"Highlights of Yad Vashem's Activities in 2013." www.yadvashem.org/press room/highlights/2013. Accessed December 5, 2016.

"Holocaust Martyrs' and Heroes' Remembrance Day." www.yadvashem .org/yv/en/remembrance/2017/previous_years.asp. Accessed November 16, 2017.

"Yad Vashem Masterplan 2001." *Yad Vashem Magazine*, Fall 1997.

Reports and Statistics

Adalah. *New Discriminatory Laws and Bills in Israel*. Adalah, June 2011.

Al-Zubaidi, Layla. *Walking a Tightrope. News Media and Freedom of Expression in the Arab Middle East*. Ramallah: Heinrich Böll Foundation, 2004.

Aman Palestine. "AMAN-Transparency Palestine." www.aman-palestine.org/en/ about-aman/about-organization. Accessed October 29, 2018.

Amnesty International. *Report 2002*. London: Amnesty International Publications, 2002.

Article 19. *Cry for Change: Israeli Censorship in the Occupied Territories*. London: Library Association Publishing, 1992.

Journalism under Occupation Israel's Regulation of the Palestinian Press. New York: Committee to Protect Journalists, 1988.

The International Centre Against Censorship and The Centre for Media Freedom in the Middle East and North Africa. Memorandum on the 1995 Press Law of the Palestinian National Authority. London: Article 19 and CMF MENA, 1999.

Auschwitz-Birkenau Museum. "Over Two Million Visitors at the Auschwitz Memorial in 2016." http://auschwitz.org/en/museum/news/over-2-million-visitors-at-the-auschwitz-memorial-in-2016,1232.html. Accessed August 8, 2017.

B'nai B'rith International. "About Us." www.bnaibrith.org/about-us.html. Accessed August 7, 2017.

B'Tselem. *Censorship of the Palestinian Press in East Jerusalem.* B'Tselem, 1990. *Discrimination in Planning, Building, and Land Expropriation.* B'Tselem, 2011. *Whitewash Protocol: The So-Called Investigation of Operation Protective Edge.* B'Tselem, September 2016.

Center for Monitoring the Impact of Peace. *Newsletter.* CMIP, September 1998.

Centre for Planning. *The Palestinian Liberation Organisation: An Analysis of the Educational Curriculum in Jordan, Lebanon and Syria.* Beirut, 1972. (In Arabic)

Coalition for Accountability and Integrity-AMAN. *Tenth Annual Report Integrity and Combating Corruption Palestine 2017.* Ramallah: Aman, 2017.

Cohen, Raphael S., David E. Johnson, David E. Thaler, Brenna Allen, Elizabeth M. Bartels, James Cahill, and Shira Efron. *From Cast Lead to Protective Edge: Lessons from Israel's Wars in Gaza.* Santa Monica: Rand Corporation, 2017.

Committee to Protect Journalists. *Attacks on the Press 1999: Israel and the Occupied Territories.* CPJ, 2000.

Council of Religious Institutions of the Holy Land. "Victims of Our Own Narratives? Portrayal of the Other in Israeli and Palestinian School Books." https://d7hj1xx5r7f3h.cloudfront.net/Israeli-Palestinian_School_Book_Study_Report-English.pdf. Accessed August 18, 2016.

Demirel, Suleyman, Thorbjoern Jagland, Warren B. Rudman, Javier Solana, and George J. Mitchell. *Sharm El-Sheikh Fact-Finding Committee Report "Mitchell Report".* The Michell Committee, 2001.

Department of State to the Committee on Foreign Relations and the Committee on International Relations. *Anti-Semitism in the United States: Report on Global Anti-Semitism.* Washington, DC, January 2005.

Economic Monitoring Report to the Ad Hoc Liaison Committee. *Palestinian Economic Prospects: Gaza Recovery and West Bank Revival.* World Bank, June 2009.

Federal Bureau of Investigation. *Hate Crime Statistics 1996.* U.S. Department of Justice Federal Bureau of Investigation, 1996.
"Incidents, Offenses, Victims, and Known Offenders by Bias Motivation, 2015." https://ucr.fbi.gov/hate-crime/2015/tables-and-data-declarations/1tab ledatadecpdf. Accessed September 11, 2017.

Foundation for Middle East Peace. *Report on Israeli Settlement in the Occupied Territories.* Foundation for Middle East Peace, November–December 2003.

Groiss, Arnon. *Jews, Israel and Peace in Palestinian School Textbooks: A Survey of the Textbooks Published by the Palestinian National Authority in the Years 2000–2001.* Center for Monitoring the Impact of Peace, 2001.

Hashomer Hachadash. *Five Year Strategic Plan 2013–2018.* Hashomer Hachadash, undated.

Hazony, Yoram, Michael B. Oren, and Daniel Polisar. *The Quiet Revolution in the Teaching of Zionist History: A Comparative Study of Education Ministry Textbooks on the 20th Century.* Shalem Press, 2000.

Human Rights Watch. *Israel, the Occupied West Bank and Gaza Strip, and Palestinian Authority Territories.* Human Rights Watch, 2002.
World Report 2008: Events of 2007. Human Rights Watch, 2008.

IMPACT. "Comments on Nurit Peled-Elhanan's Paper: The Presentation of Palestinians in Israeli Schoolbooks of History and Geography 1998–2003."

www.impact-se.org/wp-content/uploads/2016/04/NuritPeled2006.pdf. Accessed July 7, 2016.

"Peace, Tolerance and the Palestinian "Other" in Israeli Textbooks: An Analysis of State and State-Religious Textbooks for Grades 1–12, 2009–2012." www.impact-se.org/wp-content/uploads/2016/04/Israel2012 .pdf. Accessed July 6, 2016.

Institute for Palestine Studies. *The Palestinian–Israeli Peace Agreement: A Documentary Record*. Washington, DC: Institute for Palestine Studies, 1994.

Israeli Ministry of Education. "Facts and Figures in the Education System." State of Israel, Ministry of Education. http://meyda.education.gov.il/files/ minhalcalcala/facts.pdf. Accessed November 15, 2016.

Israeli Ministry of Foreign Affairs. "Agreement on Gaza Strip and Jericho Area." www.mfa.gov.il/mfa/foreignpolicy/peace/guide/pages/agreement%20on% 20gaza%20strip%20and%20jericho%20area.aspx. Accessed October 15, 2018.

"Agreement on Preparatory Transfer of Powers and Responsibilities." www .mfa.gov.il/mfa/foreignpolicy/peace/guide/pages/agreement%20on%20prepara tory%20transfer%20of%20powers%20and%20re.aspx. Accessed October 15, 2018.

"Cabinet Communique-28-Apr-2002." www.mfa.gov.il/MFA/PressRoom/ 2002/Pages/Cabinet%20Communique%20-%2028-Apr-2002.aspx. Accessed January 19, 2020.

"Declaration of Principles." www.mfa.gov.il/mfa/foreignpolicy/peace/guide/ pages/declaration%20of%20principles.aspx. Accessed October 15, 2018.

"Declaration of Principles on Interim Self-Government Arrangements September 13, 1993." www.mfa.gov.il/MFA/ForeignPolicy/Peace/Guide/ Pages/Declaration%20of%20Principles.aspx. Accessed June 20, 2017.

"The Israeli–Palestinian Interim Agreement on the West Bank and the Gaza Strip (Oslo II)." www.mfa.gov.il/mfa/foreignpolicy/peace/guide/pages/the% 20israeli-palestinian%20interim%20agreement.aspx. Accessed October 15, 2018.

"November 30: Commemorating the Expulsion of Jews from Arab Lands." www.mfa.gov.il/MFA/VideoLibrary/Pages/Jewish-refugees-from-Arab-lands .aspx. Accessed February 8, 2020.

"Pillar of Defense – Statement by DM Ehud Barak." www.mfa.gov.il/MFA/ PressRoom/2012/Pages/Pillar_of_Defense-Statement_DM_Barak_14-Nov- 2012.aspx. Accessed October 15, 2018.

"PM Sharon-s Address to the Nation-31-Mar-2002." www.mfa.gov.il/MFA/ PressRoom/2002/Pages/PM%20Sharon-s%20Address%20to%20the% 20Nation%20-%2031-Mar-2002.aspx. Accessed January 19, 2020.

"The Real Face of Hamas." www.mfa.gov.il/MFA/ForeignPolicy/Issues/Pages/ The-real-face-of-Hamas.aspx. Accessed October 15, 2018.

"Statement by Prime Minister Ehud Barak 07-Oct-2000." www.mfa.gov.il/ mfa/pressroom/2000/pages/statement%20by%20prime%20minister%20ehud %20barak%20-%2007-oct-20.aspx. Accessed October 15, 2018.

Israel-Palestine Center for Research and Information. *Report I: Analysis and Evaluation of the New Palestinian Curriculum Reviewing Palestinian Textbooks and Tolerance Education Program*. IPCRI, 2003.

Knesset. "Martyrs' and Heroes' Commemoration (Yad Vashem) Law, 5713-1953." https://knesset.gov.il/review/data/eng/law/kns2_yadvashem_eng.pdf. Accessed February 2, 2020.

Martyrs' and Heroes' Remembrance Day Law, 5719–1959. Sefer ha-Chukim 280, 1959. (In Hebrew)

"Memorial Day for Israel's Fallen Soldiers." www.knesset.gov.il/holidays/eng/memorial_day_eng.htm. Accessed January 19, 2017.

MADA, Palestinian Center for Development and Media Freedoms. *The Violations of Media Freedoms: Annual Report 2015*, Ramallah, 2015.

Middle East Media Research Institute. "Palestinians Debate Including the Holocaust in the Curriculum." *Special Dispatch* 187 (2000). www.memri.org/reports/palestinians-debate-including-holocaust-curriculum. Accessed July 26, 2017.

Mideast Mirror. *Israel Section June 19, 1996.* Mideast Mirror, 1996.

MIFTAH. *Public Discourse and Perceptions: Palestinian Media Coverage of the Palestinian–Israeli Conflict.* Ramallah: MIFTAH, 2005.

Ministry of Education. *Palestinian Curriculum: Position Paper.* Ramallah: Ministry of Education, 2002.

Nasru, Fathiyeh. *Preliminary Vision of a Palestinian Education System.* Birzeit: Birzeit University, 1993.

National Archives and Records Administration, *Public Papers of the Presidents of the United States, William J. Clinton.* Washington, DC: United States Government Printing Office, 1996.

Near East Consulting. *Survey of Palestinian Media.* Ramallah: Near East Consulting for Foundation Hirondelle, 2010.

Palestinian Authority, Ministry of Education. "The Palestinian Curriculum and Textbooks: A Clarification." www.pac-usa.org/palestinian_curriculum_and_text.htm. Accessed April 14, 2016.

Palestinian Authority, Ministry of Information. "The Palestinian People's Appeal on the 50th Anniversary of the Catastrophe 'Al-Nakba.'" www.pna.org/mininfo/nakba. Accessed July 10, 2016.

Palestinian Center for Policy and Survey Research, *CPRS Public Opinion Poll 17.* CRS, 1995.

Joint Israeli Palestinian Poll – 54. CRS, December 2014.

Joint Israeli Palestinian Poll – 56. CRS, June2015.

Joint Israeli Palestinian Poll 48, June 2013. CRS, 2013.

Joint Israeli Palestinian Poll – June 2014. CRS, 2014.

Palestinian Central Bureau of Statistics. *Access and Use of ICT by Households and Individuals by Year.* PCBS, undated.

Estimated Population in the Palestinian Territory Mid-Year by Governorate, 1997–2016. PCBS, 2016.

Localities in Jerusalem Governorate by Type of Locality and Population Estimates, 2007–2016. PCBS, 2016.

Mass Media Survey 2000 – Main Findings. PCBS, 2000.

Percentage Distribution of Persons (10 Years and Over) Who Use Computer by Internet Use and Selected Background Characteristics. PCBS, 2014.

Percentage of Persons (10 Years and Over) in the Palestine Who Use the Internet by Purpose of Use. PCBS, 2014.

Palestinian Media Watch. "About Us." www.palwatch.org/pages/aboutus.aspx. Accessed December 22, 2016.

Palestinian Ministry of Information. *The Palestinian Charter.* Palestine Ministry of Information, June 1999.

Pina, Aaron D. *Palestinian Education and the Debate over Textbooks.* Washington, DC: CRS Report for Congress, 2005.

Palestinian Elections. Washington, DC: CRS Report for Congress, 2005.

Reporters Without Borders. *Government Orders Closure of Arab Weekly.* Reporters Without Borders, December 2002.

Rocard, Michel, Henry Siegman, Yezid Sayigh, and Khalil Shikaki. *Independent Task Force Report: Strengthening Palestinian Public Institutions.* New York: Council on Foreign Relations, 1999.

Sfeir, Jacqueline and Susan Bertoni. *The Challenge of Education in Palestine: The Second Intifada.* Bethlehem University, Faculty of Education, 2003.

State of Israel: Ministry of Education. "Facts and Figures in the Education System." http://meyda.education.gov.il/files/minhalcalcala/facts.pdf. Accessed November 15, 2016.

The Peace Index, Peace Index. The Israel Democracy Institute, May 1995.

The United Nations Information System on the Question of Palestine. *Chronological Review of Events Relating to the Question of Palestine: Monthly Media Monitoring Review.* UNISPAL, January 1998.

The United Nations. *Report of the Secretary-General* Prepared Pursuant *to GA Resolution ES-10/10* (Report on Jenin) (A/ES-10/186). UN General Assembly, July 2002.

The White House. *Peace to Prosperity: A Vision to Improve the Lives of the Palestinian and Israeli People.* The White House, January 2020.

"President Bush Calls for New Palestinian Leadership." https://georgewbush-whitehouse.archives.gov/news/releases/2002/06/20020624-3.html. Accessed December 13, 2018.

United States Department of State. *Contemporary Global Anti-Semitism: A Report Provided to the United States Congress.* Washington, DC, March 2008.

United States Holocaust Memorial Museum. "Auschwitz." www.ushmm.org/wlc/en/article.php?ModuleId=10005189. Accessed September 11, 2017.

"Documenting Numbers of Victims of the Holocaust and Nazi Persecution." www.ushmm.org/wlc/en/article.php?ModuleId=10008193. Accessed October 16, 2016.

"Hajj Amin Al-Husayni: Wartime Propagandist." https://encyclopedia.ushmm.org/content/en/article/hajj-amin-al-husayni-wartime-propagandist. Accessed April 3, 2020.

Performance and Accountability Report Fiscal Year 2015. USHMM, November 2015.

"United States Policy toward Jewish Refugees, 1941–1952." www.ushmm.org/wlc/en/article.php?ModuleId=10007094. Accessed August 8, 2017.

Ya'ar, Ephraim and Tamar Herman. "Peace Index – August 2000." *Peaceindex,* August 2000. www.peaceindex.org/files/peaceindex2000_8_3.pdf. Accessed December 13, 2018.

Textbooks

Al-Dajani, Y'aqub and Yunis al-Suqi, 'Abd al-Latif al-Barguthi, 'Issa Abu Shaykha, 'Adnan Lufti, Numr al-Madi, and Ibrahim 'Uthman, *My Little Homeland*. Amman: Ministry of Education, 1966.

Al-Hababa, S. I. *National and Civic Education*. Amman: Ministry of Education, 1994.

Avieli-Tabibian, Ketzi'a. *Era of Fear and Hope 1870–1970*. Tel Aviv: Matach Publishing, 2001.

   Travel in Time: Building a State in the Middle East. Ramat Aviv: Matach Publishing, 2003.

   Travel in Time: From Peace to War and Shoah: Europe, the Mediterranean Sea and the Jews in the First Half of the 20th Century. Ramat Aviv: Matach Publishing, 2008.

Auron, Yair. *Sensitivity to Human Suffering: Genocide in the Twentieth Century*. Tel Aviv: Teacher's College, 1994.

Bar-Navi, Eli. *The Twentieth Century: Contemporary History of the Jewish People*. Tel Aviv: Tel Aviv Books, 1998.

Bar-Navi, Eli and Eyal Naveh. *Modern Times, Part II 1920–2000*. Tel Aviv: Tel Aviv Books, 1999.

Contemporary and Modern Palestinian History, Part II for the 11th Grade. Ramallah: Palestinian Authority, Ministry of Education, 2011.

Contemporary World History, Part II for the 8th Grade. Ramallah: Palestinian Authority, Ministry of Education, 1998.

Domke, Elizier. *Nationality: Building a State in the Middle East*. Jerusalem: Zalman Shazar Center, 2009.

   The World and the Jews in Past Generations, Part 2, 1920–1970. Jerusalem: Zalman Shazar Center, 1999.

Gutman, Yisrael and Chaim Schatzker. *The Holocaust and Its Meaning*. Jerusalem: Zalman Shazar Center, 1987.

Gutman, Yisrael. *Shoah and Memory*. Jerusalem: Zalman Shazar Center, 1999.

History of the Ancient Civilizations for the 5th Grade. Ramallah: Palestinian Authority, Ministry of Education, 2005.

History of the Arabs and the World in the Twentiehth Century for the 12th Grade. Ramallah: Palestinian Authority, Ministry of Education, 2012.

History of the Modern World for the 10th Grade. Ramallah: Palestinian Authority, Ministry of Education, 2010.

History of the Modern World, Part II for the 8th Grade. Ramallah: Palestinian Authority, Ministry of Education, 1999.

History of Western Civilization and the Modern World for the 11th Grade. Ramallah: Palestinian Authority, Ministry of Education, 2001/2002.

Islamic Education for the 6th Grade. Ramallah: Palestinian Authority, Ministry of Education, 2000.

Islamic Education, Part I for the 6th Grade. Ramallah: Palestinian Authority, Ministry of Education, 2011.

Keren, Nili. *Shoah: A Journey into Memory*. Tel Aviv: Tel Aviv Books, 1999.

Naveh, Eyal. *The Twentieth Century on the Verge of Tomorrow*. Tel Aviv: Tel Aviv Books, 1999.

The Twentieth Century on the Verge of Tomorrow, Teacher's Guide. Tel Aviv: Tel Aviv Books, 1999.

The Twentieth Century: The Century That Changed the World Order. Tel Aviv: Tel Aviv Books, 1994.

Naveh, Eyal, Naomi Vered, and David Shachar. *Totalitarianism and Shoah, Europe, the Mediterranean and the Jews in the First Half of the Twentieth Century*. Tel Aviv: Reches, 2009.

Msaol, Yigal. *Creating a Democratic Jewish State in the Middle East – The Establishment of the State of Israel*. Ma'ale Adumim: Hi-School Books, 2014.

Our Beautiful Language, Part I for the 5th Grade. Ramallah: Palestinian Authority, Ministry of Education, 2011.

Our Beautiful Language, Part I for the 7th Grade. Ramallah: Palestinian Authority, Ministry of Education, 2002.

Palestinian National Education for the 2nd Grade. Al-Bireh/Ramallah: Palestinian Authority, Ministry of Education, 2008.

Palestinian National Education for the 4th Grade. Al-Bireh/Ramallah: Palestinian Authority, Ministry of Education, 2004.

Palestinian National Education for the 5th Grade. Al-Bireh/Ramallah: Palestinian Authority, Ministry of Education, 2004.

Palestinian National Education for the 4th Grade. Ramallah: Palestinian Authority, Ministry of Education, 1996.

Palestinian National Education for the 5th Grade. Ramallah: Palestinian Authority, Ministry of Education, 1996.

Palestinian National Education for the 5th Grade. Ramallah: Palestinian Authority, Ministry of Education, 1998.

Palestinian National Education for the 6th Grade. Ramallah: Palestinian Authority, Ministry of Education, 2000.

Palestinian National Education for the 7th Grade. Ramallah: Palestinian Authority, Ministry of Education, 2001.

Palestinian National Education for the 8th Grade. Ramallah: Palestinian Authority, Ministry of Education, 1996.

Principles of Human Geography for the 6th Grade. Al-Bireh/Ramallah: Palestinian Authority, Ministry of Education, 2000.

Reading and Texts, Part I for the 8th Grade. Ramallah: Palestinian Authority, Ministry of Education, 2009.

Reading and Texts, Part I for the 9th Grade. Ramallah: Palestinian Authority, Ministry of Education, 2011.

Teacher's Guide: Contemporary World History, Part II for the 8th Grade. Amman: Ministry of Education, 1995.

The Geography of Palestine for the 7th Grade. Ramallah: Palestinian Authority, Ministry of Education, 2002.

The History of the Arabs and the Modern World for the 12th Grade. Ramallah: Palestinian Authority, Ministry of Education, 1994.

The History of the Arabs and the Modern World for the 12th Grade. Ramallah: Palestinian Authority, Ministry of Education, 1996.

The History of the Arabs and the Modern World for the 12th Grade. Ramallah: Palestinian Authority, Ministry of Education, 1998.

The History of the Arabs and the Modern World for the 12th Grade. Ramallah: Palestinian Authority, Ministry of Education, 2003.

The Modern and Contemporary History of the Arabs for the 9th Grade. Al-Bireh/ Ramallah: Palestinian Authority, Ministry of Education, 2003.

The Modern and Contemporary History of the Arabs for the 9th Grade. Ramallah: Palestinian Authority, Ministry of Education, 2010.

Ya'akovi, Danny. *World of Changes.* Tel Aviv: Maalot Publishing, 1999.

Palestinian Newspaper Articles

Abu Hajla, Nasir. "Bush Wants Us to Vote for Sharon." *Al-Hayat al-Jadida,* September 25, 2003.

AFP. "Dheisheh Refugees Commemorate the Nakba in the Villages from Which They Were Expelled." *Al-Quds,* May 18, 2000.

Alama, Ibrahim. "The Memory of the Pride of the Past … Celebration of the Future: A Conversation with Samih al-Qasim." *Al-Hayat al-Jadida,* May 15, 2008.

Al-Amara, Anwar. "Broad Participation in the Return March to Tirat Haifa in Commemoration of the Memory of the Nakba." *Kul al-Arab Online,* May 14, 2016. www.alarab.com/Article/747018. Accessed May 6, 2016.

Al-Bakri, Nufud. "The DFLP Calls for Social Mobilization on the Anniversary of the Nakba to Defend the Land." *Al-Hayat al-Jadida,* May 14, 2000.

"A Meeting in Gaza Demanding Support for the Right of Return and the Speedy Completion of the Reconciliation Agreement." *Al-Hayat al-Jadida,* May 15, 2014.

"Sticking to the Right of Return Based on International Resolutions and Activating Diplomatic, Media and Academic Works to Address the Refugee Issue." *Al-Hayat al-Jadida,* May 15, 2012.

Al-Barghouti, Hafez. "Our Life." *Al-Hayat al-Jadida,* May 14, 1997.

Al-Ghoul, Omar Hilmi. "The Circle of Fascism Is Complete." *Al-Hayat al-Jadida Online,* March 31, 2016. www.alhaya.ps/ar_page.php?id=125e4bby 19260603Y125e4bb. Accessed April 21, 2017.

"Dancing to the Drums of Racism." *Al-Hayat al-Jadida Online,* December 26, 2015. www.alhaya.ps/ar_page.php?id=c87891y13138065Yc87891. Accessed April 19, 2017.

"Evoking the Lessons of the Holocaust." *Al-Hayat al-Jadida Online,* May 8, 2015. www.alhaya.ps/ar_page.php?id=1496aaby21588651Y1496aab. Accessed April 19, 2017.

"Holidays Sticky with Blood." *Al-Hayat al-Jadida Online,* October 5, 2015. www.alhaya.ps/ar_page.php?id=7d3763y8206179Y7d3763. Accessed April 19, 2017.

"Netanyahu and the Holocaust of History." *Al-Hayat al-Jadida Online,* October 22, 2015. www.alhaya.ps/ar_page.php?id=8c7f1ey9207582Y8c7f1e. Accessed April 20, 2017.

"No Change to the Initiative." *Al-Hayat al-Jadida Online*, May 29, 2016. www .alhaya.ps/ar_page.php?id=15bcd60y22793568Y15bcd60. Accessed April 20, 2017.

Al-Jarwan, Seif Ali. "The Jews and [Their] Control of the Media." *Al-Hayat al-Jadida*, July 2, 1998.

Al-Kashif, Hassan. "Remembering." *Al-Hayat al-Jadida*, May 14, 1997.

Al-Masri, Tahir Taseer. "The Refugees and the Right of Return." *Al-Quds*, April 10, 1996.

Al-Qasim, Samih. "1948 … The Storm Talks … Basil Hushes." *Kul al-Arab*, May 15, 1998.

Al-Qasir, Nader. "Generations That Lived through the Nakba Are Departing and the New Generations Are Holding More Firmly to the Right of Return and the National Principles." *Al-Hayat al-Jadida*, May 15, 2012.

Al-Quds Online. "Ministry of Information: The Suffering of Our Refugees Gives Evidence of the Biggest Political Crime by Britain and the Occupation [Israel]." *Al-Quds Online*, May 15, 2016. www.alquds.com/articles/1463302 629997788600/. Accessed April 19, 2017.

"[The Number of] Palestinians Has Doubled Nine Times since the Nakba and More than One Third of Them Are Refugees. *Al-Quds Online*, May 15, 2016. www.alquds.com/articles/1463295797597400300/. Accessed April 19, 2017.

Al-Rab, Atif Abu. "Jenin, Activities and Marches Stress the Right of Return." *Al-Hayat al-Jadida*, May 16, 2001.

Al-Rahmihi, Mohammed. "The Main Challenges after 50 Years of Nakba." *Al-Quds*, May 2, 1998.

Al-Rimawi, Mustafa. "Return Is a Sacred Right to Every Expellee, There Is a Need for a Palestinian Initiative to Regain Unity." *Al-Quds*, April 6, 1994.

Amar, Khalid. "A Festival in Ramallah Commemorates the Anniversary of the Deir Yassin Massacre." *Al-Quds*, April 10, 1995.

Anbatawi, Abdul. "On the Anniversary of the Nakba: The Disaster Continues in [Our] Existence and Awareness." *Kul al-Arab Online*, May 13, 2014. www .alarab.com/Article/610876. Accessed March 7, 2017.

Anonymous. "The 66th Anniversary of the Nakba and the Bitterness of Genocide and Displacement." *Al-Hayat al-Jadida*, May 14, 2014.

"260 Protesters Were Injured in Confrontations in the Palestinian Territories during Nakba Marches." *Kul al-Arab Online*, May 15, 2012. www.alarab .com/Article/458419. Accessed May 5, 2017.

"A Martyr in Qalqilya and Hundreds Injured in a Fire in Magidu [Prison] and Dozens of Civilians Injured in Confrontations with Occupation Soldiers in Gaza, Qalqilya, Nablus and Ramallah." *Al-Hayat al-Jadida*, May 15, 2000.

"Abbas in a Speech Addressing the People in the Homeland and the Diaspora on the Anniversary of the Nakba." *Al-Quds*, May 15, 2012.

"From al-Araqib to Susiya: A Short Documentary on the Anniversary of the Nakba Calls for Justice." *Kul al-Arab Online*, May 15, 2014. www.alarab .com/Article/534646. Accessed March 7, 2017.

"Announcement by the Legislative Council on the 50th Anniversary of the Nakba." *Al-Hayat al-Jadida*, May 13, 1998.

"Arab Students at the University of Be'er Sheva Thwart an Attempt by Im Tirtzu to Prevent the Commemoration of the Nakba." *Kul al-Arab*, May 12, 2014. www.alarab.com/Article/610863. Accessed March 7, 2017.

"Archbishop Hanna in Ramallah: The Nakba Is the Reality in Which We Live and We Will Not Give up a Grain of Soil of Palestinian Soil." *Kul al-Arab Online*, May 14, 2013. www.alarab.com/Article/534462. Accessed March 6, 2017.

"Between the Nakba and the Dawn of a New Birth." *Al-Quds*, May 14, 2001.

"Call upon Our People to Commemorate the 52nd Nakba Anniversary." *Al-Hayat al-Jadida*, May 13, 2000.

"Clarification for Readers." *Al-Hayat al-Jadida*, May 15, 2000.

"Commemoration Activities to the Nakba in the Governorates." *Al-Hayat al-Jadida*, May 16, 2000.

"Confrontations in Hebron and Dozens of Injured." *Al-Hayat al-Jadida*, May 16, 2000.

"The Cultural Forum Center in Bidu Village Organizes a Massive Rally in Commemoration of the Nakba." *Al-Hayat al-Jadida*, May 10, 2008.

"The Director of the Palestinian Bureau of Statistics." *Al-Quds*, May 15, 2005.

"Dozens Injured in Clashes in Qalqilya." *Al-Hayat al-Jadida*, May 16, 2000.

"El-Sanah: Knesset's Decision on the First Reading of the Nakba Law Reflects the Failure of the Zionist Movement." *Kul al-Arab*, March 18, 2010. www.alarab.com/Article/265751. Accessed March 7, 2017.

"The Executive Council Condemns the Occupation's Repression of Peaceful Rallies and Called for a PNC Session and Valued the Prisoners' Steadfastness Highly." *Al-Hayat al-Jadida*, May 16, 2000.

"Extensive Preparations in All of the Governorates of the Homeland for the Commemoration of the Nakba Tomorrow." *Al-Quds*, May 14, 2001.

"General National Body Calls for Broad Participation in Nakba Commemoration Activities." *Al-Hayat al-Jadida*, May 13, 2000.

"The High Follow-up Committee Calls for Wide Participation in Nakba Commemoration Activities and the March of Return." *Kul al-Arab Online*, May 10, 2016. www.alarab.com/Article/746379. Accessed August 17, 2017.

"In a Statement on the Occasion of the Nakba Anniversary the Captive Leader al-Barghouti: We Bless the Reconciliation Agreement and There Is No Partner in Israel." *Al-Hayat al-Jadida*, May 15, 2014.

"Lieberman Proposes to Prevent Nakba Commemoration." *Kul al-Arab*, May 15, 2009. www.alarab.com/Article/137997. Accessed March 7, 2017.

"The March and the Meaning." *Al-Quds*, May 14, 1998.

"The Masses Commemorate the 62nd Anniversary of the Nakba." *Al-Hayat al-Jadida*, May 15, 2010.

"The Masses in Our Homeland and the Diaspora Commemorate the 57th Anniversary of the Nakba." *Al-Hayat al-Jadida*, May 15, 2005.

"More than 70 Injured in Clashes in Bethlehem." *Al-Hayat al-Jadida*, May 16, 2000.

"Nakba Removed from Textbooks." *Kul al-Arab*, July 23, 2009. www.alarab.com/Article/154553. Accessed July 10, 2017.

"The Naqab Foundation: The Crime of Demolition in Atir, a New Nakba on the Anniversary of the Nakba." *Kul al-Arab Online*, May 16, 2013. www .alarab.com/Article/534910. Accessed July 11, 2017.

"The National Committee for the Commemoration of the Nakba Calls for Broad Participation in Nakba Activities." *Al-Quds Online*, May 14, 2016. www.alquds.com/articles/1463231183412484000/. Accessed April 19, 2017.

"National Festival in Kufr Kana for the Anniversary of the Nakba and Prisoner Day." *Al-Hayat al-Jadida*, May 13, 2000.

"National Forces Call to Commemorate the Nakba with a Large Participation." *al-Quds Online*, April 23, 2016. www.alquds.com/articles/146142750087623/ 5500. Accessed March 16, 2017.

"Netanyahu: The Revival of What They Call the Nakba Leads to Incitement against Israel." *Kul al-Arab Online*, May 18, 2014. www.alarab.com/Article/ 612265. Accessed July 11, 2017.

"On the 50th Anniversary of the Nakba." *Al-Hayat al-Jadida*, May 14, 1998.

"On the 62nd Anniversary of the Nakba We Stick to the Land and There Is No Alternative to Return. Announcement by the PLO, the Higher Committee for Nakba Commemoration, Refugee Affairs Department." *Al-Hayat al-Jadida*, May 14, 2010.

"On the 62nd Nakba [Anniversary], Declaration of the Factions Assures Determination on the Right of Return." *Al-Quds*, May 15, 2010.

"On the Anniversary of the Nakba: Factions Affirm the Right of Our People to Return and Their Will for Freedom and Independence." *Al-Hayat al-Jadida*, May 15, 2016.

"Our People Commemorating the Nakba [Led to] Three Martyrs and Hundreds of Injured. One Martyr [Was] among the Security Forces in al-Bireh and Two Martyrs in Nablus and More then 600 Injured among [Palestinian] Journalists and Police Members, Occupation Forces Fire New Kinds of Weapons on Demonstrators in Gaza, Seven Occupation Forces Injured from Gun Shots among Them Two Officers in al-Bira and Jenin." *Al-Hayat al-Jadida*, May 16, 2000.

"The Palestinian Legislative Council Holds a Special Session in Commemoration of the Nakba." *Al-Hayat al-Jadida*, May 15, 2005.

"The PLO on the Anniversary of the Nakba: The Struggle for Freedom and Independence Continues." *Al-Hayat al-Jadida*, May 15, 2012.

"The President: It Is Time for the Calamity Called the Nakba of the Palestinian People to End." *Al-Hayat al-Jadida*, May 18, 2008.

"The President on the Anniversary of the Nakba: Palestinians Do Not Forget … and Will Not Forget." *Al-Hayat al-Jadida*, May 15, 2016.

"The President: Our People Will Not Forget the Situation in the Aftermath of the Nakba." *Al-Hayat al-Jadida*, May 13, 1998.

"Result of a Survey by the Site al-Arab: 90.9% Commemorate the Nakba and Do Not Recognize Israel's Independence [Day]." *Kul al-Arab* 28 April 2012. www.alarab.com/Article/453971. Accessed September 6, 2017.

"The Student Front: The University of Haifa Punishes Two Students for Commemorating the Nakba." *Kul al-Arab Online*, September 18, 2014. www.alarab.com/Article/636726. Accessed March 12, 2020.

"Today the Anniversary of the 15th of May." *Al-Quds*, May 15, 1996.

"Towards a Better Awareness on the Anniversary of the Nakba." *Al-Quds Online*, April 21, 2015. www.alquds.com/articles/1429595927270852900/. Accessed April 19, 2017.

"From the Villages That Were Destroyed—Qaqun." *Al-Quds*, June 30, 1999.

"We Remain on This Land [...] Like Olive Trees." *Al-Hayat al-Jadida*, May 15, 2012.

"Zahalka: During the Nakba Israel Occupied the Land with Weapons and Today [Israel Does It] by Legal Measures." *Kul al-Arab Online*, May 27, 2012. www.alarab.com/Article/461097. Accessed March 6, 2017.

"Zahalka in a Protest Rally in Occupied Jerusalem: The Judaization of Jerusalem Is the Biggest Nakba." *Kul al-Arab Online*, May 16, 2010. www.alarab.com/Article/300474. Accessed July 11, 2017.

Awadah, Wadiah. "Jaffa That Was." *Kul al-Arab*, May 15, 1998.

Badran, Jamama. "Witnesses of the Nakba." *Al-Quds*, May 15, 2001.

Dachbur, Ahmad. "Jew against Jew." *Al-Hayat al-Jadida*, June 24, 2003.

Darwish, Mahmoud. "Not to Begin at the End." *Al-Ahram Online*, 533, May 2001. weekly.ahram.org.eg/Archive/2001/533/op1.htm. Accessed September 21, 2017.

Farah, Najib. "Lighting a Torch on the 68th Anniversary of the Nakba in Dheisheh Camp." *Al-Quds Online*, May 14, 2016. www.alquds.com/art icles/1463256282504194700/. Accessed April 19, 2017.

Hassan, Shaker Farid. "Sixty-seven Years of the Nakba." *Kul al-Arab Online*, May 16, 2015. www.alarab.com/Article/680650. Accessed March 12, 2020.

Hawatmeh, Natif. "Nakba, Intifadah and Resistance." *Al-Hayat al-Jadida*, May 16, 2001.

Heidar, Ali. "Ongoing Nakba." *Kul al-Arab Online*, May 14, 2013. www.alarab.com/Article/534410. Accessed July 11, 2017.

Hilal, Rashid. "Natif Hawatmeh: We Move toward Holding a National Popular Conference, Return Is a Sacred Right to Palestinians, We Reject Inter-Palestinian Fighting." *Al-Quds*, April 8, 1994.

Ibrahim, Mustafa. "The Children of al-Shati and the Palestinian Nakba." *Kul al-Arab Online*, May 12, 2016. www.alarab.com/Article/746643. Accessed March 6, 2017.

Khadra, Faisal Abu. "The Palestinian People Will Not Kneel." *Al-Quds Online*, December 18, 2015. www.alquds.com/articles/1450420728492938700/. Accessed April 19, 2017.

Mansour, Chari. "Marketing Ashes." *Al-Hayat al-Jadida*, April, 13, 2001.

Meaari, Sami. "The Nakba Is Not a Memory ... It Is a Continuous State." *Kul al-Arab Online*, May 15, 2018. www.alarab.com/Article/857648. Accessed March 12, 2020.

Musa, Nanal. "The Committee for Commemoration of the Nakba Calls on the International Community to Take Responsibility." *Al-Hayat al-Jadida*, May 14, 2005.

"Villages in Ramallah Countryside Witness Central and Regional Activities on the 62nd Nakba Commemoration – Demonstrators Carried Huge Keys Sticking to the Right of Return." *Al-Hayat al-Jadida*, May 15, 2010.

Musa, Nanal and Isama Alisha. "The Occupation Suppresses Rallies against the Wall and Settlements and Uses Police Dogs to Arrest Demonstrators." *Al-Hayat al-Jadida*, May 15 2010.

Nasser, Muhasin. "Arab Leaders Are Absent from the March of Return, and Jews Participate to Affirm the Nakba." *Kul al-Arab Online*, May 13, 2011. www .alarab.com/Article/372066. Accessed March 12, 2020.

Nassar, Muhasin, Mohammed Wattad, and Rallib Qiwan. "General Strikes among Student Groups Create High Tensions in the Country's Universities." *Kul al-Arab*, May 16, 2008.

Natour, Ahmed. "The Nakba Continues." *Kul al-Arab Online*, May 2, 2015. www.alarab.com/Article/677910. Accessed March 6, 2017.

Qandeel, Lama. "The National Commemoration Committee for the Commemoration of the Nakba of 60th Anniversary Announces Its Program in the Country and the Diaspora." *Al-Hayat al-Jadida*, April 14, 2008.

Qariya, Ahmad. "Lessons of the 50th Anniversary and Options for the Future." *Al-Hayat al-Jadida*, May 12, 1998.

Razaq, Munir Abu. "The People Renew Their Allegiance with Blood and the Leader Confirms the Inevitability of Victory." *Al-Hayat al-Jadida*, May 16, 2001.

Sa'ada, Imad. "Refugees: The Anniversary of the Nakba Brings Back Our Wounds and Affection for Our Land." *Al-Quds Online*, May 13, 2016. www.alquds.com/articles/1463072654162173900/. Accessed April 19, 2017.

Sharur, Rumur. "Abu al-Adeen al-Damouni Refuses [Giving up] the Name of [His Original] Village." *Al-Hayat al-Jadida*, May 15, 2000.

Staff Editorial. "After 53 Years, the Features of the Nakba Are Embodied Once Again." *Al-Quds*, May 15, 2001.

"The Right of Return, Our National Name." *Al-Hayat al-Jadida*, May 15, 2014.

Suweitee, Hussein. "Fifty Years since the Nakba, 50 Years of struggle." *Kul al-Arab*, May 15, 1998.

"The Expellees." *Kul al-Arab*, May 15, 1998.

"The Palestinian Refugees, Regular People … But." *Kul al-Arab*, May 15, 1998.

Thahir, Walid. "The Nakba and the Dream of Return." *Kul al-Arab Online*, May 26, 2013. www.alarab.com/Article/537058. Accessed March 7, 2017.

Wafa and Correspondents. "The March of the Millions Is Launched Today in the Governorates of the Homeland." *Al-Hayat al-Jadida*, May 14, 1998.

Wafa. "A Torchlit March to Commemorate the 66th Anniversary of the Nakba in Ramallah." *Al-Hayat al-Jadida*, May 15, 2014.

"Fatah: The Right of Return Exists as Long as Palestinian Remain in Palestine." *Al-Hayat al-Jadida*, May 15, 2012.

"In Order for Our People and the World Not to Forget the Palestinian Nakba." *Al-Quds*, May 14, 1998.

"Today, the 64th Anniversary of the Nakba." *Al-Hayat al-Jadida*, May 15, 2012.

Wahib, Abu. "The Nakba Continues." *Kul al-Arab Online*, April 18, 2013. www
    .alarab.com/Article/528196. Accessed July 11, 2017.
Yunis, Abdul Rahman. "The Refugee Abu Surour: Our Relationship with the
    Jews before the Nakba Was Based on Brotherhood and Respect." *Al-Quds
    Online*, May 17, 2016. www.alquds.com/articles/1463473940780151200/.
    Accessed April 19, 2017.
    "Refugee Ali Qaraqe: They Informed Us That the Zionist Gangs Would Only
    Be [There for] a Short Visit." *Al-Quds Online*, May 17, 2016. www.alquds
    .com/articles/1463473940780151200. Accessed April 19, 2017.
    "The Refugee Mrs. al-Lahham: If We Had Known We Would Become
    Refugees, We Would Not Have Left Our Villages." *Al-Quds Online*, May
    18, 2016. www.alquds.com/articles/146355753444634 /0200/. Accessed
    April 19, 2017.

Israeli Newspaper Articles

Abebe, Danny Adino and Geul Banu. "Remember the Dead." *Yedioth Ahronot*,
    April 8, 2013.
Abebe, Danny Adino. "We Won: They Survived the Horrors of the Holocaust,
    Established Glorious Families and Chose Life." *Yedioth Ahronot*, April 15,
    2015.
Abebe, Danny Adino, Natasha Mozgovia, and Yossi Bar. "The Pain and the
    Memory." *Yedioth Ahronot*, April 16, 2007.
Adato, Edna and Zvi Singer. "Remember." *Maariv*, April 29, 2003.
AFP. "Hamas Claims Rocket Fire on Jerusalem, Tel Aviv and Haifa." *News24*,
    July 8, 2014. www.news24.com/World/News/Hamas-claims-rocket-fire-on-
    Jerusalem-Tel-Aviv-and-Haifa-20140708.
Ain, Stewart. "Barak's Gov't near Collapse." *Times of Israel*, June 16, 2000,
    https://jewishweek.timesofisrael.com/baraks-govt-near-collapse/. Accessed
    February 15, 2020.
Am-Ad, Karni. "Saour and Ibrahim." *Maariv*, May 5, 1997.
    "Top Holocaust Educator Slams Israeli Way of Remembrance." *Haaretz*, April
    26, 2016. www.haaretz.com/israel-news/.premium-top-holocaust-educator-
    slams-remembrance-1.5441419. Accessed February 15, 2020.
Anonymous. "A Safe Haven for Future Generations." *Maariv*, April 9, 2002.
    "A Second Generation of Pain." *Yedioth Ahronot*, April 19, 2004.
    "Berlin Mayor: This Is Hateful Anti-Semitism." *Yedioth Ahronot*, April 30,
    2008.
    "Carry the Torch of Life." *Maariv*, April 16, 2015.
    "Ceremony at Tel Yizhak: The Grandchildren Will Accompany the
    Torchlighters." *Yedioth Ahronot*, May 5, 2005, 3.
    "Dozens of Graves Desecrated in Germany on the Eve of Holocaust Day."
    Maariv, April 30, 2008.
    "Hate Is Increasing. 2004: Sharp Increase in Anti-Semitism." *Maariv*, May 5,
    2006.
    "Lt. Gen. Eizenkot, the Spirit of Heroism." *Yedioth Ahronot*, April 16, 2015.
    "Maariv for Kids." *Maariv*, May 2, 2000.

"Netanyahu: The West Has Not Learned a Lesson, but This Time We Will Defend Ourselves." *NRG/Maariv*, April 27, 2014. www.nrg.co.il/online/1/ART2/575/352.html. Accessed May 8, 2017.

"Never Again: The Lesson of the Holocaust Is to Fight Evil, the Prime Minister Said Last Night at Yad Vashem. However, Facing the Iranian Threat, the World Acts as It Always Had." *Maariv*, April 12, 2010.

"Personal Testimony: Holocaust Survivors and Members of the Second Generation Write Their Memories." *Yedioth Ahronot*, April 29, 2003.

"The Prime Minister Is Going to Lead the March of the Living Today in Auschwitz. 'Never will they find us not ready, never,' Sharon Promised." *Maariv*, May 5, 2006.

"Recounting." *Yedioth Ahronot*, April 4, 2012.

"Since the Holocaust There Hasn't Been Such a Strong Anti-Semitic Wave." *Maariv*, April 9, 2002.

"We Are Here." *Yedioth Ahronot*, April 8, 2013.

AP. "More Than 30 Graves Desecrated in Berlin." *NRG/Maariv*, April 29, 2008. www.nrg.co.il/online/1/ART1/727/764.html. Accessed April 18, 2017.

"They Do Not Deny, but Just Compare the [Holocaust] to the [Plight of the] Palestinians" Holocaust Painting Competition in Iran." *Ynet/Yedioth Ahronot*, May 14, 2016. www.ynet.co.il/articles/0,7340,L-4802860,00.html. Accessed April 19, 2017.

Arens, Moshe. "The Palestinian Narrative Is a Falsification of History." *Haaretz*, November 3, 2010. www.haaretz.com/the-palestinian-narrative-is-a-falsification-of-history-1.322588. Accessed August 17, 2017.

"The Palestinians Can Thank Israel for Their Skirting the Arab Catastrophe." *Haaretz*, August 14, 2016. www.haaretz.com/opinion/.premium-1.736812. Accessed August 17, 2017.

Arif, Urah. "Postal Service Issues a Special Commemoration Kit." *Yedioth Ahronot*, April 25, 1995.

Ariv, Ora. "It Is Up to Israel to Spearhead the Fight against Followers of Nazism." *Yedioth Ahronot*, April 27, 1995.

Asrovitz, Chaim. "A Rise of 40% in Violent Anti-Semitic Incidents in the World." *Maariv*, April 16, 2015.

Avnat, Ilyah. "Mother and Daughter in Torch Race." *Yedioth Ahronot*, May 5, 1997.

Avnery, Nati. "About the Holocaust and the Nakba." NRG/Maariv, May 16, 2011. www.nrg.co.il/online/1/ART2/241/319.html. Accessed April 21, 2017.

Auron, Yair. "Letter to a Palestinian Reader: Holocaust, Resurrection and Nakba." *Haaretz*, May 8, 2014. www.haaretz.com/opinion/.premium-1.589454. Accessed October 15, 2015.

Bagno, Yuval. "Holocaust Survivors and Artillery Soldiers Close the Circle." *Maariv*, May 5, 2016.

Barbibai, Orna. "We Return to the Camp as Victors." *Maariv*, April 9, 2013.

Baron, Gabi. "MK Livnat: Forbid Holding a Joint Ceremony for the Shoah and Armenians." *Yedioth Ahronot*, April 24, 1995.

Bashan, Tal. "A Healthier Mind." *Maariv*, April 16, 2015.

Beck, Eldad. "Ten percent of Jewish Cemeteries in Germany Were Desecrated in 5 Years." *Yedioth Ahronot*, January 27, 2008.

Beck, Eldad and Itamar Eichner. "In Germany Too, Netanyahu Again Blamed Mufti for His Responsibility." *Ynet*, October 21, 2015. www.ynet.co.il/art icles/0,7340,L-4714608,00.html. Accessed August 16, 2017.

Beck, Eldad, Natasha Mozgovia, and Itamar Eichner. "Munich: Carnival on International Holocaust Day." *Yedioth Ahronot*, January 27, 2008.

"Netanyahu at Auschwitz: We Will Do Everything to Prevent Another Holocaust." *Ynet/Yedioth Ahronot*, June 13, 2013. www.ynet.co.il/articles/ 0,7340,L-4392024,00.html. Accessed April 18, 2017.

"The Righteous in Sodom." *Yedioth Ahronot*, April 21, 2009.

Bender, Eric. "Zoavi Refuses to Attend a Holocaust Memorial Ceremony." *Maariv*, April 20, 2016.

Ben-Zur, Raanan. "Rabin Killer: Sharon Affected My Decision." *Ynet Online*, October 10, 2018. www.ynetnews.com/articles/0,7340,L-3615595,00.html. Accessed January 4, 2019.

Berger, Yotam. "Declassified: Israel Made Sure Arabs Couldn't Return to Their Villages." *Haaretz*, May 27, 2019. www.haaretz.com/.premium-israel-lifted-military-rule-over-arabs-in-1966-only-after-ensuring-they-couldn-t-ret-1 .7297983. Accessed February 23, 2019.

Blatman, Daniel. "Yad Vashem Is Derelict in Its Duty to Free the Shoah from Its Jewish Ghetto." *Haaretz*, May 19, 2016.

Blau, Sarah. "The Shoah Is Present." *Maariv*, April 9, 2002.

Bronstein, Eitan. "Im Tirtzu Targets Zochrot for Promoting the Return of Palestinian Refugees." *Zochrot*. http://zochrot.org/en/article/53843. Accessed September 6, 2017.

Carmel, Amos. "About the Sin That Was Not Committed." *Yedioth Ahronot*, May 5, 1997.

Chaim, Assaf and Avi Shilon. "The Shoah Is Present in Our Blood Cycle." *Maariv*, April 9, 2002.

Channel 2 News. "Government Report States: 40% of European Residents Is Anti-Semitic." *NRG/Maariv*, January 24, 2016. www.nrg.co.il/online/16/ ART2/750/278.html. Accessed April 18, 2017.

Cohen, Geula. "My Holocaust Syndrome." *Maariv*, May 2, 2000.

Danker, Amnon. "Memory." *Maariv*, May 5, 2006.

David, Achikam Moshe. "We Will Not Have Another Holocaust Because of You." *NRG/Maariv*, May 2, 2011. www.nrg.co.il/online/1/ART2/237/071 .html. Accessed May 7, 2017.

David, Ami Ben. "Unprecedented Heavy Security During the March of the Living." *Maariv*, April 9, 2002.

Doek, Nechama. "Flight A986." *Yedioth Ahronot*, April 21, 2009.

Doron, Alex. "Is Paris Burning? The Plague of Anti-Semitism in France." *NRG/ Maariv*, January 8, 2012. www.nrg.co.il/online/1/ART2/324/215.html. Accessed April 18, 2017.

Dvir, Noam. "Remember and Do Not Forget: Israel Is One with the Six Million." *Ynet/Yedioth Ahronot*, April 28, 2014. Accessed May 6, 2017. www.ynet.co.il/articles/0,7340,L-4513981,00.html.

Eglas, Ruth. "The Holocaust from the Inside Out." *Jerusalem Post Online*, January 12, 2009. www.jpost.com/Features/In-Thespotlight/The-Holocaust-from-the-inside-out. Accessed August 9, 2017.

Eichenwald, Dubi. "In the Name of the Father." *Yedioth Ahronot*, April 29, 2003.

Eichner, Itamar. "Holocaust Denial Competition: 50,000 Dollars to the Winner." *Ynet/Yedioth Ahronot*, January 12, 2016. www.ynet.co.il/articles/0,7340,L-4752001,00.html. Accessed April 19, 2017.

"Khomeini's Holocaust Denial Video: Zionists Kill Children." Ynet/Yedioth Ahronot, January 28, 2016. www.ynet.co.il/articles/0,7340,L-4759216,00.html. Accessed April 19, 2017.

"The Third Generation of Holocaust Survivors and Their Grandchildren Will Accompany Sharon." *Yedioth Ahronot*, May 5, 2005, 4.

Eichwald, Dov. "We Stood on the Cursed Land of Auschwitz and Knew We Had Won." *Yedioth Ahronot*, April 9, 2000.

Eizenkot, Gadi. "Chief of Staff's Letter Lt. Gen. Gadi Eizenkot." *Yedioth Ahronot*, May 5, 2016.

Eldar, Akiva. "Israel Defense Ministry Plan Earmarks 10 Percent of West Bank for Settlement Expansion. *Haaretz*, March 30, 2012. www.haaretz.com/israel-news/israel-defense-ministry-plan-earmarks-10-percent-of-west-bank-for-settlement-expansion-1.421589. Accessed August 21, 2017.

Elizier, Uri. "It's Still Possible." *Yedioth Ahronot*, April 21, 2006.

Elkana, Yehuda. "A Plea for Forgetting." *Haaretz*, March 2, 1988.

Eyadat, Fadi. "Surveys Finds Nearly Half of Israeli Arabs Deny Holocaust." *Haaretz*, May 18, 2009. www.haaretz.com/survey-finds-nearly-half-of-israeli-arabs-deny-holocaust-1.276206. Accessed August 30, 2017.

Fogelman, Shay. "Port in a Storm." *Haaretz*, June 3, 2011. www.haaretz.com/israel-news/port-in-a-storm-1.365729. Accessed July 10, 2017.

Freilich, Rivka. "We Are Here: The Soldiers of Yehuda." *Maariv*, May 2, 2000.

Gan, Eshel. "History Chose Us." *NRG/Maariv*, April 24, 2006. www.nrg.co.il/online/1/ART1/076/987.html. Accessed April 28, 2017.

Gilat, Amir. "This Is Me, Jork, at the Square of the Three Crosses." *Maariv*, April 9, 2002.

Golan, Asaf. "Expert: There Is a Clear Rise in Anti-Semitism in Turkey." *NRG/Maariv*, January 8, 2014. www.nrg.co.il/online/1/ART2/538/183.html. Accessed April 18, 2017.

Golan, Yehuda and Uri Arzi. "Oy to a People That Doesn't Have a National Home and Oy to a People That Doesn't Have a Defensive Force, Said Prime Minister Shimon Peres Yesterday during the Ceremony at Yad Vashem." *Maariv*, April 25, 1996.

Grayevski, Michael. "A Growth in Anti-Semitic Violence in the Last Year." *Yedioth Ahronot*, April 23, 1998.

"Israel Is the Assurance That the Holocaust Will Not Return." *Yedioth Ahronot*, April 23, 1998.

Hadad, Tamar Trabelsi, Zvi Singer, Joel Beno, and Oron Meiri. "A Third of the Youth: It Is Possible That a Second Shoah Will Happen." *Yedioth Ahronot*, April 13, 2015.

Haetzni, Elyakim. "Who Is a Good Jew." *Yedioth Ahronot*, August 3, 1999.

Halley, Jonathan. "More Than 40% of the Arabs in Israel are Holocaust Deniers." *NRG/Maariv*, May 18, 2009. www.nrg.co.il/online/1/ART1/892/038.html. Accessed April 21, 2017.

"Survey: Sixty-six percent of Israeli Arabs Reject Its Existence." *NRG/Maariv*, May 18, 2011. www.nrg.co.il/online/1/ART2/242/096.html.2011. Accessed April 21, 2017.

Hartman, Ben and Lahav Harkov. "Im Tirtzu Launches Campaign against 'Myths' of the Nakba." *Jerusalem Post*, May 13, 2011. www.jpost.com/National-News/Im-Tirtzu-launches-campaign-against-myths-of-the-Nakba. Accessed July 10, 2017.

Hoffman, Gil Stern. "Ayre Eldad to Head New Secular Right Party." *Jerusalem Post*, November 20, 2007. www.jpost.com/Israel/Arye-Eldad-to-head-new-secular-Right-party. Accessed July 10, 2017.

Ho, Spencer. "Over 80% of Palestinian Reporters Self-Censor, Study Finds." *Times of Israel Online*, October 16, 2014. www.timesofisrael.com/over-80-of-palestinian-reporters-self-censor-study-finds/. Accessed June 20, 2017.

Inbari, Itamar. "The Palestinian Nakba Is Coming to the Streets of Israel." *NRG/Maariv*, May 14, 2007. www.nrg.co.il/online/1/ART1/581/574.html. Accessed September 6, 2017.

Isaiah, Kobi. "Survey: Young People Respect Holocaust Day but Avoid Exposure." *NRG/Maariv*, April 8, 2013. www.nrg.co.il/online/16/ART2/458/624.html. Accessed August 8, 2017.

Israel News. "Gillerman at the UN Ceremony: Iran Is Preparing the Next Holocaust." *Ynet/Yedioth Ahronot*, January 2, 2006. www.ynet.co.il/articles/0,7340,L-3207235,00.html. Accessed April 19, 2017.

Kadari-Ovadia, Shira. "Israeli University Cancels Event Marking Nakba Day, Citing Violation of Law." *Haaretz*, May 16, 2019. www.haaretz.com/israel-news/.premium-in-first-israeli-university-bans-political-event-citing-violation-of-nakba-law-1.7250174. Accessed January 12, 2020.

Kalman, Aaron and Associated Press. "Netanyahu Says It's His Responsibility to Exact Price for Rockets on the South." *Times of Israel*, November 13, 2012. www.timesofisrael.com/im-responsible-states-netanyahu/?fb_comment_id=513426285335266_6329976. Accessed October 15, 2018.

Keinon, Herb. "EU Money to Be Denied for PA Schoolbooks." *Jerusalem Post*, November 2, 2001.

Keren, Nili. "The Answers Are Not in the Camps." *Haaretz*, October 10, 2013. www.haaretz.co.il/opinions/letters/1.2145706. Accessed September 27, 2017.

Keshler, Gabi. "Palestinian Suicide Bombers Are Just as Bad as the Nazis." *Maariv*, April 9, 2002.

Kinan, Amos. "Nakba, Shoah and More." *Yedioth Ahronot*, April 3, 1998.

Klein, Zvika. "70 Years of the Shoah: A Dramatic Rise in Anti-Semitism in the World." *NRG/Maariv*, April 14, 2015. www.nrg.co.il/online/1/ART2/688/943.html. Accessed May 5, 2017.

"Escaping from France: A Peak in the Immigration of Jews from Western Europe in 2015." *NRG/Maariv*. www.nrg.co.il/online/1/ART2/748/600.html. Accessed April 18, 2017.

Klinger, Noah. "Eighty-two Percent: The Shoah Will Return." *Yedioth Ahronot*, January 25, 2008.

"Not [on] Another Planet." *Yedioth Ahronot*, April 28, 2014.

"The Last [Ones]." *Yedioth Ahronot*, January 28, 2015.

Klinger, Noah, Itamar Eichner, and Danny Adino Abebe." I May Not and I Cannot Forget." *Yedioth Ahronot*, April 18, 2014.

Klinger, Noah and Zvi Singer. "Don't Forget." *Yedioth Ahronot*, May 5, 2005.

Kotz, Miriam. "How to Tell Them About This?." *Yedioth Ahronot*, April 28, 2014.

Lapid, Yair, Nava Semel, Tzipi Gonigros, Ariana Melamed, Major General Yair Naveh, and Dov Eichenwald. "Sons of Holocaust Survivors Write About the Nightmares, Hopes and Lessons." *Yedioth Ahronot*, April 19, 2004.

Lau, Meir. "Also Today, Precisely Today." *Yedioth Ahronot*, April 9, 2002.

"From Generation to Generation." *Yedioth Ahronot*, April 8, 2013.

"What Will Be When We Are No Longer Here." *Yedioth Ahronot*, May 5, 2016.

Lazaroff, Tovah. "Former Chief of Staff: Ariel Sharon Designed Gaza Disengagement to Save West Bank Settlements." *The Jerusalem Post*, August 16, 2015. www.jpost.com/Arab-Israeli-Conflict/Former-chief-of-staff-Ariel-Sharon-designed-Gaza-disengagement-to-save-West-Bank-settlements-412213. Accessed August 16, 2017.

Lipson, Nathan and Maayan Cohen. "Google Trends Presents a Very Different Picture of the Popularity of Israeli Websites." *Haaretz*, June 23, 2008. www.haaretz.com/print-edition/business/ynet-is-the-leading-israeli-internet-portal-1.248301. Accessed August 16, 2017.

"Ynet Is the Leading Internet Portal." *Haaretz*, June 23, 2008. www.haaretz.com/print-edition/business/ynet-is-the-leading-israeli-internet-portal-1.248301. Accessed September 11, 2017.

Machat, Sharon. "Effect of the Third Generation." *Maariv*, April 29, 2003.

Mahler, Maya. "Holocaust Denial? In Spain It's Okay." *Yedioth Ahronot*, January 27, 2008.

Mandel, Roi. "Naalin Holds Holocaust Exhibit." *Ynet*, January 27, 2009. www.ynetnews.com/articles/0,7340,L-3662822,00.html. Accessed January 12, 2020.

Mazori, Dalia. "About Half of the Israeli Public Fears a Second Shoah." *NRG/ Maariv*, April 13, 2015. www.nrg.co.il/online/1/ART2/688/669.html. Accessed May 8, 2017.

"Israel Bows Its Head to the Six Million." *NRG/Maariv*, April 28, 2014. www.nrg.co.il/online/1/ART2/575/456.html. Accessed April 28, 2017.

"Netanyahu: We Must Not Remain Silent in the Face of Iran's Threats." *Maariv*, April 11, 2010.

"Netanyahu: We Will Never Reach the Situation Where It Is Too Late." *Maariv*, April 9, 2013.

Mazori, Dalia and Elial Sachar. "We Salute You Who Returned to Life." *Maariv*, May 5, 2006.

Megged, Aharon. "A New Incarnation of Old Hatred." *Yedioth Ahronot*, April 29, 2003.

Menaharedt, Yiftat. "Touching Pain." *Yedioth Ahronot*, April 12, 1999.

Michaeli, Yarden. "An Awful Reminder." *Maariv*, April 30, 2008.

Morris, Benny. "Israel's Concealing of Nakba Documents Is Totalitarian." *Haaretz*, July 15, 2019. www.haaretz.com/opinion/.premium-israel-s-concealing-of-documents-on-the-nakba-is-totalitarian-1.7495203.   Accessed February 23, 2020.

Naftali, Aya Ben. "Witnesses to the Last Witness." *Yedioth Ahronot*, April 12, 2012.

News Agencies. "Iran Presents: An Exhibition of Caricatures on the Holocaust." *NRG/Maariv*, May 13, 2016. www.nrg.co.il/online/1/ART2/777/717.html. Accessed April 19, 2017.

Novick, Akiva. "Never Again." *Yedioth Ahronot*, May 2, 2011.

Paz-Melamed, Yaez. "Children of the Next Generation." *NRG/Maariv*, April 19, 2012. www.nrg.co.il/online/1/ART2/359/511.html/. Accessed April 28, 2017.

Pelter, Nurit and Michael Grayevski. "1998, a Peak Year in the Level of Anti-Semitism." *Yedioth Ahronot*, April 13, 1999.

"A Strong IDF Is the Assurance That the Holocaust Won't Return." *Yedioth Ahronot*, April 13, 1999.

"We Have an Obligation to Remember and Forget." *Yedioth Ahronot*, April 13, 1999.

Peretz, Brit. "Ganz during the March of the Living: Every Survivor and Soldier Is Part of the Victory." *Ynet/Yedioth Ahronot*, April 8, 2013. www.ynet.co.il/articles/0,7340,L-4365327,00.html. Accessed May 6, 2017.

Perry, Smadar and Itamar Eichner. "Denying the Shoah on Holocaust Memorial Day." *Yedioth Ahronot*, April 25, 2006.

Plocker, Sever. "If This Is Man." *Yedioth Ahronot*, April 7, 1994.

"Not Genocide, [but] Murder of Jews." *Yedioth Ahronot*, April 16, 2007.

Raved, Ahiya and Matan Tzuri. "Rivlin at the Holocaust Memorial Ceremony." Ynet/Yedioth Ahronot, May 5, 2016. www.ynet.co.il/articles/0,7340,L-4799903,00.html. Accessed May 5, 2017.

Regev, David, Zvi Singer, and Tamar Trabelsi Hadad. "Saving the Memory." *Yedioth Ahronot*, May 1, 2011.

Sachar, Eliel. "She Survived the Shoah [but] Was Killed in an Attack." *Maariv*, April 9, 2002.

Sagir, Dan. "In the Battalion They Knew That We Were a Killer Company." *Haaretz*, July 31, 1989.

Schultz, Elihu. "The Holocaust Is Here." *NRG/Maariv*, August 3, 2005. www.nrg.co.il/online/1/ART/966/578.html. Accessed April 19, 2017.

Segev, Tom. "Dealing with the Holocaust." *Haaretz*, September 14, 1979.

Sela, Rona. "Israel's Art Scene Is Whitewashing the Nakba." *Haaretz*, December 28, 2018. www.haaretz.com/israel-news/.premium-israel-s-art-scene-is-whitewashing-the-nakba-1.6787625?=&ts=_1547149605080.   Accessed January 10, 2019.

Senyor, Eli. "Nakba Day: 'It Is as Important to Us as the Holocaust is to Jews'." *Ynet*, May 16, 2016. www.ynet.co.il/articles/0,7340,L-3251361,00.html. Accessed May 18, 2016.

Shalev, Avner. "The Purpose of the New Museum." *YDT*, March 15, 2005.
Shapira, Michael. "Maariv Report: More Serious Anti-Semitic Attacks in 2007."
    NRG/Maariv, April 30, 2008. www.nrg.co.il/online/1/ART1/727/972.html.
    Accessed April 17, 2017.
Shavit, Ari. "Survival of the Fittest." *Haaretz*, January 8, 2004. www.haaretz
    .com/survival-of-the-fittest-1.61345. Accessed April 16, 2017.
"Top PM Aide: Gaza Plan Aims to Freeze the Peace Process." *Haaretz*,
    October 6, 2004. www.haaretz.com/1.4710372. Accessed April 16, 2017.
Shezaf, Hagar. "Burying the Nakba: How Israel Systematically Hides Evidence of
    1948 Expulsion of Arabs." *Haaretz*, July 5, 2019. www.haaretz.com/israel-
    news/.premium.MAGAZINE-how-israel-systematically-hides-evidence-of-
    1948-expulsion-of-arabs-1.7435103. Accessed February 23, 2019.
Shir, Smadar. "I Didn't Think That in Israel Another Shoah Would Happen to
    Me." *Yedioth Ahronot*, April 28, 2014.
Shor, Elkana. "The Last Generation: Holocaust Remembrance Must Come from
    Home." *NRG/Maariv*, April 28, 2014. www.nrg.co.il/online/1/ART2/575/
    582.html. Accessed April 28, 2017.
Shragal, Nadav. "From Disengagement to Reingagement." *Haaretz*, August 17,
    2005. www.haaretz.com/1.4932915. Accessed April 18, 2017.
Singer, Zvi and Noah Klinger. "Six Million Tears." *Yedioth Ahronot*, April 12,
    2010.
Singer, Zvi. "Without Education the Memory of the Shoah Will Fade." *Yedioth
    Ahronot*, April 28, 2003.
Singer, Zvi and Natasha Mozgovia. "We Won't Forget." *Yedioth Ahronot*, April
    19, 2004.
Singer, Zvi, Yossi Yehoshua, and Noah Klinger. "There Will Not Be Another
    Holocaust." *Yedioth Ahronot*, April 21, 2009.
Skop, Yarden. "Israel Unveils New Holocaust Studies Program Starting in
    Kindergarten." *Haaretz*, April 24, 2014. www.haaretz.com/israel-news/
    .premium-1.587252. Accessed April 25, 2014.
Stern, Yoav. "A Guide at Yad Vashem Is Fired after Comparing the Suffering of
    the Jews to the Suffering of the Palestinians." *Haaretz*, April 23, 2009. www
    .haaretz.co.il/news/education/1.1257108. Accessed April 25, 2014.
Stiglitz, Meir. "To Death There Was Government." *Maariv*, May 5, 1997.
Tipenbron, Aran. "500 New Members in the Neo-Nazi Party." *Yedioth Ahronot*,
    August 14, 2000.
Trabelsi, Tamar. "Livnat to Arab Schools: Give Loyalty – Get Money." *Ynet/
    Yedioth Ahronot*, August 19, 2001. www.ynet.co.il/articles/0,7340,L-
    1029929,00.html. Accessed August 22, 2017.
Triblisi-Chadad, Tamar. "A Sharp Increase in the Number of Attacks on Jews."
    Yedioth Ahronot, April 9, 2002.
"Less Anti-Semitic Incidents in the World." *Yedioth Ahronot*, April 25, 2006.
"Rise in Anti-Semitism in the World and Especially in America and Russia."
    Yedioth Ahronot, May 2, 2000.
Triblisi-Chadad, Tamar and Itamar Eichner. "[They] Hate Us More." *Yedioth
    Ahronot*, April 12, 2010.

Tuchfeld, Michael. "In Australia, There Are Fears: Anti-Semitism Is Coming Here as Well." *NRG/Maariv*, October 27, 2014. www.nrg.co.il/online/1/ART2/651/001.html. Accessed April 18, 2017.

Turjeman, Meir and Noah Klinger. "Our Holocaust." *Yedioth Ahronot*, April 28, 2016.

Tzur, Nissan. "An Extreme Right-Wing View: Anti-Semitism Is Once Again Conquering Europe." *NRG/Maariv*, April 20, 2014. www.nrg.co.il/online/1/ART2/573/804.html. Accessed April 18, 2017.

Ushpiz, Ada. "Alas, the Authority Has Finished Us." *Haaretz*, August 9, 1996.

Uzi, Abigail. "When You Grow Up." *Yedioth Ahronot*, April 19, 2012.

Watad, Mohammed S. "The Duty to Scream." *NRG/Maariv*, April 15, 2015. www.nrg.co.il/online/1/ART2/689/240.html. Accessed May 8, 2017.

Weinthal, Benjamin. "German Citizens Are No Longer Afraid to Hate Jews." *NRG/Maariv*, October 8, 2014. www.nrg.co.il/online/1/ART2/631/117.html. Accessed April 18, 2017.

Wilf, Reut. "A New Book Compares the Holocaust of European Jewry to the Nakba." *NRG/Maariv*, August 24, 2015. www.nrg.co.il/online/1/ART2/719/831.html. Accessed April 21, 2017.

Yemini, Ben-Dror. "Between Judaism and Universalism." *Maariv*, April 27, 1995.

"The Disgraceful Link Drawn between the Holocaust and the Nakba." *Ynet News*, July 29, 2015. www.ynetnews.com/articles/0,7340,L-4695275,00.html. Accessed December 18, 2019.

"The Disgrace of the Shoah and the Nakba." *Yedioth Ahronot*, August 28, 2015.

"The Holocaust and the Nakba: The Jews Turned to Construction; the Palestinians Turned to Incitement." *NRG/Maariv*, April 27, 2014. www.nrg.co.il/online/1/ART2/575/324.html. Accessed June 1, 2017.

"The Jewish Nakba: Expulsions, Massacres and Forced Conversions." *Ynet*, May 16, 2009. www.makorrishon.co.il/nrg/online/1/ART1/891/209.html. Accessed February 8, 2020.

"What about the Jewish Nakba." *Ynet*, November 28, 2014. www.ynetnews.com/articles/0,7340,L-4597344,00.html. Accessed February 8, 2020.

Yusifon, Golan and Rivka Freilich. "Weitzman: There Will Not Be Another Auschwitz." *Maariv*, May 2, 2000.

Zuroff, Efraim. "Europe Is Rewriting History and Minimizing the Holocaust." *NRG/Maariv*, April 27, 2014. www.nrg.co.il/online/1/ART2/574/844.html. Accessed April 19, 2016.

International Newspaper Articles

Abrams, Elliot. "Corruption in the Palestinian Authority." *Council on Foreign Relations*, April 5, 2018. www.cfr.org/blog/corruption-palestinian-authority.

Al-Mughrabi, Nidal. "Palestinian Unity Government Takes Office." *Reuters*, March 17, 2007. www.reuters.com/article/us-palestinians/palestinian-unity-government-takes-office-idUSL1652735820070317.

Anonymous. "Binyamin Netanyahu and the Press: 'My own Media'." *The Economist*, January 26, 2019.

"PA Selling Sort the Refugees." *Al Jazeera*, January 25, 2011. www.aljazeera.com/palestinepapers/2011/01/2011124123324887267.html. Accessed August 1, 2017.

Barker, Anne. "Violence Erupts on Israel's Borders." *ABC*, May 16, 2011. www.abc.net.au/news/2011-05-15/violence-erupts-on-israels-borders/2694524l. Accessed February 28, 2016.

Baroud, Ramzy. "The 2014 War through the Eyes of Gaza's Youth." *Al Jazeera*, September 14, 2017. www.aljazeera.com/indepth/opinion/2017/09/2014-war-eyes-gaza-youth-170912143258604.html. Accessed October 15, 2018.

Ben-Simon, Daniel. "Israel Debates Holocaust Education for First Graders." *Al-Monitor*, October 24, 2013. www.al-monitor.com/pulse/ar/originals/2013/10/holocaust-education-shai-piron-debate.html. Accessed March 16, 2020.

Booth, William. "Palestinian University Students' Trip to Auschwitz Causes Uproar." *The Washington Post*, April 12, 2014. www.washingtonpost.com/world/middle_east/palestinian-university-students-trip-to-auschwitz-causes-uproar/2014/04/12/c162ba42-c27d-11e3-9ee7-02c1e10a03f0_story.html?hpid=z5. Accessed March 10, 2016.

Bronner, Ethan. "Israel's History Textbooks Replace Myths with Facts." *The New York Times*, August 14, 1999. www.nytimes.com/1999/08/14/world/israel-s-history-textbooks-replace-mythswith-facts.html?pagewanted=all. Accessed January 15, 2016

Brulliard, Karin. "Attacks Intensify along Gaza Border." *The Washington Post*, November 16, 2012. www.washingtonpost.com/world/middle_east/3-israelis-killed-in-rocket-strike-from-gaza-intensive-israeli-assault-leaves-13-palestinians-dead/2012/11/15/22023084-2f1e-11e2-ac4a-33b8b41fb531_story.html. Accessed August 29, 2017.

Cook, Jonathan. "Why Is Israel Afraid of the Nakba's March of Return?." *Al Jazeera*, April 10, 2017. www.aljazeera.com/indepth/features/2017/04/israeli-police-block-palestinian-march-return-170409055747446.html.s. Accessed August 29, 2017.

Eldar, Akiva. "Netanyahu Invokes Holocaust to Sow Fear, Hate." *Al-Monitor*, April 12, 2018. www.al-monitor.com/pulse/originals/2018/04/israel-syria-iran-benjamin-netanyahu-bashar-al-assad-shoah.html. Accessed March 13, 2020.

Erekat, Saeb. "The Returning Issue of Palestine's Refugees." *The Guardian*, December 10, 2010. www.theguardian.com/commentisfree/2010/dec/10/israel-palestine-refugee-rights. Accessed August 16, 2016.

Erlanger, Steven. "Abbas Declares War with Israel Effectively Over." *The New York Times*, February 14, 2005. www.nytimes.com/2005/02/14/world/middleeast/abbas-declares-war-with-israel-effectively-over.html?mtrref=www.google.com. Accessed August 16, 2016.

Friedman, Thomas L. "An Intriguing Signal from the Saudi Crown Prince." *The New York Times*, February 17, 2002. www.nytimes.com/2002/02/17/opinion/an-intriguing-signal-from-the-saudi-crown-prince.html.

Haberman, Clyde. "Hundreds of Jews Father to Honor Hebron Killer." *The New York Times*, April 1, 1994.

"Israeli Arabs Say P.L.O. Pact Is a Path to First-Class Status." *The New York Times*, November 24, 1993. www.nytimes.com/1993/11/24/world/israeli-arabs-say-plo-pact-is-a-path-to-first-class-status.html?sec=&spon=&pagewanted=1. Accessed August 16, 2016.

"Major Figures on Both Sides Questioning Israel–P.L.O. Talks." *The New York Times*, April 26, 1994.

Howeidy, Amira. "PA Relinquished Right of Return." *Al Jazeera*, January 24, 2011. www.aljazeera.com/palestinepapers/2011/01/2011124121923486877.html. Accessed August 1, 2017.

Isikoff, Michael. "In Personal Plea, Top Hamas Leader Calls on Obama to Stop 'Holocaust' in Gaza." *Yahoo News*, August 25, 2014. www.yahoo.com/news/in-personal-plea–top-hamas-leader-calls-on-obama-to-stop–holocaust–in-gaza-180315615.html. Accessed October 15, 2018.

Jilani, Hina, Christine Chinkin, and Desmond Travers. "Goldstone Report: Statement Issues by Members of UN Mission on Gaza War." *The Guardian*, April 14, 2011. www.theguardian.com/commentisfree/2011/apr/14/goldstone-report-statement-un-gaza. Accessed October 15, 2018.

Joffe, Lawrence. "Faisal Husseini." *The Guardian*, May 31, 2001. www.theguardian.com/news/2001/jun/01/guardianobituaries.israel. Accessed October 15, 2018.

Malley, Robert and Hussein Agha. "Camp David: A Tragedy of Errors." *The Guardian*, July 19, 2001. www.theguardian.com/world/2001/jul/20/comment. Accessed January 19, 2019.

Nazeela, Fathi. "Iran's New President Says Israel 'Must be Wiped Off the Map'." *The New York Times*, October 27, 2005. www.nytimes.com/2005/10/27/world/middleeast/irans-new-president-says-israel-must-be-wiped-off-the-map.html?_r=0. Accessed April 18, 2017.

Odeh, Ayman. "Israel Celebrates Its Independence, We Mourn Our Loss." *The New York Times*, April 18, 2018. www.nytimes.com/2018/04/18/opinion/israel-independence-palestine-nakba.html. Accessed March 12, 2020.

O'Grady, Siobhán. "Palestinian President Says Jewish Behavior Caused the Holocaust, Sparking Condemnation." *The Washington Post*, May 2, 2018. www.washingtonpost.com/news/worldviews/wp/2018/05/02/palestinian-president-says-jewish-behavior-caused-the-holocaust-sparking-condemnation/. Accessed February 23, 2020.

Radin, Charles A. "Muslim Opens Holocaust Museum in Israel." *The Boston Globe*, May 6, 2005. http://archive.boston.com/news/world/middleeast/articles/2005/05/06/muslim_opens_holocaust_museum_in_israel/. Accessed January 12, 2020.

Reston, James. "Washington; Reagan and Begin." *The New York Times* June 23, 1982. www.nytimes.com/1982/06/23/opinion/washington-reagan-and-begin.html. Accessed August 14, 2017.

Reuters. "Israel Bans Use of Palestinian Term 'Nakba' in Textbooks." *Haaretz*, July 22, 2009. www.haaretz.com/1.5080524. Accessed February 24, 2020.

Schneider, Howard. "Hamas Objects to Possible Lessons about Holocaust in U.N.-Run Schools in Gaza." *The Washington Post*, September 2, 2009. www .washingtonpost.com/wpdyn/content/article/2009/09/01/AR2009090102496 .html?hpid=sec-world. Accessed July 26, 2017.

Sciolino, Elaine. "The Ceremony: After Decades as Enemies, Arafat and Rabin Will Meet." *The New York Times*, September 12, 1993.

Sontag, Deborah. "And Yet so Far: A Special Report; Quest for Mideast Peace: How and Why It Failed." *The New York Times*, July 26, 2001, a1.

"Clinton in the Mideast: The Overview; Clinton Watches as Palestinians Drop Call for Destruction." *The New York Times*, December 15, 1998. www .nytimes.com/1998/12/15/world/clinton-mideast-overview-clinton-watches-palestinians-drop-call-for-israel-s.html.

Tharoor, Ishaan. "The Real Reason a Palestinian Mufti Allied with Hitler? It's Not so Shocking." *The Washington Post*, October 22, 2015. www .washingtonpost.com/news/worldviews/wp/2015/10/22/the-real-reason-a-pal estinian-mufti-allied-with-hitler-its-not-so-shocking/. Accessed April 3, 2020.

UN News. "International Court of Justice Finds Israeli Barrier in Palestinian Territory Is Illegal." https://news.un.org/en/story/2004/07/108912-inter national-court-justice-finds-israeli-barrier-palestinian-territory-illegal. Accessed December 13, 2018.

Interviews

All interviews were conducted in person by the author unless stated otherwise.
Interview 1. Omar Al-Qattan. March 11, 2016.
Interview 2. Eyal Naveh. March 16 and May 15, 2016.
Interview 3. Mohammed Dajani. March 17 and April 25, 2016.
Interview 4. Ahmad Hammash. March 28 and April 13, 2016.
Interview 4. Nadim Nashif. March 29, 2016.
Interview 5. Orna Katz. March 31, 2016.
Interview 6. Khalid Al-Saifi. April 3, 2016.
Interview 7. Or Kashti. April 6, 2016.
Interview 8. Motti Neiger. April 11, 2016.
Interview 9. Umar al-Ghubari. April 12, 2016.
Interview 10. Michael Yaron. April 14, 2016.
Interview 11. Rotem Korblitt. April 17, 2016.
Interview 12. Mohammed Kaial. April 18, 2016
Interview 13. Jomama Ashqar. April 18, 2016.
Interview 14. Vered Bar-Semech. April 21, 2016.
Interview 15. Saleem Sowidan and Hanan Emseeh. April 25, 2016.
Interview 16. Fouad Moughrabi. April 26, 2016.
Interview 17. Gideon Saar. May 1, 2016.
Interview 18. Eitan Bronstein. May 3, 2016
Interview 19. Sami Adwan. May 13, 2016.

Interview 20. Ali Jarbawi. May 16, 2016.
Interview 21. Tharwat Zaid Keilani. May 26, 2016.
Interview 22. Yair Auron. May 29, 2016.
Interview 23. Rabbi Shai Piron. May 30, 2016.
Interview 24. Yitzhak Arad. June 1, 2016.
Interview 25. Wadiah Awadah. July 13 and 15, 2016.
Interview 26. Naim Abu-Hummos. July 19, 2016.
Interview 27. Noah Klinger. July 24, 2016.
Interview 28. Khalid Mahameed. August 3, 2016.
Interview 29. Eldad Beck. August 8, 2016.
Interview 30. Omar Hilmi al-Ghoul. August 15 and 16, 2016 by email.

Index

Books in the Series

For EU product safety concerns, contact us at Calle de José Abascal, 56–1°,
28003 Madrid, Spain or eugpsr@cambridge.org.

www.ingramcontent.com/pod-product-compliance
Ingram Content Group UK Ltd.
Pitfield, Milton Keynes, MK11 3LW, UK
UKHW020403140625

459647UK00020B/2619